Florida

written and researched by

Jeffrey Kennedy, Lesley Rose, Mick Sinclair and Charles Young

ROUGH
GUIDES

www.roughguides.com

Introduction to

Florida

The cut-rate package trips and photos of tanning flesh and Mickey Mouse that fill the pages of glossy holiday brochures ensure that everyone has an image of Florida – but seldom one that's either accurate or complete. Pulling in nearly sixty million visitors each year to its beaches and theme parks, the aptly nicknamed "Sunshine State" is devoted to the tourist trade, yet it's also among the least-understood parts of the US, with a history, character and diversity of landscape unmatched by any other region. Beyond the palm-fringed sands, hiking and canoeing trails wind through little-known forests and rivers, and the famed beaches themselves can vary wildly over a short distance – hordes of copper-toned revelers are often just a Frisbee's throw from a deserted, pristine strand coveted by wildlife-watchers. Variations continue inland, where busy, modern cities are rarely more than a few miles away from steamy, primeval swamps.

 In many respects, Florida is still evolving. Socially and politically, it hasn't stayed still since the earliest days of US settlement: stimulating growth has always been the paramount concern, and with an average of a thousand people a day moving to the booming state, it's currently the fourth most populous place in the nation. The changing demographics have helped overturn the common notion that Florida is dominated by retirees (though, coincidentally, the state song is a venerable spiritual entitled "Old Folks at Home"), or is part of the

Fact file

● Spanish explorers named this territory after *Pascua Florida*, the "feast of flowers" celebrated at Easter; it was during this festival in 1513 that Ponce de León and crew landed on Florida's shores.

● Florida's 447-mile-long peninsula stretches between the Gulf of Mexico and the Atlantic Ocean, and features 663 miles of beaches and about 4500 individual islands of ten acres or more.

● Five flags have been flown here: the French (1564), Spanish (1565–1763 and 1783–1821), British (1763–83), Confederate (1861–65) and US (1821–61 and from 1865 to the present). It was admitted as the 27th state in the Union in 1845; the capital is Tallahassee.

● Though 22nd in total area with 58, 560 square miles, Florida is the fourth most populous state in the US, with more than sixteen million people.

● The two major industries are tourism and agriculture; in fact, Florida produces more citrus, tomatoes, green peppers, watermelon, sweet corn and sugar than any other state.

conservative Deep South, even if elements certainly do remain. The new Floridians tend to be a younger breed, taking advantage of the economic development along the Highway 4 corridor in the center of the state – and Florida's lack of a state income tax. Immigration from outside the country is also on the increase, with Spanish- and French-Creole-speaking enclaves providing a reminder of geographic and economic ties to Latin America and the Caribbean. These links have proven almost as influential in raising the state's material wealth over the past decade as the arrival of huge domestic businesses, including sections of the film industry that have opted for central Florida in preference to Hollywood.

Not all is rosy: in the past decade, Florida vigorously fought a reputation

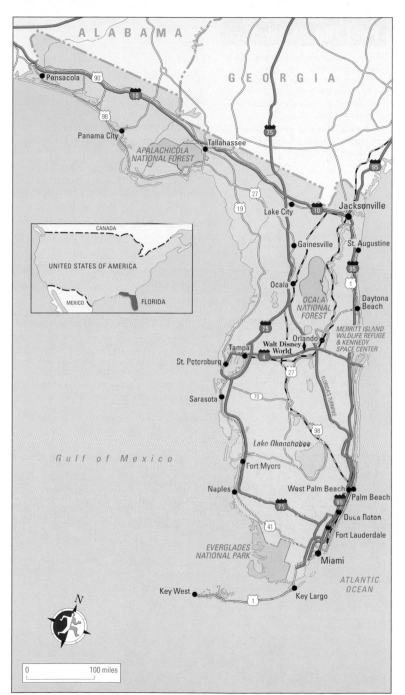

for violent crime against tourists; you're highly unlikely to encounter any trouble, but the perception still lingers on a bit. The state also served as a major political battleground for the contested presidential election in 2000, rarely putting its best face forward as legal eagles and demonstrative protesters descended here en masse for the messy proceedings. A bit more behind the scenes, Florida is engaged in a struggle to provide enough houses, schools and roads for its growing population; levels of poverty in the rural areas can be severe; and

> **Hordes of copper-toned revelers are often just a Frisbee's throw from a deserted, pristine strand coveted by wildlife-watchers.**

in an increasingly multiethnic society, racial tensions frequently surface. Expanding towns without jeopardizing the environment is another hot issue; large amounts of land are under state or federal protection, and there are signs that the conservation lobby is gaining the upper hand. Nevertheless, uncontrolled development is posing serious ecological problems – not least to the Everglades.

Cuban heritage

While evidence of Florida's **Cuban heritage** is visible in Key West and the Tampa Bay area, nowhere is it more pronounced than in Miami (see p.63). Cubans began fleeing the Batista and Castro regimes in the Fifties and Sixties, heading for the closest major city on US shores; many more were boatlifted there a few decades later. The influx has gradually reshaped the city, making it in essence a bilingual one; Hispanics, mostly of Cuban descent, now account for the majority of Miami's population, and their influence is felt in everything from the nuevo cubano cuisine in haute South Beach restaurants to local politics.

Where to go

H eat-induced lethargy is no excuse not to get out and explore
the different facets of Florida,
as the state is compact enough
to be toured easily and quickly. The
essential stop is **Miami**, whose
addictive, cosmopolitan vibe is enriched
by its large Hispanic population, and
where the much-photographed Art
Deco district of **Miami Beach**
provides an unmistakeable backdrop for
the state's liveliest nightclubs.

From Miami, a simple journey south
brings you to the **Florida Keys**, a
hundred-mile string of islands of which
each has something to call its own, be it
sport fishing, coral-reef diving, or a
unique species of dwarf deer. The single
road spanning the Keys comes to a halt
at **Key West**, a blob of land that's legendary for its sunsets and anything-
goes attitude. North from Miami,
much of the **Southeast Coast** is a disappointingly urbanized strip –
commuter territory better suited for

> **The essential stop is Miami, whose
> cosmopolitan vibe is enriched by
> its large Hispanic population.**

Theme parks

Florida's most trumpeted
attractions, its grandiose theme
parks, offer prefabricated entertainment to millions of visitors –
and locals – annually. When Walt
Disney began secretly purchasing
nearly thirty thousand acres of land
in Central Florida during the late
Sixties (see p.273), few could have
guessed the impending seismic
shift in the state's fortunes. The
vast and lucrative vacation complex
that resulted opened the floodgates
to a number of imitators, including
nearby Universal Orlando and
SeaWorld Orlando, as well as Busch
Gardens just outside Tampa; still,
Disney remains king, and constantly
tries to one-up itself with each simulated safari and futuristic video
display. Though the commercialism
never ceases, if approached with a
bit of forethought and a willingness
to give in to the frenzied spirit, it
may have you whooping just as
loudly as the kids.

living in than visiting. Alongside the busy towns, however, beaches flow for many unbroken miles and finally escape the residential stranglehold along the **Northeast Coast**, where communities are often subservient to the sands that flank them.

The coral reef

Along with the Everglades, the best evidence of Florida's natural splendor lies in its extensive **coral reef**, the only living one in the continental United States. Just offshore the Florida Keys, a string of small islands just off the southeastern corner of the state, the reef is made up of billions of tiny polyps – actually varieties of sea animals – that secrete limestone, which forms intricately shaped and vibrantly colored coral castles, and is host to a stunning array of starfish, sponges, sand dollars and angelfish, among hundreds of other species of exotic marine life. Read more about the reef, and how best to explore it, in "The Florida Keys," p.134, and in "Natural Florida," p.457.

When you tire of beach life and ocean views, make a short hop inland to **Central Florida**, whose verdant terrain features cattle farms, grassy hillsides, and isolated villages beside expansive lakes. The sole but rather dramatic disruption to this rural idyll is **Walt Disney World**, which practices tourism on the scale of the infinite. If you're in the mood, you can indulge in its ingenious fix of escapist fun; if not, the upfront commercialism may well encourage you to skip north to the deep forests of the **Panhandle**, Florida's link with the Deep South – or to the art-rich towns and sunset-kissed beaches of the **West Coast**. Explore these at your leisure as you progress steadily south to the **Everglades**, a massive, alligator-filled swathe of sawgrass plain, mangrove islands and cypress swamp, which

ix

The Florida sun

Any visitor with sensitive skin should bear in mind that Florida shares a latitude with the Sahara Desert; the power of the Florida **sun** should never be underestimated.

Time spent outdoors should be planned carefully at first, especially between 11am and 2pm, when the sun is at its strongest. A powerful **sunscreen** is essential; anything with an SPF of less than 25 is unlikely to offer the necessary protection. Light-colored, loose-fitting, lightweight clothes should protect any parts of your body not accustomed to direct sunlight. Wear a hat with a wide brim, carry sunglasses, and keep to the shaded side of the street. Drink plenty of **fluids** (but not alcohol) to prevent dehydration – public drinking-water fountains are provided for this purpose; iced tea and lemonade are the best drinks for cooling off in a restaurant.

provides as definitive a statement of Florida's natural beauty as you'll encounter.

When to go

You'll have to take into account Florida's climate – and, of course, what your goals are – when deciding on the best time for a visit. Florida is split into **two climatic zones**: subtropical in the south and warm temperate – like the rest of the southeastern US – in the north. These two zones determine the state's tourist seasons, and can affect costs accordingly.

Anywhere **south of Orlando** experiences very mild winters (November to April), with pleasantly warm temperatures and a low level of humidity. This is the peak period for tourist activity, with prices at their highest and crowds at their thickest. It also marks the best time to visit the inland parks and swamps. The southern summer (May to October) seems hotter than it really is (New York is often warmer) because of the extremely high humidity, relieved only by afternoon thunderstorms and sometimes even hurricanes (though the chances of being there during one are remote); at this time of year you'll be lucky to see a blue sky. Lower prices and fewer tourists are the rewards for braving the mugginess, though mosquitoes can render the natural areas off-limits.

> **The southern summer seems hotter than it really is because of the extremely high humidity, relieved only by afternoon thunderstorms and sometimes even hurricanes**

Winter is the off-peak period **north of Orlando**; in all probability, the only chill you'll detect is a slight nip in the evening air, though it's worth bearing in mind that at this time of year the sea is really too cold for swimming, and snow has been known to fall in the Panhandle. The northern Florida summer is when the crowds arrive, and when the days – and the nights – can be almost as hot and sticky as southern Florida.

Average temperatures (°F)

	Jan/Feb		Mar/Apr		May/Jun		July/Aug		Sept/Oct		Nov/Dec	
Jacksonville												
Avg daily temp	53	55	62	68	74	80	82	82	78	70	62	56
Key West												
Avg daily temp	70	70	74	77	81	83	85	84	83	80	76	72
Miami												
Avg daily temp	67	68	72	75	79	81	83	83	82	78	73	69
Orlando												
Avg daily temp	61	61	67	73	78	81	83	83	81	75	67	62
Pensacola												
Avg daily temp	51	54	60	67	75	80	82	82	78	69	61	54
Tallahassee												
Avg daily temp	51	53	60	66	74	80	81	81	78	68	60	53
Tampa												
Avg daily temp	60	61	67	71	77	81	82	82	81	75	68	62

things not to miss

It's not possible to see everything that Florida has to offer in one trip – and we don't suggest you try. What follows is a selective taste of the state's highlights: great beaches, outstanding national parks, spectacular wildlife – and even good things to eat and drink. It's arranged in five color-coded categories, so that you can browse through to find the very best things to see, do and experience. All highlights have a page reference to take you straight into the guide, where you can find out more.

01 **Ocean Drive** Page **86** • On weekend nights, the neon illuminations along Miami's Ocean Drive shine over a bumper-to-bumper street party.

02 **Art Deco** Page **85** • The colorful pastels of the hotels of South Beach, such as the *Leslie*, are the reason many visitors make a beeline to the area – and then stay there.

03 **Lowe Art Museum** Page 100 • Engaging displays of Spanish Old Masters and Native American artifacts make this Miami museum the top stop for art-lovers.

04 **The causeways of Miami** Page 83 • Cross Biscayne Bay via MacArthur Causeway, which connects Miami's mainland to South Beach and affords glorious views of the city skyline, especially at night.

05 **Conch fritters** Page **165** • Conch, a sort of giant freshwater sea snail prevalent just off the Keys, can be eaten raw or deep-fried as fritters.

06 **Captain Tony's Saloon** Page **166** • Relax in this rustic hangout, which Ernest Hemingway made his own during his ten raucous yet productive years in Key West.

07 **Sea turtle viewing** Page **198** • Florida's Atlantic and Gulf coasts own abundant wildlife, like numerous varieties of sea turtles, best seen when nesting in June.

08 Key deer

Page **148** • Barely larger than your average dog, the Key deer is an endearingly tame creature found only in the Keys.

09 Boca Raton Resort

Page **187** • Adam Mizner's eccentric architectural vision is most stunningly realized at this resort-cum-spectacle.

10 Fantasy Fest

Page **154** • Every October, outrageous partygoers parade in outrageous costumes along Key West's Duval Street during this gay-orientated celebration.

11 **Sunset at Sebastian Inlet** Page **133** & **317** • Sip a cocktail, dig your feet in the sand, admire the fabulous colors of a Florida sunset, perhaps best from the gulfside, but visible from near anywhere in the state.

12 **Beachcombing** Pages **171** & **206** • Whether you want to view suntanned bodies, collect shells, or just bum around in isolation, the beaches along the Atlantic Coast run the gamut – and reflect the Florida of the popular imagination.

13 **Space Shuttle launches, Cape Canaveral** Page **211** • There are few experiences more visually – or aurally – memorable than witnessing a nighttime launch at the Kennedy Space Center.

14 **Ponce Inlet Lighthouse** Page **222** • The views of Daytona and New Smyrna beaches from the top of the Ponce Inlet Lighthouse are well worth the 175-foot climb.

15 **Back to the Future, Universal Studios** Page **286** • The rides at Universal Studios trump those at Disney, perhaps none more so than the mind-bending Back to the Future.

16 **Disney's Animal Kingdom** Page **282** • Part new-age safari, part theme park, the five-hundred-acre Animal Kingdom, notably its Africa land, is many cuts above your average zoo.

17 **St Augustine's Old Town** Page **231** • Its narrow streets, preserved houses, and centuries-old fortress help St Augustine stake its claim as America's oldest city.

18 **Corkscrew Swamp Sanctuary** Page **381** • The desolate swamp landscape of the Corkscrew Swamp Sanctuary is home to the country's largest population of wood storks.

19 **Chalet Suzanne**
Page **297** • Amid the whimsical, vaguely Swiss-Arabic architecture of *Chalet Suzanne*, near Lake Wales, some of Florida's most exquisite French meals are served.

20 **Cà d'Zan**
Page **364** •
John Ringling's palatial Sarasota home and stunning art collection attest to the circus owner's enormous wealth and discriminating taste.

21 **Apalachicola National Forest** Page **412** • One of Florida's largest and most pristine national forests, Apalachicola offers endless opportunities for outdoor enthusiasts, like the thirty-mile Apalachicola Trail.

22 **Seaside** Page **427** • Take a break from the unspoiled South Walton beaches to visit the pseudo-Victorian cottages at Seaside's planned community.

23 **Fishing** Page **43** • The waters of both Florida coasts, especially the Atlantic side, teem with every fish imaginable, including deep-sea giants like marlin and tuna; hire a boat and try your luck.

24

Canoeing in the Everglades

Page **388** • Florida presents innumerable creeks and swamps for canoeing, the most impressive of which are in the Everglades.

25 **Alligator encounters** Page **392** • The "keepers of the Everglades," alligators are visible throughout the National Park, particularly along the Anhinga Trail.

contents

using the Rough Guide

We've tried to make this Rough Guide a good read and easy to use. The book is divided into five main sections, and you should be able to find whatever you want in one of them.

front section

The front colour section offers a quick tour of Florida. The **introduction** aims to give you a feel for the place, with suggestions on where to go. We also tell you what the weather is like and include a basic state fact file. Next, our authors round up their favourite aspects of Florida in the **things not to miss** section – whether it's great food, amazing sights or a special hotel. Right after this comes the Rough Guide's full **contents** list.

basics

You've decided to go and the basics section covers all the **pre-departure** nitty-gritty to help you plan your trip. This is where to find out which airlines fly to your destination, what paperwork you'll need, what to do about money and insurance, about internet access, food, security, public transport, car rental – in fact just about every piece of **general practical information** you might need.

guide

This is the heart of the Rough Guide, divided into user-friendly chapters, each of which covers a specific region. Every chapter starts with a list of **highlights** and an **introduction** that helps you to decide where to go, depending on

your time and budget. Likewise, introductions to the various towns and smaller regions within each chapter should help you plan your itinerary. We start most town accounts with information on arrival and accommodation, followed by a tour of the sights, and finally reviews of places to eat and drink, and details of nightlife. Longer accounts also have a directory of practical listings. Each chapter concludes with **public transport** details for the area covered.

contexts

Read Contexts to get a deeper understanding of how Florida ticks. We include a brief **history**, articles about **wildlife** and **environmental issues**, together with a detailed further reading section that reviews dozens of **books** relating to the state.

index + small print

Apart from a **full index**, which includes maps as well as places, this section covers publishing information, credits and acknowledgements, and also has our contact details in case you want to send in updates and corrections to the book – or suggestions as to how we might improve it.

chapter map of **Florida**

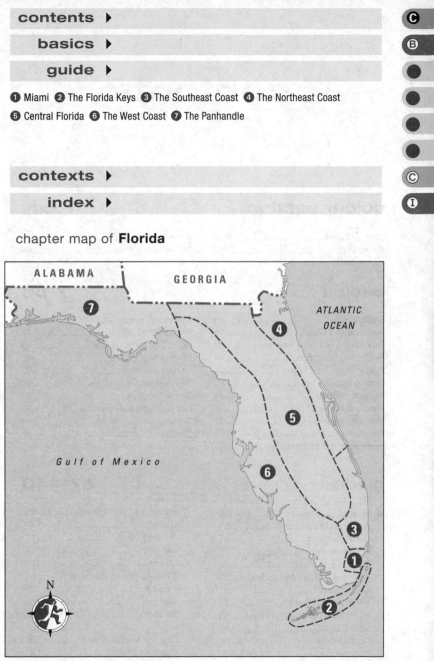

contents

colour section

basics

guide

4
■

contexts

441–474

index + small print

475–486

map symbols

symbols

maps are listed in the full index using coloured text

▭95▭	Interstate	♥	Museum
▭30▭	US Highway	🏛	Historic house
▭1▭	State Highway	⚱	Public gardens
▭707▭	Secondary State Highway	⚶	Lighthouse
=====	Track	⚓	Marina
− − −	Trail	⚶	Marshland
—+—	Railway	ⓘ	Information centre
— —	Ferry route	⊠	Post office
▪▪▪▪	State border	▪▪▪▪▪	Wall
− − −	Chapter division boundary	⬭	Stadium
———	River	◼	Building
♦	General point of interest	✛	Church
✕	Airport	⊞	Cemetery
◉	Hotel	▨	National/State park
◼	Restaurant	▨	Park
⚠	Campsite	▨	Indian reservation
⊼	Picnic area	▨	Beach
♟	Castle		

basics

basics

Getting there

While Florida has beckoned visitors since the Spanish *conquistadores* made forays in the early sixteenth century, it has never been as easily accessible as now. Both Miami and Orlando have major international airports; Fort Lauderdale, Jacksonville, Tampa/St Petersburg and Daytona Beach airports receive substancial foreign and domestic traffic; and Palm Beach, Tallahassee, Gainesville and Sarasota have regional airports. Easily reachable by car, Florida lies at the end of three major interstate highways: I-95, which runs up the East Coast to Maine; I-75, which winds through the South on the way to Ohio and Michigan; and I-10, which stretches west across Texas and finally halts at Los Angeles.

In planning your vacation, remember that airfares depend on the **season**, and Florida is split into two climatic zones (see "Introduction,"). Note also that flying on weekends is typically more expensive; price ranges quoted below assume midweek travel. You can often cut costs by going through a **specialist flight agent** – either a consolidator, who buys up blocks of tickets from the airlines and sells them at a discount, or a **discount agent**, who in addition to dealing with discounted flights may also offer special student and youth fares and a range of other travel-related services such as travel insurance, rail passes, car rentals, tours and the like. Some agents specialize in **charter flights**, which may be cheaper than any available scheduled flight, but again departure dates are fixed and withdrawal penalties are high. For some of the more popular destinations, you may even find it cheaper to pick up a bargain **package deal** from one of the tour operators listed below and then find your own accommodation when you get there. A further possibility is to see if you can arrange a courier flight, although you'll need a flexible schedule, and preferably be traveling alone with very little luggage. In return for shepherding a parcel through customs, you can expect to get a deeply discounted ticket. You'll probably also be restricted in the duration of your stay.

Booking flights online

Many airlines and discount travel Web sites offer you the opportunity to book your tick-ets online, cutting out the costs of agents and middlemen. Good deals can often be found through discount or auction sites, as well as through the airlines' own Web sites.

Online booking agents and general travel sites

Ⓦ **www.etn.nl/discount.htm** A hub of consolidator and discount agent Web links, maintained by the nonprofit European Travel Network.

Ⓦ **www.princeton.edu/Main/air800.html** Has an extensive list of airline toll-free numbers and Web sites.

Ⓦ **www.flyaow.com** Online air travel info and reservations site.

Ⓦ **www.smilinjack.com/airlines.htm** Has an up-to-date compilation of airline Web site addresses.

Ⓦ **http://travel.yahoo.com** Incorporates a lot of Rough Guide material in its coverage of destination countries and cities across the world, with information about places to eat and sleep etc.

Ⓦ **www.cheaptickets.com** Discount flight specialists.

Ⓦ **www.cheapflights.com** Flight deals, travel agents, plus links to other travel sites.

Ⓦ **www.lastminute.com** Offers good last-minute holiday package and flight-only deals.

Ⓦ **www.expedia.com** Discount airfares, all-airline search engine and daily deals.

Ⓦ **www.travelocity.com** Destination guides, hot Web fares and best deals for car hire, accommodation and lodging as well as fares. Provides access to the travel agent system SABRE, the most comprehensive central reservations system in the US.

ⓦ**www.hotwire.com** Bookings from the US only. Last-minute savings of up to forty percent on regular published fares. Travelers must be at least 18 and there are no refunds, transfers or changes allowed. Log-in required.

ⓦ**www.priceline.com** Bookings from the US only. Name-your-own-price Web site that has deals at around forty percent off standard fares. You cannot specify flight times (although you do specify dates) and the tickets are non-refundable, non-transferable and non-changeable.

ⓦ**www.skyauction.com** Bookings from the US only. Auctions tickets and travel packages using a "second bid" scheme. The best strategy is to bid the maximum you're willing to pay, since if you win you'll pay just enough to beat the runner-up regardless of your maximum bid.

ⓦ**www.travelshop.com.au** Australian Web site offering discounted flights, packages, insurance, online bookings.

ⓦ**www.uniquetravel.com.au** Australian site with a good range of packages and good-value flights.

From the UK and Ireland

Although you can fly to the US from many of Britain's regional airports, the only **nonstop scheduled flights** to Florida are from London, and all of these land either at Miami or, less often, Orlando. The **flight time** is around eight hours, leaving London around midday and arriving during the afternoon (local time). The return journey is slightly shorter, leaving in the early evening and flying through the night to arrive in London around breakfast time. A basic round-trip **economy-class ticket** will cost £200–300 for a mid-week flight in low season and £500–600 for a weekend flight in high season.

Travel agents (see below) can offer cut-price seats on direct **charter flights**. These are particularly good value if you're traveling from a British city other than London, though they tend to be limited to the summer season, be restricted to so-called "holiday destinations," and have fixed departure and return dates. Brochures are available in most high-street travel agents, or contact the specialists direct.

Many more routings use direct **one-stop** flights to Florida (a flight may be called "direct" even if it stops on the way, provided it keeps the same flight number throughout its journey). Obviously, these take a few hours longer than nonstop flights but can be more convenient (and sometimes cheaper) if you're not aiming specifically for Miami or Orlando. All the state's cities and large towns have airports – the other major one is Tampa – with good links from other US cities. Alternatively, you could take a flight to New York or **another city** on the northern East Coast and travel on from there – this won't save any money overall but is an idea if you want to see more of the country before reaching Florida. Again, travel agents have the cheapest offers.

Airlines

Alitalia ☎08705/448259 in Republic of Ireland ☎01/677 5171, ⓦwww.alitalia.it.

American Airlines ☎0845/778 9789, ⓦwww.aa.com.

British Airways ☎0845/773 3377, in Republic of Ireland ☎0141/222 2345, ⓦwww.britishairways.com.

Continental ☎0800/776464, in Republic of Ireland ☎01/814 5311, ⓦwww.flycontinental.com.

Delta ☎0800/414767, in Northern Ireland ☎028/9048 0526, in Republic of Ireland ☎1800 /414767, ⓦwww.delta.com.

United Airlines ☎0845/844 4777, in Republic of Ireland ☎1800/535300, ⓦwww.ual.com.

Virgin Atlantic Airways ☎01293/747747, in Republic of Ireland ☎01/873 3388, ⓦwww.virgin-atlantic.com.

Flight and travel agents

Apex Travel, Dublin ☎01/671 5933, ⓦwww.apextravel.ie. Specialists in flights to Australia, Africa, Far East, US, Canada.

Bridge the World ☎020/7911 0900, ⓦwww.bridgetheworld.com. Specializing in round-the-world tickets, with good deals aimed at the backpacker market.

CIE Tours International, Dublin ☎01/703 1888, ⓦwww.cietours.ie. General flight and tour agent.

Co-op Travel Care, Belfast ☎028/9047 1717. Flights and holidays around the world.

Destination Group ☎020/7400 7000, ⓦwww.destination-group.com. Good discount airfares, as well as US inclusive packages.

Flightbookers ☎020/7757 2444, ⓦwww.ebookers.com. Low fares on an extensive selection of scheduled flights.

Joe Walsh Tours, Dublin ☎01/872 2555 or 676 3053, Cork ☎021/ 277959, ⓦwww.joewalshtours.ie. General budget fares agent.

Lee Travel, Cork ℡ 021/277111,
ⓦ www.leetravel.ie. Flights and holidays
worldwide.
Liffey Travel, Dublin ℡ 01/878 8322 or 878
8063. Package tour specialists.
The London Flight Centre ℡ 020/7244 6411,
ⓦ www.topdecktravel.co.uk. Long-established
agent dealing in discount flights.
North South Travel ℡ & ⓕ 01245/608291,
ⓦ www.northsouthtravel.co.uk. Friendly,
competitive travel agency, offering discounted
fares worldwide – profits are used to support
projects in the developing world, especially the
promotion of sustainable tourism.
Premier Travel, Derry ℡ 028/7126 3333,
ⓦ www.premiertravel.uk.com. Discount flight
specialists.
Quest Worldwide ℡ 020/8547 3322,
ⓦ www.questtravel.com. Specialists in round-the-
world fares.
STA Travel ℡ 0870/160 6070,
ⓦ www.statravel.co.uk. Worldwide specialists in
low-cost flights and tours for students and under-
26s, though other customers welcome.
Student & Group Travel, Dublin ℡ 01/677 7834.
Student and group specialists, mostly to Europe.
Trailfinders ℡ 020/7628 7628, in Republic of
Ireland ℡ 01/677 7888, ⓦ www.trailfinders.com.
One of the best-informed and most efficient
agents for independent travelers; produce a very
useful quarterly magazine worth scrutinizing for
round-the-world routes.
Travel Bag ℡ 0870/900 1350,
ⓦ www.travelbag.co.uk. Discount flights to US;
official Qantas agent.
Travel Cuts ℡ 020/7255 2082,
ⓦ www.travelcuts.co.uk. Canadian company
specializing in budget, student and youth travel
and round-the-world tickets.
Usit Campus ℡ 0870/240 1010,
ⓦ www.usitcampus.co.uk. Student/youth travel
specialists, offering discount flights. Specialists in
North America travel.
USIT Now, Belfast ℡ 028/9032 7111, Dublin
℡ 01/602 1777 or 677 8117, Cork ℡ 021/270
900, Derry ℡ 028/7137 1888, ⓦ www.usitnow.ie.
Student and youth specialists for flights and trains.

Tour operators

Airtours ℡ 0870/241 2567,
ⓦ www.airtours.co.uk. Charter flights, packages
and fly-drives, mainly to Orlando.
American Adventures ℡ 01892/512700,
ⓦ www.americanadventures.com. Small-group
camping adventure trips throughout the US,

including a long-distance tour that takes in
everything between Miami and Boston.
British Airways Holidays worldwide
℡ 0870/242 4245, ⓦ www.baholidays.co.uk.
Packages, city breaks, coach tours, cruises and
tailor-mades.
Thomas Cook ℡ 08705/666222,
ⓦ www.thomascook.co.uk. Long-established one-
stop 24-hour travel agency for package holidays or
scheduled flights, with bureau de change issuing
Thomas Cook travelers' checks, own travel
insurance and car rental.
Transatlantic Vacations, 3a Gatwick Metro
Centre, Balcombe Rd, Horley, Surrey RH6 9GA (℡
01293/774441,
ⓦ www.transatlanticvacations.co.uk). Resort-
based packages in Orlando.
TrekAmerica, 4 Waterperry Court, Middleton Rd,
Banbury, Oxon OX16 4QB (℡01295 256777,
ⓦ www. trekamerica.com). Includes Florida on
some of its bus tours of the region.
Unijet, "Sandrocks", Rocky Lane, Haywards
Heath, West Sussex RH16 4RH (℡ 0870/511 4114,
ⓦ www.unijet.co.uk). Inexpensive packages, fly-
drives and charters to Orlando/Gulf Coast (all year)
as well as tailor-made packages (May–Oct)
anywhere in Florida.
Virgin Holidays, The Galleria, Station Rd,
Crawley, West Sussex RH10 1WW
(℡ 01293/617181, ⓦ www.virginholidays.co.uk).
Flights, fly-drive, tailor-mades and packages
almost anywhere in Florida.

From the US and Canada

Getting to Florida from anywhere else in
North America is never a problem, as the
region is well serviced by air, rail and road
networks. Every major and most minor US
airlines **fly to Florida**, where Miami is the
main hub, closely followed by Orlando and
Tampa. Flying remains the quickest but most
expensive way to travel; taking the **train** is a
close second; traveling by **bus** is much less
costly but also the slowest and least comfortable mode of transport.

By air

Of the **major carriers**, Delta and American
Airlines have the best links with the state's
many smaller regional airports. Flying into
any of the major airports, you can expect to
pay in the region of $250 from New York or
from Chicago. From LA the lowest fare will

be around $300, but be prepared to spend more. One of the better **smaller airlines** to check with is JetBlue, which runs flights to Orlando, Fort Lauderdale, Fort Myers, Tampa and West Palm Beach; they often run Web-only specials, so be sure to check their site before making a final purchase. Also try Air Tran Airways, based in Atlanta, which has flights to Fort Lauderdale, Fort Myers, Miami, Orlando, Sarasota and St Petersburg/Tampa from a number of Southern, Midwestern and East Coast cities.

From **Canada**, Air Canada flies direct from Toronto to Miami, Jacksonville and Tampa, as well as Fort Lauderdale and Fort Myers in winter only; from Montreal the company has direct flights to Fort Lauderdale and Miami; and from Vancouver, they offer direct flights to Miami only. From Toronto and Montreal, expect to pay a minimum of CAN$350 for a flight to Miami; CAN$450 from Vancouver. American Airlines often offers competitive, if not cheaper, fares, with flights from Toronto to Miami, Orlando and Fort Lauderdale plus several other Florida cities. They also fly to Miami from Vancouver (with a connection in Dallas).

Again, the place to find the lowest-priced fares is a **discount travel company**. If your plans are very flexible, scanning the travel pages of your local newspaper may turn up some bargains, but be sure to read the small print – many seemingly attractive deals have restrictive rules.

Airlines

Air Canada ☎ 1-888/247-2262, ⓦ www.aircanada.ca.
Air Tran Airways ☎ 1-800/AIR-TRAN, ⓦ www.airtran.com.
America West Airlines ☎ 1-800/235-9292, ⓦ www.americawest.com.
American Airlines ☎ 1-800/433-7300, ⓦ www.aa.com.
American Trans Air ☎ 1-800/435-9282, ⓦ www.ata.com.
Continental Airlines domestic ☎ 1-800/523-3273, ⓦ www.continental.com.
Delta Air Lines domestic ☎ 1-800/221-1212, international ☎ 1-800/241-4141, ⓦ www.delta.com.
Frontier Airlines ☎ 1-800/432-1359, ⓦ www.flyfrontier.com.
JetBlue ☎ 1-800/538-2583, ⓦ www.jetblue.com.
Northwest/KLM US ☎ 1-800/225-2525, in Canada ☎ 514/397-0775, ⓦ www.nwa.com.
Southwest Airlines ☎ 1-800/435-9792, ⓦ www.southwest.com.
TWA ☎ 1-800/221-2000, ⓦ www.twa.com.
United Airlines ☎ 1-800/241-6522, ⓦ www.ual.com.
US Airways ☎ 1-800/428-4322, ⓦ www.usairways.com.

Discount travel companies

Airtech ☎ 212/219-7000, ⓦ www.airtech.com. Standby seat broker; also deals in consolidator fares and courier flights.
Council Travel ☎ 1-800/226-8624 or 617/528 2091; ⓦ www.counciltravel.com. Nationwide organization that mostly, but by no means exclusively, specializes in student/budget travel.
Educational Travel Center ☎ 1-800/747-5551 or 608/256 5551, ⓦ www.edtrav.com. Student/youth discount agent.
Skylink US ☎ 1-800/AIR-ONLY or 212/573-8980, Canada ☎ 1-800/SKY-LINK. Consolidator.
STA Travel ☎ 1-800/777-0112 or 781-4040, ⓦ www.sta-travel.com. Worldwide specialists in independent travel; also student IDs, travel insurance, car rental, rail passes, etc.
Student Flights ☎ 1-800/255-8000 or 480/951-1177, ⓦ www.isecard.com. Student/youth fares, student IDs.
Travac ☎ 1-800/872-8800, ⓦ www.thetravelsite.com. Consolidator and charter broker, with offices in New York City and Orlando.
Travel Avenue ☎ 1-800/333-3335, ⓦ www.travelavenue.com. Full-service travel agent that offers discounts in the form of rebates.
Travel Cuts Canada ☎ 1-800/667-2887, US ☎ 416/979-2406. Canadian student-travel organization.
Travelers Advantage Membership Services, Inc ☎ 1-877/259-2691, ⓦ www.travelersadvantage.com. Discount travel club; annual membership fee required (currently $1 for three months' trial).
Worldwide Discount Travel Club ☎ 305/534-2642. Discount travel club.

Tour operators

American Adventures/Roadrunner Worldwide Hosteling Treks ☎ 1-800/873-5872, ⓦ www.americanadventures.com. Small-group camping adventure trips throughout the US, including a long-distance tour that takes in everything between Miami and Boston.
American Express Vacations ☎ 1-800/241-1700, ⓦ www.americanexpress.com/travel.

Packgage deals typically based around high-end resorts.

Contiki Tours ☎1-888/CONTIKI, ⓦwww.contiki.com. 18- to 35-year-olds only tour operator with plenty of long-distance trips, including one that begins in Orlando and ends in Los Angeles.

Delta Certified Vacations ☎1-800/654-6559, ⓦwww.deltavacations.com. Good for package tours to Orlando, Miami, Daytona Beach and more.

Elderhostel ☎877/426-8056, ⓦwww.elderhostel.org. Specialists in educational and activity programs, cruises and homestays for senior travelers.

Globus and Cosmos ⓦwww.globusandcosmos.com. Request brochures online or via a listed travel agent.

International Gay & Lesbian Travel Association ☎1-800/448-8550, ⓦwww.iglta.org. Offers several tours down to the Sunshine State.

Suntrek ☎1-800/SUN-TREK, ⓦwww.suntrek.com. Group travel tours, including the $500-range Florida Sunshine trip which takes in the sights from Orlando down through the Keys.

By car

How feasible it is to **drive** to Florida naturally depends on where you live and how much time you have. If you're aiming for the bustling, tourist hot spots like Orlando and Miami, you may enjoy the option of being able to spend a few days driving around the relaxing scenery of the southeast during your trip. From both New York City and Chicago, reckon on around 20 hours of actual driving to get to Miami; from Los Angeles you'll probably need around 45 hours behind the wheel.

By train

A few years ago, the deregulation of the airline industry helped make domestic air travel as cheap as train travel. In an effort to win back business, **Amtrak** (☎1-800/USA RAIL, ⓦwww.amtrak.com) has sharpened up its act all round: raising comfort levels, offering better food, introducing "Thruway" buses to link with its trains, and launching new services. Consequently, traveling to Florida by train can be enjoyable and relaxing, if not particularly inexpensive.

From **New York**, the *Silver Meteor* and the *Silver Star* traverse the eastern seaboard daily to Miami via Orlando, while the *Silver Palm*

takes a detour at Jacksonville and continues to Miami via Tampa. Fares range from specials as low as $150 to around $400 for a round-trip ticket, and the journey from New York takes between 26 and 29 hours. From **Los Angeles** to Orlando, the *Sunset Limited* crosses the southerly reaches of the US in a three-day journey. The lowest discounted round-trip fare varies according to season from $300 to $550.

If you really can't bear to be parted from your car and you live within driving distance of Lorton, Virginia (just south of Washington DC), the **Florida Auto Train** will carry you and your vehicle to Sanford, near Orlando. The journey time is 16–17 hours and passenger fares range from $85 to $170 each way; depending on its size, your vehicle will cost an additional $150–300 each way.

All the above involve overnight travel. To spare yourself a restless night, Amtrak offers various types of **sleeping accommodation**, which will set you back an extra couple hundred bucks per night.

By bus

Long-distance travel on **Greyhound** buses (☎1 800/231 2222, ⓦwww.greyhound.com) can be an endurance test but is at least the cheapest form of public transport to the Sunshine State. Also, if you have the time and inclination to include a few stopovers on the way, you'll find that Greyhound operates a more comprehensive service than do planes or trains (they also reach all but the smallest Florida towns). Scan your local newspaper or call your local Greyhound station for special fares, which are periodically offered, and remember that midweek travel is marginally cheaper than traveling on weekends.

Otherwise, the lowest round-trip fare from either Chicago or New York to Miami is currently around $120 – no refunds allowed. A more flexible ticket (allowing an 85 percent refund) costs fifty dollars more. From LA to Miami the cheaper fare is, once again, around $120 and the more flexible one $225.

From Australia and New Zealand

Because of the enormous distance, there are **no direct flights** to Florida from Australia or New Zealand. Travelers should fly to Los Angeles or San Francisco – the main points of entry to the US – and make their way from there. Of the airlines, United Airlines, Air New Zealand and Qantas are the best at arranging trouble-free connecting services through to Miami and Orlando.

A basic round-trip **economy-class ticket** on these airlines out of Sydney or Melbourne will cost around A$1400 during the low season, A$2400 high season, while from Auckland it will be NZ$1900/2900; add NZ$100 for departures from Christchurch or Wellington. Once in the States, you'll be looking at another US$350 or so. Various coupon deals, valid within the continental US, are available with your main ticket.

If you intend to take in Florida as part of a world trip, a **round-the-world** (RTW) ticket offers the greatest flexibility. Over the last couple of years, many of the major international airlines have aligned themselves with one of two globe-spanning networks: the "Star Alliance," which links Air New Zealand, Ansett Australia, United, Lufthansa, Thai, SAS, Varig and Air Canada; and "One World," which combines routes run by American, British Airways, Canadian Airlines, Cathay Pacific, LAN Chile and Qantas. Both offer RTW deals with three stopovers in each continental sector you visit, with the option of adding additional sectors relatively cheaply. Fares depend on the number of sectors required, but start at around A$2200 (low season) for a US–Europe–Asia and home itinerary. If this is more flexibility than you need, you can save $200–300 by going with an individual airline (in concert with codeshare partners) and accepting fewer stops.

Airlines

Air Canada Australia ☎ 1300/656 232 or 02/9232 5222, New Zealand ☎ 09/377 8833, ⓦ www.aircanada.ca.
Air New Zealand Australia ☎ 13 2476, New Zealand ☎ 0800/737 000 or 09/357 3000, ⓦ www.airnz.com.
American Airlines Australia ☎ 1300/650 747, New Zealand ☎ 09/309 0735 or 0800/887 997, ⓦ www.aa.com.
Continental Airlines Australia ☎ 02/9244 2242, New Zealand ☎ 09/308 3350, ⓦ www.flycontinental.com.
Delta Air Lines Australia ☎ 02/9251 3211 or 1800/500 992, New Zealand ☎ 09/379 3370 or 0800/440 876, ⓦ www.delta-air.com.
Eva Air Australia ☎ 02/9221 0407, New Zealand ☎ 09/358 8300, ⓦ www.evaair.com.

Japan Airlines (JAL) Australia ☎ 02/9272 1111, New Zealand ☎ 09/379 9906, ⓦ www.japanair.com.
KLM Australia ☎ 1300/303 747, New Zealand ☎ 09/309 1782, ⓦ www.klm.com.
Korean Air Australia ☎ 02/9262 6000, New Zealand ☎ 09/307 3687, ⓦ www.koreanair.com.
Malaysia Airlines Australia ☎ 13 2627, New Zealand ☎ 09/373 2741 or 0800/657 472, ⓦ www.malaysiaair.com.
Northwest Airlines Australia ☎ 1300/303 747, New Zealand ☎ 09/302 1452, ⓦ www.nwa.com.
Qantas Australia ☎ 13/13 13, New Zealand ☎ 09/357 8900 or 0800/808 767, ⓦ www.qantas.com.au.
Singapore Airlines Australia ☎ 13/10 11 or 02/9350 0262, New Zealand ☎ 09/303 2129 or 0800/808 909, ⓦ www.singaporeair.com.
United Airlines Australia ☎ 13/1777, New Zealand ☎ 09/379 3800, ⓦ www.ual.com.
Virgin Atlantic Airways Australia ☎ 02/9244 2747, New Zealand ☎ 09/308 3377, ⓦ www.virgin-atlantic.com.

Travel agents

Anywhere Travel Australia ☎ 02/9663 0411 or 018 401 014, ⓔ anywhere@ozemail.com.au.
Budget Travel New Zealand ☎ 09/366 0061 or 0800/808 040.
Destinations Unlimited New Zealand ☎ 09/373 4033.
Flight Centres Australia ☎ 02/9235 3522 or for nearest branch ☎ 13 1600, New Zealand ☎ 09/358 4310, ⓦ www.flightcentre.com.au.
Northern Gateway Australia ☎ 08/8941 1394, ⓔ oztravel@norgate.com.au.
STA Travel Australia ☎ 13 1776 or 1300/360 960, New Zealand ☎ 09/309 0458 or 09/366 6673, ⓦ www.statravel.com.au.
Student Uni Travel Australia ☎ 02/9232 8444, ⓔ Australia@backpackers.net.
Thomas Cook Australia ☎ 13 1771 or 1800/801 002, New Zealand ☎ 09/379 3920, ⓦ www.thomascook.com.au.
Trailfinders Australia ☎ 02/9247 7666.
Usit Beyond New Zealand ☎ 09/379 4224 or 0800/788 336, ⓦ www.usitbeyond.co.nz.

Specialist agents and tour operators

Adventure Specialists Australia ☎ 02/9261 2927. Overland and adventure tour agent.
American Town and Country Holidays Australia ☎ 03/9877 3322. Tailor-made trips,

accommodation, car rental, and city mini-stays throughout the US.

American Travel Centre/Journeys Worldwide Australia ☏07/3221 4788. All aspects of travel to the US.

Australian Pacific Tours Australia ☏03/9277 8444 or 1800/675 222, New Zealand ☏09/279 6077. Package tours and independent travel to the US.

Canada and America Travel Specialists Australia ☏02/9922 4600, ⓦwww.canada -americatravel.com.au. Wholesalers of Greyhound Ameripasses plus flights and accommodation in North America.

Creative Holidays Australia ☏02/9386 2111, ⓦwww.creativeholidays.com.au. Packages to Miami, Orlando (including Disney World) and Fort Lauderdale.

Sydney International Travel Centre ☏02/9299 8000, ⓦwww.sydneytravel.com.au. Can help with US flights, accommodation, city stays, car rental and more.

Red tape and visas

Visas

To visit the US for a period of less than ninety days, citizens of Andorra, Argentina, Australia, Austria, Belgium, Britain, Brunei, Denmark, Finland, France, Germany, Iceland, Ireland, Italy, Japan, Liechtenstein, Luxembourg, Monaco, the Netherlands, New Zealand, Norway, Portugal, San Marino, Singapore, Slovenia, Spain, Sweden and Switzerland need only a **full passport**, a **return ticket** and a **visa waiver form**. The latter will be provided either by your travel agent or by the airline during check-in or on the plane, and must be presented to immigration on arrival. Prospective visitors from parts of the world not mentioned above must have a valid passport and a **non-immigrant visitor's visa**. To obtain a visa, fill in the application form available at most travel agents and send it with a full passport to your nearest US Embassy or Consulate. Visas are not issued to convicted criminals. You'll need to give precise dates of your trip and declare that you're not intending to live or work in the US (if you are intending to do either of these things, see "Staying on," p.48).

Immigration controls

During the flight, you'll be handed an **immigration form** (and a customs declaration: see below), which must be filled out and, after landing, given up at immigration control. Part of the form will be attached to your passport, where it must stay until you leave, when an immigration or airline official will detach it.

On the form you must give details of where you are staying on your first night (if you don't know write "touring") and the date you intend to **leave** the US. You should also be able to prove that you have enough **money** to support yourself while in the US, as anyone revealing the slightest intention of working while in the country is likely to be refused admission. You may also experience difficulties if you admit to being HIV-positive or having TB.

Customs

Customs officers will relieve you of your customs declaration and ask if you have any fresh foods. You'll also be asked if you've visited a farm in the last month: if you have, your shoes may well be taken away for inspection.

The **duty-free allowance** if you're over 17 is 200 cigarettes and 100 cigars (unless they're Cuban which are prohibited) and, if you're over 21, a liter of spirits, wine or beer.

As well as foods and anything agricultural, it's also **prohibited** to carry into the country

15

Australia
Moonhah Place, Canberra (☎ 02/6214 5600,
🌐 www.usis-australia.gov).
Denmark
Dag Hammarskjölds Allé 24, 2100 Copenhagen
(☎ 35 55 31 44, 🌐 www.usembassy.dk).
Ireland
42 Elgin St, Ballsbridge, Dublin (☎ 01/688
8777).
Netherlands
Lange Voorhout 102, 2514 EJ, The Hague
(☎ 70/310 9209, 🌐 www.usemb.nl).
New Zealand
29 Fitzherbert Terrace, Thorndon, Wellington
(☎ 644/472 2068).

Norway
Drammensveien 18, Oslo (☎ 22 44 85 50).
Spain
Serrano 75, 28006 Madrid (☎ 91587-2200,
🌐 www.embusa.es).
Sweden
Dag Hammarskjölds Väg 31, SE-11589
Stockholm (☎ 08/783 5300,
🌐 www.usis.usemb.se).
UK
24 Grosvenor Sq, London W1 (☎ 020/7499
7010, 🌐 www.usembassy.org.uk).
3 Regent Terrace, Edinburgh EH7 5BW
(☎ 0131/556 8315).
Queens House, 14 Queen St, Belfast BT1 6EQ
(☎ 028/9032 8239).

any articles from North Korea, Cuba, Iran, Iraq or Libya, obscene publications, lottery tickets, chocolate liqueurs or pre-Columbian artefacts. Anyone caught carrying drugs into the country will not only face prosecution but be entered in the records as an undesirable and probably denied entry for all time. If you take prescription medicines, it may be a good idea to carry a letter from a doctor stating the exact nature of the pills you are carrying and/or prescription, in order to ease your passage through Customs.

Extensions and leaving

The date stamped on the form in your passport is the **latest** you're legally entitled to stay. Leaving a few days after may not matter, especially if you're heading home, but more than a week or so can result in a protracted – and generally unpleasant – interrogation from officials, which may cause you to miss your flight and be denied entry to the US in the future and your American hosts and/or employer to face legal proceedings.

Although not a foolproof method, one of the simplest ways to stay on is to make a quick trip to the Bahamas: the least costly way to do this is as a $100 daytrip with Seascape Ltd (☎ 1-800/327-7400), one of

many cruise companies operating from Miami and Fort Lauderdale to the Bahamas and the Caribbean – its ads are in all the local newspapers. When you re-enter the US, you may be searched, so make sure you don't have a US library card or anything else that might indicate you have an unofficial, semi-permanent US address; your diary may also be examined. All being well, you'll routinely have a new leaving date stamped in your passport.

Alternatively, you can do things the official way and get an **extension** before your time is up. This can be done by going to the nearest **US Immigration and Naturalization Service (INS)** office (in Miami at 7880 Biscayne Blvd, ☎ 305/762-3300; other addresses will be under the "Federal Government Offices" listings at the front of the phone book). They will automatically assume that you're working illegally and it's up to you to convince them otherwise. Do this by providing evidence of ample finances and, if possible, an upstanding American citizen to vouch for your worthiness. Obviously you'll also have to explain why you didn't plan for the extra time initially – saying your money lasted longer than you expected, or that a close relative is coming over, are well-worked excuses.

Information, Web sites and maps

Advance **information** for a trip to Florida can be obtained on the Internet at Ⓦ www.flausa.com. Once in Florida, you'll find most large towns have at least a Convention and Visitors Bureau ("CVB," usual hours Mon–Fri 9am–5pm, Sat 9am–1pm), offering detailed information on the local area and discount coupons for food and accommodation, but unable to book hotel or motel rooms.

In addition there are **Chambers of Commerce** almost everywhere; these are designed to promote local business interests, but are more than happy to provide travelers with local maps and information. Most communities have local free newspapers (see "Media" p.39) carrying news of events and entertainment – the most useful of which we've detailed in the Guide.

Drivers entering Florida will find **Welcome Centers**, fully stocked with information leaflets and discount booklets, at two points: on Hwy 231 at Campbellton, near the Florida–Alabama border, and off I-75 near Jennings, just south of the Florida–Georgia line. More convenient for arrivals on I-10 are the visitor information centers at Pensacola and Tallahassee, detailed in the Guide.

As for **maps**, CVBs and Chambers of Commerce give away an excellent free one of the whole state (though the Official Transportation Map does not, as its name suggests, detail public transport routes). If you're planning to drive or cycle (see "Getting around," p.23) through rural areas, use DeLorme's highly detailed 120-page *Florida Atlas & Gazetteer* ($12.95). The best commercially available city plans are published by Rand McNally (see list below).

Local **hiking maps** are available at ranger stations in state and national parks either free or for $1–2, and some camping shops carry a supply. For traveling around more of the US, the *Rand McNally Road Atlas* is a good investment, covering the whole country plus Canada and Mexico.

Members of the American Automobile Association (AAA) and its overseas affiliates (such as both the AA and the RAC in Britain) can also benefit from their maps and general assistance. They're based at 1000 AAA Drive, Heathrow, FL 32746-5063 (℡ 1-800/336-4357, Ⓦ www.aaa.com); further offices all across the state are listed in local phone books or on their Web site.

Map outlets

In US and Canada

Adventurous Traveler Bookstore, PO Box 64769, Burlington, VT 05406 (℡ 1-800/282-3963, Ⓦ www.AdventurousTraveler.com).

Book Passage, 51 Tamal Vista Blvd, Corte Madera, CA 94925 (℡ 415/927-0960, Ⓦ www.bookpassage.com).

Distant Lands, 56 S Raymond St, Pasadena, CA 91105 (℡ 1-800/310-3220, Ⓦ www.distantlands.com).

Elliot Bay Book Company, 101 S Main St, Seattle, WA 98104 (℡ 206/624-6600 or 1-800/962-5311, Ⓦ www.elliotbaybook.com).

Forsyth Travel Library, 226 Westchester Ave, White Plains, NY 10604 (℡ 1-800/367-7984, Ⓦ www.forsyth.com).

Globe Corner Bookstore, 28 Church St, Cambridge, MA 02138 (℡ 1-800/358-6013, Ⓦ www.globecorner.com).

GORP Adventure Library online only Ⓦ www2.gorp.com.

Map Link Inc, 30 S La Patera Lane, Unit 5, Santa Barbara, CA 93117 (℡ 805/692-6777, Ⓦ www.maplink.com).

Phileas Fogg's Travel Center, #87 Stanford Shopping Center, Palo Alto, CA 94304 (℡ 1-800/533-3644, Ⓦ www.foggs.com).

Rand McNally, 444 N Michigan Ave, Chicago, IL 60611 (℡ 312/321-1751, Ⓦ www.randmcnally.com); 150 E 52nd St, New York, NY 10022 (℡ 212/758-7488); 595 Market St, San Francisco, CA 94105 (℡ 415/777-3131);

around thirty stores across the US – call ☎1-800/333-0136 ext 2111 or check the Web site for the nearest store.

Travel Books & Language Center, 4437 Wisconsin Ave, Washington, DC 20016 (☎1-800/220-2665, ⓦwww.bookweb.org/bookstore/travelers).

The Travel Bug Bookstore, 2667 West Broadway, Vancouver V6K 2G2 (☎604/737-1122, ⓦwww.swifty.com/tbug).

World of Maps, 118 Holland Ave, Ottawa, Ontario K1Y 0X6 (☎613/724-6776, ⓦwww.itmb.com).

World Wide Books and Maps, 1247 Granville St, Vancouver V6Z 1G3 (☎604/687-3320, ⓦwww.worldofmaps.com).

In UK and Ireland

Blackwell's Map and Travel Shop, 53 Broad St, Oxford OX1 3BQ (☎01865/792792, ⓦwww.bookshop.blackwell.co.uk).

Florida Web sites

Travel

MetroGuide Miami
ⓦwww.miami.metroguide .net
A comprehensive listings site for Miami, with extensive dining, nightlife and local event links.

Orlando CitySearch
ⓦwww.orlando.citysearch.com
Detailed site packed with information on Orlando's best eating, drinking and entertainment spots.

Visit Florida
ⓦwww.flausa.com
Florida's official tourism site. One of the most useful areas is their suggested driving tours, including routes focused on both Cuban and Native-American history.

Media

For information on both local and national news, weather updates, sports scores and entertainment happenings, check the following sites:

Miami Herald
ⓦwww.miami.com/herald

Orlando Sentinel
ⓦwww.orlandosentinel.com

Sun-Sentinel
ⓦwww.sun-sentinel.com

Tampa Tribune
ⓦwww.tampatrib.com

Outdoor pursuits

Everglades National Park
ⓦwww.nps.gov/ever
The national park's homepage contains all the information you'll need to visit, including directions, activities, wildfire updates and more.

Florida Scuba Connection
ⓦwww.florida-scuba.com
Comprehensive site dedicated to scuba diving in and around Florida; includes hundreds of links to local dive operators.

Great Outdoor Recreation Page
ⓦwww.gorp.com
Highly recommended outdoors site, with a list of the state's best cycling spots, and a guide to paddling through the Everglades.

South Florida Board Sailing Association
ⓦwww.sfbsa.com
The homepage for the SFBS, a nonprofit organization dedicated to windsurfing issues throughout southern Florida; includes downloadable newsletters and driving directions to the best sailing spots.

Miscellaneous

Dave Barry's Columns
ⓦwww.miami.com/herald/special/features/barry/
A direct link to the latest humorous writings of Pulitzer Prize-winning *Miami Herald* columnist Dave Barry, whose topics run the gamut from politics to toxic fruitcakes.

Hemingway Days Festival
ⓦwww.hemingwaydays.com
Official site for Key West's annual Hemingway Days Festival; click on the "Hemingway Look-a-Like Society" badge to check out past Hemingway wannabes.

Hidden Mickeys of Disney
ⓦwww.hiddenmickeys.org
Obsessive fan site that points out hundreds of the hidden Mickey Mouse carvings throughout Disney World (and Disneyland Anaheim, Disneyland Paris, etc).

Easons Bookshop, 40 O'Connell St, Dublin 1
(☎ 01/873 3811, ⓦ www.eason.ie).
Heffers Map and Travel, 20 Trinity St, Cambridge
CB2 1TJ (☎ 01223/568568, ⓦ www.heffers.co.uk).
Hodges Figgis Bookshop, 56–58 Dawson St,
Dublin 2 (☎ 01/677 4754,
ⓦ www.hodgesfiggis.com).
James Thin Melven's Bookshop, 29 Union St,
Inverness IV1 1QA (☎ 01463/233500,
ⓦ www.jthin.co.uk).
John Smith and Sons, 26 Colquhoun Ave,
Glasgow G52 4PJ (☎ 0141/552 3377,
ⓦ www.johnsmith.co.uk).
The Map Shop, 30a Belvoir St, Leicester
LE1 6QH (☎ 0116/247 1400).
National Map Centre, 22–24 Caxton St, London
SW1H 0QU (☎ 020/7222 2466,
ⓦ www.mapsnmc.co.uk).
Newcastle Map Centre, 55 Grey St, Newcastle
upon Tyne NE1 6EF (☎ 0191/261 5622,
ⓦ www.traveller.ltd.uk).
Ordnance Survey of Northern Ireland, Colby
House, Stranmillis Ct, Belfast BT9 5BJ
(☎ 028/9066 1244, ⓦ www.osni.gov.uk).
Ordnance Survey Service, Phoenix Park, Dublin

8 (☎ 01/820 6100, ⓦ www.irlgov.ie/osi/).
Stanfords, 12–14 Long Acre, London WC2E
9LP (☎ 020/7836 1321,
ⓦ www.stanfords.co.uk); maps by mail or
phone order are available on this number and
via ⓔ sales@stanfords.co.uk. Other branches
within British Airways offices at 156 Regent St,
London W1R 5TA (☎ 020/7434 4744), and 29
Corn St, Bristol BS1 1HT (☎ 0117/929 9966).
The Travel Bookshop, 13–15 Blenheim
Crescent, London W11 2EE (☎ 020/7229 5260,
ⓦ www.thetravelbookshop.co.uk).

In Australia and New Zealand
The Map Shop, 6 Peel St, Adelaide (☎ 08/8231
2033, ⓦ www.mapshop.net.au).
Mapland, 372 Little Bourke St, Melbourne
(☎ 03/9670 4383, ⓦ www.mapland.com.au).
Mapworld, 173 Gloucester St, Christchurch
(☎ 03/374 5399, ⓕ 03/374 5633,
ⓦ www.mapworld.co.nz).
Perth Map Centre, 1/884 Hay St, Perth
(☎ 08/9322 5733, ⓦ www.perthmap.com.au).
Specialty Maps, 46 Albert St, Auckland
(☎ 09/307 2217, ⓦ www.ubd-online.co.nz/maps).

Health and insurance

Even though EU health care privileges apply in Florida, residents of the **United Kingdom** would do well to take out an insurance policy before traveling to cover against theft, loss and illness or injury. Before paying for a new policy, however, it's worth checking whether you are already covered: some all-risks home insurance policies may cover your possessions when overseas, and many private medical schemes include cover when abroad. In **Canada**, provincial health plans usually provide partial cover for medical mishaps in the US, while holders of official student/teacher/youth cards in Canada and the US are entitled to meager accident coverage and hospital in-patient benefits. Students will often find that their student health coverage extends during the vacations and for one term beyond the date of last enrollment.

After exhausting the possibilities above, you might want to contact a specialist travel insurance company, or consider the travel insurance deal we offer (see box, overleaf). A typical travel insurance policy usually provides cover for the loss of baggage, tickets and – up to a certain limit – cash or checks, as well as cancellation or curtailment of your journey. Most of them exclude so-called dangerous sports unless an extra premium is paid: in Florida, this can mean scuba diving and windsurfing. Many policies can be chopped and changed to exclude coverage you don't need – for example, sickness and accident benefits can often be excluded or included at will. If you do take medical coverage, ascertain whether benefits will be paid as treatment proceeds or only after return home, and whether there is a 24-hour medical emergency number. When securing baggage cover, make sure that the per-article limit will cover your most valuable possession. If you need to make a claim, you should keep receipts for medicines and medical treatment, and in the event you have anything stolen, you must obtain an official theft report from the police.

Health

If you have a serious **accident** while in Florida, emergency medical services will get to you quickly and charge you later. For **emergencies** or ambulances, dial ☏911 (or whatever variant may be on the information plate of the pay phone). If you have an accident but don't require an ambulance, we've listed casualty departments in the Guide; ditto for **dental treatment.**

Should you need to see a doctor, lists can be found in the Yellow Pages under "Clinics" or "Physicians and Surgeons." A basic consultation fee is $50–100, payable in advance. Medication isn't cheap either – keep receipts for all you spend and claim it back on your insurance policy when you return.

The most common minor aggravations found in Florida are **sunburns** and **mosquito bites**. To avoid painful – and potentially dangerous – sunburns, apply liberal amounts of sunscreen whenever outside. Those with fair skin should wear a wide-brimmed hat and think about staying out of the sun entirely during its brightest period (11am–3pm). For more on mosquitoes, see p.45 of "The backcountry."

Rough Guide travel insurance

Rough Guides offers its own travel insurance, customized for our readers by a leading UK broker and backed by a Lloyds underwriter. It's available for anyone, of any nationality, travelling anywhere in the world.

There are two main Rough Guide insurance plans: **Essential**, for basic, no-frills cover; and **Premier** – with more generous and extensive benefits. Alternatively, you can take out **annual multi-trip insurance**, which covers you for any number of trips throughout the year (with a maximum of sixty days for any one trip). Unlike many policies, the Rough Guides schemes are calculated by the day, so if you're traveling for 27 days rather than a month, that's all you pay for. If you intend to be away for the whole year, the Adventurer policy will cover you for 365 days. Each plan can be supplemented with a "Hazardous Activities Premium" if you plan to indulge in sports considered dangerous, such as skiing, scuba diving or trekking. Rough Guides also does good deals for older travelers, and will insure you up to any age, at prices comparable to SAGA's.

For a policy quote, call the Rough Guide Insurance Line on UK freefone ☏0800/015 09 06; US freefone ☏1-866/220-5588 or, if you're calling from elsewhere ☏+44 1243/621 046. Alternatively, get an online quote at ⓦ www.roughguides.com/insurance

Costs, money and banks

To help with planning your Florida vacation, this book contains **detailed price information** for lodging and eating throughout the region. Unless otherwise stated, the **hotel price codes** given (explained on p.29) are for the cheapest double room in high season, exclusive of any local taxes which may apply, while meal prices include food only and not drinks or tip. Naturally, as time passes after the publication of the book, you should make allowances for inflation.

If you're coming from elsewhere in the States, you'll likely not find Florida any more or less expensive, save in the resorts and big cities. For foreign visitors, even when the **exchange rate** is at its least advantageous (see box overleaf), you'll find virtually everything – accommodation, food, gas, cameras, clothes and more – to be better value in the US than it is at home.

Your biggest single expense is likely to be **accommodation**. Few hotel or motel rooms in cities cost under $35 – around $50 is more usual – and rates in rural areas are little cheaper. Although hostels offering dorm beds – usually for $15–25 – exist, they are not widespread and in any case represent only a very small saving for two or more people traveling together. Camping, of course, is cheap, ranging from free to perhaps $18 per night.

As for **food**, $15 a day is enough to get you an adequate life-support diet, while for a daily budget of around $25 you can dine pretty well. Beyond this, everything hinges on how much sightseeing, taxi-taking, drinking and socializing you do.

The rates for traveling around using buses, trains and even planes, may look cheap on paper, but costs soon mount up. For a group of two or more, renting a car can be a very good investment.

Sales tax of 6.5 percent is added to virtually everything you buy in shops, but it isn't part of the marked price.

Cash and travelers' checks

US dollar travelers' checks are the best way to carry money, for both American and foreign visitors; they offer the great security of knowing that lost or stolen checks will be replaced. You should have no problem using the better-known checks, such as American Express and Visa, in shops, restaurants and filling stations (don't be put off by "no checks" signs, which only refer to personal checks). Be sure to have plenty of the $10 and $20 denominations for everyday transactions.

Major Florida banks – such as Bank of America, Barnett, First Florida, Southeast and Sun – will (with considerable fuss) change travelers' checks in other currencies and foreign currency. Commission rates tend to be lower at exchange bureaux like Deak-Perera and Thomas Cook; airport exchange offices can also be reasonable. Hotels rarely, if ever, change money.

Banking hours in Florida are generally 10am until 3pm Monday to Thursday and 10am to 5pm on Fridays.

The usual fee for travelers' check sales is one or two percent, though this fee may be waived if you buy the checks through a bank where you have an account. Make sure to keep the purchase agreement and a record of check serial numbers safe and separate from the checks themselves. In the event that checks are lost or stolen, the issuing company will expect you to report the loss forthwith to their offices (most companies claim to replace lost or stolen checks within 24 hours); see p.47 for more on what to do if your travelers' checks are lost or stolen.

Credit and debit cards

If you have a **Visa, Mastercard, Diners Club, Discover** or **American Express** card

Money: a note for foreign travelers

Regular upheaval in the world's money markets causes the relative value of the US dollar against the currencies of the rest of the world to vary considerably. Generally speaking, one pound sterling will buy between $1.45 and $1.70; one Canadian dollar is worth between 76¢ and 85¢; one Australian dollar is worth between 67¢ and 88¢; and one New Zealand dollar is worth between 55¢ and 72¢.

US currency comes in notes worth $1, $5, $10, $20, $50 and $100, plus various larger (and rarer) denominations. Confusingly, all are the same size and same green color, making it necessary to check each note carefully. The dollar is made up of 100 cents in coins of 1 cent (known as a penny), 5 cents (a nickel), 10 cents (a dime) and 25 cents (a quarter). Look out for the new "state" quarter designs being introduced one month at a time, and also the new golden "Sacagawea" dollar coin, named after the Native American women who assisted Lewis and Clark on their expeditions through the uncharted West. Very occasionally, you might come across the JFK half-dollars (50¢), Susan B. Anthony dollar coins, or a two-dollar bill. Change (quarters are the most useful) is needed for buses, vending machines and telephones, so always carry plenty.

you really shouldn't leave home without it. Almost all stores, most restaurants and many services will take some kind of plastic. In addition, hotels and car rental companies will ask for a card either to establish your credit-worthiness, or as security, or both.

With most cards it is also possible to **withdraw cash** at any bank displaying relevant stickers, or from appropriate automatic teller machines (**ATMs**) – though note you'll be charged a commission by some, which the machine will tell you. Diners Club cards can be used to cash personal checks at Citibank branches. American Express cards can only get cash, or buy travelers' checks, at American Express offices (check the Yellow Pages) or from the travelers' check dispensers at most major airports. Most Canadian credit cards issued by home-town banks will be honored in the US, as will other credit cards issued abroad.

Thanks to a relaxation in interstate banking restrictions, American holders of ATM cards from out of state are likely to discover that their cards work in the machines of select Florida banks (check with your bank before you leave home). Not only is this method of financing safer, but at around only a dollar fifty per transaction it's economical as well. Foreign travelers can also use their ATM cards, as long as they're linked to international networks such as **Cirrus** and **Plus** – though it's important to check the latest details with your credit card company before departing, as otherwise the machine may simply gobble up your plastic friend. Overseas visitors should also bear in mind that fluctuating exchange rates may result in spending more (or less) than expected when the item eventually shows up on a statement.

Wiring money

Having money wired from home using one of the companies listed below is never convenient or cheap, and should be considered a last resort. It's also possible to have money wired directly from a bank in your home country to a bank in Florida, although this is somewhat less reliable because it involves two separate institutions. If you go this route, your home bank will need the address of the branch bank where you want to pick up the money and the address and telex number of their head office, which will act as the clearing house; money wired this way normally takes two working days to arrive, and costs around £25/$40 per transaction.

Money-wiring companies

American Express Moneygram ☎ 1-800/926-9400, ⓦ www.moneygram.com.
Thomas Cook US ☎ 1-800/287-7362, Canada ☎ 1-888 /8234-7328, ⓦ www.us.thomascook.com.
Western Union ☎ 1-800/325-6000, ⓦ www.westernunion.com.

Youth and student discounts

Various official and quasi-official **youth/student ID cards** soon pay for themselves in savings. Full-time students are eligible for the International Student ID Card (ISIC), which entitles the bearer to special air, rail and bus fares and discounts at museums, theaters and other attractions. For Americans there's also a health benefit, providing up to $3000 in emergency medical coverage and $100 a day for sixty days in a hospital, plus a 24-hour hotline to call in the event of a medical, legal or financial emergency. The card costs $22 for Americans; CAN$16 for Canadians; A$16.50 for Australians; NZ$21 for New Zealanders; and £6 in the UK.

You only have to be 26 or younger to qualify for the **International Youth Travel Card**, which costs US$22/£7 and carries the same benefits. Teachers qualify for the **International Teacher Card**, offering similar discounts and costing US$22, CAN$16, A$16.50 and NZ$21. All these cards are available in the US from Council Travel, STA, Travel Cuts and, in Canada, Hostelling International (see p.12 for addresses); in Australia and New Zealand from STA or Campus Travel; and in the UK from Usit Campus and STA.

Several other travel organizations and accommodation groups also sell their own cards, good for various discounts. A university photo ID might open some doors, but is not as easily recognizable as the ISIC cards although the latter are often not accepted as valid proof of age, for example in bars or liquor stores.

Getting around

Travel in the surprisingly compact state of Florida is rarely difficult or time-consuming. Crossing between the east and west coasts, for example, takes only a couple of hours and even the longest possible trip – between the western extremity of the Panhandle and Miami – can just about be accomplished in a day. With a car you'll have no problems, but traveling by public transport requires adroit planning: cities and larger towns have bus links – and, in some cases, an infrequent train service – but many rural areas and some of the most enjoyable coastal sections are much harder to reach.

Buses

Buses are the cheapest way to travel. The only long-distance service is **Greyhound**, which links all major cities and many smaller towns. In isolated areas buses are fairly scarce, sometimes only appearing once a day, if at all – so plot your route with care. Between the big cities, buses run around the clock to a fairly full timetable, stopping only for meal breaks (almost always fast-food dives) and driver changeovers. Any sizeable community will have a Greyhound station; in smaller places the local post office or gas station doubles as the stop and ticket office.

In the Florida Keys, the bus makes scheduled stops but can also be flagged down anywhere along the Overseas Highway.

Fares – for example $39 one way between Miami and Orlando – are relatively inexpensive, and can be reduced by 15 percent if you're a student or buy your ticket at least one week in advance. If you plan on doing a lot of traveling, Greyhound's **Discovery Passes** for domestic travelers are good for unlimited travel nationwide for 7 days ($209 adult/$188 student or senior), 15 days ($319/$287), 30 days ($429/$386) and 60 days ($599/$539); the reduced rates for foreign travelers are given in the box on p.25.

Their **Web site** (ⓦ www.greyhound.com) has a useful searcheable timetable; otherwise, information can be obtained from local terminals. The phone numbers for the larger Greyhound stations are given in the Guide.

By train and Tri-Rail

A much less viable way of getting about is by **train** (run by Amtrak). Florida's railroads were built to service the boom towns of the Twenties and, consequently, some rural nooks have rail links as good as the modern cities. The actual trains are clean and comfortable, with most routes in the state offering two services a day. In some areas, Amtrak services are extended by buses, usable only in conjunction with the train.

Fares are only slightly more than the bus – $45 one way between Miami and Orlando is typical, though again there are student and advance purchase (one week) discounts.

The Tri-Rail

Designed to reduce road traffic along the congested Southeast Coast, the elevated Tri-Rail system came into operation in 1989, ferrying commuters between Miami and West Palm Beach with twelve stops on the way. The single-journey flat fare is a very cheap $2.50; the only drawback is the fact that almost all services run during rush hours – meaning a very early start, or an early evening arrival, and only six services on a Sunday.

> For Amtrak information: ☎ 1-800/USA RAIL, ⓦ www.amtrak.com.
> For Tri-Rail information: ☎ 1-800/874-7245, ⓦ www.tri-rail.com.

By plane

Provided your plans are flexible and you use the special cut-rate fares which are regularly advertised in local newspapers, off-peak plane travel within Florida is not much more expensive than taking a bus or train – and will also, obviously, get you there more quickly. Typical cut-rate one-way fares are around $75 for Miami–Orlando and $120 for Miami–Tallahassee; full fares are much higher.

For toll-free airline numbers, see p.12.

Driving and car rental

As a major vacation destination, Florida is one of the cheapest places in the US in which to **rent a car**, thanks to a very competitive market. Drivers are supposed to have held their licenses for at least one year (though this is rarely checked), and people **under 25** may very well encounter problems or restrictions when renting, usually having to pay an extra $10–25 a day. If you are under 25, always call ahead. If your are under 21 you will not be able to rent a car, period.

Car rental companies will also expect you to have a **credit card**; if you don't have one they may let you leave a hefty deposit (at least $300–500) but don't count on it. The likeliest tactic for getting a good deal is to phone the major firms' toll-free 800 numbers for their best rates – most will try to beat the offers of their competitors, so it's worth haggling. Booking through your credit card is also another way of getting good deals as many have deals with car rental companies, so give them a call as well.

In general, the **lowest rates** are available at the airport branches. Always be sure to get free unlimited mileage and be aware that leaving the car in a different city than the one in which you rent it may incur a drop-off charge of as much as $200 – though many firms do not charge drop-off fees within Florida.

Alternatively, a number of **local companies** rent out new – and not so new – vehicles: Rent-a-wreck have several offices in Florida including Orlando and Fort Lauderdale (☎ 1-800/944-7501, ⓦ www.rent-a-wreck.com), and in Miami try Alva (☎ 305/444-3923) or Inter-America Car Rental (☎ 1-800/871-3030). Other companies are listed in the Yellow Pages. Rates in Miami range from $25 to $50 a day, and $150 to $180 a week with unlimited mileage. Again, you should always check that free mileage is included in the rental cost.

When you rent a car, read the small print carefully for details on **Collision Damage Waiver** (CDW), a form of insurance which often isn't included in the initial rental charge but is well worth considering. This specifically covers the car that you are driving yourself – you are in any case insured for damage to other vehicles. At $12 to $20 a day, it can add substantially to the total cost, but

All the main American airlines (and British Airways in conjunction with USAir) offer air passes for visitors who plan to fly a lot within the US: these have to be bought in advance, and in the UK are usually sold with the proviso that you cross the Atlantic with the relevant airline. All the deals are broadly similar, involving the purchase of at least three coupons (around $375–450; with $60–100 for each additional coupon up to a maximum of ten; all depending on season and carrier), each valid for a flight of any duration in the US. Read the small print before you buy as some companies will count a connection flight as one coupon whereas some don't.

The Visit USA scheme entitles foreign travelers to a 30 percent discount on any full-priced US domestic fare, provided you buy the ticket before you leave home – but this isn't a wise choice for travel within Florida, where full-priced fares are very high.

Greyhound Discovery Passes

Foreign visitors intending to travel virtually every day by bus (which is unlikely), or to venture further around the US, can buy a Greyhound Discovery Pass, offering unlimited travel within a set time limit, before leaving home: most travel agents can oblige. Costs for adults/students are: $185/167 (7-day), $285/246 (15-day), $385/345 (30-day) or $509/458 (60-day). The passes are available from USIT or STA.

The first time you use your pass, it will be dated by the ticket clerk (this becomes the commencement date of the ticket), and your destination is written on a page which the driver will tear out and keep as you board the bus. Repeat this procedure for every subsequent journey.

Amtrak rail passes

Rail travel can't get you around all Florida, but overseas travelers have a choice of three rail passes. The least expensive, the East Region Pass, available in 15- and 30-day forms, costs £141 (£174 June–Aug) and £177 (£214) respectively. Alternatively, the National Pass entitles you to travel throughout the US, again for 15 or 30 days, for a price of £197 (£294 June–Sept 7) or £257 (£367) respectively. By combining rail with some other form of travel, you could take advantage of the 30-day Coastal Pass, permitting unlimited train travel on the country's East and West coasts; this pass costs £157 (£191 June–Aug). There is no 15-day option on the Coastal Pass.

On production of a passport issued outside the US or Canada, the passes can be bought at Amtrak stations in the US. In the UK, you can buy them from Amtrak's UK agent, Leisure Rail (☎0870/750 0222).

Car rental

UK nationals can drive in the US on a full UK driving license (International Driving Permits are not regarded as sufficient). Fly-drive deals are good value if you want to rent a car (see opposite), though you can save up to 60 percent simply by booking in advance with a major firm or booking through your credit card company. You can choose not to pay until you arrive, but make sure you take a written confirmation of the quoted price with you. Remember that it's safer not to rent a car straight off a long transatlantic flight; and that standard rental cars have automatic transmissions.

It's also easier and cheaper to book RVs (see overleaf) in advance from abroad. Most travel agents who specialize in the US can arrange RV rental, and usually do it cheaper if you book a flight through them as well. A price of £550–650 for a five-berth van for a fortnight is fairly typical.

without it you're liable for every scratch to the car – even those that aren't your fault. Some credit card companies (AMEX for example) offer automatic CDW coverage to anyone using their card to pay in full for the rental; read the fine print beforehand in any case. You'll also be charged a Florida surcharge of $2.05 per day. Be warned that many airport branches of car companies levy additional charges of up to ten percent onto the rental price – Miami doesn't, but most other Florida airports do.

If you decide to hire a bottom-of-the-range model, when you go to pick up the vehicle you will invariably be asked if you want to upgrade to a better-quality car for an apparently small extra charge. Although it may sound like a good deal, bear in mind two things: firstly, if the company has already hired out all of their bottom-of-the-range cars, they are duty-bound to give you a better car at no extra charge (a fact that they will not necessarily inform you of before asking you to upgrade); secondly, the mark-up price for a better-quality car is quoted at a daily rate, which may sound reasonable at first but quickly escalates when totaled for your entire trip, and does not include extras such as tax.

When collecting your car, ensure that it has a **full tank of gas**, as this is part of the agreement. Likewise, you are expected to return the car with a full tank, and if you don't you will probably end up paying for a whole tank even if you left it half full. Again, check the terms. Finally, check to see if it is cheaper to arrange car hire and insurance from your own country rather than to wait until you reach the US.

Car rental agencies

In North America

Alamo ☎1-800/522-9696, ⓦwww.alamo.com.
Auto Europe US ☎1-800/223-5555, Canada ☎1-888/223-5555, ⓦwww.autoeurope.com.
Avis US ☎1-800/331-1084, Canada ☎1-800/272-5871, ⓦwww.avis.com.
Budget ☎1-800/527-0700, ⓦwww.budgetrentacar.com.
Dollar ☎1-800/800-6000, ⓦwww.dollar.com.
Enterprise Rent-a-Car ☎1-800/325-8007, ⓦwww.enterprise.com.
Hertz US ☎1-800/654-3001, Canada ☎1-800/263-0600, ⓦwww.hertz.com.

National ☎1-800/227-7368, ⓦwww.nationalcar.com.
Thrifty ☎1-800/367-2277, ⓦwww.thrifty.com.

In Australia

Avis ☎13 6333, ⓦwww.avis.com.
Budget ☎1300/362 848, ⓦwww.budget.com.
Dollar ☎02/9223 1444 or 1800/358 008, ⓦwww.dollarcar.com.au.
Hertz ☎1800/550 067, ⓦwww.hertz.com.
National ☎13 1908.
Thrifty ☎1300/367 227, ⓦwww.thrifty.com.au.

In New Zealand

Avis ☎09/526 5231 or 0800/655 111, ⓦwww.avis.com.
Budget, ☎0800/652 227 or 09/375 2270, ⓦwww.budget.com.
Hertz ☎09/309 0989 or 0800/655 955, ⓦwww.hertz.com.
National ☎09/537 2582.
Thrifty ☎09/309 0111, ⓦwww.thrifty.com.nz.

In the UK

Autos Abroad ☎0870/066 7788, ⓦwww.autosabroad.co.uk.
Avis ☎0870/606 0100, ⓦwww.avisworld.com.
Budget ☎0800/181181, ⓦwww.go-budget.co.uk.
Hertz ☎0870/844 8844, ⓦwww.hertz.co.uk.
Holiday Autos ☎0870/400 0000, ⓦwww.holidayautos.com.
National ☎0870/536 5365, ⓦwww.nationalcar.com.
Thrifty ☎01494/751600, ⓦwww.thrifty.co.uk.

In Ireland

Avis Northern Ireland ☎028/9442 3333, Republic of Ireland ☎01/605 7555, ⓦwww.avis.co.uk.
Budget Northern Ireland ☎0800/181 181, Republic of Ireland ☎01/878 7814, ⓦwww.budgetcarrental.ie or www.budget-ireland.co.uk.
Hertz Northern Ireland ☎028/9442 2533, Republic of Ireland ☎0903/27711, ⓦwww.hertz.co.uk.
Holiday Autos ☎01/872 9366, ⓦwww.holidayautos.ie.

Renting an RV

Besides cars, Recreational Vehicles (or **RVs**) – those huge juggernauts that rumble down the highway complete with multiple bedrooms, bathrooms and kitchens – can be rented from around $350 per week for a basic camper on the back of a pickup truck.

These are good for groups or families traveling together, but they can be quite unwieldy on the road.

Rental outlets are not as common as you might expect, as people tend to own their own RVs. On top of the rental fees you have to take into account mileage charges, the cost of gas (some RVs do twelve miles to the gallon or less) and any drop-off charges. In addition, it is rarely legal simply to pull up in an RV and spend the night at the roadside; you are expected to stay in designated RV parks – some of which charge $35–50 per night.

The Recreational Vehicle Rental Association, 3930 University Drive, Fairfax, VA 22030 (☎703/591-7130 or 1-800/336-0355, ⊛www.rvamerica.com) publishes a newsletter and a directory of rental firms. A couple of the larger companies offering RV rentals are Cruise America (☎1-800/327-7799, ⊛www.cruiseamerica.com) and Go! Vacations (☎1-800/845-9888).

Roads

The best **roads** for covering long distances quickly are the wide, straight and fast **Interstate Highways**, usually at least six lanes and always prefixed by "I" (for example I-95) – marked on maps by a red, white and blue shield bearing the number. Even-numbered Interstates usually run east–west and those with odd numbers north–south.

A grade down are the **State and US highways** (for example Hwy-1), sometimes divided into scenic off-shoots such as Hwy-A1A, which runs parallel to Hwy-1 along Florida's east coast. There are a number of toll roads, by far the longest being the 318-mile Florida's Turnpike; tolls range from 25¢ to $6 and are often graded according to length of journey – you're given a distance marker when you enter the toll road and pay the appropriate amount when you leave. You'll also come across toll bridges, usually charging 10–25¢ to cross, sometimes as much as $3.

Even major roads in cities are technically State or US highways but are better known by their local name. Part of Hwy-1 in Miami, for instance, is more familiarly known as Biscayne Boulevard. Rural areas also have much smaller County Roads (given as Routes in the Guide, such as Route 78 near Lake Okeechobee); their number is preceded by a letter denoting their county.

Rules of the road

Although the law says that drivers must keep up with the flow of traffic, which is often hurtling along at 70mph, the **official speed limit** in Florida is 55mph (65mph on some Interstate stretches), with lower signposted limits – usually around 30-35mph – in built-up areas. A minimum speed limit of 40mph also applies on many Interstates and highways. There are no spot fines; if you get a ticket for speeding, your case will come to court and the size of the fine will be at the discretion of the judge; $75 is a rough minimum. If the police do flag you down, don't get out of the car and don't reach into the glove compartment as they may think you have a gun. Simply sit still with your hands on the wheel and turn on the inside light if it's dark; when questioned, be polite and don't attempt to make jokes.

Apart from the obvious fact that Americans drive on the right, various rules may be unfamiliar to foreign drivers. US law requires that any alcohol be carried unopened in the trunk of the car; it's illegal to make a U-turn on an Interstate or anywhere where a single unbroken line runs along the middle of the road; it's also illegal to park on a highway, and for front-seat passengers to ride without fastened seatbelts.

Motoring organizations

In North America
American Automobile Association (AAA). Each state has its own club – check the phone book for local address and phone number (or call ☎1-800/222-4357; ⊛www.aaa.com).
Canadian Automobile Association (CAA) ☎613/247-0117, ⊛www.caa.com. Each region has its own club – check the phone book for local address and phone number.

In the UK and Ireland
RAC ☎0800/550055, ⊛www.rac.co.uk.
AA ☎0800/444500, ⊛www.theaa.co.uk.
AA Travel, Dublin ☎01/617 9988, ⊛www.aaireland.ie.

In Australia and New Zealand
Australian Automobile Association ☎02/6247 7311.
New Zealand Automobile Association ☎09/377 4660.

At junctions, you can turn right on a red light if there is no traffic approaching from the left; and some junctions are four-way stops: a crossroads where all traffic must stop before proceeding in order of arrival.

It can't be stressed too strongly that **Driving Under the Influence** (DUI) is a very serious offence. If a police officer smells alcohol on your breath, he/she is entitled to administer a breath, saliva or urine test. If you fail, they'll lock you up with other inebriates in the "drunk tank" of the nearest jail until you sober up – and, controversially, in some parts of the state they're empowered to suspend your driving license immediately. Your case will later be heard by a judge, who can fine you $200 or, in extreme (or repeat) cases, imprison you for thirty days.

Parking

Parking meters are common in cities; their charge for an hour ranges from 25¢ to $1. Parking lots generally charge $2–3 an hour, $6–10 per day. If you park in the wrong place (such as within ten feet of a fire hydrant) your car is likely to be towed away, or wheel-clamped – a sticker on the windscreen will tell you where to pay the $30–45 fine. Whenever possible, **park in the shade**; if you don't, you might find the car too hot to touch when you return to it – temperatures inside cars parked in the full force of the Florida sun can reach 140°F.

Breakdowns

If you **break down** in a rented car, there'll be an emergency number pinned to the dashboard. Otherwise you should sit tight and wait for the Highway Patrol or State Police, who cruise by regularly. Raising the hood of your car is recognized as a call for assistance, though women traveling alone should, obviously, be wary of doing this. Another tip, for women especially, is to rent a mobile telephone from the car hire agency – you often have to pay only a nominal amount until you actually use it, but having a phone can be reassuring and even a potential life-saver.

Hitching

Where it's legal, **hitching** may be the cheapest way to get around but it is also the most unpredictable and potentially very dangerous, especially for women traveling alone. We don't advise it, but if you're going to, follow some common-sense rules: make sure you sit next to a door that's unlocked, keep your luggage within reach, refuse the ride if you feel unsure of the driver and demand to be let out if you become suspicious of his/her intentions.

Hitching is illegal in Miami and on the outskirts of many other cities and in whole counties; indeed, it is always prohibited to wait for a lift by standing on the road (as opposed to beside it on the pavement or grass verge) or by a freeway entrance sign – rules which are enforced. On Interstates, thumb from the entrance ramps only. Another, slightly less risky, technique is to strike up a conversation with likely-looking drivers in roadside diners or gas stations. Safer still is to scrutinize the "ride boards" on university campuses, though drivers found this way will usually expect a contribution towards fuel costs.

Cycling

Cycling is seldom a good way to get around the major cities (with the exception of some sections of Miami), but many smaller towns are quiet enough to be pleasurably explored by bicycle, there are many miles of marked cycle paths along the coast, and long-distance bike trails crisscross the state's interior. Cycling is gaining popularity among Floridians, too, and a free monthly magazine, *Florida Bicyclist,* is aimed at the growing band of devoted pedalers; find it in bookshops and bike shops or on street corners.

Bikes can be **rented** for $8–15 a day, $35–70 a week, from many beach shops and college campuses, some state parks and virtually any place where cycling is a good idea; outlets are listed in the Guide.

The best cycling areas are in North Central Florida, the Panhandle and in parts of the Northeast Coast. By contrast, the southeast coastal strip is heavily congested and many south Florida inland roads are narrow and dangerous. Wherever you cycle, avoid the heaviest traffic – and the midday heat – by doing most of your pedaling before noon.

For free biking information and detailed maps ($2–15) of cycling routes, write to the State Bicycle Program, Florida Department of Transportation, 605 Suwannee St, Tallahassee, FL 32399-0450 (☎805 /488-3111, ⑩www.dot.state.fl.us/safety/ ped-bike/ped-bike.htm). You can get the same maps from most youth hostels.

Accommodation

Accommodation costs inevitably account for a significant proportion of the expenses for any traveler in Florida, though you often get good value for what you pay. If you're on your own, it's possible to pare costs by sleeping in dormitory-style hostels, where a bed can cost from $15 to $25. Youth hostels in Florida, however, are few and far between, with just two affiliated to the IYHA (International Youth Hostel Association), in Key West and Clearwater, for the whole west coast; there's also a non-affiliated hostel just outside the Everglades.

Groups of two or more will find it little more expensive to stay in the far more plentiful motels and hotels, where basic rooms away from the major cities typically cost anything upwards of $40 a night. Many hotels will set up a third single bed for around $5–10 on top of the regular price, reducing costs for three people sharing. By contrast, the lone traveler will have a hard time of it: "singles" are usually double rooms at an only slightly reduced rate. Prices quoted by hotels and motels are almost always for the actual room rather than for each person using it.

Motels are plentiful on the main approach roads to cities, around beaches and by the main road junctions in country areas. High-rise **hotels** predominate along the popular sections of the coast and are sometimes the only accommodation in city centers. In major cities **campgrounds** tend to be on the outskirts, if they exist at all.

Wherever you stay, you'll be expected to **pay in advance**, at least for the first night and perhaps for further nights too, particularly if it's high season and the hotel's expecting to be busy. Payment can be in cash or in dollar travelers' checks, though it's more common to give your credit card number and sign for everything when you leave. **Reservations** are only held until 5pm or 6pm unless you've told the hotel you'll be arriving late. Most of the larger chains have an advance booking form in their brochures and will make reservations at another of their premises for you – in any case, you should book ahead wherever possible, especially in big cities and popular stretches of coast.

Accommodation price codes

It's a fact of Florida resort life that the plain and simple motel room, which costs $30 on a weekday in low season, is liable to cost two or three times that amount on a weekend in high season. To further complicate matters, high and low season vary depending on whether you're in north or south Florida, and some establishments that depend on business travelers for their trade (such as those in downtown areas, distanced from the nearest beach) will actually be cheaper on weekends than on weekdays. Local events – such as a Space Shuttle launch on the Space Coast, or Spring Break in Panama City Beach – can also cause prices to increase dramatically.

Throughout the book, we've graded accommodation prices according to the cost of the least expensive double room throughout most of the year – but do allow for the fluctuations outlined above.

❶ up to $40 ❸ $60–80 ❺ $100–130 ❼ $175–250
❷ $40–60 ❹ $80–100 ❻ $130–175 ❽ $250 and upwards

Hotels and motels

While **motels** and **hotels** essentially offer the same things – double rooms with bathroom, TV and phone – motels are often one-off affairs run by their owners and tend to be cheaper (typically $30–45) than hotels ($45–75), which are likely to be part of a nationwide chain. All but the cheapest motels and hotels have pools for guests' use and many offer cable TV and free local phone calls. Under $60, rooms tend to be similar in quality and features; spend $60–70 in rural areas or $80–100 in the cities and you get more luxury – a larger room and often additional facilities such as a tennis court, gym and golf course. Paying over $150 brings all the above, plus likely an ocean view and some upmarket trappings.

Alternatively, there are a number of unexciting but dependable **budget-priced chain hotels**, which, depending on location, cost around $40–60; the cheapest are Days Inn, Econo Lodge, Hampton Inns, Knights Inns and Red Carpet Inns. Higher up the scale are mid-range chains like Best Western, Howard Johnson's (now usually abbreviated to HoJo's), TraveLodge and La Quinta – though if you can afford their prices (usually $75–125), there's normally somewhere nicer to stay.

On your travels you'll also come across **resorts**, which are motels or hotels equipped with a restaurant, bar and private beach – on average these cost $70–110; and efficiencies, which are motel rooms adapted to offer cooking facilities – ranging from a stove squeezed into a corner to a fully equipped kitchen – usually for $10–15 above the basic room rate.

There are of course – especially in cities – plenty of **high-end establishments**, which can cost just about any amount of money, depending on the luxury – we've pointed out which ones are atmospheric and worthwhile in the Guide.

Since inexpensive diners are everywhere, very few hotels or motels bother to offer **breakfast**, though there's a trend towards providing free coffee (from paper cups) and sticky buns on a self-service basis from the lobby.

Discount options

During **off-peak periods** many motels and hotels struggle to fill their rooms and it's worth **haggling** to get a few dollars off the asking price. Staying in the same place for more than one night will bring further reductions. In addition, pick up the many **discount coupons** that fill tourist information offices and welcome centers (see p.17), and look out for the free *Traveler Discount Guide*. Read the small print, though: what appears to be an amazingly cheap room rate sometimes turns out to be a per-person charge for two people sharing and limited to midweek.

Many of the higher-rung hotel chains offer **pre-paid discount vouchers**, which in theory save you money if you're prepared to pay in advance. To take advantage of such schemes, British travelers must purchase the vouchers in the UK, at a usual cost of £50–70. Most rooms are one voucher per night (for one–four people), though some posher places charge two, and others two during high season. However, it's hard to think of a good reason to buy them; you may save a nominal amount on the fixed rates, but better-value accommodation is not exactly difficult to find in the US, and you may well regret the inflexibility imposed upon your travels. Most UK travel agents will have details of the various voucher schemes. The cheapest is the "Liberty Hotel Pass" deal offered by Days Inn, Howard Johnson's, Knights Inn, Ramada and TraveLodge; the UK sales office is at Stamford House, Woodbridge Rd, Guildford, Surrey GU1 4QD (℡01483/440470, ⓦwww.libertyhotelpass.co.uk). They can supply you with a directory of hotels in the scheme and can make reservations for you.

Bed and breakfasts

Typically, **bed and breakfast** inns, as they're usually known, are restored buildings in the smaller cities and more rural areas. If you're a fan, be aware that they are often not recommended by visitor centers (especially if they lack the amenities of more modern and more mundane motels), so you'll need to specifically ask for bed and breakfast listings. Most towns throughout Florida have a so-called historic section, and it is worth driving around to discover bed and breakfasts in the most serene surroundings. Even the larger establishments tend to have less than ten rooms, sometimes without TV and phone but always with flowers, stuffed cushions and an almost contrived homely atmosphere; others may just be a couple of furnished rooms in someone's home.

While always including a huge and wholesome breakfast (five courses are not unheard of), prices vary greatly: anything from $45 to $200 depending on location and season; most cost between $60 and $80 per night for a double. Bear in mind, too, that most are booked well in advance, making it sensible to contact either the inn directly (details are given throughout the Guide) or one of the agents below at least a month ahead – longer in high season.

YMCA/YWCAs and hostels

At around $14–18 (a few dollars more for non-members) per night per person, **hostels** are clearly the cheapest accommodation option other than camping. There are two main kinds of cheap, hostel-like accommodation in the US: **YMCA/YWCA hostels** (known as "Ys"), offering accommodation for both sexes or, in a few cases, women only; and official **American Youth Hostels (AYH)**. In Florida you'll find AYH youth hostels in Miami Beach, Daytona Beach, St Augustine, Fort Lauderdale, Key West, Orlando and Clearwater near St Petersburg. You can make reservations through the International Booking Network (IBN), and for a small booking fee the Hostelling International association in your home country can reserve accommodation before leaving home (see boxes below and overleaf for contact information). This has the advantage of putting a confirmation slip in your hand, which you won't have if telephone-booking long distance once in the United States.

Particularly if you're traveling in high season, it's advisable to book ahead through one of the specialist travel agents or international youth hostel offices. Some hostels will allow you to use a sleeping bag, though officially they should (and many do) insist on a sheet

---

Youth Hostel Associations

USA
Hostelling International-American Youth Hostels (HI-AYH), 733 15th St NW, Suite 840, PO Box 37613, Washington, DC 20005 (☎202/783-6161, ⓦwww.hiayh.org). Annual membership for adults (18–55) is $25, for seniors (55 or over) is $15, and for under-18s is free. Lifetime memberships are $250.

Canada
Hostelling International/Canadian Hostelling Association, Room 400, 205 Catherine St, Ottawa, Ontario K2P 1C3 (☎1-800/663-5777 or 613/237-7884, ⓦwww.hostellingintl.ca). Rather than sell the traditional one- or two-year memberships, the association now sells one Individual Adult membership with a 28- to 16-month term. The length of the term depends on when the membership is sold, but a member can receive up to 28 months of membership for just $35. Membership is free for under-18s and you can become a lifetime member for $175.

England and Wales
Youth Hostel Association (YHA), Trevelyan House, 8 St Stephen's Hill, St Albans, Herts AL1 2DY (☎0870/870 8808, ⓦwww.yha.org.uk and www.iyhf.org, ⓔcustomerservices@yha.org.uk). Annual membership £12.50, for under-18s £6.25.

Scotland
Scottish Youth Hostel Association, 7 Glebe Crescent, Stirling FK8 2JA (☎0870/1553 255, ⓦwww.syha.org.uk). Annual membership £6, for under-18s £2.50.

Ireland
An Óige, 61 Mountjoy St, Dublin 7 (☎01/8304555, ⓦwww.irelandyha.org). Adult (and single parent) membership IR£10; family (two parents and children under 16) IR£4; under-18s IR£4.
Hostelling International Northern Ireland, 22–32 Donegall Rd, Belfast BT12 5JN (☎028/9032 4733, ⓦwww.hini.org.uk). Adult membership £10, under-18s £6; family £20.

Australia
Australia Youth Hostels Association, 422 Kent St, Sydney (☎02/9261 1111, ⓦwww.yha.com.au). Adult membership rate A$49 for the first twelve months and then A$32 each year after.

New Zealand
New Zealand Youth Hostels Association, 173 Gloucester St, Christchurch (☎03/379 9970, ⓦwww.yha.co.nz). Adult membership NZ$40 for one year, NZ$60 for two and NZ$80 for three.

sleeping bag, which can usually be rented at the hostel. The maximum stay at each hostel is technically three days, though this is again a rule that is often ignored if there's space. Few hostels provide meals, but most have cooking facilities, and there's sometimes a curfew of around midnight: alcohol, smoking and, of course, drugs are banned.

The informative *American Youth Hostel Handbook* ($5) is available from hostels in the US, or direct from the AYH national office (see p.31). For overseas hostelers, the *International Youth Hostel Handbook* provides a full list of hostels. In Britain it's available from the Youth Hostel Association headquarters (see p.31). Handbooks and membership are also available from the privatized YHA shops – find your nearest by looking on the Internet at ⓦ www.yhaadventure.com.

IBN booking centers

Australia (Sydney) ☎ 02/9261 1111
Canada (Ontario) ☎ 1-800/663-5777
UK (London) ☎ 020/ 7836 1036
New Zealand (Auckland) ☎ 09/309 2802

Camping

Florida **campgrounds** range from the primitive (a flat piece of ground that may or may not have a water tap) to others that are more like open-air hotels with shops, restaurants and washing facilities. Naturally, prices vary according to amenities, ranging from nothing at all for the most basic plots to up to $35 a night for something comparatively luxurious. There are plenty of campgrounds but often plenty of people intending to use them: take special care over plotting your route if you're camping during public holidays or weekends, when many sites will be either full or very crowded. By contrast, some of the more basic campgrounds in state and national parks will often be completely empty

midweek. For camping in the wilderness, there's a nightly charge of $3 payable at the area's administrative office.

Privately run campgrounds are everywhere, their prices ranging from $8 to $35, and the best are listed throughout the Guide; for a fuller list, write for the free *Florida Camping Directory* to the Florida Campground Association, 1340 Vickers Drive, Tallahassee, FL 32303-3041 (☎ 904/562-7151, ⓦ www .floridacamping.com). State parks – there are over 300 in Florida – are often excellent places to camp; sites cost $5–20 for up to four people sharing. Never more than half the space is reserved, the rest goes on a first-come first-served basis (bear in mind that park offices close at sunset; you won't be able to camp there if you arrive later). Reservations can be made within two months of arrival by phone only, and stays are limited to fourteen days. Reservations won't be held after 5pm unless previously arranged. If you're doing a lot of camping in state parks, get the two free leaflets, *Florida State Parks Camping Reservations Procedures* and *Florida State Parks Fees Schedule* from any state park office, or by writing to the Department of Natural Resources, Division of Recreation and Parks, 3900 Commonwealth Blvd, Tallahassee, FL 32399 (☎ 850/488-9872, ⓦ www.myflorida .com/communities/learn/stateparks/index .html).

Similarly priced campgrounds exist in National Parks and National Forests – see the details throughout the Guide, or contact the National Park Service, PO Box 2416, Tallahassee, FL 32316 (☎ 850/580-3011, ⓦ www.nps.gov) and the US Forest Service, 325 John Knox Rd, Suite F-100, Tallahassee, FL 32303 (☎ 850/922-2103, ⓦ www.fs.fed.us/recreation/).

However desolate it may look, much of undeveloped Florida is, in fact, private land and rough camping is illegal. For **permitted rough camping**, see "The backcountry" p.43.

Food and drink

Florida has a mass of restaurants, fast-food outlets, cafés and coffee shops on every main street, all trying to outdo one another with their cut-price daily specials. In every town mentioned in this book you'll find reviews of the full range of eating options.

Fresh fish and **seafood** are abundant all over Florida, as is the high-quality produce of the state's cattle farms – served as ribs, steaks and burgers – and junk food is as common as anywhere else in the country. But the choice of what to eat is influenced by where you are. In the northern half of the state, the accent is on wholesome cooking – traditional Southern dishes such as grits, cornbread and fried chicken. As you head south through Florida, this gives way to the most diverse and inexpensive gathering of Latin American and Caribbean cuisines to be found anywhere in the US – you can feast on anything from curried goat to mashed plantains and yucca.

Breakfast

For the price (on average $3–5) breakfast makes a good-value, very filling start to the day. Go to a **diner**, **café** or **coffee shop**, all of which are very similar and usually serve breakfast until at least 11am (some continue all day) – though there are special deals at earlier times, say 6–8am, when the price may be even less.

Lunches and snacks

The Florida workforce takes its lunch break between 11.30am and 1.30pm, during which hours all sorts of low-cost **set menus** and all-you-can-eat specials are on offer – generally excellent value. Most Cuban restaurants and fishcamps (see "Dining Out," overleaf) are exceptionally well priced all the time and you can get a good-sized lunch in one for $4–5. **Buffet restaurants** – most of which also serve breakfast and dinner – are found in most cities and towns; $6–8 lets you pig out as much as you can from a wide variety of hot dishes.

As you'd expect, there's also **pizza**; count on paying $7–12 for a basic two-person pizza at national chains and local outlets. If it's a warm day and you can't face hot food, find a deli (see below) with a salad bar, where you can help yourself for $3. Frozen yogurt or ice cream may be all you feel like eating in the midday heat: look for exotic versions made with mango and guava sold by Cuban vendors.

Snacks

For **quick snacks**, many **supermarket deli** counters do ready-cooked meals for $4–5,

Free food and brunch

Some **bars** are used as much by diners as drinkers, who fill up on the free **hors d'oeuvres** laid out by a lot of city bars between 5pm and 7pm Monday to Friday – an attempt to nab the commuting classes before they head off to the suburbs – and sometimes by beachside bars to grab beach-goers before they head elsewhere for the evening. For the price of a drink you can stuff yourself with chilli, seafood or pasta.

Brunch is another deal to look out for: indulged in on weekends between 11am and 2pm. For a set price ($8 and up) you get a light meal (or even a groaning buffet) and a variety of complimentary cocktails or champagne. We've listed the most interesting venues in the Guide.

as well as a range of salads and sandwiches. Bagels are also common, while **street stands** sell hot dogs, burgers or a slice of pizza for around $1–2; in Miami, **Cuban fast-food stands** serve crispy pork sandwiches and other spicy snacks for $2–3, and most shopping malls have ethnic fast-food stalls, often pricier than street stands but usually with edible and filling fare. Bags of fresh oranges, grapefruit and watermelons are often sold from the roadside in rural areas, as are **boiled peanuts** – a dollar buys a steaming bagful. Southern **fast-food chains** like Popeye's Famous Fried Chicken and Sonny's Real Pit Bar-B-Q will satisfy your hunger for $3–4, but are only marginally better than the inevitable burger chains. **Coffee shops** appear all through Florida, providing a huge array of basic cooking in relaxed surroundings.

Dining out

Even if it sometimes seems swamped by the more fashionable regional and ethnic cuisines, traditional **American cooking** is found all over Florida. Portions are big and you start with salad, eaten before the main course arrives; look out for heart of palm salad, based around the delicious vegetable at the heart of the sable palm tree. Main dishes are dominated by enormous steaks, burgers, piles of ribs or half a chicken. Vegetables include French fries or a baked potato.

Southern cooking makes its presence felt throughout the northern half of the state. Vegetables such as okra, collard greens, black-eyed peas, fried green tomatoes and fried eggplant are added to staples such as fried chicken, roast beef and **hogjaw** – meat from the mouth of a pig. Meat dishes are usually accompanied by cornbread to soak up the thick gravy poured over everything; with fried fish, you'll get **hush puppies** – fried corn balls with tiny bits of chopped onion. Okra is also used in gumbo soups, a feature of **Cajun** cooking, which originated in nearby Louisiana as a way of using up leftovers. A few (usually expensive) Florida restaurants specialize in Cajun food but many others have a few Cajun items (such as red beans and rice and hot and spicy shrimp and steak dishes) on their menu.

Alligator is on many menus: most of the meat comes from alligator farms, which cull a certain number each year. The tails are deep-fried and served in a variety of styles – none of which makes much of a mark on the bland, chicken-like taste. **Frogs' legs** also crop up occasionally.

Regional *nouvelle cuisine* is largely too pretentious and expensive for the typical Floridian palate, although some restaurants in the larger cities do extraordinary and inspired things with local fish and the produce of the citrus farms, creating small but beautifully presented affairs for around $40–50 a head.

Almost wherever you eat you'll be offered **Key Lime Pie** as a dessert, a dish which began life in the Florida Keys, made from the small limes that grow there. The pie is similar to lemon meringue but with a sharper taste. Quality varies greatly; take local advice to find a good outlet and your tastebuds will tell you why many swear by it.

Fish and seafood

Florida excels with **fish and seafood** – which is great news for non-meat-eaters. Even the shabbiest restaurant is likely to have an excellent selection, though fish comes freshest and cheapest at **fishcamps**, rustic places right beside the river where your meal was swimming just a few hours before; a fishcamp lunch or dinner will cost around $5–9. Catfish tends to top the bill, but you'll also find grouper, dolphin (the fish not the mammal, sometimes known by its Hawaiian name, mahimahi), mullet, tuna and swordfish, any of which (except catfish, which is nearly always fried) may be boiled, grilled, fried or "blackened" (charcoal-grilled). Of **shellfish**, the tender claws of **stone crabs**, eaten dipped in butter, raise local passions during their mid-October to mid-May season; spiny (or "Florida") lobster is smaller and more succulent than its more famous Maine rival; oysters can be extremely fresh (the best come from Apalachicola) and are usually eaten raw (though best avoided during summer, when they carry a risk of food poisoning) – many restaurants have special "raw bars," where you can also consume meaty shrimp, in regular and jumbo sizes. Another popular crustacean is the very chewy **conch** (pronounced "konk"); abundant throughout the Florida Keys, they usually come deep-fried as fritters served up with various sauces, or as a chowder-like soup.

Ethnic cuisine

Florida's **ethnic cuisines** become increasingly exotic the further south you go. In Miami, **Cuban food** is extremely easy to find and can be very good value. Most Cuban dishes are meat-based: frequently pork, less often beef or chicken, always fried (including the skin, which becomes a crispy crackling) and usually heavily spiced, served with a varying combination of yellow or white rice, black beans, plantains (a sweet, banana-like vegetable) and yucca (cassava) – a potato-like vegetable completely devoid of taste. Seafood crops up less often, most deliciously in thick soups, such as *sopa de mariscos* – shellfish soup. Unpretentious Cuban diners serve a filling lunch or dinner for under $6, though a growing number of upmarket restaurants will charge three times as much for identical food. In busy areas, many Cuban cafés have street windows where you buy a thimble-sized cup of sweet and rich *café Cubano* – Cuban coffee – strong enough to make your hair stand on end; also available is *café con leche*, coffee with warm milk or cream, though it's strictly for the unadventurous and regarded by Cubans as a children's drink. If you want a cool drink in Miami, look out for roadside stands offering *coco frio* – coconut milk sucked through a straw directly from the coconut, for $1.

Although nowhere near as prevalent as Cuban cooking, foods from other parts of the **Caribbean** and **Latin America** are easily located around Miami: Haitian, Argentinian, Colombian, Nicaraguan, Peruvian, Jamaican and Salvadorean restaurants also serve the city's diverse migrant populations – at very affordable prices.

Service and tipping

Foreign travelers should note to top up the bill in restaurants by 15–20 percent; a little less perhaps at a bar.

Other ethnic cuisines turn up all around the state, too. **Chinese** food is everywhere and often very cheap, as is **Mexican**, though many Mexican restaurants are more popular as places to knock back margaritas than to eat in; **Japanese** is more expensive; **Italian** food is popular but can be expensive once you leave the simple pastas and explore the more gourmet-inclined Italian regional cooking in the major cities. **French** food, too, is widely available, though pricey. **Thai**, **Korean** and **Indonesian** food is similarly city-based, though usually cheaper; Indian restaurants, on the other hand, are thin on the ground just about everywhere. More plentiful are well-priced, family-run **Greek** restaurants, and a smattering of **Minorcan** places are evidence of one of Florida's earliest groups of European settlers.

Drinking

Most drinking in Florida is done in restaurant or hotel lounges, at fishcamps (see "Dining Out," opposite) or in "tiki bars," open-sided straw-roofed huts beside a beach or hotel pool. Some beachside bars, especially in Daytona Beach and Panama City Beach, are split-level, multi-purpose affairs with discos and stages for live bands – and take great pride in being the birthplace of the infamous wet T-shirt contest (nowadays sometimes joined by G-string

Latin American food terms

Ajiaco criollo	Meat and root vegetable stew	*Pan*	Bread
Arroz	Rice	*Pan con lechon*	Crispy pork sandwich
Arroz con leche	Rice pudding	*Piccadillo*	Minced meat, usually beef, served with peppers and olives
Bocadillo	Sandwich		
Chicarones de pollo	Fried chicken crackling		
Frijoles	Beans	*Pollo*	Chicken
Frijoles negros	Black beans	*Puerca*	Pork
Maduros	Fried plantains	*Sopa de mariscos*	Shellfish soup
Masitoas de puerca	Fried spiced pork	*Sopa de plantanos*	Meaty, plantain soup
Morros y Christianos	Literally "Moors and Christians," black beans and white rice	*Tostones*	Fried mashed plantains
		Vaca	Beef

and "best legs" shows), an exercise in unrestrained sexism that shows no signs of declining in popularity among a predominantly late-teen and twenty-something clientele.

To buy and consume alcohol **you need to be 21** and could well be asked for ID even if you look much older. Recent clampdowns have resulted in bars "carding" anyone who looks 30 and under. Licensing laws and drinking hours vary from area to area, but generally alcohol can be bought and drunk in a bar, nightclub or restaurant any time between 10am and 2am. More cheaply, you can usually buy beer, wine or spirits in supermarkets and, of course, liquor stores, from 9am to 11pm Monday to Saturday and from 1pm to 11pm on Sundays. Note that it is illegal to consume alcohol in a car, on most beaches and in all state parks, with a possible fine of $100 or more.

Beer

A small band of Florida **microbreweries** (tiny, one-off operations) create interesting beers, though rarely are these sold beyond their own bar or restaurant. It's more common for discerning beer drinkers to stick to imported brews, the most widely available of which are the Mexican brands Bohemia, Corona and Dos Equis. Don't forget that in all but the more pretentious bars, several people can save money by buying a quart or half-gallon **pitcher** of beer. If bar prices are a problem, you can stock up with **six-packs** from a supermarket at $5–7 for domestic, $8–12 for imported brews.

Wine and cocktails

If **wine** is more to your taste, try to visit one of the state's fast-improving wineries: several can be toured and their products sampled for free. One of the most successful is Chautauqua Vineyards, in De Funiak Springs in the Panhandle (see p.418). In a bar or restaurant, however, beside a usually threadbare stock of European wines, you'll find a selection from Chile and California. Cabernet Sauvignon is certainly worth trying – a light, drinkable red; other reds typically available include Burgundy, Merlot and Pinot Noir. Among the whites, Chardonnay is very dry and full of flavor and generally preferred to Sauvignon Blanc or Fumé Blanc, though these have their devotees. It's fairly inexpensive: a glass of wine in a bar or restaurant costs from around $4–6, a bottle $15–30. Buying a bottle from a supermarket can prove cheaper still.

Cocktails are extremely popular, especially rich fruity ones consumed while gazing over the ocean or into the sunset. Varieties are innumerable, sometimes specific to a single bar or cocktail lounge, and most will cost $5–10. Cocktails and all other drinks come cheapest during **happy hours** (usually 5–7pm; sometimes much longer) when many are half-price and there might be a buffet thrown in.

Mail, phones and email

It won't be hard to make contact with anyone back at home when in Florida, though the laid-back attitude prevalent in the Florida Keys may get through to the postal system there.

Mail

Post offices are usually open Monday to Friday 9am–5pm and Saturday 9am–noon, and there are blue mail boxes on many street corners. Ordinary mail within the US costs 34¢ for a letter weighing up to an ounce; addresses must include the zip code (postal code), as well as the sender's address on the envelope. **Air mail** between Florida and Europe generally takes about four days to a week to arrive. Postcards, aerograms and letters weighing up to an ounce (a single sheet) cost 80¢.

Letters can be sent c/o General Delivery (what's known elsewhere as poste restante) to any post office in the state but must include the post office's zip code and will only be held for thirty days before being returned to sender – so make sure there's a return address on the envelope. If you're receiving mail at someone else's address, it should include "c/o" and the regular occupant's name; otherwise it, too, is likely to be returned.

Rules on sending parcels are very rigid: packages must be in special containers bought from post offices and sealed according to their instructions, which are given at the start of the *Yellow Pages*. To send anything out of the country, you'll need a customs declaration form, available from a post office. Postal rates for sending a parcel airmail, weighing up to 1lb, are $16.50 to Europe, $14.50 to Australasia – by land prices are about a third and take six times as long to get there.

Telephones

Florida's **telephones** are run by several companies, the largest being Southern Bell, all of which are linked to the AT&T network.

Public telephones invariably work and are easily found – on street corners, in train and bus stations, hotel lobbies, bars, restaurants – and they take 25¢, 10¢ and 5¢ coins. The cost of a **local call** from a public phone varies according to the actual distance being called. The minimum is 25¢ for the first three minutes and a further 10¢ for each additional three minutes – when necessary, a voice will come on the line telling you to pay more.

More expensive are **non-local calls** ("zone calls"), to numbers within the same area code (commonly, vast areas are covered by a single code) but costing much more and sometimes requiring you to dial 1 before the seven-digit number. Pricier still are **long-distance calls** (ie to a different area code), for which you'll need plenty of change. If you still owe money at the end of the call, the phone will ring immediately and you'll be asked for the outstanding amount (if you don't cough up, the person you've been calling will get the bill). Non-local calls and long-distance calls are far cheaper if made between 6pm and 8am, and calls from **private phones** are always much cheaper than those from public phones.

Florida area codes

305 Miami and the Florida Keys
386 Daytona Beach
407 Orlando and surrounds and the central section of the East Coast
561 The Southeast Coast north of Palm Beach
850 All the Panhandle east of and including Tallahassee
904 Most of the Northeast Coast, North Central Florida, and some of the northern parts of the West Coast
941 Most of the West Coast and parts of South Central Florida including Dade and DeSoto counties

Making telephone calls from **hotel rooms** is usually more expensive than from a payphone (and there are usually payphones in hotel lobbies). On the other hand, some budget hotels offer free local calls from rooms – ask when you check in. An increasing number of phones accept **credit cards** – simply swipe the card through the slot and dial. Another way to avoid the necessity of carrying copious quantities of change everywhere is to obtain a pre-paid **AT&T charge card** (information on ☏ 1-800/361-4470).

Many government agencies, car rental firms, hotels and other services have **toll-free numbers**, for which you don't have to pay anything: these numbers have the prefix 1-800, 1-877 or 1-888. Some lines, such as ☏ 1-800/777-HEAT to get the latest on the Miami Heat basketball team, employ the letters on the push-button phones as part of their "number."

Phoning home

One of the most convenient ways of phoning home is via a **telephone charge card**, with which you can make calls from most hotel, public and private phones that will be charged to your own account. While rates are always cheaper from a residential phone at off-peak rates, that's normally not an option when you're traveling (if you do use a calling card in conjunction with a residential phone, when you're staying as a guest, for instance, you will be paying the calling card company's rates, which will usually be more expensive than the local operator's). You

may be able to use it to minimize hotel phone surcharges, but don't depend on it. However, the benefit of calling cards is mainly one of convenience, as rates aren't necessarily cheaper than calling from a public phone and can't compete with the discounted off-peak times many local phone companies offer. But since most major charge cards are free to obtain, it's certainly worth getting one at least for emergencies.

In **the UK and Ireland**, British Telecom (☏ 0800/345144, ⓦ www.chargecard.bt.com) will issue free to all BT customers the BT Charge Card, which can be used in 116 countries; AT&T (Dial ☏ 0800/890011, then 888 641 6123 when you hear the AT&T prompt to be transferred to the Florida Call Centre, free 24 hours) has the Global Calling Card; while Cable & Wireless (☏ 0500/100505) issues its own Global Calling Card, which can be used in more than sixty countries abroad, though the fees cannot be charged to a normal phone bill.

To call **Australia and New Zealand** from overseas, telephone charge cards such as Telstra Telecard or Optus Calling Card in Australia, and Telecom NZ's Calling Card, can be used to make calls abroad, which are charged back to a domestic account or credit card. Apply to Telstra (☏ 1800/038 000), Optus (☏ 1300/300 937), or Telecom NZ (☏ 04/801 9000).

Mobile phones

US and Canadian **mobile phone** users will likely find that their phones work fine throughout most of Florida. But, before leaving home, be sure to check with your service provider to make sure that costly roaming charges don't apply. Quite often, you can change your service plan to fit your traveling needs if necessary.

Calling home from overseas

Australia: international access code + 61+ city code
New Zealand: international access code + 64 + city code
UK and Northern Ireland: international access code + 44 + city code
Republic of Ireland: international access code + 353 + city code

If you're coming from abroad and want to use your **mobile phone**, you'll need to check with your phone provider whether it will work abroad, and what the call charges are. Unless you have a tri-band phone, it is unlikely that a mobile bought for use outside the US will work inside the States, with many only working within the region designated by the area code in the phone number ie 212, 415 etc. They tend to be expensive to own in the US, too, as users are billed for both incoming and outgoing calls. Calling a US mobile, however, costs no more than making a call to a landline in that area code. For details of which mobiles will work outside the US, contact your mobile service provider.

Most mobiles in Australia and New Zealand use **GSM**, which works well in Southeast Asia and Europe, but not usually in the US – check with your provider.

In the UK, for all but the very top-of-the-range packages, you'll have to inform your phone provider before going abroad to get international access switched on. You may get charged extra for this depending on your existing package and where you are travelling to. You are also likely to be charged extra for incoming calls when abroad, as the people calling you will be paying the usual rate. If you want to retrieve messages while you're away, you'll have to ask your provider for a new access code, as your home one is unlikely to work abroad. Most UK mobiles use GSM too, which gives access to most places worldwide, except the US. Tri-band phones will automatically switch to the US frequency, but these can be pricey, so you may want to rent a phone if you're traveling to the US. For further information about using your phone abroad, check out ⓦwww.telecomsadvice.org.uk/features /using_your_mobile_abroad.htm.

Email

One of the best ways to keep in touch while traveling is to sign up for a **free Internet email** address that can be accessed from anywhere, for example YahooMail or Hotmail – accessible through ⓦwww.yahoo.com and ⓦwww.hotmail.com. Once you've set up an account, you can use these sites to pick up and send mail from any Internet café, or hotel with Internet access.

If you're toting along a **lap-top**, check the useful ⓦwww.kropka.com for details on how to plug your lap-top in when abroad, on phone country codes around the world, and information about electrical systems in different countries.

The media

Newspapers

The best-read of Florida's **newspapers** is the *Miami Herald*, providing in-depth coverage of state, national and world events; the *Orlando Sentinel* and *Tampa Tribune* are not far behind and, naturally enough, excel at reporting their own areas. Overseas newspapers are often a preserve of specialist bookshops, though you will find them widely available in major tourist areas.

Every community of any size has at least a few **free newspapers**, found in street distribution bins or just lying around In piles. It's a good idea to pick up a full assortment: some simply cover local goings-on, others provide specialist coverage of interests ranging from long-distance cycling to getting ahead in business – and the classified and personal ads can provide hours of entertainment. Many of them are also excellent sources for bar, restaurant and nightlife information, and we've mentioned the most useful titles in the Guide.

TV

Florida's **TV** is pretty much the standard network sitcom and talk-show barrage you get all over the country, with frequent interruptions for hard-sell commercials.

Game shows fill up most of the morning schedule; around lunchtime you can take your pick of any of a dozen daily soaps. Slightly better are the cable networks, to which you'll have access in most hotels and which include the around-the-clock news of CNN and MTV's non-stop circuit of mainstream pop videos.

Especially in the south, Spanish-language stations provide services for the Hispanic communities.

Radio

Most of Florida's **radio stations** stick to the usual commercial format of retro-rock, classic pop, country, or easy-listening.

In general, except for news and chat, the occasional fire-and-brimstone preacher, and Latin and Haitian music, stations on the AM band are best avoided in favor of the FM band, in particular the public and college stations on the air in Tallahassee, Gainesville, Orlando, Tampa and Miami, found on the left of the dial (88–92FM). These invariably provide diverse and listenable programming, whether it be bizarre underground rock or abstruse literary discussions, and they're also good sources for local nightlife news.

Festivals and public holidays

Someone somewhere is always celebrating something in Florida, though few festivities are shared throughout the region. Instead, there is a disparate multitude of local annual events: art and craft shows, county fairs, ethnic celebrations, music festivals, rodeos, sandcastle-building competitions and many others of every description. The most interesting of these are listed throughout the Guide and you can phone the visitor center in a particular region ahead of your arrival to ask what's coming up. For the main festivities in Miami and Miami Beach see p.124 and in Key West p.154.

The biggest annual event to hit Florida is **Spring Break**: a six-week invasion (late February through March and early April) of tens of thousands of students seeking fun in the sun before knuckling down to their summer exams. Times are changing, however: one traditional Spring Break venue, Fort Lauderdale, has successfully encouraged the students to go elsewhere; another, Daytona Beach, is planning to do likewise. Panama City Beach, though, welcomes the carousing collegiates with open arms and Key West – despite its lack of beach – is fast becoming a favorite Spring Break location. If you are in Florida during this time, it'll be hard to avoid some signs of Spring Break –

a mob of scantily clad drunken students is a tell-tale sign – and at the busier coastal areas you may well find accommodation costing three times the normal price; be sure to plan ahead.

Public holidays

The biggest and most all-American of all the **public holidays** is **Independence Day** on the Fourth of July, when most of Florida grinds to a standstill as people salute the flag and take part in firework displays, marches, beauty pageants and more, all in commemoration of the signing of the Declaration of Independence in 1776. The large amusement parks, particularly Disney World, are completely swamped during this time. More sedate is **Thanksgiving Day**, on the last Thursday in November, which is essentially a domestic affair, when relatives return to the familial nest to stuff themselves with roast turkey, and (supposedly) fondly recall the first harvest of the Pilgrims in Massachusetts – though in fact Thanksgiving was already a national holiday before anyone thought to make that connection.

On the national public holidays listed below, banks and offices are liable to be closed all day, and shops may reduce their hours.

January 1	**New Year's Day**
January 15	
	Martin Luther King Jr's Birthday
Third Monday in February	**Presidents' Day**
Varies (usually early April)	**Easter Monday**
Last Monday in May	**Memorial Day**
July 4	**Independence Day**
First Monday in September	**Labor Day**
Second Monday in October	**Columbus Day**
November 11	**Veterans' Day**
Last Thursday in November	
	Thanksgiving Day
December 25	**Christmas Day**

Sports and ocean activities

Florida is as fanatical about sports as the rest of the US, but what's more surprising is that collegiate sports are often, especially among lifelong Floridians, more popular than their professional counterparts. This is because Florida's professional teams are comparatively recent additions to the sporting scene and have none of the traditions and bedrock support that the state's college sides enjoy. Seventy thousand people attending an inter-college football match is no rarity. Other sports less in evidence include soccer, volleyball, greyhound racing and Jal Alai – the last two chiefly excuses for betting.

Baseball

Until April 1993 Florida had no professional baseball team of its own – now, the state has two. In 1997, the first Florida team to come along, the **Florida Marlins**, became the youngest expansion team in history to win the World Series, shelling out millions of dollars to attract star-quality players. After taking the championship, the team slashed its budget, lost most of its marquee names, and is now a young, developing team. The Marlins play at **Pro Player Stadium**, sixteen miles northwest of downtown Miami: tickets are available from Ticketmaster (see p.129) or direct from the box office (☎ 305/626-7400, ⓦ www.floridamarlins.com) – most seats are in the range $5–55.

The Marlins, though, still generally play better ball than the bottom-of-the-barrel **Tampa Bay Devil Rays**, who joined the league in 1998 and have yet to have a winning season. The Devil Rays play at Tropicana Stadium (☎ 727/825-3137, ⓦ www.devilrays.mlb.com), which is actually located in St. Petersburg – most seats are $5–75.

The major league **baseball season** runs from April to early October, with the league championships and the World Series, the final best-of-seven playoff, lasting through the end of the month.

Spring training

Even if the local pro team is slumping, Florida has long been the home of **spring training**

(Feb and March) for a multitude of professional ball clubs – and thousands of fans plan vacations so that they can watch their sporting heroes going through practice routines and playing in the friendly matches of the Grapefruit League (the Cactus League plays out in Arizona). Much prestige is attached to being a spring training venue and the local community identifies strongly with the team that it hosts – in some cases the link goes back fifty years. Turn up at 10am to join the crowds watching the training (free); the twenty-odd sides who come to train in Florida include the following: the Boston Red Sox, City of Palms Park, Fort Myers (☎1-877/RED-SOXX); the Detroit Tigers, Joker Marchant Stadium, Lakeland (☎863/688-7911); the LA Dodgers, Holman Stadium, Vero Beach (☎561/569-6858); the NY Mets, Thomas J. White Stadium, Port St. Lucie (☎561/871-2115); and the NY Yankees, Legends Field, Tampa (☎813/287-8844).

Football

Of the state's three **professional football** teams, the **Miami Dolphins** have been the most successful, appearing five times in the Superbowl and, in 1972, enjoying the only undefeated season in NFL history. They, like the Marlins, play at Pro Player Stadium (see p.41; ⊛www.miamidolphins.com; most tickets around $30–50). The **Jacksonville Jaguars**, who entered the league in 1995, have stolen a bit of the Dolphins' thunder; they've already been in the playoffs four times, twice coming within one game of the Super Bowl. They play their games at Alltel Stadium (☎904/633-6000, ⊛www.jaguars.com; most tickets around $30–50). The **Tampa Bay Buccaneers** have also had recent success; they play in Raymond James Stadium (☎813/879-BUCS, ⊛www.tampabaybucs.com; tickets $15–65).

Even greater fervor is whipped up by both the **University of Florida Gators** (in Gainesville) and the **Florida State University Seminoles** (in Tallahassee). Both play around eleven games a season, the former in the Southeast Conference, and the latter in the rival Atlantic Coast Conference. Third among the college teams in terms of support but successful nevertheless, the **University of Miami Hurricanes** play in the Big East Conference. Tickets to college games generally run around $100 and are difficult to come by. Further details are given in the Guide.

The **football season** for both the professional and collegiate levels begins in late summer and lasts through January.

Basketball

The state's two **professional basketball** teams have enjoyed intermittent success in the National Basketball Association. The **Miami Heat**, who joined the NBA in 1988, play at the American Airlines Arena (☎786/777-HEAT, ⊛www.miamiheat.com), while the **Orlando Magic**, who joined joined two years later play at the Orlando Arena (☎407/839-3900, ⊛www.orlandomagic.com). Tickets for both teams are in the range $14–70.

Top among the **college teams** are the Florida University Gators (☎1-800/34-GATOR, ⊛www.gatorzone.com) and the Miami University Hurricanes (☎1-800/GO-CANES, ⊛www.hurricanesports.com).

Ice hockey

Florida boasts two teams in the National Hockey League (NHL): the **Florida Panthers** (☎305/530-4444; ⊛www.flpanthers.com), who play at the National Car Rental Center in Sunrise near Fort Lauderdale, and the **Tampa Bay Lightning** (☎813/301-6600; ⊛www.tampabaylightning.com), who play in the grandly named Ice Palace. The **NHL season** runs between October and June, and tickets for both teams are $15–75 and are available from Ticketmaster or on the spot from the each team's booking office.

Watersports

Even non-swimmers can quickly learn to **snorkel**, which is the best way to see one of the state's finest natural assets: the living **coral reef** that curls around its southeastern corner and along the Florida Keys. Many guided snorkeling trips run to the reef, costing $25–50 – further details are given throughout the Guide. More adventurous than snorkeling is loading up with air-cylinders to go **scuba diving**. You'll need a Certified Divers Card to do this; if you don't already have one you'll be required to take a course, which can last anything from one hour to a day and costs $50–100. Get details from diving shops, always plentiful near good diving areas, which can also provide equipment, maps and general information.

When you snorkel or dive, observing a few underwater precautions will increase enjoyment and safety: wear lightweight shoes to avoid treading on jellyfish, crabs, or sharp rocks; don't wear any shiny objects, as these are likely to attract hungry fish such as the otherwise harmless barracuda; never dive alone; always leave your boat by diving into the current – by doing this, the current will help glide you back to the boat later; always display the red and white "diver down" flag. And, obviously, never dive after drinking alcohol.

The same reefs that make snorkeling and diving so much fun cause **surfing** to be less common than you might expect, limiting it to a few sections of the east coast. Florida's biggest waves strike land between Sebastian Inlet and Cocoa Beach, and surfing tournaments are held here during April and May. Lesser breakers are found at Miami Beach's First Street Beach, Boca Raton's South Beach Park and around the Jacksonville Beaches. Surfboards can be rented from local beach shops for $10–15 a day.

If you prefer to cut a (usually) more gentle passage through water, many of the state's rivers can be effortlessly navigated by **canoe**; see "The backcountry" for more details.

Fishing

Few things excite higher passions in Florida than **fishing**: the numerous rivers and lakes and the various breeds of catfish, bass, carp and perch that inhabit them bring eager fishermen from all over the US and beyond. Saltwater fishing is no less popular, with barely a coastal jetty in the state not creaking under the strain of weekend anglers. The most sociable way to fish, however, is from a "party boat" – a boatload of people putting to sea for a day of rod-casting and boozing; these generally cost $25–30 and are easily found in good fishing areas. Sportsfishing – heading out to deep water to do battle with marlin, tuna and the odd shark – is much more expensive. In the prime sportsfishing areas, off the Florida Keys and off the Panhandle around Destin, you'll need at least $200 a day for a boat and a guide. To protect fish stocks, a highly complex set of rules and regulations governs where you can fish and what you can catch. For the latest facts, get the free *Florida Fishing Handbook* from the Florida Fish and Wildlife Conservation Commission, 620 Meridian Street, Tallahassee, FL 32399-1600 (℡ 850/488-1960, ⓦ www.state.fl.us/fwc).

The backcountry

Despite the common notion that Florida is entirely composed of theme parks and beaches, much of the state is undeveloped land containing everything from scrubland and swamps to shady hardwood hammocks and dense forests streaked by gushing rivers. Hiking and canoe trails make the wilderness accessible and rewarding – miss it and you're missing Florida.

The **US's protected backcountry** areas fall into several potentially confusing categories. **State parks** are the responsibility of individual states and usually focus on sites of natural or historical significance. **National parks** are federally controlled, preserving areas of great natural beauty or ecological importance. Florida's three **national forests**

are also federally administered but enjoy much less protection than national parks.

Hiking

Almost all state parks have undemanding **nature trails** intended for a pleasant hour's ramble; anything called a **hiking** or **back-**

packing trail – plentiful in state and national parks, national forests and through some unprotected land as part of the **1300-mile Florida Trail** – requires more thought and planning.

Many hiking trails can easily be completed in a day, the longer ones have rough camping sites at regular intervals (see "Camping," below), and most periodically pass through fully equipped camping areas – giving the option of sleeping in comparative comfort. The best time to hike is from late fall to early spring: this avoids the exhausting heat of the summer and the worst of the mosquitoes (see "Wildlife", opposite) and reveals a greater variety of animals. While hiking, be extremely wary of the **poisonwood tree** (ask a park ranger how to identify it); any contact between your skin and its bark can leave you needing hospital treatment – and avoid being splashed by rainwater dripping from its branches. Be sure to carry plenty of drinking water, as well as the obvious hiking prerequisites.

In some areas you'll need a **wilderness permit** (free or $1) from the local park ranger's or wilderness area administration office, where you should call anyway for maps, general information on the hike and a weather forecast – sudden rains can flood trails in swampy areas. Many state parks run organized hiking trips, details of which are given throughout the Guide. For general hiking information, write to or check the Web site of the Florida Department of Natural Resources, 3900 Commonwealth Blvd, Tallahassee, FL 32399 (℡850/488-0406, ⓦwww.floridadep.org) or the Florida Trail Association, PO Box 13708, Gainesville, FL 32604 (℡1-800/343-1882, ⓦwww.florida-trail.org), with the latter's Web site giving details of most trails and being constantly updated.

Canoeing

One way to enjoy natural Florida without getting blisters on your feet is by **canoeing**. Canoes can be rented for around $15–20 a day wherever conditions are right: the best of Florida's rivers and streams are found in north Central Florida and the Panhandle. Many state and national parks have canoe runs, too; the **Florida Canoe Trails System** comprises 36 marked routes along rivers and creeks, covering a combined distance of nearly a thousand miles.

Before setting off, get a canoeing **map** (you'll need to know the locations of access points and any rough camping sites) and check **weather conditions** and the river's **water level**: a low level can expose logs, rocks and other obstacles; a flooded river is dangerous and shouldn't be canoed; coastal rivers are affected by tides. Don't leave the canoe to walk on the bank, as this will cause damage and is likely to be trespassing. When a **motorboat** approaches, keep to the right and turn your bow into the wake. If you're **camping**, do so on a sandbar unless there are designated rough camping areas beside the river. Besides food, carry plenty of drinking water, a first-aid kit, insect repellent and sunscreen.

Several small companies run canoe trips ranging from half a day to a week; they supply the canoe and take you from the end of the route back to where you started. Details are given throughout the Guide; or look out for the free *Canoe Florida* leaflet, available from most state parks and some local tourist information offices. For more on the Florida Canoe Trails System, pick up the free *Florida Recreational Trails System Canoe Trails* (available from the **Department of Natural Resources**, address above) or simply look on the Internet at ⓦ www.myflorida.com/communities/learn/trails/canoe/.

Camping

All hiking trails have areas designated for **rough camping**, with either very limited facilities (a handpump for water, sometimes a primitive toilet) or none at all. Traveling by canoe (see "Canoeing", above), you'll often pass sandbars, which can make excellent overnight stops. It's preferable to cook by stove, but otherwise start fires only in permitted areas – indicated by signs – and use deadwood. Where there are no toilets, bury human waste at least four inches in the ground and a hundred feet from the nearest water supply and campground. Burn rubbish carefully, and what you can't burn, carry away. Never drink from rivers and streams, however clear and inviting they may look (you never know what unspeakable acts people – or animals – further upstream performed in them), or from the state's many natural springs; water that isn't from taps should be boiled for at least five minutes or cleansed with an iodine-based purifier before you drink it. Always get advice, maps and a weather forecast from the park ranger's or wilderness area adminstration office – often you'll need to fill in a wilderness permit, too, and pay a small nightly camping fee.

Wildlife

Though you're likely to meet many kinds of **wildlife** on your travels, only mosquitoes and, to a much lesser extent, alligators and snakes, will cause any problems.

From June to November, **mosquitoes** are a tremendous nuisance and virtually unavoidable in any area close to fresh water. During these months, insect repellent (available for a few dollars in most camping shops and supermarkets) is essential, as is wearing long-sleeved shirts and long trousers. It's rare for mosquitoes to carry diseases, though during 1991 Florida was hit by an outbreak of viral encephalitis, a mosquito-borne disease that can cause paralysis and death. As each generation of mosquitoes dies out during the winter, it's unlikely that this will be repeated – at least not for many years.

The biggest surprise among Florida's wildlife is the apparent docility of **alligators** – almost always they'll back away if approached by a human (though this is not something you should put to the test) – and the fact that they now turn up all over the place, despite being decimated by decades of uncontrolled hunting. These days, not only is it unlawful to kill alligators (without a license), but feeding one can get you two months in prison and a hefty fine: an alligator fed by a human not only loses its natural fear of people but comes to associate them with food – and lacks the brainpower to distinguish between food and feeder. The only truly dangerous type of alligator is a mother guarding her nest or tending her young. Even then, she'll give you plenty of warning, by showing her teeth and hissing, before attacking.

Like alligators, Florida's **snakes** don't go looking for trouble, but several species will retaliate if provoked – which you're most likely to do by standing on one. Two species are potentially deadly: the coral snake, which has a black nose and bright yellow and red rings covering its body, and usually spends the daylight hours under piles of rotting vegetation; and the cottonmouth moccasin (sometimes called the water moccasin), dark-colored with a small head, which lives around rivers and lakes. Less harmful, but still worth avoiding, are two types of rattlesnake: the easily identified diamond-back, whose thick body is covered in a diamond pattern, and which turns up in dry, sandy areas and hammocks; and the grey-colored pygmy, so small it's almost impossible to spot until it's too late. You're unlikely to see a snake in the wild and snake attacks are even rarer, but if bitten you should contact a ranger or a doctor immediately. It's a wise precaution to carry a snakebite kit, available for a couple of dollars from most camping shops.

For more on Florida's wildlife and its habitats, see "Natural Florida" in Contexts.

Crime and personal safety

No one could pretend that Florida is trouble-free, though outside of the urban centers crime is often remarkably low-key. Even the lawless reputation of Miami is in excess of the truth, though several clearly defined areas are strictly off limits. At night you should always be cautious – though not unduly frightened – wherever you are. All the major tourist and nightlife areas in cities are invariably brightly lit and well policed. By being careful, planning ahead and taking good care of your possessions, you should, generally speaking, have few real problems.

Car crime

When **driving**, under no circumstances stop in any unlit or seemingly deserted urban area – and especially not if someone is waving you down and suggesting that there is something wrong with your car. Similarly, if you are "accidentally" rammed by the driver behind, do not stop immediately but drive on to the nearest well-lit, busy and secure area (such as a hotel, toll booth or gas station) and phone the emergency number (℡ 911) for assistance. Keep your doors locked and windows never more than slightly open (as you'll probably be using air-conditioning, you'll want to keep them fully closed anyway). Do not open your door or window if someone approaches your car on the pretext of asking directions. Even if the person doing this looks harmless, they may well have an accomplice ready to attack you from behind. Hide any valuables out of sight, preferably locked in the trunk or in the glove compartment (any valuables you don't need for your journey should be left in your hotel safe).

Always take care when planning your route, particularly through urban areas, and be sure to use a reliable map such as the ones we've recommended on p.17. Particularly in Miami, local authorities are making efforts to add directions to tourist sights and attractions to road signs, thereby reducing the possibility of visitors unwittingly driving into dangerous areas. Needless to say, you should always heed such directions, even if you think you've located a convenient short cut. Having said all this, it's important not to spend your time in Florida in fear. Outside the problem areas of Miami,

there is an easy-going and essentially safe atmosphere on roads throughout the state.

Street crime and hotel burglaries

After car crime, the biggest problem for most travelers in Florida is the threat of **mugging**. It's impossible to give hard-and-fast rules about what to do if you're confronted by a mugger. Whether to run, scream or fight depends on the situation – but most locals would just hand over their money.

Of course, the best thing is simply to avoid being mugged, and there are a few basic rules worth remembering: don't flash money around; don't peer at your map (or this book) at every street corner, thereby announcing you're a lost stranger; even if you're terrified or drunk (or both), don't appear so; avoid dark streets and never start to walk down one that you can't see the end of; and in the early hours stick to the roadside edge of the pavement so it's easier to run into the road to attract attention.

Some emergency numbers

American Express (TCs) ℡ 1-800/221-7282; (credit cards) ℡ 1-800/528-4800
Diners Card ℡ 1-800/234-6377
Mastercard/Access (credit cards) ℡ 1-800/826-2181
Thomas Cook/Mastercard (TCs) ℡ 1-800/223-7373
Visa (TCs) ℡ 1-800/227-6811; (credit cards) ℡ 1-800/336-8472

Losing your passport

Few disasters create bigger headaches for foreign travelers than **losing your passport**. You can't get home without it, and it can be an extremely tough process to get a new one. The British Consulate in Florida – which can (very grudgingly) issue passports – is in Miami at Suite 2800, 1001 S Bayshore Drive, Coconut Grove, FL 33131 (℡305/374-1522, ℻305/374-8196). Expect to spend around $40 on fees and waste at least a week. If you are a "Briton in distress," which includes losing your passport, you can call the very helpful British Consulate General in Atlanta, Georgia (℡404/524-5856), who can help organize emergency passports quickly. The office is open Monday to Friday 9am–5pm. Make sure you have at least $50 and photographs of yourself ready.

If the worst happens and your assailant is toting a gun or (more likely) a knife, try to stay calm: remember that he (for this is generally a male pursuit) is probably scared, too. Keep still, don't make any sudden movements – and hand over your money. When he's gone you'll be shocked, but try to find a cab to take you to the nearest police station. Here, report the theft and get a reference number on the report to claim insurance (see "Health and Insurance," p.19) and travelers' check refunds. If you're in a big city, ring the local Travelers Aid (their numbers are listed in the phone book) for sympathy and practical advice.

Another potential source of trouble is having your hotel room burgled while you're out. Some Orlando area hotels are notorious for this and many such break-ins appear to be inside jobs. Always store valuables in the hotel safe when you go out; when inside keep your door locked and don't open it to anyone who seems suspicious; if they claim to be hotel staff and you don't believe them, call reception on the room phone to check.

Lost travelers' checks

Lost travelers' checks are a common problem. Keep a record of the numbers of your checks separately from the actual checks and, if you lose them, ring the issuing company on their toll-free number. They'll ask you for the check numbers, the place you bought them, when and how you lost them and whether it's been reported to the police. All being well, you should get the missing checks reissued within a couple of days – and perhaps an emergency advance to tide you over.

Staying on

Far from being the land of the "newly wed and the nearly dead" as many comedians have described the state, Florida's immaculate climate has persuaded people from all over the US and the rest of the world to arrive in search of a subtropical paradise. The following suggestions for finding work are basic and, if you're not a US citizen, represent the limits of what you can do without the all-important Social Security number (without which, legally, you can't work at all).

Finding work

Since the federal government introduced fines of up to $10,000 for illegal employees, employers have become understandably choosy about whom they hire. Even the **usual casual** jobs – catering, restaurant and bar work – have tightened up for those without a **Social Security number**. If you do find work it's likely to be of the less visible, poorly paid kind – as washer-up rather than waiter. **Agricultural work** is always available on Central Florida farms during the October to May citrus harvest; check with the nearest university or college, where noticeboards detail what's available. There are usually no problems with papers in this kind of work, though it often entails working miles from major centers and is wearying "stoop" (continually bending over) labor in blistering heat. If you can stick it out, the pay is often good and comes with basic board and accommodation. House-cleaning and baby-sitting are also feasible, if not very well-paid options.

Publications and Web sites

Another pre-planning strategy for working abroad is to get hold of *Overseas Jobs Express* (Premier House, Shoreham Airport, West Sussex BN43 5FF; ☎ 01273/699611, ⓦ www.overseasjobs.com), a fortnightly publication with a range of job vacancies, available by subscription only. Vacation Work also publishes books on summer jobs abroad and how to work your way around the world; call ☎ 01865/241978 or visit ⓦ www.vacationwork.co.uk for their catalogue. Travel magazines like the reliable *Wanderlust* (every two months; £2.80) have a Job Shop section which often advertises job opportunities with tour companies.

Au pair visas

For young women (in most cases) working as an **au pair** is a viable option. Applicants for au pair visas to the US who will be looking after babies under two will have to prove that they have at least 200 hours' experience with infants, 24 hours' training in child development and 8 hours' child safety training. Applicants will also have to undergo testing to provide a personality profile. The prospective employers must provide a written description of the job they expect their au pair to perform, so there is protection on both sides. Au Pair in America (see below), can arrange visas and placements.

Study and work programs

From the UK and Ireland

British Council, 10 Spring Gardens, London SW1A 2BN (☎ 020/7930 8466). Produces a free leaflet which details study opportunities abroad. The Council's Central Management Direct Teaching (☎ 020/7389 4931) recruits TEFL teachers for posts worldwide (check ⓦ www.britishcouncil.org/work/jobs.htm for a current list of vacancies), and its Central Bureau for International Educational and Training (☎ 020/7389 4004; publications ☎ 020/7389

Opportunities for foreign students

Foreign students wishing to **study in Florida** can either try the long shot of arranging a year abroad through their own university, or apply directly to a Florida university (being prepared to stump up the painfully expensive fees).

The Student Exchange Visitor Program, for which participants are given a J-1 visa enabling them to take a job arranged in advance through the program, is not much use since almost all the jobs are at American summer camps – of which the state has none. If you're interested anyway, organizations to contact in the UK include BUNAC; see below for details.

4880; ⓦ www.centralbureau.org.uk) enables those who already work as educators to find out about teacher development programs abroad. It also publishes a book *Year Between* aimed principally at gap-year students detailing volunteer programs, and schemes abroad.

BUNAC (British Universities' North America Club), 16 Bowling Green Lane, London EC1R 0QH (ⓣ 020/7251 3472, ⓦ www.bunac.org). Organizes working holidays in the US for students, typically at summer camps or training placements with companies.

Council Exchange, 52 Poland St, London W1F 7AB (ⓣ 020/7478 2000). International study and work programs for students and recent graduates.

Work Experience USA, Green Dragon House, 64–70 High Street, Croydon CR0 9XN (ⓣ 020/8688 9051, ⓦ www.campcounselors.com). For full-time students only, a chance to live and work in a regular job in the US; £695 covers flights, insurance, guaranteed job offer, orientation and help with tax forms and other paper work. Minimum ten weeks, maximum four months, plus one month's travel. They also offer a scheme as above but you find your own job in the US for £595.

From Australia and New Zealand

Australians Studying Abroad, 1/970 High St, Armadale, Melbourne (ⓣ 1800/645 755 or 03/9509 1955, ⓦ www.asatravinfo.com.au). Study tours focusing on art and culture.

Council on International Educational Exchange, Level 8, University Centre, 210 Clarence St, Sydney (ⓣ 02/9373 2730, ⓦ www.councilexchanges.org.au). International student exchange programs.

Finding a place to live

Apartment hunting in Florida is not the nightmare it is in, say, New York: accommodation is plentiful and not always expensive, although the absence of housing associations and co-ops means that there is very little really inexpensive accommodation anywhere except in country areas. Accommodation is almost always rented unfurnished; in general, expect to pay $500–800 a month for a studio or one-bedroom apartment, $900 upwards per month for two to three bedrooms in Miami, Tampa or Orlando, a lot less in rural areas. Most landlords will expect one month's rent as a deposit, plus one month's rent in advance.

There is no statewide organization for accommodation so you'll have to check out the options in each place. By far the best way to find somewhere is to ask around. Otherwise, rooms for rent are often advertised in the windows of houses and local papers have "Apartments For Rent" sections. In Miami, the best source is *New Times*, although you should also scan the *Miami Herald* classifieds. In Tampa and Orlando check out the *Tampa Tribune* and *Orlando Sentinel* respectively.

Women's Florida

Though this is the state that invented the wet T-shirt contest and which still promotes itself with photos of bikini-clad models draping themselves around palm trees, practically speaking, a woman traveling alone in Florida is not usually made to feel conspicuous, or liable to attract unwelcome attention. Outside of Miami and the seedier sections of the other major cities, much of the state can feel surprisingly safe. But as with anywhere, particular care has to be taken at night. Use common sense at all times: walking through unlit, empty streets is never a good idea; take a cab if you've got any qualms.

In the major urban centers, provided you listen to advice and stick to the better parts of town, going into bars and clubs alone should pose few problems: there's generally a pretty healthy attitude towards women who do so and your privacy will be respected. Gay and lesbian bars are usually a trouble-free and welcoming alternative.

However, small towns tend not to be blessed with the same liberal or indifferent attitudes towards lone women travelers. People seem to jump immediately to the conclusion that your car has broken down, or that you've suffered some terrible tragedy; in fact, you may get fed up with well-meant offers of help. If your vehicle breaks down in a country area, walk to the nearest house or town for help; on Interstate highways or heavily traveled roads, wait in the car for a police or highway patrol car to arrive. One increasingly available – and handy – option is to rent a portable telephone with your car, for a small additional charge

Rape statistics in the US are outrageously high, and it goes without saying that you should never hitch alone – this is widely interpreted as an invitation for trouble and there's no shortage of weirdos to give it. Similarly, be wary of picking someone up for a ride. Avoid traveling at night by public transport – deserted bus stations, if not actually threatening, will do little to make you feel secure – and where possible you should team up with a fellow traveler. There really is security in numbers. On Greyhound buses, make a point of sitting as near to the front – and the driver – as possible. Should disaster strike, all major towns have some kind of rape counseling service; if not, the local sheriff's office will make adequate arrangements for you to get help, counseling and, if necessary, get you home.

Specific women's contacts are listed in the city sections of the Guide, but for detailed country-wide info, read the annual *Index/Directory of Women's Media* (published by the Women's Institute for the Freedom of the Press, 3306 Ross Place NW, Washington, DC 20008-3332; ⓦwww.wifp.org), which lists women's publishers, bookshops, theater groups, news services and media organizations and more, throughout the country.

Travelers with disabilities

Travelers with mobility problems or other physical disabilities are likely to find Florida to be in tune with their needs. All public buildings must be wheelchair-accessible and have suitable toilets, most city street corners have dropped curbs, and most city buses are able to "kneel" to make access easier and are built with space and handgrips for wheelchair users.

When organizing your holiday, read your travel insurance small print carefully to make sure that people with a pre-existing medical condition are not excluded. A medical certificate of your fitness to travel, provided by your doctor, is also extremely useful; some airlines or insurance companies may insist on it. Make sure that you have extra supplies of prescription drugs – carried with you if you fly – and a prescription including the generic name in case of emergency. Carry spares of any clothing or equipment that might be hard to find; if there's an association representing people with your disability, contact them early in the planning process.

Use your travel agent to make your journey simpler: airline or bus companies can cope better if they are expecting you. With at least a day's notice, domestic airlines, and most transatlantic airlines, can do much to ease a disabled person's journey; wheelchairs can be provided at airports, staff primed to help, and, if necessary, a helper will usually be permitted free travel.

On the ground, the major car rental firms can, given sufficient notice, provide vehicles with hand controls (though these are usually only available on the more expensive makes of vehicle); Amtrak will provide wheelchair assistance at its train stations, adapted seating on board and a 15 percent discount on the regular fare, provided they have 72 hours notice; Greyhound buses, despite the fact that they lack designated wheelchair space, will allow a necessary helper to travel free.

Many of Florida's hotels and motels have been built recently, and disabled access has been a major consideration in their construction. Rarely will any part of the property be difficult for a disabled person to reach, and often several rooms are specifically designed to meet the requirements of disabled guests.

The state's major theme parks are also built with disabled access in mind, and attendants are always on hand to ensure that a disabled person gets all the necessary assistance and derives maximum enjoyment from their visit. Even in the Florida wilds, facilities are good: most state parks arrange programs for disabled visitors; the Apalachicola National Forest has a lakeside nature trail set aside for the exclusive use of disabled visitors and their guests; and, in the Everglades National Park, all the walking trails are wheelchair-accessible, as is one of the backcountry camping sites.

For further information, get the free *Florida Services Directory for Physically Challenged Travelers* from the Florida Division of Tourism (see "Information, Web sites and maps" on p.18 for the address).

Contacts and resources

In the UK and Ireland

Access Travel, 6 The Hillock, Astley, Lancashire M29 7GW (☎ 01942/888844, ⊛ www .access-travel.co.uk). Tour operator that can arrange flights, transfers and accommodation. This is a small business, personally checking out places before recommendation. They can guarantee accommodation standards in Florida.

Disability Action Group, 2 Annadale Ave, Belfast BT7 3JH (☎ 028/9049 1011). Provides information about access for disabled travelers abroad.

Holiday Care, 2nd Floor, Imperial Building,

Victoria Rd, Horley, Surrey RH6 7PZ
(℡ 01293/774535, Minicom ℡ 01293/776943;
ⓦ www.holidaycare.org.uk). Provides free lists of
accessible accommodation abroad.
Irish Wheelchair Association, Blackheath
Drive, Clontarf, Dublin 3 (℡ 01/833 8241, Ⓕ 833
3873, ⓔ iwa@iol.ie). Useful information provided
about traveling abroad with a wheelchair.
Tripscope, Alexandra House, Albany Rd, Brentford
TW8 0NE (℡ 08457/585641,
ⓦ www.justmobility.co.uk/tripscope,
ⓔ tripscope@cableinet.co.uk). This registered
charity provides a national telephone information
service offering free advice on transport for those
with a mobility problem.

In the US and Canada

Access-Able (ⓦ www.access-able.com). Online
resource for travelers with disabilities.
Directions Unlimited, 123 Green Lane, Bedford
Hills, NY 10507 (℡ 1-800/533-5343 or 914/241-
1700). Tour operator specializing in custom tours
for people with disabilities.
Mobility International USA, 451 Broadway,
Eugene, OR 97401 (Voice and TDD ℡ 541/343-
1284, ⓦ www.miusa.org). Information and referral
services, access guides, tours and exchange
programs. Annual membership $35 (includes
quarterly newsletter).
**Society for the Advancement of Travelers
with Handicaps (SATH)**, 347 5th Ave, New York,
NY 10016 (℡ 212/447-7284, ⓦ www.sath.org).

Non-profit educational organization that has
actively represented travelers with disabilities
since 1976.
Travel Information Service (℡ 215/456-9600).
Telephone-only information and referral service.
Twin Peaks Press, Box 129, Vancouver, WA
98661 (℡ 360/694-2462 or 1-800/637-2256,
ⓦ www.twinpeak.virtualave.net). Publisher of the
Directory of Travel Agencies for the Disabled
($19.95), listing more than 370 agencies
worldwide; *Travel for the Disabled* ($19.95); the
Directory of Accessible Van Rentals ($12.95) and
Wheelchair Vagabond ($19.95), loaded with
personal tips.
Wheels Up! (℡ 1-888/389-4335,
ⓦ www.wheelsup.com). Provides discounted
airfare, tour and cruise prices for disabled
travelers, also publishes a free monthly newsletter
and has a comprehensive Web site.

In Australia and New Zealand

**ACROD (Australian Council for Rehabilitation
of the Disabled)**, PO Box 60, Curtin, ACT 2605
(℡ 02/6282 4333); 24 Cabarita Rd, Cabarita, NSW
2137 (℡ 02/9743 2699). Provides lists of travel
agencies and tour operators for people with
disabilities.
Disabled Persons Assembly, 4/173–175
Victoria St, Wellington, New Zealand (℡ 04/801
9100). Resource center with lists of travel
agencies and tour operators for people with
disabilities.

Senior travelers

For many senior citizens, retirement brings the opportunity to explore the world
in a style and at a pace that is the envy of younger travelers. As well as the obvious advantages of being free to travel for longer periods during the quieter,
more congenial and less expensive seasons, anyone over the age of 62 can
enjoy the tremendous variety of discounts available, but must produce suitable
ID. Both Amtrak and Greyhound, for example, and many US airlines, offer (small-
ish) percentage reductions on fares to older passengers. Museums, art galleries
and even hotels offer small discounts as well, and since the definition of Senior
can drop as low as 55, it is always worth asking.

Any US citizen or permanent resident aged 62 or over is entitled to free admission for life to all national parks, monuments and historic sites using a **Golden Age Passport**, for which a once-only $10 fee is charged; it can be issued at any such site. This free entry also applies to any accompanying car passengers in their car or, for those hiking or cycling, the passport-holder's immediate family. It also gives a 50 percent reduction on fees for camping, parking and boat launching.

Contacts and resources

American Association of Retired Persons, 601 E St, NW Washington, DC 20049 (☏ 1-

800/424-3410, membership hotline ☏ 1-800/515-2299 or 202/434-2277, ⓦ www.aarp.org). Can provide discounts on accommodation and vehicle rental. Membership open to US and Canadian residents aged 50 or over for an annual fee of US$10 or US$27 for three years. Canadian residents only have the annual option.
Elderhostel, 75 Federal St, Boston, MA 02110 (☏ 1-877/426-8056, ⓦ www.elderhostel.com). Runs an extensive worldwide network of educational and activity programs, cruises and homestays for people over 60 (companions may be younger). Programs generally last a week or more and costs are in line with those of commercial tours.

Gay and lesbian Florida

The biggest gay and lesbian scene in Florida is in Key West, at the very tip of the Florida Keys. The island town's live-and-let-live tradition has made it a holiday destination favored by American gays and lesbians for decades, and many arrivals simply never went home: instead, they've taken up permanent residence and opened guesthouses, restaurants and other businesses – even running gay and lesbian snorkeling and diving trips.

Miami and Fort Lauderdale's networks of gay and lesbian resources, clubs and bars are quite extensive – within certain areas – and it's not hard to pick up on the scene. There are smaller levels of activity in the other cities, and along developed sections of the coast a number of motels and hotels are specifically aimed at gay travelers – Fort Lauderdale, for example, has over forty gay hotels. Predictably, attitudes to gay and lesbian visitors get progressively worse the further you go from the populous areas. Being open about your sexuality in the rural regions is likely to provoke an uneasy response if not open hostility. There are also active and relaxed gay scenes in Pensacola and, to a lesser extent, Tallahassee.

For a complete rundown on local resources, bars and clubs, see the relevant headings in individual cities. Of the statewide

publications to look out for, by far the best is the free *TWN* (*The Weekly News*; ☏ 305/757-6333), packed with news, features and ads for Florida's gay bars and clubs. Also look out for the *Southern Exposure Guide* (☏ 305/294-6303) and the South Beach scene's *Wire* (☏ 305 /538-3111). On the Internet, ⓦ www .gay-guide.com has a wide range of useful information about gay and lesbian travel in Florida.

Contacts and resources

In the UK

ⓦ www.gaytravel.co.uk Online gay and lesbian travel agent, offering good deals on all types of holiday. Also lists gay- and lesbian-friendly hotels.
Dream Waves, Redcot High St, Child Okeford,

Blandford DT22 8ET (☎ 01258/861149, ℮ Dreamwaves@aol.com). Specializes in exclusively gay holidays, including summer sun packages.

In the US and Canada

Damron Company, PO Box 422458, San Francisco, CA 94142 (☎ 1-800/462-6654 or 415/255-0404, Ⓦ www.damron.com). Publisher of the *Men's Travel Guide*, a pocket-sized yearbook full of listings of hotels, bars, clubs and resources for gay men; the *Women's Traveler*, which provides similar listings for lesbians; the *Road Atlas*, which shows lodging and entertainment in major US cities; and *Damron Accommodations*, which provides detailed listings of over 1000 accommodations for gays and lesbians worldwide. All of these titles are offered at a discount on the Web site. No specific city guides – everything is incorporated in the yearbooks.

Ferrari Publications, PO Box 37887, Phoenix, AZ 85069 (☎ 1-800/962-2912 or 602/863-2408, Ⓦ www.ferrariguides.com). Publishes *Ferrari Gay Travel A to Z*, a worldwide gay and lesbian guide; *Inn Places*, a worldwide accommodation guide; the guides *Men's Travel in Your Pocket* and *Women's Travel in Your Pocket*, and the quarterly *Ferrari*

Travel Report. Also gay guides to Paris and Mexico.

International Gay/Lesbian Travel Association, 4331 N Federal Hwy, Suite 304, Fort Lauderdale, FL 33308 (☎ 1-800/448-8550, Ⓦ www.iglta.org). Trade group that can provide a list of gay and lesbian owned or friendly travel agents, accommodation and other travel businesses.

In Australia and New Zealand

Gay and Lesbian Travel (Ⓦ www.galta.com.au). Directory and links for gay and lesbian travel worldwide.

Gay Travel (Ⓦ www.gaytravel.com). The site for trip planning, bookings, and general information about international travel.

Parkside Travel, 70 Glen Osmond Rd, Parkside, SA 5063 (☎ 08/8274 1222 or 1800/888 501, ℮ hwtravel@senet.com.au). Gay travel agent associated with local branch of Hervey World Travel; all aspects of gay and lesbian travel worldwide.

Silke's Travel, 263 Oxford St, Darlinghurst, NSW 2010 (☎ 02/9380 6244 or 1800/807 860, ℮ silba@magna.com.au). Long-established gay and lesbian specialist, with the emphasis on women's travel.

Traveling with children

Much of Florida is geared towards kid-friendly travel, what with the theme parks, water slides, beaches and so on, so you're unlikely to encounter too many problems with children in tow.

Hotels and **motels** almost without exception welcome children: those in major tourist areas such as Orlando often have a games room and/or a play area, and allow children below a certain age (usually 14, sometimes 18) to stay free in their parents' room.

In all but the most formal restaurants, young diners are likely to be presented with a **kids' menu** – liberally laced with hot dogs, dinosaur burgers and ice cream – plus crayons, drawing pads and assorted toys.

Activities

Most large towns have at least one child-orientated **museum** with plenty of interactive educational exhibits – often sophisticated enough to keep even adults amused for hours. Virtually all museums and other tourist attractions have reduced rates for kids under a certain age.

Florida's **theme parks** may seem the ultimate in kids' entertainment but in fact are much more geared towards entertaining adults than most people expect. Only Walt Disney World's Magic Kingdom is tailor-made for young kids (though even here, parents are warned that some rides may frighten the very young); adolescents (and adults) are likely to prefer Disney-MGM Studios or Universal Studios.

Away from the major tourist stops, **natural Florida** has much to stimulate the young. In the many state parks and in the Everglades National Park, park rangers specialize in tuning formative minds in to the wonders of nature – aided by an abundance of alligators, turtles and all manner of brightly colored birds. A boat trip in dolphin-inhabited waters – several of these are recommended in the Guide – is another likely way to stimulate curiosity in the natural world.

On a more cautious note, adults should take great care not to allow young flesh to be exposed to the Florida sun for too long: even a few minutes' unprotected exposure can cause serious **sunburn**.

No matter how you go, once you get there take special care to keep track of one another – it's no less terrifying for a child to be lost at Walt Disney World than it is for him or her to go missing at the shopping mall. Whenever possible agree a meeting place before you get lost, and it's not a bad idea, especially for younger children, to attach some sort of wearable ID card and for toddlers to be kept on reins.

A good idea in a major theme park is to show your child how to find (or how to recognize and ask uniformed staff to take them to) the **"Lost Kids Area."** This designated space not only makes lost kids easy to locate but provides supervision plus toys and games to keep them amused until you show up. Elsewhere, tell your kids to stay where they are and not to wander; if you get

lost, you'll have a much easier time finding each other if you're not all running around anxiously.

Getting around

Children under two years old **fly** for free – though that doesn't mean they get a seat – and when aged from two to twelve they are usually entitled to half-price tickets.

Most families choose to travel by car, and while this is the least problematic mode of transport, it's worth planning ahead to assure a pleasant trip. Don't set yourself unrealistic targets if you're hoping to enjoy a driving vacation with your kids. Pack plenty of sensible snacks and drinks; plan stops every couple of hours; arrive at your destination well before sunset; and if you're passing through big cities, avoid traveling during rush hour. Also, it can be a good idea to give an older child some responsibility for route-finding – having someone "play navigator" is good fun, educational and often a real help to the driver. If you're doing a fly-drive vacation, note that car rental companies can usually provide kids' car seats for around $5 a day. You would, however, be advised to take your own, as they are not always available.

Contacts and resources

Rascals in Paradise, 2107 Van Ness Ave, Suite 403, San Francisco, CA 94109 (ⓣ 415/921-7000 or 1-800/872-7225, ⓦ www.rascalsinparadise.com). Can arrange scheduled and customized itineraries built around activities for kids.
Travel With Your Children, 40 Fifth Ave, New York, NY 10011 (ⓣ 212/477-5524 or 1-888/822-4388). Publish a regular newsletter, *Family Travel Times* (ⓦ www.familytraveltimes.com), as well as a series of books on travel with children including *Great Adventure Vacations With Your Kids*.

Directory

ADDRESSES Generally speaking, roads in built-up areas are laid out to a grid system, creating "blocks": addresses of buildings refer to the block, which will be numbered in sequence from a central point usually somewhere downtown; for example, 620 S Cedar will be six blocks south of this downtown point. In small towns and parts of larger cities, "streets" and "avenues" often run north–south and east–west respectively; streets are usually named (sometimes alphabetically), avenues generally numbered.

CIGARETTES AND SMOKING Smoking is universally forbidden on public transport and flights, and restaurants are typically divided into smoking and nonsmoking sections. Cigarettes are, however, still widely sold. A packet of twenty costs around $2.50, though most smokers buy cigarettes by the carton for around $18.

DEPARTURE TAX None: airport tax is included in the price of your ticket.

DONATIONS Many museums request donations rather than an admission fee; usually you'll be expected to put $2–3 or so into the collection as you enter. If you don't, you won't be turned away but will suffer the indignity of being considered a complete cheapskate.

DRUGS Despite the widely accepted fact that much of the marijuana and cocaine consumed in the US arrives through Florida, the state's laws regarding possession of drugs are among the toughest in the country. Bluntly put, it isn't worth the risk of being caught in possession of any illegal substance in any quantity whatsoever.

ELECTRICITY 110V AC. All plugs are two-pronged and rather insubstantial. Some travel plug adapters don't fit American sockets. British-made equipment won't work unless it has a voltage-switching provision.

FLEA MARKETS Beside almost any major road junction, you'll find something touting itself as "Florida's Biggest Fleamarket." The genuinely big ones usually take place on Fridays and weekends, with hundreds of booths selling furniture, household appliances, ornaments, clothes – often hideous and always cheap.

HURRICANES Despite the much publicized onslaught of Hurricane Andrew in August 1992, statistically it's highly improbable that a hurricane will hit during your visit, and even if it does there will be plenty of warning – accurate tracking of potential hurricanes brewing around the Gulf of Mexico and the Caribbean from June to November (regarded as the hurricane season) being a feature of every TV weather bulletin. Local services are well equipped, most buildings are (supposedly) hurricane-proof, evacuation routes are signposted, and even phone books carry tips on how to survive – and, as shown by mass evacuations prior to the near-miss of Hurricane Floyd in 1999, Floridians have become much less blasé in their attitude to hurricanes. A more likely source of danger is thunderstorms; see opposite.

ID Should be carried at all times. Two pieces should suffice, one of which should have a photo: a passport and credit card(s) are your best bets.

LAUNDRY All but the most basic hotels will wash laundry for you, but it'll be a lot cheaper for a wash (about $1.50–2) and tumble dry ($1–1.50) in a laundromat – found all over; take plenty of quarters.

MEASUREMENTS AND SIZES The US has yet to go metric, so measurements are in inches, feet, yards and miles; weight in ounces, pounds and tons. Liquid measurements differ, too: American pints and gallons are about four-fifths of British ones. US clothing sizes can be calculated by subtracting two from

British sizes; thus, a British women's size 12 is a US size 10. Shoe sizes are one and a half more than the equivalent British size.

PUBLIC TOILETS Don't exist as such in most areas. Bars, restaurants and fast-food outlets are the places to go, though technically you should be a customer.

TAX Be warned that 6.5 percent sales tax is added to virtually everything you buy in a shop.

THUNDERSTORMS Subtropical southern Florida has frequent, very localized thunderstorms throughout the summer. Obviously, if possible you should shelter inside a building to avoid being struck by lightning (which, on average, kills eleven people a year). If you're caught in the open, stay away from metallic objects and don't make a dash for your car – most people who are struck are doing this.

On the plus side, the air after a storm is refreshingly free of humidity.

TICKETS For music, theater and sports, use Ticketmaster (ⓦ www.ticketmaster.com), whose plentiful offices are listed in the phone book and through whom you can buy tickets over the phone with your credit card.

TIME Most of Florida runs on Eastern Standard Time; the section of the Panhandle west of the Apalachicola River, however, is on Central Standard Time – one hour behind the rest of Florida.

TIPPING You shouldn't depart a bar or restaurant without leaving a tip of at least 15 percent (unless the service is utterly disgusting). About the same amount should be added to taxi fares – and round them up to the nearest 50¢ or dollar. A hotel porter

Florida terms

Barrier island A long, narrow island of the kind protecting much of Florida's mainland from coastal erosion, comprising sandy beach and mangrove forest – often blighted by condos (see below).

Condo Short for "condominium," a tall and usually ugly block of (normally) expensive apartments.

Cracker Nickname given to Florida farmers from the 1800s, stemming from the sound made by the whip used in cattle round-ups (or possibly from the cracking of corn to make grits). These days it's also a common term for the state's conservative ruralites: surly, insular types who prefer the company of wild hogs to people they don't already know.

Crackerbox Colloquial architectural term for the simple wooden cottage lived in by early Crackers (see above), ingeniously designed to allow the lightest breeze to cool the whole dwelling.

Florida ice Potentially hazardous mix of oil and water on a road surface following a thunderstorm.

Hammocks Not open-air sleeping places but patches of trees. In the south, and especially in the Everglades, hammocks often appear as "tree islands" above the flat wetlands. In the north, hammocks are larger and occur on elevations between wetlands and pinewoods. All hammocks make excellent wildlife habitats and those in the south are composed of tropical trees rarely seen elsewhere in the US.

Intracoastal Waterway To strengthen coastal defenses during World War II, the natural waterways dividing the mainland from the barrier islands (see above) were deepened and extended. The full length, along the east and southwest coasts, is termed the "Intracoastal Waterway."

Key Derived from the word "cay" – literally an island or bank composed of coral fragments.

No see'ums Tiny, mosquito-like insects; near-impossible to spot until they've already bitten you.

Snowbird Term applied to a visitor from the northern US coming to Florida during the winter to escape sub-zero temperatures – usually recognized by their sunburn.

should get roughly $1 per item for carrying your baggage to your room. When paying by credit or charge card, you're expected to add the tip to the total bill before filling in the amount and signing.

VIDEOS The standard format used for video cassettes in the US is different from that used in Britain. You cannot buy videos in the US compatible with a video camera bought in Britain.

guide

guide

Miami

CHAPTER 1 # Highlights

* **Art Deco architecture** The core of South Beach is an amazing display of preserved Deco buildings, mostly hotels, from the 1930s and 1940s. **P.85**

* **Ocean Drive** The scene on South Beach begins and ends here, amidst a sea of perfectly tanned bodies. **P.85**

* **The Fontainebleau Hotel** Check out the ornate lobby chandeliers and the rock grottoes and waterfalls of the swimming pool at this luxury playground. **P.90**

* **Calle Ocho** This is the main strip of Miami's Little Havana, a perfect place for exploring Cuban culture – and enjoying a strong Cuban coffee. **P.93**

* **Coral Gables** This elegant district of Spanish and Italian-style architecture is announced by a series of finely wrought entrances. **P.96**

* **Lowe Art Museum** The Spanish Masters are the highlights in Miami's most highly acclaimed museum. **P.99**

* **Restaurants** Many talk about the local club scene, but Miami has great restaurants too, from cheap and plentiful Cuban food to excellent seafood at places like *Joe's Stone Crabs*. **P.110**

Miami

Far and away the most exciting city in Florida, **MIAMI** is a stunning and often intoxicatingly beautiful place. Set beside the cool blue waters of Biscayne Bay, with roads lined by lush tropical foliage, the state's major urban center is awash with sunlight-intensified natural colors and the delicious scent of jasmine. An emerging city with a sharp, contemporary style (and some glaring social problems), there are moments, such as when the downtown skyline glows in the warm night and the beachside palm trees sway in the evening breeze, when a more beautiful city is hard to imagine.

The climate and landscape may be near-perfect, yet it's the people that make Miami unique. In direct contrast to the traditional Anglo-American-dominated US metropolis, two-thirds of Miami's over two million population is of Hispanic origin, of which the majority are Cubans. They form easily the most visible – and powerful – ethnic group in a city that's home to dozens from all over Latin America and the Caribbean. Spanish is the main language in most areas, and news from Havana, Caracas or Bogotá frequently gets more attention than the latest word from Washington. The city is no melting pot, however. Ethnic divisions and tensions are often all too evident. Since the black ghettos first erupted in the Sixties, violent expressions of rage have been a periodic feature of Miami life.

Some sections are still rather dangerous, but Miami has cleaned itself up considerably since 1980, when it was plagued by the highest murder rate in the country. It has also grown rich as a key gateway for US-Latin American trade, to which the glut of expensively designed banks and financial institutions bears witness. Strangely enough, another factor in Miami's revival was the mid-Eighties cop show *Miami Vice*, which was less about crime than designer clothes and subtropical scenery; set in Miami Beach's **Art Deco** district, the series helped make this a popular location for fashion shoots.

Miami has very little history to look back on, and little is known of indigenous Tequesta people who were virtually wiped out by the Spanish *conquistadores* led by **Juan Ponce de León** who arrived in 1513. The new invaders had no interest in developing southern Florida, being far more interested in Cuba, and built only a few small settlements along the Miami River and around Biscayne Bay. The whole of the region was finally sold by Spain to the British in 1763, and up until a century ago Miami was a swampy outpost where a hodgepodge of a thousand mosquito-tormented settlers commuted by boat around a trading post and a couple of coconut plantations.

The area code for Miami and Miami Beach is ☏ 305 and has to be added even if dialing from within Miami.

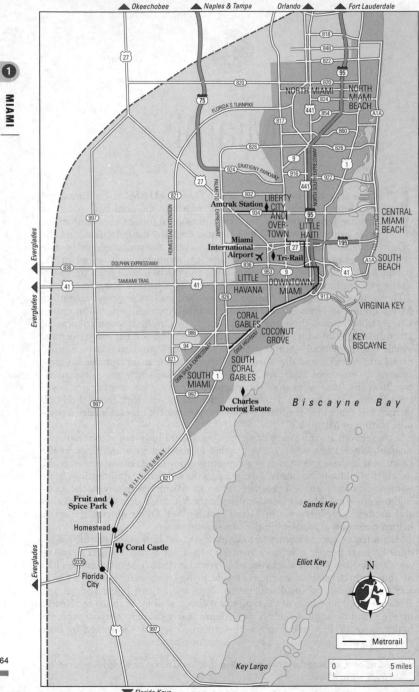

▲ Okeechobee   ▲ Naples & Tampa   Orlando ▲   ▲ Fort Lauderdale

818
848
822
95
NORTH MIAMI   NORTH MIAMI BEACH
820
824
441
854
A1A
817
860
826
826
1
924   GRATIGNY PARKWAY
916   922
441
9
832
LIBERTY CITY AND OVER-TOWN
Amtrak Station
934
LITTLE HAITI
95
CENTRAL MIAMI BEACH
195
MARTIN LUTHER KING AVENUE
SOUTH BEACH
Miami International Airport ✈
Tri-Rail
A1A
836   DOLPHIN EXPRESSWAY
953
DOWNTOWN MIAMI
41   TAMIAMI TRAIL
41
LITTLE HAVANA
9
41
826
913   VIRGINIA KEY
CORAL GABLES
COCONUT GROVE
986
KEY BISCAYNE
94
SOUTH CORAL GABLES
821
DON SHULA EXPRESSWAY
SOUTH MIAMI
1
992
Charles Deering Estate
Biscayne Bay
27
US 27
820
75   FLORIDA'S TURNPIKE
821
HOMESTEAD EXTENSION
PALMETTO EXPRESSWAY
997
Everglades ◄
Everglades ◄
Everglades ◄
Everglades ◄
997

S DIXIE HIGHWAY
821
Fruit and Spice Park
Homestead
Coral Castle
9336
Florida City
1   997

Sands Key
Elliot Key
Key Largo

N

Metrorail
0 _____ 5 miles

▼ Florida Keys

The first mention of the **"Village of Miami"** comes after the Second Seminole War ended in 1842, when a man called William English re-established a plantation once owned by his uncle, and started selling plots of land – making him Miami's first property developer. The construction by Henry Flagler of the railroad in 1896 (though only after being given vast swathes of land in the city) gave Miami its first fixed land link with the rest of the country, and literally cleared the way for the Twenties property boom. This saw entire communities, such as George Merrick's **Coral Gables**, appear almost overnight and form the basis of the city you see today.

During the Fifties, **Miami Beach** established itself as a celebrity-filled resort, while at the same time – and with much less fanfare – thousands of Cubans fleeing the successive Batista and Castro regimes began arriving on mainland Miami. The Sixties and Seventies brought decline, as Miami Beach's celebrity cachet waned and it became a haven for retirees. The city's tourist industry was damaged still further by the Liberty City Riot of 1980, which marked a low-point in Miami's black-white relations.

Since then, with the strengthening of Latin American economic links and a younger, more cosmopolitan breed of visitor energizing Miami Beach – where the fashionable district of **South Beach** holds much of the city's interest for lounging during the day and indulging at night – the city is enjoying a surge of optimism and affluence. As Latino immigration drastically alters the demography of the nation, today's Miami could well be a preview of tomorrow's US.

Arrival and information

However and whenever you arrive in Miami, grasping initial bearings will not be difficult. All points of entry are within a few miles of the center, and public transport links are generally reliable. Numerous offices around the city dispense general tourist information and advice.

By air

All passenger **flights** land at Miami International Airport (☏ 876-0970), a chaotic complex six miles west of downtown Miami. Once through the gate, it's a simple matter to get across the city.

Some of the main **car rental firms** (see "Driving and car rental," p.67) have desks close to the baggage reclaim area and provide free transport to collect a vehicle. Otherwise, you have to grab your luggage, leave the terminal and flag down a bus belonging to your rental company. If you're arriving in Miami after dark, especially after a long flight, consider spending your first night at an airport hotel; the rental parking lots are located in a none-too-safe area, and it can be confusing for first-time visitors to make their way onto the city- or beach-bound highways. **Local buses** depart from several points beside the airport's concourse; take #7 (every 40min; Mon–Fri 5.30am–8.30pm, Sat & Sun 7am–7pm) to downtown Miami (40–50min), or the #J bus (every 30min; daily 5.30am–11.30pm) for the slightly longer journey to Miami Beach. City Bus and Tri-Rail Shuttle signs opposite the airport's E departure gates indicate the bus stop. A short cab ride from the airport will deliver you to the

Miami West Greyhound station, with links to other parts of Miami (see below) and beyond.

Quicker, if more expensive, than public transport, the **SuperShuttle** minivans (grandly calling themselves "limos") run around the clock and will deliver you to any address in or around Miami, with per-person rates of between $7.50 (for downtown) and $17.50 (for Key Biscayne). Their representatives are easy to spot as you leave the baggage reclaim area. Taxis are in plentiful supply outside the airport building; there are flat rates from the airport: $18 to downtown, $24 to South Beach, $29 to Miami Beach, $31 to Key Biscayne and $34 to Bal Harbour.

By bus

Of several **Greyhound** (☎1-800/231-2222, ⊛www.greyhound.com) stations in Miami, the busiest is **Miami West**, near the airport, at 4111 NW 27th St (☎871-1810). Most Greyhound buses, however, including those to and from Key West, also stop at the **Downtown** station, 100 NW Sixth St (☎379-7403). This is the nearest stop to downtown Miami and South Beach (take the Metrorail from the adjacent Overtown station to Government Center and change to a bus for either) – it's worth noting that Overtown is not a pleasant place to arrive during the day, let alone after dark. Local bus services are detailed on p.68.

By train and Tri-Rail

The **train** station, 8303 NW 37th Ave (☎1-800/872-7245), is seven miles northwest of downtown Miami, with an adjacent **Metrorail** stop that provides access to downtown Miami and beyond; bus #L stops here on its way to Central Miami Beach. The Tri-Rail (☎1-800/TRIRAIL), the cheap commuter service running between Miami and West Palm Beach (see Basics p.24), links directly with the Metrorail at 1149 E 21st St, also seven miles northwest of downtown Miami. Fares range from $3.50–9.25. For more information on the Metrorail, see p.69.

By car

Most of the major **roads** into Miami take the form of elevated expressways that – accidents and rush hours permitting – make getting into the city simple and quick, though potentially hair-raising. From the north, **I-95** (also called the **North-South Expressway**) streaks over the downtown streets before joining **Hwy-1** (also called **South Dixie 1**), an ordinary road that continues on through South Miami. Crossing the Everglades from the west coast, **Hwy-41** (also called the **Tamiami Trail**) enters Miami along SW Eighth Street, and you'll save time by turning off north along the Florida's Turnpike (coming from the north and skirting the city's western periphery) to reach the **Dolphin Expressway (Hwy-836)**, which meets I-95 just south of downtown Miami. Hwy-27, the main artery from Central Florida, becomes the **Robert Frost Expressway** close to the airport and intersects with I-95 just north of the downtown area. The slower, scenic coastal route, **Hwy-A1A**, enters the city at the northern tip of Miami Beach.

Information

Although Miami has no single office devoted to tourist **information**, several useful outlets for leaflets, free tourist magazines and general practical advice dot the city. In **downtown Miami**, outside Bayside Marketplace, The Greater Miami Convention and Visitors Bureau, 701 Brickell Ave, Suite 2700, (Mon–Fri

8.30am–6pm; ☎ 539-3063, Ⓦ www.TropicoolMiami.com), has an information stand open from 11.30am-8pm; at **Miami Beach**, the Miami Beach Chamber of Commerce, 1920 Meridian Ave (Mon–Fri 9am–6pm, Sat & Sun 10am–4pm; ☎ 672-1270, Ⓦ www.miamibeachchamber.com), is a good stop, with a kiosk located at the intersection of Lincoln Road Mall and Washington Avenue (Mon–Fri 9.30am–4pm). Also at Miami Beach is the Art Deco Welcome Center, 1001 Ocean Drive, where the Art Deco Preservation League furnishes information on South Beach's historic Art Deco district and organizes tours (daily 9am–5pm; ☎ 672-2014, Ⓦ www.mdpl.org). Useful **chambers of commerce** in other districts are detailed throughout the Guide. If you're spending time in **Homestead**, the Everglades, or just passing through, be sure to stop at the area's excellent Tropical Everglades Visitor Information Center, 160 Hwy-1 (Mon–Sat 8am–4.45pm; ☎ 1-800/388-9669, Ⓦ www.tropicaleverglades.com).

Most of the free **maps** are useful for only very basic route searches; it's worth spending $3.95 on the street-indexed *Trakker* map of Miami, available from most newsstands and many shops. Miami's only daily **newspapers** are the *South Florida Sun-Sentinel*, which usually has an extensive international news section, and the slightly less informative *Miami Herald* (both: weekdays 35¢; Sunday editions $1). The latter also has a Spanish-language version, *El Nuevo Herald*.

Getting around

While designed for the car, Miami is an easily navigable city boasting a comprehensive public transit system that provides a sound alternative for daytime travel.

Driving and car rental

Driving around Miami is both practical and a piece of cake, especially once you've got the hang of the one-way-street grid system. Traffic in and out of Miami can be heavy, but the city's **expressways** (see "Arrival" above) will carry you swiftly from one area to another. Before setting off on a journey, plan your route carefully so as not to stray into an unsafe area, and if you do get lost, ask for directions at a gas station. Use ordinary streets and avenues for short journeys only, as they're often clogged by local traffic and may have confusing one-way systems. **Rush hour** (7–9am & 4-6pm) should also be avoided if possible. Driving between Miami and Miami Beach is straightforward using one of six causeways; each is well marked and quickly accessed from the main arteries.

There is plenty of provision for **street parking** in Miami, though actually finding an empty space can prove difficult, particularly at night in Coconut Grove and the South Beach. Parking meters are everywhere and usually require 50¢ per half-hour; save every quarter you get as you'll need vast quantities. Parking at public **parks and beaches** normally costs $2–3 per day; **parking lots** generally charge $3 an hour, $10 per day. Those in the downtown shopping district charge exorbitant rates, and if you must park in the city, aim for the tiny, reasonably priced parking lot situated across from the Gesú Church (on NE First Ave between Second and Third streets; $9 per day). With the exception of Bayside Marketplace, shopping mall parking lots seldom charge, but may have a two-hour time limit. Note that parking in a marked residential area will incur a ticket.

Miami media

Publications

The following are free magazines and newspapers that provide entertainment and arts information about the Greater Miami area. All can be picked up at tourist information centers, street machines or hotels:

Beach Buzz ☏893-8838, ⓦwww.beachesfoundation.org/beachbuzz. Get it before you get naked. Naturist news and listings for South Florida.

New Times ☏372-0004, ⓦwww.newtimes.com. The best weekly listings paper in Miami; food, drink, entertainment and – to a lesser extent – the arts. Published Thursdays.

One Heart ☏561/781-6677. Listings, articles and classifieds for those in need of New Age spiritual therapy.

Outlook ☏954/567-1306. Looks a bit like a porno mag, but stuffed full of the latest notices about gay (though not lesbian) nightlife and entertainment.

Showtime Reliable Friday listings section of the *Sun-Sentinel*.

South Florida Gourmet ☏668-6270. Purportedly a restaurant listings paper, though actually not very strong on restaurant listings. It does include a useful list of happy hours and tastings, however.

Street Miami ☏523-7878. Reasonable listings and editorials; not as in-depth as *New Times* but not as unwieldy either.

Sun Post ☏538-9700. Fairly vacuous news and gossip about South Beach.

TWN The Weekly News ☏757-6333. *The* gay and lesbian newspaper.

Wet ☏758-9700. Astonishingly vacuous, though one of the best sources of info on the ever-changing South Beach club scene.

What's Happening ☏376-2735. Arts and cultural events listings booklet published by the Greater Miami Convention and Visitors Bureau.

Most of the major **car rental** companies have booking desks at the airport and provide free transportation from the terminals to their offices, where your car will be waiting. Many companies also have offices along Collins Avenue in South Beach: Alamo, 3355 NW 22nd St (☏1-800/327-9633, ⓦwww .goalamo.com); Arena, 1300 Collins Ave (☏672-9890, ⓔarenacar@bellsouth .net); Avis, 2330 NW 37th St & 2318 Collins Ave (☏1-800/831-2847, ⓦwww.avis.com); Budget, 3901 NW 28th St (☏871-2722, ⓦwww.budget.com); Hertz, 3755 NW 21st St & 441 Collins Ave (☏871-0300, ⓦwww.hertz.com); and Thrifty, 2875 NW 42nd Ave & 2310 Collins Ave (☏1-800/367-2277, ⓦwww.thrifty.com). Charges – including taxes – are around $40–50 a day or $150–300 a week for an economy car, with an insurance premium of $20–30 depending on the type of cover. Depending on the fine print, smaller firms can be cheaper, but be on the lookout for special offers and discount vouchers from the big boys. With any company, be aware that they don't rent to under-21s and if you are under 25, you'll be charged a hefty additional fee ($10–25 per day). Some firms also require you to have a credit card, so give them a call first.

Public transport

An integrated **public transport** network of buses, trains and a monorail run by Metro-Dade Transit covers Miami, making the city easy – if time-consuming – to get around by day. Night travel is much harder, especially in South Beach.

Bus routes cover the entire city, most emanating from downtown Miami, and run from 4am to 2.30am daily. The flat-rate one-way **bus fare** is $1.25, payable on board by dropping the exact amount in change or notes into a machine beside the driver. If you need to transfer to another bus, say so when you get on; the driver will give you a **transfer** ticket, which you hand over to the driver of the next bus. Transfer tickets are route- and time-stamped to prevent you lingering too long between connections or taking scenic detours (if you do so, you'll be charged the full fare again).

Considerably quicker, the **Metrorail** is a single elevated railroad that links the northern suburbs with South Miami. Trains run every five to twenty minutes between 6am and midnight. Useful stops are Government Center (for downtown), Vizcaya, Coconut Grove and Douglas Road or University (for Coral Gables). Stations do, however, tend to be awkwardly situated, and you'll often need to use Metrorail services in conjunction with a bus. One-way **Metrorail fares** are $1.25; buy a token from the machines (insert five quarters) at the station and use it to get through the turnstile. Transfers between buses and Metrorail cost 25¢ from the bus driver or a Metrorail station transfer machine.

Downtown Miami is ringed by the **Metromover** (sometimes called the "People Mover"), a monorail loop (6am–midnight) that doesn't cover much ground but gives a bird's-eye view of downtown Miami. The flat fare is 25¢, payable into the machines at the stations. Transfers to Metromover from Metrorail (at Government Center and Brickell Avenue stations) are free; to transfer from Metromover to Metrorail, insert $1 in coins into the turnstile between the respective platforms.

One way to get around South Beach is via the **Electrowave** – an air-conditioned shuttle that runs solely on electricity. The shuttle runs north–south on Washington Avenue, between Seventeenth Street and Fifth Street from the Colony Theater to the Miami Beach Marina (every 10–15min; Mon–Wed 8am–2am, Thurs–Sat 8am–4am, Sun & holidays 10am–2am; 25¢, exact change only; ☎843-9106).

If you're sticking around for a while, consider a **Metropass**, which gives unlimited rides on all services for a calendar month. The Metropass costs $60 from any shop displaying the Metro-Dade Transit sign and is on sale from the 20th of each month.

For **information** and **free route maps and timetables**, go to the Transit Service Center (Mon–Fri 8am–6pm) inside the Metro-Dade Center in downtown Miami, or phone ☎770 3131 (Mon–Fri 6am–10pm, Sat & Sun 9am–5pm). Individual route maps and timetables can usually be found on buses.

Miami addresses and orientation

Miami's **street naming and numbering system** takes some getting used to. The city splits into quadrants, divided by Flagler Street and Miami Avenue (which intersect downtown). **Streets** run east–west and **avenues** north–south, their numbers getting higher the further you go from downtown Miami – each block has a hundred numbers so, for example, 940 Washington Ave is between Ninth Street and Tenth Street, which run perpendicular. **Roads** are less common and run northwest or southeast. Streets and avenues change their compass-point prefix when crossing into a new quadrant. For example, SE First Street becomes SW First Street after crossing Miami Avenue, and NW Second Avenue becomes SW Second Avenue after crossing Flagler Street.

In some areas the pattern varies, most obviously in Coral Gables, where streets have names instead of numbers, and avenues are numbered in sequence from Douglas Avenue.

Metro-Dade Transit, from downtown Miami to:
Coconut Grove #48
Coral Gables #24
Key Biscayne #B
Little Havana #8
Miami Beach #C, #K or #S (along Alton Rd)
Miami International Airport #7

Greyhound within Miami, from downtown Miami to:
Homestead (3 daily; 1hr 15min)
Miami Beach (18 daily; 25–45min)
Miami West (18 daily; 15–45min)
North Miami Beach (18 daily; 20–45min)

Besides the official services, **privately run minibuses** (known as "Jitneys") link busy areas for a flat fare of $1. They generally pull up at regular bus stops, but can be waved down practically anywhere. Look for their destination boards on the front. Note that such buses are unregulated and are rarely insured to carry passengers – you take them very much at your own risk.

Taxis

Taxis are abundant and often the only way to get around at night without a car. **Fares** are $1.50 for the first quarter mile and $2 a mile after that. From downtown Miami you'll pay around $12 to Coconut Grove and $16 to Miami Beach. An empty cab will stop if the driver sees you waving, but it's more common to phone: Central Cab (☎532-5555), Metro Taxi (☎888-8888), Yellow (☎444-4444) and Flamingo Taxi (☎885-7000) are all fairly reliable.

Cycling

Although you won't be able to see all of Miami by **cycling**, Coral Gables and Key Biscayne are perfectly suited to pedal-powered forays, and there's a fifteen-mile cycle path through Coconut Grove and into South Miami. For details, get hold of the free leaflet *Miami on Two Wheels* from the Greater Miami Convention and Visitors Bureau (see "Information" p.66).

You can **rent a bike** for $10–20 per day from several outlets including: in Coconut Grove, Grove Cycle Shop, 3216 Grand Ave (☎444-5415); or in Key Biscayne, Mangrove Cycles, The Square, 260 Crandon Blvd (☎361-5555). Helmets are usually included in the price, though you may have to pay an extra $1 per day for the lock. For cruising around Miami Beach, you can beat exorbitant hotel bike-rental charges by going to the Miami Beach Bicycle Center, 601 Fifth St (☎674-0150). They also have weekly rates ($70) and arrange guided bicycle tours of the Art Deco district; trips leave at 10.30am on the third Sunday of the month and cost $10 for the tour plus $10 for the bike – phone ahead to reserve your place.

Walking tours and rollerblading

Miamians consider **walking** anywhere a bizarre concept, but some of the city's more enjoyable areas are compact enough to cover on foot – though too far apart to walk between. For an informative and entertaining stroll, take one of

Dr Paul George's Walking Tours (daily 10am–4.30pm; ☎375-1621, ⓦwww.historical-museum.org), which are offered in conjunction with the Historical Museum of Southern Florida and take in a number of areas, including downtown Miami, Coconut Grove, Coral Gables, Little Havana, South Beach and the Miami Cemetery. There are 25 different itineraries, and walks last two to three hours and cost $15.

Elsewhere, you shouldn't miss the ninety-minute **Art Deco Walking Tour** of South Beach. A perfect introduction to the area's phenomenal architecture, the tour begins each Saturday at 10.30am and Thursday at 6.30pm from the Art Deco Welcome Center, 1001 Ocean Drive ($10; ☎672-2014, ⓦwww.mdpl.org).

A speedier means of getting around is **rollerblading**, or in-line skating, particularly popular in South Beach; see "Listings" for rental (or sales) details.

Bus, boat and helicopter tours

Scores of travel companies run **guided bus tours** around Miami's obvious points of tourist interest, but most are overpriced ($30-50 for a day) and only mildly informative. Some of the best vehicular tours are operated by Dr Paul George's Walking Tours (see opposite); boat ($35), bus ($35) and bike ($15) tours of Miami are available from September to June. Leaflets for these and other tours are available from any hotel or Chamber of Commerce.

If you prefer water to dry land – and the downtown skyline is undoubtedly most striking from across the water – several small craft moored along the jetty at the Bayside Marketplace offer **boat tours** around Biscayne Bay; check the posted departure times and prices (usually $22 per person for an hour) to find the best deal. Other cruises include: *Sea Kruz*, 300 Alton Rd, Miami Beach Marina (☎538-8300), which has four- to five-hour day (1pm) and evening (7.30pm) cruises with casino gambling and live entertainment; and *Island Queen*, Bayside Marketplace (☎379-5119), has an awesome, high-speed boat called the *Bayside Blaster* that zooms up the Government Cut waterway on the weekends (1.30–9.30pm, every 2hrs; $12) – they also do $14 yacht trips round Bayside that depart hourly between 11am and 6pm and last an hour and a half.

Accommodation

Finding a place to stay in Miami is only a problem over New Year's and important holiday weekends such as Memorial Day and Labor Day. The city is

---

Reservation services

The following services can often find you rooms at discounted rates:
Central Reservation Service (☎1-800/226-4866, ⓦwww.roomconnection.net)
Hotel Discount Hotline (☎1-888/429-4290, ⓦwww.HotelResService.com)
Unlimited Consolidators (☎1-800/781-9131, ⓦwww.members.aol.com/UnltdConso)

Accommodation price codes

All accommodation prices in this book have been coded using the symbols below. Note that prices are for the least expensive double rooms in each establishment. For a full explanation see p.29 in Basics.

❶ up to $40   **❸** $60–80   **❺** $100–130   **❼** $175–250
❷ $40–60   **❹** $80–100   **❻** $130–175   **❽** $250+

small enough that you can stay just about anywhere and not feel isolated, though the lion's share of **hotels** and **motels** are on **Miami Beach**: an ideal base for nightlife, beachlife and seeing the city. Prices vary from $35 to $300, but you can anticipate spending at least $40–75 during the summer, and $60–100 during the winter (or upwards of $100 per night in the ultra-chic South Beach hotels).

Away from Miami Beach, choice is reduced and costs increase. **Downtown Miami** – interesting by day but dull at night – has few affordable rivals to its expense-account chain hotels; distinctive character and architecture make Coral Gables appealing, but its rooms are seldom cheap; the stylish high-rise hotels of Coconut Grove are a jet-setter's preserve; and in **Key Biscayne** you'll need $150 a night for the plainest oceanside room. Only in **South Miami** and along SW Eighth St, unremarkable in themselves but a feasible base if you're driving, will you find a good assortment of no-frills motels for $40–60 a night. The **airport** area hotels should only be considered if you're catching a plane at an unearthly hour or arriving late and want to avoid driving into Miami after dark.

During the winter you'd be well advised to **reserve ahead**, either directly or through an agent. Between May and November, however, you'll save by going for the best deals on the spot (though you may want to arrange your first night in advance). Don't be afraid to **bargain**, as this can result in a more than a few dollars being lopped off the advertised rate – especially if you're staying for more than a few days, though **single** rooms are rarely cheaper than **doubles**. Prices below are for the winter season; all will be lower during the summer. Many places will also put extra beds in your room – usually up to a total of four – for a small surcharge.

Hotels and motels

Downtown Miami

Best Western Marina Park, 340 Biscayne Blvd (☎371-4400, ☏ 372-2862). A bland exterior shields a much warmer, more welcoming interior, with views across the Port of Miami and the neighboring parks. **❹–❺**

Hampton Inn-Downtown, 2500 Brickell Ave (☎854-2070, ☏ 856-5055, ⓦwww.hampton-inn@hotmail.com). A generic but perfectly adequate chain motel, a mile from the center of downtown Miami. **❺**

Inter-Continental Miami, 100 Chopin Plaza (☎577-1000, ☏ 577-0384, ⓦwww.interconti.com). Wicker chairs and a Henry Moore sculpture improve the atmosphere of this

multinational chain hotel. Very classy and comfortable. **❻–❽**

Miami River Inn, 118 SW South River Drive (☎325-0045, ☏ 325-9227, ⓦwww.miamiriverinn.com). Most of the buildings making up the inn date to 1908 and provide comfortable accommodations in a unique environment a short walk across the Miami River from the center of town or the Brickell Avenue banking district. Rooms have stunning views of either the city or the inn's garden and pool. **❺–❻**

Miami Sun Hotel, 226 NE First Ave (☎375-0786, ☏ 375-0296). The cheapest rooms in downtown Miami; pay for five days, get two free. **❶**

Wyndham Biscayne Bay Hotel, 1600 Biscayne Blvd (☎374-0000, Ⓕ 374-0020, ⓦwww.wyndham .com). Just another hotel catering to wealthy business types. If you can't afford a room, take a peek at the glamorous lobby and subterranean shopping mall. ④–⑧

South Beach

Blue Moon, 944 Collins Ave (☎673-2262, Ⓕ 534-1546). Small, lavish hotel remodeled in cool blue and white tones. ⑦

Brigham Gardens Guesthouse, 1411 Collins Ave (☎531-1331, Ⓕ 538-9898, ⓦwww.brighamgardens .com). Large rooms with either basic or fully equipped kitchens. A tropical garden patio and friendly atmosphere contribute to make this one of the most pleasant places to stay in South Beach. Ten percent discount for seven days or more. ⑤–⑥

Cadet Hotel B&B, 1701 James Ave (☎672-6688, Ⓕ 532-1676, ⓦwww.cadethotel.com). A quaint B&B in the heart of South Beach – Clark Gable stayed here. Parking and breakfast included. ⑤–⑥

Cavalier, 1320 Ocean Drive (☎604-5064, Ⓕ 531-5543, ⓦwww.islandoutpost.com). Recently and completely revamped 1930s Art Deco hotel, now featuring neo-Moorish decor. ⑦–⑧

Colony, 736 Ocean Drive (☎1-800/2-COLONY, Ⓕ 532-0762, ⓦwww.colonyhotel-sobe.com). This beautifully refurbished Art Deco delight is the most photographed hotel in South Beach. ⑥–⑦

Delano, 1685 Collins Ave (☎672-2000, Ⓕ 532-0099). South Beach's most chic lodgings mix Art Deco with minimalist modernism (eg, lots of white) and all-round luxury. Gauzy white curtains billow in the lobby, and it's style, style, style from then on in. Celebrities and the rich lounge around on expensive sofas, here or around the pool, and the hotel incorporates *Blue Door* – an acclaimed and very, very expensive restaurant– and the *Rose Bar*. Incidentally, Madonna once had an interest in *Blue Door*, and for this reason the Delano is universally known by taxi-drivers as "Madonna's Hotel." ⑧

Essex House, 1001 Collins Ave (☎1-800/553-7739, Ⓕ 532-3827, ⓦwww.southbeachresorts.com). Warm atmosphere and one of the more tastefully restored Art Deco hotels. Price includes breakfast. ④–⑧

Leslie, 1244 Ocean Drive (☎1-800/OUTPOST, Ⓕ 672-5611, ⓦwww.islandlife.com). Excellently located on the beachside Art Deco strip, with striking interior design – bright colors and mirrors at crooked angles. ⑤–⑧

Marlin, 1200 Collins Ave (☎604-5063, Ⓕ 673-9609, ⓦwww.themarlinhotel.com). Eleven costly

but cozy suites brightly decorated with a Caribbean-islands theme, plus a rooftop sun deck. If you can't afford to stay here, at least have a drink at the futuristic bar. ⑦–⑧

Mermaid, 909 Collins Ave (☎538-5324, Ⓕ 538-2822). Cost-effective rooms – one with kitchenettes – in a colorfully-painted Caribbean-style cottage with a bar on the patio. ⑤–⑥

Park Central, 640 Ocean Drive (☎538-1611, Ⓕ 534-7520, ⓦwww.theparkcentral.com). Largest of the Art Deco options, and one of the few with a pool. ⑦–⑧

Peter Miller Hotel, 1900 Collins Ave (☎531-7611). Slightly shabby Art Deco hotel, but one of the least expensive places on South Beach. Large, cool rooms, friendly service and negotiable rates. ②–③

Raleigh, 1775 Collins Ave (☎1-800/848-1775, Ⓕ 538-8140, ⓦwww.raleighhotel.com). The 1990s refurbishment aped the original 1940s look, but added state-of-the-art electronics in every room. Probably the best-run and currently the most glamorous hotel in South Beach. ⑦–⑧

Shelley, 844 Collins Ave (☎531-3341, Ⓕ 535-0077). An original Art Deco hotel with impeccably clean rooms and just across the street from Ocean Drive and the beach. Pastries and juice in the mornings in the lobby. Rooms can hold up to four people. Breakfast included. ⑥

Villa Paradiso, 1415 Collins Ave (☎532-0616, Ⓕ 673-5874). Fully equipped studios and one-bedroom apartments with kitchens, just one block away from the beach. ⑤–⑥

Waldorf Towers, 860 Ocean Drive (☎531-7684, Ⓕ 672-6836, ⓦwww.waldorftowers.com). Another Art Deco landmark, facing the ocean and right in the throng of the fashionable strip. ④–⑧

Central Miami Beach

Alexander, 5225 Collins Ave (☎1-800/327-6121, Ⓕ 341-0554, ⓦwww.alexanderhotel.com). Well equipped suites in this swanky four-star hotel. Two pools in a garden terrace overlooking their private beach. You won't want to leave. ⑧

Bay Harbor Inn, 9660 E Bay Harbor Drive, Bay Harbor Islands (☎868-4141, Ⓕ 867-9094, ⓦwww.bayharborinn.com). Low-key elegance in an upmarket residential neighborhood a few minutes' walk from the beach and fifteen minutes' drive from downtown. The most attractive rooms are those with views onto Indian Creek, which fronts the inn. Price includes breakfast. ⑥

Eden Roc Resort & Spa, 4525 Collins Ave (☎531-0000, Ⓕ 674-5555, ⓦwww.edenrocresort .com). A landmark on the Beach since the 1950s, this has been refurbished to the last detail and again ranks amongst Miami's most luxurious hotels. Most of the rooms command spectacular views. Besides the two pools, there's a health spa offering everything from shiatsu massage to seaweed and salt scrubs. ❽

Fontainebleau Hilton, 4441 Collins Ave (☎538-2000). Once the last word in glamour, now it is elaborately refurbished with period furniture and fittings and regaining its lost esteem; a staff of up to two thousand attends your every whim. ❽

The Golden Sands, 6910 Collins Ave (☎1-800/932-0333, ℱ 886-0187, ⓦwww.goldensands.com). Nothing flashy and mostly filled by package-touring Europeans, but likely to turn up some of the cheapest deals with a pool in this pricey area. ❹

Normandy Plaza, 6979 Collins Ave (☎866-6669). This is the cheapest deal in the area, and although having no pool (and so-so rooms) you won't get a sea view for less anywhere in Miami. ❷–❸

North Miami Beach

Paradise Inn, 8520 Harding Ave (☎865-6216, ℱ 865-9028, ⓔparadiseinn85@hotmail.com). Neatly tucked into Surfside's main street, this is one of the best bargains around. ❸

Thunderbird Resort, 18401 Collins Ave (☎1-800/327-2044, ℱ 932-7521, ⓦwww.dezerhotels.com). No frills, but handy for both Miami and Fort Lauderdale. Like most hotels around here, you can step straight out of your room into the pool or onto the beach. ❷–❺

Coral Gables

Biltmore, 1200 Anastasia Ave (☎1-800/727-1926, ℱ 913-3162, ⓦwww.biltmorehotel.com). A landmark, Mediterranean-style hotel that has been pampering the rich and famous since 1926. Show up to pace the echoey corridors and sink into the lobby armchairs, even if you can't afford to stay here. ❽

Gables Inn, 730 S Dixie Hwy (☎661-7999, ℱ 665-7981). Basic but clean and the least expensive in the area. ❸

Omni Colonnade, 180 Aragon Ave (☎441-2600, 445-3929, ⓦwww.omnihotels.com). Marble floors, oriental rugs and brass lamps fill this showpiece of Mediterranean Revival architecture. ❽

Place St Michel, 162 Alcazar Ave (☎444-1666, ℱ 529-0074, ⓦwww.hotelplacestmichel.com). Small, romantic hotel just off the Miracle Mile, with modernized rooms, Laura Ashley decor and copious European antiques. Rates include continental breakfast. ❺–❼

Riviera Courts, 5100 Riviera Drive (☎1-800/368-8602, ℱ 667-8993). Simple, homely motel

equipped with a pool, close to the University of Miami and the Miracle Mile. ❸–❹

Coconut Grove

Doubletree at Coconut Grove, 2649 S Bayshore Drive (☎858-2500, ℱ 858-9117). Elegant high-rise surrounded by banyan trees, with cozy rooms and great views – just a quarter of an hour's walk from the area's cafés and bars. ❺–❼

Grand Bay, 2669 S Bayshore Drive (☎1-800/327-2788, ℱ 859-2026, ⓦwww.grandbay.com). Expense-account elegance with marble floors, antiques, grandiose artwork. ❼–❽

Mayfair House, 3000 Florida Ave (☎441-0000, ⓦwww.mayfairhousehotel.com). Luxurious all-suite hotel, complete with rooftop swimming pool. ❻–❽

South Miami

A1 Budget Motel, 30600 S Dixie Hwy, South Miami (☎247-7032, ℱ 247-9090, ⓔsparthsan@cs.com). Basic and clean rooms, with some non-smoking rooms and a laundry next door. ❷

Deluxe Inn Motel, 28475 S Dixie Hwy, South Miami (☎248-5622). Maybe it's not truly "deluxe," but it offers good, clean rooms at a fair price. ❶

Katy's Place B&B, 31850 SW 195th Ave, South Miami (☎247-0201). Pleasant bed and breakfast with a pool, hot-tub, laundry facilities and home-cooked breakfast. ❹–❺

Key Biscayne

Sheraton Royal, 555 Ocean Drive (☎373-6000, ℱ 374-2279, ⓦwww.sheraton.com). Upper-bracket beachside hotel with all the amenities you can think of, and some good off-season reductions. ❼

Silver Sands Oceanfront Motel, 301 Ocean Drive (☎361-5441, 361-5477, ⓦwww.silversandsmiami.com). Fairly standard rooms unexceptional for the price, but you get to watch the marine iguanas who have colonized their botanical garden and occasionally swim in the pool. ❼–❽

Sonesta Beach, 350 Ocean Drive (☎1-800/SONESTA, ℱ 365-2082, ⓦwww.sonesta.com). High-rise resort with luxurious rooms, sports facilities, bars and a prime stretch of private beach. ❻–❽

Homestead

Best Western Gateway to the Keys, 411 S Krome Ave, Homestead (☎246-5100, ℱ 242-0056, ⓔgatewaybw@aol.com). One of the most comfortable places to stay hereabouts, and usefully located between the Keys, Miami and the

Everglades. All rooms are non-smoking. **4**

Coral Roc, 1100 N Krome Ave, Homestead (℡247-4010, ℻ 242-1580). Unexciting but fully functional and clean motel. **2**

Everglades Motel, 605 S Krome Ave, Homestead (℡247-4117, 242-1580). Despite its slightly run-down exterior, the rooms are okay and there's a coin-operated laundry for guests. **2**

At the airport

Hampton Inn-Miami Airport, 777 NW 57th Ave (℡1-800/HAMPTON, ℻ 262-5488, ⓦwww.hampton-inn.com). Branch of a good-value hotel chain two miles from the airport, offering some of the best rates in the area. Twenty-four-hour courtesy bus available to airport. **6**

MIA, Miami International Airport (℡1-800/327-1276, ℻ 871-0800, ⓦwww.miahotel.com). There's no excuse for missing your plane if you stay here; this stylishly designed and fully equipped hotel is located inside the airport, but you'll pay for the convenience. **7**

Miami Airways Motel, 5001 36th St (℡883-4700, ℻ 888-8072). Recently renovated modern rooms and easily the cheapest in the area. One mile from airport. **2**

Quality Inn, 2373 NW Le Jeune Rd (℡871-3230, ℻ 871-1106, ⓦwww.qualitymia.com) Well-presented chain hotel just across the road from the airport, with a beckoning pool. **3**

Hostels

All of the following are in South Beach.

AYH Youth Hostel, at the *Clay Hotel*, 406 Española Way (℡534-2988). Impeccably posi-tioned in the heart of South Beach, with clean dorms for $16 ($17 for non-IYHA-members) as well as private single and double rooms for $42–62.

Banana Bungalow, 2360 Collins Ave (℡1-800/7-HOSTEL, ℻ 531-3217, ⓦwww.bananabungalow .com). Biggest hostel in Miami, boasting a large pool, inexpensive Internet facilities ($6/hour), a (slightly grubby) kitchen, organized tours and flight reservation, and the cheapest tropical-style bar on the strip. Guests can lounge pool-side while gabbing with (or more usually, trying to pick up) fellow travelers from around the globe – being so far from the center of the SoBe action this is where most guests pass the evenings. Dorm beds are $14–19, though at $95–105 the private rooms aren't worth it. If you're in the dorm, remember you'll need your own padlock for the locker.

Ninth Street Hostel, 236 Ninth St (℡534-0268, ℻ 534-5862, ⓦwww.sobehostel.com). Friendly hostel with beds in four-person dorms for $16 ($17 for non-IYHA-members), as well as private singles and doubles ($50–62), centrally positioned in South Beach. Has Internet facilities, kitchen, laundry, a comfortable movie-lounge and books tours.

The Tropics Hotel and Hostel, 1550 Collins Ave (℡531-0361, ℻ 531-8676, ⓦwww.tropicshotel.com). Housed in a stylish Art Deco building this is more of a hotel than a hostel and more genteel than any of the above. Spotless and comfortable four- or six-person dorms for $18 a person, with doubles also available for a reason-able $50. A clean kitchen, swimming pool, laundry facilities and airport shuttle are all available. Attracts a more mature crowd.

The city and the beaches

Despite its relatively small population, **Miami** is a highly diverse city. Many of its districts are officially cities on their own, and each has a distinctive back-ground and character. Some are compact enough to explore on foot, but you'll need a car, or local buses, to travel between them – though the city doesn't stretch far inland because of the natural barrier of the Everglades swamps, dis-tances between northern and southern reaches are considerable. Beware that the mood within a district can switch dramatically from one block to another, making it easy to stray into hostile territory if you don't stay alert.

The obvious starting point is **downtown Miami**, the small, bustling nerve center of the city. Its streets are lined by garishly decorated shops and filled with a startling cross-section of people, bringing a lively human dimension to an area overlooked by futuristic office buildings. Close to the **downtown area** are regions of marked contrast. Those to the north - with a few exceptions – are run-down and dangerous, infamous for their outbreaks of violent racial unrest. To the south are the international banks signifying Miami's new wealth – and the state-of-the-art residential architecture that comes with it.

It's the small island, **Miami Beach,** that commands the most attention. Three miles offshore, sheltering Biscayne Bay from the Atlantic Ocean, Miami Beach was an ailing fruit farm in the 1910s when its Quaker owner, John Collins, formed an unlikely partnership with a flashy entrepreneur called Carl Fisher. With Fisher's money, Biscayne Bay was dredged, and the muck raised from its murky bed provided the landfill that transformed the island into the sculptured landscape of palm trees, hotels and tennis courts that – by and large – it is today.

In varying degrees, all twelve miles of Miami Beach are worth seeing – and its firm, crushed-coral-rock beach offers excellent sunbathing and swimming opportunities – though only **South Beach**, a fairly small area at the southern end, will hold your attention for long. Here, rows of tastefully restyled Thirties Art Deco buildings have become chic gathering places for the city's fashionable faces and the stamping ground of Miami's more creative and unconventional elements. It's no fluke that many of Florida's leading art galleries, trendsetting restaurants and much of its raucous club scene are found in this compact area. Heading north, **Central Miami Beach** was where Fifties screen stars had fun in the sun and helped cement Miami's international reputation as a glamorous vacation spot. Oddly enough, it's the monolithic hotels remaining from these times that give the area a modicum of appeal. Further on, **North Miami Beach**, despite splitting into several distinctive communities, has even less to kindle the imagination – a long way from the action and mostly overrun by package tourists – but makes a good back route if you're heading north from Miami towards Fort Lauderdale.

Beyond the environs of downtown Miami, the city spreads out in a broad arc to the west and south. The first of Miami's Cubans settled a few miles west in (what became) **Little Havana**. This is still one of the more intriguing parts of Miami, rich with Latin American looks and sounds but far less solidly Cuban than it used to be. Immediately south, Little Havana's street grid gives way to the spacious boulevards of **Coral Gables**, whose finely wrought Mediterranean-style architecture – a far cry from cheap pastiches elsewhere – is as impressive now as it was in the 1920s when it set new standards in town planning. South of the downtown area, **Coconut Grove** vies with South Beach for the title of Miami's trendiest quarter; beautifully placed alongside **Biscayne Bay**, it boasts a plethora of neatly appointed streetside cafés as well as mansions and shops from a bygone era.

Beyond Coconut Grove and Coral Gables, **South Miami** is a lackluster residential sprawl with little of note, fading into farming territory towards **Homestead** on Miami's southern edge, and into the barren expanse of the Everglades to the west. **Key Biscayne** is a more attractive destination: a classy, secluded island community with some exquisite beaches, five miles off the mainland but easily reached by causeway.

Downtown Miami and around

DOWNTOWN MIAMI is not a place in which to relax: humanity storms down its short streets, rippling the gaudy awnings of countless cut-price electronics, clothes and jewelry stores, easing up only to buy imported newspapers or to gulp down a spicy snack and a mango juice from a fast-food stand.

Since the early Sixties, when newly released Cuban Bay of Pigs veterans came here to spend their US Government back pay, the predominantly Spanish-speaking businesses of the downtown square mile have reaped the benefits of any boost in South or Central American incomes. Affluent Latinos pour into Miami International Airport and move downtown in droves, seeking the goods they can't find at home. Minorities in this throng include dazed-looking European tourists, clean-cut Anglo-Americans with local government jobs, and street people of indeterminate origin dragging their worldly possessions with them. Only some solid US public architecture and whistle-blowing traffic cops remind you that you're still in Florida and not on the main drag of a busy, slightly chaotic Latin American capital.

The nerve-jangling streets (safe by day), and the feeling they induce of being at the crossroads of the Americas, are reason enough to spend half a day in

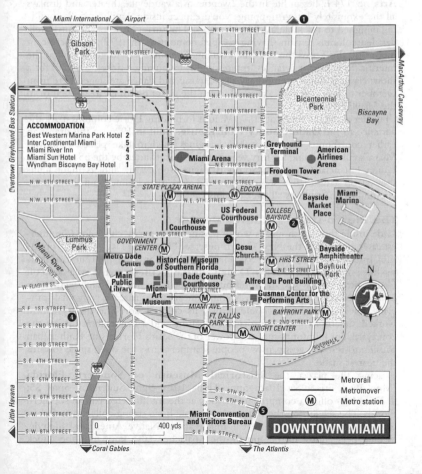

downtown Miami, but added attractions are an excellent historical collection at the **Historical Museum of Southern Florida**, the well-stocked **Main Public Library** and the Neoclassical **Federal Courthouse**, which contains some large, impressive murals. When the street melange becomes too much, you can revive your senses with a quick *café Cubano* in one of the many small Cuban cafés (see "Eating," p.110).

Flagler Street and the Metro-Dade Cultural Center

Nowhere gives a better first taste of downtown Miami than **FLAGLER STREET**, by far the loudest, brightest, busiest strip, and long the area's main attraction. Start at the eastern end by glancing inside the 1938 **Alfred Du Pont Building**, no. 169 E, which currently houses the Florida National Bank (whose first floor is open to the public), to find fanciful wrought-iron screens, bulky brass fittings and frescoes of Florida scenes epitomizing the decorative style popular with US architects at the end of the Depression.

Nearby, the even less restrained **Gusman Center for the Performing Arts**, no. 174 E, began life in the Twenties as a vaudeville theater, and displays all the exquisitely kitsch trappings you'd expect inside a million-dollar building designed to resemble a Moorish palace. The turrets, towers and intricately detailed columns remain (having escaped demolition in 1972), and a crescent moon still flits across the star-filled ceiling. The only way to get a look at the interior (the exterior is far less interesting) is by buying a ticket ($15–30) for a show: classical and contemporary plays, music and dance are staged here from October to June; details are available from the ticket booth (☎ 372-0925) or in the *Miami Herald*.

Further along the street, at no. 73 W, four forbidding Doric columns mark the entrance to the **Dade County Courthouse.** Built in 1926 on the site of an earlier courthouse – where public hangings used to take place – this was Miami's tallest building for fifty years (until it was dwarfed by the 55-story First Union Financial Center on South Biscayne Boulevard), and its night lights showed off a distinctive stepped pyramid peak that beamed out a symbolic warning to wrongdoers all over the city.

The Metro-Dade Cultural Center

Little inside the courthouse is worth passing the security check for (the juiciest cases are tried in the New Courthouse; see "North of Flagler Street" opposite). Instead, you should cross SW First Avenue towards the giant, air-raid shelter-like building of the **Metro-Dade Cultural Center**, entered via a ramp off Flagler Street. This was an ambitious attempt by renowned architect Philip Johnson to create a postmodern Mediterranean-style piazza, a congenial gathering place where Miami could display its cultural side. The theory almost worked: superb art shows, historical collections and a major library frame the courtyard, but Johnson forgot the power of the south Florida sun. Rather than pausing to rest and gossip, most people scamper across the open space towards the nearest shade.

Facing the piazza, the **Historical Museum of Southern Florida** (Mon–Wed, Fri & Sat 10am–5pm, Thurs 10am–9pm, Sun noon–5pm; $5; ☎ 375-1492) offers a comprehensive look at the multifaceted past of southern Florida. The section on the indigenous people has a strong collection of photographs and artifacts that reveal much about Native Americans' lifestyle. Fleeing persecution further north, the Apalachee (also known as the Creek

Indians) began arriving during the eighteenth century in what was then Spanish-ruled southern Florida, followed (under similar circumstances) by the Seminoles a century later. Unfortunately, little evidence or information remains of the indigenous Tequesta peoples who had been killed off by disease, murder or enslavement by the time the British (who kept records) took over from the Spanish (who didn't), though the foundations of a *chickee* hut were found recently on a downtown building site. Another fine display covers the trials and tribulations of early Miami settlers, enabling you to put faces to names such as Tuttle and Brickell that crop up as street, park or bridge titles all over the city. Also well chronicled are the fluctuating fortunes of Miami Beach: from its early days as a celebrities' vacation spot – with amusing photos of Twenties Hollywood greats – through to the renovation of the Art Deco district. Recent history is also covered, with considerable space devoted to the arrival of Cuban refugees and immigrants.

A few yards from the historical museum, the **Miami Art Museum of Miami-Dade County** (Tues–Fri 10am–5pm, Sat & Sun noon–5pm; $5; ☎375-5000) showcases outstanding international traveling exhibitions, with a particular strength in Latin American works from 1940 to the present. Directly opposite the museum is the **Main Public Library** (Mon–Wed, Fri & Sat 9am–6pm, Thurs 9am–9pm, Sun 1–5pm; closed Sun in summer), which, besides the usual lending sections, has temporary exhibitions on art and literary themes as well as a massive collection of Florida magazines and books.

Adjoining the Cultural Center, the **Metro-Dade Center** (also called the Government Center) chiefly comprises county government offices, but useful bus and train timetables can be gathered from the **Transit Service Center** (daily 7am–6pm; ☎770-3131) by the Metrorail entrance at the eastern side of the building.

North of Flagler Street

The tempo drops and storefronts become less brash as you head **north of Flagler Street**. A busy Hispanic procession passes in and out of the 1925 Catholic **Gesú Church**, 118 NE Second St, whose Mediterranean Revival exterior and stylishly decorated innards make a pleasing splash, but otherwise there's nothing else to slow you down until you reach the Neoclassical **US Federal Courthouse**, 300 NE First Ave (Mon–Fri 8.30am–5pm), a few minutes' walk away.

Finished in 1931, the building first functioned as a post office; Miami's then negligible crime rate required just one room on the second floor for judicial purposes. The room did acquire a monumental **mural**, however: *Law Guides Florida's Progress*, by Denman Fink (the designer behind much of Coral Gables, see p.96), a 25-foot-long depiction of Florida's evolution from swampy backwoods to modern state; if the courtroom's locked, see if the security guard will grant you a peek. In 1985, fresco artist David Novros was commissioned to decorate the building's medieval-style inner **courtyard**, to which his bold, colorful daubs make a lively addition.

By the late Sixties, Miami's crime levels became too much for the old courthouse to handle, and the building of the $22 million **New Courthouse** was started next door (main entrance on N Miami Ave; Mon–Fri 8.30am–5pm). A gruesome creation of concrete and glass, the major advantage of the new courthouse – other than size – is that jurors can pass in and out unobserved: "Getting them out without getting them dead," as one judge commented.

Bayside Marketplace and north

Typical Miamian consumerism is on display at the **BAYSIDE MARKET-PLACE**, 401 N Biscayne Blvd (Mon–Sat 10am–10pm, Sun 11am–9pm; restaurants and bars stay open later), a large, pink shopping mall providing pleasant waterfront views from its terraces. Enlivened by street musicians and some choice international food stands, the place is less hideous than might be expected, but is clearly aimed at tourists. A number of pleasure trips around the bay begin here (see "Bus, boat and helicopter tours," p.71) .

To the north of the Bayside Marketplace, endless lines of container trucks turning into Port Boulevard attest to the importance of the **Port of Miami** – now one of the world's biggest cargo and cruise ship terminals. Just beyond, the perpetual flame of the John Kennedy Memorial Torch of Friendship symbolizes good relations between the US and its southern neighbors, and guards the entrance to **Bicentennial Park,** filled with markers to various US-approved Central American luminaries.

Between Bicentennial Park and Bayside Marketplace is the **American Airlines Arena**, home of the Miami Heat basketball team, with restaurants and shops linked to Bayside by a pedestrian bridge.

Freedom Tower and around

Across Biscayne Boulevard, the **FREEDOM TOWER**, originally home to the now defunct *Miami News*, earned its current name by housing the Cuban Refugee Center, which began operations in 1962. Most of those who left Cuba on the "freedom flights"★ got their first taste of US bureaucracy here. The 1925 building, modeled on the Giralda bell tower in Seville in Spain, has been closed for some years owing to ongoing restoration – its Mediterranean features are more impressive from a distance, anyway. There are plans to reopen it as a museum of Cuban culture once it is complete.

Beyond the Freedom Tower, there's little more to see within walking distance, and you're on the fringe of some of the city's most impoverished – and dangerous – neighborhoods. You might venture a few blocks further to the **City of Miami Cemetery**, on the corner of North Miami Avenue and NE Eighteenth Street, though this should only be undertaken with a **walking tour** ($15; ☎ 375-1625 for details). There are historical stories aplenty here, such as Julia Tuttle's, whose claim to fame as "mother of the city" is that she and the Brickell family bribed Henry Flagler to bring the railway to Miami. Alas, many of the graves are littered with used syringes, anything valuable has been stolen and the family vaults of early Miami bigwigs have had their doors torn off by the homeless seeking shelter.

Little Haiti and the Police Museum

About 200,000 **Haitians** live in Miami, forming one of the city's major ethnic groups – albeit it far smaller than the Cuban population. Roughly a third of them live in what's become known as **LITTLE HAITI**, a two-hundred-block area (formerly known as Lemontown) that centers on NE Second

---

★ Between December 1965 and June 1972, ten empty planes a week left Miami to collect Cubans – over 250,000 in total – allowed to leave the island by Fidel Castro. While US propaganda hailed them as "freedom fighters," most of the arrivals were simply seeking the fruits of capitalism, and, as Castro astutely recognized, those who were seriously committed to overthrowing his regime would be far less troublesome outside Cuba.

Avenue, north of 42nd Street (buses #9 or #10 from the downtown area). Aside from hearing Haitian Creole on the streets (almost all Miami's Haitians speak English as a third language after Creole and French), you'll notice the colorful shops, offices and restaurants. For a taste of the culture, visit the **Caribbean Marketplace**, 5927 NE Second Ave (Tues–Sun 9am–8pm), a large building designed to resemble the French Colonial Iron Market in Port au Prince, which contains stalls and small stores selling Haitian handicrafts, books, records and food such as goat-stew. Established in 1990 to encourage local entrepreneurs and create a commercial focal point for the community, the Marketplace has been largely unsuccessful, with much of the space unused. **The Haitian Refugee Center**, 32 NE 56th Ave, will give you a greater insight into why Haitians remain one of the more oppressed immigrant groups in Miami, most scraping their living as taxi-drivers or hotel maids, hindered by poor education and English-language skills, and by the often racist attitudes of Anglos, Cubans and black Americans alike.

Close to Little Haiti (buses #3, #16, or "Biscayne Max" from downtown Miami), the **American Police Hall of Fame & Museum**, 3801 Biscayne Blvd (daily 10am–5.30pm; $6; ℡573-0070, ⓦwww.aphf.org), occupies the former local FBI headquarters – a shrine to law and order located near to Liberty City and Overtown, scene of some of Miami's most desperate living. You can easily while away a spare hour here: besides CIA baseball caps, a robo-cop (from the film) and the car from the film *Blade Runner*, the first floor is devoted to a somber memorial to slain police officers. Upstairs you'll find information on gangsters; a dope addict's kit; an arsenal of weapons found on highways; the chain gang leg-irons still used in Tennessee; and moments of humor, including a signed photo of Keith Richards, a member of the museum's celebrity advisory board. Bad taste abounds throughout – you can even have your photograph taken in the electric chair or a gas chamber.

Liberty City and Overtown

These two neighborhoods are part of the Seventeenth District, which has the highest proportion of black residents in the state and has been the site of numerous black expressions of rage at racial injustice. In December 1979, after a prolonged sequence of unpunished assaults by white police officers on members of the African-American community, a respected black citizen, Arthur MacDuffie, was dragged off his motorbike in **LIBERTY CITY** and beaten to death by a group of four white officers. Five months later, an all-white jury acquitted the accused officers, sparking off what became known as the Liberty City Riot. On May 18, 1980, the night after the trial, the whole of Miami was ablaze, from Carol City in the far north to Homestead in the south. The violence began on Sunday, roadblocks sealed off African-American neighborhoods until Wednesday, and a citywide curfew lasted until Friday. In the final tally, eighteen were dead, hundreds injured, and damage to property was estimated at over $200 million. Reports of shooting, stone throwing and whites being dragged from their cars and attacked or even burned alive, were rife in the press, though the majority of the victims were actually African Americans killed by police and National Guardsmen.

Incredibly, what has been seen as the "worst racial paroxysm in modern American history" (not the first nor likely to be the last violent expression of Miami's racial tensions) caused no harm to Miami's broader fortunes, coming just as the city was establishing itself as a hub of Latin American finance and on the brink of becoming fashionable. Even Liberty City soon found a chic international fashion district (see "Shopping," p.126) springing up in the disused warehouses on its periphery – the western edge of Little Haiti. Nonetheless, Miami's African Americans have remained at the bottom of the city's social heap, and there were further (less serious) riots in 1989 after a Latino police officer beat a black man to death in the same area – little had changed in nine years (and to the present) and Miami's reaction might well be taken as an example of how not to address such social problems.

From the earliest days, Coloredtown, as **OVERTOWN** was previously known, was divided by train tracks from the white folks of downtown Miami, and by the Thirties – when its jazz clubs thrilled multiracial audiences – conditions were so bad and overcrowding so extreme that Liberty City was built in an adjoining area to ease the strain.

In recent decades, Miami's black–white relations have been complicated by the extraordinary scale of Hispanic immigration, which has caused the city's African Americans to miss out even on the menial jobs that elsewhere in the US are their traditional preserve. This unique form of political dispossession was borne out by an official snub delivered by the city's Cuban American mayor, Xavier Suarez, to the June 1990 visit of Nelson Mandela. This incident, which stemmed from Mandela's refusal to denounce Fidel Castro, stimulated a well-organized **African American boycott** of the City's lucrative tourist industry, causing African American professional organizations around the US to cancel conventions planned for Miami. Dubbed the "quiet riot," the boycott cost the city millions of dollars in lost revenue.

Needless to say, these areas are not only depressing but also dangerous, and your very presence may be seen as provocative, particularly if you're white. If you do unwittingly find yourself driving through the area, keep your windows closed, doors locked, be wary when stopping at lights, and do not leave your car.

If you've a serious interest in the African American contribution to Miami and Florida, head for the **Black Archives History and Research Foundation of South Florida**, in Building C, Suite 101, 5400 NW 22nd Ave (Mon–Fri 9am–5pm; free; ☏636-2390, ⓦwww.theblackarchives.org), a resource center that also arranges guided tours of black historical areas. Currently the tours are only for a minimum of ten people, though more tourist-orientated bus and walking tours are being planned – phone or check the Web site for the latest info.

Miami River and Brickell Avenue

Fifteen minutes' walk south from Flagler Street, the **MIAMI RIVER** marks the southern limit of downtown. If your crossing is delayed by the drawbridge being raised to allow a ship through, glance westwards to the concrete modernity of the *Hotel Inter-Continental*, at the river's mouth, built on the site where Henry Flagler's *Royal Palm Hotel* stood at the turn of the century. At the behest of Miami's biggest landowners, Flagler – a millionaire oil baron whose railroad opened up Florida's east coast and brought wealthy wintering socialites to his string of smart hotels – extended the rail line here from Palm Beach. His luxury hotel and subsequent dredging of Biscayne Bay to accommodate cruise ships did much to put Miami on the map.

Brickell Avenue Banks and the Atlantis

One landowner, William Brickell, ran a trading post on the south side of the river, an area now dominated by **BRICKELL AVENUE.** Beginning immediately across the SE Second Avenue Bridge and running to Coconut Grove (see p.102), Brickell Avenue was *the* address in 1910s Miami, easily justifying its "millionaires row" nickname. While the original grand homes have largely disappeared, money is still Brickell Avenue's most obvious asset: over the bridge begins a half-mile parade of banks, the largest group of international **banks** in the US, whose imposing forms are softened by fore-courts filled with sculptures, fountains and palm trees. Far from being places to change a travelers' check, these institutions are bastions of international high finance. From the late Seventies, Miami emerged as a corporate banking center, cashing in on political instability in South and Central America by offering a secure home for Latin American money, some of which needed laundering.

The sudden rise of the Brickell banks was matched by new condominiums of breathtaking proportions but little architectural merit a few blocks further along. In their pastel-shaded midst, these astronomically priced abodes include the most stunning modern building in Miami: the **Atlantis**, at no. 2025. First sketched on a napkin in a Cuban restaurant and finished in 1983, the Atlantis crowned several years of innovative construction by a small architectural firm called Arquitectonica, whose style – variously termed "beach-blanket Bauhaus" and "ecstatic modernism" – fused postmodern thought with a strong sense of Miami's eclectic architectural heritage. The building's focal point is a gaping square hole through its middle where a palm tree, a Jacuzzi and a red-painted spiral staircase tease the eye. You won't be allowed inside unless you know someone who lives there, which might be just as well: even its designers admit the interior doesn't live up to the exuberance of the exterior, and claim the building to be "architecture for 55mph" – in other words, seen to best effect from a passing car.

South Beach (SoBe)

Miami Beach's most exciting area is **SOUTH BEACH**, which occupies the southernmost three miles. Filled with pastel-colored Art Deco buildings, up-and-coming art galleries, modish diners and suntanned beach addicts, it attracts multinational swarms of photographers and film crews who zoom in on one of the hottest high-style backdrops in the world.

Approaching Miami Beach: the causeways and islands

The six **causeways** crossing Biscayne Bay between Miami and Miami Beach offer striking views of the city, especially at night when the lights of buildings downtown twinkle over the bay's dark waters. Some of the causeways also provide the only land access to the artificial residential islands that shelter the rich and famous from unwanted attention.

Best pickings are along **MacArthur Causeway**, running from just north of downtown Miami into Miami Beach's South Beach. A mile into it, **Watson Island Park** harbors the **Japanese Garden**, bequeathed to the city by a Japanese industrialist in 1961; pride of place goes to an eight-ton statue of Hotei – the Japanese god of prosperity. On subsequent islands are the former homes of gangster Al Capone (Palm Island), author Damon Runyon (Hibiscus Island) and actor Don Johnson (Star Island).

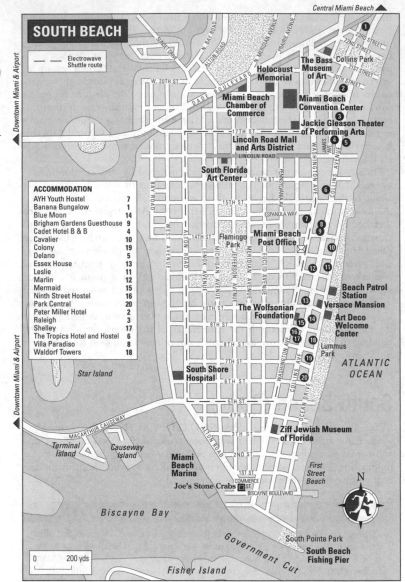

Socially, South Beach is unsurpassed. By day, fine-bodied hunks soak up the rays on the beach, and by night the ten blocks of Ocean Drive are the heart and soul of the biggest party in Miami: chic terrace cafés spill across the wide sidewalk amid a procession of fashion models, tropical-shirted existentialists, wide-eyed tourists, tarot card readers and middle-aged trendies. Places worth frequenting are listed under "Nightlife," see p.118. Ocean Drive is also the scene of the Miami Beach cruise; see the box on p.86.

Not all South Beach is so sensuous. Just a few blocks from Ocean Drive, the streets still bear the scars of the area's poverty-stricken Seventies, and the arrival in 1980 of the "Marielitos," Fidel Castro's gift to the US of Cuban criminals and misfits (see "Little Havana," p.92), many of whom ended up here. Provided you stick to the main streets and exercise the usual caution, however, none of South Beach is unduly dangerous.

The Art Deco district

As much as the beach and the social life, it's the **Art Deco district**, containing the world's greatest concentration of Art Deco architecture, that brings people to South Beach. Art Deco here is a smorgasbord rather than a gourmet experience; there are no great buildings, just a great number of them – numbering in the hundreds between 5th and 23rd streets between Ocean Drive and Lennox Avenue - built during the late Thirties in a style that became known as "Miami Beach Art Deco."

Ocean Drive and the Art Deco hotels

Painstaking restoration notwithstanding, little of the Art Deco district looks today quite like it did in the Thirties. Nowhere is this more apparent than in

MIAMI | South Beach

Art Deco in Miami Beach

Art Deco's roots go back to the Paris of 1901, though in the US it only began to take hold as a building style in the Thirties. With it, the nation shook off the restraints of Classical Revivalism and the gloom of the Depression. Thrilling and new, Art Deco architecture embraced technology, borrowing streamlined contours from the aerodynamic designs of futuristic cars, trains and planes. It also incorporated playful and humorous themes, employing wacky ornamentation and vivid colors, as well as new materials, such as aluminum, chrome and plastic. Often derided as vulgar, Art Deco nonetheless became a symbol of a country emerging from economic catastrophe to become the first twentieth-century superpower.

In the late Thirties, a small group of architects built prolifically – and fast – in Miami Beach. Employing the hallmarks of Art Deco, they used local limestone and stucco to produce buildings that were cheap (and often cramped and uncomfortable) but instantly fashionable - defining the look of the nation's fun-and-sun mecca with a style soon dubbed **Miami Beach Art Deco** (sometimes called **Tropical Deco**). Recognizable Florida motifs, such as herons, pelicans, blooming flowers and blazing sunsets, soon decorated facades and porches. Nautical themes were prevalent, too: windows resembled portholes, balconies stretched out like luxury liner sundecks, and any ungainly bulges on roofs were disguised as ships' funnels. Many of the buildings were painted stark white, reflecting the force of the Florida sun with matching intensity.

It's a sobering thought that Miami Beach almost lost all of these significant structures, which fell into decline from the late Fifties and were sought after by property developers wishing to replace them with anonymous high-rise condominiums. In the mid-Seventies, the **Miami Beach Art Deco Preservation League** (see "Information") – whose first meeting drew just six people – was born with the aim of saving the buildings and raising awareness of their architectural and historical importance. The league's success has been dramatic – a major turning point was convincing the buck-hungry developers of the earning potential of such a unique area. The driving force of the movement, the late Barbara Capitman, failed in her attempt at a similar initiative in Opa-Locka, a socially blighted district in northwest Miami, nowadays better known for its crack dealers than its zany, arabesque architecture.

The Miami Beach cruise

A bumper-to-bumper procession of horn-honking, passenger-swapping autos along Ocean Drive between Fifth and Fourteenth streets, the **Miami Beach cruise** – part unofficial street party, part pick-up exercise – takes place on Fridays and Saturdays from around 7pm to 4am, and on Sunday from noon to 7pm. Join in if you dare!

the colors – "a palette of Post Modern cake-icing pastels now associated with *Miami Vice*," according to disgruntled Florida architecture chronicler Hap Hatton – that appeared in 1980 when local designer Leonard Horowitz started adorning the buildings. Furthermore, the details of restoration reflect the tastes of the buildings' owners more than historical accuracy – but Miami Beach Art Deco of the new millennium is a sight to behold in its own right.

Examples of the Art Deco style are too numerous to list (or view) in full; just stroll around and keep your eyes open. For a more structured investigation, try the **walking tour** from the Art Deco Welcome Center or the **cycling tour** from Miami Beach Bicycle Center (see p.70).

The district's contemporary look should be assessed from Ocean Drive, where a line of revamped hotels have exploited their design heritage; you can venture into the lobbies for a look, and many are worth visiting for their bars or restaurants (see "Eating" and "Nightlife"). Among them, the **Park Central**, no. 640, is a geometric *tour de force*, with octagonal windows, sharp vertical columns and a wrought-iron decorated stairway leading up to the mezzanine level, which displays monochrome photos of Miami Beach in the Twenties. Nearby, at no. 850, a corner of the **Waldorf Towers** is topped by an ornamental lighthouse. Just across the street in Lummus Park (the grassy patch that separates Ocean Drive from the beach), and more honestly redolent of the old days, stands the boat-shaped **Beach Patrol Station**, unmistakeable for its vintage oversized date and temperature sign, and still the base of the local lifeguards.

Just ahead are two buildings at the center of the controversy currently raging through South Beach: should the area's Art Deco buildings be decorated only in the pastel colors approved by the Art Deco Preservation League, or can they be allowed to evolve a particularly 1990s South Beach style that uses much more vivid tones. The purple and orange frontage of the **Cardozo**, no. 1300, and the intense yellow exterior of the **Leslie**, no. 1244, are the recent work of Barbara Hulanicki, who founded London's scene-setting clothes store Biba in the 1960s. Hulanicki's exuberant tones have upset many South Beach purists, but seem set to be the look of South Beach to come.

Walk at least once after dark along the beach side of **Ocean Drive**. This frees you from the crowds and enables a clear view of the Art Deco hotels' **neon illuminations**, casting shimmering circles and lines of vivid blues, pinks and greens around the contours of the buildings.

Away from the image-conscious trappings of Ocean Drive, perhaps the district's most enduring relic, an example of the less ornate Depression Moderne style, is the **Miami Beach Post Office**, 1300 Washington Ave (lobby Mon–Fri 6am–6pm, Sat 6am–4pm). Inside, streaming sunlight brightens the murals sweeping around a rotunda; there can be few more enjoyable places to buy a stamp.

South of Fifth Street: South Pointe Park and around

South of Fifth Street, a small and shabby area called **South Pointe** is being revamped by a major redevelopment project: more, it seems, to exploit the commercial potential of the location than to benefit the community. A marina and several restaurants have been added, and the luxury 26-story South Pointe Towers leaps skyward from South Pointe Park (see below), dwarfing the stucco-fronted boxes in which most local people live. The best route through South Pointe is the mile-long shorefront boardwalk, beginning near the southern end of Lummus Park, and finishing by the 300-foot-long jetty lined with people fishing off First Street Beach, the only surfing beach in Miami and alive with tanned, athletic bodies even when the waves are calm. You can swim and snorkel here, too, but bear in mind that the big cruise ships frequently pass close by and stir up the current.

South Pointe Park

On its inland side, the boardwalk skirts **South Pointe Park** (daily 8am–sunset), whose handsome lawns and tree-shaded picnic tables offer a respite from the packed beaches. The park is a good place to be on Friday evenings when its open-air stage is the venue for enjoyable free **music events** (details are posted up around South Beach).

Seats on the southern edge of the park give you a view of **Government Cut**, a waterway first dredged by Henry Flagler at the turn of the century and now, substantially deepened, the route for large cruise ships beginning their journeys to the Bahamas and Caribbean. You might also witness an impounded drug-running vessel being towed along by the authorities. Don't be surprised, either, to hear the neighing of horses: Miami Beach's police horses are stabled on the eastern side of the park.

North along Washington Avenue

Running through South Beach parallel to Ocean Drive is **Washington Avenue**, much of it lined by small, Cuban-run supermarkets, trendy restaurants and boutiques, run-down retirement homes, and a string of nightclubs. Two of Miami Beach's museums are located here, while a third lies just to the west.

Ziff Jewish Museum of Florida

During the 1920s and 1930s, South Beach became a major destination for Jewish tourists escaping the harsh northeastern winters. In response, many of the hotels placed "Gentiles Only" notices at their reception desks, and the slogan "Always a view, never a Jew" appeared in many a hotel brochure. Despite this, by the 1940s South Beach had a largely Jewish population and, though today the center of the community has moved north along the Beach to around 40th and 50th streets, a considerable number of elderly Jews still come here to live out their last years. The **Ziff Jewish Museum of Florida**, 301 Washington Ave (Tues–Sun 10am–5pm; $5, free Sat; ☎672-5044, ⓦwww.jewishmuseum.com), bears testimony to Jewish life not only in Miami Beach, but in all of Florida. Housed in an elegant 1936-built Art Deco building, which served as an Orthodox synagogue for Miami Beach's first Jewish congregation, the museum documents Florida's Jewish heritage from the eighteenth century to the present day. Apart from its permanent collection, the museum hosts visiting exhibitions on Jews in Florida, the Caribbean and elsewhere.

Wolfsonian Foundation

Seventy thousand late-nineteenth century and twentieth century decorative arts and crafts from Europe and the Americas have been assembled in a Mediterranean-Revival building by Mitchell Wolfson Jr at the **Wolfsonian**

Foundation, 1001 Washington Ave (Tues & Thurs–Sat 11am–6pm, Sun noon–5pm; $5; ☎ 531-1001). Anyone with a passing interest in decorative, architectural or politically inspired art ought to be able to find something of interest in the galleries, which also provide a wonderfully cool haven from the shadeless avenue outside.

Española Way

Other than the Miami Beach Post Office (described above under "The Art Deco district"), nothing along Washington Avenue need delay you until you reach **Española Way**, between Fourteenth and Fifteenth streets. While renowned for its Art Deco, Miami Beach also boasts several examples of the Mediterranean Revival architecture found across much of Miami; most of these are situated on this slender street overhung by narrow balconies and striped awnings.

Completed in 1925, Española Way was grandly envisaged as an artists' colony, but only the rumba dance craze of the Thirties – said to have started here, stirred up by Cuban bandleader Desi Arnaz★ – came close to fitting the bill. Following South Beach's social rise in the Eighties, however, a group of browsable commerical art galleries and art supply stores have revived the original vision; they now fill the first-floor rooms, while above them, small top-floor apartments are optimistically marketed as artists' lofts.

Lincoln Road Mall and the Lincoln Road Arts District

A short walk further north, between Sixteenth and Seventeenth streets, the pedestrianized **Lincoln Road Mall** was considered the flashiest shopping precinct outside of New York during the Fifties, its jewelry and clothes stores earning it the label "Fifth Avenue of the South." Today, run-of-the-mill consumer durable stockists fill the section closest to Washington Avenue, and the focus of interest has shifted a few blocks west to the **Lincoln Road Arts District**, around Lenox Avenue. Here, among a number of private art galleries breathing life into what were, a few years ago, fairly seedy offices and shops, the studios (viewing hours are displayed on their doors) and showrooms of the **South Florida Art Center, Inc**, 810 Lincoln Rd, will tune you into the burgeoning South Beach arts scene. The area's increasingly cultured mood is reflected in the many restaurants and cafés along the mall (see "Eating"), and it is a favorite place for evening strolls.

The Jackie Gleason Theater and the Miami Beach Convention Center

The first of two public buildings immediately north of Lincoln Road Mall, the 3000-seat **Jackie Gleason Theater of Performing Arts**, fronted by Pop artist Roy Lichtenstein's expressive *Mermaid* sculpture, stages Broadway shows and classical concerts. However, it is best known to middle-aged Americans as the home of exuberant entertainer Jackie Gleason's immensely popular TV show, *The Honeymooners*, which began in the Fifties and ran for twenty years.

On the far side of the theater, sunlight bounces off the white exterior of the massive **Miami Beach Convention Center**, which occupies a curious niche in US political history. At the Republican Convention held here in August 1968, Richard Nixon won the nomination that would take him to the White

★Arnaz (later to find wider fame as the husband of Lucille Ball and co-star of *I Love Lucy*) and his band often performed in the *Village Tavern*, inside the *Clay Hotel*, which is now the city's youth hostel; see "Accommodation."

House. Nixon counted his votes oblivious to the fact that the first of Miami's Liberty City riots had just erupted (see "Liberty City and Overtown" p.81).

The Holocaust Memorial

It is hard not to be moved by Kenneth Treister's **Holocaust Memorial**, 1933–1945 Meridian Ave (daily 9am–9pm; free; ☎538-1663), completed in 1990 and dedicated to Elie Wiesel. Depicting a 42-foot-high bronze arm tattooed with an Auschwitz number reaching towards the sky. Life-sized figures of emaciated, tormented people attempt to climb this deeply emotive sculpture, which rises from a lily pond in the center of a plaza, around which are graphic images recalling the Nazi genocide against the Jews.

The Bass Museum of Art

A little further north, within a sculpture-studded garden, is the fetching coral-rock building of the **Bass Museum of Art**, 2121 Park Ave (Tues, Thurs–Sat 10am–5pm, Wed 10am–9pm, Sun 1–5pm; $6; ☎ 673-7530, ⓦ www.bassmuseum .org), whose major expansion, completed in 1995, was overseen by the acclaimed Japanese architect Arata Isozaki. The museum's permanent collection – dominated by worthy European works mostly from the fifteenth to seventeenth centuries, with Rubens, Rembrandt and Dürer heading the cast – is a notch above anything else you'll find in the state. For those who are not fine-art buffs, the contemporary visiting exhibitions offer greater stimulation.

Central Miami Beach

The energy of South Beach fades dramatically as you travel north of 23rd Street to **CENTRAL MIAMI BEACH**. Collins Avenue charts a five-mile course through the area, between Indian Creek – across which are the golf courses, country clubs and secluded palatial homes of Miami Beach's seriously rich – and the swanky hotels around which the Miami Beach high life revolved during the glamorous Fifties. These often madly ostentatious establishments are the main attraction of Central Miami Beach; the strand itself is largely the preserve of families and older folk, and is backed by a long and lovely boardwalk that stretches over a mile from 21st Street.

Along Collins Avenue

The southern edge of Central Miami Beach is defined by the garbage-clogged **Collins Canal**, cut in the 1910s to speed the movement of farm produce through the mangrove trees that then lined Biscayne Bay. The canal is a dismal sight, but improves as it flows into the luxury-yacht-lined **Indian Creek**, and along Collins Avenue you'll see the first of the sleek condos and hotels that characterize the area.

Unlike their smaller Art Deco counterparts in South Beach, the later **hotels** of Central Miami Beach are massive monuments to the Fifties. When big was beautiful, these state-of-the-art pleasure palaces drew the international jet set by offering much more than mere accommodation: a price that few could afford also bought access to exclusive bars, restaurants and lounges where film and TV stars cavorted to the envy of the rest of the US. Yet the good times were short-lived. As everyone tried to cash in, cheap imitations of the pace-setting hotels formed an ugly wall of concrete along **Collins Avenue**; quality sank, service deteriorated and the big names moved on. By the Seventies, many of the hotels looked like what they really were: monsters from another age. The

Eighties saw Miami's social star re-emerge, and a revival was soon under way. Many of the polished-up hotels are now occupied by well-heeled Latin American tourists – along with gray-haired swingers from the US for whom Miami Beach never lost its cachet.

The Fontainebleau Hilton

Before Central Miami Beach became a celebrities' playground, the nation's rich and powerful built rambling shorefront mansions here. One of them, the winter home of tire-baron Harvey Firestone, was demolished in 1953 to make room for the **Fontainebleau Hilton**, 4441 Collins Ave, a dreamland of kitsch and consumerism that defined the Miami Beach of the late Fifties and Sixties. Gossip-column perennials, such as Joan Crawford, Joe DiMaggio, Lana Turner and Bing Crosby, were Fontainebleau regulars, as was crooner Frank Sinatra who, besides starting a scrambled-egg fight in the coffee shop, shot many scenes here as the private-eye hero of the Sixties film *Tony Rome*. Drop in for a look around the curving lobby overhung by weighty chandeliers, and venture through the tree-filled grounds to a swimming pool complete with rock grottoes and waterfalls.

Even if you find the bellhops lurking in the lobby daunting, one feature you shouldn't miss is Richard Haas' 13,000-square-foot trompe l'oeil mural on one of the exterior walls. Approaching from the south, Collins Avenue veers left just before the hotel, passing beneath the mural. Unveiled in 1986, it creates the illusion of a great hole in the wall exposing the hotel directly behind – one of the biggest driving hazards in Miami.

More hotels and luxury homes

Truth be told, there's not much more to see in Central Miami Beach. For its place in local folklore, the *Fontainebleau Hilton* is easily the most tempting of the hotels, though you might snatch glances inside the *Shawnee*, no. 4343, and the *Castle Beach Club*, no. 5445, both Fifties survivors that have undergone stylized renovation, with marble floors, indoor fountains and etched glasswork. Meanwhile, the ultra-swish *Alexander*, no. 5225, has become a watering hole for Miami's present-day smart set.

Many of the rich people who live in Miami Beach have gracefully appointed homes up pine-tree-lined drives on the other side of Indian Creek. Cross the water on Arthur Godfrey Road and drive (or cycle) around the exclusive La Gorce Drive and Alton Road for an eyeful of what money can buy.

From further down Collins Avenue to North Miami Beach, hotels dominate the scene. In 1968, an unrestrained Norman Mailer wrote of the area: "Moorish castles shaped like waffle irons, shaped like the baffle plates on white plastic electric heaters, and cylinders like Waring blenders, buildings looking like giant op art and pop art paintings, and sweet wedding cakes, cottons of kitsch and piles of dirty cotton stucco. . ."

North Miami Beach and inland

Collins Avenue continues for seven uninspiring miles through **NORTH MIAMI BEACH**, enriched only by a few noteworthy beaches and parks. Confusingly, owing to the machinations of early property speculators, the four small communities that make up this northern section of Miami Beach lack a collective name, and the area officially titled "North Miami Beach" is actually inland, across Biscayne Bay.

Surfside, Bal Harbour and Haulover Beach

Untouched for years as big-money developments loomed all around, the low-rise buildings of **Surfside** – the pleasant North Shore Park marks the community's southern limit – retain a rather appealing old-fashioned ambience, though the community is currently in the throes of gradual gentrification, and only the neighborhood's **beach**, between 91st and 95th streets, will make you want to stick around; incidentally, it's one of the few in Miami Beach to allow topless sunbathing.

Directly north, **Bal Harbour** – its aspirations of "Olde Worlde" elegance reflected in its anglicized name – is similar in size to Surfside but entirely different in character: an upmarket area filled with the carefully guarded homes of some of the nation's wealthiest people. The exclusive Bal Harbour Shops, 9700 Collins Ave, packed with outrageously expensive designer stores, sets the tone for the area.

A better place to spend time, especially if you can lose your inhibitions easily, is **Haulover Beach Park**, just to the north, whose reputation as a nudist beach doesn't overshadow the sprawling vegetation that backs onto more than a mile of pristine sand. There's also a great view of the Miami Beach skyline from the end of the pier. To get there take buses #H, #K or #S up Collins Avenue and get off at the coastguard station, where there are also parking facilities ($3). From here turn right for the regular beach or left for the "clothing optional" one, which starts at beach watch-station 24. Note that stations 27–29 are predominantly gay – and fairly cruisey at that.

Sunny Isles and Golden Beach

Beyond Haulover Park, **Sunny Isles** is as lifeless as they come: a place where European travel agencies dump unsuspecting package tourists and where, owing to bargain-basement prices, French Canadian tourists choose to return year after year, dominating the fast-food restaurants and tacky souvenir shops along Collins Avenue. You'll quickly get a tan on Sunny Isles' sands (if you can stay out of the shadows cast by enormous hotel blocks), but everything around is geared to low-budget, package tourism, and, if you're staying here without a car, you're likely to feel trapped. Of passing interest, however, are some architecturally excessive hotels erected during the Fifties: along Collins Avenue, watch out for the camels and sheikhs guarding the *Sahara*, no. 18335; the crescent-moon-holding maidens of the *Blue Mist*, no. 19111; and the Moorish-Polynesian-Deco-Ulua-Bad-Kitsch of the *Marco Polo*, no. 19200.

By the time you reach **Golden Beach**, the northernmost community of Miami Beach, much of the traffic pounding Collins Avenue has turned inland on the Lehman Causeway (192nd Street), and the anachronistic hotels have given way to quiet shorefront homes. Public beach access here is negligible, and unless you're intending to leave Miami altogether (Collins Avenue, as Hwy-A1A, continues north to Fort Lauderdale), there's a bigger draw to be found directly inland.

Inland: the Ancient Spanish Monastery

The Sunny Isles Causeway (163rd Street, Dixie Highway) leads across to North Miami Beach, on the mainland. Despite its name, this area is a continuation of the depressed suburbs north of downtown Miami, and not a place to linger unless you're visiting the **Ancient Spanish Monastery** (Mon–Sat

The coastal route, Hwy-A1A (Collins Avenue), and the mainland Hwy-1 (Biscayne Boulevard), both continue into Hollywood, at the southern edge of the Fort Lauderdale area, fully described in Chapter Three, "The Southeast Coast."

10am–4pm, Sun 1–5pm; $5; ☎945-1461). Publishing magnate William Randolph Hearst came across the twelfth-century monastery in Spain in 1925, bought it for $500,000, broke it into numbered pieces and shipped it to the US – only for it to be held by customs, who feared that it might carry foot-and-mouth disease. Photos in the monastery's entrance room show the 11,000 boxes that contained the monastery when it came ashore – and a docker standing over them, scratching his head.

The demands of tax officials left Hearst short of ready funds, and the monastery lingered in a New York warehouse until 1952, when the pieces were brought here and reassembled as a tourist attraction. The job took a year and a half, and was done largely by trial and error thanks to incorrect repackaging of the pieces. Pacing the cloisters, as Cistercian monks did for 700 years, you can see the uneven form of the buttressed ceilings and rough, honey-colored walls. Now used as an Episcopal church, the monastery is a model of tranquility, its peacefulness enhanced by a lush garden setting.

If you're not driving, **getting to the monastery** is relatively easy with buses #E, #H and #V from Sunny Isles or #3 from downtown Miami. Get off at 163rd Street, and it's a ten-minute walk – look out for the signpost.

Little Havana

Unquestionably the largest ethnic group in Miami, the impact of **Cubans** on the city over the last four decades has been incalculable. Unlike most Latino immigrants to the US, who trade one form of poverty for another, Miami's first Cuban arrivals in the late Fifties had already tasted affluence. They rose quickly through the social strata and nowadays wield considerable clout in the running of the city, and indeed the state.

The first Miami Cubans settled a few miles west of downtown Miami in what became known as **LITTLE HAVANA**. According to tourist brochures, the streets are filled with old men in *guayaberas* (billowing cotton shirts) playing dominoes, and exotic restaurants whose walls vibrate to the pulsating rhythms of the homeland. The reality is more subdued: Little Havana's parks, memorials, shops and food stands all reflect the Cuban experience – and as such shouldn't be missed – but the streets are quieter than those of downtown Miami (except during the Calle Ocho Festival in early March – see "Miami festivals," p.124) and no more attractive than any poor inner-city area. Like their US peers, as soon as the early settlers acquired sufficient dollars, they gave up the tightly grouped, modest homes of Little Havana for fully fledged suburban living, returning only for political demonstrations and dining out in the area's costly (but excellent) Spanish eateries.

For all the powerful emotions stirred up by its politics, there's not an awful lot to see in Little Havana; the appeal of the place is almost all atmospheric. On the graffitied streets, the prevailing mood is one of a community carrying on its daily business, and while the sights, smells and sounds are distinctly Cuban, most of the people you'll pass – at least those under 50 – are less likely to be Cuban than Nicaraguan, Honduran or Colombian, the latest immigrant groups in Miami to use Little Havana as a first base.

Only the neighborhood's main strip, SW Eighth Street, or **Calle Ocho,** offers more than houses: tiny cups of sweet Cuban coffee are sold from street-side counters, the odors of cigars being rolled and bread being baked waft across the sidewalk, shops sell Santería (see box below) ephemera beside six-foot-high models of Catholic saints, and you'll spot the only branch of Dunkin' Donuts to sell guava-filled doughnuts.

Along Calle Ocho

The most pertinent introduction to Little Havana is the **Brigade 2506 Memorial**, between Twelfth and Thirteenth avenues along Calle Ocho. Inscribed with the brigade crest, topped by the Cuban flag and an eternal flame, this simple stone remembers those who died at the Bay of Pigs on April 17, 1961, during the attempt by a group of US-trained Cuban exiles to invade the island and wrest control from Castro.

Depending on who tells the story, the outcome was the result of either ill-conceived plans, or the US's lack of commitment to Cuba – to this day, sections of the Cuban community hate Kennedy only slightly less than Fidel Castro. Every anniversary, veterans clad in combat fatigues and carrying assault rifles gather here to make pledges of patriotism throughout the night.

A more recent addition to the Memorial is a picture of the mother of Elián González with an inset of the boy himself, a fresh reminder of the community's most recent scrap with Castro. Elián fled Cuba with his mother on a raft in 2000; she drowned en route, he was picked up by the Coast Guard. This led to the most infamous of custody battles between his mother's Miami-based relatives and the father who remained in Cuba. Though he was offered considerable sums to come to the US to bring Elián up there, the father eventually won custody and took his son back to Cuba.

A less emotionally charged gathering place is **Máximo Gómez Domino Park** (daily 8am–6pm), a few yards away on a corner of Fourteenth Avenue; access to its open-air tables is (quite illegally) restricted to men over 55, and this is one place where you really will see old men in *guayaberas* playing dominoes.

Santería

Near the Brigade 2506 Memorial stands a statue of the Virgin Mary underneath a massive ceiba tree that has chicken bones and brightly colored bundles of cloth adorning its roots. These are sacrificial objects left by local practitioners of Santería, a religion of African origin that incorporates elements from the Catholic faith. Originating with the Yoruba peoples in West Africa, Santería was brought by them to Cuba and the rest of the Americas when they were enslaved. The Catholic slave-owners outlawed its practices, and it only survived by identifying its *orishas* (emissaries of Olorun, the one true god) with Catholic saints – hence the name Santería ("the way of the saints"). Similar to Voodoo in Haiti or Macumba in Brazil, its practitioners can get *orishas* to give magical aid and guidance through plant, food, or animal sacrifices offered during chants and dancing initiations. While there are an estimated three million Santería adherents in Cuba, it's thought there are 800,000 devotees, of various nationalities, in the US. It's little understood here, and the animal (and alleged human) sacrifices have brought them into conflict with animal-rights activists – though a court case in Miami's Hialeah district in 1993 confirmed the constitutional rights of adherents to practice their religion.

Proximity to the Caribbean island has long made Florida a place of refuge for Cuban activists and economc migrants. A raft ride from Cuba's northern shore, propelled by prevailing currents, can take four days to arrive in South Florida. From José Martí in the 1890s to Fidel Castro in the early Fifties, the country's radicals arrived to campaign and raise funds, and numerous deposed Cuban politicians have whiled away their exile in Florida. However, until comparatively recent times, New York, not Miami, was the center of Cuban émigré life in the US.

During the mid-Fifties, when opposition to the Batista dictatorship in Cuba – and the country's subservient role to the US – began to assert itself, a trickle of Cubans started arriving in the predominantly Jewish section of Miami called Riverside, moving into low-rent properties vacated as the extant community grew wealthier and moved out. The trickle became a flood when Castro took power, and as Cuban businesses sprang up on SW Eighth Street and Cubans began making their mark on Miami life, the area began to be known as **Little Havana.**

Those who left Cuba derived largely from the affluent white middle and upper classes with most to lose under communism. Many regarded themselves as the entrepreneurial sophisticates of the Caribbean, and stories are plentiful of formerly high-flying Cuban capitalists who arrived penniless in Little Havana, took menial jobs and, over the course of two decades – and aided by a formidable network of old ex-pats – toiled, wheeled and dealed their way steadily upwards to positions of power and influence (and not just locally – leading Miami Cubans also have considerable influence over the US government's policy towards Cuba) with their 800,000 votes and hefty campaign contributions.

The second great Cuban influx into Miami was of a quite different social nature and racial composition: the **Mariel boatlift** in May 1980 brought 125,000 predominantly black islanders from the Cuban port of Mariel to Miami. Unlike their more worldly predecessors, these arrivals were largely poor and uneducated, and a fifth of them were fresh from Cuban jails – incarcerated for criminal rather than political crimes. Bluntly put, Castro had dumped his criminals and misfits on Miami. Only a few of them wound up in Little Havana: most "Marielitos" settled in South Beach where they proceeded to terrorize the local community, thereby becoming a source of embarrassment to Miami's longer-established and determinedly respectable (and white) Cubans.

Eight blocks west along Calle Ocho from here you'll find the small, newly opened **Latin American Art Museum** at no. 2206 (Tues–Fri 11am–5pm, Sat 11am–4pm; free; ☎ 644-1127), which has permanent exhibitions of contemporary Latin American artists (including many Cubans) and incorporates two private galleries if you wish to buy artworks.

Further west, the peaceful greenery of **Woodlawn Cemetery**, between 32nd and 33rd avenues (daily sunset–dusk), belies the scheming and skulduggery that some of its occupants indulged in during their lifetimes. Two former Cuban heads of state are buried here: Gerardo Machado, ousted from office in 1933, is in the mausoleum, while one of the protagonists in his downfall, Carlos Prío Socarras, president from 1948 to 1952, lies just outside. Also interred in the mausoleum (and marked only by his initials) is **Anastasio Somoza**, dictator of Nicaragua until overthrown by the Sandinistas in 1979, and later killed in Paraguay.

Around Calle Ocho

With nondescript, low-income housing to the north and modest Spanish Revival Twenties bungalows to the south, there's little to draw you away from

Exile politics

However much Miami Cubans have prospered in the US, for many the liberation of their country is rarely far from their minds. Some older Cubans – driven by a fanatical hatred of Fidel Castro and communism – still consider themselves as exiles, though few would seriously think about giving up their comfortable lifestyles to return, whatever regime governs Cuba.

Within the complexities of Cuban exile politics, there's a major rift: one school of thought holds that the US sold Cuba out to the USSR, beginning when President Kennedy* withheld air support from the invading Brigade 2506 at the Bay of Pigs in 1961, and favors a violent overthrow of the communist regime with a return to the survival-of-the-fittest ethic of the old days. The more pragmatic line runs that the Cuban clock can't be turned back, and that the only way for exiled Cubans to be usefully involved is to face up to the present situation and use their economic muscle to bring about changes.

Fueled by a mix of machismo and hero-worship of early Cuban independence fighters, passions run high, and action – usually violent – has been prized more than words. In Miami, Cubans even *suspected* of advocating dialogue with Castro have been killed; one man had his legs blown off in the Eighties for suggesting violence on the streets was counterproductive, and the Cuban Museum of the Americas was bombed for displaying the work of Castro-approved artists.

In 1995, however, there was a break in the violence, as the hostility between exile factions was directed instead towards President Clinton and his policies of returning all future economic refugees to Cuba; for the first time since Castro came to power, Cubans had lost their special status, and instead were treated as any other economic migrant seeking to enter the US illegally. With George W. Bush's election as president, however, things will probably change, especially since his brother Jeb relies on the predominantly Republican Cuban vote to remain governor.

*In 1978, the US government's House Select Committee on Assassinations listed a (still active) Miami-based Cuban "action group," Alpha 66, as having "the motivation, capability, and resources" to have assassinated President Kennedy, and various, if unsubstantiated, links to the alleged assassin, Lee Harvey Oswald.

Calle Ocho. One possible detour is the **Cuban Museum of the Americas**, 1300 SW Twelfth Ave (Tues–Fri 10am–5pm, weekends by appointment, ☏529-5400, ⓦwww.ohwy.com/fl/c/cumuamer), which was established by Cuban exiles. Its exhibitions of contemporary work have to be carefully chosen to avoid inflaming local passions; the museum suffered a bomb attack in 1989 for displaying the works of artists living in Cuba, regarded as collaborators by extreme anti-Castro exiles.

You might also drop into *La Esquina de Tejas* restaurant, 101 SW Twelfth Ave, where you can mull over the signed photos of Ronald Reagan. It was in this otherwise ordinary Cuban eatery that the president, seeking re-election, took a well-publicized lunch in 1983 in an effort to harness the powerful Cuban vote in Miami. Four years later, George Bush called by for a swift *café Cubano* and a drawn-out photo call. Aside from his right-wing domestic policies, Reagan gained immense popularity among Miami Cubans for his support of the Nicaraguan Contras, viewed as kindred spirits in the guerrilla struggle against communism. (It's widely acknowledged that the Contras ran their anti-Sandinista operation from offices in Miami and trained for combat in the Everglades.) The community's affection was demonstrated by the renaming of Twelfth Avenue as Ronald Reagan Boulevard.

There's no point in actually going there (except for a sports event; see "Listings"), but from here you can see the rising hump of the 70,000-seat **Orange Bowl** stadium, about ten blocks north. This is home to the University of Miami's football team, the Hurricanes, but is best remembered by older Cubans as the place where, on a December night in 1962, John Kennedy took the Brigade 2506 flag and vainly promised to return it "in a free Havana."

Coral Gables

Though all of Miami's constituent cities are quick to assert their individuality, none has a greater case than **CORAL GABLES**, south of Little Havana. With twelve square miles of broad boulevards and leafy streets lined by elaborate Spanish- and Italian-style architecture, it makes the much more famous Art Deco district (see p.85) seem decidedly shabby.

Whereas Miami's other early property developers built cheap and fast in search of a quick buck, the creator of Coral Gables, a local man named **George Merrick**, was as much of an aesthete as an entrepreneur. Taking Mediterranean Europe as his inspiration, Merrick raided street names from a Spanish dictionary – coincidentally, many of today's residents are wealthy, Spanish-speaking Cubans – and enlisted his artist uncle, Denman Fink, and architect Phineas Paist to plan the plazas, fountains and carefully aged stucco-fronted buildings that would be built on the 3000 acres of citrus groves and pineland he inherited from his father.

Coral Gables: the entrances

To make a strong first impression on visitors to Coral Gables, Merrick planned eight grand **entrances** on the main access roads, of which only four were completed before the bust. The three most impressive are to the north, along a two-and-a-half-mile stretch of SW Eighth Street.

The million-dollar **Douglas Entrance** (junction with Douglas Road) was the most ambitious, consisting of a gateway and tower with two expansive wings of shops, offices and artists' studios. During the Sixties it was almost bulldozed to make room for a supermarket, but survived to become a well-scrubbed business area, still upholding Merrick's Mediterranean themes in its architecture. Further west, the sixty-foot-high vine-covered **Granada Entrance** (junction with Granada Boulevard) is based on the entrance to the city of Granada in Spain. A better appetizer for Coral Gables is the **Country Club Prado Entrance** (junction with Country Club Prado), the expensive recreation of a formal Italian garden bordered by freestanding stucco-and-brick pillars topped by ornamental urns and lamps with wrought-iron brackets.

The "Villages"

Driving (or cycling) around the less busy parts of Coral Gables, you'll catch glimpses of several "**Villages**," small pockets of residential architecture intended to diversify the area's Mediterranean looks. These include the brightly colored roofs and ornately carved balconies of the **Chinese Village**, on the "5100" block of Riviera Drive; the timber-beamed town houses of the **French Normandy Village**, on the "400" block of Vizcaya Avenue, at Le Jeune Road; and, perhaps strangest of all, the twisting chimneys and scroll-work arches of the **Dutch South African Village**, also on the "400" block of Vizcaya Avenue.

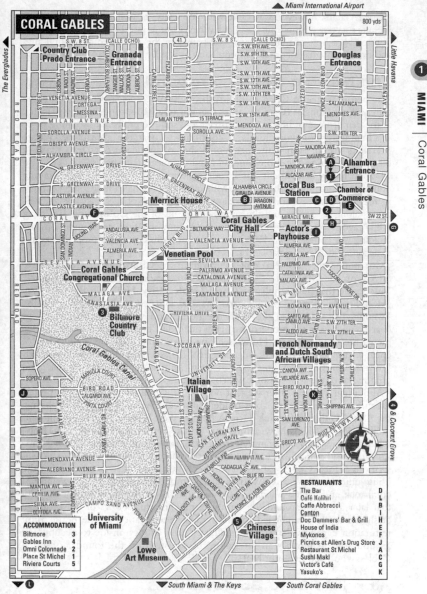

CORAL GABLES

Miami International Airport

The Everglades

Little Havana

Country Club Prado Entrance

Granada Entrance

Douglas Entrance

SW 8 ST. (CALLE OCHO)
S.W. 8 ST. (CALLE OCHO)
S.W. 9TH ST.
S.W. 9TH TER.
S.W. 10TH AVE.
S.W. 11TH AVE.
S.W. 12TH AVE.
S.W. 13TH AVE.
S.W. 13TH TER.
S.W. 14TH AVE.
S.W. 15TH AVE.

LISBON ST. EL PASO ST. MADRID ST.
TANGIER ST. WALLACE ST. CORDOVA ST.
MESSINA ST.
VENETIA AVENUE
ORTEGA
MESSINA
MILAN AVENUE
SOROLLA AVENUE
OBISPO AVENUE
ALHAMBRA CIRCLE
N. GREENWAY DRIVE
S. GREENWAY DRIVE
ASTURIA AVENUE
CASTILE AVENUE

COLUMBUS STREET
CAPRI STREET
PIZARRO STREET
CORTEZ STREET
S.W. 45TH AVE
S.W. 44TH AVE
SEGOVIA STREET
HERNANDO AVENUE
LE JEUNE ROAD
SALZEDO STREET
PONCE DE LEON BLVD

MILAN TERR.
15 TERRACE
SOROLLA AVE.
MENDOZA AVE.

S.W. 16TH TER.
MAJORCA AVE.
NAVARRE AVE.
MINORCA AVE.
ALCAZAR AVE.

SALAMANCA AVE.
MENORES AVE.

GALIANO ST.
DOUGLAS ROAD

Alhambra Entrance

A
1
Local Bus Station
B
C D
E
Chamber of Commerce

ALHAMBRA CIRCLE
GIRALDA AVENUE
ARAGON AVENUE

CORDOVA ST.
CASTILA STREET
ALHAMBRA CIRCLE
N. GREENWAY DRIVE

Merrick House

COLUMBUS BOULEVARD
GRANADA BOULEVARD
CORDOVA ST.
DESOTO BLVD
BILTMORE WAY

CORAL WAY

Coral Gables City Hall

Actor's Playhouse

MIRACLE MILE
SW 22 ST

2
H
I

Venetian Pool

Coral Gables Congregational Church

F

ANDALUSIA AVE.
VALENCIA AVE.
ALMERIA AVE.
SEVILLA AVENUE
MALAGA AVE.
ANASTASIA AVE.

BILTMORE WAY
VALENCIA AVENUE
SEVILLA AVENUE
PALERMO AVENUE
CATALONIA AVENUE
MALAGA AVENUE
SANTANDER AVENUE
RIVIERA DRIVE

S.W. 43RD AVE.
HERNANDO AVE.

ALMERIA AVE.
SEVILLA AVE.
PALERMO AVE.
CATALONIA AVE.
MALAGA AVE.

ROMANO AVENUE
SARTO AVE.
CAMILO AVE. S.W. 27TH TER.
ALEDO AVE. S.W. 27TH LA.

PONCE DE LEON BLVD
UNIVERSITY DRIVE
COCONUT GROVE DR.

G

3
Biltmore Country Club

SEVILLA AVENUE
SAN DOMINGO ST.
INDIAN MOUND TRAIL

ESCOBAR AVE.

French Normandy and Dutch South African Villages

CANDIA AVE.
VELARDE AVE.
BIRD ROAD
LAGUNA AVE.
SAN LORENZO AVE.
GRECO AVE.

S.W. 38TH AVE.
S.W. 38TH CT.
ESTANZA
SHIPPING AVE.

DOUGLAS ROAD
DIXIE HIGHWAY

4 & Coconut Grove

Coral Gables Canal

SOPERO AVE.

J

MARIOLA COURT
BIRD ROAD
ALGARDI AVE.
PINTA COURT

ALHAMBRA CIRCLE
SAN AMARO DR.
SANTA MARIA DR.
GRANADA BOULEVARD
UNIVERSITY DRIVE
TOLEDO STREET
UNIVERSITY DR.
SEGOVIA STREET S.W. 45TH AVE.
RIVIERA DRIVE
LE JEUNE ROAD (S.W. 42ND ST)

Italian Village

A
AURORA

N

MENDAVIA AVENUE
ALEGRIANO AVENUE
BLUE ROAD

MANTUA AVE.
CECILIA AVE.
SIENA AVE.
OCTONA AVE.

RED ROAD
FERDINAND ST.

SAN ESTEBAN AVE.
GERONIMO DRIVE
MAGGIORE ST.
PAMPLONA ST.
MADEIRA AVE.

CAMPO SANO AVENUE
PARMA AVE.
ZAGUA AVE.
PADUA AVE.
PICINO DR.
BILTMORE DR.
VILABELLA AVE.
ALMINAR AVE.
CADAGUA AVE.
RONDA AVE.
RIVIERA DR.
BLUE RD.

ALMINAR AVE.
VILABELLA AVE.
PONCE DE LEON BLVD
LOS PINOS AVE.

1

University of Miami

Lowe Art Museum

5
Chinese Village

L

South Miami & The Keys

South Coral Gables

ACCOMMODATION
Biltmore	3
Gables Inn	4
Omni Colonnade	2
Place St Michel	1
Riviera Courts	5

RESTAURANTS
The Bar	D
Café Kolibri	L
Caffe Abbracci	B
Canton	I
Doc Dammers' Bar & Grill	H
House of India	F
Mykonos	E
Picnics at Allen's Drug Store	J
Restaurant St Michel	A
Sushi Maki	C
Victor's Café	G
Yasuko's	K

0   800 yds

Coral Gables land started selling overnight, with the five years following the first sale in 1921 bringing in $150 million, a third of which was channeled into the biggest advertising campaign ever seen. The layout and buildings of Coral Gables quickly took shape, but the sudden end of Florida's property boom in 1926 (see "History" in Contexts for the full account) wiped Merrick out. He ran a fishing camp in the Florida Keys until that was destroyed by a hurricane, and wound up as Miami's postmaster until his death in 1942.

Coral Gables, however, was built with longevity as well as beauty in mind. Despite successive economic crises, it has never lost its good looks, and these days, boosted by a host of multinational companies in the renovated office buildings and by its very image-conscious population, it is still a lovely place to explore.

The Miracle Mile and around

The best entrance to Coral Gables is through SW 22nd Street, which on the other side of Douglas Road becomes the **Miracle Mile**, conceived by Merrick as the centerpiece of his business district and still the preferred shopping place of community-conscious locals. It continues to bear the imprint of George Merrick's vision, even if the occasional spot of mundane Art Deco makes a bizarre addition to the more fanciful Mediterranean trimmings.

Dominated by department stores, Latin American travel agents and a staggering number of bridal shops, the Miracle Mile (actually only half a mile long) becomes increasingly expensive and exclusive as you head west. Notice the arcades and balconies along its course, and the spirals and peaks of the **Colonnade Building** (180 Aragon Ave). Now a smart hotel (see "Accommodation," p.74) and shops, the building was completed in 1926 – just a few months before the property crash – to accommodate Merrick's land sales office.

Cut around the corner to collect info from the **Chamber of Commerce**, 50 Aragon Ave (Mon–Fri 8.30am–5pm; ☎446-1657), and complete the Miracle Mile inside the grandly pillared **Coral Gables City Hall**, 405 Biltmore Way (Mon–Fri 8am–5pm), whose corridors are adorned with posters from the Twenties that advertised the "City Beautiful" and with newspaper clippings bearing witness to the property mania of the time. There's also a case full of oddments from the Biltmore Hotel (see opposite), which fall some way short of encapsulating the moneyed elegance that characterized Merrick's spa resort. From the third floor landing you can view Denman Fink's impressive blue and gold mural of the four seasons, which decorates the interior of the bell tower.

About half a mile further west, at no. 907 on Coral Way – a typically peaceful and tree-lined Coral Gables residential street - Merrick's childhood home, the **Coral Gables Merrick House** (Sun & Wed 1–4pm; $2, by appointment only; ☎460-5361), is now a museum charting his family's history. In 1899, when George was 12, his family arrived here from New England to run a 160-acre fruit and vegetable farm – and, in the case of George's father, to deliver sermons at local Congregational churches. The farm was so successful that the house quickly grew from a wooden shack into a modestly elegant dwelling of coral rock and gabled windows (the inspiration behind the name of the city that later grew up around the family farm). The dual blows of the property crash and a citrus blight led to the gradual deterioration of the house, until restoration began in the Seventies. There's only enough inside to occupy half an hour, but it provides an interesting background on the founder of Coral Gables, who lived here until 1916.

Along De Soto Boulevard

There's no reason to continue along Coral Way, so backtrack instead to the junction with **De Soto Boulevard**, named for the conquistador Hernando de Soto, who led an expedition to Florida from Cuba in 1539. The boulevard curls southwards to three of Merrick's most notable achievements.

While his property-developing contemporaries left ugly scars across the city after digging up the local limestone, Merrick had the foresight – and the help of Denman Fink – to turn his biggest quarry into a sumptuous swimming pool. **The Venetian Pool**, 2701 De Soto Blvd (June–Aug Mon–Fri 11am–7.30pm, Sat & Sun 10am–4.30pm; Sept, Oct, April & May Tues–Sun 11am–5.30pm; Nov–March Tues–Sun 10am–4.30pm; $5; ☎460-5356), an elaborate conglomeration of palm-studded paths, Venetian-style bridges and coral-rock caves, was opened in 1924. Despite its ornamentation, the pool was never designed with the social elite in mind; admission was cheap and open to all, and even today's local residents get a special discount.

A few minutes' walk further south, on land donated by Merrick, stands the **Coral Gables Congregational Church**, 3010 De Soto Blvd (Mon–Fri 8am–4pm; ☎448-7421), a bright Spanish Revival flurry topped by a barrel-tiled roof and enhanced by Baroque features. The building's excellent acoustics make it a popular venue for jazz and classical **concerts**; ask for details at the church office, just inside the entrance.

The Biltmore Hotel

Merrick's crowning achievement – aesthetically if not financially – was the **Biltmore Hotel**, 1200 Anastasia Ave (☎445-1926), which wraps its broad wings around the southern end of De Soto Boulevard. The 26-story tower of the hotel can be seen across much of low-lying Miami: if it seems similar to the Freedom Tower (see p.80), it's because they're both modeled on the Giralda bell tower of Seville Cathedral in Spain. The *Biltmore* was hawked as "the last word in the evolution of civilization," and everything about it was outrageous: 25-foot-high frescoed walls, vaulted ceilings, a wealth of imported marble and tiles, immense fireplaces and custom-loomed rugs. To mark the opening in January 1926, VIP guests were brought in on chartered, long-distance trains, fed on pheasant and trout and given the run of the casino. The following day, they could fox-hunt, play polo or swim in the US's largest pool – whose first swimming instructor was Johnny Weissmuller, future Olympic champion and the original screen Tarzan.

Although high-profile celebrities, such as Bing Crosby, Judy Garland and Ginger Rogers, kept the *Biltmore* on their itineraries, the end of the Florida land boom and the start of the Depression meant that the hotel was never the success it might have been. In the Forties, many of the finer furnishings were lost when the hotel became a military hospital, and decades of decline followed. The future looked rosier in 1986, when $55 million was lavished on a restoration program, but the company hired went bust, and the great building remained closed. Only in 1993 did it finally reopen, after another multimillion dollar refit. Now once again it is functioning as a hotel; you can step inside to admire the elaborate architecture, take afternoon tea in the lobby for $15, or join the free historical tours beginning at 1.30pm, 2.30pm and 3.30pm every Sunday in the lobby.

The neighboring **Biltmore Country Club**, also open to the public, has fared better. You can poke your head inside for a closer look at its painstakingly renovated Beaux Arts features, but most people turn up to knock a ball along the lush fairways of the **Biltmore Golf Course**, which, in the glory days of the hotel, hosted the highest-paying golf tournament in the world.

South of the Biltmore: the Lowe Art Museum

One of the few parts of Coral Gables where Mediterranean-style architecture doesn't prevail is on the campus of the **University of Miami**, whose dismal, box-like buildings about two miles south of the Biltmore have traditionally been filled by students with wealthy parents rather than healthy intellects. In recent years, the university has undergone something of a renaissance and now attracts top faculty in many fields and a more academically orientated student body.

The sole reason to visit the campus is the **Lowe Art Museum**, 1301 Stanford Drive (Tues, Wed, Fri, Sat 10am–5pm; Thurs 12–7pm; Sun noon–5pm; $5; ☎284-3535, ⓦwww.loweartmuseum.org). Established in 1950, the Lowe underwent major renovation and extension work in 1995 and now constitutes Miami's foremost art museum. The diverse permanent collection contains Renaissance and European Baroque art, Spanish Old Masters, nineteenth-century European paintings and a considerable number of contemporary American works. Non-Western art is also well represented, including varied pre-Columbian, African and East Asian collections, Guatemalan textiles, and one of the finest Native American art collections in the country. The Lowe also hosts some excellent national and international touring exhibitions; to find out what's on, check the *New Times*, its Web site or phone.

South Coral Gables

Much as his Venetian Pool was a cleverly converted quarry, Merrick turned the construction ditches that ringed the infant Coral Gables into a network of canals, calling them the "Miami Riviera" and floating gondolas on them. Although the idea never really took off, the placid waterways remain, running between the university campus and a secluded residential area on Biscayne Bay, just south of Coconut Grove (described below).

Dividing Coconut Grove and South Miami (see overleaf), the **Matheson Hammock Park**, 9601 Old Cutler Rd (6am–sunset; $3.50 parking fee), was a coconut plantation before becoming a public park in 1930. On the weekends, thousands decant here to picnic, use the marina and take a dip in the artificial lagoon, great for small children but with little to offer adults; the rest of the sizeable park is much less crowded, and you can easily while away a few hours strolling around the wading pond – popular with people catching crabs – or along the winding trails above the mangrove swamps.

Virtually next door, the **Fairchild Tropical Garden**, 10901 Old Cutler Rd (daily 9.30am–4.30pm; $8; ☎667-1651, ⓦwww.ftg.org), turns the same rugged terrain into lawns, flowerbeds and gardens decorated by artificial lakes. A good way to begin exploring the 83-acre site – the largest tropical botanical gardens in the continental United States – is to hitch a ride on the free tram (departing hourly, on the hour, from inside the garden's entrance) for a forty-minute meander along the trails, with a live commentary on the various plants.

The tropical habitats reproduced here – some more successfully than others – range from desert to rainforest, though there's relatively little space devoted to fauna endemic to southern Florida. As a research institution, Fairchild works with scientists all over the world to preserve the diversity of the tropical environment; many of the plant species here, such as Cape Sable Whiteweed and Alvaradoa, are extinct in their original environments, and efforts have been made to re-establish them in their places of origin.

Some two-thirds of Fairchild's plants were destroyed or badly damaged on August 24, 1992, by Hurricane Andrew, which led to extensive restructuring of the gardens, including an impressive new rainforest section. This area is not part of the tram-ride, but a walk-through is very congenial, with a waterfall and river surrounded by orchid-covered trees.

Food can be brought into the gardens to be consumed in a special picnic area, though you'll need to stock up before entry as there are no shops nearby. Otherwise, there's only a small **café** (9.30am–4.30pm) serving overpriced sandwiches and snacks.

Coconut Grove

A stamping ground of down-at-heel artists, writers and lefties through the Sixties and Seventies, today's **COCONUT GROVE** is a glitterati hangout thanks to business-led revitalization. Art galleries, fashionable restaurants and towering bay-view apartments mark its central section – clear signs of a neighborhood whose fortunes keep rising. But Coconut Grove, finely placed along the shores of Biscayne Bay, also retains much of value from its formative years. A century ago, a strange mix of Bahamian settlers and New England intellectuals searching for spiritual fulfillment laid the foundations of a fiercely idiosyncratic community, separated from the fledgling city of Miami by a dense, jungle-like wedge of tropical foliage. The distance between Coconut Grove and the rest of Miami is still very much apparent: cleaner and richer than ever, but continuing to fan the flames of liberalism – and boasting the best batch of **drinking and music** locales outside of Miami Beach.

Villa Vizcaya

In 1914, farm-machinery mogul James Deering followed his brother, Charles (of Charles Deering Estate fame, see "South Miami," p.105), to south Florida and blew $15 million recreating a sixteenth-century Italian villa within the belt of vegetation between Miami and Coconut Grove. A thousand-strong workforce completed his **Villa Vizcaya**, 3251 S Miami Ave (daily 9.30am–4.30pm; gardens open until 5pm; $10; ☏250-9133), in just two years. The lasting impression of the grandiose structure is that both Deering and his designer (the crazed Paul Chalfin, who was hell-bent on becoming an architectural legend) had more money than taste: Deering's madly eclectic art collection and his belief that the villa should appear to have been inhabited for 400 years, resulted in a thunderous clash of Baroque, Renaissance, Rococo and Neoclassical fixtures and furnishings, and even the landscaped **gardens**, with their fountains and sculptures, weren't spared his pretensions. Nonetheless, Villa Vizcaya is one of Miami's more sought-out sights, with many diverting details – Chinese figures casting shadows across the tearoom, and a Georgian library, for instance. It's also a popular wedding reception venue, hence the brigades of beaming Cuban brides being photographed here. **Guided tours** of the first floor (45min; last tour 3pm) leave frequently from the entrance loggia – dominated by a second-century marble statue of the Roman god Bacchus – and provide solid background information, after which you're free to explore at your leisure.

The rest of Coconut Grove

Straight across South Miami Drive from Villa Vizcaya, the **Museum of Science and Space Transit Planetarium**, 3280 S Miami Ave (daily 10am–6pm; last admission 5pm; $10; ☏854-4200, ⓦ www.miamisci.org), sets a different mood entirely. Its interactive exhibits provide a good two-hour family diversion, though a stronger reason to visit is the collection of wildlife at the museum's rear. Vultures and owls are among a number of injured birds seeing out their days here, a variety of snakes can be viewed at disturbingly close quarters and the resident tarantula is happy to be handled. The adjoining **planetarium** (shows hourly on the hour) has the usual trips-around-the-cosmos shows and hosts headbanging rock music laser shows (Fri & Sat nights 9pm, 10pm, 11pm & midnight; $6; ☏646-4420). Details are available by phone or from the ticket office inside the museum.

Where South Miami Drive becomes Bayshore Drive, close to Mercy Hospital, the road off to the left leads to the **Church of Ermita de la Curidad** (daily 9am–9pm), erected by Miami Cubans. A mural behind the altar traces the island's history, and the conical-shaped church is angled to allow worshipers to look out across the bay in the direction of Cuba.

Back on Bayshore Drive, for the next two miles or so you'll catch glimpses of limestone jutting through the greenery on the inland side. It was on this ridge, known as **Silver Bluff**, that several early settlers established their homes, later joined by the well-heeled notables of 1910s Miami; a few of their houses still stand, though none is open to the public. The area has remained a preserve of the rich, whose opulent abodes are shielded from prying eyes by carefully maintained trees.

Central Coconut Grove

The suggestion of major money around Silver Bluff yields to blatant statements of wealth once you draw closer to central Coconut Grove. Bayshore Drive continues between expensive, high-rise condos and jogger-filled, landscaped parks. Turning left up Pan American Drive will take you to the **marina** on **Dinner Key**, a picnic spot for settlers at the turn of the nineteenth century and now a mooring for lines of hundred-thousand-dollar yachts.

Next door, the **Coconut Grove Exhibition Center** is nowadays a popular venue for top-of-the-line car and interior furnishing shows. Its forerunner was the Dinner Key Auditorium, where in 1969 the rock legend Jim Morrison, singer with the Doors, dropped his leather pants to expose himself during the band's first – and last – Florida show; this caused Miami's police to clamp down on local rock clubs, and increased the band's fame and notoriety a hundredfold.

The gigantic Exhibition Center overshadows the more cheerful **Miami City Hall**, 3400 Pan American Drive (Mon–Fri 8am–5pm), the small and unlikely seat of local government. The blue-and-white-trimmed Art Deco building used to be an airline terminal: in the Thirties, passengers checked in here for the Pan American Airways seaplane service to Latin America, and the sight of the lumbering craft taking off used to draw thousands to the waterfront. In front of the City Hall a small plaque records the fact that Dinner Key was the place that veterans of the Bay of Pigs stepped ashore after their release from Cuba in 1962.

Peacock Park, at the end of Bayshore Drive beside MacFarlane Road, was a notorious hippie haunt at the time of Morrison's misdemeanor in Coconut Grove. More recently it's been cleaned up to fit the area's present smart, sophisticated image, and now features tennis courts and some peculiar abstract rock sculptures. The **Coconut Grove Chamber of Commerce**, 2820 MacFarlane Rd (Mon–Fri 9am–5pm; ☎444-7270, ⊛www.coconutgrove.com), on a corner of the park, has copious selections of free leaflets and maps of the area.

Along Main Highway

At the end of MacFarlane Road you hit **Main Highway** and Coconut Grove as most Miamians see it: several blocks of trendy cafés, galleries and boutiques. Though less enjoyable than South Beach, it's a fine place for a stroll, if only to watch the neighborhood's affluent fashion victims going through their paces. You can eat, drink and pose at **CocoWalk** (for other places to do all three, see "Eating" and "Drinking," p.110 and p.117) – an enjoyable collection of open-air restaurants and bars, and yet more stylish shops – located between Main Highway and Virginia Street, at 3000 Grand Ave. Or for a taste of sheer exclusivity, drop into **Streets of Mayfair** (Mon, Thurs & Fri 10am–9pm, Tues, Wed

& Sat 10am–7pm, Sun noon–5.30pm), at the corner of MacFarlane Road and Grand Avenue, a designer shopping mall whose zigzagging walkways – decorated by fountains, copper sculptures, climbing vines and Romanesque concrete doodles – wind around three floors of expense-account stores.

Heading south down Main Highway you'll come across the beige and white **Coconut Grove Playhouse**, at no. 3500 (see "Theater," p.122). Opened in 1927 and still going strong on a mixed diet of Broadway blockbusters and less mainstream offerings, this is the best of the area's several examples of Mediterranean Revival architecture, but warrants only a passing glance as you move on to the most enduring historic site in Coconut Grove, at the end of a path right across Main Highway from the playhouse.

The Barnacle

The tree-shaded track leads to a tranquil bayside garden and a century-old house known as the **Barnacle** (Fri–Sun, 10am–4pm; $1; ☎448-9445), built by "Commodore" Ralph Middelton Munroe: sailor, brilliant yacht-designer and a devotee of the Transcendalist Movement (which advocated self-reliance, a love of nature and a simple lifestyle). The Barnacle was ingeniously put together in 1891 with local materials and tricks learned from nautical design. Raising the structure eight feet off the ground in 1908 improved air circulation and prevented flooding, a covered verandah enabled windows to be opened during rainstorms, and a skylight allowed air to be drawn through the house – all major innovations that alleviated some of the discomforts of living all year in the heat and humidity of south Florida. More inventive still, when Munroe needed more space for his family he simply jacked up the single-story structure and added a new floor underneath. Only with the guided tour (10am, 11.30am, 1pm & 2.30pm) can you see inside the house, where many original furnishings remain alongside some of Munroe's intriguing photos of pioneering Coconut Grovers. The grounds, however, you are free to explore on your own. The lawn extends to the shore of Biscayne Bay, while behind the house are the last remnants of the tropical hardwood hammock that extended throughout the Miami area.

Charles Avenue and Black Coconut Grove

The Bahamian settlers of the late 1800s, who later provided the labor that went into building Coconut Grove and nearby areas, mostly lived along what became **Charles Avenue** (off Main Highway, close to the playhouse), in small, simple wooden houses similar to the "conch houses" that fill Key West's Old Town (see "The Florida Keys" p.131). You'll find a trio of these still standing on the "3200" block, though be warned that they are on the edge of **Black Coconut Grove** (not a name you'll find on maps, but one which everyone uses), a run-down area stretching westwards to the borders of Coral Gables. The fact that such a derelict district exists within half a mile of one of the city's most fashionably upmarket areas provides a stark reminder of the divisions between Miami's haves and have-nots.

South Coconut Grove

South of the playhouse, the outlook along Main Highway soon reverts to expansive older homes set back from the street. A couple of easily found minor sights are the only reasons to stop as you pass through towards South Miami. After half a mile, you'll spy the **Ransom Everglades School**, 3575 Main Highway, founded in 1903 for boarding pupils who split the school year between New York's Adirondack Mountains and here. Oddly enough, the main schoolroom was a Chinese-style **pagoda** (Mon–Fri 9am–5pm; free), which still stands incongruously in the middle of what's now an upper-crust prep school. Inside the green-painted pine structure are a few amusing relics from the school's past.

A little further on, near the corner of Devon Road, the 1917 **Plymouth Congregational Church** (Mon–Fri 9am–4pm) has a striking, vine-covered, coral-rock facade; remarkably, this finely crafted exterior was the work of just one man. Note, too, the 375-year-old main door, hand-carved in walnut, which looks none the worse for its journey from an early seventeenth-century monastery in the Spanish Pyrenees. If the church door beside the parking lot is locked, try the church office, on the other side of Devon Road.

South Miami

South of Coral Gables and Coconut Grove, monotonous middle-class suburbs consume almost all of **SOUTH MIAMI**, an expanse of cozy but dull family homes reaching to the edge of the Everglades, interrupted only by golf courses and a few contrived tourist attractions. Mini-malls, gas stations, cut-price waterbed outlets and bumper-to-bumper traffic are the star features of its primary thoroughfare, Hwy-1. You can't avoid this route entirely, but from South Coral Gables a better course is Old Cutler Road, which makes a pleasing meander from Coconut Grove through a thick belt of woodland (see also Matheson Hammock Park, p.100 and Fairchild Tropical Garden, p.100) between Biscayne Bay and the suburban sprawl. Cutting inland from Hwy-1 is unrewarding (and unthinkable without a car), since there are no stops of any major importance.

The Charles Deering Estate

Long before modern highways scythed through the city, **Old Cutler Road** was the sole road between Coconut Grove and Cutler, a small town that went into terminal decline in the 1910s after being bypassed by the new Flagler railroad. A wealthy industrialist and amateur botanist, Charles Deering (brother of James, the owner of Villa Vizcaya; see "Coconut Grove," p.102), was so taken with the natural beauty of the area that he purchased all of Cutler and, with one exception, razed its buildings to make way for the **Charles Deering Estate**, 16701 SW 72nd Ave (10am–5pm; $6; ☎235-1668, ⓦ www.co.miami-dade.fl.us/parks/deering, completed in 1922. Deering maintained the Richmond Inn, Cutler's only hotel, as his own living and dining quarters. Its pleasant wooden form now stands in marked contrast to the limestone mansion he erected alongside, whose interior – echoing halls, dusty chandeliers and checker-board-tile floors – is Mediterranean in style but carries a Gothic spookiness. More impressive than the buildings are the 420-acre **grounds**, where signs of human habitation dating back 10,000 years have been found amid the pine woods, mangrove forests and tropical hardwood hammocks. Ticket price includes a free one-hour historical tour of the interior and a half-hour tour of the grounds.

Visitor information

While in this vicinity, you should take advantage of the excellent **Tropical Everglades Visitor Information Center** (daily 8am–6pm; ☎1-800/388-9669 or 245-9180), located at 160 Hwy-1, close to the junction with Hwy-9336 (344th Street); it offers a wealth of information and is particularly strong on the Everglades.

Parrot Jungle

Parrot Jungle, 11000 SW 57th Ave (daily 9.30am–6pm; adults $16.99, children 3–10 $11.66; ℡666-7834), has parrots and macaws of rainbow plumage swapping squawks as visitors wander along delightfully shaded pathways past their cages. The gardens are designed to protect both residents and visitors from the hot Florida sun and include hundreds of varieties of plants, waterfalls and a lake with Caribbean pink flamingos. Apart from birds, the park is home to numerous species of alligators (including albinos) and crocodiles, giant tortoises, chimpanzees and other primates. Even if you don't intend to enter Parrot Jungle, the *Parrot Café* (8am–5pm) offers views of the park and makes a useful stop if you're coming from the nearby Fairchild Tropical Garden (see p.100).

Metrozoo

A more extensive display of wildlife – assuming you're not opposed to zoos on principle – is the **Metrozoo**, 12400 SW 152nd St (daily 9.30am–5.30pm; last admission 4pm; adults $8, children $4; ℡251-0400). Even so, while psychological barriers such as moats and small hills are employed instead of cages, it's hard to imagine that many of the animals enjoy baking in the heat and humidity any more than their audience; both tend to spend their time here pursuing shade and a cool drink. If you do come, the snow-white Bengal tigers are the prize exhibit. Avoid visiting during the sweltering midday temperatures of summer, and when it rains – most of the zoo is outdoors.

Gold Coast Railroad Museum

Sharing the zoo's entrance, the **Gold Coast Railroad Museum** (Mon–Fri 11am–3pm, Sat & Sun 11am–4pm; adults $5, children $3; ℡253-0063, ⓦwww.goldcoast-railroad.org) houses a small but intriguing collection of old locomotives that can be clambered upon for closer inspection. With them is the *Ferdinand Magellan*, a luxury Pullman car that was custom-built in 1928 for presidential use and features escape hatches and steel armor plating. Harry S. Truman traveled 21,000 miles in it on his 1948 re-election campaign, giving three hundred speeches from the rear platform.

Key Biscayne and around

A compact, immaculately manicured community five miles off the Miami shore, **KEY BISCAYNE** is a great place to live – if you can afford it. Seeking relaxation and creature comforts away from life in the fast lane, the moneyed of Miami fill the island's upmarket homes and condos: even Richard Nixon had his presidential winter house here, and singer Sting has recuperated between tour dates in one of the luxury shorefront hotels. For visitors, Key Biscayne offers a couple of inviting beaches, a third within a state park, and a fabulous cycling path running the full length, but cheap eats and lodgings are in predictably short supply.

Virginia Key and around

Without a private yacht, the only way onto Key Biscayne is via **Rickenbacker Causeway**, a four-mile-long continuation of SW 26th Road just south of downtown Miami; it soars high above Biscayne Bay, allowing shipping to glide underneath, and provides a breathtaking view of the Brickell Avenue skyline

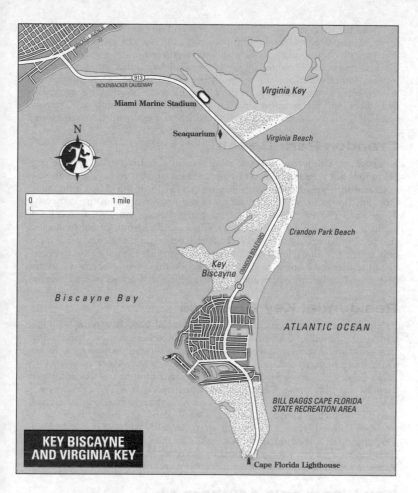

**KEY BISCAYNE
AND VIRGINIA KEY**

(see p.82). Drivers have to pay a $1 toll; otherwise you can cross the causeway by bus (#B), bike or even on foot.

The first land you'll hit is the unexceptional and sparsely populated **VIR-GINIA KEY**. The Miami Marine Stadium is the prominent building on the left, but this is now closed owing to disrepair and underuse. A few yards beyond it is the beginning of a two-mile lane that winds through a cluster of Australian pines to **Virginia Beach** (daily 8am–sunset; cars $2). During the years of segregation, this was set aside for Miami's black community (chosen, cynics might say, for its proximity to a large sewage works). Later, flocks of hippies became seriously laid-back around the secluded coves, which still provide a private setting for nude sunbathing. Nowadays it's also something of a windsurfers' paradise here, and they swarm off-shore and all along Rickenbacker Causeway. It's usually possible to hire windsurfboards from stands along the beach.

In contrast, on the right of the main road, the **Miami Seaquarium** marine park (daily 9.30am–6pm; adults $23, children under 10 $18; parking costs extra; ☎361-5705) is a bustling place where you can while away three or four hours watching the usual roster of performing seals and dolphins. Be sure not to miss Lolita, the 8000-pound star of the spectacular killer-whale show (daily, noon). The park's most important work – undertaking breeding programs to preserve Florida's endangered sea life and serving as a halfway house for injured manatees and other sea creatures – goes on behind the scenes. Though the park, which served as the backdrop for the *Flipper* TV series, is enjoyable, remember that there are plenty more marine parks in Florida, such as Orlando's SeaWorld, and much more in Miami on which to spend your time and money.

Crandon Park Beach

Not content with living in one of the best natural settings in Miami, the people of Key Biscayne also possess one of the finest landscaped beaches in the city – **Crandon Park Beach** (8am–sunset; cars $4; ☎361-5421), a mile along Crandon Boulevard (the continuation of the main road from the causeway). Three miles of golden beach fringe the park, and you can wade out at knee-depth to a sandbar far from the shore. Filled by the sounds of boisterous kids and sizzling barbecues on weekends, at any other time the park is disturbed only by the occasional jogger or holidaymaker straying from the private beaches of the expensive hotels nearby. Relax beside the lapping ocean waters and keep a look out for manatees and dolphins, which are both known to swim by.

Residential Key Biscayne

Besides its very green, manicured looks, **residential Key Biscayne**, beginning with an abrupt wall of apartment buildings at the southern edge of Crandon Park Beach, has little to offer visitors. You'll need to pass through, however, on the way to the much more rewarding Bill Baggs Cape Florida State Recreation Area (see below), and while doing so should pick up information on the area at the very friendly and informative **Chamber of Commerce** at 87 West McIntyre St (Mon–Fri 9am–5pm; ☎361-5207, ⊛www.keybiscaynechamber.org). Afterwards, loop along **Harbor Drive**, where at no. 485 W stands the former home of ex-president Richard Nixon, who picked up his *Miami Herald* here one morning in 1972 to read of a break-in at the Watergate Complex in Washington; the seemingly insignificant event (only featured by the paper because two Miami Cubans were involved) led to Nixon's resignation two years later.

Key Biscayne's southern tip

Crandon Boulevard terminates at the entrance to the 400-acre **Bill Baggs Cape Florida State Recreation Area** (daily 8am–sunset; cars $4, pedestrians and cyclists $1; ☎361-5811), which covers the southern extremity of Key Biscayne. An excellent swimming **beach** lines the Atlantic-facing side of the park, and a boardwalk cuts around the wind-bitten sand dunes towards the **Cape Florida Lighthouse**, built in the 1820s. Only with the ranger-led tour for the first ten people to arrive (Thurs–Mon at 9.30am & 12.30pm; free) can you climb through the 95-foot-high structure, which offers fantastic views of of the whole island and Miami in the distance. It was attacked by Seminole Indians in 1836 and seized by Confederate soldiers to disrupt Union shipping during the Civil War. The lighthouse remained in use until 1878, and now serves as a navigation beacon.

Stiltsville

Looking out from the park across the bay, you'll spy the grouping of fragile-looking houses known as **Stiltsville**. Held above water by stilts, these wooden dwellings were built and occupied by fishermen in the Forties and Fifties, and enraged the authorities by being outside the jurisdiction of tax collectors. Stiltsville's demise is attested to by a recent law forbidding repair work on the ramshackle structures, whose state of disrepair was compounded by the destruction wrought by Hurricane Andrew in 1992; only seven of the fourteen original houses are still standing, used largely for parties or boyscout trips. Locals are now trying to preserve the area and more info can be found at ⓦwww.stiltsville.org.

Homestead and around

Suburbia yields to agriculture as you leave South Miami along Hwy-1, where broad, fertile fields grow fruit and vegetables for the nation's northern states. Aside from offering as good a taste of Florida farm life – the region produces the bulk of America's winter tomatoes – as you're likely to find so close to its major city, the district can be a money-saving stop (see "Accommodation") en route to the Florida Keys or the Everglades National Park.

HOMESTEAD is the agricultural area's main town, and the least galvanizing section of Miami. Krome Avenue, just west of Hwy-1, slices through the center, but besides a few restored 1910s–1930s buildings (such as the Old City Hall, no. 43 N), there's little to detain you other than the **Florida Pioneer Museum**, no. 826. Here you'll find two yellow-painted train station buildings, store photos and objects from Homestead's formative years – this end-of-the-line town was planned by Flagler's railroad engineers in 1904. To the rear, a 1926 caboose keeps moderately entertaining railroad mementos. It is currently closed, so phone the city hall (ⓉT247-8221) to find out if it's open.

Around Homestead

Time is better spent around Homestead than actually in it, with plenty of diversions just a few minutes' drive from the town. You can also gather your own dinner in this area; keep an eye out for **"pick your own"** signs, where, for a few dollars, you can take to the fields and load up with peas, tomatoes and a variety of other crops.

The Coral Castle

The one essential stop in these parts is the **Coral Castle**, 28655 S Dixie Hwy (daily 9am-6pm; adults $8, children $5; ⓉT248-6344), whose bulky coral-rock sculptures can be found about six miles northeast of Homestead, beside Hwy-1, at the junction with 286th Street. Remarkably, these fantastic creations, whose delicate finish belies their imposing size, are the work of just one man – the enigmatic **Edward Leedskalnin**. Jilted in 1913 by his 16-year-old fiancée in Latvia, Leedskalnin spent seven years working his way across Europe, Canada and the US before buying an acre of land just south of Homestead. Using a profound – and self-taught – knowledge of weights and balances, he raised enormous hunks of coral rock from the ground, then used a workbench made from car running boards and handmade tools fashioned from scrap to refine the blocks into chairs, tables and beds. It is thought the castle was intended as a love nest to woo back his errant sweetheart. Leedskalnin died here in 1951.

You can wander around the slabs, sit on the hard but surprisingly comfortable chairs, swivel a nine-ton gate with your pinkie, and admire the numerous coral representations of the moon and planets that reflect Leedskalnin's interest in astronomy and astrology; also on display is his twenty-foot-high telescope. But you won't be able to explain how the sculptures were made. No one ever saw the secretive Leedskalnin at work, or knows how, alone, he could have loaded 1100 tons of rock onto the rail-mounted truck that brought the pieces here in 1936.

Fruit and Spice Park, Monkey Jungle

The subtle fragrances of the **Fruit and Spice Park**, 24801 SW 187th Ave (daily 10am–5pm; $3.50; ☎247-5727), tickle your nostrils as soon as you enter. Rare exotica, such as star fruit and the aptly named Panama candle tree, are the highlights of a host of tropical peculiarities; there are daily guided tours (10am, 1.30pm & 2pm; included with entry) that will give you a good introduction to the secret lives of spices.

To the north of Homestead, at 14805 SW 216th St, **Monkey Jungle** (daily 9.30am–5pm; last admission 4pm; adults $14.50, children 4-12 $9; ☎235-1611, ⓦ www.monkeyjungle.com) is one of the few places of protection in the US for endangered primates. Covered walkways keep visitors in closer confinement than the monkeys, and lead through a steamy hammock where baboons, orang-utans, gorillas and 35 species of monkeys move through the vegetation. Despite a fair amount of freedom, the animals don't appear to be a terribly happy bunch, possibly because of overcrowding. The monkeys spend most of their time scrounging food from visitors – take care not to get bitten or, just as unpleasant, relieved on by inmates angry if there are no treats on offer.

Biscayne National Park

If you're not going to the Florida Keys, make a point of visiting **Biscayne National Park** (daily 8am–sunset; ☎230-1144), at the end of Canal Drive (328th Street), east of Hwy-1. The bulk of the park lies beneath the clear ocean waters, where stunning formations of living coral provide a habitat for shoals of brightly colored fish and numerous other creatures too delicate to survive on their own. For a full description of the wondrous world of the living coral reef, see John Pennekamp State Park, in "The Florida Keys", p.137.

The lazy way to view it is on the three-hour **glass-bottomed boat** trip from the National Park Service concession near the entrance at Convoy Point (daily at 10am; adults $20 plus tax, children under 12 $13; reservations ☎230-1100, ⓦ www.nps.gov/bisc/), but for a fuller encounter you should embark on one of their three-hour snorkel tours (daily 1.30pm; $30 including all equipment). They also rent out canoes ($8/hr) and two-person kayaks ($16/hr). Maps and information about the park are available at the **visitor center** next door (daily 8.30am–5pm; ☎230-7275). For tours and dives, phone at least a day ahead to make reservations.

Another option is to visit the Park's **barrier islands**, seven miles out. A tour boat leaves for **Elliot Key** from Convoy Point at 1.30pm on Sundays between December and May – tickets ($20 return) can be bought from NPS. Once ashore, besides calling at the **visitor center** (Sat & Sun 10am–4pm) and contemplating the easy six-mile hiking trail along the island's forested spine, there's nothing to do on Elliot Key except sunbathe in solitude.

Eating

With everything from the greasiest hot-dog stand to the finest gourmet restaurant vying for business, **eating** in Miami is a buyer's market. Anywhere that serves breakfast is usually open at 6am or 7am, most restaurants do business between noon and midnight or 1am, some closing between lunch and dinner, and a few operate around the clock (see box on p.114). Be on the look out, too, for the reduced-price food offered at happy hours (see overleaf), and the ample buffets that constitute **Sunday brunch** (see p.116).

The big fast-food franchises and pizza chains are as plentiful here as elsewhere across the country, and "typical" **American** food, such as thick, juicy burgers and sizeable sandwiches, is easily found. Recent years have seen the development of a **New Floridian** style of cooking, which successfully combines *nouvelle cuisine* methods and presentation with Caribbean ingredients, such as tropical fruit and fish. Yet Miami is too cosmopolitan for a single food style to be dominant, and only **seafood**, every bit as plentiful and good as you would expect so close to fish-laden tropical waters, is a common feature among the city's myriad of cuisines drawn from every corner of the Americas – and beyond. Much of what is out there is rather affordable, at least by American big-city standards, so you'll rarely need an expense account to dine out on a giant mess of stone-crab claws – a regional specialty – or fresh-picked lobsters. More than five hundred species of fish thrive offshore, both run-of-the-mill and exotic; basically, if you can't find it on your plate somewhere, it hasn't evolved yet.

Ethnic cuisine

Cuban food is what Miami does best. A sizeable lunch or dinner in one of the innumerable small, family-run Cuban diners (always pleased to show off their culinary skills to non-Spanish-speaking customers) will cost an absurdly low $4–7, a fraction of the prices charged by fancier Cuban restaurants - mostly in Little Havana and Coral Gables - now lauded by the nation's food critics thanks to the development of a lighter, more attractive **Nuevo Cubano** style of cooking that is essentially Cuban food cooked with olive oil, better presented and with a much larger bill. **Haitian** cooking is slowly gaining popularity in Miami, and the restaurants in Little Haiti, just north of downtown Miami, are just some of the places in which to sample it. **Argentine**, **Jamaican**, and **Peruvian** eateries bear witness to the city's strong Caribbean and Latin American elements, though aside from Cuban food, for sheer quality and value for money it's hard to better the many **Japanese** outlets, most north of downtown Miami and a few in South Miami – all much cheaper than their European counterparts – while in South Beach, expensive but good-quality sushi is the current rage. Chinese and Thai places are abundant, too, as are **Italian**. By contrast, **Indian** food is having a hard time taking root despite a couple of commendable restaurants in Coral Gables, and Mexican food is far less common than in most other parts of the US.

Eating practicalities

In the listings below, the price of an average dinner – excluding drinks, taxes and tips – is assumed to be around $15–20 ($20–25 for fish) unless otherwise stated. Always check your bill when you get it, especially around the South Beach tourist drags – and remember they'll often automatically add a 15 percent gratuity which you can cross off if you're not happy with the service.

Downtown and around

Big Fish, 55 SW Miami Ave Rd (☎373-1770). Lively spot on the Miami River, with folding chairs, benches and picnic tables. Menu includes home-cooked Italian fish dishes with vegetarian options. Fairly pricey, but the main dishes can easily feed two. Mon–Sat noon–3.30pm & 6.30–11.30pm, Sun noon–midnight.

Cisco's Cafe, 5911 NW 36th St (☎871-2764). Though the place resembles a fast-food chain, its ordinary Mexican fare is enlivened by quite extraordinary appetizers piled high on rainbow plates. Try the butter guacamole and homemade corn tortillas. Daily 11.15am–11.15pm.

Edelweiss, 2655 Biscayne Blvd (☎573-4421). Hearty German and Swiss food with traditional

Almost every restaurant in Miami has a **happy hour**, usually on weekdays from 5pm to 8pm, when drinks are cheap and usually come in tandem with discounted food – varying from chicken wings to fresh seafood – or free hors d'oeuvres. Watch for the signs outside or scan the numerous newspaper ads for the best deals – or try one of the following listings, which are consistently among the best in the city.

Doc Dammers' Bar & Grill, inside the *Colonnade Hotel*, 180 Aragon Ave, Coral Gables (℡441-2600). Where the young(ish) and unattached of Coral Gables mingle after work to the strains of a pianist. Mon–Thurs 5–8pm & Fri 6–10pm, free hors d'oeuvres. See "Eating" p.115.

Firehouse Four, 1000 S Miami Ave (℡371-3473). Rip-roaring 5-7pm daily happy hour (except Mon) with hundreds of people enjoying the salsa rhythms, $1 off all drinks and free hors d'oeuvres. Thurs sees $3 cocktails, and Wed free champagne for the ladies. See "Eating" below.

Les Deux Fontaines, 1230 Ocean Drive, Miami Beach (℡672-7878, ⓦwww .lesdeuxfontaines.com). Lousy service, but worth turning up for the 2-4-1 happy hour (4–7pm) when you can pick up a half-pound of prawns and a couple of martinis for about 12 bucks. See "Live music" p.120.

Monty's Raw Bar, 2550 S Bayshore Drive, Coconut Grove (℡858-1431). Half-price cocktails and reduced-price beer washed down with discounted seafood complement the bay view at Coconut Grove's best happy hour. Mon–Fri 4–8pm.

Rusty Pelican, 3201 Rickenbacker Causeway, Key Biscayne (℡361-3818). Complimentary hors d'oeuvres and reduced drinks prices (daily 4.30–7pm) happily coincide with the best sunset you can see in Miami.

schnitzel, bratwurst and excellent strudel desserts. Daily 5–11pm.

Firehouse Four, 1000 S Miami Ave (℡371-3473). Italian pasta, seafood and tapas at slightly above-average prices and served in a very stylish interior. See "Happy hours." Daily noon–midnight.

Fishbone Grille, 650 S Miami Ave (℡530-1915). A busy but friendly restaurant serving the finest budget seafood in Miami. Located next to *Tobacco Road* (see "Drinking" and "Live music," p.117) where many of the diners move on to. Daily 5.30–10pm.

Gourmet Diner, 13951 Biscayne Blvd (℡947-2255). Always a line for a winning French-Continental daily menu at moderate prices. Daily 11am–11pm.

Hiro, 17516 Biscayne Blvd (℡948-3687). Miami's only late-night sushi bar, and where the city's sushi chefs hang out after work. Open until 3.30am.

Joe's Seafood Restaurant, 400 NW Fourth St (℡638-8602 or 374-5637). The river side setting improves the only-adequate seafood. Not to be confused with *Joe's Stone Crabs* (see opposite). Daily 11am–10/11pm.

La Ideal, 188 NE Third Ave, near Bayside Marketplace (℡358-2501). Inexpensive Latin food in an informal setting. Not the widest of menus, but you can fill up for under ten bucks. Also has occasional live Latin rhythms in the evening. Daily 8am–midnight.

Lombardi's, S-125 at the Bayside Marketplace, 401 Biscayne Blvd (℡381-9580). Mid-price range Italian

and American favorites served inside the Neoclassical Italian interior with stylish Italian art and furniture or outside by the Tiki bar which has live salsa bands playing from 8pm onwards. Daily 11am–11pm.

Orlando's Seafood Restaurant and Fish Market, 501 NW 37th Ave (℡642-6767). Large, airy restaurant serving fresh, well-cooked Cuban seafood dishes. Fantastic service and not too pricey. Daily 11am–11pm.

S & S Diner, 1757 NE Second Ave (℡373-4291). This established eatery proffers platefuls of meatloaf, turkey, stuffed cabbage, beef stew, shrimp Creole or pork chops for less than $8. Counter service only. Closed Sun.

Tobacco Road, 638 S Miami Ave (℡381-8970). The restaurant section of this bar (see "Drinking" and "Live music") offers hamburgers, fries and sandwiches, which are consumed by relaxing yuppies and the occasional biker. Daily 11.30am–2am.

South Beach and around

Blue Door, inside the *Delano Hotel*, 1685 Collins Ave (℡672-2000). Very expensive French cuisine – it's overseen by super-chef Claude Troisgros – with added touches of flavor from Asia, Italy and the Americas. Anyone for a *foie gras* burger? Daily 7am–midnight.

Café Efesus, 1339 Washington Ave (℡674-0078). Authentic Turkish cuisine in intimate surroundings with live belly-dancing (see "Live music," p.121) Fri & Sat from 10.30pm onwards. Vegetarian options available. Daily 6pm–2am (or later).

Casona De Carlitos, 2232 Collins Ave (T) 534-7013). Hearty, inexpensive ($8 lunch specials) Italian-Argentine food and live music with lots of Latin-style pasta and grilled red meat. Daily noon–1am.

Da Leo Trattoria, 819 Lincoln Rd (T) 674-0354). A reliable high-quality Italian restaurant serving authentic fare at not too expensive prices. Very popular, so reservation recommended. Daily 1pm–midnight.

David's Coffee Shop, corner of Meridian and Lincoln Ave (T) 534-8736). Low-priced Latin food served all day and night to a crowd that's sleazy but discerning.

El Rancho Grande, 1626 Pennsylvania Ave (T) 673-0480). Low-cost, authentic Mexican food is served with a smile in this cozy colorfully painted restaurant, handily placed just off Lincoln Road. Daily noon–midnight.

Eleventh Street Diner, 1065 Washington Ave (T) 534-6373). All-American fare served around the clock; eat inside in cozy booths or outside on the terrace.

Grillfish, 1444 Collins Ave (T) 538-9908). Immensely popular fish restaurant (they sauté as well as grill fish and meat) serving much better fare than most places on Ocean Drive at much better prices. Always full, so reservation recommended. Daily noon–midnight/1am.

Joe's Stone Crabs, 227 Biscayne St (T) 673-0365). Only open from October to May when Florida stone crabs are in season; expect long lines of tourists waiting (usually a couple of hours) to pay $20 for a succulent plateful.

Lario's on the Beach, 820 Ocean Drive (T) 532-9577). Better known for being owned by singer Gloria Estefan than for such sophisticated Nuevo Cubano food as *vaca frita* served in a Latin nightclub atmosphere; when the live band strikes up, the diners dance (Thurs–Sat 10pm onwards). Daily noon–midnight.

Las Americas, 450 Lincoln Rd Mall (T) 673-0560). No-frills but tasty Cuban food in a cafeteria-style atmosphere – cheapest on Lincoln. Daily noon–1am.

Maiko Japanese Restaurant, 1255 Washington Ave (T) 531-6369). Highly imaginative sushi creations are what make this moderately priced restaurant so popular. Daily 1pm–midnight.

New Sushi Hana, 1131 Washington Ave (T) 604-0300). Large portions of beautifully presented Japanese food at unusually affordable prices. Daily noon–midnight/1am.

News Café, 800 Ocean Drive (T) 538-NEWS). Utterly fashionable sidewalk café with extensive mid-price breakfast, lunch and dinner menu and front-row

seating for the South Beach promenade. 24hr.

Pacific Time, 915 Lincoln Rd (T) 534-5979). Modern American cooking with strong East Asian influences producing excellent results, though fairly pricey. Daily 6pm–midnight.

Palace Bar & Grill, 1200 Ocean Drive (T) 531-9077). One of the few trendy places for breakfast, from 8am–5pm. Otherwise general, inexpensive fare including good burgers. Weekday half-price happy hour 4–7pm. Daily 8am–1am.

Puerto Sagua, 700 Collins Ave (T) 673-1115). Where local Cubans meet gringos over espresso coffee, beans and rice. Cheap, filling breakfasts, lunches and dinners. Daily 8am–2am.

Rumba, 2008 Collins Ave. Basic Cuban diner offering $4 plates of plain, but very filling food (meat or fish, rice, beans and salad) and $2.50 breakfasts with genuinely friendly service. Attracts a very broad mix of Cubans, construction workers, street-people and crazies. 24hrs, but eating not advised late at night unless you have a very strong stomach.

Smith & Wollensky's, 1 Washington Ave, Miami Beach (T) 673-2800). Popular and pricey American steakhouse where you can sit either in the large interior or on the terrace overlooking Government Cut. Has an extensive and impressive wine list with bottles of wine from $30 to $1500. Reservation recommended. Daily noon–1.30am.

Tantra, 1445 Pennsylvania Ave (T) 672-4765). The sensual French/Mediterranean flavors offered up here are no mistake – the restaurant's theme, enhanced by muted lighting, is based on Tantric philosophies and aphrodisiac ingredients. Enjoy. Food daily 7pm–2am.

Tap Tap Haitian Restaurant, 819 Fifth St (T) 672-2898). The tastiest and most attractively presented Haitian food in Miami, at very reasonable prices. Wander around the restaurant to admire the Haitian murals, and visit the upstairs gallery where exhibits on worthy Haitian themes are held. Daily 5–11pm.

Thai Toni, 890 Washington Ave (T) 538-8424). Tasty Thai food at moderate prices in this bamboo-themed fashionable hangout. 6pm–12.30am.

Wolfie's, 2038 Collins Ave (T) 538-6626). Long-established deli drawing an entertaining mix of New York retirees and late-night clubbers – all served in generous, if somewhat overpriced, helpings of fried favorites and sweet desserts. Open 24 hours, and serving better-priced specials throughout the day.

World Resources, 719 Lincoln Rd (T) 535-8987). Excellent, Thai and Japanese food served in an informal sidewalk café setting. Try the economical $9.50 *bento sushi* boxes. Daily noon–1am.

Yuca, 501 Lincoln Rd (T) 532-9822). Still the rave of food critics up and down the land, serving

Nuevo Cubano cuisine in a gourmet-diner setting; great stuff, but expect to pay about $50 per person. Reserve at the weekend. Daily 1pm–1am.

North Central and Miami Beach and around

Al Amir, 12953 Biscayne Blvd (℡892-6500). Authentic Middle Eastern cuisine at good prices.

Bangkok Orchid, 5563 NW 72nd Ave (℡887-3000). Delicious Thai meals along a stretch lacking any other remotely exotic eateries.

Café Prima Pasta, 414 71st St (℡867-0106). One of the best pasta restaurants in Miami – and one of the least expensive in its class. The place is tiny, so arrive early. Cash only. Mon–Sat noon–midnight, Sun 5pm–midnight.

Chef Allen's, 19088 NE 29th Ave (℡935-2900). Outstanding "New Floridian" cuisine, such as yellowtail smothered in a coconut-milk-and-curry sauce and Caribbean antipasto, is created here by Allen Susser, widely rated as one of America's greatest chefs. Only dine here if money's not a problem.

Rainforest Café, 12801 W Sunrise Blvd, inside Sawgrass Mills Mall (℡851-1015). Theme restaurant complete with growling safari sounds, thunderstorms and tasty New World food. Daily 8am–9pm.

Rascal House, 17190 Collins Ave (℡947-4581). Largest, loudest and most authentic New York deli in town; huge portions and cafeteria ambience. Daily 6.30am–2am.

Little Havana

Ayestaran, 706 SW 27th Ave (℡649-4982). Long a favorite Cuban restaurant among those in the know, especially good value for its $5–8 daily specials. Daily 7am–1am.

Casa Juancho, 2436 SW Eighth St (℡642-2452). Generally pricey, but the Castilian tapas are good value at $6–8, and there's a convivial mood as strolling Spanish musicians serenade the wealthy Cuban clientele. Has one of the best-stocked Spanish wine cellars in the country. Daily noon–midnight.

Casa Panza, 1620 SW Eighth St (℡643-5343). Less formal and more Iberian than many of the other Spanish restaurants hereabouts, with authentic *tapas*, *raciones* and main dishes prepared in a mainly

madrileño (Madrid) style. Above-average prices, but you get to watch free flamenco on Tues & Thurs–Sat from 8pm onwards. Open lunch and dinner.

Covadonga, 6480 SW Eighth St (℡261-2406). Fairly pricey Cuban seafood specialties abound in this nautical-themed restaurant frequented by a local clientele. Daily 11am–11pm.

El Bodegon de Castilla, 2499 SW Eighth St (℡642-0505). Iberian flavors embellish the local grouper, snapper and sole seafood dishes. A bit on the pricey side. Daily noon–midnight.

El Padrinito, 3494 SW Eighth St (℡442-4510). Excellent Dominican entrées like grouper steak smothered in coconut sauce served in a homestyle setting. Lunch and dinner.

Exquisito, 1510 SW Eighth St (℡643-0227). Inexpensive family-run Cuban restaurant serving *Creole-Cubana* dishes to Cubans rather than tourists in an unpretentious atmosphere. Daily 7am–midnight.

Hy-Vong, 3458 SW Eighth St (℡446-3674). Tiny, dinner-only Vietnamese restaurant; a favorite of hip yuppies and Vietnam vets. No frills, slow service, but damn good food. Tues–Sun 6–11pm.

Islas Canarias, 285 NW 27th Ave (℡649-0440). Tucked away inside a drab shopping mall. Gargantuan piles of fine, unpretentious Cuban food at unbeatable prices. Daily 7am–11pm.

La Carreta, 3632 SW Eighth St (℡444-7501). The real sugar cane growing around the wagon wheel outside is a good sign: inside, homestyle Cuban cooking is served at moderate prices. 24hr.

La Esquina de Tejas, 101 SW Twelfth Ave (℡545-0337). Where Reagan and Bush Senior both courted the Hispanic vote. A dependable address for Cuban lunches and dinners.

La Palacio de los Jugos, 5721 W Flagler Ave (℡264-1503). A handful of tables at the back of a Cuban produce market, where the pork sandwiches and shellfish soup from the takeout stand are the tastiest for miles. Daily 7am–9pm.

Versailles, 3555 SW Eighth St (℡444-0240). Chandeliers, mirrored walls, a great atmosphere and wonderful inexpensive Cuban food. Daily 8am–1am or later.

24-hour eats

The five below, all in South Beach, are places where you can get reasonably priced food all night. See the South Beach listings for fuller details.

David's Coffee Shop, corner of Eleventh St and Collins Ave (℡534-8736)

Eleventh Street Diner, 1065 Washington Ave (℡534-6373)

News Café, 800 Ocean Drive (℡538-6397)

Rumba, 2008 Collins Ave

Wolfie's, 2038 Collins Ave (℡538-6626)

Coral Gables

The Bar, 172 Giralda Ave (☎ 442-2730). Mainly a bar, but notable for the good-value daily lunch specials ($6–7). Mon–Sat 11am–2am Sun 5.30pm–midnight. See "Drinking."

Café Kolibri, 6901 Red Rd (☎ 665-9051). Bakery with gourmet, lowfat and vegan entrées. Also doubles as a restaurant with delicious Tuscan specialties.

Caffe Abbracci, 318 Aragon Ave (☎ 441-0700). Original dishes like pasta stuffed with pumpkin hold the attention of a fashionable crowd as they sip their vintage wine.

Canton, 2614 Ponce de León Blvd (☎ 448-3736). Hub of Eastern flavors of Cantonese, Mandarin and Szechuan, known for huge portions of honey garlic chicken. Good sushi bar as well. Moderate.

Doc Dammers' Bar & Grill, inside the *Omni Colonnade Hotel*, 180 Aragon Ave (☎ 561-6511). Affordable eating in a ssaloon; serving breakfast, lunch and dinner, and pacious, Twenties-style offering a happy hour in its piano bar. See the "Happy hours" box on p.112.

House of India, 22 Merrick Way (☎ 444-2348). Quality catch-all Indian food including some excellently priced lunch buffets. Daily noon–3pm & 7pm–midnight.

Mykonos, 1201 Coral Way (☎ 856-3140). Greek food in an unassuming atmosphere: *spinakopita*, lemon chicken soup, *gyros*, *souvlaki* and huge Greek salads. Good vegetarian options. Mon–Thurs 11am–10pm, Fri & Sat till 11pm, Sun 5–10pm.

Picnics at Allen's Drug Store, 4000 Red Rd (☎ 665-6964). Low-priced, homestyle cooking, such as freshly made burgers in an old-fashioned drugstore complete with a jukebox that blasts golden oldies.

Restaurant St Michel, in *Hotel Place St Michel*, 2135 Ponce de León Blvd (☎ 446-6572). Outstanding French and Mediterranean cuisine amid antiques and flowers. Not cheap, but very alluring.

Sushi Maki, 2334 Ponce de León Blvd (☎ 443-1884). Excellent mid to high-priced sushi, supplemented by cooked Thai and Vietnamese dishes. Daily 11am–10/11pm.

Victor's Café, 2340 SW 32nd Ave (☎ 445-1313). Latin musicians (Thurs–Sat) make for lively dining, but the Cuban food – while good – tends to be slightly overpriced. Daily noon–11pm/midnight.

Yasuko's, 4041 Ponce de León Blvd (☎ 444-6622). Intimate mid-price Japanese restaurant with an outstanding sushi bar and usually packed with students from the nearby University of Miami. Daily 5.30–10pm.

Coconut Grove

Café Med, 3015 Grand Ave, inside CocoWalk (☎ 443-1770). Delicious Mediterranean cuisine in an excellent people-watching location. Get the *sapori di mare* – linguine with lobster and mixed seafood.

Café Tu Tu Tango, inside CocoWalk, 3015 Grand Ave (☎ 529-2222). A quirky and entertaining spot themed as an artist's garret; lengthy menu of good-quality food served in tapas-sized portions and at high speed. 11am–midnight, later on weekends.

Cheesecake Factory, inside CocoWalk, 3015 Grand Ave (☎ 447-9898). You'll need plenty of time to choose from the book-thick menu, which is an assortment of traditional American fare, innovative appetizers and 42 varieties of cheesecake. Daily 11am–midnight.

Chrysanthemum, 2911 Grand Ave (☎ 443-6789). Superb Peking and Szechuan cooking at fairly moderate prices; a surprise in a city not known for quality Chinese food.

Greenstreet Café, 3110 Commodore Plaza (☎ 567-0662). Quaint sidewalk café with eclectic assortment of low- to mid-priced cuisine ranging from Middle Eastern to Jamaican. Daily 7am–midnight.

Le Bouchon du Grove, 3430 Main Hwy (☎ 448-6060). Don't let the chi-chi name fool you. Here you'll find unpretentious award-winning French food, with fabulous Kir Royales and freshly prepared desserts at reasonable prices. Great place for coffee and a croissant in the morning too. Daily 8am–midnight. Reservation required for dinner.

Paulo Luigi's, 3324 Virginia St (☎ 445-9000). Supposedly this is the favorite haunt of local NBA players who come for the deliciously inventive (and relatively inexpensive) homestyle pasta and meat dishes. Meat and poultry tend to be a better bet than the seafood dishes.

Scotty's Landing, 3381 Pan American Drive (☎ 854-2626). Tasty, inexpensive seafood and fish'n'chips consumed at marina-side picnic tables in a simple setting. Daily 11am–11pm.

Señor Frog's, 3480 Main Hwy (☎ 448-0999). Broad selection of reasonably priced Mexican food, but most people come to gulp down $8 margaritas. Daily 11.30am–2am.

Taurus Steak House, 3540 Main Hwy (☎ 443-5553). A carnivore's heaven. Meat is the main dish in this creaking old steakhouse that's been open for years. Daily 8.30pm–2am. See also "Drinking."

Tuscany Café, 3484 Main Hwy (☎ 445-0022). Fine, well-presented Italian food made with authentic ingredients. Relaxed ambience with tables on the terrace for watching the world stroll by. Daily noon–midnight.

Brunch

Sunday **brunch** in Miami is usually a more upmarket affair than its equivalent in New York or Los Angeles; high-quality buffet food is laid out in a stylish setting, and usually accompanied by cheap drinks or, at the swankier establishments, complimentary champagne. Served from around 11am to 3pm, brunch costs $10–50 depending on the quality of the food; again, check the newspapers for up-to-the-minute offers, or simply show up with a big appetite at one of the establishments listed.

Bice Restaurant, at the *Grand Bay Hotel*, 2669 S Bayshore Drive, Coconut Grove (℡858-9600). *Bice* attracts the well-heeled glutton, serving fine food, including some Italian additions, in large portions in a very chic dining room.

Colony Bistro, 736 Ocean Drive, South Beach (℡673-6776). Gourmet brunch served in a small but stylish sidewalk café that is great for people-watching.

Franz & Josephs, 3145 Commodore Plaza, Coconut Grove (℡448-2282). Best-value brunch in the Grove, which includes champagne and plenty of pampering by Franz.

The Gordon Lobby Bar, at the *Fontainebleau Hilton*, 4441 Collins Ave, South Beach (℡538-2000). Gargantuan eighty-foot buffet and doting service; also a sneaky way to glimpse the inside of this Fifties landmark hotel (for $32).

Sundays on the Bay, 5420 Biscayne Blvd, Key Biscayne (℡361-6777). The biggest and most enjoyable brunch in Miami ; make a reservation to avoid waiting in line.

1200 Restaurant, at the *Biltmore Hotel*, 1200 Anastasia Ave, Coral Gables (℡445-1926). At over fifty bucks a head, this is Miami's most expensive and elaborate brunch in the city's most historic hotel (see p.74); overpriced but a worthwhile indulgence.

South Miami

Akashi, 5830 S Dixie Hwy (℡665-6261). Generous sushi boats and tender chicken teriyaki make this restaurant trip worthwhile. The cooked food isn't bad either - try the *ton katsu* (a Japanese fried pork chop).

Caravan, 10827 SW 40th St (℡551-1099). Good Iranian meat-based food in a simple setting. Tues–Sun 11am–10.30pm.

Chifa Chinese Restaurant, 12590 N Kendall Drive (℡271-3823). In all probability the only restaurant in Florida specializing in Peruvian-Cantonese cuisine. Tasty deep-fried appetizers, run-of-the-mill main courses, plus a range of Chinese and Peruvian beers are served up at mid-range prices.

El Toro Taco, 1 S Krome Ave (℡245-8182). Excellent family-run Mexican restaurant serving generous portions at a great price. A gem in the center of Homestead that makes a good place to stop en route to the Keys.

Old Cutler Inn, 7271 SW 168th St (℡238-1514). A neo-rustic country inn that's a neighborhood fave for its steaks, shrimps and delicious desserts. Daily 11am–10.30pm.

Sakura, 8225 SW 124th St (℡238-8462). Tiny, good-value sushi bar and restaurant that's always packed. Mon–Fri 12.30–2.30pm & daily 5.30–10/11pm.

Sango Jamaican and Chinese Restaurant, 9485 SW 160th St (℡252-0279). Somewhat of a strange combination, but fine Jamaican favorites, such as curried goat and jerk chicken, can be had here at great prices. Mainly a takeout joint, it does have some informal seating and the constant procession of customers in and out makes for an interesting accompaniment to the food. Don't bother with the Chinese fare. Daily noon–1am.

Shorty's Bar-B-Q, 9200 S Dixie Hwy (℡670-7732). Sit at a picnic table, tuck a napkin in your shirt and graze on barbecued ribs, chicken and corn on the cob – pausing only to gaze at the cowboy memorabilia on the walls. Daily 11am–10/11pm.

Su Shin, SW 88th St, Kendall (℡271-3235). Great teriyakis, daily specials and sushi chefs with a sense of humor. Fairly expensive. Mon–Fri 11.30am–2.30pm & 5–11pm, Sat & Sun 5–11pm.

Wagons West, 11311 S Dixie Hwy (℡238-9942). Maximum cholesterol breakfasts and other unhealthy fare are consumed in this always crowded, budget-priced shrine to cowboys and the Wild West. Mon–Sat 6.30am–9pm, Sun 6.30am–2.30pm.

Key Biscayne

Bayside Seafood Restaurant, 3501 Rickenbacker Causeway (℡361-0808). Atmospheric Tiki bar populated with stray cats and hungry boaters. Highlights include the fresh seafood and tasty seasoned french fries. See "Drinking" and "Live music." Daily noon–10/11pm.

Mad Fish House, 3301 Rickenbacker Causeway (℡ 365-9391). Fish specialities in a gorgeous outdoor setting on the water. Daily noon–10pm.

Rusty Pelican, 3201 Rickenbacker Causeway

(℡ 361-3818). The American, Italian and seafood dishes are only okay, but you mainly want to come here for the absolutely breathtaking views of the bay as you dine. Daily 11am–11pm/midnight. See "Happy hours," p.112.

Sundays on the Bay, 5420 Crandon Blvd (℡ 361-6777). Marina seafood eatery catering to the boats and beer set. Very casual. See "Live music."

Drinking

Miami's **drinking** is more commonly done in restaurants, nightclubs and discos than in the seedy bars so beloved of American filmmakers. One or two dimly lit dives do capture the essence of the archetypal US bar, however, and a handful of Irish and British pubs stock imported ales. But boozing in restaurant lounges, back rooms of music spots or shorefront hotel bars is more in keeping with the spirit of the city. Most places where you can drink are open from 11am or noon until midnight or 2am, with the liveliest hours between 10pm and 1am. Among the following listings, some are suited to an early evening, pre-dinner tipple, while others – especially those in Coconut Grove and Miami Beach – make prime vantage points for watching the city's poseurs come and go. Prices are broadly similar, though the most pose-worthy places sometimes charge way above the average.

Downtown and around

Churchill's Hideaway, 5501 NE Second Ave (℡ 757-1807). A British enclave within Little Haiti, with big-screen live soccer matches and UK beers on tap. See also "Live music."

Tobacco Road, 626 S Miami Ave (℡ 374-1198). Crusty R&B venue (see "Live music") that sees plenty of serious boozing in its downstairs bar.

South Beach

The Abbey Brewing Company, 1115 Sixteenth St (℡ 538-8110). Small, unpretentious, pub-like microbrewery serving the best beers on SoBe. Acclaimed for their creamy Oatmeal Stout, with $1 off all beers during the happy hour (Mon–Fri 1–7pm). Open daily till 5am.

Banana Cabana, at the *Banana Bungalow Hostel*, 2360 Collins Ave (℡ 1-800/7-HOSTEL). Tiki bar setting by the pool, where drinks start at a dirt-cheap $2 during happy hour (5–8pm). Daily noon–midnight (when you will be thrown out on the dot).

Clevelander, 1020 Ocean Drive (℡ 531-3485). The ultimate poolside sports bar, with pool tables, sports-tuned TVs and partially clothed athletic physiques attacking the brews. Daily 11am–5am.

Club Deuce Bar & Grill, 222 Fourteenth St (℡ 531-6200). Raucous neighborhood bar open until 5am, with a CD jukebox, pool table and a clientele that includes cops, transvestites, artists and models.

Irish House, 1430 Alton Rd (℡ 534-5667). Old neighborhood bar with two well-used pool tables and serving inexpensive draught beers. Open till 2am, 4am on weekends.

Marlin Hotel, 1200 Collins Ave (℡ 604-5000). Sleek and futuristic hotel bar smack in Art Deco central, with a mixed bag of live music and top-notch martinis ($7.50). 5pm–2/3am.

The Playwright, 1265 Washington Ave (℡ 534-0667). More Irish than most "Irish" bars – ie decent Guinness and six-deep at the bar on a Friday night – with televised international sports (that means soccer, rugby and cricket) and live Irish or blues music on most nights.

Ted's Hideaway South, 124 Second St (℡ 532-9869). Laid-back local sports bar with two happy hours (noon–7pm & 1–3am) for $2 bottles of beer. Daily noon–5am.

Zeke's Road House, 625 Lincoln Rd, Miami Beach (℡ 532-0087). Laid-back beer bar boasting an enormous range of quality domestic and foreign imported beers; all $2 a bottle or $4 a pint, all day. Old movie photos on the walls and blues tunes on the inside, with open-air seating out on Lincoln. Recommended. Daily noon–1am.

Coral Gables

The Bar, 172 Giralda Ave (℡ 442-2730). Busy, fairly upmarket drinking place with a surprisingly mellow, tavern-like atmosphere.

Duffy's Tavern, 2108 SW 57th Ave (☎264-6580). Large TV screen beaming American sports events for the athletically minded drinker. Daily beer specials for $2 a pint. Open 10am–1am.

John Martin's, 253 Miracle Mile (☎445-3777). Irish pub and restaurant with occasional folk singers and harpists accompanying a good batch of imported brews. See "Live music."

Titanic Brewing Company, 5818 Ponce de León Blvd (☎667-2537). The latest addition to the microbrewery craze, serving six types of stouts and ales brewed on the premises. Very popular with students and has live rock music at the weekends.

Coconut Grove

Fat Tuesdays, inside CocoWalk, 3015 Grand Ave (☎441-2992). Part of a chain of bars famous for fruit-flavored frozen daiquiris, which you can imbibe while observing the milling crowds.

Monty's Bayshore Restaurant, 2550 S Bayshore Drive (☎858-1431). Drinkers often outnumber the diners (see "Eating"), drawn here by the gregarious mood and the views across the bay.

Sail Bar, 3064 Grand Ave (☎444-5270).

Californian sports bar and restaurant with a youngish crowd and surfboards aplenty. Inexpensive Baja-Californian food during the day with happy tunes and a good party atmosphere at night. It could have something to do with "Hurricane Category Five" cocktails which are the house speciality – and mighty potent they are too. Daily till 3am.

Taurus, 3540 Main Hwy (☎448-0633). Old Coconut Grove drinking institution, with a burger grill on weekends and a nostalgic rock-loving crowd.

Tavern in the Grove, 3416 Main Hwy (☎447-3884). Down-to-earth locals' haunt with bouncy jukebox and easy-going mood.

Key Biscayne

Bayside Hut, 3501 Rickenbacker Causeway (☎361-0808). Friendly beer-drinking crowd beside the bay. See "Eating" and "Live music," p.116 and p.121.

The Sandbar, at *Silver Sands Motel & Villas*, 301 Ocean Drive (☎361-5441). The poolside bar is a prime site for sipping cocktails as the ocean crashes close by.

Nightlife

Miami's **nightlife** has taken a slight turn for the worse since the glory days of the mid to late-Nineties. Although there are a lot of **clubs** in South Beach's Art Deco strip, the scene has become somewhat jaded and many places are all too similar – any winning formula is quickly copied, and there isn't a great deal of variety either in musical styles or atmosphere. Still there are few places in the world where you'll find such a sheer concentration of nightlife, and it remains an integral part of the Miami experience. Read *New Times,* published on Thursdays, for the latest raves or, better still, quiz any groover you encounter around the cafés and bars of South Beach.

If you don't give a fig for fashion and just want to dance your socks off, there are plenty of mainstream **discos** where you can do just that – many can be found in Coconut Grove. More adventurously, track down one of the city's **salsa** or **merengue** (a slinky dance music from the Caribbean) clubs, hosted by Spanish-speaking DJs.

Not surprisingly, Fridays and Saturdays are the busiest, but there's a decent choice on any night and some of the mainstream discos boost their midweek crowds by offering cut-price drinks, free admission for women and bizarre asides such as aerobics shows and amateur strip contests. Most places open at 10pm, but don't even think of turning up before midnight as they only hit a peak between then and 2am – although some continue until 7am or 8am and provide a free breakfast buffet for survivors. Usually there's a **cover charge** of $5–30 and a **minimum age of 21** (it's normal for ID to be checked). Be prepared to empty your wallet (or should that be have it emptied?), though there's a new trend of $20 (less if you're a girl or in a large group) all-you-can-drink nights. Some of these evenings are organized by Mike and Margarita, South

Beach's hosts with the most, who move from club to club (latest info ℡ 286-4890), though the free bar tends only to have one bartender, so you may have to wait quite a long time when you want a drink.

Obviously you should dress with some sensitivity to the style of the club, but only by turning up in rags at the smartest door are you ever likely to be turned away on account of your clothes. There are a number of places with velvet ropes and large bouncers, and to get in you'll typically need to have reservations, be on the guest list, be a young female, or use a liberal dose of bluff. Many of the clubs below present gay nights during the week; for gay- and lesbian-specific clubs, see p.123.

All the following are in South Beach unless otherwise stated.

Clubs and discos

Amnesia, 136 Collins Ave (℡ 531-5535). Open-air deep-house and hip-hop club popular with the younger crowd. Daily; $10–20 cover.

Bash, 655 Washington Ave (℡ 538-2274). Co-owned by Sean Penn and Simply Red's Mick Hucknall, many revelers get no further than the salsa grooves in the garden dance-patio. Inside there's an intimate bar and a thumping dance-floor playing techno. Daily; $10–20 cover.

Blue, 222 Española Way (℡ 534-1009). Small, popular club/bar playing deep-house, funk and soul daily from 10pm onwards; no cover. Recommended.

Club 609, 3342 Virginia St, Coconut Grove (℡ 444 6096). The Grove's only real club and it's always jam-packed - maybe something to do with the male clientele who all appear to be about four-foot wide at the shoulders. Two hot, dark and sweaty dance-floors pump out hip-hop and salsa, and this season's color is definitely black, with thick gold chains de rigueur for men.

Crobar, inside the Cameo Theater, 1445 Washington Ave (℡ 531-8225). One of the nicest clubs in South Beach, being more of a place to have a good time than pose - though they still have a large VIP area. The venue is great (high ceiling and airy) and the hip-hop and techno music good. Occasionally hosts dance-bands. Closed Tues; $5–25 cover.

Level, 1235 Washington Ave (℡ 532-1525). Largest club in South Beach featuring prog-house on the cavernous main dance-floor, with two smaller ones playing Ibiza sounds and hip-hop. Presently very hip and attracting lots of celebs to its large VIP areas. Associated with the Ministry of Sound in London and Pacha in Ibiza. Thurs–Sat; $20 cover.

Mango's, 900 Ocean Drive (℡ 673-4422). Just follow the thumping bass to this slightly cheesy – but fun – oceanside club, where scantily-clad dancers prefer the bar top to the floors. Cover charge after 9pm of $5–10. Also see "Live music." 3pm–5am.

ShadowLounge, 1532 Washington Ave (℡ 531-9411). Large psychedelic interior playing techno for a more mature crowd. Thurs-Sun; $15–30 cover charge.

Zanzibar, 615 Washington Ave (℡ 538-6688). The theme nights here are as wild as the dancers, and the lines stretch around the block. Has an outside dance-floor and mixes techno, reggae, hip-hop and Latin grooves depending on the night. Wed–Sun 11pm 5am; cover charge $5–10.

Salsa and merengue clubs

Bonfire Club, 1060 NE 79th St, Little Haiti (℡ 261-2394). Smooth and very danceable salsa sounds. Wed-Sun; $2–5.

Club Tipico Dominicano, 1344 NW 36th St, Little Havana (℡ 634-7819). Top merengue DJs hosting the sessions Fri–Sun; $5 cover.

Club Tropigala, 4441 Collins Ave, in the Fontainebleau Hilton (℡ 672-7469). Dine to the rhythms of hot Latin sounds in the glamorous (or cheese-tastic, depending on your point of view) setting of the landmark Fontainebleau Hotel; $35 including dinner.

El Palenque, 981 SW Eighth St, Little Havana (℡ 856-4565). Restaurant-nightclub serving inexpensive Mexican and Salvadorian cuisine during the day, and Latin grooves at night - including occasional bachata, the rhythmic music of Santo Domingo. Daily 11am–6pm & 9pm–5am; usually no cover.

Live music

In a city that still goes crazy over the studio-based Latin-pop of local girl Gloria Estefan, you might not expect to find a **live music** scene at all. However, a large number of **locales** - many of them poky clubs or the backrooms of restaurants or hotels – host bands throughout the week, though it's often a matter of quantity over quality.

If you're imagining you might be able to catch some good **Cuban** music, forget it. None of the native Cuban musicians can come here and local talent is thin on the ground. The best you can do is catch one of the bands playing the same set night after night on Ocean Drive, or find a Cuban with a Casio organ singing *bolero* (a type of mournful Cuban music) in Little Havana's restaurants.

Be they glam, goth, indie or metal, the City's **rock bands** tend to be pale imitations of the better-known US and European groups that periodically add Miami to their tour schedules. **Jazz** fans fare slightly better, and there's a trustworthy **R&B** scene plus a very minor **folk** one. It's reggae, however, that's most worth seeking out; aside from acts flying in from Jamaica, the musicians among Miami's sizeable Jamaican population appear regularly at several small spots. Finding them is a slight problem, though, and unless you have a particular address, it isn't advised to wander around North Miami or Perrine (in the South) looking for them as they aren't the safest of areas. There's a rare chance to hear live **Haitian** music in Miami, but for **country** sounds, you'll have to leave the city altogether.

Other than for megastar performers (see below), to see a band you've heard of, expect to pay $20 upwards; for a local act, admission will be $5–10 or free. Most places open up at 8pm or 9pm, with the main band going onstage around 11pm or midnight.

The most comprehensive music **listings** are in the weekly *New Times*, but if you can't decide where to go on a Friday night, go along to South Pointe Park (see "Miami Beach," p.87), where there's entertainment and usually a **free concert** to be heard; look for the posters strewn all over South Beach.

Miami also gets its share of **big performances**, as the venues listed in box opposite – none of which has much atmosphere – attract top names in rock, soul, jazz, reggae and funk; tickets are $20-35 from a branch of Ticketmaster (see "Listings"), over the phone or on the Internet by credit card.

Latin music

Hoy Como Ayer, 2212 SW Eighth St (☎ 541-2631). About the only place to hear decent Cuban music in Miami, this dark, smoky joint is plastered with black-and-white photos of Cuban crooners past. Has a mix of live *bolero*, salsa, and rumba and is indeed a place saturated in nostalgia. Wed–Sat 9am–3am; $10 cover Fri & Sat.

Mambos, 1020 Ocean Drive (☎ 538-9029). Nightly live salsa and merengue from 7pm. No cover but the dancers will hit you – and hit you hard – for tips.

Mango's, 900 Ocean Drive (☎ 673-4422). It's hard to stand still when the Brazillian, reggae or Cuban bands that play here strike up; $5–10 cover after 9pm. See "Nightlife."

Jazz

Jazid, 1342 Washington Ave, Miami Beach (☎ 673-9372). Its ambience bordering on the club scene, this comfortable venue features smooth vocalists and hot tunes daily. Recommended. Daily 9pm–5am; $5 cover after 10pm.

Les Deux Fontaines, 1230 Ocean Drive, Miami Beach (☎ 672-7878,

ⓦ www.lesdeuxfontaines.com). Features mainly Dixieland swing jazz. Daily from 8pm.

Rock, blues and R&B

Churchill's Hideaway, 5501 NE Second Ave, Little Haiti (☎ 757-1807). Good place to hear local hopeful rock and indie bands. Cover $10–15. See "Drinking."

The Grind, 12573 Biscayne Blvd, North Miami

Big performance venues

James L. Knight Center, 400 SE Second Ave, downtown Miami (☎372-4633, ⓦ www.jlknightcenter.com)
Miami Arena, 701 Arena Blvd, downtown Miami (☎673-3330, ⓦ www.nws.org)
Pro Player Stadium, 2269 Dan Marino Blvd, 16 miles northwest of downtown Miami – bus #27 (☎623-6100, ⓦ www.proplayerstadium.com)

(☎899-9979). College nights and indie rock with local eccentric bands. In the process of changing hands so phone before you go.
Scully's Tavern, 9809 Sunset Drive, South Miami (☎271-7404). Rock and blues bands play here for beer-drinking, pool-playing regulars; no cover.
Tobacco Road, 626 S Miami Ave, downtown Miami (☎374-1198). Earthy R&B from some of the country's finest exponents; free–$8. See "Drinking."

Reggae

Bayside Hut, 3501 Rickenbacker Causeway, Key Biscayne (☎361-0808). Free bayside open-air reggae jams on Fri and Sat at 8pm.
Studio One 83, 2860 NW 183 St, Overtown (☎621-7295). Powerful hip-hop, soul and reggae, yet located in a dangerous area north of downtown Miami; cover $5–15.
Sundays on the Bay, 5420 Crandon Blvd, Key Biscayne (☎361-6777). Unlikely but lively setting

for live reggae (as well as occasional salsa and merengue). Thurs–Sun; free entrance. See "Eating."

Folk and Arabic

Café Efesus, 1339 Washington Ave (☎674-0078). Live belly dancing and Arabic music Fri & Sat from 10.30pm onwards at this Turkish restaurant. See "Eating," p.112.
John Martin's, 253 Miracle Mile, Coral Gables (☎445-3777). Spacious Irish bar (see "Drinking") and restaurant with Irish folk music several evenings a week; free.
Luna Star Café, 775 NE 125th St, North Miami (☎892-8522). Open-mic nights and poetry readings. Phone before you go as it has erratic opening hours.

Haitian music

Tap Tap, 819 Fifth St, South Beach (☎672-2898). Best known for its excellent restaurant (see "Eating"), interesting gallery and regular live Haitian music – phone ahead for details.

Classical music, dance and opera

To find out **what's on**, read the listings in the free *New Times* (published on Thursdays). The Miami-based New World Symphony Orchestra, 541 Lincoln Rd (☎673-3331, ⓦ www.nws.org), offers concert experience to some of the finest graduate **classical** musicians in the US. Its season runs from October to May with most performances at the Lincoln Theater; tickets $22–62 or for $12 you can see rehearsals (see Web site for dates). For better-known names, look out for top-flight soloists guesting with the Miami Chamber Symphony (☎858-3500) at the Gusman Concert Hall or the Lincoln Theater; tickets $15–30.

The city's two major professional **dance** companies, the Miami City Ballet, 2200 Liberty Ave, South Beach (☎532-4880, ⓦ www.miamicityballet.org) and the Ballet Theater of Miami (☎442-4840), appear at the Gusman Center for the Performing Arts; tickets are $15–45, but the Miami City Ballet also holds cut-price dress rehearsals at the Colony Theater for under $10. A third troupe is the Ballet Flamenco La Rosa, 555 Seventeenth St (☎757-8475, ⓦ www .panmiami.org), whose frenetic Latin dance productions also take place at the Colony Theater; tickets $10–20.

Opera is the poor relation of classical music and dance in Miami despite the efforts of the Florida Grand Opera, 1200 Coral Way (☎854-1643, ⓦ www.fgo.org), which brings impressive names to a varied repertoire at the Miami-Dade County Auditorium; tickets $10–60.

Colony Theater, 1040 Lincoln Rd, Miami Beach (℡ 674-1026)
Gusman Center for the Performing Arts, 174 E Flagler St, downtown Miami (℡ 372-0925)
Gusman Concert Hall, 1314 Miller Drive, University of Miami (℡ 284-2438 or 284-6477)
Jackie Gleason Theater of the Performing Arts, 1700 Washington Ave, South Beach (℡ 673-7300)
Lincoln Theater, 541 Lincoln Rd, South Beach (℡ 673-3331)
Miami-Dade County Auditorium, 2901 W Flagler St, near 27th Ave (℡ 547-5414)

Comedy

Whether it's the difficulty of finding jokes to span Miami's multicultural population, or simply its geographical distance from the stand-up comedy hotbeds of New York and Los Angeles, the city is very short of **comedy clubs**, although the ones it does have draw enthusiastic crowds and often comparatively big names. Admission is $5–10; phone for show times.

Comedy clubs

Improv Comedy Club, 3390 Mary St, Coconut Grove (℡ 441-8200). One of the nationwide chain of Improv comedy clubs and the best place in Miami for comedy, despite the rather formal atmosphere. Opens at 9 pm; reservations required.

New Theater, 65 Almeira Ave, Coral Gables (℡ 461-1161). Fri & Sat nights showcase the hilarious talents of the Laughing Gas Comedy Improv Company. Shows start at 11pm.

Theater

Though small, Miami's **theater** scene is of an encouragingly high standard. Winter is the busiest period, though something worth seeing crops up almost every week on the alternative circuit. If you're fluent in Spanish, make a point of visiting one of the city's **Spanish-language theaters**, whose programs are listed in *El Nuevo Herald* (the Spanish-language version of the *Miami Herald* newspaper): Bellas Artes, 1 Herald Plaza (℡ 325-0515), Teatro Martí (the longest-running Latin theater in the city), 420 SW Eighth Ave (℡ 545-7866) and Teatro Trail, 3717 SW Eighth St (℡ 448-0592), are three of the best; tickets are $12–15.

Major and alternative theaters

Coconut Grove Playhouse, 3500 Main Hwy, Coconut Grove (℡ 442-2662). Comfortable and well-established mainstream theater that bucks up its schedule with many interesting experimental efforts; $20–45.

New Theater, 65 Almeira Ave, Coral Gables (℡ 443-5909). Sitting neatly between mainstream and alternative, a nice place for a relaxing evening; $10–20.
Ring Theater, at the University of Miami, 1380 Miller Drive (℡ 284-3355). Assorted offerings year-round from the drama students of the University of Miami. Closed Oct–March; $5–18.

Film

Except for the **Miami Film Festival** (℡ 377-FILM), ten days and nights of new films from far and wide in February at the Gusman Center for the Performing Arts (see above), Miami is barren territory for film buffs. That said, at one point in American history, Florida might have rivaled Hollywood as the film capital of the world (see "Contexts" for more information). Most **film** theaters are multiscreen affairs inside shopping malls showing first-run American features. Look at the "Weekend" section of the Friday *Miami Herald* for complete listings, or call the Movie Hotline (☎888-FILM). The main theater locations are the AMC Theater (☎448-2088), at 1601 Biscayne Blvd; Cinema 10, in the Miracle Center Mall, 3301 Coral Way; the eight-screen AMC in the CocoWalk, 3015 Grand Ave; and Movies at the Falls, in the Falls Mall, SW 136th St (☎255-2500); admission is $5-10.

For arthouse films try: the Absinthe House Cinematique, 235 Alcazar Ave, Coral Gables, for high-brow foreign films (☎446-7144); Alliance Cinema, 927 Lincoln Rd, Suite 119, South Beach, for contemporary independent offerings (☎531-8504); or Astor Art Cinema, 4120 Laguna St, off Le Jeaune in downtown, for quirky underground films.

For **arthouse**, **foreign-language** or fading monochrome **classic** films, many libraries have screenings, as does the Bass Museum of Art, 2121 Park Ave (☎673-7530), on Tuesdays – newspaper listings carry details.

Gay and lesbian Miami

Miami's **gay** and **lesbian** communities are enjoying the city's boom times as much as anyone else, with a growing number of gay-owned businesses, bars and clubs opening up around the city. The scene, traditionally focusing on Biscayne Boulevard, has become more focused on South Beach in the late Nineties. In either of these areas, most public places are friendly and welcoming towards gays and lesbians – though attitudes in other parts of Miami can sometimes be considerably less enlightened. The key sources of info – mainly entertainment – are the free *TWN* (*The Weekly News*), *Outlook* or *Scoop*, available from any of the places listed below and from many of the mixed bars and clubs around South Beach.

Resources

Gay Community Book/Video Store, 7545 Biscayne Blvd (☎754-6900). Copious books, magazines, newspapers and videos of gay and lesbian interest. Mon–Sat 11am–9pm, Sun noon–8pm.

Bars, clubs and discos

Cactus, 2041 Biscayne Blvd (☎438-0662, Ⓦwww.thecactus.com). Happy hours aplenty (daily 4–9pm) and daily tropical-drinks specials at its Tiki bar make it one of the liveliest gay bars in the area.

Laundry Bar, 721 N Lincoln Lane (☎531-7700). Relaxed lesbian/gay/straight bar with low lighting and an un-cruisey scene. Hosts DJ's at the weekends and yes, you can do your laundry here. Open daily 10am–5am.

Ozone, 6620 SW 57th Ave and Red Rd (☎667-2888). Features "Adorable Wednesdays," with two-for-one drinks all night. No cover.

Salvation, 1771 West Ave (☎673-6508, Ⓦwww.salvationsobe.com). Giant warehouse converted into an anything-goes club with the shirtless and rippled partying to thumping techno beats.

Twist, 1057 Washington Ave (☎538-9478, Ⓦwww.twistsobe.com). Longest-running gay bar on SoBe and a bit of an institution. Now featuring six different environments with comfy lounges, an outdoor terrace and two packed techno dancefloors. No cover and daily two-for-one happy hour 1–9pm.

Warsaw Ballroom, 1450 Collins Ave, Miami Beach (☎1-800/9-WARSAW). Fridays this is the busiest and biggest gay disco in town. $15–25 cover.

Women's Miami

Though it lacks the extended networks of Los Angeles or New York, Miami is steadily becoming a better place for **women** seeking the support and solidarity

Miami festivals

The precise dates of the festivals listed below vary from year to year; check the details at any tourist information office or Chamber of Commerce.

January

Early *Miami Jazz Festival*: international jazz performances in and around downtown, including contemporary, traditional and Latin jazz, as well as blues and gospel (☎ 858-8545, ⓦ www.miamijazzfestival.com).

Mid *Art Deco Weekend*: talks and free events focus on South Beach architecture. On Ocean Drive (☎ 672-2014).

Taste of the Grove: pig out on food and free music in Coconut Grove's Peacock Park (☎ 444-7270).

Key Biscayne Art Festival: enjoy music, arts and crafts and fresh seafood along Crandon Boulevard (☎ 365-0120).

February

Early *Homestead Championship Rodeo*: professional rodeo cowboys compete in steer-wrestling, bull-riding, calf-roping and bareback riding (☎ 247-3515).

Miami Film Festival: latest US and overseas films premiere in downtown Miami's Gusman Center for the Performing Arts (☎ 377-3456).

Mid *Coconut Grove Arts Festival*: hundreds of (mostly) talented unknowns display their works in Coconut Grove's Peacock Park and on nearby streets (☎ 447-0401).

March

Early *Carnival Miami*: an offshoot of the Calle Ocho Festival, with Hispanic-themed events across the city culminating in a parade at the Orange Bowl on the first Saturday of the month (☎ 644-8888).

Mid *Calle Ocho Festival*: massive festival of Cuban arts, crafts and cooking along the streets of Little Havana on the second Sunday of the month (☎ 644-8888).

Ericksson Open: men and women compete in the world's largest tennis tournament held at the Crandon Park Tennis Center in Key Biscayne (☎ 446-2200).

April

Early *Miracle Mile Festival*: parades and floats along the Miracle Mile sing the praises of Coral Gables.

South Beach Film Festival: local and non-resident film directors debut short films at the Colony Theater, 1040 Lincoln Rd (☎ 532-1233).

May

The Great Sunrise Balloon Race & Festival: held at Homestead Air Force Base (☎ 273-3051).

---

of other women in business, artistic endeavors, or simply looking for a reliable and inexpensive source of medical care.

Women's organizations

Women's Chamber of Commerce of Dade County, 7700 SW 88th St, Suite 310 (☎ 446-6660). Promoting women-owned and women-run businesses throughout south Florida.

Health care and counseling centers

Eve Medical Center, 3900 NW 79th Ave, Doral (☎ 591-2288). Low-cost medical care and abortions in serene, supportive environment.

June
Early *Goombay Festival*: a spirited bash in honor of Bahamian culture, in and around Coconut Grove's Peacock Park (☎238-6186).
Art in the Park: arty stalls and displays in the Charles Deering Estate in South Miami.

July
4 July *America's Birthday Bash*: music, fireworks and a laser-light show celebrate the occasion at Bayfront Park in downtown Miami (☎358-7550).
Tropical Agricultural Fiesta: enjoy fresh mangoes along with exotic fruits and other ethnic foods at the Fruit and Spice Park (☎246-3311).

August
Early *Miami Reggae Festival*: celebration on the first Sunday of the month of Jamaican Independence Day with dozens of top Jamaican bands playing around the city (☎891-2944).

September
Mid *Festival Miami*: three weeks of performing and visual arts events organized by the University of Miami, mostly taking place in Coral Gables (☎284-4940).

October
Hispanic Heritage Festival: lasts all month and features innumerable events linked to Latin American history and culture (☎541-5023).
Mid *Caribbean-American Carnival*: a joyous cavalcade of soca and calypso bands in Bicentennial Park.
Columbus Day Regatta: Florida's largest watersports event is a race commemorating Columbus's historic voyage. At Key Biscayne (☎858-3320).

November
Mid *Miami Book Fair International*: a wealth of volumes from across the world spread across the campus of Miami-Dade Community College in downtown Miami (☎237-3258).
Harvest Festival: a celebration of southern Florida's agricultural traditions, including homemade crafts, music and re-enactments at the Fair/Expo Center on Coral Way (☎375-1492).

December
26–1 Jan *Indian Arts Festival*: Native American artisans from all over the country gather at the Miccosukee Village – 27 miles west of Miami – to display their work (☎223-8380).
30 *King Mango Strut*: a very alternative New Year's Eve celebration, with part-time cross-dressers and clowns parading through Coconut Grove (☎445-1865).
31 *Orange Bowl Parade*: mainstream climax of the New Year's bashes all over the city, with floats, marching bands and the crowning of the Orange Bowl Queen at the Orange Bowl (☎371-4600).

Miami Women's Healthcenter, at North Shore Medical Center, 1100 NW 95th St (☎835-6165). Education, information, support and discussion groups, physician referrals, mammograms, seminars and workshops.
Planned Parenthood of Greater Miami: 681 NE 125th St, North Miami (☎895-7756); 1699 SW 27th Ave (☎285-5535 ext 7); Goulds Shopping Center 11621 SW 216th St (☎238-8344); 3333 Overseas Highway, Suite 140, Marathon (☎289-9499). Economical health care for men and women, including birth control supplies, pregnancy testing, treatment of sexually transmitted diseases and counseling. 24hr info-line (☎285-2061).
Women and Teens Community Health Center, 1990 NE 163rd St, North Miami Beach (☎895-1274,

@ www.braithwaite.yourmd.com). Health care for women and teens.
Women's Resource & Counseling Center, 111 Majorca Ave, Coral Gables ☎ 448-8325,

@ www.miamicounseling.com). Friendly clinic providing individual, marriage, group and family counseling, psychotherapy and assertiveness training.

Shopping

Shopping for the sake of it isn't the big deal in Miami that it is in some American cities, though there's plenty of opportunity for eager consumers to exercise their credit cards. Bizarre as it may seem, Miami leads the field in **shopping mall** architecture, blowing millions of dollars on environments intended subtly to soften the hard commercialism of the stores which fill them – several malls are worthy of investigation for this reason alone. These days, traditional **department stores**, such as the dependable Macys and Sears Roebuck & Co, generally show up inside the malls too, but Miami has one dignified survivor, Burdines, that stands alone.

The closer you get to the beach, the wackier Miami's **clothes** shops become – look out for zebra-print bikinis and Art Deco shirts. However, the best places for quality togs at discounted rates are the designer outlets of the **fashion district**, on Fifth Avenue between 25th and 29th streets, just north of downtown Miami; here you'll find classy outfits – most of Latin American origin – at slashed prices. With less finesse, there can be finds amid the discarded garb filling the city's **thrift stores**.

Unless you're existing on a shoestring budget – or are preparing a picnic – you won't need to shop for **food and drink** at all, although supermarkets like Publix and Winn-Dixie, usually open until 10pm, are plentiful – flip through the phone book to locate the nearest one. You can buy alcohol from supermarkets and, of course, from the many **liquor stores**, but if you're looking for quality grub or booze, only the largest of the supermarkets and a few specialist suppliers will oblige.

Gun shops have long outnumbered **bookshops** in Miami, but large discount chains like B. Dalton's and Waldenbooks have arrived, with branches in shopping malls, and there are also a few local outlets stocking quality reading material. Some of the city's record shops make good browsing territory, too, their contents spanning everything from doo-wop rarities to the smoothest salsa hits.

Malls and department stores

Aventura Mall, 19501 Biscayne Blvd, North Miami Beach ☎ 935-1110). One of the largest air-conditioned malls in the state, boasting virtually every major department store: Macys, Sears, J C Penney. Pick up a map on entry or you'll never find your way out.
Bal Harbour Shops, 9700 Collins Ave, Miami Beach ☎ 866-0311). Don't come to buy but to watch designer-shopping in this temple of upmarket consumerism.
Bayside Marketplace, anchored at 400 Biscayne Blvd, near downtown Miami ☎ 577-3344). Squarely aimed at tourists, but a good blend of diverse stores – selling everything from Art Deco ashtrays to bubblegum – beside the

bay, with some excellent food stands.
Burdines, 22 E Flagler St, downtown Miami ☎ 577-2312). Run-of-the-mill clothes, furnishings and domestic appliances, but Miami's oldest department store – circa 1936 – is an entertaining place to cruise. Daily 10am–6pm.
CocoWalk, 3015 Grand Ave, Coconut Grove ☎ 444-0777). In the heart of Coconut Grove, this open-air complex has a relatively small range of stores, some good places to eat and a decent sixteen-screen multiplex cinema.
Dadeland Mall, 7535 N Kendall Drive, South Miami ☎ 665-6226). More top-class department stores and speciality shops in a totally enclosed, air-conditioned environment conducive to passionate shopping.
The Falls, Hwy-1 and SW 136th St, South

Miami (℡255-4570). Sit inside a gazebo and contemplate the waterfalls and the rainforest that prettify suburban Miami's classiest set of shops. Ask about the tourist saving scheme.

Lincoln Road Mall, Lincoln Rd and Sixteenth, South Beach (℡673-7010). Not a shopping mall in the usual sense of the word, but, between Washington Ave and Alton Road, a pedestrian-only road lined with stores. Many are given over to art galleries, but there's also a whole range of trendy clothes stores and many excellent side-walk cafés and restaurants.

Prime Outlets, 250 E Palm Drive, Florida City (℡248-4727). Located where the Florida's Turnpike meets Hwy-1 and conveniently located for people traveling to the Keys or Everglades. Dedicated shoppers will find huge savings on name brands.

Streets of Mayfair, 2911 Grand Ave, Coconut Grove (℡448-1700). The expensive stores take second place to the landscaped tropical foliage and the discreetly placed classical sculptures.

Clothes and thrift stores

Coral Gables Congregational Church Thrift Shop, 3010 De Soto Blvd, Coral Gables (℡445-1721). After viewing the church (see "Coral Gables"), drop in on the wide variety of stock at the thrift store next door. Mon–Fri 10am–2pm.

Miami Twice, 6562 SW 40th St, South Beach (℡666-0127). Department store specializing in vintage clothing, accessories and some furniture. Mon–Sat 10am–7pm, Sun noon–6pm.

One Hand Clapping, 7165 SW 47th St, Miami Beach (℡661-6316). Amid a wondrous assortment of antique junk, there are hats, dresses and scarves here to delight the time-warped flapper.

Food and drink

Epicure Market, 1656 Alton Rd, South Beach (℡672-1861). Tasty morsels for the gourmet palate and a mouthwatering array of hot foods for immediate consumption. Mon–Fri 10am–8pm, Sat 10am–7pm, Sun 10am–6pm.

Estate Wines and Gourmet Foods, 92 Miracle Mile, Coral Gables (℡442-9915). Alongside the fine foods, an exquisite stock of wines chosen with the connoisseur in mind. Mon–Fri 10am–5pm, Sat 10am–4pm.

Perricone's Marketplace, 15 SE Tenth St, downtown Miami (℡374-9693). Italian market with imported meats and cheeses, a homemade bakery, and a mid-price restaurant (opening at 11.30am) on the premises. Daily 7am–11pm.

Books

Books & Books, 296 Aragon Ave, Coral Gables (℡442-4408) and a small branch at 933 Lincoln Rd, Miami Beach (℡532-3222). Excellent stock of general titles but especially strong on Floridian art and design, travel and new fiction; also has author signings and talks: ℡444-9044 for the latest events. Daily 10am–11pm.

Cervantes Book Store, 1898 SW Eighth St, Little Havana (℡642-5222). Spanish-speakers will find here a wide selection of Spanish-language fiction and nonfiction – as well as a few English books. Mon–Sat 9am–7pm.

Downtown Book Center, 247 SE First St, downtown Miami (℡377-9939). Adequate selection ranging from the latest blockbusters to esoteric and academic tomes. Also stocks European newspapers and magazines. Mon–Fri 9am–5.30pm, Sat 9am–2pm.

Kafka's Kafe, 1464 Washington Ave, South Beach (℡673-9669). Used-book store with café and Internet connection. It might take you a while to find something decent, but it's a good place to pick up some inexpensive reading for the beach. Also stocks foreign newspapers. Daily 9am–8pm.

The 9th Chakra, 811 Lincoln Rd, South Beach (℡538-0671). Gifts for the soul, dreamcatchers and a plethora of reading materials ranging from simple meditation to reiki and spiritual instruction. Tues–Thurs noon–9pm, Fri & Sat noon–11pm, Sun 1–9pm.

Records, CDs and tapes

Lily's Records, 1260 SW Eighth St, Little Havana (℡856-0536). Unsurpassed stock of salsa, merengue and other Latin sounds. Mon–Sat 9am–9pm, Sun 10am–6pm.

Spec's Music, 501 Collins Ave, South Beach (℡534-3667). Mix of contemporary and hard-to-find music of all types. Daily 10am–midnight.

Yesterday & Today Dance Music, 1614 Alton Rd, Miami Beach (℡534-8704). Specialist dance-music shop. Daily noon–8pm.

Cuban curios

Botanica Esperanza, 901 SW 27th Ave at SW Ninth St, Little Havana (℡642-2488). Santería supplies, like religious candles, bead necklaces, animal skins and Mexican good-luck charms.

Coral Way Antiques, 3127 SW 22nd St, Coral Gables (℡567-3131). Old postcards, books, military items and other Cuban collectibles. Daily 1–6pm.

Listings

AIDS Hotline (T) 667-7855).

Airlines Air Canada, Airport Concourse "G" (T) 1-888-247-2262); American Airlines, 150 Alhambra Plaza (T) 1-800/433-7300); British Airways, 354 SE First St (T) 1-800/247-9297); Continental, Airport Concourse "C" (T) 871-1400); Delta, 201 Alhambra Circle (T) 448-7000); Northwest Airlines/KLM, 150 Alhambra Plaza (T) 1-800/225-2525); TWA, Airport Concourse "G" (T) 1-800/221-2000); United, 178 Giralda Ave (T) 1-800/241-6522); US Airways, 150 Alhambra Plaza (T) 1-800/428-4322); Virgin Atlantic, 225 Alhambra Circle (T) 1-800/862-8621).

Airport Miami International, six miles west of downtown Miami (T) 876-7000). Take local bus #7 from downtown Miami (around 30–45min) or local bus #J from Miami Beach (around 40–50min). There are also privately-run SuperShuttle buses (T) 871-2000). More details on p.65.

American Express Main hotline (T) 1-800/325-1218. Offices around the city: in downtown Miami, Suite 100, 330 Biscayne Blvd (T) 358-7350); in Coral Gables, 32 Miracle Mile (T) 446-3381); in Miami Beach, at Bal Harbour Shops, 9700 Collins Ave (T) 865-5959).

Amtrak 8303 NW 37th Ave (T) 1-800/872-7245).

Area Code (T) 305.

Banks See "Money exchange."

Bike rental See p.70.

Boat rental Skim over Biscayne Bay in a motor boat. Equipped with 90–2000hp engines, such vessels can be rented for 2–8hr – rates start at $99 for two hours – from Boat Rentalplus, 2400 Collins Ave, Miami Beach (T) 534-4307, (W) www.boatrentalplus.com).

Coastguard (T) 535-4368.

Consulates Canada, 200 S Biscayne Blvd, Ste. 1600 (T) 579-1600); Denmark, PH 1D, 2655 Le Jeune Rd, CG (T) 446-0020); France, 2 S Biscayne Blvd, Ste. 1710 (T) 372-9799); Germany, Suite 2200, 100 N Biscayne Blvd (T) 358-0290); Netherlands, 800 Brickell Ave, Ste. 918 (T) 789-6646); Norway, Suite 305, 1007 North American Way, Port of Miami (T) 358-4386); Spain, 2655 Le Jeune Rd, CG (T) 446-5511); UK, 1001 Brickell Ave, Ste. 918 (T) 374-1522).

Crisis Hotline (T) 358-4357.

Dentists To be referred to a dentist: (T) 947-7999.

Doctor To find a physician: (T) 324-8717.

Emergencies Dial (T) 911 and ask for relevant emergency service.

Everglades daytrips In the absence of public transport, almost every tour operator in Miami runs half- or full-day trips ($25–35) to the Everglades,

but these seldom involve more than a quick gape at an alligator and an air-boat ride – or even enter the Everglades National Park.

Hospitals with emergency rooms. In Miami: Jackson Memorial Medical Center, 1611 NW Twelfth Ave (T) 585-1111); Mercy Hospital, 3663 S Miami Ave (T) 854-4400). In Miami Beach: Mt Sinai Medical Center, 4300 Alton Rd (T) 674-2121); South Shore Hospital, 630 Alton Rd (T) 672-2100).

Internet cafés are available all over Miami and South Beach in particular. Prices are generally around $7–9 per hour, or $1 for five minutes. On South Beach the least expensive places are the *Banana Bungalow* (see "Accommodation").

Laundromats Check the Yellow Pages for the nearest; handiest for South Beach are: Wash Club of South Beach, 510 Washington Ave (T) 534-4298; 6am–midnight) and Bianca's Coin Laundry & Dry Cleaning, 211 Twentieth St (T) 672-3784; 6am–10pm). If you fancy a drink while you wash, try the *Laundry Bar* (see "Gay and lesbian Miami"p.123).

Left Luggage At the airport, some Greyhound terminals (phone to be sure) and the Amtrak station.

Library The biggest is Miami-Dade County Public Library, 101 W Flagler St (Mon–Sat 9am–6pm, Thurs until 9pm; Oct–May also Sun 1–5pm; (T) 375-2665, (W) www.mdpls.org) - see p.74.

Lost and found For something lost on Metro-Dade Transit, phone (T) 375-3366 (Mon–Fri 8am–4.30pm). Otherwise call the police (T) 673-7960).

Money exchange Using your bank/credit card at an ATM is the easiest and safest way. Otherwise bring US dollar travelers' checks or cash, but if you need to change money, facilities are available at the airport, at American Express, and the following: Barnett Bank, 701 Brickell Ave or call (T) 350-7143 for the nearest branch; First Union National Bank, 200 S Biscayne Blvd (T) 599-2265); Suntrust Bank, 777 Brickell Ave (T) 592-0800); NationsBank, 701 Brickell Ave (T) 1-800/299-2265), and 1300 Brickell Ave (T) 372-0800); Citibank International, 1685 Washington Ave & 401 Arthur Godfrey Rd, South Beach and1790 Biscayne Blvd, downtown Miami (T) 1-800/627-3999).

Parking fine for an expired meter $18, for parking in a residential area $23 – both increasing to $45 if not paid within thirty days. You'll find the addresses where you can pay on the back of the ticket (T) 673-PARK).

Pharmacies Usually open from 8am or 9am until 9pm or midnight. 24-hour pharmacy branches of Eckerd at 1825 Miami Gardens Drive (T) 932-5740); 1549 SW 107th Ave (T) 220-0147); 2235

Collins Ave (☎ 673-9514); 200 Lincoln Rd (☎ 673-9502).

Police Non-emergency: ☎ 673-7900; emergency: ☎ 911. If you are robbed anywhere on Miami Beach, report it at the station at 1100 Washington Ave and the report (for insurance purposes) can usually be collected within 3–5 days (records office Tues–Fri 8am–3pm; ☎ 673-7100).

Post offices In downtown Miami, 500 NW Second Ave; in Coral Gables, 251 Valencia Ave; in Coconut Grove, 3191 Grand Ave; in Homestead, 739 Washington Ave; in Key Biscayne, 59 Harbor Drive; in Miami Beach, 1300 Washington Ave and 445 W 40th St. All open Mon–Fri 8.30am–5pm, Sat 8.30am–12.30pm, or longer hours.

Rape hotline ☎ 549-585-7273.

Rollerblading Hugely popular in Miami, especially in South Beach. Fritz Skate & Bikes, at 726 Lincoln Rd (☎ 532-1954), both sell and rent out rollerblades and safety gear, as well as offering free lessons on Sundays at 10.15am (weather permitting). Rental costs around $8 per hour, $24 per day, or $15 overnight (6pm–noon); to buy, prices range from $90 to $300.

Sports The Miami Dolphins (☎ 954-452-7000, Ⓦ www.miamidolphins.com) and the Florida Marlins (☎ 626-7400, Ⓦ www.floridamarlins.com) play at Pro Player Stadium, 2269 NW 199th St, sixteen miles northwest of downtown Miami: tickets are available from TicketMaster (see below) or the box office (Mon–Fri 8.30am–5.30pm) – most seats are around $30 for football and $4–55 for baseball. The football season lasts August through December, and the baseball season April through September. The Miami Heat basketball team plays NBA games downtown at the American Airline Arena, 601 Biscayne Blvd (info on ☎ 577-HEAT, Ⓦ www.heat.com); tickets $8–200 from TicketMaster or the box office (Mon–Fri 10am–5pm). The basketball season lasts November through April. The University of Miami's football, basketball and baseball teams are all called the Miami Hurricanes: game and ticket (usually $5–99) info Mon–Fri 8am–6pm on ☎ 284-2263 or Ⓦ www.hurricanesports.com.

State-road information ☎ 470-5277.

TicketMaster Tickets for arts and sports events, payable by credit card: ☎ 358-5885, Ⓦ www.ticketmaster.com.

Weather information ☎ 229-4522.

Western Union Offices all over the city; call ☎ 1-800/325-6000 to find the nearest branch.

TRAVEL DETAILS

Trains (AMTRAK ☎ 1-800/USA-RAIL, Ⓦ www.amtrak.com)

Miami to: New York (3 daily; 26hr 25min–28hr 40min); Ocala (1 daily; 7hr 39min); Sebring (3 daily; 3hr 15min); Orlando (2 daily; 5hr 15min); St. Petersburg (1 daily; leaves 7am to Orlando 5hr 33min, and buses depart Orlando 12.23pm for St. Petersburg at 1.05pm (2hr 40min)); Tampa (1 daily; leaves at 5pm and takes 5hr 15min); Washington DC (3 daily; 22hr 7min–24hr 34min); Winter Haven (3 daily; 4hr).

Tri-Rail (5–15 daily)

Miami to: Boca Raton (1hr); Delray Beach (1hr 7min); Fort Lauderdale (31min); Hollywood (16min); West Palm Beach (1hr 34min).

Buses (GREYHOUND ☎ 1-800/231-2222, Ⓦ www.greyhound.com)

Miami to: Daytona Beach (3 daily; 7hr 5min–7hr 55min); Fort Lauderdale (hourly; 55min); Fort Myers (4 daily; 4hr–4hr 45min); Fort Pierce (8–9 daily; 3hr–3hr 30min); Jacksonville (8 daily; 7hr 30min–8hr); Key West (3–4 daily; 4hr 40min); Orlando (7 daily; 6hr); Sarasota (4 daily; 6hr 30min–7hr); St. Petersburg (7 daily; 7–8hr); Tampa (5 daily; 7–9hr); West Palm Beach (7–8 daily; 2hr).

The Florida Keys

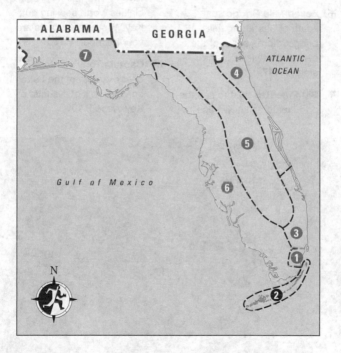

CHAPTER 2 Highlights

* **John Pennekamp State Park** Snorkel or dive around the living coral reef to spot shipwrecks and exotic marine life. **P.133**

* **Swimming with dolphins** You can take to the waters with these intelligent creatures while in Key Largo. **P.135**

* **Seven Mile Bridge** Just south of Marathon, this bridge affords some of the best sunset views in the state. **P.147**

* **Big Pine Key** Just to see the odd creatures known as Key

deer; the pines are merely an added bonus. **P.148**

* **Whitehead Street** Down-to-earth and manageable, this street offers some top Key West attractions, like Papa Hemingway's House. **P.161**

* **Key lime pie and conch fritters** Two fine local specialties worth seeking out; Key West's restaurants are your best bet. **P.165**

* **Captain Tony's Saloon** The best example of the bohemian vibe, as it still exists, on Key West. **P.166**

The Florida Keys

A string of over ten thousand small islands of which less than fifty are inhabited, the **FLORIDA KEYS**★ emerge just off the southeastern corner of the state to form a hundred-mile long arc that trails off within ninety miles of Cuba. The Keys' main attraction is the **Florida Reef**, a great band of living coral just a few miles offshore whose range of color and dazzling array of ocean life – including dolphins and loggerhead turtles – are exceptional sights. Throughout the Keys, and especially for the first sixty-odd miles, fishing, snorkeling and diving dominate – and are ruthlessly hawked at every opportunity – and if you're not planning to indulge in watersports, you'll be hard-pressed to find much else to fill your time. Here and there, houses built around the turn of the nineteenth century by Bahamian settlers and seedy waterside bars run by refugees from points north hint at the islands' history. And while there are some stunning natural areas and worthwhile ecology tours, the whole stretch is primarily a build-up to **Key West**, the real pearl on this island strand.

One of the better places to visit the reef is the **John Pennekamp State Park**, one of the few interesting features of **Key Largo** on the **Upper Keys**. Like **Islamorada**, further south, Key Largo is rapidly being populated by suburban Miamians, moving here for the sailing and fishing but unable to survive without shopping malls. Islamorada is the best base for fishing, and also has some natural and historical points of note – as does the next major settlement, **Marathon**, which is at the center of the **Middle Keys** and thus makes a useful short-term base. Thirty miles on, the **Lower Keys** get fewer visitors and less publicity than their neighbors. Don't dismiss them, though; in many ways these are the most unusual and appealing of the Keys. Covered with dense forests, they are home to a tiny and endangered species of Key deer as well as mud turtle, mangrove terrapin and mole slink, and, at **Looe Key**, offer a tremendous departure point for trips to the Florida Reef.

Key West, the final dot of the North American continent before a thousand miles of ocean, is the end of the road in every sense. Shot through with an intoxicating aura of abandonment, it's a small but immensely vibrant place. The only part of the Keys with a real sense of history, Key West was once – unbelievably – the richest town in the US and the largest settlement in Florida. There are old homes and museums to explore and plenty of bars in which to while away the hours.

The area code for all numbers in this chapter is ☎305.

★ Derived from the Spanish word "cayo," which means a small island, a key is a small island or bank composed of coral fragments. The Florida Keys are the largest such grouping in the US, but keys are common all along the state's southerly coastlines.

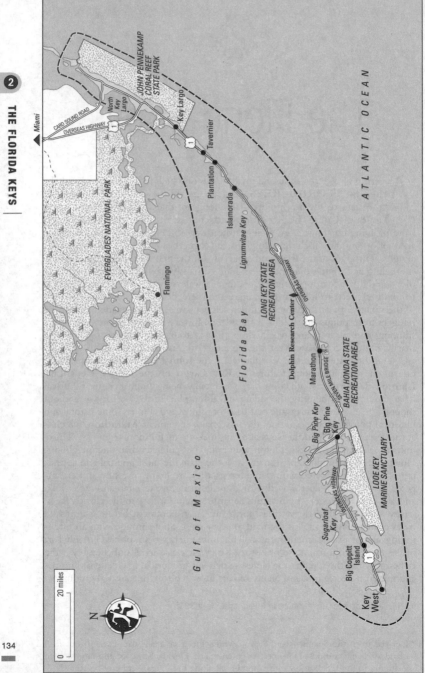

Key West also has a couple of small **beaches**, something noticeably missing else-where owing to the reef. But the meager sand and surf are easily made up for by the Keys' spectacular **sunsets**. As the nineteenth-century ornithologist John James Audubon once rhapsodized: "a blaze of refulgent glory streams portal of the West and the masses of vapour assume the semblance of mountains of molten gold."

Practicalities

Traveling through the Keys could hardly be easier as there's just one route all the way through to Key West: the **Overseas Highway (Hwy-1)**. This is punctuated by **mile markers (MM)** – posts on which mileage is marked, starting with MM127, just south of Homestead (see p.109), and finishing with MM0, in Key West. Almost all places of business use mile markers as an address, and throughout this chapter they are tagged with an "MM" (for example, "the *Holiday Inn*, at MM100"). Bear in mind that U-turns are not always possible on the Overseas Highway, so stay alert to avoid missing exits.

Traveling from Miami presents two options. Either take the I-95 south to Hwy-1 or, for a shorter route, take the Florida's Turnpike Extension toll route south and pick up Hwy-1 at Florida City. Most motels and restaurants are strung along the highway, often using the mile markers as addresses. Public transport consists of three daily Greyhound **buses** between Miami and Key West (see "Travel details" at the end of the chapter), and a skeletal local bus service in Key West.

Accommodation is abundant but more expensive than on the mainland. During high season, November–April, budget for *at least* $50–85 a night, and $35–55 the rest of the year. **Camping** is considerably less expensive and is well catered for throughout the Keys.

Note that throughout this chapter only the most basic diving information is given. Always take local advice before venturing into the water. (See "The Backcountry" on p.43 for information on outdoor safety).

The Upper Keys

The northernmost portion of the Florida Keys, the **UPPER KEYS** are roughly made up of three major communities – Key Largo, Tavernier and Islamorada – between which lies a scattering of small islands, most of which are accessible only by boat. **Key Largo** is the biggest, though not the prettiest, of the Keys and boasts the **John Pennekamp Coral Reef State Park** as its main attraction. Further on, the little town of **Tavernier** is really a place to pass through on the way to bigger and livelier **Islamorada**, which is mostly made up of a string of state parks.

North Key Largo

The best way to arrive in the Keys by car is with Card Sound Road (Hwy-905A; $1 toll), which branches off Hwy-1 a few miles south of Homestead. Doing so avoids the bulk of the tourist traffic and, after passing through the desolate southeastern section of the Everglades, gives soaring views of the mangrove-dotted waters of Florida Bay (where a long wait and a lot of luck might be rewarded with a glimpse of a rare American crocodile) – and a glimpse of the Keys as they would all have looked long ago before commercialism took hold.

Swimming with dolphins

Long before the Sixties TV show *Flipper* brought about a surge in their popularity, **dolphins** – marine mammals smaller than whales and differentiated from porpoises by their beak-like snout – were the subject of centuries of speculation and mythology. According to the wildest speculations, dolphins once lived on land but became so disenchanted by the course of civilization during ancient times that they took to the sea, vowing to bide their time until humankind was ready to receive their wisdom. Whatever the truth, there's no disputing that dolphins are extremely intelligent, with brains similar in size to those of humans. They communicate in a **language** of clicks and whistles, and use a sonar technique called echolocation to detect food in dark waters and, perhaps, to create "sound pictures" for one another.

The world's dolphin population has been reduced by several factors, including the nets of tuna fishermen, but they are a common sight around the Florida Keys and are the star attraction of the state's many marine parks – though watching them perform somersaults in response to human commands gives just an inkling of their potential. However, there is some attempt at preservation, and the **Dolphin Research Center** (address below; Wed–Sun 9am–4pm, closed Mon & Tues) rescues and rehabilitates sick or wounded dolphins and other sea mammals found around the Keys – using these opportunities to further expand their ongoing sea-mammal research. At the center, dolphins are used in therapy programs for cancer sufferers and mentally handicapped children; the exceptional patience and gentleness displayed by the dolphins (all of which are free to swim out to sea whenever they want) in this work suggest that their sonar system may allow them to make an X-ray-like scan of a body to detect abnormalities and perhaps even to "see" emotions. Take a **tour** (Wed–Sun at 10am, 11am, 12.30pm, 2pm, & 3.30pm; $12.50, age 4–12 $7.50) of the research center to become better informed on these remarkable – and still barely understood – mammals. The Dolphin Research Center is also one of four places in the Florida Keys where, by booking well ahead, you can **swim with dolphins** ($125 for around twenty minutes). Averaging seven feet in length, dolphins look disconcertingly large at close quarters – and will lose interest in you long before you tire of their company – but if you do get the opportunity to swim in them, it's an unforgettable experience.

In Key Largo: **Dolphins Plus**, MM100 (☎ 451–1993, ⊛ www.pennekamp.com /dolphins-plus) and **Dolphin Cove**, MM102 (☎ 451-4060, ⊛ www.dolphinscove.com). In Islamorada: **Theater of the Sea**, MM84.5 (☎ 664-2431, ⊛ www.theaterofthesea.com). In Marathon: **Dolphin Research Center**, MM59 (☎ 289-1121, ⊛ www.dolphins.org).

The bulk of **North Key Largo**, where Hwy-905 touches ground, is free of development, and human habitation is marked only by the odd shack amid a rich endowment of trees. Despite elaborate plans to turn the area into a city called Port Bougainvillea, with high-rise blocks and a monorail (a plan mercifully dashed by sudden bankruptcy), much of the land here is now owned and protected by the state. Horror stories about drug smugglers and practitioners of the voodoo-like Santería seem designed to ward off visitors, but in reality, although it goes on, there's probably no more drug smuggling here than anywhere else in the Keys, and magic merchants come not to sacrifice innocent tourists but to gather weird and wonderful herbs for use in rituals. There's probably more danger from the exclusive *Ocean Reef Club*, whose golf course you'll spot after a few miles if you turn left where Hwy-905 splits; it's regarded by the FBI as the country's most secure retreat for such very important people as Colin Powell – watch out for nervous, armed men in dark suits. If you want to explore North Key Largo at length, you'll have to eat and sleep in Key Largo or Tavernier (see below).

Further south, Hwy-905 merges with Hwy-1 near MM109. Known from here on as the **Overseas Highway**, Hwy-1 is the only road all the way to Key West.

John Pennekamp Coral Reef State Park

The one essential stop as you approach Key Largo is the **John Pennekamp Coral Reef State Park**, at MM102.5 (daily 8am–sunset; cars and drivers $3.75 plus 50¢ per passenger, pedestrians and cyclists $1.50; ☏451-1202, Ⓦwww.pennekamppark.com). At its heart is a protected 78-square-mile section of living coral reef, part of the reef chain that runs from here to the Dry Tortugas, five miles off of Key West (see p.169).

Just a few decades ago, great sections of the reef were dynamited or hauled up by crane to be broken up and sold as souvenirs. These days, collecting Florida coral is illegal, and any samples displayed in tourist shops have most likely been imported from the Philippines.

Despite the damage wrought by ecologically unsound tourism, experts still rate this as one of the most beautiful reef systems in the world. Whether you opt to visit the reef here – one of the better spots – or elsewhere in the Keys (such as Looe Key, see "The Lower Keys," p.149), make sure you do visit it – the eulogistic descriptions you'll hear are rarely exaggerations.

Seeing the reef: practicalities

Since most of the park lies underwater, the best way to see it is with a **snorkeling tour** (9am, noon & 3pm; 1hr 30min; adults $24.95, under-18s $19.95, plus $5 for equipment; ☏451-1621) or, if you're qualified, a **guided scuba dive** (9.30am & 1.30pm; 1hr 30min; $37, plus minimum of $20.50 for equipment; diver's certificate required; ☏451-6322). If you prefer to stay dry, a remarkable amount of the reef can be enjoyed on the two-and-a-half-hour **glass-bottomed boat tour** (9.15am, 12.15pm & 3pm; adults $18, under-12s $10; ☏451-1621). You can also rent a boat, ranging from a single-person kayak to a 22-foot power boat – canoes cost $10 per hour ($30 per half-day), 12-foot sailboats $20 per hour ($60 per half-day) and power boats $30 or $40 per hour. Note that only during the summer are you likely to get a place on these tours or obtain a boat without booking ahead. To be sure, call to make a reservation, or drop into Sundiver Station, MM103 (☏451-2220). If there's no room, try one of the numerous local diving shops: American Diving Headquarters,

MM106 (☎1-800/322-3483 or 451-0037), and Captain Slate's Atlantis Dive Center, at MM106.5 (☎1-800/331-DIVE, ⓦwww.pennekamp.com/atlantis), are just two that operate their own trips out to the reef – and cover a larger area than park tours – at around the same rates.

At the reef

Only when you're at **the reef** does its role in providing a sheltered environment for a multitude of crazy-colored fish and exotic sea life become apparent. Even from the glass-bottomed boat you're virtually guaranteed to spot lobsters, angelfish, eels and wispy jellyfish shimmering through the current, shoals of minnows stalked by angry-faced barracudas – and many more less easily identified aquatic curiosities.

Despite looking like a big lump of rock, the **reef**, too, is a delicate living thing, composed of millions of minute coral polyps that extract calcium from the seawater and grow from one to sixteen feet every 1000 years. Coral takes many shapes and forms, resembling anything from staghorns to a bucket, and comes in a paint-box variety of colors due to the plants, zooxanthellae, living within the coral tissues. Sadly, it's far easier to spot signs of death rather than life on the reef: white patches show where a carelessly dropped anchor or a diver's hand have scraped away the protective mucus layer and left the coral susceptible to lethal disease.

This destruction got so bad at the horseshoe-shaped **Molasses Reef**, about seven miles out, that the authorities sank two obsolete coastguard cutters nearby to create an alternative attraction for divers. In as much as the destruction has slowed, this plan worked and today you'll enjoy some great snorkeling around the reef and the cutters. If you prefer diving and **wrecks**, head for **the Elbow**, a section of the reef a few miles northeast of Molasses, where a number of intriguing, barnacle-encrusted nineteenth-century specimens lie; like most of the Keys' diveable wrecks, these were deliberately brought here to bolster tourism in the Seventies, which lessens their allure somewhat, and you definitely won't find any treasure.

By far the strangest thing at the reef is the **Christ of the Deep**, a nine-foot bronze statue of Christ intended as a memorial to perished sailors. The algae-coated creation, twenty feet down at Key Largo Dry Rocks, is a replica of Guido Galletti's *Christ of the Abyss*, similarly submerged off the coast of Genoa, Italy – and is surely the final word in Florida's long-time fixation with Mediterranean art and architecture. Glass-bottomed boat trips, by the way, don't visit the Elbow or the statue.

Back on land: the visitor center

Provided you visit the reef early, there'll be plenty of time left to enjoy the terrestrial portion of the park. The ecological displays at the **visitor center** (daily 8am–5pm) provide an inspiring introduction to the flora and fauna of the Keys and will give you a practical insight into the region's transitional zones: the vegetation changes dramatically within an elevation of a few feet. The park's tropical **hardwood hammock**★ trails meander through red mangroves, pepper trees, and graceful franzipannes. Raccoon, heron and fiddler crab tracks are everywhere, and hairy-legged, golden orb spiders dangle from many a branch.

★ Cropping up all over Florida, hammocks are pockets of woodland able to flourish where the ground elevation rises a few feet above the surrounding wetlands. For a fuller explanation, see "Natural History" in Contexts.

The park also boasts some fine man-made beaches (you won't find any more – man-made or not – until Key West), but note that the coral is very unforgiving to bare feet. Another option for exploring the park is to rent a canoe (single $10 per hour, double $15 per hour; $50/$75 per day) and glide around the mangrove-fringed inner waterways.

Key Largo

Thanks to the 1948 film in which Humphrey Bogart and Lauren Bacall grappled with what were then Florida's best-known features – crime and hurricanes – almost everybody has heard of **KEY LARGO**. Ironically, the film's title was chosen for no other reason than it suggested somewhere warm and exotic, and, though set here, the film was almost entirely shot in Hollywood – hoodwinking countless millions into thinking that paradise was a town in the Florida Keys.

Recognizing a potential tourist bonanza, business people here soon changed the name of their community from Rock Harbor to Key Largo (a title that until then had applied to the whole island, derived from *Cayo Largo* – Long Island – the name given to it by early Spanish explorers), and tenuous links with Hollywood are maintained even today. The steam-powered boat that was used in *The African Queen* is moored (when not on promotional tours) in the marina of the *Holiday Inn*, MM100, and the hotel's lobby displays a selection of stills of Bogart and co-star Katharine Hepburn acting their hearts out – in England and Africa.

Clinging to an image based more in movies than reality, Key Largo proper is really a jumble of filling stations, shopping plazas and fast-food outlets. There are one or two low-key attractions, and the offshore islands may persuade you to stay for a night or two. If you're in more of a hurry and are here in the early evening, at least make time to hop off the Overseas Highway to enjoy the sunset.

There are two places in on the key where you can swim with dolphins. The first is **Dolphins Plus**, just south of MM100 (daily 9am–5pm; ☎451-1993), a dolphin education and research facility that has twelve of them for you to indulge in a "dolphin encounter." The price of a "structured" half-hour swim (with one of these) is $150 (to observe only $10, under-15s $5) or there is also an "unstructured" swim with wild dolphins which is $100 – though with the latter, contact is not guaranteed. The other venue is **Dolphin Cove** (daily 8am–5pm; ☎451-4060, ⓦwww.dolphinscove.com), a five-acre marine environment research center at MM102. If you qualify (which entails having a swimsuit, a towel and $150), sessions are on Saturday and Sunday only at 9am, 1pm & 3.30pm. If you can't afford a close encounter, $20 (under-16s $15) gets you in as a non-swimming observer. Dolphin Cove is also the departure point for Captain Sterling's Crocodile Tours (☎1-888/224-6044, Ⓔcaptserl@pennekamp.com; reservation required), one of the more knowledgeable in the area.

Information and accommodation

If you didn't stop at the well-stocked Visitor Information Center near Homestead (see "Miami," p.67), pull up at the new and highly informative **Key Largo Chamber of Commerce**, 106000 Overseas Highway, at MM106 (daily 9am–6pm; ☎1-800/822-1088). The colonial-style center has piles of brochures, money-saving vouchers and hotel booking information. Don't confuse the visitor center with the **Key Largo Tourist Center**, 103360 Overseas Highway (daily 9am–7pm; ☎453-0066, ⒻGF453-9197), which promotes only the area's ritziest hotels.

Islands off Key Largo

The tiny, uninhabited **islands** just off Key Largo make glorious forays, and there's no better way of exploring them than hiring a boat or catamaran. Signs abound for boat rentals, but the most reliable and user-friendly option is Robbie's Boat Rentals and charters, located bayside at MM77.5 (☏664-9814). A rugged, Hemingwayesque personality, Captain Tim (everyone goes by their first name in the Keys) will take good care of you whether you rent a boat to explore Indian Key or to snorkel in Alligator Reef with Captain Keith, a self-styled "jellyfish warrior." They can take you out, but if you decide to go it alone, do heed their advice about the varying shades of shallow waters to avoid grounding your boat. If a glass-bottomed boat tour is more up your alley, head to the *Holiday Inn* docks at MM100 (☏451-4655) where the *Key Largo Princess* makes two-hour cruises at 10am, 1pm and 4pm ($25).

In addition to beds, plenty of **motels** offer diving packages. Look for signs or try: *Economy Efficiency* (also known as *Ed & Ellen's*), 103365 Overseas Highway (☏451-9949; ❷), which is basic but clean; *Largo Lodge*, 101740 Overseas Highway (☏451-0424 or 1-800/INTHESUN, ⓦwww.largolodge.com; ❺), offers comfortable apartments in a lovely garden setting right on the beach, though children aren't allowed; and though not plush, *Seafarer*, MM97.8 (☏852-5349; ❸), has spotless cottages and daily diving tours to the local marine sanctuaries. Next door, prices go up at the *Kona Kai Resort* (MM98), 97802 Overseas Highway (☏852-4629; ❹–❺), but the chalets are huge and stylish, a dozen strains of banana grow in the garden and the hotel has its own art gallery. Very costly but one-of-a-kind, *Jules' Undersea Lodge*, at 51 Shoreland Drive (☏1-800/858-7119 or 451-2353; ❽), is a tiny "hotel" thirty feet below the ocean's surface. It is more theme park than a place to stay and is always booked well in advance. The two-bedroom accommodations are perfectly safe and are linked to land by an intercom system. The overnight, two-person luxury option ($1000) comes with such amenities as caviar and flowers. Just remember your diver's certificate – otherwise you'll have to take the hotel's three-hour crash course ($95) before you'll be allowed to unpack.

Of the many **campgrounds** in and around Key Largo, the cleanest and cheapest is the John Pennekamp Coral Reef State Park (☏451-1202; see above), though for high season you'll need to book several months ahead. *The Key Largo Kampground*, MM101 (☏451-1431), is a reasonable alternative but has no grass pitches.

Eating and drinking

Far enough south for fine Caribbean cuisine, but close enough to the Everglades for a taste of 'gator, Key Largo is a fine place to **eat**. The best breakfasts are found at *Ballyhoo's Grill and Grog*, MM97.8 (☏852-0822), opposite the *Seafarer* hotel (see above). Opened 25 years ago by a couple of fishermen, it features pancakes, omelettes, croissants dipped in orange and egg and a wide selection of grilled food (and of drink). *Ganim's Restaurant*, 99696 Overseas Highway (☏451-2895), has cheap breakfasts and lunches. Try the "Sealegs Supreme" salad of crabmeat, tuna and fruit in honey mustard and the huge portions of sweet pies. *Frank Keys Café*, 100211 Overseas Highway (☏453-0310), in an attractive cottage hidden away in the trees off the highway, offers slightly more sophisticated – and considerably more expensive – seafood and other dishes. If you've got a hankering for 'gator, a good spot is *Snappers Raw Bar*,

MM94.4 at 139 Seaside Ave (☎852-5956). Enjoy the waterside, candlelit setting with an alligator starter, or swing by for the Sunday champagne jazz brunch (10am–2pm). *Mrs Mac's*, MM99.4 (☎451-3722), provides bowls of ferociously hot chilli and other home-cooked goodies, and *The Fish House Restaurant and Seafood Market*, MM102.4 (☎451-4665, Ⓦwww.fishhouse.com), is a must for all seafood lovers.

If you are undaunted by bikers in leather jackets and tropical shorts, check out the *Caribbean Club*, MM104 (☎451-4466), for a lively **drink** (it also offers cheap jet-ski rentals during the day). For a mellower crowd, visit *Coconuts,* the bar at the *Marina del Mar Resort*, MM100 (☎451-4107). And if you'd like to relax with some good conch fritters and a beer, head up to *Alabama Jack's,* just north of the toll booth on the Card Sound Road (Hwy-905A). This former bordello is now something of an institution.

Tavernier

Just ten miles south of Key Largo on the Overseas Highway is **TAVERNIER**, a small, homely town that was once the first stop on the Flagler railway (the Keys' first link to the mainland, see "The Seven Mile Bridge" p.147). There's not a whole lot here, but Tavernier's historic buildings and decent *café Cubano* (see "Practicalities" below) make it a worth a short stop.

Just before crossing into Tavernier, at MM93.6, is the **Florida Keys Wild Bird Rehabilitation Center** (daily 8.30am–5.30pm; donations suggested; ☎852-5339), an inspirational place where volunteers rescue and rehabilitate birds that have been orphaned or have met with other common catastrophes like colliding with cars or power lines. A wooden walkway is lined with huge enclosures, and signs detail the birds' histories.

If you drop into Harry Harris Park, off the Overseas Highway along Burton Drive, on a weekend, you could well find an impromptu party and free live music – locals sometimes drop by with instruments and station themselves on picnic tables for jam sessions.

A rarity in the Keys outside of Key West, the old buildings of the historic district, between MM91 and MM92 deserve stopping for. In addition to the plank walls and tin roofs of the turn-of-the-century Methodist Church (now functioning as a small visitor center) and post office, you'll see some of the Red Cross buildings erected after the 1935 Labor Day hurricane, which laid waste to a good chunk of the Keys. Built of foot-thick walls of concrete and steel, the new buildings were supposedly invincible to nature's fiercest poundings. Unfortunately, the use of seawater in the construction caused the walls to crumble, leaving only rusting steel frames. To find the historic center, turn down the side of the *Tavernier Hotel,* and then take the first right up Atlantic Circle Drive. More quaint than spectacular, it's the sort of place where the Waltons might have had a retreat.

Practicalities

Despite its dismal exterior, the *Sunshine Café*, at MM91.8 (no phone and no English spoken), is really a hidden gem. It serves top-notch *café Cubano* for $1 and trays of Cuban food such as the requisite black beans and rice. For really cheap, wholesome food, the *Sunshine Supermarket*, at MM 91.8 (☎852-7216), which is attached to the cafeteria, sells hot Cuban sandwiches and roasted pig. Next door, *The Copper Kettle* is a cozy English-style tea room that features candlelit dinners of honey Cajun shrimp and other regional delights. The restaurant is owned by the *Tavernier Hotel*, MM91.8 (☎852-4131, ⓦwww .tavernierhotel.com; ➍), a quaint **hotel** painted gum-pink that was originally built as an open-air theater but has been a hotel for the past seventy years.

Islamorada

Once over Tavernier Creek, you're at the start of a twenty-mile strip of islands: Plantation, Windley, and Upper and Lower Matecumbe, which are collectively known as **ISLAMORADA** (pronounced "eye-la-more-ah-da). More than any other section of the Keys, fishing is headline news here. Tales of monstrous tarpon and blue marlin captured off the coast are legendary, and there's no end to the smaller prey routinely hooked by total novices. (Even former president George Bush successfully cast a line or two in these waters.)

If you'd like to head out to sea, you'll be well provided for. There's no problem renting fishing boats, or, for much less, joining a fishing party boat from any of the local marinas. The biggest docks are at the Holiday Isle, 84001 Overseas Highway (☎664-2321 ext 641), and Bud 'n' Mary's Marina and Dive Center, MM80 (☎1-800/742-7945).

There's notable **snorkeling** and **diving** in the area, too. Crocker and Alligator reefs, a few miles offshore, both have near-vertical sides, whose cracks and crevices provide homes for a lively variety of crabs, shrimp and other small creatures that in turn attract bigger fish looking for a meal. Nearby, the wrecks of the *Eagle* and the *Cannabis Cruiser* provide a home for families of gargantuan amberjack and grouper. Get full snorkeling and diving details from the marinas (see above) or any dive shop on the Overseas Highway – expect to pay $40 for a half-day of snorkeling.

Back on dry land, you might want to pass a couple of hours at the **Theater of the Sea**, MM84.5 (daily 9.30am–4pm; adults $16.75, under-13s $10.25; ☎664-2431, ⓦwww.theaterofthesea.com), but only if the somewhat steep price doesn't deter you and you're not planning to visit any of the other marine parks in Florida, which are better. Sea lions, dolphins and a half-dozen tanks full of assorted fish and crustaceans are introduced by a knowledgeable staff, and, if you reserve ahead, you can swim with the dolphins (minimum age 10; $95; see p.136).

For non-fishing folk, there's little in Islamorada to warrant an extended stay. **The Chamber of Commerce**, at MM82.5 (Mon–Fri 9am–5pm; ☎664-4503 or 1-800/322-5397), is packed with general information and details on the latest cut-rate accommodation deals (see p.144). Half a mile further south, the Art Deco **Hurricane Monument** marks the grave of the 1935 Labor Day hurricane's 425 victims, killed when a tidal wave hit the train that was attempting to evacuate them. The unkempt state of the stone is perhaps an indication of modern Keys dwellers' nonchalant attitude to the threat of a repeat disaster.

Islamorada's state parks

Indian Key, **Lignumvitae Key** and **Long Key** – three state parks at the southern end of Islamorada – offer a broader perspective of the area than just fishing and diving. The **guided tours** to Indian Key and Lignumvitae Key are particularly enchanting, and reveal a near-forgotten chapter of the Florida Keys' history and a virgin forest respectively. The Indian Key tour (Thurs–Mon 8.30am & 12.30pm) departs from Robbie's Marina, MM77.5 (☎664-9814; $15; children $10), as does the Lignumvitae Tour (9.30am & 1.30pm; $15, children $10). A tour of both keys is available for $25.

Indian Key

You'd never guess from the highway that **Indian Key**, one of many small, mangrove-skirted islands off Lower Matecumbe Key, was once a busy trading center, given short-lived prosperity – and notoriety – by a nineteenth-century New Yorker called Jacob Houseman. After stealing one of his father's ships, Houseman sailed to Key West looking for a piece of the lucrative wrecking (or salvaging) business. Mistrusted by the close-knit Key West community, he bought Indian Key in 1831 as a base for his own wrecking operation. In the first year, Houseman made $30,000 and furnished the eleven-acre island with streets, a store, warehouses, a hotel and a population of around fifty. However, much of his income was not honestly gained: Houseman was known to lead donkeys with lanterns along the shore to lure ships towards dangerous reefs, and he eventually lost his wrecking license for "salvaging" from an anchored vessel.

In 1838, Indian Key was sold to physician-botanist Henry Perrine, who had been cultivating tropical plants here with an eye to their commercial potential. A Seminole attack in 1840 burnt every building to the ground and ended the island's habitation, but Perrine's plants survive and today form a swath of flowing foliage that includes sisal, coffee, tea and mango plants. Besides allowing ample opportunity to gaze at the flora, the two-hour tour takes you around the one-time streets, up the observation tower and past Houseman's grave – his body was brought here after he died working on a wreck off Key West.

Lignumvitae Key

By the time you finish the three-hour tour of **Lignumvitae Key,** you'll know a strangler fig from a gumbo limbo and will instantly be able to recognize many more of the hundred or so species of tropical trees – "lignumvitae" is Latin for "wood of life" – in this two-hundred-acre hammock. Further treats are the sizeable spiders, such as the golden orb, whose silvery web regularly spans the pathway. The trail through the forest was laid out by a wealthy early Miamian, W. J. Matheson, whose 1919 limestone **house** is the island's only sign of habitation and shows the deprivations of early island living – even for the well-off. The house actually blew away in the 1935 hurricane, but was found and brought back.

Long Key State Recreation Area

Many of the tree species found on Lignumvitae can be spotted at **Long Key State Botanical Site**, MM67.5 (Thurs–Mon 8am–sunset; cars $3.75 plus 50¢ per passenger; pedestrians and cyclists $1.50; ☎664-4815). There's a nature trail that takes you along the beach and on a boardwalk over a mangrove-lined lagoon and guided tours to take you round (info on ☎664 9814). Or, better still, you can rent a canoe ($7 per hour) and follow the simple **canoe trail** through the tidal lagoons in the company of mildly curious wading birds. **Camping** in the park costs $25.75 (info on ☎664-483).

The backcountry

If you've access to a boat or sufficient money (at least $200 a day) to rent one with a guide, Islamorada makes a good base for exploring the fish-laden waters and bird-filled skies of the **backcountry**. This is the term for the countless small, uninhabited islands that fill Florida Bay, beginning about eighteen miles west and constituting the edge of the Everglades National Park – more fully described in "The West Coast," p.383 Ask at any Islamorada marina for more details.

Practicalities

You're unlikely to find **accommodation** in Islamorada for under $70 a night, although price wars among the bigger hotels can reveal occasional finds. The popular *Holiday Isle Beach Resort*, 84001 Overseas Highway, MM84 (☎1-800/327-7070; ❺), is a psychedelic trip: vivid citrus-colored plastics and tiki huts fill this vacation village. The atmosphere is young and friendly and the hotel itself is very comfortable. Otherwise, the best bets are *Drop Anchor*, MM85 (☎664/4863; ❹), *Key Lantern*, MM82 (☎664-4572; ❸), and the *Islamorada Motel*, MM87.8 (☎852-9376; ❹). If you have a tent, use either Long Key State Recreation Area (see above) or the RV-dominated *KOA* **campground** on Fiesta Key, MM70 (☎664-4922).

Provided you avoid the obvious tourist traps, you can **eat** well and fairly cheaply. Best of all is the excellent-value fare at *Islamorada Fish Company*, MM81 (☎1-800/258-2559), whose fresh seafood is exported all over the world. Despite a constant full house (try to get here before 6pm), the staff are particularly friendly. *Manny & Isa's*, MM81.5 (☎664-5019), serves high-quality, mid-price Cuban food; *Whale Harbor Inn*, MM84 (☎664-4959), proffers massive seafood buffets to devil-may-care gluttons; the ramshackle but justifiably pricey *Green Turtle Inn*, MM81.5 (☎664-9031; closed Mon), has glorious chowders; and the *Hungry Tarpon*, at MM77.5 Lower Matecumbe Key (☎664-0535), serves superb fish from local recipes in a converted 1940s bait shop. For more elegant surroundings, try the seafood and Italian dishes at *Little Italy Restaurant*, MM 68.5, Long Key (☎664-4472); open for breakfast, lunch and dinner, it offers main courses that start at around $8.50.

When it comes to **nightlife**, many people get no further than the huge tiki bar at *Holiday Isle Beach Resort* (see above), which always throbs on weekends to the sound of insipid rock bands. Alternatively, investigate the nightly drink specials at *Lor-e-lei's*, MM82 (☎664-4656), where nightly sunset celebrations reel in the crowds. For raunchy blues and boozing, visit the much less touristy *Woody's*, MM82 (☎664-4335), which picks up steam after 11pm.

The Middle Keys

The Long Key Bridge (alongside the old Long Key Viaduct) points south from Long Key and leads to the **Middle Keys**. The largest of these islands, which stretch from Duck Key to Bahia Honda Key, is Key Vaca – once a shantytown of railway workers – which holds the area's major settlement, **MARATHON**. On first sight this is a town as commercialized and uninspiring as Key Largo, but it does have some worthwhile features, hidden just off the Overseas Highway.

Marathon

If you didn't get your fill of tropical trees at Lignumvitae Key (see "Islamorada" above), turn right onto 55th Street at MM50.5 (opposite the K-Mart), which leads to 63 steamy acres of subtropical forest at **Tropical Crane Point Hammock** (Mon–Sat 10am–5pm, Sun noon–5pm; $8.95; ☎743-9100). A free booklet gives details of the trees you'll find along the one-mile **nature trail**, and you'll also pass one of the last examples of Bahamian architecture in the US: a house built in 1903 by Bahamian immigrants.

The hammock's excellent **Museum of Natural History of the Florida Keys** (same hours and admission) offers a thought-provoking rundown of the area's history – starting with the Caloosa Indians (who had a settlement on this site until they were wiped out by disease brought by European settlers in the 1700s) and continuing with the story of early Bahamian and American settlers. Not to be missed is the motley collection of artifacts near the museum shop, including a raft made of inner tubes that carried four Cuban refugees across ninety miles of ocean in the early 1990s.

A large section of the museum features interactive displays designed to introduce kids to the wonders of the Keys' subtropical ecosystems, including the hardwood hammocks and reefs. Much the same ground is covered at the adjoining **Florida Keys Children's Museum** (same hours and admission), which houses a tropical aquarium, a terrarium and an artificial saltwater lagoon where you can feed the fish. The hammock's resident mosquitoes are a painful nuisance, so consider investing in the bug sprays available at the pharmacy directly across the highway.

Snorkeling, diving, fishing and sailing

The choice locale for the pursuits of **snorkeling** and **scuba diving** is around **Sombrero Reef**, marked by a 142-foot-high nineteenth-century lighthouse, whose nooks and crannies provide a safe haven for thousands of darting, brightly colored tropical fish. The best time to go out is early evening when the reef is most active, since the majority of its creatures are nocturnal. The pick of local dive shops is Hall's Diving and Snorkeling Center (☎1-800/331-4255, ⊛www .hallsdiving.com), at 1994 Overseas Highway (MM48). Five-day Basic Open Water Scuba Certificate courses ($395) are offered to novice divers, and night diving, wreck diving and Instructor's Certificate courses are available to the experienced. Once certified, you can rent equipment ($50 and upwards) and join a dive trip (9am, 1pm & 5.30pm; $40).

Around Marathon, **spearfishing** is permitted a mile offshore (there's a three-mile limit elsewhere), and the town hosts four major **fishing tournaments** each year: in early May (for tarpon); late May (dolphin, the fish not the mammal); early October (bonefish); and early November (sailfish). Precise dates are available from the **Chamber of Commerce** (see overleaf). You may fancy your chances, but entering costs several hundred dollars and only the very top anglers participate. Just being around during a tournament, however, will give you an insight into the Big Time Fishing mentality, and if you feel inspired to put to sea yourself, wander along one of the marinas and ask about chartering a boat. Boats take out up to six people and charge between $400 and $850 for a full day's fishing (7am–4pm), including bait and equipment. If you can't get a group together, join one of the countless group boats for about $40 per person for a full day's fishing – remember, though, that it's easier to catch fish with fewer people aboard.

Although most of the boats at the local marinas are large power vessels designed for anglers, Marathon is also a major **sailboat** base, offering vessels for charter – with or without a captain – as well as sailing courses. A reliable source of both is the Faro Blanco Marina Resort, MM48.5 (see overleaf).

Marathon Information

For one-stop information on the surrounding area and accommodation, head to the **Chamber of Commerce** at MM53.5 bayside (℡743-5417 or 1-800/262-7284, ⓦwww.floridakeysmarathon.com).

For a closer look at the Keys' marine life, take the **glass-bottomed boat tour** (daily 10am; $20; ℡743-4795, ⓦwww.snorkelcenter.com/glassbottomboat /index) from the marina of the $200-a-night *Hawks Cay Resort* on Duck Key, reached by way of a causeway at MM61. Led by a radically minded local naturalist, the two-hour trip will furnish you with a wealth of information on the make-up of the reef and the creatures who live there.

If you have more sedate activities in mind, Marathon has a couple of small beaches. **Sombrero Beach**, along Sombrero Beach Road (off the Overseas Highway near MM50), is a slender strip of sand with good swimming waters and shaded picnic tables. Four miles north, **Key Colony Beach**, a man-made island dredged into existence during the Fifties for the building of pricey homes, is prettier and quieter.

Just east of Marathon is the **Dolphin Research Center**, MM59 at Grassy Key (Wed–Sun, 9am–4pm; ℡289-1121, ⓦwww.dolphins.org). For $125 you can learn about and swim with dolphins in an "encounter program," but you must book at least a month in advance (by phone only ℡289-0002). The center's escorted walk (10am, 11am, 12.30pm, 2pm, & 3.30pm; $12.50, age 4–12 $7.50) is less expensive, but also less fun.

Accommodation

There's decent mid-range accommodation around Marathon. The only **campground** permitting tents (others are designed for motor homes and trailers only) is *Knights Key Park*, MM47 (℡743-4343).

Banana Bay, 4590 Overseas Highway (℡1-800/226-2621). Good-value beachside resort, with well-equipped rooms and a freshwater swimming pool – plus the requisite Tiki bar – which is romantically surrounded by palm trees. ❺
Faro Blanco Marine Resort, 1996 Overseas Highway (℡1-800/759-3276, ⓦwww.spottswood.com/faroblanco). This resort has small cottages and houseboats offer beautiful views of the mangroves. ❹

Flamingo Inn, MM59 at Grassy Key (℡289-1478). Very comfortable beds, big clean rooms, a pool and good deals. ❹
Sea Dell, 5000 Overseas Highway (℡1-800/648-3854, ⓦwww.floridakeys.net/seadell). The least costly of the plentiful supply of cheaper motels. ❸
Seaward, 8700 Overseas Highway (℡743-5711). Best motel rooms for the price in the area, and it's also got the added bonus of a pool. ❹
Sombrero, 19 Sombrero Blvd (℡1-800/433-8660). Similar accommodation to the *Faro Blanco* . ❸

Eating

Marathon will definitely be your base for eating in this stretch of the Middle Keys, and it's not a bad one at that. It does go to sleep early; the only place with a hint of nightlife is the tiki bar of *Shuckers Raw Bar and Grill*, 725 11th St (℡743-8686), which is also a prime vantage point for sipping a drink as the sun goes down.

Castaway, on 15th Street at MM47.8 (℡743-6348). This hidden gem serves wonderful and cheap seafood and scrumptious honey-drenched buns.
Crocodiles on the Water, on 15th Street (℡743-9018). Just across from *Castaway* and part of the

classy *Faro Blanco Marine Resort* (see above), this restaurant specializes in Cuban fish and oyster dishes. Desserts include frozen turtle pie – which just means praline ice cream served in a breezy, friendly atmosphere.

Don Pedro Restaurant, MM53 (☏743-5247).
This establishment offers good Cuban fare at reasonable prices.
Herbie's, 6350 Overseas Highway, MM50.5
(☏743-6373). The inexpensive seafood here keeps it generally busy.
Pancho's Steak House, MM48 (☏289-1629).
This is a good retreat for true carnivores if they're "seafooded out," serving Latin-style strips of steak with all the trimmings.

Porky's, MM47.5 (☏743-6637). Platefuls of beef and chicken are the speciality here.
The Seven Mile Grill, 1240 Overseas Highway
(☏743-4481). Locals flock here for fine conch chowders and shrimp steamed in beer. The empty cans seem to have been used as decoration.
Village Café, at the gulf-side Village Plaza, 5800 Overseas Highway (☏743-9090). Quality Italian dishes can be enjoyed in this simple setting.

The Seven Mile Bridge and Pigeon Key

In 1905, Henry Flagler, whose railway opened up Florida's East Coast, undertook the extension of its tracks to Key West. The Overseas Railroad, as it became known (though many called it "Flagler's folly"), was a monumental task that took seven years to complete and was marked by the appalling treatment of the railworkers.

Bridging the Middle Keys gave Flagler's engineers some of their biggest headaches. North of Marathon, the two-mile-long Long Key Viaduct, a still-elegant structure of nearly two hundred individually cast arches, was Flagler's personal favorite and was widely pictured in advertising campaigns. Yet a greater technical accomplishment was the **Seven Mile Bridge** (built from 1908 to 1912) to the south, linking Marathon to the Lower Keys. At one point, every US-flagged freighter on the Atlantic was hired to bring in materials – including special cement from Germany – while floating cranes, dredges and scores of other craft set about a job that eventually cost the lives of 700 laborers. When the trains eventually started rolling (doddering over the bridges at 15mph), passengers were treated to an incredible panorama: a broad sweep of sea and sky, sometimes streaked by luscious red sunsets or darkened by storm clouds.

The Flagler bridges were strong enough to withstand everything that the Keys' volatile weather could throw at them, except for the calamitous 1935 Labor Day hurricane, which tore up the railway. The bridges were subsequently adapted to accommodate a road: the original Overseas Highway. Tales of hair-raising bridge crossings (the road was only 22 feet wide), endless tailbacks as the drawbridges jammed – and the roadside parties that ensued – are part of Keys folklore. The later bridges, such as the $45-million new **Seven Mile Bridge** between Key Vaca and Bahia Honda Key that opened in the early Eighties, certainly improved traffic flow but also ended the mystique of traveling the old road – and its walls are just high enough to hide the fabulous view.

The old bridges, intact but for the mid-sectional cuts to allow shipping to pass, now make extraordinarily long fishing piers and jogging strips. A section of the former Seven Mile Bridge also provides the only land access to **Pigeon Key**, which served as a railway work camp from 1908 to 1935, and until recently was used by the University of Miami for marine science classes. Its seven original wooden buildings have been restored as **Historic Pigeon Key** (daily 10am–4pm; $7.50; ☏289-0025, Ⓦwww.pigeonkey.com), whose museum helps visitors understand the hardships routinely suffered by the workers. Cars are not permitted access to Pigeon Key, which contributes to the serene atmosphere of the place – though they now have one of those bogus-train tours to take you round (every hour, on the hour). A shuttle bus leaves hourly (9am–4pm; $4) from the Pigeon Key Visitor's Center at MM48.

The Lower Keys

Starkly different to their northerly neighbors, the **LOWER KEYS** are quiet, heavily wooded and predominantly residential. Aligned north-south and resting on a limestone rather than a coral base, these islands have flora and fauna that are very much their own. Such species as the key deer, the Lower Keys cotton rat and the Cudjoe Key rice rat – all of which are endangered – live here, though mainly tucked away miles from the Overseas Highway. Most visitors speed through the area on the way to Key West, just forty miles further, but the area's lack of rampant tourism and easily found seclusion make this a good place to linger for a day or two. The main settlement is **Big Pine Key**, where the **Lower Keys Chamber of Commerce**, at MM31 (Mon–Fri 9am–5pm, Sat 9am–3pm, ☏1-800/872-3722), is packed with information on the area.

Bahia Honda State Recreation Area

While not officially part of the Lower Keys, the first place of consequence you'll hit after crossing the Seven Mile Bridge is the 300-acre **Bahia Honda State Recreation Area** (daily 8am–sunset; cars $4 with 50¢ for each additional person; pedestrians and cyclists $1.50; ☏872-2353), one of the Keys' prettiest spots. The northeasterly section of the park rings a lagoon with a natural beach and inviting, two-tone ocean waters.

While here, you should ramble on the **nature trail**, which loops from the shoreline through a hammock of silver palms, geiger and yellow satinwood trees, passing rare plants, such as dwarf morning glory and spiny catesbaea. Keep a lookout for white-crowned pigeons, great white herons, roseate spoonbills and giant ospreys (whose bulky nests are plentiful throughout the Lower Keys, often atop telegraph poles). Nature programs start at 11am and you can ask about special **walks** such as the Flagler Story Walk, though it's all pleasant enough without a guide.

The waters at the park's southern end are good for swimming (beware, though, that currents here can be very swift), as well as for snorkeling, diving and especially windsurfing – rent equipment from the Bahia Honda marina's dive shop. You'll also notice the two-story **Flagler Bridge**. The unusually deep waters here (Bahia Honda is Spanish for "deep bay") made this the toughest of the old railway bridges to construct, and widening it for the road proved impossible: the solution was to put the highway on a higher tier. It's actually far safer than it looks and there's a fine view from the top of the bridge over the Bahia Honda channel towards the forest-coated Lower Keys.

Facilities in the park include a campground and cabins, a snack bar, and a dive shop offering reef snorkel trips, scuba trips and boat rental.

Big Pine Key and around

The eponymous trees on **Big Pine Key** are less of a draw than its **Key deer**, delightfully tame creatures that enjoy the freedom of the island; don't feed them (it's illegal), and be cautious when driving – signs alongside the road state the number of road-kills to date during the year. The deer, no bigger than large dogs, are related to the white-tailed deer and arrived long ago when the Keys were still joined to the mainland; they provided food for sailors and Key West residents for many years, but hunting and the destruction of their natural habitat led to near-extinction by the late Forties. **The National Key Deer Refuge** was set up here in 1954 to safeguard the animals – one refuge manager went so far as to burn the cars and sink the boats of poachers – and their population has now stabilized between 250 and 300.

Pick up factual information on the deer from the **refuge headquarters** (Mon–Fri 8am–5pm; ☏872-2239), at the western end of Watson Boulevard, off Key Deer Boulevard. To see them, drive along Key Deer Boulevard or turn east onto No Name Key. You should spot a few; they often amuse themselves in domestic gardens. Your chances are best in the cooler temperatures of early morning or late afternoon.

Also on Key Deer Boulevard, the **Blue Hole** is a freshwater lake with a healthy population of soft-shelled turtles and at least one alligator, which now and then emerges from the cool depths to sun itself – parts of the lakeside path may be closed if it has staked out a patch for the day. Should the 'gator get your adrenalin pumping, take a calming stroll along the short **nature trail**, a quarter of a mile further south along Key Deer Boulevard.

The rest of the Lower Keys

An even more peaceful atmosphere prevails on the Lower Keys south of Big Pine Key, despite the efforts of property developers. **The Torch Keys**, so-named for their forests of torchwood – used for kindling by early settlers – can be swiftly bypassed on the way to **Ramrod Key**, where Looe Key Marine Sanctuary is a terrific place for viewing the coral reef.

Perhaps the most expensive thing you'll see anywhere in the Keys, if not in all of Florida, is the balloon-like "aerostat" hovering 10,000 feet above **Cudjoe Key**. With an annual budget of over $23 million, it is used by the US government to beam TV images and radio broadcasts of American-style freedom – "unbiased news", sitcoms and soap operas – to Cuba. Called TV Martí and Radio Martí, the stations were named after the late-nineteenth-century Cuban independence fighter, José Martí, and are under the control of the US Broadcasting Board of Governors. Castro and the Cuban government allegedly expend a lot of effort trying to jam the TV signal.

Looe Key Marine Sanctuary

Keen underwater explorers should home in on **Looe Key Marine Sanctuary**, clearly signposted from the Overseas Highway on Ramrod Key. Named after *HMS Looe*, a British frigate that sank here in 1744, this five-square-mile area of protected reef is in every part the equal of the John Pennekamp Coral Reef State Park (see above). The crystal-clear waters and reef formations create an unforgettable spectacle: rays, octopus and a multitude of gaily colored fish flit between tall coral pillars, big brain coral, complex tangles of elk and staghorn coral, and soft corals like purple seafans and sea whips.

The sanctuary office (Mon–Fri 8am–5pm; ☏292-0311) can provide free maps and information. You can only visit the reef itself on a trip organized by one of the many diving shops throughout the Keys; the nearest is the neighboring Looe Key Dive Center (☏1-800/942-5397, ⓦwww.diveflakeys.com/full/index.html).

If you're here around the second Saturday in July, you may consider donning your flippers and checking out the annual **Lower Keys Underwater Music Festival**. The music is broadcast via special speakers suspended beneath boats positioned above the reef. The music ranges from the Beatles' *Yellow Submarine* to Handel's *Water Music*, and there's quite a carnival atmosphere, with many people dressing up before they go down. There's no actual charge, though you'll have to pay for the boat and diving equipment at the sanctuary office. For more info call ☎872-9100.

Perky's Bat Tower

On Sugarloaf Key, fifteen miles from Ramrod Key, the 35-foot **Perky's Bat Tower** stands as testimony to one man's misguided belief in the mosquito-killing powers of bats. A get-rich-quick book of the Twenties, *Bats, Mosquitoes and Dollars*, led Richter C. Perky, a property speculator who had recently purchased the island, into thinking that bats would be the solution to the Keys' mosquito problem. With much hullabaloo, he erected this brown cypress lath tower in 1929 and dutifully sent away for the costly "bat bait," which he was told would lure an army of bats to the tower. It didn't work: no bat ever showed up, the mosquitoes stayed healthy, and Perky went bust soon after. The background story is far more interesting than the actual tower, but if the tale tickles your fancy, you can view it from the bumpy road just beyond the sprawling *Sugarloaf Lodge*, at MM17.

Practicalities

For what they offer, **motels** in the Lower Keys are expensive. *Looe Key Reef Resort*, MM27.5 (☎872-2215; ❹–❺), is ideal for visiting the marine sanctuary, or there's *Parmer's Resort*, off MM28.5 at 565 Barry Ave (☎872-2157; ❹). For a real splurge, stay at the idyllic *Little Palm Island*, MM28.5, Little Torch Key (☎872-2524, ⓦ www.littlepalmisland.com; no children; ❾), whose thatched cottages are set in lush gardens a few feet from the beach. They also have a fantastic and truly expensive fish restaurant. **Campgrounds** are plentiful; try the Bahia Honda State Recreation Area's *Big Pine Key Fishing Lodge*, MM33 (☎872-2351), *Sea Horse*, MM31 (☎872-2443), and *Sugar Loaf Key KOA*, MM20 (☎745-3549). Three **bed and breakfast inns** on Big Pine Key make cozy alternatives, but book early: *Deer Run*, 1985 Long Beach Drive, MM33 (☎872-2015, ⓦ www.floridakeys.net/deer; ❺); *Barnacle*, 1557 Long Beach Drive, MM33 (☎872-3298 or 1-800/465-9100; ❹); and the adult-only *Casa Grande*, 1619 Long Beach Drive, MM33 (☎872-2878, ⓦ www.floridakeys.net/casagrande; ❺).

The best place to eat in the Lower Keys is *Mangrove Mama's*, at MM20 on Sugarloaf Key (☎745-3030; closed Sept), for its rustic atmosphere, great seafood and home-baked bread. A real locals' joint is *Big Pine Coffee Shop*, MM30 (☎872-2790), where you can sit at formica tables and gorge on crab salads and steamed shrimp by the half-pound. Otherwise, try *Bobalu's Southern Café*, MM 10 (☎296-1664), on Big Coppitt Key for good cholestoral-filled Southern cooking fare breakfast through to dinner, or grab a sandwich at *Dip N'Deli*, MM31 at the *Big Pine Motel* (☎872-9090).

Nightlife is not a strong suit; when locals want to live it up they go to Key West. Take a shot at the *No Name Pub*, at the eastern end of Watson Boulevard on Big Pine Key (☎872-9115), for a variety of beers, food and occasional live bands; the *Looe Key Reef Resort* (see above) for weekend drinking; or, if desperate, the lounge of the *Cedar Inn*, MM31 (☎872-4031).

Key West

Much closer to Cuba than mainland Florida, **KEY WEST** can often seem very far removed from the rest of the US. Famed for their tolerant attitudes and laid-back lifestyles, its 30,000 islanders seem adrift in a great expanse of sea and sky. Despite the million tourists who arrive each year, the place resonates with an anarchic and individualist spirit that hits you the instant you arrive. Locals (known as Conchs – after the giant sea snails eaten by early settlers – if they're long-term residents of Key West, or Freshwater Conchs if they're more recent arrivals) ride bicycles, shoot the breeze on street corners and smile at complete strangers.

Yet as wild as it may at first appear, Key West today is far from being the misfits' mecca that it was just a decade or so ago. Much of the sleaziness has been gradually brushed away through a steady process of what some might see as rather cutesy restoration and revitalization – it takes a lot of money to buy a house here now – paving the way for a sizeable vacation industry that at times seems to revolve around party boats and heavy drinking. Not that Key West is near to losing its special identity; it's still nonconformist, and don't dare suggest otherwise. The liberal attitudes have attracted a large influx of gay people, estimated at two in five of the population, who take an essential role in running the place and sink thousands of dollars into its future.

The sense of isolation from the mainland – much stronger here than on the other Keys – and the camaraderie of the locals are best appreciated by adjusting to the mellow pace and joining in. Amble the side streets, make meals last for hours, and pause regularly for refreshment in the numerous bars. Key West's knack for tourism can be gaudy, but depending on what you want, it's quite simple to bypass the commercial traps and discover an island as unique for its present-day society as for its remarkable past.

The secret to discovering Key West's magical qualities is simple: sidestep the areas that, until the mid-Eighties, made up the so-called core of the island, but have since fallen prey to the tourist tribes who come to buy T-shirts and drink themselves silly.

The tourist epicenter is on **Duval Street**, whose northern end is marked by **Mallory Square**, a historic landmark that is now home to a brash chain of bars that entirely ignores the whimsical, freethinking spirit of the island. But just a few steps east of here is the historic section, a network of streets teeming with rich foliage and brilliant blooms draped over curious architecture. This area boasts many of the best guesthouses, many eateries and wacky galleries; not to mention the streets themselves, which are peopled with characters straight out of the wildest of imaginations.

To the west of Duval Street, just off Whitehead Street, lies Bahama Village, an area of dusty lanes where cockerels wander and birds screech into the night. This unique enclave boasts some of the best-hidden restaurants on the island, although developers are already speculating on the area's future.

Some history

Piracy was the main activity around Key West – first settled in 1822 – before Florida joined the US and the navy established a base here. This cleared the way for a substantial **wrecking industry**. Millions of dollars were earned by lifting people and cargo off shipwrecks along the Florida reef, and by the mid-nineteenth century, Key West was the wealthiest city in the US.

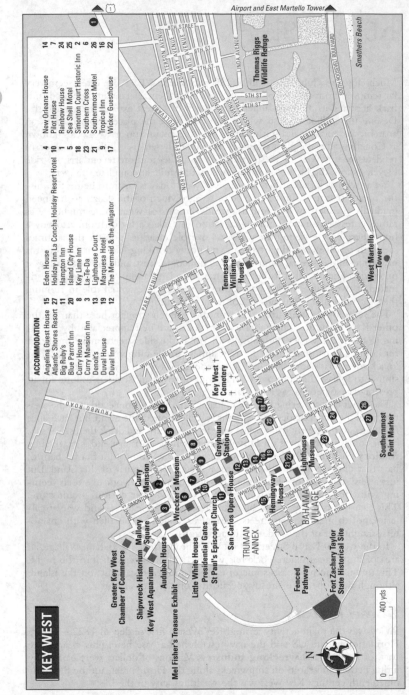

KEY WEST

Airport and East Martello Tower

Thomas Riggs
Wildlife Refuge

Smathers Beach

ACCOMMODATION

Angelina Guest House	15	Eden House	4
Atlantic Shores Resort	27	Holiday Inn La Concha Holiday Resort Hotel	10
Big Ruby's	11	Hampton Inn	5
Blue Parrot Inn	20	Island City House	18
Curry House	8	Key Lime Inn	3
Curry Mansion Inn	3	La-Te-Da	13
Denoit's	13	Lighthouse Court	21
Duval House	19	Marquesa Hotel	9
Duval Inn	12	The Mermaid & the Alligator	17
New Orleans House	14		
Pilot House	7		
Rainbow House	24		
Sea Shell Motel	25		
Simonton Court Historic Inn	2		
Southern Cross	6		
Southernmost Motel	26		
Tropical Inn	16		
Wicker Guesthouse	22		

THUMBO ROAD

Tennessee
Williams'
House

West Martello
Tower

Key West
Cemetery

Greyhound
Station

Greater Key West
Chamber of Commerce

Shipwreck Historium

Mallory
Square

Key West Aquarium

Audubon House

Mel Fisher's Treasure Exhibit

Curry
Mansion

Wrecker's Museum

Little White House

Presidential Gates

St Paul's Episcopal Church

San Carlos Opera House

Lighthouse
Museum

Hemingway
House

BAHAMA
VILLAGE

TRUMAN
ANNEX

Fenced
Pathway

Fort Zachary Taylor
State Historical Site

Southernmost
Point Marker

N

0   400 yds

The Conch Republic

In April 1982 the US Border Patrol set up a roadblock on US Highway 1 at the *Last Chance Saloon* in Florida City, ostensibly to prevent illegal aliens (and drugs) entering the US mainland. This effectively cut off the Florida Keys at the confluence of the only two roads out to the mainland, leading to seventeen-mile tailbacks and a sudden, sharp decline in tourist numbers – as well as causing massive disruption to basic services. The mayor of Key West (with the backing of other community leaders), after failing to remove the checkpoint through legal means, formed the "Conch Republic" and seceded from the US in Mallory Square on April 23 – and declared war on Washington for good measure. The first shots fired were of stale Cuban bread broken over the head of a man dressed in an admiral's uniform – though some claim there were more concrete targets in the form of Federal spies who had quickly descended upon the town. The new prime minister then surrendered to the US navy – and demanded US foreign aid and war reparations of one billion dollars. Washington didn't respond directly (at least with an aid package), though it did quietly remove the offending checkpoint. The event is now celebrated annually at the Conch Republic Independence Celebration (see overleaf) and is a great excuse for making a weeklong party as well as a humorous but serious political point: the community – already separated geographically from the mainland – will always strive to maintain a social distance as well.

The building of reef lighthouses sounded the death knell for the wrecking business, but Key West continued to prosper. Many **Cubans** arrived bringing cigar-making skills, and migrant **Greeks** established a lucrative sponge enterprise (the highly absorbent sea sponges, formed from the skeletons of tiny marine creatures, were the forerunners of today's synthetic sponges). Industrial unrest and a sponge-blight drove these businesses north to Tampa and Tarpon Springs, and left Key West ill-prepared to face the **Depression**. Diehard Conchs, living on fish and coconuts, defied any suggestion that they move to the mainland, but by the summer of 1934 they were finally driven into bankruptcy. Under Franklin Roosevelt's New Deal, Key West was tidied up and readied for tourism, yet the 1935 Labor Day hurricane blew away the Flagler railway – Key West's only land link to the outside world. Luckily, the bridges were used for the construction of the Overseas Highway, which first saw use in 1938.

An injection of naval dollars during World War II eventually saved Key West by providing the backbone for its economy, while the island's geographical location made it an ideal vantage point from which to survey communist Cuba in the Sixties. **Tourists** started arriving in force during the Eighties, just as a taste for independence was rising among the locals and a strange chain of events led to the formation of the "**Conch Republic**" (see box, above).

Arrival, information and getting around

The Overseas Highway, the only road into Key West, runs through the bland eastern section of the island to the infinitely more interesting Old Town. On the way you'll pass the information-packed **Welcome Center** (Mon–Sat 9am–7.30pm, Sun 9am–6pm; ☎292-8962) at 3840 North Roosevelt Blvd. If you don't feel like stopping here, press on and use the **Greater Key West Chamber of Commerce**, next to Mallory Square at 402 Wall St (Mon–Fri 8am–6pm, Sat & Sun 8am–5pm; ☎294-2587), for free tourist pamphlets and discount vouchers. Four miles east of town is the **Key West International**

Airport (☎296-5439), whose name belies its services – it only handles flights from Miami and other Florida cities. There are no buses from the airport to town, and a taxi costs around $10. Greyhound **buses** stop only once in town (at the junction of Simonton and Virginia streets) before carrying on to the airport.

For **getting around** the narrow, pedestrian-filled streets of the Old Town, you're far better off walking or cycling than driving. If street signs appear curiously absent, you'll find them painted vertically on the base of each junction lamppost, though many are peeling off. If you're planning to venture further afield, **rent a bike** ($7–10 per day) or moped ($25–30 per day) from one of Adventure Scooter & Bicycle Rentals two locations: 708 and 925 Duval St, or the *Key West International Hostel* (see "Accommodation"). Remarkably, there is a **bus service** (☎292-8164) on Key West: two routes, clockwise and counterclockwise, loop around the tiny island roughly every fifteen minutes between 7am and 9am, and 2.30pm and 5.30pm. You'll also notice the new **cycle-rickshaws** who'll pedal you around (in their highest gear) and charge $1 a minute – that's about $20 from one end of Duval Street to the other.

The oft-plugged, ninety-minute guided tours of the island's main sights are a fair option, but only if you're really pushed for time and won't be able to explore on your own. The **Conch Tour Train** (Mallory Square; every 20–30min, 9am–4pm; $18, age 4–12 $9; ☎294-5161) or the **Old Town Trolley** (board at any of the marked stops around the Old Town; every 30min, 9am–4.30pm; $18, age 4–12 $9; ☎296-6688) dole out loud-speakered information, but the tours don't really foster an appreciation of the island's atmosphere.

Key West festivals

Early January *Key West Literary Festival.* Four-day celebration of the island's famous four – Tennessee Williams, Ernest Hemingway, Robert Frost, and Thornton Wilder. Includes seminars, discussions and readings with well-known living authors as well as special tours (☎1-888/293-9291).

January–May *Old Island Days.* Tours, talks, concerts, flower shows and art festivals celebrating Key West's history (☎294-9501).

Late April *Conch Republic Independence Celebration.* A party in Mallory Square with a symbolic raising of the Conch Republic flag, commemorating the declaration of the Keys' independence from the US in 1982 (see "Some history") (☎296-0213).

Mid-July *Hemingway Days.* Literary seminars, writers' workshops, daft trivia competitions, arm-wrestling and lookalike contests commemorate Ernest Hemingway, Key West's best-known writer (☎294-4440).

Early September *WomenFest.* Key West's only dedicated lesbian-orientated event, with art shows, theater and other assorted happenings (☎296-2491).

Late October *Goombay Festival.* Caribbean street party in Bahama Village (☎293-8305).

Late October *Fantasy Fest.* A gay-dominated version of Mardi Gras, with outrageous costumes paraded throughout the night along Duval Street – if you want a room at this time you'll need to book well in advance (☎296-1817, ⓦwww.fantasyfest.net).

Early November *Cuban-American Heritage Festival.* A celebration of all things Cuban American, including a street fiesta as well as more serious discussions at a symposium (☎295-9665, ⓦwww.cubanfest.com).

Mid-December *Lighted Boat Parade.* Lighted boats sail in and around Key West Harbor (☎292-9520).

Get **precise dates** on all of these from the Chamber of Commerce or Welcome Center (addresses above) or check Web sites where given.

A number of easily found **free publications** list current events: *Solares Hill* (monthly) is the most informative, but look out also for *Island Life* (weekly), *The Conch Republic* (monthly), and the gay-orientated gossip sheet *What's Happening* (weekly).

Getting connected to the **Internet** is not cheap in Key West, and the majority of cybercafés charge $9 and upwards for an hour's worth – and some charge as much as $20, so ask before you start. The least expensive is Down Under, 1970 North Roosevelt Blvd (daily 11am–4pm; $5/hr).

Accommodation

Unless you're traveling with children or in a group, choosing one of the excellent guesthouse/bed-and-breakfasts is far more fun than staying in a hotel – most hotels are either stationed on the bland road that leads to the island, or are overhyped and priced to match.

Accommodation costs in Key West are always high – particularly from November to April when the simplest motel room will be in excess of $90 per night. Prices drop considerably at other times, but expect to pay at least $70 wherever you stay. Genuine **budget options** are limited to pitching a tent or renting a basic cottage at *Jabour's Trailor Court*, 223 Elizabeth St (℡294-5723) or the seaside (but out of town) *Boyd's Campground,* 6401 Maloney Ave, (℡294-1465). The *Key West International Hostel*, 718 South St (℡296-5719, ℮keyshostel@aol.com; members $18, non-members $22), has small, grubby dorms but is the only hostel on the island.

Wherever you stay, a reservation is essential from November to April, and would be a sensible precaution for weekend stays at any other time. If you arrive in October during Fantasy Fest, a hugely popular gay and lesbian Mardi Gras, expect a hike in room cost – if you can get one at all.

Many of the restored villas operating as guesthouses in the historic district are gay- and lesbian-run, and while most welcome all adults, few accept young children. A handful (listed below) are exclusively gay male, while only one is for lesbians only.

Guesthouses

Angelina Guest House, 302 Angela St (℡1-800/874-7326, ℮info@dolphintrul.com). Well-priced rooms in a restored former 1920s bordello with a great wrap-around veranda. Right in Bahama Village. ❸

Blue Parrot Inn, 916 Elizabeth St (℡1-800/231-2473, ℗www.blueparrotinn.com). The friendly owners of this 1884 house in the heart of the historic district serve excellent breakfasts in a lush, courtyard garden. No children. ❺

Curry Mansion Inn, 511 Caroline St (℡1-800/253-3466 or 294-5349; ℱ 294-4093, ℗www.currymansion.com). Pricey but worth it for a night in this landmark Victorian home (see below). Enjoy the antiques, superb breakfasts, complimentary cocktail parties and use of the pool and showers all day after check-out. ❻

Denoit's, 512 Angela St (℡294-6324, ℗www.key-westsoaps-linens.com). Just four rooms round a small patio behind a linen shop, but very clean and homely. Rooms are comfortable and individually decorated with original artworks and furniture from the Caribbean. No children or smoking. ❺

Duval House, 814 Duval St (℡294-1666; ℱ 292-1701). The lower-priced rooms are excellent value, and a bit more gets you a four-poster bed and a balcony overlooking the grounds. One of the few places with ample parking. ❻

Duval Inn, 511 Angela St (℡295-9531 or 1-877/418-6900, ℗www.duvalinn.com). Though the new management is planning renovations once it has taken over, some of the current rooms are still very basic and all have shared bathrooms; be sure to look before paying, though some might find the old rooms do have a certain charm. ❹

Island City House, 411 William St (℡1-800/634-8230, ℗www.islandcityhouse.com). This grand mansion, built in the 1880s for a Charleston merchant family, offers studios and one- or two-bedroom apartments overlooking the pool and tropical gardens. Children welcome. ❻

Key Lime Inn, 725 Truman Ave (☎294-6222 or 1-800/201-6222). Choose from the tiny cottages or the chain-style rooms in the nineteenth-century house. Lots of lovely trees and a pool make up for the lack of space and over-renovation of the interior. ❼

La-Te-Da, 1125 Duval St (☎1-800/528-3320). This pastel-interior 1894 house is at the center of gay social life. The tree-studded complex includes several bars, discos and the classy *Alice's* restaurant (see "Eating"). While very popular with gays, the clientele is mixed. Prices drop by half out of season. ❻

Marquesa Hotel, 600 Fleming St (☎292-1919 or 1-800/869-4631, ⓕ 294-2121, ⓦwww.marquesa .com). A grand guesthouse (built in 1884) with a formal clientele and lush green surroundings. Pop in to view the old photographs of Key West's past, though avoid the restaurant, which borders on pompous. ❽

The Mermaid & the Alligator, 729 Truman Ave (☎294-1894 or 1-800/773-1894, ⓕ 295-9925, ⓦwww.kwmermaid.com). A gem of a house (built in 1904) with stunning interior decor. Fabulous gardens, a pool, and wine served each evening make for a deeply relaxing stay. No children under 16. ❻–❻

Simonton Court Historic Inn, 320 Simonton St (☎1-800/944-2687, ⓕ 293-8446, ⓦwww.simontoncourt.com). Renovated from an old cigar factory, the main house has a wide selection of rooms, and well-equipped cottages dot this historic compound. No children. ❼

Tropical Inn, 812 Duval St (☎294-9977). Large, airy rooms in a charming restored Conch house at the center of the action. Most of the rooms sleep three, and the more expensive ones have balconies. Ask about the neighboring cottages with hot-tubs and kitchens. No children. ❹

Wicker Guesthouse, 913 Duval St (☎296-2475 or 1-800/880-4275, ⓦwww.wickerhousekw.com). One of the least expensive guesthouses on Key West. Comprised of four restored Conch houses. The cheaper rooms lack TVs and air-conditioning (but have ceiling fans). There is a communal Jacuzzi, a pool and fine complimentary breakfasts are served in the garden. ❻

Exclusively gay guest-houses

Big Ruby's, 409 Appelrouth Lane (☎296-2323 or 1-800/477-7829, ⓕ 296-0281, ⓦwww.bigrubys.com). Delightful, peaceful yet vibrant and social. There's lots of extras, like splendid Sunday brunches, free drinks, design-conscious rooms and the friendliest of staffs. Book

in advance. The $320 a night penthouse suite is exceptional. ❻

Curry House, 806 Fleming St (☎294-6777 or 1-800/633-7439; ⓕ 294-5322, ⓦwww.vtsmall.com). The oldest all-male gay guesthouse in the area. Clean, comfortable and well liked. ❺

Eden House, 1015 Fleming St (☎1-800/533-KEYS; ⓕ 294-1221, ⓦwww.edenhouse.com). One of Key West's most relaxing hideaways and one of the few Art Deco hotels on the island. Peaceful rooms surround the pool where Goldie Hawn filmed *Criss Cross* in 1990. There's a quiet area of hammocks under a giant tree, and there are big reductions off season. ❹

Lighthouse Court, 902 Whitehead St (☎294-9588, ⓕ 294-6861, ⓦwww.lighthousecourt.com). A very social address in the shadow of the lighthouse just opposite Hemingway's house. It's not cheap and service can vary, but it's hugely popular with the "in" crowd. ❺

New Orleans House, 724 Duval St (☎293-9800 or 1-888/293-9873; ⓕ 293-9870, ⓦwww .bourbonstreetcomplex.com). Huge, very clean rooms with full kitchens are a highlight at this centrally located, if not too cozy, new guesthouse. The facade overlooks Duval Street, so ask for a room at the back if you want to sleep before 3am. Huge discounts out of season. ❺

Pilot House, 414 Simonton St (☎1-800/648-3780 or 294-8719; ⓕ 294-9298, ⓦwww .pilothousekeywest.com). Sharing the same owners as *New Orleans House* (above), this guesthouse has contemporary suites in a classic, though over-renovated, Victorian house. The house was once owned by Joseph Otto, a prominent Prussian surgeon, who happens to have the maddest grave in Key West cemetery (see below). Great pools, breakfasts and a peaceful, convenient location. ❼

Rainbow House, 525 United St (☎292-1450 or 1-800/749-6696). The lone lesbian-only guesthouse on the island, this attractive former cigar factory serves breakfast and has two pools and hot-tub. ❺

Hotels and motels

Atlantic Shores Resort, 510 South St (☎296-2491 or 1-800/526-3559, ⓦwww.atlanticshoresresort .com). Open to all, this Art Deco resort is hugely in vogue with the gay crowd for its Sunday "tea-dances" (see "Gay and lesbian Key West" below). Both men and women enjoy the clothing-optional sundecks overlooking the ocean. ❺

Hampton Inn, 2801 N Roosevelt Blvd (☎1-800/HAMPTON). A large branch of a reliable (and usually low-cost) hotel chain, with spacious rooms, a bar and a pool; rates, however, are far higher than most Hampton Inns. ❺

Holiday Inn La Concha Holiday Resort Hotel, 430 Duval St (☎1-800/745-2191 or 296-2991, ⓕ 294-3283, ⓦwww.keywest.com/laconcha.html). Now a link in the chain, this colorful hotel first opened in 1925 and has been refurbished to retain some of its Twenties-style decor. Big pluses for most guests are the large swimming pool and bar overlooking the town. ❼

Sea Shell Motel, 718 South St (☎296-5719, ⓔkeyshostel@aol.com). If the adjoining youth hostel is full or doesn't appeal, this offers standard motel rooms at the lowest rates in the neighborhood. ❹

Southern Cross, 326 Duval St (☎1-800/533-4891, ⓔdhakeeper@aol.com). Key West's oldest hotel offers no-frills rooms; get one at the rear if you want to avoid the night-time hubbub along Duval Street. ❸

Southernmost Motel, 1319 Duval St (☎1-800/354-4455, ⓕ 294-8272). The rooms at the US's most southerly motel are decked out in tropical shades; its two poolside tiki bars are the ideal place to meet other guests before taking the ten-minute walk to the heart of Key West. ❺

The Old Town

The square mile of the **Old Town** contains a good portion of what you'll want to see and is certainly the best place for imbibing Key West's finest feature: its atmosphere. Tourists are plentiful around the main streets, but the relaxed, casually hedonistic mood affects everyone, no matter if you've been here twenty years or twenty minutes. All of the Old Town can be seen on foot in a couple of days, though you should allow at least three – dashing about isn't the way to enjoy the place.

Along Duval Street

Anyone who saw Key West two decades ago would now barely recognize the main promenade, **Duval Street**, which cuts a mile-long swathe right through the Old Town, making it easy to regain bearings after exploring the side streets. Teetering precariously on the safe side of seedy for many years, much of the street has been transformed into a well-manicured strip of boutiques; beachwear and Israeli-run T-shirt shops cater to the vacationing middle-aged of Middle America. Yet its colorful "local characters" and round the clock action mean that Duval Street is still an interesting place to hang out.

Other than shops and bars, few places on Duval Street provide a break from tramping the pavement. One, however, is the **Oldest House Museum** (daily 10am–4pm; $5, children $1; ☎294-9502), at no. 322, in, fittingly, one of the oldest houses in Key West. The exhibits here give some background to the wrecker industry on which Key West's earliest good times were based: salvaging cargo from foundering vessels. In the days before radio and radar, wrecking crews simply put out in bad weather and sailed as close as they dared to the menacing reefs, hoping to spot a grounded craft. Judging by the choice furniture that fills the museum, Captain Watlington, the wrecker who lived here during the 1830s, did pretty well. On the top floor modern cartoons recount several Key West folk tales, including the sea dunking of a preacher who dwelled too long on the evils of drinking.

Swarms of children wander through **Ripley's Believe It or Not Odditorium,** at no. 257 (daily 9am–11pm; $10.95, age 4–12 $8.95; ☎293-9694), a museum of trivia crammed with fanciful facts and figures about a myriad of unrelated subjects. A hologram of founder Robert Ripley bleats out the "believe it or not" mantra throughout the museum, provoking yawns from anyone over 10.

A few blocks on, **St Paul's Episcopal Church**, at no. 401, is worth entering briefly for its rich stained-glass windows. If overwhelmed by piety, you might scoot around the corner for a look at the **Old Stone Methodist Church**, 600 Eaton St. The oldest church in Key West, it was built in 1877 and is shaded by a giant Spanish laurel tree in its front yard.

At 516 Duval St, the **San Carlos Opera House** (daily 9am–5pm; $3; ☏294-3887) has played a leading role in Cuban exile life since it opened (on a different site) as the San Carlos Institute in 1871. It was from here in 1892 that Cuban Revolutionary hero José Martí welded the Cuban exiles together into a force that would topple the regime in 1902. Financed by a $100,000 grant from the grateful new Cuban government, the present building dates from 1924, and Cuban architect Francisco Centurion designed the two-story building in the Cuban baroque style of the period. The soil on its grounds is from Cuba's six provinces, and a cornerstone was taken from Martí's tomb. Following the break in diplomatic ties between the US and Cuba in 1961, the building fell on hard times – and was briefly used as a cinema, much to the annoyance of local Cubans – until it was revived by a million-dollar restoration project. Now, besides staging opera in its acoustically excellent auditorium and maintaining a well-stocked research library (including, most notably, the records of the Cuban consulate from 1886 to 1961), it has a first-rate permanent exhibition on the history of Cubans in the US and, in particular, Key West.

You'll know when you get near the southern end of Duval Street because, whether it's a house, motel, filling station or restaurant, everything advertises itself as being "the southernmost" of its kind. In case you're interested, the true **southernmost point** in Key West, and consequently in the continental US, is to be found at the intersection of Whitehead and South streets – only 90 miles from Cuba.

Mallory Square and around

In the early 1800s, thousands of dollars' worth of marine salvage was landed at the piers, stored in the warehouses and sold at the auction houses on **Mallory Square**, just west of the northern end of Duval Street. The square's present-day commerce, however, is based on tourism, and little remains from the old days. By day, the square is a plain souvenir market selling overpriced ice cream, trinkets and T-shirts. But at night it is transformed for the sunset celebration. Jugglers, fire-eaters and assorted loose-screw types create a merry backdrop to the sinking of the sun. The celebration, which began in the Sixties as a hippie excuse for a smoke-in, is lively and fun, though it too is slowly succumbing to commercialization.

Key West Aquarium

More entertaining than the square during the day is the small gathering of sea life inside the adjacent **Key West Aquarium**, 1 Whitehead St (daily 10am–6pm; adults $8, age 4–12 $4; ☏296-2051), where ugly creatures such as porcupine fish and longspine squirrel fish leer from behind glass, and sharks (the smaller kinds such as lemon, blacktip and bonnethead) are known to jump out of their open tanks during the half-hour **guided tours and feedings** (11am, 1pm, 3pm & 4.30pm). If you intend to eat conch, a rubbery crustacean sold as fritter or chowder all over Key West, do so before examining the live ones here – they're not the world's most aesthetically pleasing creatures.

Mel Fisher's Treasure Exhibit and around

In the wild, the aquarium's fish might make their homes around the remains of sunken galleons that plied the trade route between Spain and its New World colonies during the sixteenth and seventeenth centuries. In **Mel Fisher's Maritime Heritage Society Museum**, 200 Greene St (daily 9.30am–5pm; adults $6.50, age 13–18 $4; ℡294-2633), you'll get a good look at skillfully crafted decorative pieces, a highly impressive emerald cross, a liftable gold bar, plus countless vases and daggers alongside the obligatory cannon, all salvaged from two seventeenth-century wrecks. As engrossing as the collection is, it's really a celebration of an all-American rags-to-riches story. Now the high priest of Florida's many treasure-seekers, Fisher was running a surf shop in California before he arrived in the Sunshine State armed with old Spanish sea charts. In 1985, after years of searching, he discovered the *Nuestra Señora de Atocha* and the *Santa Margarita*, both sunk during a hurricane in 1622, forty miles southeast of Key West – they yielded a haul said to be worth millions of dollars. Among matters you won't find mentioned at the exhibit is the raging dispute between Fisher and the state and federal governments over who owns what, and the ecological disturbance that uncontrolled treasure-seeking has wrought upon the keys. This conflict led to the recent change of name, from "Treasure Exhibit" to "Heritage Museum."

At Greene and Front streets, the imposing, Romanesque **Customs House** (℡296-3913) was built in 1891 and used as a post office, customs office and federal court house. Long derelict, the building is being gradually renovated for use as a local history museum – call ahead for details on exhibits and opening hours.

Just a block up Wall Street from Mallory Square (in front of the waterfront Playhouse Theater) is the **Historic Sculpture Garden** (open all the time; ℡294-4192), a bizarre, pretend graveyard full of sculpted heads of the men and women who have influenced Key West, such as Asa Tift and Henry Flagler. It looks more like a waxwork chamber of horrors than an austere tribute, but the information plates disclose the interesting origins of the island's road names and the whole experience makes for a fun history lesson. The grounds are paved with engraved bricks, and, for $60, you can help preserve the area and know that thousands of tourists are trampling on – and maybe even reading – your name.

The Truman Annex and Fort Zachary Taylor

The old naval storehouse that contains the Fisher trove was once part of the **Truman Annex** (daily 8am–6pm; free), a decommissioned section of a naval base established in 1822 to keep a lid on piracy around what had just become US territory. Some of the buildings subsequently erected on the base, which spans a hundred acres between Whitehead Street and the sea, were – and still are – among Key West's most distinctive. The dreamy Customs House (see above) is a fine example.

The most famous among them, however, is the comparatively plain **Harry S. Truman Little White House Museum** (daily 9am–5pm; adults $7.50, under-13s $3.75), by the junction of Caroline and Front streets. This house earned its name by being the favorite holiday spot of President Harry S. Truman (for whom the Annex was named), who first visited in 1946 and allegedly spent his vacations playing poker, cruising Key West for doughnuts, and swimming. Primitive plumbing meant that no one in the house was allowed to flush the toilet during his visits. The house is now a museum that chronicles the Truman years with an immense array of memorabilia.

In 1986, the Annex passed into the hands of a young property developer who purchased it for $17.25 million. The developer made a lot of fast friends by throwing open the weighty Presidential Gates on Caroline Street (which had previously parted only for heads of state) and encouraging the public to walk or cycle around the complex. If you feel so inclined, get the free **walking**

2

guide from the well-marked sales office and embark on a building-by-building tour – the buildings' interiors, unfortunately, are closed to the public.

The Annex also provides access, along a fenced pathway through the operating naval base, to the less interesting **Fort Zachary Taylor State Historical Site** (daily 8am–sunset; cars $3.25, plus $1 per person; pedestrians and cyclists $1.50), built in 1845 and later used in the blockade of Confederate shipping during the Civil War. Over ensuing decades, the fort simply disappeared under sand and weeds. Excavation work has gradually revealed much of historical worth, though it's hard to comprehend the full importance without joining the 45-minute **guided tour** (daily at noon & 2pm). Most locals pass by the fort on the way to the best **beach** in Key West – a place yet to be discovered by tourists, just a few yards beyond.

Whitehead Street

A block west of crowded Duval Street, **Whitehead Street** is much quieter, has a range of sights and, with its mix of rich and poor homes, reveals a more diverse side of Key West.

At the junction of Whitehead and Wall streets is the **Shipwreck Historium** (☎ 292-8990; daily shows start at 9.45am and run every 30 min until 4.45pm; $8). Enthusiastic guides attempt in vain to enlist audience participation as they recount the history of wrecking in Key West before letting visitors loose on the museum. The collection boasts some fine cargo from the *Isaac Allerton*, which sank in 1856 and remained untraced until 1985. Better still is the panoramic view from the top of the reconstructed viewing tower.

On the corner with Greene Street, the **Audubon House and Tropical Gardens** (daily 9.30am–5pm; $7.50, age 6–12 $3.50, ☎ 1-877/281-2473, ⓦ www.audubonhouse.com) was the first of Key West's elegant Victorian-style properties to get a thorough renovation in 1958 – its success encouraged a host of others to follow suit and sent housing prices soaring. The house's name is taken from famed ornithologist John James Audubon, who actually had nothing to do with the place. Audubon spent a few weeks in Key West in 1832, scrambling around the mangrove swamps (now protected as the Thomas Riggs Wildlife Refuge, see p.164), looking for the birdlife he later portrayed in his highly regarded *Birds of America* portfolio. Audubon's link to the house goes no further than the lithographs that decorate the walls and staircase. Original Audubon prints, hand-colored under his instruction, are for sale here at a few hundred to a few thousand dollars.

The man who actually owned the property was a wrecker named John Geiger. In addition to twelve children of their own, Geiger and his wife took in many others from shipwrecks and broken marriages. Self-guided **tours** through the house require the visitor to wear a personal stereo system, which broadcasts the ghostly voices of Mrs Geiger and the children chatting at you about how life was back in their day and pointing out some of the house's fine nineteenth-century European furniture and antiques.

The Ernest Hemingway Home and Museum

It may be the biggest tourist draw in Key West, but to the chagrin of Ernest Hemingway fans, guided tours of **The Ernest Hemingway Home and Museum**, 907 Whitehead St (daily 9am–5pm; adults $8, children 6–12 $5; ☎ 294-1136, ⓦ www.hemingwayhome.com), deals more in fantasy than fact. Although Hemingway owned this large, vaguely Spanish-Colonial-style house for thirty years, he lived in it for barely ten, and the authenticity of the furnishings – a motley bunch of tables, chairs and beds about which the guide is rather smug – was hotly disputed by Hemingway's former secretary.

Hemingway bought the house in 1931, not with his own money but with an $8000 gift from the rich uncle of his then wife, Pauline. Originally one of the grander Key West homes, built for a wealthy nineteenth-century merchant, the dwelling was seriously run-down by the time the Hemingways arrived. It soon acquired such luxuries as an inside bathroom and a swimming pool, and was filled with an entourage of servants and housekeepers.

Hemingway produced some of his most acclaimed work in the deer-head-dominated study, located in an outhouse, which the author entered by way of a homemade rope bridge. Here he penned the short stories *The Short Happy Life of Francis Macomber* and *The Snows of Kilimanjaro*; the novella *The Old Man and the Sea* and the novels *A Farewell to Arms* and *To Have and Have Not*, the latter describing Key West life during the Depression.

Among the highlights of the tour are pictures of the author's four wives and a lovely ceramic sculpture of a cat by Picasso. Hemingway's studio is a colorful affair, with a quarry-tiled floor and deer heads that look onto his old Royal typewriter. In the garden, a water trough for the cats is supposedly a urinal from *Sloppy Joe's* (see "Nightlife"), where the big man downed many a pint. When Hemingway divorced Pauline in 1940, he boxed up his manuscripts and moved them to a back room at *Sloppy Joe's* before heading off to a house in Cuba with his new wife, journalist Martha Gellhorn.

To see inside the house (and the study) you have to join the half-hour **guided tour** (ten daily), but afterwards you're free to roam at leisure and play with some of the fifty-odd cats. The story that these are descendants from a feline family that lived here in Hemingway's day is yet another dubious claim: the large colony of inbred cats once described by Hemingway was at his home in Cuba.

The Lighthouse Museum and the Bahama Village

From the Hemingway House, you'll easily catch sight of the **Lighthouse Museum**, 938 Whitehead St (daily 9am–5pm; adults $6, under-12s $2; ⊤294-0012), simply because it is an 86-foot lighthouse – one of Florida's first, raised in 1847, and still functioning. There's a tiny collection of lighthouse junk and drawings at ground level, and it's possible (if tedious) to climb the 88 steps to the top of the tower, though the views of Key West are actually better from the top-floor bar of the *Holiday Inn La Concha* hotel (see "Accommodation"). Most of the pictures taken here are not of the lighthouse but of the massive Chinese banyan tree at the base. But you can ogle the lighthouse's huge lens (installed in 1858): a twelve-foot high, headache-inducing honeycomb of glass.

The narrow streets around the lighthouse and to the west of Whitehead Street constitute **Bahama Village**, an engaging area relatively devoid of tourists and glossy restoration jobs. Most of the squat, slightly shabby homes – some of them once small cigar factories – are occupied by people of Bahamian and Afro-Cuban descent. Not only does this area have some of the best and most authentic eateries around, but it also just about holds onto the laid-back Key West atmosphere waning elsewhere on the island. Sadly, the little tour trains are now running close by, and property developers are slowly bringing Bahama Village up to speed with touristy areas to the east. For now, though, the place is still relatively untouched: locals still dress up on Sundays and file into the unusual, flaking churches, and the village teems with energy day and night. A more modern attraction here is the community swimming pool at the corner of Catherine and Thomas streets, an Olympic-size pool with fantastic ocean views.

Caroline and Greene streets

At the northern end of Duval Street turn right onto **Caroline Street** or **Greene Street**, and you'll come across numerous examples of late-1800s "Conch houses," built in a mix-and-match style that fused elements of Victorian, Colonial and Tropical architecture. The houses were raised on coral slabs, and rounded off with playful "gingerbread" wood trimming. Erected quickly and cheaply, Conch houses were seldom painted, but many here are bright and colorful, evincing their recent transformation in the last fifteen years from ordinary dwellings to hundred-thousand-dollar winter homes.

In strong contrast to the tiny Conch houses, the grand three-story **Curry Mansion**, 511 Caroline St (daily 10am–5pm; adults $5, under-12s $1; ☎ 294-5349), was built in 1869 and once the abode of William Curry, Florida's first millionaire. Inside, amid a riot of Tiffany glass and sensational bird's-eye maple panelling, is a heady stash of strange and stylish fittings that include an antique Chinese toilet bowl and a lamp designed by Frank Lloyd Wright.

What sets this museum apart is that it is also the present-day home of Al and Edith Amsterdam. The owners for the past 25 years, the Amsterdams are personable hosts when not at their similar mansion in upstate New York. Much of the memorabilia and photographs are from their own younger days, including a Westley Richards gun belonging to Hemingway and given to Mrs Amsterdam by one of the author's wives. Exploring this sensational house is made all the more pleasurable by the Amsterdams' friendly, open-door policy. Clamber up into the attic and you'll be rewarded with a fairy-tale assortment of antique furniture, including a crazy, sequin-covered bed. Climbing even higher to the beautiful **Widows Walk** (a walkway around the rooftop where sailors' wives looked for signs of their husbands' return), affords terrific views over the town. Other highlights of the house include the still-used 1940 Doverlift elevator and the eighteenth-century furnishings of the music room.

Heritage House Museum

A delightful hour or two can be spent at the charming **Heritage House Museum**, 410 Caroline St (Mon–Sat 10am–5pm, Sun 11am–4pm; tours $6, under-12s free; ☎ 296-3573). This double-veranda, Colonial-style home has been in the same family for seven generations, and the present owner, Jean Porter, lives in an annexe. Jean's mother, Jessie Porter, who died in 1979, was the great-granddaughter of William Curry (see above), and Miss Jessie, as she was known, was at the hub of Key West's efforts to preserve the historic section of town. Among the luminaries she counted as friends were Tallulah Bankhead, who visited with Tennessee Williams, Gloria Swanson and Thornton Wilder; their photographs are mounted in the hallway. Robert Frost also came and lived in a cottage in the garden. While you can wander about the garden, the cottage itself is off limits.

Other highlights include an enticing music room where you can play the 1865 French piano, a library of rare books, and a dining room twinkling with crystal and colorful dining chairs taken from a Spanish shipwreck. Outside, recordings of Robert Frost reading his poetry are played in the lush gardens upon request.

The dockside area

Between Williams and Margaret streets, the **dockside** area has been spruced up into a shopping and eating strip called **Land's End Village**, with a couple of enjoyable bars (see "Nightlife," p.166). One with more than drinking to offer is *Turtle Kraals*, in business as a turtle cannery until the Seventies, when harvesting turtles became illegal. There are tanks of touchable sea life inside the restaurant and, just along the short pier, a grim gathering of the gory machines used to slice and mince green turtles – captured off the Nicaraguan coast – into a delicacy known as "Granday's Fine Green Turtle Soup." Apart from pleasure cruisers and shrimping boats along the docks, you might catch a fleeting glimpse of a naval hydrofoil – vessels of unbelievable speed employed on anti-drug-running missions from their base a mile or so along the coast.

Key West Cemetery

Leaving the waterfront and heading inland along Margaret Street for five blocks will take you to the **Key West Cemetery** (daily sunrise–6pm; free), which dates back to 1847, and whose residents are buried in vaults above ground (a high water table and solid coral rock prevents the traditional six-feet-under inter-ment). Despite the lack of celebrity stiffs, the many witty inscriptions ("I told you I was sick") suggest that the island's relaxed attitude toward life also extends to death. Most visitors wander about without guides, but a far better plan is to call local historian and preservationist **Sharon Wells** (1hr 30min; $20; ⊤294-8380, ⓔsharon@seekeywest.com). Her informative tour includes the grave of an E. Lariz, whose stone reads "devoted fan of singer Julio Iglesias," and the resting place of Thomas Romer, a Bahamian born in 1789. He died 108 years later and was "a good citizen for 65 of them." Look out also for the fenced grave of Dr Joseph Otto. Included on the plot is the grave of his pet deer, Elphina, and three of his Yorkshire terriers, one of whom is described as being "a challenge to love."

A fifteen-minute walk from the cemetery, at 1431 Duncan St, is the modest two-story clapboard **house** kept by **Tennessee Williams**, which is not open to the public. Unlike his more flamboyant counterparts, Williams – Key West's longest-residing literary figure, made famous by his steamy evocations of Deep South life in plays such as *A Streetcar Named Desire* and *Cat on a Hot Tin Roof* – kept a low profile during his 34 years here (he arrived in 1941 and died in 1985).

The rest of Key West

There's not much more to Key West beyond its compact Old Town. Most of the **eastern section** of the island – encircled by the north and south sections of Roosevelt Boulevard – is residential, but Key West's longest beach is located here, and there are several minor points of botanical, natural and historical interest.

At the southern end of White Street, **West Martello Tower** is one of two Civil War lookout points complementing Fort Zachary Taylor (see p.161). Despite its original military purpose, it's now filled by the intoxicating colors and smells Though it makes a nice outdoor break, a more worthwhile target is the tower's of a **tropical garden** (Wed–Sun 9.30am–3.30pm; free; ⊤294-3210). Though it makes a nice outdoor break, a more worthwhile target is the tower's sister fort, East Martello Tower, which now incorporates a museum (see opposite).

From the tower, Atlantic Avenue quickly intersects with South Roosevelt Boulevard, which skirts on one side the lengthy but slender Smathers Beach – the weekend parade ground of Key West's most toned physiques and a haunt of windsurfers and parasailors – and on the other side the forlorn salt ponds of the **Thomas Riggs Wildlife Refuge**. From a platform raised above the refuge's mangrove entanglements, you should spot a variety of wading birds prowling the grass beds for crabs and shrimp. Save for the roar of planes in and out of the nearby airport, the refuge is a quiet and tranquil place; to gain admission you have to phone the Audubon House (⊤294-2116) to learn the combination of the locked gate.

Half a mile further, just beyond the airport, the **East Martello Museum and Gallery** (daily 9.30am–5pm; adults $3, under-13s $1) is the second of the two Civil War lookout posts. The solid, vaulted casements now store a fascinating assemblage on local history, plus the wild junk-sculptures of legendary Key Largo scrap dealer Stanley Papio, and the Key West scenes created in wood by a Cuban-primitive artist called Mario Sanchez. There are also displays on local writers, and memorabilia from films shot in Key West; the island's old houses and dependable climate have made it a popular location – in recent years, the final scenes of Sydney Pollack's *Havana* were shot here.

Eating

While there are some excellent places to thrill the palate – and despite the abundant **restaurants** and **snack stands along** the main streets – it's difficult to eat cheaply in Key West. There's no shortage of chic venues for fine French, Italian and Asian cuisine, but if you want really good, inexpensive food and don't want to resort to fast-food chains, visit any of the **Cuban sandwich shops**, which also do filling, tasty meals at a fraction of the price of a main-street pizza. Explore streets off the beaten path and understand that the less a place is hyped, the better the quality will normally be. Most menus, not surprisingly, feature fresh **seafood**, and you should sample **Conch fritters** – a Key West speciality – at least once.

Cafés, bakeries and sandwich shops

Blond Giraffe, 629 Duval St (☎293-6667). Great place to try award-winning Key Lime pie (you can even watch them make it) as well as gourmet coffees and, surprisingly, Argentine (though they claim it's Brazilian) *mate* tea – and the benches are perfectly positioned for people-watching.

Blue Heaven Bake Shop, 309 Petronia St (☎296-0867). This remains the funkiest café on the island, with superb muffins, sweet pies, gateaux and breads. A taste of Sixties hedonism in Bahama Village. See also *Blue Heaven Café* overleaf.

Camille's, 703 Duval St (☎296-4811). Laid-back lunches and (more expensive) dinners, but renowned for its locally acclaimed breakfasts, splendid atmosphere and luscious, casual food. Try a brunch of shrimp cakes, blueberry pancakes or French toast with mango coconut cream sauce for $6. For what you get, at around $20–25, dinner is slightly overpriced.

Conch Shop, 308 Petronia St, next to Johnson's Grocery (☎294-4140). Basic formica tables and a staff sweating over bubbling oil makes this down-to-earth eatery (serving "soul & sea food" since 1953) appear kind of gritty. Be brave – the fritters, served with potato salad and iced tea or jungle punch are excellent and very well priced. Erratic opening hours, especially on the weekend.

Croissants de France, 816 Duval St (☎294-2624). Once known for its freshly baked cream cakes and pastries, this still-popular address is now hit and miss – they still have good coffee, though.

Dennis Pharmacy, 1229 Simonton St (☎294-1890). A real drugstore dining experience with superb *café con leche* and set breakfasts. The service is no-frills, but there's plenty of local gossip to overhear while you sip. Only open until 5pm.

Dining in the Raw, 800 Olivia St (☎295-2600). There isn't much room to sit, but the exquisite mid-priced vegetarian (mostly vegan) dishes can be prepared for takeout. Desserts are to die for and include non-dairy pecan pie, raw apple cobbler and iced herbal teas to wash it all down. You can call ahead to place takeout orders.

Five Brothers Grocery, intersection of Southard and Grinnell streets (☎296-5205). Expect long lines at this age-old grocery store, perfect for strong Cuban coffee and cheap Cuban sandwiches. This is a real neighborhood find – locals love it.

Johnson's Grocery, 800 Thomas St in Bahama Village (☎294-8680). Stop here for an ice-cold beer and the freshest sandwiches in town. Their small café also does great breakfasts and lunches. Closed Sun.

Just for Loco's, just off Duval at 517 Truman Ave (☎296-1177). Tiny, inexpensive diner serving authentic Cuban, Mexican and Tropical dishes that'll fill you up. Great *café Cubano* and outstanding tacos. Daily 8am–4pm.

Sandy's Café, 1026 White St (☎295-0193). A deliciously dingy shack serving terrific, cheap Cuban sandwiches. Try the Cuban-mix sandwich, $3.50.

Restaurants

A&B Lobster House, 700 Front St (☎294-5880). Overlooking the town's harbor, there could hardly be a more scenic setting for indulging in a luxury fresh seafood dinner. If you find the prices too rich (or want to eat at lunchtime), try *Alonso's* raw bar upstairs that is run by the same people at about half the price.

Alice's at La-Te-Da, 1125 Duval St (☎292-4888). This place has great walnut fritters and an eclectic menu that ranges from passionfruit salad to rack of lamb. Quite pricey and attracts a mainly gay crowd.

Antonia's, 615 Duval St (☎294-6565). Excellent northern Italian cuisine served in a formal though friendly environment; dinner only – expensive but worth it.

Around the World, 627 Duval St (☎296-2115). Dishes drawn from every corner of the globe; if nothing appeals, tuck into the sizeable salads and sample the extensive selection of wines and beers.

Blue Heaven Café, corner of Thomas and Petronia streets (☎296-0867). Sit in this dirt yard in Bahama Village, watch the roosters wander from table to table, and enjoy the superb, fresh local fish dishes. It's not cheap but it's a must.

BO's Fish Wagon, 801 Caroline St (☎294-9272). The over-the-counter fish'n'chips and Conch frit-

ters claim to be the cheapest in town. Closed Sun.

Café des Artistes, 1007 Simonton St (☎294-7100). Pricey but fine tropical-French cuisine, serving the freshest local seafood, lobster and steak. Dinner only; reservation recommended.

Café Marquesa, 600 Fleming St (☎292-1244). Attractive small café offering an imaginative new American-style vegetarian-based menu at moderate prices.

Caribe Soul, 425 Grinnell St (☎296-0094). Moderately priced Caribbean dishes, well presented in laid-back surroundings – try the shrimp eggs Benedict for breakfast.

Duffy's Steak & Lobster House, 1007 Simonton St (☎296-4900). Usually packed. As the name suggests, there's an immense selection of steak and lobster dishes, all at around $20–30 a head.

El Siboney, 900 Catherine St (☎296-4184). Inexpensive traditional Cuban dishes and a casual atmosphere. Open for breakfast, lunch and dinner. Recommended.

Mangia Mangia, 900 Southard St (☎294-2469). Best-value Italian restaurant on the island, with fine fresh pasta (you can watch them making it in their front window), a nice atmosphere and good prices.

Mangoes, 700 Duval St (☎292-4606). Eat indoors or outdoors under huge umbrellas; high-quality seafood and steaks served in sumptuous sauces, and a variety of vegetarian dishes created with a Caribbean slant. Excellent service.

Seven Fish Restaurant, 632 Olivia St (☎296-2777). Not cheap, but not hyped up for the tourist market either. The food, primarily fish, is excellent and very fresh.

Nightlife

The carefully cultivated "anything goes" nature of Key West is exemplified by the **bars** that make up the bulk of the island's **nightlife**. Gregarious, rough-and-ready affairs, often open until 4am and offering a cocktail of yarn-spinning locals, revved-up tourists and (often) live blues, funk, country, folk or rock music. The mainstream bars are grouped around the northern end of Duval Street, no more than a few minutes' stagger apart. Much of Key West's best nightlife, though, revolves around its eateries, and the best are far from Mallory Square's well-beaten path.

Bars, clubs and live music venues

The Afterdeck at Louie's Backyard, junction of Vernon and Waddell streets (☎295-1061) Peacefully located far from Duval Street, this is a classy and sophisticated hangout on the water, behind a classy and expensive restaurant. Open until 2am.

The Bull, 224 Duval St (☎296-4565). This bar is loud and rowdy, featuring the best of local musicians each night – mainly blues and R & B. Check the list on the door to see who's playing – or just turn up to drink. Open till 4am nightly.

Captain Tony's Saloon, 428 Greene St (☎294-1838). This rustic saloon was the original *Sloppy*

Joe's (see below), a renowned hangout of Ernest Hemingway – he met his third wife, Martha Gellhorn, here. Live music of various kinds every night.

El Meson de Pepe, next to Mallory Square at 410 Wall St (☏295-2620). Cuban-style restaurant/bar in a converted warehouse, funkily decked out with brightly colored murals and the obligatory black-and-white photos of 1950s Havana. Has a pleasant tiki bar in the garden (great at sunset), and nightly live Cuban music to which some of the patrons attempt to dance. Serves reasonably tasty Cuban-Conch (that's Cuban food made more palatable to mid-Westerners).

Epoch, 623 Duval St (☏296-8521). On the site of the fabled *Copa*, which burned down in 1995, this techno-loud disco is the biggest in town, and aimed at the younger crowd – special offers run along the lines of "puke all you can for $20."

Green Parrot Bar, 601 Whitehead St (☏294-6133). A Key West landmark since 1890, this bar draws local characters to its pool tables, dart-board and pinball machine, and offers various types of live music on weekends.

Hog's Breath Saloon, 400 Front St (☏292-2032). Very popular as a result of endless hype, this is a place to drink yourself silly and then buy a T-shirt to prove it. Nightly live rock, blues or funk bands play for a nominal cover charge.

Margaritaville, 500 Duval St (☏292-1435). Owner Jimmy Buffett – a Florida legend for his rock ballads extolling a laid-back life in the sun – occasionally pops up to join the live country bands that play here nightly.

Rumrunners, 201 Duval St (☏294-1017). A multi-level entertainment complex showcasing live rock, with both indoor and open-air dance-floors where DJs play a wide range of musical styles. Cheap and tasty food too.

Schooner Wharf, at the marina end of William St (☏292-9520). A large, dark dance-floor, unusual music styles and lots of cocktails fill this laid-back bar.

Sloppy Joe's, 201 Duval St (☏294-5717). Despite the memorabilia on the walls and the hordes of tourists, this bar – with live rock or blues nightly – is not the one made famous by Ernest Hemingway's patronage. For the real thing, see *Captain Tony's Saloon*, opposite.

Turtle Kraals, Land's End Village, end of Margaret St (☏294-2640). A locals' hangout, offering fine views over the marina and mellow blues on Friday and Saturday nights from the second-story *Tower Bar*.

Two Friends, 512 Front St (☏296-3124). A small, friendly restaurant/bar with live jazz every night but Monday.

Virgilio's, adjoining *La Trattoria* at 524 Duval St (☏296-1075). Very, very classy lounge-bar, with the best cocktails and live jazz around. As expensive as the Italian restaurant it shares the building with.

Wax, 42 Appleworth Lane (☏296-6667). Intimate, low-lit dance-bar playing grown-up techno and extensively patronized by what the locals refer to as "Euro-trash." Open daily 9pm–4am; usually free.

Gay and lesbian Key West

Gay life in Key West is always vibrant and attracts frolicking hordes from North America and Europe. The party atmosphere is laid-back, sometimes outrageous, and there's an exceptional level of integration between the straight and gay communities. Unlike other Florida gay centers like South Beach, Key West does a fine job at keeping the catwalk-strutting – and hand-holding – at bay (though it's always lurking at poolsides in the sun). Outside the Old Town, though, it's not always a good idea to be openly gay and there have unfortunately been reports recently of gay-bashing late at night in these areas.

The tragedy of AIDS has hit Key West hard since the mid-1980s. Many of those stricken have come to soak up the temperate climate and the very evident camaraderie of the locals. A somber but important trip to the ocean at the end of White Street reveals a striking AIDS memorial, where blocks of black granite are engraved with a roll call of those in Key West who have been struck down.

Just about all the gay bars and hotels – all from Duval Street's 800 block southwards – are male-orientated, though most are welcoming to women. Also nearby is the Gay and Lesbian Community Center at C14 Duval Square – entrance 1075 Duval St – (☏292-3223, ⓦwww.glcckeywest.org), which has all the latest information as well as literary seminars, gay–interest video screenings and lesbian social events on Fridays.

Bars

Atlantic Shores Beach Club, 511 South St (☏296-2491). Due to its wild tea-dance extrava-ganzas, this is now the place to go every Sunday. The masses – both men and women – bronze in the sun, and about thirty percent of them are nude. If you're not staying at the attached hotel (see "Accommodation" above), there's a $3 fee for a lounger and towel. Perfect for sunset watching.
Bourbon St Pub, 724 Duval St (☏296-1992). A friendly, busy bar with a huge cocktail bar where bare-but-for-G-string model boys dance till their pouches are full of dollar bills.
Divas, 711 Duval St (☏292-8500). Popular for dancing and its regular drag shows (Fri–Sun; $1–3), this is becoming a mainstay on the circuit.
Eight-O-One Bar, 801 Duval St (☏294-4737). Known for its zany daily drag shows (nightly 8.15pm; $10) in its upstairs bar. The downstairs bar is more of a pick-up joint.
La-Te-Da, 1125 Duval St (☏294-8435). The vari-ous bars and discos of this hotel complex have long been a favorite haunt of locals and visitors. Very friendly and more casually upscale (OK, expensive) than its neighbors.
One Saloon of Key West, 1 Appelrouth Lane (☏296-8118). A small, dark bar full of youngish men watching blue videos, which are a secondary attraction to the real flesh strutting on the bars.

Listings

Airport Four miles east of the Old Town, on South Roosevelt Blvd (☏296-5439). No public transport link to the Old Town; a taxi will cost around $10.
American Airlines (☏1-800/433-7300; from Miami), Delta (☏1-800/354-9822; from Orlando and Tampa), Gulfstream International (☏1-800/992-8532; from Miami and Tampa) and USAir (1-800/428-4322; from Miami, Fort Lauderdale, Orlando and Tampa) fly into Key West. Flights between Key West and Miami start at around $150 return (depending on season and availability).
Bike rental From Adventure Scooter & Bicycle Rentals, at 1 and 601 Duval St (plus five other locations around the Old Town ☏293-9933) and the *Youth Hostel*, 718 South St (☏296-5719).
Bookstores Best of all is the Key West Island Bookstore, 513 Fleming St (☏294-2904; daily 10am–9pm), packed with the works of Key West authors and Keys-related literature, and with an excellent selection of rare and second-hand books. Blue Heron at 1014 Truman Ave (☏ 296-3508,

Mon–Sat 9am–9pm, Sun if owners feel like it) is very knowledgeable and friendly. Specializing in gay studies and the works of local authors, it also has a good general stock. Flaming Maggies, 830 Fleming St (☏294-3931; daily 10am–6pm), stocks gay- and lesbian-interest books and also serves excellent coffee. Bargain Books, 1028 Truman Ave (☏294-7446; daily 7am–10pm), has a massive stock of second-hand books, usually at half the cover price.
Buses Local information ☏292-8160.
Car rental Only worth it if you're heading off to see the other Keys. All companies are based at the airport: Alamo (☏294-6675); Dollar (☏296-9921); Hertz (☏294-1039); Tropical (☏294-8136).
Cigars Key West used to be a major producer of cigars. Now they can only be purchased at La Tabaqueria in the lobby of the *Southern Cross Hotel* at 326 Duval St; on Fri, Sat & Sun you can see them being rolled.
Dive shops Diving and snorkeling trips and equip-ment rental can be arranged all over Key West. Try the highly acclaimed Southpoint Divers, 714 Duval St (☏1-800/891-DIVE, ⓦwww.southpointdivers.com), or the less expen-sive Seabreeze Reef Raider, 617 Front St (☏1-800/370-7745, ⓦwww.keywestscubadive.com). (See also "Reef trips" and "Ecology tours" below.)
Ecology tours Dan McConnell, based at Mosquito Coast Island Outfitters, 1107 Duval St (☏294-7178; ⓦwww.key-west.com/tours/mosquito), runs six-hour kayak tours of backcountry mangroves ($45 per person) filled with facts on the ecology and history of the Keys; there's also an opportunity to snorkel in this unique environment at 8.45am and return at 3.00pm. To explore the reef by boat, join the informative half- or full-day tours aboard the 65-foot schooner *Reef Chief* (☏292-1345 or check ⓦwww.reefchief.com for details).
Greyhound Office at airport (☏296-9072).
Hospitals 24-hour casualty department at Lower Florida Keys Medical Center, 5900 College Rd, Stock Island (☏294-5531).
Late food shops Owls, 712 Caroline St, daily until 11pm; Sunbeam Market, 500 White St, never closes.
Library 700 Fleming Ave (☏292-3395); book sale on the first Saturday of each winter month.
Newsagents L. Valladares & Son, 1200 Duval St, stocks British and Irish newspapers and a vast selection of magazines from the US and elsewhere.
Parking 24-hour parking is available at the corner of Caroline and Grinnell streets ($1.25/hr, $8/day; ☏293-6426).

Police Emergency ☎911, non-emergency ☎296-2424.

Post office 400 Whitehead St (Mon 8.30am–5pm, Tues–Fri 9.30am–5pm, Sat 9.30am–noon; ☎294-2257; zip code 33040).

Reef trips *The Discovery* glass-bottomed boat makes three two-hour trips a day from the northern tip of Duval St to the Florida Reef; around $20, phone for times and price (☎293-0099). For snorkeling and diving, see "Dive shops," above.

Supermarket Fausto's Food Palace, 522 Fleming St (Mon–Sat 8am–8pm, Sun 8am–6pm) or, for big supermarkets, head for the Overseas Market between N.Rooservelt Blvd and Paterson Ave.

Taxi Unlikely to be necessary except to get to the airport (see above); try Five (☎296-6666) or Friendly Cab (☎292-0000).

Watersports Jetskiing, waterskiing and parasailing are all possible, in the right conditions, using outlets set up alongside Smathers Beach. For more details phone Sunset Watersports (☎296-2554) or Seabago Watersports (☎294-5687).

Beyond Key West: the Dry Tortugas

Seventy miles west of Key West in the Gulf of Mexico is a small group of islands that the sixteenth-century Spaniard Juan Ponce de León named the **Dry Tortugas** for the large numbers of turtles (*tortugas* in Spanish) he found there – the "dry" was added later to warn mariners of the islands' lack of fresh water. Comprising Garden Key and its neighboring reef islands, the entire area has been designated a wildlife sanctuary to protect the nesting grounds of the sooty tern – a black-bodied, white-hooded bird that's unusual among terns for choosing to lay its eggs in scrubby vegetation and bushes. From early January, these and a number of other winged rarities show up on Bush Key, and they are easily spied with binoculars from Fort Jefferson on Green Key (see below)

Fort Jefferson

Green Key is the last place you'd expect to find the US's largest nineteenth-century coastal fortification, but **FORT JEFFERSON** (daily during daylight hours), which rises mirage-like in the distance as you approach, is exactly that. Started in 1846 and intended to protect US interests on the gulf, the fort was never completed, despite thirty years of building. Instead it served as a prison, until intense heat, lack of fresh water, outbreaks of disease and savage weather made the fort as unpopular with its guards as its inmates; in 1874, after a hurricane and the latest yellow fever outbreak, it was abandoned.

Following the signposted **walk** around the fort and viewing the odds and ends in the small museum won't take more than an hour – and spare time should be allocated to **swimming** and **snorkeling**: get a free map of the best locations from the park ranger's office by the entrance.

You can **get to the fort** by air in half an hour with *Seaplane of Key West* from Sunset Marina, 5603 Junior College Rd, Stock Island ($179 half-day, $305 full day; ☎294-6978) – a beautiful trip that takes you low over the turquoise water. Less expensive and more relaxed is the Tortugas high-speed ferry, *Yankee Freedom II*, which leaves from the Key West Sea Port on Monday, Wednesday and Saturday at 8am (☎1-800/YANKEECAT; $95, under-15s $60). The price includes breakfast, lunch, guided tour and snorkel gear. After a few leisurely hours at the fort, the ferry returns at 5.30pm. Avid birdwatchers can **camp** at Fort Jefferson for up to twenty days, though given its lack of amenities you have to come well prepared with your own supplies of water and food; only in an emergency can you count on help from the park ranger. A round-trip ferry ticket including tent camping costs $109, under-15s $79.

TRAVEL DETAILS

Buses

Three Greyhound buses a day run between Miami and Key West. Scheduled stops are listed below, though the bus can be waved down at other stops – stand by the side of the Overseas Highway and jump about like a maniac when you see the bus coming.

Scheduled stops are in: North Key Largo (Central Plaza, 103200 Overseas Highway; ☏451-6280); Islamorada (Burger King, MM82; ☏852-4266); Marathon (6363 Overseas Highway; ☏743-3488); Big Pine Key (MM30.2; ☏872-4022); Key West (junction Duval, Simonton and Virginia streets; and Key West International Airport (☏296-9072).

From Miami to: Big Pine Key (3hr 50min); Islamorada (2hr 20min); Key West (4hr 30min); Marathon (3hr 20min); North Key Largo (1hr 55min).

Ferries

A passenger-only ferry service operated by X-press (☏1-800/650-5397, ⓦ www.xp2kw.com) will take you from Key West across to Fort Myers on the Gulf of Mexico side of mainland Florida (see "West Coast" chapter p.371). The ferry leaves from the A & B Marina on Front Street, and is a good way of getting to Florida's west coast without zigzagging back across the Keys and through the Everglades. The ferry runs daily – weather permitting – only at 5.30pm and ticket prices are $70 one way, or $119 for a round-trip – though there's a $10 surcharge on return tickets if you don't come back the same day.

Planes

A more sensible option is to fly on an island hopper and Cape Air (☏1-800/352-0714, ⓦ *www.flycapeair.com*) flies to Naples, Fort Meyers and Fort Lauderdale from Key West daily.

The Southeast Coast

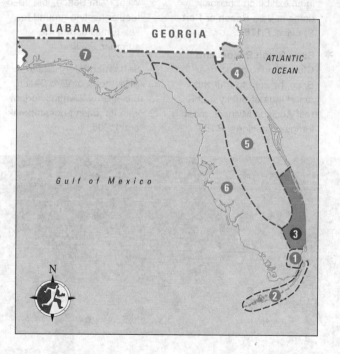

CHAPTER 3

Highlights

* **Fort Lauderdale** The town's reputation as a haven for teens and retirees has begun to diminish, and some lovely buildings and a fine museum make its downtown an inviting target. **P.176**

* **Spring training** If you're here in the springtime, take in an exhibition baseball game at Vero Beach or Port St Lucie. **P.178**

* **Boca Raton Resort and Club** If you're going near Boca, be sure to tour this resort, one of quirky architect Addison Mizner's most intriguing designs. **P.187**

* **Morikami Museum and Japanese Gardens** You'll feel like you've been transported to Japan after stepping into an intricate tea ceremony here. **P.189**

* **Hobe Sound National Wildlife Refuge** This refuge on Jupiter Island, north of West Palm Beach, is a spectacular nesting ground for sea turtles during the summer. **P.200**

* **Sebastian Inlet** Sixteen Miles north of Vero Beach, this inlet challenges surfers with its roaring ocean breakers. **P.205**

The Southeast Coast

Stretching from the fringes of northern Miami along almost half of Florida's Atlantic shoreline, the 130-mile **SOUTHEAST COAST** is the sun-soaked Florida of the popular imagination, with bodies bronzing on palm-dotted beaches as warm ocean waves lap idly against silky-soft sands. Roughly half the region forms one of the fastest-growing residential areas in the state, however, leaving many of the once spectacular ocean strips walled by unappealing high-rises. While you can drop your beach towel just about anywhere, don't spend all your time on the Southeast Coast cultivating a tan. Take the time to explore some of the towns and seek out the undeveloped, protected sections, where you'll experience the Florida coastline as nature intended it. The **Gold Coast**, the first fifty-odd miles of the Southeast Coast up to Palm Beach, lies deep within the sway of Miami and comprises back-to-back conurbations often with little to tell them apart. However, the first and largest, **Fort Lauderdale**, is certainly distinctive: the reputation for rowdy beach parties – stemming from its years as a student Spring Break destination – is well out of date; the town has cultivated a cleaner-cut, sophisticated and posher image, aided by an excellent art museum and an ambitious downtown improvement project. Further north, diminutive **Boca Raton**, which possesses some of the Gold Coast's finest beaches, is renowned for its 1920s Mediterranean Revival buildings. Boca Raton was shaped by the unconventional architect Addison Mizner, but the latter is best remembered for his work in **Palm Beach**, which is now inhabited almost exclusively by multimillionaires, yet accessible to visitors of all budgets.

North of Palm Beach, the population thins, and nature asserts itself forcefully throughout the **Treasure Coast**. Here, rarely crowded beaches flank long, pine-coated barrier islands such as Jupiter and Hutchinson islands, whose miles of untainted shoreline are quiet enough for sea turtles to come ashore and lay their eggs.

By car, the scenic route along the Southeast Coast is **Hwy-A1A**, which sticks wherever possible to the ocean side of the **Intracoastal Waterway**. Beloved of Florida's boat owners, this stretch was formed when the rivers dividing the mainland from the barrier islands were joined and deepened during World War II to reduce the threat of submarine attack. When necessary, Hwy-A1A turns inland and links with the much less picturesque **Hwy-1**. The speediest road in the region, **I-95**, runs about ten miles west of the coastline, splitting the residential sprawl from the wide-open Everglades, and is only worthwhile if you're in a hurry.

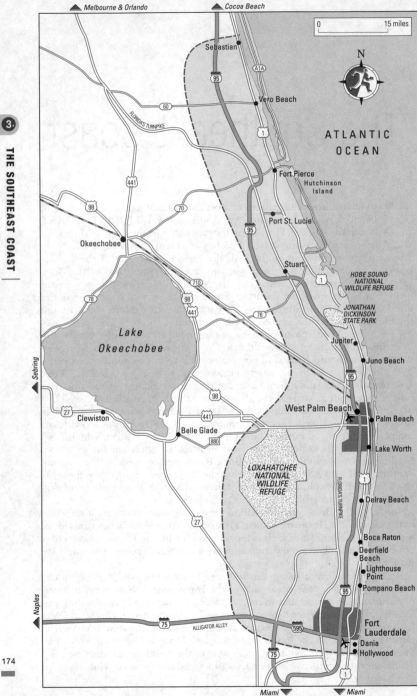

Melbourne & Orlando

Cocoa Beach

0   15 miles

N

Sebastian

A1A

95

60

Vero Beach

1

FLORIDA'S TURNPIKE

ATLANTIC
OCEAN

441

Fort Pierce

Hutchinson
Island

98

70

95

Port St. Lucie

Okeechobee

1

Stuart

HOBE SOUND
NATIONAL
WILDLIFE REFUGE

710

98
441

76

JONATHAN
DICKINSON
STATE PARK

78

Lake
Okeechobee

Jupiter

95

Juno Beach

98

Sebring

West Palm Beach

27

Clewiston

441

Palm Beach

Belle Glade

880

Lake Worth

LOXAHATCHEE
NATIONAL
WILDLIFE
REFUGE

FLORIDA'S TURNPIKE

Delray Beach

1

Boca Raton

27

Deerfield
Beach

Lighthouse
Point

95

Pompano Beach

Naples

75

ALLIGATOR ALLEY

595

Fort
Lauderdale

75

Dania

Hollywood

Miami

Miami

Frequent Greyhound connections link the bigger towns, and a few daily services run to the smaller communities. Local **buses**, plentiful from the edge of Miami to West Palm Beach, are nonexistent in the more rural Treasure Coast. Along the Gold Coast, there's the additional option of the dirt-cheap Tri-Rail rush-hour service, while Amtrak has two daily **trains** running as far north as West Palm Beach.

The Gold Coast

The widely admired beaches and towns occupying the fifty-mile commuter corridor north of Miami make the **GOLD COAST** – named for the booty washed ashore from sunken Spanish galleons – one of the most heavily populated and tourist-besieged parts of the state. The sands sparkle, the nightlife rocks, and many of the communities have an assertively individualistic flavor – but if you're seeking peace and seclusion, look elsewhere.

Hollywood

From Miami Beach, Hwy-A1A runs through undistinguished Hallandale before reaching **HOLLYWOOD** – founded and named by a Californian in 1924 – with a generous beach and a more cheerful persona than the better-known and much larger Fort Lauderdale, ten miles north. Allocate an hour to the three-mile-long pedestrian-only **Broadwalk**, parallel to Hwy-A1A (known here as Ocean Drive), whose snack bars and skateboarders enliven a casual amble, and the **Art and Culture Center of Hollywood**, 1650 Harrison St (Tues–Sat 10am–4pm, Sun 1–4pm; $3; ☎954/921-3274), which exhibits works by emergent Florida artists.

Modestly priced **motels** line Hollywood's oceanside streets. For good value try the *Stardust Motel*, 915 N Ocean Drive (☎1-800/354-1718; ❸), or the *Dolphin*, 342 Pierce St (☎1-800/922-4498, ⓦwww.thedolphinhotel.com; ❸). As usual, you'll save a few dollars by staying further inland, where the *Shell Motel*, 1201 S Federal Hwy (☎954/923-8085, ⓦwww.shellmotelhollywood.com; ❷), has the best rates.

On the whole, Hollywood's **nightlife** has plenty to enjoy. Solid blues and R&B (with occasional jazz) are the staple of *Club M*, 2037 Hollywood Blvd (☎954/925-8396), as well as at the mellow *O'Hara's Jazz Pub*, 722 E Las Olas Blvd (☎954/524-1764). Raunchy rock and roll prevails at the *J&S Restaurant* *and Lounge,* 5701 Johnson St (℡ 954/966-6196), on Friday and Saturday nights; live blues (Thurs–Sun) and Japanese food (daily) are on offer, for dinner only, at the small and rather pricey *Sushi Blues*, 1836 S Young Circle (℡ 954/929-9560); and if you fancy a drink right on the beach, accompanied by live jazz and Jamaican food, make for *Sugar Reef Tropical Bar and Grill*, 600 N Surf Rd (℡ 954/922-1119; closed Tues in summer).

A cheap, intimate place to **eat** Thai food is *Try My Thai*, 2003 Harrison St (℡ 954/926-5585). You may also want to try *Dave & Busters*, 3000 Oakwood Blvd (℡ 954/923-5505), for standard American fare with plenty of hi-tech bar games, or the awesome techno decor but pricier food at *Revolution 2029*, 2029 Harrison St (℡ 954/920-4748). For a shoreside **drink**, you can't beat *Ocean's Eleven Lounge*, 3111 N Surf Rd (℡ 954/927-5549), a bit of a hike from the center but much the better for it – they also do breakfasts from 8am onwards.

Dania

Ocean Drive continues north into **DANIA**, whose prime asset isn't the grouping of pseudo-English antique shops along Hwy-1 but the pine trees and sands of the **John U Lloyd Beach State Recreational Area**, 6503 N Ocean Drive (daily 8am–sunset; cars $3.25, pedestrians and cyclists $1). Situated on a peninsula jutting out into the entrance to the shipping terminal of Port Everglades, the 251-acre park provides an enjoyable, 45-minute nature trail around its mangrove, seagrape and guava trees. If you're around during June and July (Wed & Fri 9pm), you can find out about loggerhead turtle watching; trips include a twenty-minute slide presentation and a visit to a nest if one is available, but try to book a month or so in advance as they are immensely popular – and take plenty of insect repellent. Check with a park ranger (℡ 954/923-2833) for details on this and other scheduled activities.

With more time to spare, visit the **Graves Museum of Archaeology and Natural History**, 481 S Federal Hwy (Tues–Sat 10am–4pm, Thurs until 8pm, Sun 1–4pm; $5; ℡ 954/925-7770), where copious Tequesta Indian artifacts that were unearthed locally mark an excellent pre-Columbian collection, augmented by items from Africa and Egypt.

Towards Fort Lauderdale: by boat, car or bus

To continue north without a car you can use local bus #1 (which you can catch at any BCT stop on Hwy-1), or the pricier Greyhound, 1707 Tyler St in Hollywood (℡ 954/922-8228). Alternatively, if you're not weighed down by luggage, call the Water Taxi (℡ 954/467-6677) to ferry you from the recreational area to any dockable part of Fort Lauderdale – see "Fort Lauderdale" p.178 for more details.

Fort Lauderdale

A thinly populated riverside trading camp at the turn of the century, **FORT LAUDERDALE** came to be known as "the Venice of America" when its mangrove swamps were fashioned into slender canals during the Twenties.

The area code for Hollywood, Dania and Fort Lauderdale is ℡ 954.

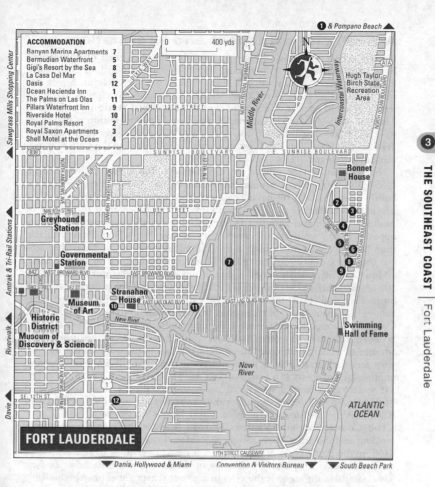

ACCOMMODATION

Banyan Marina Apartments	7
Bermudian Waterfront	5
Gigi's Resort by the Sea	8
La Casa Del Mar	6
Oasis	12
Ocean Hacienda Inn	1
The Palms on Las Olas	11
Pillars Waterfront Inn	9
Riverside Hotel	10
Royal Palms Resort	2
Royal Saxon Apartments	3
Shell Motel at the Ocean	4

FORT LAUDERDALE

From the Thirties on, intercollegiate swimming contests drew the nation's youth here, a fact seized upon by the 1960 teen-exploitation film, *Where the Boys Are*, which instantly made Fort Lauderdale the US's number one Spring Break venue. Hundreds of thousands of students congregated around the seven miles of sand for a six-week pre-exam frenzy of underage drinking and lascivious excess, earning the place a global reputation for rambunctious beach life. By the late Seventies, the students were also bringing six weeks of traffic chaos, and proving a deterrent to regular tourists. Fighting back, the local authorities began a negative advertising campaign across the country's campuses in the early Nineties, enacting strict laws to restrict boozing and wild behavior around the beach.

Subsequently, Fort Lauderdale has emerged as an affluent business, historical and cultural center dominated by a mix of wealthy retirees and affluent yuppies keen to play down the beach-party tag and play up the town's settler-period history. It's a pleasant place (with a flourishing gay scene, see "Gay Fort Lauderdale" below), and a long way from the social inferno you might have been led to expect.

Arrival, city transport and information

Known as Federal Highway, Hwy-1 plows through the center of **downtown Fort Lauderdale**, three miles inland from the coast. Just south of downtown, **Hwy-A1A** veers oceanwards off Hwy-1 along SW Seventeenth Street and runs through beachside Fort Lauderdale. All the long-distance public transport terminals are in or near downtown: the Greyhound **bus station** is at 515 NE Third St (☏954/764-6551), while the **train** and Tri-Rail station is two miles west at 200 SW 21st Terrace (Amtrak ☏1-800/872-7245, ⓦwww.amtrak.com; Tri-Rail ☏1-800-TRI-RAIL, ⓦwww.trirail.com), linked to the center by regular buses #10 and #22.

The handiest service offered by the thorough **local bus** network (BCT ☏954/357-8400, ⓦwww.brouard.org/bct) is the #11, which runs twice hourly along Las Olas Boulevard between downtown Fort Lauderdale and the beach; **timetables** are available from Governmental Center, at the corner of Andrews Avenue and Broward Boulevard, or from the bus terminal directly opposite. If you are using the buses, remember to buy a **Buz Pass** (available from bus drivers; $2.50), which allows unlimited travel on the buses throughout Broward County – otherwise it's $1 a journey and there are no transfers.

More expensive than buses – but more fun – are **water taxis** (daily 10am–midnight; ☏954/467-6677, ⓦwww.watertaxi.com, a series of small boats that will pick up and deliver you almost anywhere along Fort Lauderdale's many miles of waterfront, from Broward up to Seventeenth Street Causeway. Though these taxis are without a doubt the best way to see the city, be aware that they can often run late, and you must be sure to call well in advance of midnight in order to assure a ride home (if you're eating out, ask your server to arrange a pick-up after your meal). An all-day pass, allowing unlimited usage, costs $16 (single tickets are $7.50).

If you'd rather have a structured water tour of the city, the *Jungle Queen* (☏954/462-5596) offers dinner cruises and riverboat tours of Millionaire's Row, the Venetian Isles and the New River Jungles.

The **Convention and Visitors Bureau** is inside the port administration building at 1850 Eller Drive, Suite 303 (Mon–Fri 8.30am–5pm; ☏954/765-4466) in the Port Everglades area, which is nearly impossible to find without a car. You're better off picking up a copy of the free *CityLink* magazine or *New Times* (available throughout the city) to find out what's going on. Also available is a free **tourism and cultural hotline** (☏954/527-5600), staffed by operators fluent in five languages. Unlike most of Florida, Fort Lauderdale also has a

---

Professional sports venues

Sports enthusiasts will find the Greater Fort Lauderdale area a hub of professional athletic activity: you can catch the spring training (in March) of baseball's Baltimore Orioles at Fort Lauderdale Stadium (☏954/938-4890) and, during the regular season, watch the Florida Marlins (☏305/626-7400, ⓦwww marlins.mlb.com) at Pro Player Stadium, 2269 NW 199th St, sixteen miles northwest of downtown Miami. August sees the preseason training of NFL's Miami Dolphins (☏305/620-2578, ⓦwww.miamidolphins.com) in nearby Davie; during the regular season they, too, play in Pro Player Stadium. The National Car Rental Center at 2555 Panther Parkway, just west of Fort Lauderdale in Sunrise, is home to the Florida Panthers hockey team (☏954/835-7000, ⓦwww.floridapanthers.com). It's also not far to the Miami Areana, 701 Arena Blvd, to see the Miami Heat (☏305/530-4444, ⓦwww.nba.com/heat) play professional basketball.

number of good **bookstores**, including The Book Rack (Mon–Sat 10am–6pm) at 1374 SE Seventeenth St, which sells and exchanges its vast stock of fiction paperbacks. For **Internet** access, try the nearby Calling Station ($6/hr) at no. 1366, which caters to the nautical folk's communication needs.

Accommodation

A handy free booklet, *Superior Small Lodgings Guide*, is available from the Convention and Visitors Bureau (see opposite), and lists reasonably priced accommodation. Options for staying in downtown Fort Lauderdale are relatively limited, but the scores of **motels** clustered between the Intracoastal Waterway and the ocean can be exceptionally good value. If money is tight there are three **hostels** in town, mainly frequented by out-of-work deck hands: near the beach is the *Florida Beach Hostel* at 2115 N Ocean Blvd (☎954/567-7275, ⓦ www.fortlauderdalehostel.com; $16), which is clean and offers free parking, food, snorkel gear, has a pleasant rooftop patio and will pick you up from anywhere in Fort Lauderdale during the day; less centrally located are the friendly *Floyd's International Youth Hostel and Crew House*, near the junction of Hwy-1 and Seventeenth Street at 445 SE Sixteenth St (☎954/462-0631, ⓦ www.floydshostel.com; $17); and the less boisterous (and smoking-prohibited) *Villa Hostel*, over the road at 506 SE Sixteenth St (☎954/524-4681, ⓦ www.villahostel.com; $17). The closest **campground** is *Easterlin*, corner of 1000 NW 38th St and Tenth Avenue, Oakland Park (☎954/938-0610; $15 per person), three miles north of downtown and reached by bus #14.

Banyan Marina Apartments, 111 Isle of Venice (☎ 1-800/524-4431, ⓦ www.banyanmarina.com). These apartments (with a few double rooms) are on a waterway a short drive from the beach and close to Las Olas Boulevard. ❹

Bermudian Waterfront, 315 N Birch Rd (☎954/467-0467). North of the center but handy for the sea, this hotel offers one- and two-bed suites boasting fully equipped kitchens. ❸

La Casa Del Mar, 3003 Granada Blvd (☎954/467-2037). Though this attractive B&B caters mainly to a gay clientele, all are welcome to enjoy wine and cheese afternoons by the pool, and the water taxi can pick you up from a block away. Ask for the "Judy Garland Room" where the actual Munchkins slept during a film festival. ❶

Ocean Hacienda Inn, 1924 N Atlantic Blvd (☎1-800/562-8467, ⓦ www.oceanhacienda.com). This great oceanfront hotel features a tropical garden, a heated pool facing the ocean and surprisingly inexpensive rooms across the road. ❹

Pillars Waterfront Inn, 111 N Birch Rd (☎1-800-7666, ⓦ www.pillarshotel.com). This quiet, relaxing British-colonial-style hotel, with luxurious rooms, antique furniture and a pool, is only half a block from the ocean. ❼

Riverside Hotel, 620 E Las Olas Blvd (☎1-800/325-3280). Elegant, comfortable, well-placed but overpriced downtown option. ❹

Royal Saxon Apartments, 551 Breakers Ave (☎954/566-7424). Fresh flowers and fruit in every room, and a ten-minute walk to restaurants and shopping. One of the best-value finds in Fort Lauderdale. ❹

Sholl Motel at the Ocean, 3030 Bayshore Drive (☎954/463-1723, ⓦ www.shelmotel.com). This cheerful, well-equipped motel is a stone's throw from the beach. ❸

Downtown Fort Lauderdale

Tall, anonymous, glass-fronted buildings make an uninspiring first impression, but **downtown Fort Lauderdale** has an outstanding modern art museum and a number of restored older buildings to usefully occupy several hours. Because of a multi-million-dollar effort to prettify the district, parks and promenades are linked by the pedestrian-only, one-and-a-half-mile **Riverwalk** along the north bank of the New River, which ends at the state-of-the-art Museum of Discovery and Science.

The Museum of Art

In a postmodern structure shaped like a slice of pie, the **Museum of Art**, 1 E Las Olas Blvd (Tues–Sat 10am–5pm, Sun noon–5pm, $15; guided tours Tues, Thurs & Fri 1.30pm, free; ☎954/525-5500, ⊛www.museumofart.org), provides ample space and light for the best art collection in the state, with an emphasis on modern painting and sculpture. The strongest exhibits are drawn from the museum's hoard of works from the **CoBrA** movement, which began in 1948 with a group of artists from Copenhagen, Brussels and Amsterdam (hence the acronym). CoBrA's art is typified by bright expressionistic canvases combining playful innocence with deep emotional power. Important names to look for include Asger Jorn, Carl Henning-Pedersen and Karel Appel, though many later adherents of the movement also produced formidable works, and there are plenty of them here to admire. Another attraction is the William Glackens wing, named after the early nineteenth-century American impressionist who painted most of the pieces exhibited here while in France.

The historic district and the Stranahan House

For a quick look at Fort Lauderdale's past, walk a few blocks west from the Art Museum to the **historic district**, at the center of which is the **Historical Society**, on Riverwalk at 219 SW Second Ave (Tues–Fri 10am–4pm; $3; ☎954/463-4431). Here you can pick up details on walking tours past (and sometimes inside) three of the oldest buildings in Fort Lauderdale, located nearby and in the process of being spruced up for the public: the 1907 **King-Cromartie House** (currently Sat only, with tours at 1pm, 2pm & 3pm), whose many then-futuristic fixtures include the first indoor bathroom in Fort Lauderdale; the three-story 1905 **New River Inn** (Tues–Sun noon–5pm; $5), which was the first hotel here and also contains a small museum of period artifacts; and the 1905 **Philomen Bryan House** (Tues–Fri 10am–4pm; free), once the home of the Bryan family, who constructed many other buildings in this area. To give perspective on the old buildings and the town's past in general, the Historical Society mounts informative temporary displays and stocks plenty of historical books and free pamphlets.

A few minutes' walk east stands a more complete reminder of early Fort Lauderdale life: the carefully restored **Stranahan House** (Mon–Sat 10am–5.30pm, Sun 1–5.30pm; $5; ☎954/524-4736, ⊛www.stranahanhouse .com), behind the Hyde Park Market on Las Olas Boulevard. Erected in 1901, with high ceilings, narrow windows and wide verandas, the building is a fine example of Florida frontier style, and served as the home and trading post of a turn-of-the-century settler, Frank Stranahan. An occasionally hokey-sounding recording tells the story of Stranahan, a prosperous dealer in otter pelts, egret plumes and alligator hides, which he purchased in 1901 from Seminole Indians trading along the river. Financially devastated by the late-Twenties Florida property crash, Stranahan drowned himself in the same waterway.

The Museum of Discovery and Science

Directly west from the historic district, and marking the end of Riverwalk, the gleaming **Museum of Discovery and Science**, 401 SW Second St (Mon–Sat 10am–5pm, Sun noon–6pm; $12.50; ⊛www.mods.org, is among the best of Florida's ample number of child-orientated science museums. However, childless adults shouldn't think twice about coming (though they should aim to avoid weekends and school holidays, when the place is packed) because the exhibits present the basics of science in numerous ingenious and entertaining ways. You can even pretend to be an astronaut, rising in an air-powered chair to realign an orbiting satellite, or making a simulated trip to the moon. The museum also contains a towering 3-D IMAX film theater (daily shows – check admission booth for times; $9 or else buy a $12.50 combination ticket for both museum and film; ☎954/467-6637).

Around Las Olas Boulevard and the beach

Downtown Fort Lauderdale is linked to the beach by **Las Olas Boulevard** – on the cutting edge of fashion, art and food (from restaurants to sidewalk cafés) – and then by the Isles, well-tended canal-side land where residents park their cars on one side of their mega-buck properties and moor their luxury yachts on the other. Once across the arching Intracoastal Waterway Bridge, about two miles on, you're within sight of the ocean and the mood changes appreciably: where Las Olas Boulevard ends, **beachside Fort Lauderdale** begins – T-shirt, sunscreen and swimwear shops are suddenly everywhere.

Along the seafront, **Ocean Boulevard** bore the brunt of Spring Break partying until the clean-up of the Eighties. The whole area has benefited from a multi-million-dollar facelift, and now only a few beachfront bars bear any trace of the carousing of the past, though the sands, flanked by graciously aging coconut palms and an attractive promenade, are by no means deserted or dull; joggers, rollerbladers and cyclists create a stereotypical beach scene, and a fair number of whooping students still turn up here each spring.

Since the bulk of Fort Lauderdale's accommodation is here, you'll have no difficulty exploring the beach, the bars, and a few other items of interest in either direction along the main strip.

South along Ocean Boulevard

A short way south of the Las Olas Boulevard Junction, the **International Swimming Hall of Fame**, 1 Hall of Fame Drive (Mon–Sat 9am–7pm, Sun 11am–4pm; $3; ☎954/462-6536), salutes aquatic sports with a collection even dedicated non-swimmers will enjoy. The two floors are stuffed with medals, trophies and press cuttings pertaining to the muscle-bound heroes and heroines of swimming, diving and many more obscure watery activities.

For a few hours of solitude, thread through the residential streets a mile further south to the placid **South Beach Park**, a restful spot at the tip of Fort Lauderdale's coastline.

North along Ocean Boulevard

The lackluster commercial complex called **BeachPlace** sits just north of the Las Olas Boulevard Junction. Here you'll find three levels of predictable shops (such as Banana Republic, Gap, Speedo) with a smattering of bars and restaurants, including *Howl at the Moon* and *Sloppy Joe's*. The good thing about BeachPlace is that you can hop up from the sand to grab a bite to eat, buy souvenir paraphernalia, or go to the rest room. Otherwise it's just another overhyped mall with a spectacular waterfront location.

Further north, in the midst of the high-rise hotels and apartment blocks that dominate the beachside area, Fort Lauderdale's pre-condo landscape can be viewed in the jungle-like 35-acre grounds of **Bonnet House**, 900 N Birch Rd (tours Wed–Fri 10.30am, 11.30am, 12.30pm & 1.30pm; Sat & Sun 12.30pm, 1.15pm, 1.45pm & 2.30pm; $9; ☎954/563-5393), a few minutes' walk off Ocean Boulevard. Turn up fifteen minutes before your chosen tour time to assure yourself a spot. The house and its surroundings – including a swan-filled pond and resident monkeys – were designed by Chicago muralist Frank Clay

Bartlett and completed in 1921. The tours of the vaguely plantation-style abode highlight Bartlett's eccentric passion for art and architecture – and for collecting ornamental animals, dozens of which fill virtually all of the thirty rooms.

Another green pocket is nearby: beside Sunrise Boulevard, the tall Australian pines of the **Hugh Taylor Birch State Recreation Area** (daily 8am–sunset; cars $3.25, pedestrians and cyclists $1) form a shady backdrop for canoeing on the park's mangrove-fringed freshwater lagoon – a good way to perk yourself up after a morning spent prostrate on the beach.

Eating

Fort Lauderdale has many affordable, enjoyable **places to eat**, featuring everything from Asian creations to homemade conch chowder. Restaurants are grouped in different sections of the town, however, and traveling between them can be difficult without a car. Note that if you take the Water Taxi (advisable, especially if you'll be drinking; see p.178), make sure to tell your server when your meal is over so they can arrange for the taxi to pick you up.

Café Europa, 726 E Las Olas Blvd (℡ 954/763-6600). Funky moderately priced café, always packed, with a mouth watering display of desserts, unusual pizza toppings and a wall full of city-skyline. Daily 10am–11.30pm/midnight.

Casablanca Café, intersection of Alhambra and Ocean blvds, opposite the beach (℡ 954/764-3500). An American piano bar in a Moroccan setting with a good, eclectic menu with moderate prices. Expect large portions of Mediterranean specialities, such as paella and Greek salad. Daily 11.30am–11.30pm.

Coconuts, 429 Seabreeze Blvd, directly on the Intracoastal Waterway (℡ 954/467-6788). Best place to watch the sunset in Fort Lauderdale, serving mid-price giant portions of prime rib, award-winning bay scallops and delicious coconut bread. Daily 11.30am–10pm.

Durty Harry's, 1368 Seventeenth St (℡ 954/524-7263). Excellent-value and filling subs, pizzas and seafood main dishes are served by cheerful waitresses at this unpretentious bar/restaurant with a mixed crowd of – mainly mature – locals and slumming boatsmen attracted by the $2.95 pitchers of beer and inexpensive nibbles that accompany them. Daily 11am–2/3am.

Ernie's BBQ Lounge, 1843 S Federal Hwy (℡ 954/523-8636). The scruffy but likeable moderately priced *Ernie's*, south of downtown, is a local legend for its glorious conch chowder (add sherry to taste). Daily 11am–2am.

The Floridian, 1410 E Las Olas Blvd (℡ 954/463-4041). Reasonable, inespensive downtown 24-hour coffee shop with a cozy diner style, where many go for the mammoth breakfasts. Lunch and dinner aren't too shabby either.

Franco & Vinny's Mexican Cantina, 2870 E Sunrise Blvd (℡ 954/565-3839). Mexican favorites are served at giveaway prices near the beach, with live music Fri and Sat nights. Daily 4pm–11pm/midnight.

Japanese Village, 716 E Las Olas Blvd (℡ 954/763-8163). Good Japanese food graces this central location at reasonable prices. Mon–Fri noon–2pm & 5.30–10.30pm.

Lester's Diner, 250 State Rd 84 (℡ 954/525-5641). Cheap diner food, with the added bonus of a kickstart of coffee served in a 32-ounce cup, is available here 24 hours a day.

Mangos, 904 E Las Olas Blvd (℡ 954/523-5001). Good mid-price pants-stuffing portions and a breezy outside dining area, perfect for listening to the roaring live jazz inside and for people watching along Las Olas Boulevard. Daily 11am–1am.

Shooters Waterfront Café, 3033 NE 32nd Ave (℡ 954/566-2855). Popular beachside restaurant drawing large crowds for its generous – though fairly pricey – portions of seafood, burgers and salads. Good place for Sunday brunch. Mon–Sat 11.30am–3am, Sun 11am–4pm.

Southport Raw Bar, 1536 Cordova Rd (℡ 954/525-CLAM). This boisterous local bar offers succulent crustaceans and well-prepared fish dishes. Daily 11.30am–2am.

Sukhothai, at Gateway Plaza, 1930 E Sunrise Blvd (℡ 954/764-0148). Tasty, moderately spiced (and priced) Thai dishes. Daily 11.30am–2.30pm & 5–10pm.

Drinking

Some of the restaurants above, particularly *Shooters* and the *Southport Raw Bar*, are also notable drinking spots. Other promising libation locations near the beach are the listed below.

Elbo Room, 241 S Fort Lauderdale Beach Blvd (☎954/463-4615). Once a Spring Break favorite, this is now the ideal place for an evening drink as the ocean breeze ruffles your hair.

Kim's Alley Bar, 1920 E Sunrise Blvd in Gateway Plaza (☎954/804-2244). A 22-foot-long African mahogany bar dominates this popular watering hole.

Parrot Lounge, 911 Sunrise Lane (☎954/563-1493). This easygoing bar specializes in oversized pitchers of beer.

Quarterdeck, 1541 Cordova Rd (☎524-6165). Nautically themed neighborhood bar that attracts locals and deck hands from the nearby hostels for its beer specials (Mon and Thurs) when you get five domestic beers for five dollars.

Shakespeare's Pub & Grille, 1015 NE 26th St (☎954/563-7833). This is the local favorite pub from which most crawls originate.

Nightlife and entertainment

To find out who's playing where, call the free Entertainment Hotline (☎954/527-5600), pick up the free *CityLink* or *New Times* magazines from newsstands or consult the "Showtime" segment of the Friday edition of the local *Sun-Sentinel* newspaper. For high culture in town, you might check out the **Broward Center for the Performing Arts**, 201 SW Fifth Ave (ticket information ☎954/462-0222, ⓦwww.curtainup.com), a pleasant, modern, waterfront building that houses Broadway shows and more offbeat productions in its intimate Amaturo Theater.

Baja Beach Club, 3200 N Federal Hwy (☎954/561-2432). If you're seeking the drunken hedonism of Spring Break, you will enjoy the regular drink specials and bikini contests here.

Bierbrunnen, 425 S Ocean Blvd (☎954/462-1008). This is a reliable venue for a variety of musical styles (Sat only) as well as German beer and bratwurst.

Cheers, 941 E Cypress Creek Rd (☎954/771-6337). Rock and roll brings the house down until 4am.

The Chilli Pepper, 200 W Broward Blvd (☎954/525-5996). The mix of techno and rock puts this among the dance venue favorites.

Desperado's Nightclub, 2520 S Miami Rd (☎954/463-2855). This joint, complete with a mechanical bull in the corner, attracts country lovers.

O'Hara's Pub, 722 E Las Olas Blvd (☎954/524-1764). This is a stylish venue for hearing jazz.

Poor House, 110 SW Third Ave (☎954/522-5145). Smoky blues and the occasional swing band are featured here.

Gay and lesbian Fort Lauderdale

Fort Lauderdale has been one of **gay** America's favorite holiday haunts for years and is often referred to as San Francisco-by-the-Sea. Like the rest of Fort Lauderdale, the scene has quieted down considerably over recent years, but there's still plenty going on. For more information, contact the Gay and Lesbian Community Center at 1717 N Andrew's Ave (Mon–Sat 10am–10pm, Sun noon–5pm; ☎954/463-9005, Ⓔglccvoice@aol.com); or pick up free copies of *Scoop* and *Hot Spots* magazines, located throughout the area.

Accommodation

Fort Lauderdale has over forty **guesthouses** aimed at gay men : the comfortable and friendly *Gigi's Resort by the Sea*, 3005 Alhambra St (☎954/463-4827, ⓦwww.gigisresort.com; ❸), clothing-optional *The Palms on Las Olas*, 1760 E Las Olas Blvd (☎1-800/550-7656, ⓦwww.palmsonlasolas.com; ❹), and the swankier *Royal Palms Resort*, 2901 Terramar St (☎954/564-6444, ⓦwww.royalpalms.com; ❼). Of the mixed motels, try *La Casa Del Mar* (see "Accommodation" p.179), or the *Oasis*, 1200 S Miami Rd (☎954/523-3043; ❸), whose inland location keeps its prices down.

Bars and clubs

Gay **bars** and **clubs** in Fort Lauderdale fall in and out of fashion; read the statewide free gay weekly newspaper, *The Weekly News*, or the free *CityLink* magazine for the latest hotspots. Usually among the pacesetters are: *Cathode Ray*, 1105 E Las Olas Blvd (℡ 954/462-8611), a video bar that steadily warms up as the evening wears on; *The Copa*, 2800 S Federal Hwy (℡ 954/463-1507), a long-running dance club that draws all ages; and *Georgie's Alibi*, 2266 Wilton Drive (℡ 954/565-2526), which is currently one of the most popular. For **eating** as well as drinking, try *Legends Café*, 1560 NE Fourth Ave (℡ 954/467-2233), a restaurant/bar that fills up quickly (it's best to make a reservation); and *Chardees*, 2209 Wilton Drive (℡ 954/563-1800), which has a lively piano bar and a fabulous Sunday brunch. The biggest – and some say best – **disco** is *The Collusion*, 2520 S Miami Rd (℡ 954/832-0100), which plays techno sounds and is open till late every weekend.

Inland from Fort Lauderdale: Davie and around

Away from its beach and downtown area, Fort Lauderdale lapses into dismal suburbia all the way to the Everglades. Most people only pass through to reach "Alligator Alley" – the familiar name for **I-75**, which speeds arrow-straight towards Florida's West Coast a hundred miles distant (see "The West Coast," p.315).

An exception to the prevailing factories, housing estates and freeway interchanges, **DAVIE** lies twenty miles from the coast on Griffin Road, surrounded by citrus groves, sugar cane and dairy pastures. Davie's 40,000 inhabitants are besotted with the Old West: jeans, plaid shirts and Stetsons are the order of the day, and there's even a hitching post (for tethering horses) outside the local McDonald's. Davie's cowboy origins go back to settlers who came here in the 1910s to herd cattle and work the fertile black soil. If you're charmed by the attire, stock up in Grifs Western, 6211 SW 45th St (℡ 954/587-9000), a leading purveyor of boots, hats and saddles; otherwise simply turn up for the rodeo, held most Saturdays at 8pm at the Davie 5 Star Rodeo, Davie Arena, 4271 Davie Rd (℡ 954/384-7075, ⓦ www.5starrodeo.com; $12) – look for the rearing white horse sign. A smaller rodeo takes place most Wednesday evenings.

Like its counterparts elsewhere in the state, the **Native Village** at the Seminole Reservation (daily 9am–4pm; $5 for a self-guided tour; $8 for a guided tour; $10 for guided tour with alligator-wrestling show; ℡ 954/961-4519), a mile south of Davie on Hwy-441, is a depressing place where plastic tomahawks are flogged to tourists. There is some sensitivity to be found, however, in the paintings by Guy LaBree, a local white man who spent time on Seminole reservations during his childhood and whose work is intended to pass legends and history on to younger Seminole generations. More likely, it's the bingo hall across the road from the village that attracts most white people: laws against high-stakes bingo don't apply to Indian reservations, and you can win $100,000 or more here. You can buy your fill of tax-free cigarettes, too.

A more entertaining attraction on the Seminole Reservation is **Billie Swamp Safari** (daily 8.30am–6.30pm; ℡ 1-800/949-6101). Hydroplane buggies resembling inflated army jeeps take visitors cruising high above the Everglades (25min $10, 1hr $20), where alligators, egrets and American buffalo are sure to be seen. An all-day pass that includes a buggy tour with an educational package on snakes and alligators is $36. You can also experience a traditional overnight camp-out in a native-style *chickee* (an open-sided, palm-thatched hut) and listen to ancient Seminole tales (a two-person *chickee* is $35 per night, eight-person dorm $65).

Twelve miles northeast of Davie at Coconut Creek, **Butterfly World**, 3600 W Sample Rd (Mon–Sat 9am–5pm, Sun 1–5pm, last admission 4pm; $13; ☏954/977-4400), stocks, as its name suggests, a massive collection of butterflies. Many are hatched here from larvae – which you'll see in the laboratory – and flap out their short lives around nectar-producing plants inside several aviaries. Exhibits include the colorful Hummingbird Habitat and the fragrant Rose Garden. Spotting Ecuadorian metalmarks, Malay sulpurs and their equally exotic peers will keep amateur lepidopterists amused for hours.

North of Fort Lauderdale

Stay on Hwy-A1A **north from Fort Lauderdale**, which is a far superior route to Hwy-1 and passes through several sedate beachside communities. One of these, **Lauderdale-by-the-Sea,** lies around four miles up the coast, and is one of the best places to don scuba-diving gear and explore the reefs.

There are two pleasant **B&Bs** here: *Blue Seas Courtyard*, 4525 El Mar Drive (☏954/772-3336; **❷**); and the excellent *A Little Inn by the Sea*, 4546 El Mar Drive (☏1-800/492-0311; **❺**), with luxurious linens and gourmet breakfasts. You'll soon find the best eateries, among them the *Aruba Beach Café*, 1 E Commercial Blvd (☏954/776-0001), where you can tickle your tastebuds with Caribbean and New World cuisine.

Pompano and Deerfield beaches

Pompano Beach, centered on Pompano Square, is just two miles on from Lauderdale-by-the-Sea. This is one of the larger beach towns, with a moderately good ocean strip. Still, there's not too much to occupy you, unless you have a particular penchant for greyhound racing. **The Pompano Harness Track**, 1800 SW Third St (☏954/972-2000, ⓦwww.pompanopark.com), is Florida's only such arena and features racing from November to early April.

Three miles further, Hwy-A1A crosses the Hillsboro Inlet, whose 1907 light house gives its name to the posh canal-side community of **Lighthouse Point**. There's nothing to detain you here except the offshore *Cap's Place* (☏954/941-0418), which can only be reached by ferry from 2765 NE 28th Court right on the Intracoastal Waterway; follow directions from NE 24th Street. The food – fresh seafood at affordable prices – is one attraction, but the fact that the restaurant doubled as an illegal gambling den during Prohibition is another: Franklin Roosevelt, Winston Churchill and the Duke of Windsor, remembered by fading photos, are just three of those who relaxed in the company of owner Cap Knight, a one-time rumrunner whose family presides over the restaurant.

More offbeat history is attached to **Deerfield Beach**, four miles on. As Hwy-A1A twists to the right, you'll catch a glimpse of the triangular Deerfield Island Park in the Intracoastal Waterway. During the Thirties, the island was almost purchased by Al Capone, who, along with gangster colleagues, frequented the swanky *Riverview Restaurant*'s casino, underneath the Hillsboro Boulevard Causeway at 1741 Riverview Rd. Capone's property bid was thwarted by his arrest for tax evasion, and the island, untarnished by development, is occupied today by raccoons and armadillos. Its two walking trails are reachable only with the free ferry from the *Riverview* on Wednesday and Saturday mornings; call ☏954/360-1320 for times.

Boca Raton and around

Directly north of Deerfield Beach, Hwy-A1A and Hwy-1 both enter Palm Beach County, the latter becoming the Stars-and-Stripes-decorated **Blue Memorial Highway**: "a tribute to the armed forces that have served the United States of America," confirming the general conservatism of the region. You can practically smell the money crossing into the county's southernmost town, **BOCA RATON** (literally "the mouth of the rat"), where smartly dressed valets park your car at supermarkets, and golf-mad retirees and executives from numerous hi-tech industries – most notably computer giant IBM – hibernate year-round. More noticeably, Boca Raton has an abundance of Mediterranean Revival architecture, a style prevalent here since the Twenties and preserved by strict building codes – the town's newer structures are obligated to incorporate arched entrance ways, fake bell towers and red-tiled roofs whenever possible. Other than the architecture, the town features some under-recognized beaches and parks.

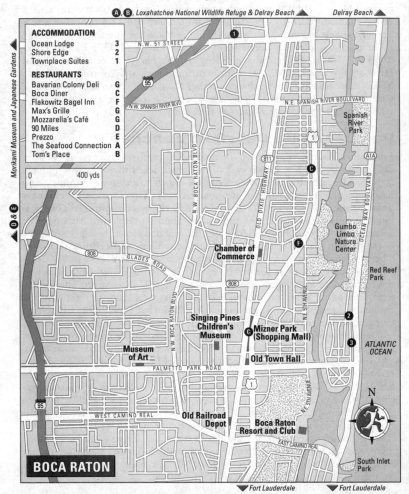

A, B, *Loxahatchee National Wildlife Refuge & Delray Beach* ▲   *Delray Beach* ▲

ACCOMMODATION

Ocean Lodge	3
Shore Edge	2
Townplace Suites	1

RESTAURANTS

Bavarian Colony Deli	G
Boca Diner	C
Flakowitz Bagel Inn	F
Max's Grille	G
Mozzarella's Café	G
90 Miles	D
Prezzo	E
The Seafood Connection	A
Tom's Place	B

0 ——— 400 yds

N.W. 51 STREET

95

N.W. SPANISH RIVER BLVD.   N.E. SPANISH RIVER BOULEVARD

Spanish River Park

N.W. BOCA RATON BLVD.   OLD DIXIE HIGHWAY   811   A1A

OCEAN WAY BOULEVARD

Gumbo Limbo Nature Center

GLADES ROAD   808   **Chamber of Commerce**   F

Red Reef Park

N.E. 5TH AVENUE

808

N.W. BOCA RATON BLVD.   **Singing Pines Children's Museum**   G **Mizner Park (Shopping Mall)**   2   ATLANTIC OCEAN   3

Museum of Art   **Old Town Hall**

PALMETTO PARK ROAD   1

95   WEST CAMINO REAL   **Old Railroad Depot**   **Boca Raton Resort and Club**   N.E. 5TH AVENUE   N

EAST CAMINO REAL

South Inlet Park

BOCA RATON

▼ *Fort Lauderdale*   ▼ *Fort Lauderdale*

Downtown Boca Raton

The origins of Boca Raton's Mediterranean-flavored architecture, which you see all over the **downtown** area, go back to **Addison Mizner**, the "Aladdin of architects" (a nickname given because of the almost magical flare in his designs, which were influenced by the Moorish styles of southern Spain), who furnished the fantasies of Palm Beach's fabulously wealthy (see p.000) through the Twenties. Unable to give reign to his megalomaniacal desires elsewhere, Mizner swept into Boca Raton on the tide of the Florida property boom after World War I, bought 1600 acres of land and began selling plots of a future community "beyond realness in its ideality." Envisaging gondola-filled canals, a luxury hotel and a great cathedral dedicated to his mother, Mizner's plans were nipped in the bud by the economic crash of 1926, and he went back to Palm Beach with his tail between his legs.

The few buildings that Mizner did manage to complete left an indelible mark on Boca Raton. His million-dollar *Cloister Inn* grew into the present **Boca Raton Resort and Club**, 501 E Camino Real (☎561/447-3000, ⓦwww.bocaresort.com ❽), a pink palace of marble columns, sculptured fountains and carefully aged wood (the centuries-old effect accomplished by the hobnailed boots of Mizner's workmen) that still claims the 160-foot-wide Camino Real – carrying traffic between Hwy-A1A and downtown Boca Raton – as its private driveway. With $200-a-night rooms, the resort might be most affordably viewed on its guided tours (Dec–April Tues 1.30pm; $5; ☎561/395-6766) run by the Boca Raton Historical Society, though staying here is certainly a treat, too.

For its part, the Historical Society resides in Mizner's more accessible dome-topped **Old Town Hall**, 71 N Federal Hwy (Mon–Fri 10am–4pm; ☎561/395-6766), completed in 1927. The society's library, detailing Mizner's times and the rest of Boca Raton's past, is worthy of scrutiny; turn left along the corridor as you enter the building. Nearby, the old railroad depot, at the junction of Dixie Highway and SE Eighth Street, is another seminal Mizner-era building but without much allure; the depot (the Count de Hoernle Pavilion) is only opened for wedding receptions and meetings, and a couple of post-Mizner streamlined locomotives stand outside.

Boca's downtown museums

The well-heeled of Boca Raton can pay homage to Mizner at Mizner Park, off Hwy-1 between Palmetto Park Road and Glades Road, not a park at all, but one of several stylish, open-air shopping malls that improved downtown Boca Raton in the Nineties. Decorated by palm trees and waterfalls, and packed with *haute couture* stores and several affordable places to eat (see "Practicalities," p.189), Mizner Park contains an open amphitheater for concerts, and is also home to the **International Museum of Cartoon Art**, 201 Plaza Real (Tues–Sat 10am–6pm, Sun noon–6pm; adults $8, students $6; ☎561/391-2200), which is a must for anyone interested in cartoon art, from Daffy Duck to political cartoons to graphic novels. The museum holds over 160,000 drawings as well as a video library.

To escape the Mizner influence altogether, go to the beaches (see overleaf) or turn west onto Palmetto Park Road for the **Singing Pines Children Museum**, 498 Crawford Blvd (Tues–Sat noon–4pm; $1; ☎561/368-6875).

Housed in a driftwood cracker cottage – the simple abode of early Florida farmers (see Contexts p.451) – the museum stocks entertaining remnants from the pioneer days alongside exhibitions aimed at kids. A mile further, the **Museum of Art**, 801 W Palmetto Park Rd (Tues, Thurs & Fri 10am–4pm, Sat & Sun noon–4pm; suggested donation $3; ℡561/392-2500), has benefited from generous patrons and inspired curatorship to become one of Florida's finest small art museums. Besides its temporary exhibitions on leading Florida artists, the museum has a permanent collection that includes the Mayers Collection of drawings by modern masters – Degas, Matisse, Picasso and Seurat are among those represented – and a formidable trove of African art.

Sports fanatics will revel in the **Sports Immortals Museum**, 6830 N Federal Hwy (Mon–Sat 10am–6pm, open Sun in summer only; $5; ℡561/997-2575), which houses an overwhelming assortment of sporting mementos, from Muhammad Ali's championship belt to the baseball that killed the ballplayer Ray Chapman in 1920.

Boca Raton's beaches

All four of Boca Raton's beaches are open to the public, but they are walled in by tall rows of Australian pine, so it is unlikely that you'll stumble across them. They tend, therefore, to be the preserve of select Floridians rather than long-distance travelers (for more detailed information contact Palm Beach County Parks and Recreation; ℡561/966-6600).

The southernmost patch, **South Inlet Park**, is the smallest and quietest of the quartet, often deserted in midweek save for a few people fishing along its short jetty. To reach it, watch for a track turning sharply right off Hwy-A1A, just beyond the Boca Raton Inlet. **South Beach Park**, a mile north, is a surfers' favorite, though the actual beach is a fairly tiny area of coarse sand. **Red Reef Park**, a mile further, is far better for sunbathing and swimming – activities that should be combined with a walk around the **Gumbo Limbo Nature Center** (Mon–Sat 9am–4pm, Sun noon–4pm; donations suggested; ℡561/338-1473), directly across Hwy-A1A, whose wide boardwalks take you through a tropical hardwood hammock and a mangrove forest beside the Intracoastal Waterway. Keep your eyes peeled for ospreys, brown pelicans and the occasional manatee lurking in the warm waters. Between May and July you can join the center's nightly tours to watch sea turtles. These can be extremely popular, however, so you'd be well advised to book as far in advance as possible.

Boca Raton's most explorable beachside area, however, is **Spanish River Park** (daily 8am–sunset; cars $8 weekdays, $10 weekends & holidays, pedestrians and cyclists free), a mile north of Red Reef Park on Hwy-A1A. Here you'll find fifty acres of lush vegetation, most of which is only penetrable on secluded trails through shady thickets. Aim for the forty-foot observation tower for a view across the park and much of Boca Raton. The adjacent beach is a slender but serviceable strip, linked to the park by several nifty tunnels beneath Hwy-A1A.

Boca Raton is also a good place from which to visit Loxahatchee National Wildlife Refuge (see p.197). It's located about ten miles north of here, just off Hwy-441 and two miles south of Boynton Beach Boulevard/Route 804. Also available is the chance to see the Everglades from an airboat. Head for **Loxahatchee Everglades Tours**, West End Lox Road, due west of Boca Raton off State Road 7/Route 441 (daily 9am–5pm; $17.50 per person for three hours; ℡1-800/683-5873).

Practicalities

The nearest Greyhound **bus** terminals are in Pompano Beach, 2190 NE Fourth St (℡954/946-7067) and Delray Beach, 402 SE Sixth Ave (℡561/272-6447). The Tri-Rail station is near the Embassy Suites, off Yamato Road and I-95 (℡1-800/TRI-RAIL), and their shuttle buses connect with the town center. The Palm Tran bus #91 (℡561/233-4BUS) operates from Monday to Saturday and runs from Mizner Park through downtown to the Sandalfoot Shopping Center; the fare is $1 one way.

The **Chamber of Commerce**, 1800 N Dixie Hwy (Mon–Thurs 8.30am–5pm, Fri 8.30am–4pm; ℡561/395-4433), supplies the usual information on area hotels and such. You can stay in relative luxury at places like the *Boca Raton Resort and Club* (see "Downtown Boca Raton); otherwise, the cheapest **motels** near the beaches are *Shore Edge*, 425 N Ocean Blvd (℡561/395-4491; ❹), and *Ocean Lodge*, 531 N Ocean Blvd (℡561/395-7772; ❹), which also has kitchen units. During the low season you'll save money by sleeping slightly inland at the *Townplace Suites,* 5110 NW Eighth Ave (℡561/994-7232; ❷).

As for a place to **eat**, *Prezzo*, 7820 Glades Rd #175 (℡561/451-2800), tucked away inside the Arvida Parkway Center, looks a bit like a chain but features succulent homemade pastas and oak-oven pizza specialities, which are worth shelling out for. At Mizner Park, the *Bavarian Colony Deli*, 435 Plaza Real (℡561/393-3980), serves excellent moderately priced sandwiches, while the reasonably priced American dishes at *Mozzarella's Café*, 409 Plaza Real (℡561/750-3580), are equally worth trying. *Max's Grille*, 404 Plaza Real (℡561/368-0080), is slightly upscale with a unique blend of American food that reflects various ethnic delicacies. There's more choice a mile or two further north on the N Federal Highway: Greek and Italian fare at the *Boca Diner*, no. 2801 (℡561/750-6744); barbecued ribs and steaks at *Tom's Place*, no. 7251 (℡561/997-0920); tasty sea fare at *The Seafood Connection*, no. 6998 (℡561/997-5562); great Cuban (but avoid the Mexican) dishes at *90 Miles*, 7860 Glades Rd (℡561/218-9090); and, for a good-value breakfast, head for the Jewish food at *Flakowitz Bagel Inn*, 1999 N Federal Hwy (℡561/368-0666), which offers excellent bagels as well as lamb shanks and sautéed chicken livers for more substantial meals.

The Morikami Museum and Japanese Gardens

South Florida might be the last place you'd expect to find a formal Japanese garden complete with a Shinto shrine, a teahouse and a museum recording the history of a Japanese agricultural colony, but ten miles northwest of Boca Raton at the **Morikami Museum and Japanese Gardens**, 4000 Morikami Park Rd (Tues–Sun 10am–5pm; adults $7, children 6–18 $4; ℡561/495-0233, ⓦwww.morikami.org), you'll find all three. These are reminders of a group of Japanese farmers who came here at the turn of the nineteenth century at the behest of the Florida East Coast Railway to grow tea and rice and farm silkworms in a colony called Yamato, but wound up selling pineapples until a blight killed off the crop in 1908.

Artifacts and photographs within the Morikami's older set of buildings remember the colony. Across the beautifully landscaped grounds, the newer portion of the museum stages themed exhibitions drawn from an enormous archive of Japanese objects and art, and has user-friendly computers ready to impart information about various aspects of Japan and Japanese life. A traditional **teahouse**, assembled here by a Florida-based Japanese craftsman, is periodically used for tea ceremonies.

North towards Palm Beach

Most of the shoulder-to-shoulder towns **north of Boca Raton** that are connected by Hwy-A1A have a nice patch of beach, and a couple are putting their modest histories on display, but none should be considered lengthy stops. If you're reliant on public transport, you can take the local CoTran bus #1S, which runs every hour through towns between Boca Raton and West Palm Beach.

Delray Beach

Five miles north of Boca Raton, **Delray Beach** justifies a half-day visit: its powdery-sanded **municipal beach**, at the foot of Atlantic Avenue, is rightly popular, and is one of the few in Florida to afford a view of the Gulf Stream – a cobalt-blue streak about five miles offshore.

Nipping a short way inland along Atlantic Avenue, you'll find more to pass the time. On the corner with Swinton Avenue, an imposing schoolhouse dating from 1913 forms part of **Old School Square** (Tues–Sat 11am–4pm, Sun 1–4pm; free; ℡561/243-7922), a group of buildings restored and converted into a cultural center. The spacious first floor of the former school hosts temporary art exhibitions, though a peek upstairs reveals several one-time classrooms still furnished with desks and black-painted walls used to avoid the exorbitant cost of slate blackboards. Within sight, just across NE First Street, the **Cason Cottage** (Tues–Fri 10am–3pm; free), erected in 1920 for Dr John Cason, member of an illustrious local family, warrants a look for its simple woodframe design based on pioneer-era Florida architecture.

Delray Beach makes a sensible lunch stop. At the municipal beach, *Boston's on the Beach*, 40 S Ocean Blvd (℡561/278-3364, ⓦwww.bostonsonthebeach.com), serves incredibly fresh seafood at reasonable prices. Among less expensive beachside **accommodation**, the *Bermuda Inn*, 64 S Ocean Blvd (℡561/276-5288; ❺), and *Wright by the Sea*, 1901 S Ocean Blvd (℡561/278-3355; ❻), are your best bets.

Lake Worth

If you're pressing on by car, a more inspiring option than Hwy-1 is Hwy-A1A, which charts a picturesque course along twenty-odd miles of slender barrier islands, ocean views on one side and the Intracoastal Waterway – plied by luxury yachts and lined with opulent homes – on the other. Whichever route you take, make a quick stop at **Lake Worth** (not to be confused with the actual lake of the same name that divides Palm Beach from West Palm Beach), ten miles north of Delray Beach, for the entertaining clutter of the **Historical Museum**, in the Utilities Department Buildings at 414 Lake Ave (Tues–Fri 10am–2pm; free). Plant-filled bathtubs, artistically arranged rusting tools and picks aplenty from bygone decades are all infectiously doted over by the museum's curator.

The newest attraction in the area is the recently relocated **Hibel Museum of Art**, 701 Lake Ave (Tues–Sat 10am–5pm, Sun 1–5pm; free; ℡561/533-6872, ⓦwww.hibel.org). Forget Warhol and Rothko, the most commercially successful artist in the US is Edna Hibel, an octagenarian resident of Singer Island (just north of Palm Beach, see p.198), whose works fill this deep-carpeted museum. Inspired by "love," Hibel has been churning out coy, sentimental portraits, usually of serene Asian and Mexican women, since the late Thirties, often working seven days a week to meet demand. Pay a visit, though, if only to admire the unflappable devotion of the guides, and to figure out why Hibel originals change hands for $50,000.

Otherwise, there's nothing to hinder your progress to Palm Beach (with Hwy-A1A) or West Palm Beach (with Hwy-1) just a few miles north. For a bite to eat before you move on, try the steak sandwich on garlic bread for $7.95 at *Rosie's Key West Grill*, 612 Lake Ave (℡561/582-1330).

Palm Beach

A small island town of palatial homes, pampered gardens and streets so clean you could eat your dinner off them, **PALM BEACH** has been synonymous for nearly a century with the kind of lifestyle only limitless loot can buy. A bastion of conspicuous wealth, whose pomposity – banning clothes lines, for example – knows no bounds, Palm Beach is, for all its faults, irrefutably unique.

The nation's upper crust began wintering here in the 1890s, after Standard Oil magnate Henry Flagler brought his Florida East Coast Railway south from St Augustine and built two luxury hotels on this then-secluded, palm-filled island. Throughout the Twenties, Addison Mizner began a vogue for Mediterranean-style architecture, covering the place with arcades, courtyards and plazas – and the first million-dollar homes. Since then, corporate tycoons, sports heroes, jet-setting aristocrats, rock stars and CIA directors have flocked here, eager to become part of the Palm Beach elite and enjoy its aloofness from mainland life.

Summer is very quiet and easily the least costly time to stay here. The pace heats up between November and May, with the winter months a whirl of elegant balls, fund-raising dinners and charity galas – local residents give more to tax-deductible causes in a year than most people earn in a lifetime. Winter also brings the polo season – watching a chukka or two is the one time Palm Beach denizens show themselves in the less particular environs of West Palm Beach (on the mainland), where the games are held.

Even by walking – much the best way to view the moneyed isle – you'll get the measure of Palm Beach in a day. Either drive in along Hwy-A1A from the south, or use one of the two bridges over Lake Worth from West Palm Beach, the nearest bus and train stop.

The waters off the beach also merit investigation; artificial reefs were created here in the 1960s to protect the coastline by preventing erosion of the natural reef. These are now a spectacular draw for divers; contact the Palm Beach County Chamber of Commerce (see p.195) for further information.

Approaching Palm Beach: the south of the island

Though near-neighbors like to think otherwise, Palm Beach as a byword for wealth, extravagance and exclusivity begins about five miles north of the town of Lake Worth on Hwy-A1A, by the junction with Southern Boulevard (Hwy-98). Here, the **Palm Beach Bath and Tennis Club** is the first of the community's strictly members-only watering holes; its arched windows give sweeping ocean views – passers-by see just the club's guarded entrance. Likewise, for the

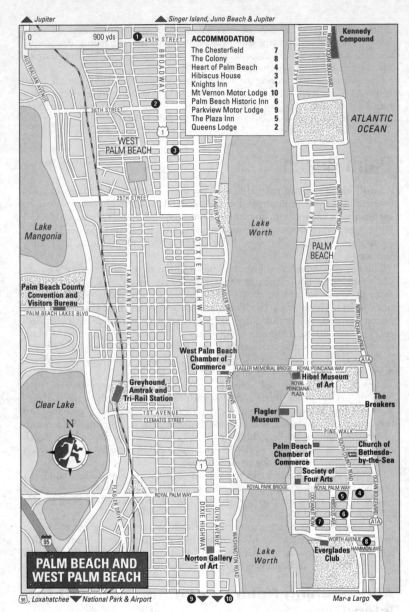

ACCOMMODATION

The Chesterfield	7
The Colony	8
Heart of Palm Beach	4
Hibiscus House	3
Knights Inn	1
Mt Vernon Motor Lodge	10
Palm Beach Historic Inn	6
Parkview Motor Lodge	9
The Plaza Inn	5
Queens Lodge	2

PALM BEACH AND WEST PALM BEACH

next couple of miles along this busy two-lane highway (a bad place to cycle or walk, or even stop your car) the high-class homes are shielded from prying eyes by walls of hedges.

You should have no trouble, however, spotting the red-roofed Italianate tower topping **Mar-a-Largo**. Finished in 1926, this was the $8-million winter abode of breakfast cereal heiress Marjorie Merriweather-Post, queen of Palm Beach high society for nearly forty years. On Merriweather-Post's death in 1973,

Mar-a-Largo's 118 rooms and eighteen-acre grounds were bequeathed to the US government – which couldn't afford the upkeep. Instead, "Florida's most sybaritic private residence" was sold to property tycoon Donald Trump and it remains a very private residence.

Further on, close to the Via La Selva turning, a sprawling Colonial-style property once owned by John Lennon and Yoko Ono can just be glimpsed. Hardly a place to enhance the ex-Beatle's anti-establishment credentials, it belonged earlier to turn-of-the-century multi-millionaire Cornelius Vanderbilt. Half a mile north, Hwy-A1A becomes Ocean Boulevard as it enters the town of Palm Beach.

Palm Beach: the town

The main residential section of Palm Beach – **the town** – is where you should spend most of your time, and **Worth Avenue**, cruised by classic cars and filled with designer stores and privately owned high-class art galleries, is a good place to start your stroll, even if you can only afford to window-shop.

Other than expense-account acquisition, the most appealing aspect of the street is its architecture: stucco walls, crafted Romanesque facades and narrow passageways leading to small courtyards where miniature bridges cross non-existent canals and spiral staircases climb to higher levels. On the top floor of one of the courtyard buildings, Via Mizner, situated on the corner with Hibiscus Avenue, sits the former pied-à-terre of the man responsible for the Mediterranean look replicated all over Palm Beach – the flamboyant architect **Addison Mizner**. Unfortunately, it is not open to the public.

After heading up to Worth Avenue's western end to gawk at the vessels moored on Lake Worth – rows of ocean-going yachts with more living space than most people's homes – you should explore the rest of the town along Cocoanut Row or County Road.

Palm Beach's architect: Addison Mizner

A former miner and prizefighter, **Addison Mizner** was an unemployed architect when he arrived in Palm Beach in 1918 from California to recuperate following the recurrence of a childhood leg injury. Inspired by the medieval buildings he'd seen around the Mediterranean, Mizner, financed by the heir to the Singer sewing machine fortune, built the **Everglades Club**, at 356 Worth Ave, which is off limits to the public. Described by Mizner as "a little bit of Seville and the Alhambra, a dash of Madeira and Algiers," the Everglades Club was the first public building in Florida in the Mediterranean Revival style, and fast became the island's most prestigious social club.

The success of the club, and the house he subsequently built for society bigwig Eva Stotesbury, won Mizner commissions all over Palm Beach as the wintering wealthy decided to swap their suites at one of Henry Flagler's hotels for a "million-dollar cottage" of their own.

Brilliant and unorthodox, Mizner's loggias and U-shaped interiors made the most of Florida's pleasant winter temperatures, while his twisting staircases to nowhere became legendary. Pursuing a medieval look, Mizner used untrained workmen to lay roof tiles crookedly, sprayed condensed milk onto walls to create an impression of centuries-old grime, and fired shotgun pellets into wood to imitate worm holes. By the mid-Twenties, Mizner had created the Palm Beach Style – which Florida architecture buff Hap Hatton called "the Old World for the new rich." Mizner later fashioned much of Boca Raton (see p.187).

Cocoanut Row

Four blocks north from its junction with Worth Avenue, **Cocoanut Row** crosses Royal Palm Way close to the stuccoed buildings of the **Society of the Four Arts**, at 2 Four Arts Plaza (Mon–Sat 10am–5pm, Sun 2–5pm; suggested donation $3; ☎561/655-7226), which presents art shows and lectures of an impressive standard between early December and mid-April, and whose library is worth browsing.

Half a mile further along Cocoanut Row you'll notice the white Doric columns fronting **Whitehall**, also known as the Henry Morrison Flagler Museum (Tues–Sat 10am–5pm, Sun noon–5pm; last tour leaves between 3.15pm and 3.30pm; $10; ☎561/655-2833, ⓦwww.flagler.org). The most overtly ostentatious home on the island, Whitehall was a $4-million wedding present from Henry Flagler to his third wife, Mary Lily Kenan, whom he married (after controversially persuading the Florida legislature to amend its divorce laws) in 1901. Like many of Florida's first luxury homes, Whitehall's interior design was created by pillaging the great buildings of Europe: among the 73 rooms are an Italian library, a French salon, a Swiss billiard room, a hallway modeled on the Vatican's St Peter's and a Louis XV ballroom. All are richly stuffed with ornamentation but – other than their mutual decadence – lack any aesthetic cohesion. Flagler was in his seventies when Whitehall was built, 37 years older than his bride and not enamored of the banquets and balls she continually hosted. He often sloped off to bed using a concealed stairway, perhaps to ponder plans to extend his railway to Key West – a display on the project fills his former office. From the 110-foot hallway, informative but not compulsory 45-minute **free guided tours** depart continuously and will leave you giddy with the tales – and the sights – of the earliest Palm Beach excesses. Don't miss the authentic railroad car, outside the exit to the gift shop, and the spectacular views of West Palm Beach from Flagler's enormous backyard.

Whitehall was built beside Flagler's first Palm Beach resort, the *Royal Poinciana Hotel*: a six-story, Colonial-style structure of 2000 rooms, which became the world's largest wooden building on its completion in 1894. A small plaque marks the spot, but only the remains of a grand ballroom are left of the hotel, whose hundred-acre grounds spread to what's now Royal Poinciana Way.

County Road

In terms of things to see, **County Road** is the poor relation of Cocoanut Row – to which it runs parallel – but is still worth a stroll. Along it, two blocks north of Worth Avenue, Mizner's Mediterranean Revival themes are displayed in Palm Beach's very tidy local administration offices and bank buildings. By contrast, the 1926 **Church of Bethesda-by-the-Sea**, a fifteen-minute walk further north, is a handsome imitation-Gothic pile replacing the island's first church (see "The North of the Island"): the large stained-glass windows depict Christianity around the world, but ignore them and walk instead through the echoing cloisters to the **Cluett Memorial Gardens** (daily 9am–5pm; free), a peaceful spot in which to take a stone pew and tuck into a picnic lunch.

A little further north, County Road is straddled by the golf course of *The Breakers* hotel, erected in 1926 and the last of Palm Beach's swanky resorts. Inside, the lobby is filled with tapestries, chandeliers, huge fireplaces and painted ceilings; at 3pm on Wednesdays there's a free guided tour of the premises.

The north of the island

The limited points of interest beyond Royal Poinciana Way are best viewed from the three-mile **Lake Trail**, a bicycle and pedestrian path skirting the edge of Lake Worth, almost to the northern limit of the island. A bicycle is the ideal

THE SOUTHEAST COAST | Palm Beach

mode of transport here: rent one from Palm Beach Bicycle Trail Shop, 223 Sunrise Ave (℡561/659-4583), for $20 a day.

Most locals use the trail as a jogging strip, and certainly there's little other than exercise and fine views across the lake to make it worthwhile. Keep an eye out, though, for "Duck's Nest," the oldest remaining home in Palm Beach, built in 1891, and the **original Church of Bethesda-by-the-Sea**, at Barton Avenue and South Country Road, which dates from 1889. Serving a congregation of early homesteaders across a 125-mile stretch of coast, all of whom had to get here by boat, the shingled church is now a private house, but easily spotted by the clockface hanging from its short tower.

The Lake Trail expires a few minutes' pedal south of the Lake Worth Inlet, a narrow cut separating Palm Beach from the high-rise-dominated Singer Island. To get to the inlet – for a sight of the neighboring island and a modest sense of achievement – weave on through the short residential streets.

For variation, cycle back to central Palm Beach along Ocean Drive (take care as there's no marked cycle path), which passes the two-acre former **Kennedy Compound**, at 1095 N Ocean Blvd, bought by Joe Kennedy – father of John, Robert and Edward – in 1933. The Kennedys never fully integrated into ultra-conservative Palm Beach life; feeling unwelcome at the Everglades Club, Joe upset the establishment by joining the rival Palm Beach Country Club – and it's said that few Palm Beach tears were shed in 1963 when John was assassinated. In April 1991, Palm Beach was rocked by the arrest here of William Kennedy Smith, nephew of Senator Edward Kennedy, on charges of sexual battery (Florida's legal term for rape). He was later acquitted.

Practicalities

In a town that is often wary of tourists, the **Chamber of Commerce**, 45 Cocoanut Row (Mon–Fri 9am–4.30pm in winter, 10am–4.30pm in summer; ℡561/655-3282, ⓦwww.palmbeachchamber.com), is a welcome provider of free maps and reliable **information**.

You'll need plenty of money to stay in Palm Beach: comfort and elegance are the key words, and prices can vary so greatly depending on the time of year that in some cases we've noted both high- and low-season prices below. *Palm Beach Historic Inn*, 365 S County Rd (℡561/832-4009; ❻), is a friendly bed-and-breakfast spot with the best rates in town, but you'll need to book early. Otherwise, to save money, come between May and December, when the prices on the island are lowest. Try the opulent *Chesterfield*, 363 Cocoanut Row (℡1-800/243-7871, ⓦwww.redcarnationhotels.com; ❾), which serves tea each afternoon; the luxurious *Colony*, 155 Hammon Ave (℡1-800/521-5525; ❺-❾); the homely *Heart of Palm Beach*, 160 Royal Palm Way (℡1-800/523-5377; ❻-❽); and the modern *Plaza Inn*, 215 Brazilian Ave (℡1-800/233-2632; ❹-❻). Obviously, it's far cheaper to stay outside Palm Beach and visit by day – easily done from West Palm Beach even without a car; see overleaf.

Luckily, you can **eat** relatively cheaply. *TooJay's*, 312 Royal Poinciana Plaza (℡561/659-7232), is a top-notch bakery and deli open from breakfast onwards, where you can choose from a wide selection of food, including scrumptious omelets for less than $6; *The Ocean Grand Hotel Dining Room*, 2800 S Ocean Blvd (℡561/582-2800), has organic and some vegetarian dishes; and *Hamburger Heaven*, 314 S County Rd (℡561/655-5277, but no reservations), dispenses delicious ground-beef burgers. More expensive options include *Testa's*, 221 Royal Poinciana Way (℡561/832-0992), which serves exquisite seafood and pasta at between $10 and $15; and *Charley's Crab*, 456 S

Ocean Blvd (☎561/659-1500), overlooking the dunes, which serves up a mean shrimp cocktail among other scrumptious seafood (and a killer Sunday brunch). If money is no object (you'll spend at least $50 a head) and you're dressed to kill, make for the super-elegant French restaurant *Café L'Europe*, 150 Worth Ave (☎561/655-4020). Alternatively, the Publix supermarket at 265 Sunset Ave is useful if the above are closed or you just want picnic fare.

West Palm Beach and around

Founded to house the workforce of Flagler's Palm Beach resorts, **WEST PALM BEACH** has long been in the shadow of its glamorous neighbor across the lake. Only during the last two decades has the town gained a life of its own, with smart new office buildings, a scenic lakeside footpath – and less seemly industrial growth sprouting up on its western edge. Above all, West Palm Beach holds the promise of accommodation and food at a lower price than in Palm Beach, and is the closest you'll get to the island using public transport – CoTran buses from Boca Raton and Greyhound services stop here, leaving a few minutes' walk to Palm Beach over one of the Lake Worth bridges.

Information, public transport and accommodation

The **Chamber of Commerce**, 401 N Flagler Drive, at the corner of Fourth Street (Mon–Fri 8.30am–5pm; ☎561/833-3711, ⓦwww.pbol.com), has stacks of free leaflets, and can answer questions on the whole Palm Beach County area. The West Palm Beach train (☎1-800/872-7245), Tri-Rail (☎1-800/TRI-RAIL) and Greyhound (☎561/833-8534) stations are all located at 201 S Tamarind Ave, and linked by regular shuttle buses to the downtown area. Most local CoTran bus (☎561/233-1111) routes converge at Quadrille Road.

Most budget chain motel prices in West Palm Beach are inflated. The best deals are to be found at *Queens Lodge*, 3712 Broadway (☎561/842-1108; ❷); *Parkview Motor Lodge*, 4710 S Dixie Hwy (☎1-800/523-8978; ❸); *Mt Vernon Motor Lodge*, 310 Belvedere Rd (☎1-800/545-1520; ❸); or *Knights Inn*, 2200 45th St (☎1-800/843-5644, ⓦwww.knightsinn.com; ❸). For a real treat that doesn't bust your wallet, try the charming *Hibiscus House*, 501 30th St, just off Flagler Street (☎561/863-5633; ❹). Loaded with kitsch alongside beautiful antiques – including a baby grand piano – it has balconies in practically every room and a delightful pool where homemade breakfasts are served. The owner is a virtual encyclopedia of Palm Beach, and is more than happy to impart his knowledge.

Downtown West Palm Beach

Other than tending to basic needs, one of the few reasons to linger in **downtown West Palm Beach** is the fine collections of the **Norton Museum of Art**, 1451 S Olive Ave (Tues–Sat 10am–5pm, Sun 1–5pm; $6, children 13–21 $2; ☎561/832-5194, ⓦwww.norton.org), a mile south of the downtown area. Together with some distinctive European paintings and drawings by Gauguin, Klee, Picasso and others, the museum, which expanded in 1997, boasts a solid grouping of twentieth-century American works: Mark Tobey's study of stifling urban motion, *The Street*, and Stuart Davis' *New York Mural* are most impressive. Among a sparkling roomful of Far Eastern pieces are seventh-century sculpted Buddhas, absorbingly complex amber carvings and a collection of tomb jades dating from the period 1500–500 BC .

In the late Fifties the boom of shopping malls in Palm Beach practically shut down the small boutiques and cafés on Clematis Street, turning it into another bland area of downtown West Palm Beach. Today, thanks to a major renovation project during the late Nineties, Clematis Street is once again home to a diverse mix of restaurants, shops, privately owned galleries and an exciting schedule of cultural activities. Daytime lunch concerts, the Thursday evening "Clematis by Night" events and a continual parade of food and arts-and-crafts vendors has brought the area to life. The second Tuesday of the month heralds "Clematis Backstage," which can range from concerts to holiday celebrations in the spacious outdoor Meyer Amphitheater, and on Saturday mornings the street turns green with a farmer's market. Colorfully landscaped, Clematis Street stretches from the Intracoastal Waterway to the heart of downtown, culminating with the interactive fountain in Centennial Square, which shoots jets of water into the air amidst dripping and squealing adults and children.

Eating, drinking and nightlife

The majority of good places to eat are congregated on Clematis Street. Try *Bimini Bay Café*, at no. 104 (☎561/833-9554), a casual yet fairly pricey restaurant with spectacular views of the Intracoastal Waterway; *My Martini Grille*, at no. 225 (☎561/832-8333), which serves American grill specialities and a variety of designer martinis; the intimate *Pescatore*, at no. 200 (☎561/837-6633), for inexpensive Italian seafood dishes; and *Dax Key West Grill*, at no. 300 (☎561/833-0449), which cools you down with frozen cocktails and its second-floor, deckside view. Inexpensive grilled food can be found at *Roxy's Bar & Grille*, at no. 319 (☎561/833-2402); from there, an evening might easily lead to dancing at the industrial-themed *Liquid Room* (☎561/655-2332), a few doors down at no. 313. For something on the lighter side, go to *Robinson's Pastry Shop*, at no. 215 (☎561/833-4259), which sells wonderful freshly baked snacks and sandwiches during the day, or try the *Respectable Street Café*, at no. 518 (☎561/832-0706) with its immaculate Japanese garden. It is also good for an evening drink and – quite incongruously – drum'n'bass nights on weekends from 11pm until very late.

Away from Clematis Street, *Sushi Rok*, at 106 N Olive Ave (☎561/835-0086), has tasty, reasonably priced Japanese dishes; and for food with a side order of laughs, visit *The Comedy Corner*, 2000 S Dixie Hwy (☎561/833-1812; Wed–Sun), which has a bar, inexpensive beer and stand-up comics from 8pm onwards ($10 admission).

Inland from West Palm Beach

West Palm Beach makes a good stepping-off point for the **Loxahatchee National Wildlife Refuge**, 10216 Lee Rd in Boynton Beach (daily

6am–7.30pm; cars $3.25, pedestrians and cyclists $1; visitor center open Wed–Sun; ☎561/732-3684). Travel west along Hwy-80 for about five miles, then turn south along Hwy-441, and the well-signposted main entrance is twelve miles ahead. The 200 square miles of sawgrass marshes – the northerly extension of the Everglades (see p.383) – are only marginally penetrable on two easy walking trails from the visitor center. One meanders through a cypress hammock, and the other is a boardwalk that leads over the marshes to an observation tower. On either, you'll probably see a few snakes and alligators and get a firm impression of what undeveloped inland Florida is like – and how incredibly flat it is. It's also possible to go on guided canoe trails, airboat rides, bird walks and "night prowls."

African and Asian wildlife is the star attraction of **Lion Country Safari** (daily 9.30am–5.30pm; last vehicles admitted 4.30pm; $15.50, children under 9 $10.50; ☎561/793-1084, ⓦwww.lioncountrysafari.com), on Southern Boulevard W (eighteen miles west of I-95 and before the junction of Hwy-98 and Hwy-441). Lions, elephants, giraffes, chimpanzees, zebras and ostriches are among the creatures roaming a 500-acre plot in which human visitors are confined to their cars. It's awkward to reach and expensive to visit, but if you can't leave Florida without photographing a flamingo, Lion Country Safari could well be for you.

Venturing further inland to the Lake Okeechobee area (described in "Central Florida," p.299), Hwy-80 from West Palm Beach runs the forty miles to the lakeside town of Belle Glade.

The Treasure Coast

West Palm Beach marks the northern limit of Miami's hinterland and the end of the Southeast Coast's heavily touristed sections. Aside from some small and uninspiring towns, the next eighty miles – dubbed the **TREASURE COAST** simply to distinguish it from the Gold Coast – missed out entirely on the expansion seen to the south and to the north, leaving wide open spaces and some magnificent swathes of quiet beach that attract Florida's nature lovers and a small band of well-informed tan-seekers.

Singer Island and Juno Beach

North of West Palm Beach, Hwy-A1A swings back to the coast at **SINGER ISLAND**. The beaches are perfectly adequate but the place lacks life and is predominantly residential, with little budget-range **accommodation**; the *Days Inn Oceanfront Resort*, 2700 N Ocean Drive (☎561/848-8661; ❹), is the least expensive option. Nearby, on Hwy-A1A, is the **John D. MacArthur Beach State Park** (daily 8am–sunset; visitor center open Wed–Sun 9am–5pm; cars $3.25, pedestrians and cyclists $1; ☎561/624-6950), one of the few beach state parks with worthwhile nature trails and swimming areas.

The area code for the parts of the Treasure Coast mentioned in this chapter is ☎561.

The next few miles are mostly golf courses and planned retirement communities, but one good stop is **JUNO BEACH**, where Hwy-A1A follows a high coastal bluff and, with luck, you'll find one of the unmarked paths down to the uncrowded sands.

Alternatively, keep going until you reach the beachside Loggerhead Park, also the site of the **Marine Life Center** (Tues–Sat 10am–3pm; free), intended for kids but good for adults brushing up on their knowledge of marine life in general and sea turtles in particular. There's a turtle hatchery here and displays on their life cycles. The only time turtles give up the security of the ocean is between June and July, when they steal ashore to lay eggs under cover of darkness. This is one of several places along the Treasure Coast where expeditions are led to watch them; get the details at the museum or on ☎561/627-8280. Reservations are essential and taken from May onwards.

Jupiter and Jupiter Island

Splitting into several anodyne districts around the wide mouth of the Tequesta River, **JUPITER**, about six miles north of Juno Beach, was a rumrunners' haven during the Prohibition era; these days it's better known as the home town of Florida's favorite son, actor Burt Reynolds. Most symbols of "Burtness" have gone under, such as his restaurant, the museum on his ranch and the Jupiter Theater. The Burt Reynolds Park, beside Hwy-1 near the town center, is a nice enough park that carries the man's name, but only the most zealous fan should seek it out.

A visit to the **Florida History Center and Museum**, 805 N Hwy-1 (Tues–Fri 10am–4pm, Sat & Sun 1–4pm; $4; ☎561/747-6639), describes pioneer life on and around the Tequesta River long before Burt's time. To gain more insight into how the pioneers lived, you can walk through an original home located on the grounds (Wed & Sun 1–4pm; $2). The only other thing in Jupiter that merits consideration is the red-brick lighthouse built in 1860 – making it the oldest building in Palm Beach County – on the north bank of the Jupiter Inlet, with a small museum devoted to nineteenth-century nautical paraphernalia in the **Jupiter Lighthouse Park** (Sun–Wed 10am–4pm; $5, free Sun afternoons; last tour 3.15pm; ☎561/746-3101). The lighthouse can be seen from Beach Road, the route Hwy-A1A takes back to the coast after looping through the town. This route skirts the Jupiter Inlet Colony – a wealthy community whose roads are guarded by photo-electric beams, enabling police to check any suspicious traffic cruising the deadend streets – before heading north along Jupiter Island. If you're feeling hungry, a great, albeit pricey, place to **eat** (order from the appetizer menu – portions are just as big) seafood is *Charley's Crab*, 1000 N Hwy-1 (☎561/744-4710), on the Jupiter Inlet.

Jupiter Island

Two miles into **Jupiter Island** on Hwy-A1A, pull up at the **Blowing Rocks Nature Preserve** (daily 9am–4.30pm; $3; ☎561/747-3113, ⓦwww.tnc.florida .org), where a limestone outcrop covers much of the beach and powerful incoming tides are known to drive through the rocks' hollows, emerging as gusts of spray further on. At low tide, it's sometimes possible to walk around the outcrop and peer into the rock's sea-drilled cavities. Guided nature walks are available, though if you fancy a swim, note that no lifeguards are present.

Seven miles further north, the shell-strewn Hobe Sound Beach marks the edge of the 960-acre **Hobe Sound National Wildlife Refuge** (daily sunrise–sunset; free), which occupies the remainder of the island. Having achieved spectacular success as a nesting ground for sea turtles during the summer (turtle hikes available Jan–March Tues & Thurs; ☎ 561/546-2067), the refuge is also rich in birdsong, with scrub jays among its tuneful inhabitants. To find out more about the refuge's flora and fauna, visit the small **interpretive center** (Mon–Fri 9am–3pm; ☎ 561/546-2067; $1), on the mainland where Hwy-A1A meets Hwy-1.

The northern end of Jupiter Island comprises **St Lucie Inlet State Preserve** (daily 8am–sunset; cars $3.25, pedestrians and cyclists $1; ☎ 561/744-7603), whose 928 acres include mangrove-lined creeks and over two miles of beach accessible by boat ($2) from Hobe Sound Beach. It's occasionally possible to see manatees feeding in the grass beds north of the dock, though the boardwalk is notable primarily for the skunk-like aroma emitted by the aptly named shite-stopper, a tropical tree.

Inland: the Jonathan Dickinson State Park

Two miles south of the Hobe Sound interpretive center on Hwy-1, the **Jonathan Dickinson State Park** (daily 8am–sunset; cars $3.25, pedestrians and cyclists $1; ☎ 561/546-2771, ⓦ www.abfla.com) preserves a natural landscape quite different from what you'll see at the coast. Step up to the observation platform atop **Hobe Mountain**, an 86-foot-high sand dune, and survey the pines, palmetto (a stumpy, tropical palm fan) flatlands and the mangrove-flanked course of the winding Loxahatchee River. The intrepid can obtain hiking maps from the entrance office and set off along the nine-mile Kitchen Creek Trail, which starts from the park's entrance and finishes in a cypress hammock at some basic campgrounds; beware that campground space must be booked in advance (tents for one to four people May–Nov $14, Dec–April $17; cabins $65–85 a night for a minimum of two nights; ☎ 561/546-2771 or 1-800/746-1466).

Anyone more adventurous should rent a canoe from the people who rent out the cabins (see above) and paddle along the Loxahatchee River – don't be put off by the preponderance of alligators – to the **Trapper Nelson Interpretive Center**, named for a Quaker washed ashore near here in 1697. Another way to get there is by taking the two-hour cruise aboard the *Loxahatchee Queen II* (four daily Wed–Sun, 9am–3pm; $12; reservations ☎ 561/746-1466), which leaves from the park's pier.

Stuart and Hutchinson Island

HUTCHINSON ISLAND, another long barrier island, lies immediately north of Jupiter Island. To reach it (with either Hwy-1 or Hwy-A1A), you'll first pass through **STUART**, a neat and tidy, but rather boring, town on the south bank of the St Lucie River. Stuart has a number of century-old wooden buildings proudly preserved on and around Flagler Avenue – pick up a free walking guide from the **Chamber of Commerce**, 1650 S Kanner Hwy (Mon–Fri 8.30am–5pm; ☎ 561/287-1088, ⓦ www.goodnature.org) – and a Greyhound station at 757 SE Monterey Rd (☎ 561/287-7777), but not much else to keep you engaged. There is a **bike rental** outlet, however, Pedal Power, 1211 SE Port St Lucie Blvd (☎ 561/335-1310), which you'll need (if you don't have a car) to make the four-mile trip along Hwy-A1A, over the Intracoastal Waterway and to Hutchinson Island (though the cycle path only begins at

Jensen Beach – see below). For a bite to **eat** in downtown Stuart, try the *Riverwalk Café*, 201 SW St Lucie Ave (T 561/221-1511), or *The Flagler Grill*, 47 SW Flagler Ave (T 561/221-9517).

Hutchinson Island

Largely hidden behind thickly grouped Australian pines, several beautiful beaches line the twenty-mile-long **Hutchinson Island**, located to the east of Stuart along Hwy-A1A (also known as Ocean Boulevard). Keep your eyes peeled for the public access points. It would be hard, however, to miss **Stuart Beach**: facing Hwy-A1A it is a low-key stretch of brown sand where tourists are heavily outnumbered by locals – a fine venue for a few hours of ray absorption.

Close by, at 825 NE Ocean Blvd, the **Elliott Museum** (daily 1–5pm; $4; T 561/225-1961) exhibits a sizeable hodgepodge of mechanical objects and ornaments, few of which seem to be the work of Sterling Elliott, whom the place is intended to commemorate. A talented inventor active during the 1870s, Elliott's creations displayed here include an automatic knot-tier and the first addressing machine, while his quadricycle – a four-wheeled bicycle – solved many of the technical problems that hindered the development of the car. It's hard, therefore, to fathom why much of the museum is given over to reconstructed turn-of-the-century shops, Victorian fashion accessories and a hangar full of vintage cars – not to mention autographed memorabilia of members of the Baseball Hall of Fame and various Seminole artifacts.

A mile south at 301 SE MacArthur Blvd, **Gilbert's Bar House of Refuge** (Tues–Sun 1–5pm; $4; T 561/225-1875) is a better stop: a convincingly restored refuge for wrecked sailors that was one of ten erected along Florida's east coast during 1875. Furnished in a Victorian style, the rooms of the refuge are best understood with the free guided tour (starting when you're ready, every day except Saturday). There's more evidence of the refuge's importance in the entrance area – lifeboat equipment, ship's logs and a modern weather station – along with reminders of the building's more recent function as a sea turtle hatchery.

Pushing on north, roughly halfway along the island, **Jensen Beach** has the only road to the mainland between Stuart and Fort Pierce, as well as a small but pleasant beach. Move on if you feel like eating because the pickings are pretty slim here. For **accommodation**, try the *Dolphin Motor Lodge*, 2211 NE Dixie Hwy (T 561/334-1313; ❹). Jensen Beach also marks the start of a cycle path, which continues – passing one of Florida's two nuclear power stations (which has a visitor center with interactive exhibits; Tues–Fri & Sun 10am–4pm, T 561/468-4111; free) – to the Fort Pierce Inlet, which divides Hutchinson Island in two. To reach the northern half (known as North Hutchinson Island), you'll need to pass through the area's biggest town, Fort Pierce.

Fort Pierce

A number of rustic motels, bars and restaurants grouped along Hwy-A1A beside a more than adequate beach make the first taste of **FORT PIERCE** a favorable one. The bulk of the town (looped through by Hwy-A1A) lies two miles away across the Intracoastal Waterway, where tourism plays second fiddle to processing and transporting the produce of Florida's citrus farms. The convivial coastal section makes an amenable base for island exploration, but the mainland town has only a few features likely to detain you for long. Scuba diving off the coast is, however, an entirely different prospect, giving you a chance to explore reefs and wrecks dating back to the time of the Spanish galleons.

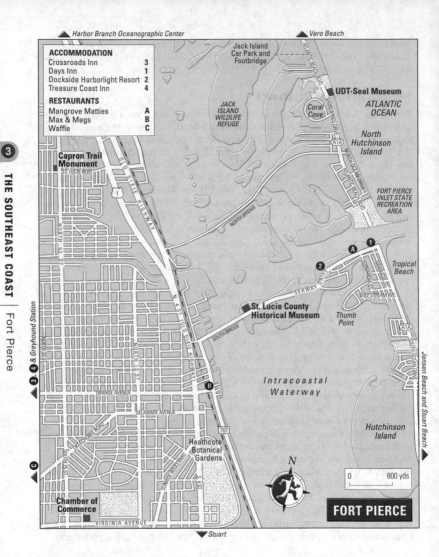

Harbor Branch Oceanographic Center — Vero Beach

ACCOMMODATION
Crossroads Inn — 3
Days Inn — 1
Dockside Harborlight Resort — 2
Treasure Coast Inn — 4

RESTAURANTS
Mangrove Matties — A
Max & Megs — B
Waffle — C

Jack Island Car Park and Footbridge

UDT-Seal Museum

ATLANTIC OCEAN

JACK ISLAND WILDLIFE REFUGE

Coral Cove

North Hutchinson Island

Capron Trail Monument
ST LUCIE BLVD

OLD DIXIE HIGHWAY

NORTH BRIDGE

FORT PIERCE INLET STATE RECREATION AREA

NORTH 52 ST

N AST OLD DIXIE HIGHWAY

Tropical Beach

SEAWAY DRIVE

St. Lucie County Historical Museum

Thumb Point

SOUTH BRIDGE

Intracoastal Waterway

ORANGE AVENUE

DELAWARE AVENUE

Hutchinson Island

OKEECHOBEE ROAD

Heathcote Botanical Gardens

SUNRISE BOULEVARD

SOUTH 25 ST

N

0 — 800 yds

Chamber of Commerce

VIRGINIA AVENUE

FORT PIERCE

Stuart

The Historical Museum

Beside Hwy-A1A, close to the Intracoastal Waterway bridge at 414 Seaway Drive, the **St Lucie County Historical Museum** (Tues–Sat 10am–4pm, Sun noon–4pm; $2; ☎561/468-1795) keeps a cogent assembly of relics. Among them are a full-sized Seminole Indian *chickee* (a palm-thatched hut) and a solid account of the Seminole Wars, including the 1835 fort from which Fort Pierce took its name, and a re-creation of P.P. Cobb's general store, the hub of the turn-of-the-century town. Outside the museum, **Gardner House**, a 1907 "cracker" cottage can be glanced at long enough to note the tall ceilings and many windows that allowed the muggy Florida air to circulate in the days before air-conditioning. The museum also contains an exhibition gallery and a fully restored 1919 fire engine.

Downtown Fort Pierce and around

Entering **downtown Fort Pierce**, your gaze is held by a sewage treatment works and the towers of a cement factory, which provide a stark contrast to Hutchinson Island's raging vegetation. If you've time, however, Hwy-A1A quickly escapes oceanwards to North Hutchinson Island. Don't bother with the downtown area but make an excursion a few miles north along Hwy-1. From mid-November to early April you may catch sight of manatees in the Indian River Lagoon. A viewing area is located at Moore's Creek at the marina, where Avenue C and North Indian River Drive meet.

The Capron Trail Monument and Indian River Drive

A couple of miles north of downtown Fort Pierce, Hwy-1 crosses St Lucie Boulevard, and a left turn along here leads to a memorial (by the junction with 25th Street) recalling the nineteenth-century soldiers who inched their way from here towards Fort Brooke – the site of present-day Tampa. Their machetes hacked out the **Capron Trail**, one of the first east–west cross-Florida routes. Driving back, stay on St Lucie Boulevard as it crosses Hwy-1 and turn left along **Indian River Drive**, where gracious, rambling wooden homes dating from the early 1900s line the Intracoastal Waterway.

The Heathcote Botanical Gardens

At 210 Savanna Rd, off Hwy-1 and north of Jefferson Plaza, the **Heathcote Botanical Gardens** (Tues–Sat, 9am–5pm; also Nov–April Sun 1–5pm; $3; ☎561/464-4672), is an oasis in an otherwise gray setting, providing a relaxing and surprisingly cool place to while away a couple of hours amid a well-laid-out display of tropical flowers and trees as well as a small Japanese garden.

The Harbor Branch Oceanographic Institution

Five miles north of St-Lucie Boulevard, the **Harbor Branch Oceanographic Institution**, 5600 N Hwy-1 (daily 10am–5pm; $5; ☎1-800/333-4264), is a phenomenally well-equipped deep-sea research and education center. The highly informative tours (Mon–Sat noon & 2pm; land tour $10, boat tour $19, combo $25) depart from the visitor center and cover such highlights as full-scale models of research submersibles and an "Aquaculture" exhibit featuring interactive displays and videos to show you how seafood can be specially cultured for human consumption and thus help to satisfy our increasing demand on the seas. You'll also get the chance to eat in the research center's canteen: a good feed for $7 – try the meatloaf and, of course, the seafood.

Practicalities

The Fort Pierce Greyhound **bus station** (☎561/461-3299) is six miles from downtown at 7005 Okeechobee Rd, near the junction of Hwy-70 and Florida's Turnpike; a cab (try Gray Taxi Service, ☎561/461-7200) from here to the beach will cost around $15–20. A group of ordinary but inexpensive **accommodation** options are available close to the station. For rooms, try *Days Inn*, 6651 Darter Court off I-95 (☎561/466-4066, ⓦwww.daysinn.com; ❸), the *Treasure Coast Inn*, 7025 Okeechobee Rd (☎561/460-9855; ❷), or *Crossroads Inn*, 7050 Okeechobee Rd (☎561/465-8600; ❷).

Otherwise, sleeping (with the exception of camping) and dining are best done close to the beach, two miles east of downtown Fort Pierce. Most motels are geared up for stays of several nights and many rooms include cooking facilities. Try the *Days Inn*, 1920 Seaway Drive (☎561/461-8737, ⓦwww.daysinn.com;

4), which features a pool and cable TV, or join the fishing folk at the more basic *Dockside Harborlight Resort*, 1152 Seaway Drive (**☎**1-800/286-1745, **ⓦ**www.docksideinn.com; **2**). There are further choices along Seaway Drive and the northern part of Ocean Drive; ask on the spot for the best deals. For **camping**, head inland and seven miles south of downtown Fort Pierce along Route 707 to *Savannah's* (**☎**561/464-7855), a sizeable square of reclaimed marshland beside the Intracoastal Waterway where you can pitch a tent for $10. To explore this unspoiled landscape, take one of the nature trails or hire a canoe.

Eating options in Fort Pierce include lots of seafood options with *Max & Megs*, 122 N Second St (**☎**561/467-0065), one of the less expensive ones. If you're feeling flush, you can always visit the more refined *Mangrove Matties*, 1640 Seaway Drive (**☎**561/466-1044), which offers such dishes as coconut shrimp and conch chowder and has a great waterside location. Family-style food is available at the *Waffle* next to the bus station, and seafood at *The Galley Grille*, 927 N Hwy-1 (**☎**561/468-2081).

You can get general **information** from the **Chamber of Commerce**, 2200 Virginia Ave (Mon–Fri 8.30am–5pm; **☎**561/595-9999, **ⓦ**www.stluciechamber .org). There are various diving packages on offer, among them Dixie Divers, 621 N Second St (**☎**561/460-1771) and Deep 6 Dive, 2323 S Hwy-1 (**☎**561/465-4114), who both charge around $25 for a 24-hour package.

Port St Lucie

Adjacent to and merging with southern Fort Pierce lies **Port St Lucie**. The chief attractions here are the marina and the St Lucie County Sport Complex, at 527 NW Peacock Loop (**☎**561/871-2115), where the **New York Mets** baseball team holds its spring training – if you're around in February or March it's worth checking out the goings-on. It's also the regular home of the St Lucie Mets, a Florida State League baseball team, whose season opens in April. At the close of the ninth inning you can rest your head in the nearby *Best Western*, 7900 S Hwy-1 (**☎**561/878-7600, **ⓦ**www.bestwestern.com; **4**).

North Hutchinson Island

Covering 340 acres at the southern tip of North Hutchinson Island, **Fort Pierce Inlet State Recreation Area** (daily 8am–sunset; cars $3.25, pedestrians and cyclists $1; **☎**561/468-3985), at 905 Shorewinds Drive, off Hwy-A1A, overlooks the Fort Pierce Inlet and the community's beach. Its location makes it a scenic setting for a picnic, as well as a launch site for local surfers. A mile north, on Hwy-A1A, a footbridge from the parking lot of the **Jack Island State Preserve** (same times and fees as above) leads onto the mile-long Marsh Rabbit Run, a boardwalk trail cutting through a thick mangrove swamp to an observation tower on the edge of the Indian River. Great blue herons and ospreys are among birdlife to watch out for.

Concern for the environment is not something shared by the **UDT-SEAL Museum** (**☎**561/595-5845; Tues–Sat 10am–4pm, Sun noon–4pm; $3), at 3300 N Hwy-A1A between the recreation area and the wildlife refuge, dedicated to the US Navy's frogman demolition teams who've been exploding seamines and beach defenses since the Normandy landings. During World War II, the UDTs (Underwater Demolition Teams) trained on Hutchinson Island – like most of Florida's barrier islands, it was off limits to civilians at the time. The more elite SEALs (Sea Air Land) came into being during the Sixties. The museum covers the technicalities of establishing beachheads, though jingoism is predictably apparent – anyone who can't keep doubts over US foreign policy to themselves should steer clear.

Vero Beach and around

For the next fourteen miles north, Australian pines mar Hwy-A1A's ocean view until North Hutchinson Island imperceptibly becomes **Orchid Island** and you reach **VERO BEACH**, the area's sole community of substance and one with a pronounced upmarket image. It makes an enjoyable hideaway, however, with a fine group of beaches around Ocean Drive, parallel to Hwy-A1A. There's little to tempt you from the sands, but it's worth taking the trouble to view the *Driftwood Resort*, 3150 Ocean Drive (℡561/231-0550; ➏), a Thirties hotel, now fully equipped apartments, erected from a jumble of driftwood, flea-market finds and pieces of Palm Beach mansions demolished to avoid taxes.

Practicalities

Three miles from the coast, **inland Vero Beach** has a Greyhound terminal at the Texaco filling station, 1995 Hwy-1 (℡561/562-6588), and a **Chamber of Commerce at** 1216 21st St (Mon–Fri 9am–5pm; ℡561/567-3491). At the beach, exceptions to priccy **accommodation** are the *Riviera Inn*, 1605 S Ocean Drive (℡561/234-4112; ➍), and *Sea Spray Gardens*, 965 E Causeway Blvd (℡561/231-5210; ➌), both with great deals off season. Good-value **eateries** include the *Beachside Restaurant*, opposite the Driftwood Resort, at 3125 Ocean Drive (℡561/234-4477), which serves a fine crabmeat quiche; *Nino's Café*, 1006 Easter Lily Lane (℡561/231-9311), which features large protions of pasta; and *Tangos*, 925 Bougainvillea Lane, between Ocean and Cardinal drives (℡561/231-1550), which is renowned for both its baked crab, brie and artichoke dip and its lobster quesadillas entrées.

North of Vero Beach: Sebastian Inlet

Tiny beachside communities dot the rest of the island, but you'll find most activity – and campgrounds ($17 Dec–April, $15 May–Nov) – around the **Sebastian Inlet State Recreation Area**, 9700 S Hwy-A1A (open 24 hours; cars $3.25, pedestrians and cyclists $1, ℡407/984-4852), sixteen miles north of Vero Beach. Roaring ocean breakers lure surfers here, particularly over Easter when contests are held, and anglers cram the jetties for the East Coast's finest fishing. Without a board or a rod, you can amuse yourself by keeping an eye out for the endangered birdlife making sorties from nearby Pelican Island, the oldest wildlife refuge in the country and off limits to humans. For a bit of dolphin and manatee watching, the *Inlet Explorer* (located inside Inlet Marina; $18, children under 12, $12; ℡407/724-5424 or 1-800/952-1126) offers two-hour tours of the Indian River Lagoon. Alternatively, head a couple of miles south of the inlet to the **McLarty Museum**, at 13180 N Hwy-A1A (daily 10am–4.30pm; $1; ℡561/589-2147), where you can view treasure salvaged from a Spanish fleet that perished in a hurricane in 1715.

Beyond Sebastian Inlet you reach the outskirts of the **Space Coast**, which is covered in "The Northeast Coast," p.211.

TRAVEL DETAILS

Buses

Fort Lauderdale to: Delray Beach (2 daily; 1hr 10min); Fort Pierce (12 daily; 2hr 50min); Stuart (4 daily; 3hr 15min); Vero Beach (5 daily; 3hr 55min); West Palm Beach (14 daily; 2hr).

Hollywood to: Fort Lauderdale (11 daily; 10–30min); Orlando (8 daily; 5–6hr).

West Palm Beach to: Belle Glade (1 daily; 55min); Fort Pierce (7 daily; 1hr); Stuart (4 daily; 45min); Tampa (5 daily; 7hr–8hr 30min); Vero Beach (4 daily; 2hr 30min).

Tri-Rail

Mon–Fri 14 daily, Sat 7 daily, Sun 6 daily; $2.50; ☏1-800/874-7245, ⊛www.trirail.com.

Trains

Hollywood to: Boca Raton (39min); Delray Beach (51 min); Fort Lauderdale (15min); West Palm Beach (1hr 16min).

The Northeast Coast

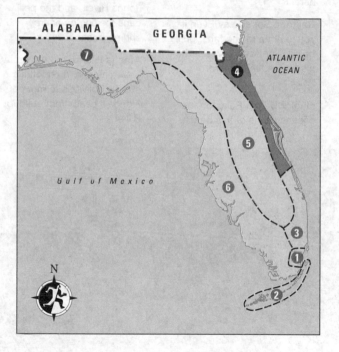

CHAPTER 4

Highlights

* **Kennedy Space Center** Watch nighttime space-shuttles being launched against the clear sky – and feel a part of history. **P.211**

* **Merritt Island National Wildlife Refuge** An incredible array of wildlife, birds especially, can be found here. **P.215**

* **Daytona Speedway** Even if you're not a racing fan, you'll be hard-pressed to resist the high-speed thrills here. **P.226**

* **Flagler Beach** Relax on the pristine sands of this beach, just fourteen miles from more crowded Daytona. **P.227**

* **St Augustine** America's oldest city, so little else should need to be said. **P.228**

* **Mayport Ferry** Enjoy the excellent views of the St Johns River –and the pelicans feeding on nearby shrimp boats. **P.243**

* **Amelia Island** Another great beach area, and one that's slightly oblivious to most of Florida's beachfront buildup. **P.244**

The Northeast Coast

Substantially free of commercial exploitation, with washed-up sharks' teeth sometimes more evident on its beaches than people, the 190 miles of Florida's **NORTHEAST COAST** are tailor-made for leisurely exploration. You'll often feel like doing nothing more strenuous than settling down beside the ocean, but throughout the region signs of the forces that have shaped Florida – from ancient Native American settlements to the launch site of the Space Shuttle – are easy to find and worth exploring. When planning your trip, remember that, owing to the less tropical climate, the Northeast Coast's tourist **seasons** are the reverse of those of the Southeast Coast: the crowded time here is the summer, when accommodation is more expensive and harder to come by than during the winter months.

Besides sharing a shoreline, the towns of the Northeast Coast have surprisingly little in common. Those making up the **Space Coast**, the southernmost area, primarily serve the hordes passing through to visit the impressively efficient **Kennedy Space Center**, birthplace and still the launching pad of the nation's space exploits. Its public image is unrelentingly positive, but the Space Center is definitely worth a visit, as is the wildlife refuge that surrounds it. Seventy miles north of the Space Coast lies **Daytona Beach**, a small town with a big strand, where the legendary excesses of Spring Break gained international notoriety in the Eighties until local authorities began to discourage all sorts of teenage carousing. The result is that things are mellower, almost downbeat, in Daytona now.

Along the northerly section of the coast, the plentiful evidence of Florida's early European landings is best displayed in the comprehensively restored town of **St Augustine**, where sixteenth-century Spaniards established North America's earliest foreign settlement. In addition to the attractions of the town itself, there's the surrounding coast, part of a divine strand stretching to the **Jacksonville Beaches**, twenty miles north, where lying in the sun and tuning into the sprightly local nightlife will waste a few decadent days. Just inland, the city of **Jacksonville**, struggling to shrug off its gray industrial image, merits only a cursory glance, if any, as you strike out towards the state's northeastern extremity. Here, overlooking the coast of Georgia, slender **Amelia Island** is fringed by gorgeous silver sands and features a quirky, posh Victorian-era main town.

The **road network** is very much a continuation of the Southeast Coast's system: **Hwy-A1A** hugs the coastline, with occasional breaks, while **Hwy-1** charts a less appealing course on the mainland and is a lot slower than **I-95**, which divides the coastal area from the eastern edge of Central Florida. Greyhound **buses** are frequent along Hwy-1 between the main towns, but, as with the rest of Florida, the best way to get around is by car. Forget the **train** – only Jacksonville has a station.

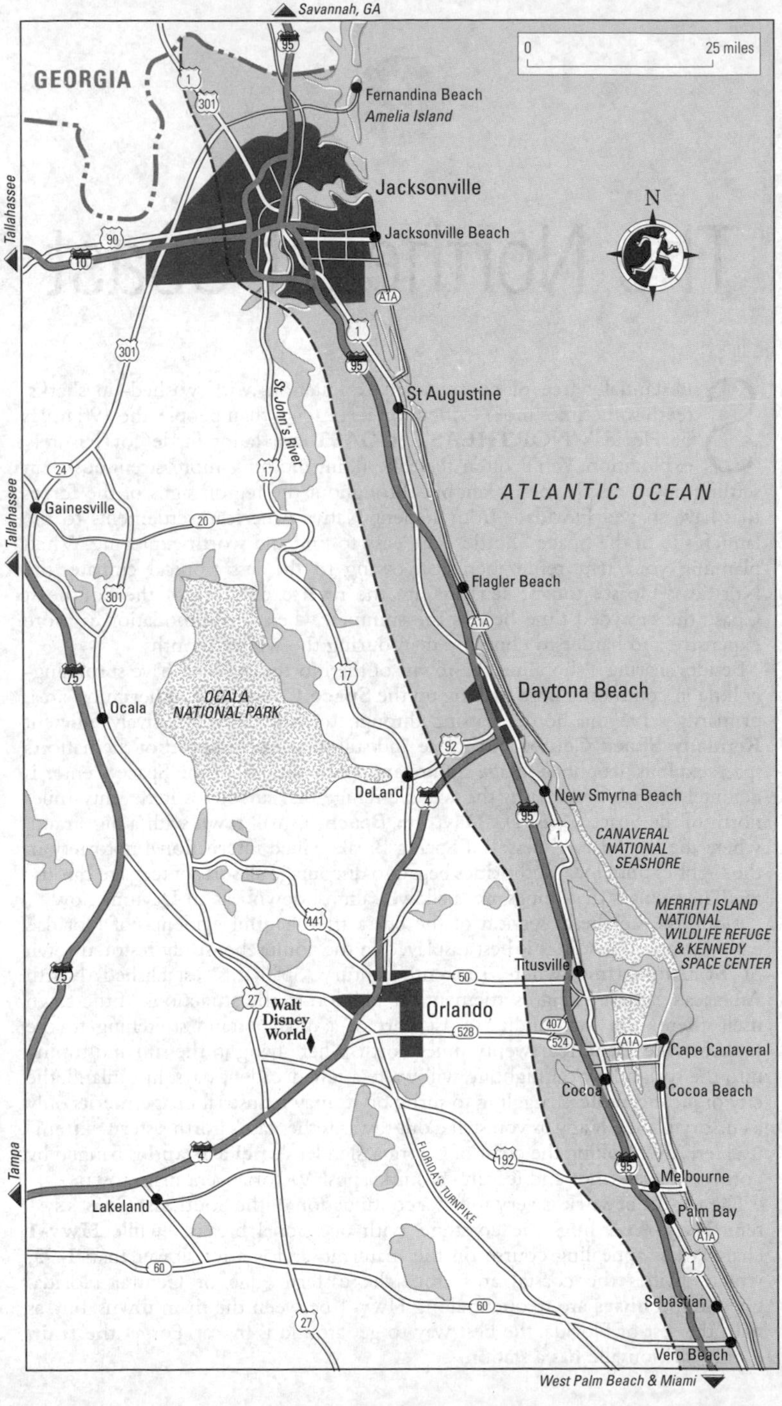
Savannah, GA
0
25 miles
GEORGIA
Fernandina Beach
Amelia Island
Jacksonville
N
Jacksonville Beach
Tallahassee
St Augustine
St. John's River
ATLANTIC OCEAN
Gainesville
Tallahassee
Flagler Beach
Daytona Beach
OCALA NATIONAL PARK
Ocala
DeLand
New Smyrna Beach
CANAVERAL NATIONAL SEASHORE
MERRITT ISLAND NATIONAL WILDLIFE REFUGE & KENNEDY SPACE CENTER
Titusville
Walt Disney World
Orlando
Cape Canaveral
Cocoa
Cocoa Beach
FLORIDA'S TURNPIKE
Tampa
Melbourne
Lakeland
Palm Bay
Sebastian
Vero Beach
West Palm Beach & Miami
1
301
95
90
10
A1A
301
17
24
20
301
75
17
92
4
441
50
27
528
407
524
192
60
27
75

The Space Coast

The barrier islands that dominate the Treasure Coast (see "The Southeast
Coast," p.198) continue north into what's known as the **SPACE COAST**, the
base of the country's space industry and site of the Kennedy Space Center,
which occupies a flat, marshy island bulging into the Atlantic just fifty miles east
of Orlando. Many of the visitors who flock here are surprised to find that the
land from which the Space Shuttle leaves earth is also a sizeable wildlife refuge
framed by several miles of rough coastline. Except for the beach-orientated
communities on the ocean, the towns of the Space Coast are of little interest
other than for low-cost overnight stops on the way to St Augustine or points
north, or for meal breaks. The new 24-hour Space Coast general information
hotline is ☎321/452-INFO, or from outside the area, ☎1-800/93-OCEAN.

The Kennedy Space Center

Justifiably the biggest attraction in the area, the **Kennedy Space Center** is the
nucleus of the US space program: it's here that space vehicles are developed,
tested and blasted into orbit. The first launches actually took place across the
water at the US Air Force base on Cape Canaveral (renamed Cape Kennedy
in 1963 and changed back to the original in 1973), from which rockets still lift
off. After the space program was expanded in 1964 and the Saturn V rockets
proved too large to launch from there, the focus of activity was moved to
Merritt Island, positioned between Cape Canaveral and the mainland and
directly north of Cocoa Beach.

The Space Center is well worth a visit for its solid documentation of US
achievements, revealing how closely success in space is tied to the nation's sense
of well-being.

The Kennedy Space Center Visitor Complex

Everything at the **KSC Visitor Complex** is within easy walking distance of
the parking lot, as is the departure point for the bus tour (see overleaf). The
complex will keep anyone with the faintest interest in space exploration entertained for a good hour. Everything you might expect to see is here: actual mission capsules, space suits, lunar modules, a granite memorial to those who gave
their lives in the quest to explore space, a full-sized, walk-through mock-up of
the Space Shuttle, and an interactive exhibit on the 1997 Pathfinder mission to
Mars, where scientists may have discovered signs of possible extraterrestrial bac-
terial life embedded in rocks. The rockets standing outside the museum in the
Rocket Garden are deceptively simple in appearance and far daintier than the
gigantic Saturn V (only seen on the bus tour) that launched the Apollo missions.

The area code for Cocoa Beach and the Space Coast is ☎321.

Next door to the complex, the IMAX **theater** shows two films, using 70mm film projected onto a five-story screen. Highlighting dramatic shots from an orbiting space shuttle, *The Dream Is Alive* (37min) captures the sensations of space flight as well as the daily business of living in space; *L5: First City in Space* (35min) is a 3-D film that constructs a future space settlement using real NASA footage and data, and depicts plans for the international space station, which is being created by thirteen countries and is explained on the bus tour. A couple of new offerings are the **Astronaut Encounter**, a daily chance to meet a real live astronaut, and **Exploration in the New Millennium**, a futuristic exhibit tracing the history of mankind's urge to go where no man has gone before, an educational journey that includes the chance to touch an actual piece of the planet Mars.

As far as **eating** goes, there are four canteens and various snack bars scattered around the Visitor Complex that provide standard pizza and hot-dog fare at down-to-earth prices. Though convenient for snacks and drinks (you can eat futuristic ice cream in solid-pellet form called "space dots"), you might be better off packing a cooler and eating in the aptly named "Lunch Pad."

The Kennedy Space Center Tour

The **bus tour** (daily 9.30am–5pm; every 15min; included with your Maximum Access Badge) around the rest of the Merritt Island complex provides a dramatic insight into the colossal grandeur of the space program. After zooming through the main gate and passing countless gators on the side of the road, the 52-story **Vehicle Assembly Building** (where the Shuttles, like Apollo and Skylab before them, are put together and fitted with payloads) looms ahead. Unfortunately, access is prohibited, but if a door is open you'll catch a glimpse inside one of the world's largest structures. Equivalent in volume to three and a half Empire State Buildings, the VAB is the second largest in the world and the first stop for the "crawlerway" – the huge tracks along which Space Shuttles are wheeled to the launch pad.

With luck, a Space Shuttle will be in place for take-off when the bus takes a loop around the **launch pad** – no different in reality from what you've seen on TV, and no more interesting than any other large pile of scaffolding if a Shuttle isn't present (obviously, when a countdown is under way there are no

---

The Kennedy Space Center: practical info and tips

The only **public entry roads** to the Kennedy Space Center are Hwy-405 from Titusville, and Route 3 off Hwy-A1A between Cocoa Beach and Cocoa: on either approach, follow signs for the Kennedy Space Center **Visitor Complex** (daily 9am–dusk; free), which underwent a massive revamping in late 2000 and contains a museum, a life-size Space Shuttle Explorer replica, the Universe Theater, exhibit halls, the Astronaut Memorial, the Rocket Garden and an IMAX film theater.

Arrive early to avoid the crowds, which are thinnest on weekends and during May and September. To take the bus tour or to see one of the two IMAX films, you should **buy tickets** from the ticket pavilion as soon as you arrive (Maximum Access Badge $24, children $15).

To **see a launch** from the Space Center, phone ☎321/449-4444 or 321/452-2121 for recorded schedule information, **launch dates** and times, or you can get all your tickets online at ⊛www.KennedySpaceCenter.com. Note, however, that the sheer magnitude of the blast delivers an extraordinary, unforgettable experience from anywhere within a forty-mile radius of the launch pad. The night launches are the most spectacular.

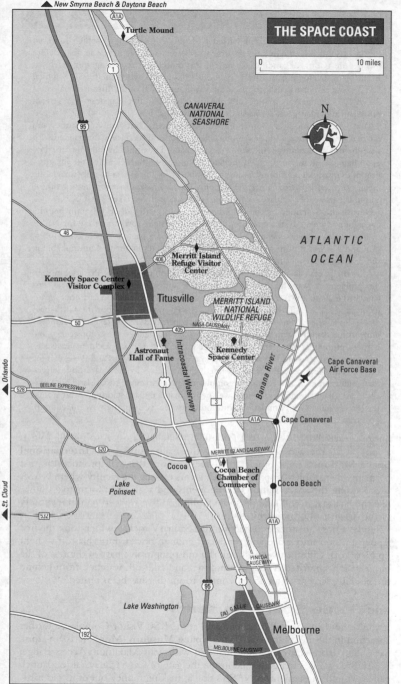

New Smyrna Beach & Daytona Beach

Turtle Mound

A1A

1

95

CANAVERAL
NATIONAL
SEASHORE

THE SPACE COAST

0   10 miles

N

46

ATLANTIC
OCEAN

Merritt Island
Refuge Visitor
Center

406

Kennedy Space Center
Visitor Complex

Titusville

MERRITT ISLAND
NATIONAL
WILDLIFE REFUGE

50

405

NASA CAUSEWAY

Orlando

Astronaut
Hall of Fame

Intracoastal Waterway

Kennedy
Space Center

Banana River

Cape Canaveral
Air Force Base

528

BEELINE EXPRESSWAY

1

3

A1A

Cape Canaveral

St. Cloud

520

MERRITT ISLAND CAUSEWAY

532

Cocoa

Lake
Poinsett

Cocoa Beach
Chamber of
Commerce

Cocoa Beach

A1A

PINEDA
CAUSEWAY

95

1

Lake Washington

EAU GALLIE CAUSEWAY

Melbourne

192

MELBOURNE CAUSEWAY

213

Fort Pierce & Miami

Fort Pierce

The growth of the Space Coast started with the **"Space Race,"** which followed President John F. Kennedy's declaration in May 1961 to "achieve the goal, before the decade is out, of landing a man on the moon and returning him safely to Earth." This statement came in the chill of the Cold War, when the USSR – which had just put the first man into space following its launch of the first artificial satellite in 1957 – appeared scientifically ahead of the US, a fact that dented American pride and provided great propaganda for the Soviets.

Money and manpower were pumped into **NASA** (National Aeronautics and Space Administration), and the communities around Cape Canaveral expanded with a heady influx of scientists and would-be astronauts. The much-hyped Mercury program helped restore prestige, and the later Apollo moonshots captured the imagination of the world. The moon landing by Apollo 11 in July 1969 not only turned the dreams of science-fiction writers into reality, but also meant that for the first time – and in the most spectacular way possible – the US had overtaken the USSR.

During the Seventies, as the incredible expense of the space program became apparent and seemed out of all proportion to its benefits, pressure grew for NASA to become more cost-effective. The country entered a period of economic recession and NASA's funding was drastically slashed; unemployment – unthinkable in the buoyant Sixties – threatened many on the Space Coast.

After the internationally funded Skylab space station program, NASA's solution to the problem of wasteful one-use rockets was the reusable **Space Shuttle**, first launched in April 1981, and able to deploy commercial payloads and carry out repairs to orbiting satellites. The Shuttle's success silenced many critics, but the Challenger disaster of January 1986 – when the entire crew perished during take-off – not only imbued the country with a deep sense of loss but highlighted the complacency and corner-cutting that had crept into the space program after many accident-free years.

Despite numerous satisfactory missions since, technical problems and the exercising of stringent safety procedures have caused serious delays to the Space Shuttle program, illustrating what a colossal accomplishment the manned moon landings actually were. Of equal significance may well be the manned space station in orbit around the earth, planned for completion within the first few years of the new millennium.

bus tours; see the box on p.212 for launch-watching tips). Also on the tour is a look at all the activity surrounding the realization of the **International Space Station**, a joint project of sixteen nations that will produce the first permanently inhabitable space station. Visitors can see the facility where NASA is processing the space station's components and soak up informative tidbits, like the fact that it will take 38 space flights and five years to haul the entirety of the space station into orbit.

Besides a nose-to-nozzle inspection of a Saturn V rocket, which took the first Apollo mission into space and produced enough power upon blastoff to light up New York City for over an hour, the most impressive part of the rest of the bus tour is a simulated Apollo countdown and take-off, watched from behind the blinking screens of an actual control room that has been retired.

Air Force Space Museum

If you've not had your fill of space travel at the KSC Visitor Complex, a further attraction in the area is the **Air Force Space Museum** (Mon–Fri 10am–2pm, Sat & Sun 10am–4pm; an additional $20 with your Maximum Access Badge; ☎321/853-9171), situated a mile inside the gate of Cape Canaveral (on launch pad 26A), and a testament to NASA's skill at making money out of its old hardware. The museum consists of a large expanse of land rather akin to the Rocket Garden at the KSC Visitor Complex (see p.211), and two buildings containing exhibits and information on rocket development, some of which proves fascinating: one such nugget is the fact that all the extraordinary developments of the space program stem from V2 rockets, which were originally fired by Nazi Germany against Britain in the closing years of the World War II— and were subsequently launched into orbit by America in 1950.

For yet another angle on space travel, visit the **Astronaut Hall of Fame** (see Titusville, p.218), just down the road from the Kennedy Space Center.

Merritt Island National Wildlife Refuge

NASA shares its land with the **Merritt Island National Wildlife Refuge** (daily sunrise–sunset; free), entered via Route 402 from Titusville. Here you'll find alligators, armadillos, raccoons, bobcats and one of Florida's greatest concentrations of birdlife living alongside some of the world's most advanced technology.

Even if you're only coming for a day at the Space Center, it would be a shame to pass up such a spectacular place – though it has to be said that Merritt Island, on first glance, looks anything but spectacular, comprising acres of estuaries and brackish marshes interspersed by occasional hammocks of oak and palm, and pine flatwoods where a few bald eagles construct nests ten feet in circumference. Winter is the **best time to visit**, when the island's skies are alive with thousands of migratory birds from the frozen north, and when mosquitoes are absent. At any other period, and especially in summer, the island's Mosquito Lagoon is worthy of its name; bring ample insect repellent.

Seeing the refuge

Seven miles east of Titusville on Route 406, the six-mile **Black Point Wildlife Drive** gives a solid introduction to the basics of the island's ecosystem. At the entrance you can pick up a highly informative free leaflet that describes specific stops along the route. From one you'll spot a couple of bald eagle nests, while another by the mudflats affords a good vantage point for watching a wide variety of wading and shore birds swooping on their dinner.

Be sure to do some walking within the refuge, too. Off the wildlife drive, the five-mile **Cruickshank Trail** weaves around the edge of the Indian River. If the whole length is too strenuous for you, there's an observation tower just a few minutes' walk from the parking lot. For a more varied landscape, drive a few miles further east along Route 402 – branching from Route 406 just south of the wildlife drive – passing the **visitor center** (Mon–Fri 8am–4.30pm, Sat & Sun 9am–5pm; closed Sun Mar–Oct; ☎321/861-0667), and tackle the half-mile **Oak Hammock Trail** or the two mile **Palm Hammock Trail**, both accessible from the same parking lot.

The Canaveral National Seashore

A slender, 25-mile-long beach dividing Merritt Island's Mosquito Lagoon from the Atlantic Ocean, the **Canaveral National Seashore** (winter 6am–6pm, summer 6am–8pm; $5) begins at **Playalinda Beach** on Route 402, seven miles east of the refuge's visitor center. The National Seashore's entire length is top-notch beachcombing and surfing territory, and also suitable for swimming. Except when rough seas and high tides submerge it completely, you should take a wind-bitten ramble along the palmetto-lined path to wild **Klondike Beach**, north of Playalinda Beach, often coated with intriguing shells and marked from May through September by the tracks left by sea turtles crawling ashore at night to lay eggs. The Space Coast is the second largest **turtle nesting** area in the world and turtle-watching is a popular local pastime. Call ☎800/936-2326 for more information.

At the northern tip of the National Seashore, on **Apollo Beach** (accessible only by road from New Smyrna Beach, eight miles north of Apollo, see "Heading north: New Smyrna Beach," p.219), is **Turtle Mound**. This is a "midden," or a 35-foot heap of oyster shells and other refuse left by the Timucua Indians over several generations of living here. The site became prominent enough over time to be marked on maps by Florida's first Spanish explorers, being visible several miles out to sea. Take a few minutes to walk along the boardwalks, through the dense, fragrant vegetation to the top of the mound.

Cocoa Beach

A few miles south of the Kennedy Space Center, **Cocoa Beach** comprises just a ten-mile strip of shore and a few residential streets off Atlantic Avenue (Hwy-A1A). As well as being unquestionably the best base from which to see the Space Coast, it's also a favored haunt of surfers, who are attracted here by some of the most "radical" waves in Florida. Major (and minor) surfing contests are held here during spring and summer, and throughout the year the place has a perky, youthful feel. There's also a big beach volleyball contingent here, setting and spiking on four permanent courts. On weekends there's often free music around the pier and beachside parks, and to get an idea of the community's prime concerns you need only take a walk around the original *Ron Jon Surf Shop*, 4151 N Atlantic Ave (☎321/799-8820 or 1-888/RJ SURFS), a virtual surfing theme park with its colorful, high-energy vibes, and its branch a stone's throw away (the Water Sports Store). Both are open 24 hours a day and packed with surfboards (rental per day is $20 for a fiberglass board), bicycles ($5 for two hours or $50 per week), kites and extrovert beach attire.

Information and transport

The Cocoa Beach **Chamber of Commerce** is located on Merritt Island at 400 Fortenberry Rd (Mon–Fri 9am–5pm; ☎321/459-2200). A local **bus** service (SCAT; ☎321/633-1878) runs regularly to and from Cape Canaveral through Cocoa Beach (#9), and #6 runs from downtown Cocoa to Cocoa Beach; both routes cost $1 one way. The Cocoa Beach Shuttle (☎321/784-3831) runs to and from Orlando International Airport for $18 one way; call to be collected from any hotel on Hwy-A1A. To get around the beach area, rent a **bike** from the *Ron Jon Surf Shop* (details above). The nearest Greyhound station is on the mainland in Cocoa at 302 Main St (☎321/636-6531).

Accommodation

Accommodation bargains are rare in Cocoa Beach. You can expect prices to be highest during February, July and August – and during Space Shuttle launches. The lowest rates for motels are at the *Fawlty Towers*, 100 E Cocoa Beach Causeway (☎321/784-3870; ❸) and the spartan *Motel 6*, 3701 N Atlantic Ave (☎321/783-3103; ❷). Or you can try the pleasant *Days Inn Cocoa Beach*, 5500 N Atlantic Ave (☎321/784-2550 or 1-888/799-1631; ❺); and, for a good-priced bed and breakfast, check out *Luna Sea*, 3185 N Atlantic Ave (☎1-800/586-2732; ❹). For a longer stay, try the *Econo Lodge Resort*, 1275 N Atlantic Ave (☎1-800/795-2252; ❹), with its great pool; this is especially good value for several people sharing. To relax in style, stay at *Sea Esta Villas*, 686 S Atlantic Ave (℡1-800/872-9444, ⓦwww.seaestavillas.homestead.com; ❺), with its homely, upscale suites, or go for the plush *Ocean Suite Hotel*, 5500 Ocean Beach Blvd (℡1-800/367-1223; ❺), located within walking distance of the famous Cocoa Beach Pier. The most tent-friendly **campground** is *Jetty Park*, 400 Jetty Drive (℡321/783-7111; $14.85), five miles north at Cape Canaveral.

Eating and nightlife

Many inland restaurants strive to undercut each other, resulting in some good **eating** deals if you have your own transportation; see "Inland" below for suggestions and scan free magazines (found in motels and at the Chamber of Commerce) such as *Restaurant Dining Out, The Dining Out Guide* and *Space Coast* for money-saving coupons. Close to the beach, the options are fewer. For great oysters and a $5 lunch buffet, head for *Rusty's Seafood & Oyster Bar,* 628 Glen Cheek Drive at Port Canaveral (℡321/783-2033). A great dinner option is *The Pier Restaurant*, on the pier (℡321/783-7549), which has a quality (and somewhat expensive) menu especially strong on seafood and features a Sunday champagne brunch. Or you can opt for the cheaper *Old Fish House*, 249 W Cocoa Beach Causeway (℡321/799-9190), with its all-you-can-eat specials.

Nightlife is most enjoyable if you start early at one of the beachside **happy hours**: try *Marlins' Good Time Grill*, also part of the pier complex (℡321/783-7549), or *Surfside Café*, on the beach at 211 E Cocoa Beach Causeway (℡321/799-9977), which features live Southern rock bands and a full menu. As the evening draws on, the *Pig and Whistle*, 801 N Atlantic Ave (℡321/799-0724), offers TV soccer and overpriced English bitter, while *Coconuts*, 2 Minuteman Causeway (℡321/784-1422), has drinking and **live music** on the beach.

Inland: Palm Bay, Melbourne, Cocoa and Titusville

The chief attractions of the Space Coast's sleepy **inland towns**, strung along Hwy-1, are cheaper accommodation and food than at the beaches, plus areas of historical interest that provide relief from the usual tourist drag.

Palm Bay

The southernmost town is **Palm Bay**, thirty miles north of Vero Beach (see p.205). Despite boasting a higher population than any of its neighbors, it's the least geared to tourism, being largely a commuter belt town for Space Coast employees. There's little to detain you here apart from the small **Turkey Creek Sanctuary**, 1502 Port Malabar Blvd (daily 7am–sunset; free), whose short boardwalk trail winds through three distinct (and simulated) native habitats – hardwood hammock, sand and pine scrub, and wet hardwood forest – that support endangered species of flora and fauna.

Melbourne

Just a few miles north of Palm Bay lies the pretty yet dull town of **Melbourne**. You can take in the **Brevard Zoo**, 8225 Wickham Rd (daily 10am–5pm; $5.50; ℡321/254-WILD), with its Latin American, Australian and native Floridian fauna, or the collections at the **Brevard Museum of Art and Science**, 1463 Highland Ave (Tues–Sat 10am–5pm, Sun 1–5pm; $5; ℡321/242-0737, ⓦwww.artandscience.org). Melbourne's **restaurants** aren't bad: *Conchy Joe's*, 1477 Pineapple Ave (℡321/253-3131), has seafood, live reggae in the evenings and great views of the Indian River; *Durango Steakhouse*, 6767 N Wickham Rd (℡321/259-2934), serves up juicy Southwest-style steaks; and the friendly, busy *New England Eatery*, 5670 Hwy-A1A (℡321/723-6080), has fresh seafood at terrific prices. After eating, stroll along **Crane Creek**, a stretch of water between the Hwy-1 road bridge and the railway bridge, which is a **manatee-watching** area, though the viewing opportunites further north are better. A shoreline boardwalk, lined with oak trees and sabal palms, provides an attractive spot from which to glimpse these shy, endangered creatures.

If you're **staying** overnight, try the comfortable *Holiday Inn*, 420 S Harbor City Blvd (℡321/723-5320; ❸), with its pool and exercise room. When it's time to move on and you don't have your own wheels, catch a Greyhound **bus** at 460 S Hwy 1 (℡321/723-4323).

Cocoa

In **Cocoa**, thirty miles north of Melbourne and eight miles inland from Cocoa Beach, the brick-paved sidewalks and turn-of-the-nineteenth-century buildings of **Cocoa Village** fill several small blocks south of King Street (Hwy-520) and make for a relaxing stroll. Among the twee antique shops and boutiques, seek out the Porcher House, 434 Delannoy Ave (Mon–Fri 9am–5pm; free; ℡321/631-9075), a grand Neoclassical abode built in 1916.

For a greater insight into the town's origins, head a few miles west to the **Brevard Museum of History and Natural Science**, 2201 Michigan Ave (Tues–Sat 10am–4pm, Sun 1-4pm; $4; ℡321/632-1830), whose displays recount Cocoa's birth as a trading post when the first settlers arrived in the 1840s by steamboat and mule. There's also a respectable exhibit of Florida wildlife and some informative leaflets that are particularly useful if you're planning to visit the Merritt Island National Wildlife Refuge (see p.215).

The **Astronaut Memorial Hall and Planetarium**, 1519 Clearlake Rd (Tues, Fri & Sat 6.30–10pm; $12; ℡321/634-3732), which offers planetarium shows, I-Works movies and laser shows, is a halfhearted attempt to attract tourist dollars from the overflow of the nearby Kennedy Space Center and will interest only the most devoted of space enthusiasts.

If you're **staying** in Cocoa, there are some small and uninviting motels lining Cocoa Boulevard. The best option is the *Econo Lodge Space Center* at no. 3220 N (℡321/632-4561 or 1-888/721-9423; ❷), which has a pool and allows pets. For **eating**, try *Norman's Food and Spirits*, 3 Forrest Ave (℡321/632-8782), offering great lunch specials and entertaining karaoke in the evenings; alternatively, *Café Margaux*, 220 Brevard Ave (℡321/639-8343), is a stylish spot for a pasta lunch.

Titusville

If you don't visit the Kennedy Space Center, you'll at least get a great view of the towering Vehicle Assembly Building from **Titusville**, twenty miles north of Cocoa. If you find you have time on your hands here, visit the **Valiant Air Command Museum**, 6600 Tico Rd (daily 10am–6pm; $6; ℡321/268-1941), a celebration of slightly more pedestrian flying machines than those at the Kennedy Space Center. Originally formed to commemorate the US Air Force's involvement in preventing Japan's invasion of mainland China in 1941, the museum today exhibits lovingly restored planes, with examples from all wars since that date. The best way to see them is in March, when the VAC holds an air show and most of these war veterans take to the skies.

Apart from this, all that's commendable about Titusville is its ease of access to the Kennedy Space Center (via Hwy-405) and the Merritt Island National Wildlife Refuge (via Hwy-402). On the way to either place, visit the

Astronaut Hall of Fame (daily 9am–5pm; $13.95, children $9.95; ☎321/269-6100, ⓦwww.astronauthalloffame.com), one of Florida's most entertaining interactive museums. Simulation rides allow visitors to experience stomach-churning g-forces, weightlessness and 360-degree spins. There's also a mock Space Shuttle and tours of **SpaceCamp USA**, where young wannabe astronauts spend several weeks spinning about in contraptions designed to simulate the extreme g-forces of space travel.

For **food**, search out the seafood and steaks at *Janet's Café Orleans*, 605 Hopkins Ave (☎321/269-6020), or the seafood at locally famous *Dixie Crossroads*, 1475 Garden St (☎321/268-5000). Inexpensive **motels** are plentiful along Washington Avenue (Hwy-1): *South Wind*, no. 1540 S (☎321/267-3681; ❸), and *Siesta*, no. 2006 (☎321/267-1455; ❸), are just two. Otherwise, try the *Best Western Space Shuttle Inn*, 3455 Cheney Highway (☎321/269-9100; ❹), which also offers eco-tourism packages for exploring the unique flora and fauna of the area, such as sawgrass, loggerhead turtles and idigo snakes. For moving on, the Greyhound **bus** station is at 212 S Washington Ave (☎321/267-8760).

Heading north: New Smyrna Beach

After the virgin vistas of the Canaveral National Seashore, the tall beachside hotels of **New Smyrna Beach**, thirty miles north of Titusville on Hwy-1, create the impression of a likeable low-key beach community, where the sea – protected from dangerous currents by offshore rock ledges – is perfect for **swimming** and **surfing**, especially at Smyrna Dunes State Park, located on the south side of Ponce Inlet, to the north. To reach the beach (or the northern section of the Canaveral National Seashore, see p.215), you have to pass through the inland section of the town, before swinging east on Hwy-A1A.

A wealthy Scottish physician, Andrew Turnbull, bought land here in the mid-1700s and set about creating a Mediterranean colony, recruiting Greeks, Italians and Minorcans to work for seven years on his plantation in return for fifty acres of land each. The colony, named after his Greek wife's home town in what is now actually Turkey,. didn't last: bad treatment, language barriers, culture clashes, disease and financial disasters hastened its demise, and many of the settlers moved north to St Augustine (see p.228).

The immigrants worked hard, however (by most accounts, they had little choice), laying irrigation canals, building a sugar mill and commencing work on what was to be a palatial abode for Turnbull. Close to Hwy-1, the **ruins** of the mill (at the junction of Canal Street and Mission Road) and his unfinished house (at Riverside Drive and Julia Street) are substantial enough to merit a look. The nearby **Visitor Center**, 2242 State Rd 44, just off I-95 (Mon–Fri 9am–6pm, Sat 9am–5pm, Sun 1-4pm; ☎1-866/397-6976 or 386/428-1600, ⓦwww.newsmyrnabeachonline.com), has a handy historical brochure, as well as the usual local information. You can also stop by the **Chamber of Commerce** downtown, closer to the remains of the fort, at 115 Canal St (☎1-800/541-9621).

From Orlando International Airport, you can get a round-trip shuttle service with DOTS buses (fifteen round-trips per day; ☎1-800/231-1965) for $160 per couple – or Greyhound **buses** will drop you here at Steil's Gas Station, 600 Canal St (☎386/428-8211) – and then you can use the local Votran (☎386/424-6800)

The area code for Daytona Beach and New Smyrna Beach is ☎386.

to get around. If you want to stay over, the two cheapest, and most basic, **motels** are on Hwy-1 (locally called the Dixie Freeway): *Smyrna Motel*, no. 1050 N (☏386/428-2495 or 1-800/362-1841; ❷), which has an eagle's nest on its property, and the even more spartan *Shangri-La*, no. 805 N (☏386/428-8361; ❶). If you're in the mood for a truly luxurious and super-welcoming bed and breakfast, don't bypass the *Night Swan Intracoastal B&B*, within walking distance of downtown at 512 S Riverside Drive (☏1-800/465-4261 or 386/423-4940, ⓦwww.nightswan.com; ❹), with its own dock, the perfect spot for viewing Shuttle launches. Stay a few days to soak up the gracious hospitality. Across the arching causeway bridge and out to the beach itself, the pink stucco *Sea Vista Ocean Front Resort*, 1701 S Atlantic Ave, Hwy A1A (☏1-800/874-3917 or 386/428-2210, ⓦwww.seavistaresort.com; ❷), has its own pool and a beachside Tiki bar with cocktails, munchies and a full menu. The rouper sandwich is a coastal favorite. For the area's finest upscale **dining**, there's *Norwood's*, on the beach side of the causeway at 400 Second Ave (☏386/428-4621); maybe you'll be lucky enough to stop by when they're offering one of their famous wine-tastings, to complement the mouthwatering seafood.

Continuing north from New Smyrna Beach, Hwy-A1A joins with Hwy-1 for ten miles before splitting off oceanwards near Ponce Inlet, five miles south of mainland Daytona Beach.

Daytona Beach

The consummate Florida beach town, with rows of airbrushed-T-shirt shops, amusement arcades and wall-to-wall motels, **DAYTONA BEACH** owes its existence to twenty miles of light brown sand where the only pressure is to relax and enjoy yourself.

For decades, Daytona Beach was invaded by half a million college kids going through the Spring Break ritual of underage drinking and libido liberation. In the mid-Nineties, the town ended its love affair with the nation's students and tried to emulate Fort Lauderdale (see "The Southeast Coast, p.176") by cultivating a more refined image – an attempt that has been only partially successful, to say the least, since now it seems to cater mainly to bikers and race-car fanatics. In fact, Daytona Beach presents a decidedly seedy air these days. It's as if the rowdy kids have moved on and no one at all has come to replace them – except for the rowdy adults.

The resort is the center of three major annual events: the world-famous **Daytona 500** stock-car meeting, held at the Daytona International Speedway; **Bike Week**, when thousands of leather-clad motorcyclists converge for races at the Speedway; and the relatively new **Biketoberfest**, which is much the same idea (see box on p.226 for more info on all three events).

Even before the students and bikers, the beach was a favorite with pioneering auto enthusiasts such as Louis Chevrolet, Ransom Olds and Henry Ford, who came here during the early 1900s to race their prototype vehicles beside the ocean. The land speed record was regularly smashed, five times by millionaire British speedster Malcolm Campbell who, in 1935, roared along at 276mph. As a legacy of these times, Daytona Beach is one of the few Florida towns where the dubious thrill of **driving on the beach** is permitted: pay $5 at any beach entrance, stick to the marked track, observe the 10mph speed limit, park at right-angles to the ocean – and beware of high tide.

Arrival and getting around

As Ridgewood Avenue, **Hwy-1** steams through **mainland Daytona Beach**, passing the Greyhound station, at no. 138 S (☎386/255-7076 or 1-800/231-2222). By car, you should keep to **Hwy-A1A** (known as Atlantic Avenue), which enters the beachside area – filling a narrow sliver of land between the ocean and the Halifax River (part of the Intracoastal Waterway) a mile from the mainland.

Local buses (Votran ☎386/761-7700) connect the beaches with the mainland and the Greater Daytona Beach area, though there is no night or Sunday service (buses run until 6pm daily). The bus terminal is at the junction of US-1 and Bethune Boulevard in mainland Daytona Beach. At the beach, **trolleys** run until midnight along the central part of Atlantic Avenue from January to August only. A **taxi** between the airport and the beach will cost around $10; cab companies include AAA Metro Taxi (☎386/253-2522) and Yellow Cab (☎386/255-5555).

Don't leave mainland Daytona Beach without stopping by the **Convention and Visitors Bureau** in the Chamber of Commerce building at 126 E Orange Ave (calls answered Mon–Fri 9am–9pm, Sat & Sun 10am–4pm; ☎1-800/854-1234, ⓦwww.daytonabeach.com), for a wealth of free information.

Accommodation

From mid-May to November, scores of small **motels** on Atlantic Avenue slash their rates to $35–45 for a double – cheaper for two people sharing than staying at the youth hostel (see below). These rates go up by $10–15 from December to February, and soar to $80-plus during March and April (though the demise of Spring Break may stabilize prices between December and mid-May). Pick up the free *Superior Small Lodging Guide* from the Convention and Visitors Bureau for helpful hints on where to stay.

Hotels, motels and bed and breakfasts

Coquina Inn, 544 S Palmetto Ave (☎386/254-4969 or 1-800/805-7533). This homely bed and breakfast is located a little inland. ❹

Cove, 1306 N Atlantic Ave (☎1-800/828-3251). The *Cove* affords guests comfort and easy access to the beach. ❷

The Driftwood Beach Motel, 657 S Atlantic Ave (☎386/677-1331 or 1-800/490-8935). This beachfront motel accommodates limited budgets. ❷

Hampton Inn Oceanfront, S Atlantic Ave 3135 (☎1-800/822-7707, ⓦwww.avistahotels.com). One of the more luxurious options, offering private balconies, a large pool and a Jacuzzi. ❺

Live Oak Inn, 444-448 S Beach St (☎386/252-4667 or 1-800/881-4667). This Colonial-style inland bed and brekfast comes equipped with a Jacuzzi. ❹

Robin Hood, 1150 N Atlantic Ave (☎386/252-8228). A comfortable stay and easy access to the beach are available at this hotel. ❹

Streamline, 140 S Atlantic Ave (☎386/258-6937). The closest the area has to a youth hostel, the *Streamline* has received reviews from travelers ranging from OK to horrible. ❶

Sunglow Resort, 3647 S Atlantic Ave (☎1-800/225-3399, ⓦwww.sunglowresort.com). This resort is ideal if you want to be right next to the Sunglow Pier and enjoy the private pool. ❹

Tropical Manor Motel, 2237 S Atlantic Ave (☎1/800-253-4920). This friendly, roomy beachfront motel is the best deal of the bunch. ❷

The Villa, 801 N Peninsula Drive (☎386/248-2020, ⓦwww.thevillabb.com). This inland bed and breakfast is situated in a Spanish-style mansion. ❺

Camping

Nova Family Campground, 1190 Herbert St , ten miles south of mainland Daytona Beach (☎386/767-0095). Accessible by bus #17A, #17B or #7. $16 to pitch a tent.

Tomoka State Park, seven miles north of mainland Daytona Beach (☎386/676-4050). Take bus #1B, which stops a mile down the road; $8–16 to pitch a tent with rates highest in February.

If you're enjoying yourself at the beach but have to fly home from Orlando, you can take advantage of the **Daytona-Orlando Transit Service** (DOTS; ☎1-800/231-1965), whose shuttle buses run every ninety minutes (4.30am–9.30pm) from the corner of Nova Road and Eleventh Street to Orlando International Airport. On request, the buses also make stops in DeLand and Sanford. The one-way fare is $27 ($49 round-trip). Call ahead for details and reservations.

The beach and around

Without a doubt, the best thing about Daytona Beach *is* the **beach**: a seemingly limitless affair – 500 feet wide at low tide and, lengthways, fading dreamily into the heat haze. There's little to do other than develop your tan, take the occasional ocean dip or observe one of the many pro volleyball tournaments that set up camp during the summer. Even the **pier**, at the end of Main Street, isn't a source of action: you can loiter in one of two characterless bars; enjoy panoramic views of the town from the Space Needle ($2); take the Sky Ride, a run-down cable-car-like conveyance that ferries you slowly from one end of the pier to the other over the heads of patient anglers; try the Sky Coaster Ride, a 60mph amusement arcade affair; or go for a whirl on the rather dubious-looking bungee ride just to the north of the pier.

Nearby, Main Street and Seabreeze Boulevard have better bars and cafés (see "Eating" and "Nightlife"), but for more diverse pursuits – such as rambling around sand dunes, climbing an old lighthouse or discovering Daytona Beach's history – you need to head twelve miles south to Ponce Inlet, three miles north to Ormond Beach or cross the Halifax River to the mainland.

South to Ponce Inlet

Traveling south along Atlantic Avenue (buses #17A or #17B; only the former goes all the way to Ponce Inlet), small motels and fast-food dives give way to the towering beachside condos of affluent Daytona Beach shores. As you approach **Ponce Inlet**, four miles ahead, the outlook changes again, this time to single-story beach homes and large sand dunes.

Here, at the end of Peninsula Drive – parallel to Atlantic Avenue – the 175-foot-high **Ponce Inlet Lighthouse** (daily 10am–9pm; $4; ☎386/761-1821) illuminated the treacherous coast from the late 1800s until 1970, giving seaborne access to New Smyrna Beach (see p.219). Stupendous views make climbing the structure worthwhile, and the outbuildings hold engaging artifacts from its early days, as well as mildly interesting displays on US lighthouses in general. Several **nature trails** scratch a path through the surrounding scrub-covered dunes to a (usually) deserted **beach**; pick up a map from the **ranger station** at the end of Riverside Drive. Once you've trekked up an appetite, drop into the eccentric *Lighthouse Landing* (see "Eating," p.226), beside the lighthouse, whose cheap seafood is brought ashore at the adjoining marina.

North to Ormond Beach

In 1890, planning to bring his East Coast railway south from St Augustine, oil baron Henry Flagler bought the local hotel, built a beachside golf course and helped give **Ormond Beach** (Chamber of Commerce Office, 165 W Granada Blvd; ☎386/677-3454, ⓦ www.ormondchamber.com), three miles north of Main Street (buses #1A or #1B; the latter runs only as far as Granada Blvd); the refined tone that it retains to this day. Millionaires like John D. Rockefeller

DAYTONA BEACH

Tomoka State Park & Bulow Ruins ▲   ▲ St. Augustine

◄ St. Augustine

GRANADA BLVD
Ormond Beach
Art Gallery
The
Casements
A
1

ROCKEFELLER DR.
Ormond Beach

TOMOKA AVENUE

NORTH RIDGEWOOD AVENUE

NOVA ROAD

FLEMING AVENUE

Halifax River

NORTH ATLANTIC AVENUE

PLAZA BLVD.

NORTH HALIFAX AVENUE

A1A

SEAVIEW AVE.

TLOMISH AVENUE

RIVERSIDE DRIVE

Holly Hill

UNIVERSITY BLVD

SEABREEZE BLVD.

SOUTH ATLANTIC AVENUE

Pier

NORTH BEACH STREET

MAIN STREET

Daytona
Beach

FAIRVIEW AVE.

BROADWAY

SOUTH RIDGEWOOD AVENUE

Mary McLeod
Bethune Foundation

CYPRESS STREET

INTERNATIONAL SPEEDWAY BLVD

Greyhound
Station

ORANGE AVE.

NOVA ROAD

MASON AVENUE

Convention
and Visitors
Bureau

Silver Beach

Halifax
Historical
Museum

Museum of
Arts and Sciences

BELLE VUE AVENUE

OLD DE LAND ROAD

Daytona
International
Speedway

▼ Klassix Auto Museum   ▼ Airport

ATLANTIC
OCEAN

N

2
B
3
C
4 **D**
E
5
F

G
8
H
10

6
7
9

11 ▲
& Ponce Inlet

0   800 yds

ACCOMMODATION

Atlantic Waves Motel	6
Coquina Inn B & B	10
Cove Motel	2
Driftwood Beach Motel	5
Hampton Inn	9
Live Oak Inn	8
Robin Hood Motel	3
Sunglow Resort	11
Tropical Manor Motel	7
The Villa B & B	4
Youth Hostel	1

RESTAURANTS & CAFÉS

Aunt Catfish's	L
Checkers	E
Clocktower	B
Inlet Harbor	K
Julian's	A
Lighthouse Landing	J
Mainstreet Pier	F
McK's Tavern	G
Rio Bravo Cantina	H
St Regis Restaurant and Patio Bar	D
Sapporo	I
Shells	C

wintered here, and the car-happy fraternity of Ford, Olds and Chevrolet used Flagler's garage to fine-tune their autos before powering them along the beach. Note, however, that beach driving is now prohibited in Ormond Beach, from North Granada Boulevard.

Facing the Halifax River at the end of Granada Boulevard, Flagler's **Ormond Hotel** stood until 1993, when it was demolished to much public mourning. However, the **Casements** (Mon–Fri 10am–2.30pm, Sat 10–11am;

free), a three-story villa on the other side of Granada Boulevard that was bought by Rockefeller in 1918 is in fine shape (all the original furniture, though, was sold, and what remains was donated by neighbors). **Guided tours** of the house (which, oddly enough, now holds displays of Hungarian folklore and Boy Scouts of America bric-a-brac) run every thirty minutes from 10am and tell you more than you'll ever need to know about Rockefeller and his time here, which was mostly spent playing golf and pressing dimes into the hands of passers-by.

At 78 Granada Blvd, the Polynesian-style **Ormond Memorial Art Museum and Gardens** (Mon–Fri 10am–4pm, Sat & Sun noon–4pm; free) puts on reasonable temporary art shows – if they don't appeal, the gallery's jungle-like **gardens**, with shady pathways winding past fishponds to a gazebo, just might.

The mainland

When you're tired of the sands or nursing your sunburn, cross the river to **mainland Daytona Beach**, where several waterside parks and walkways contribute to a relaxing change of scene, and four museums will keep you out of the sun for a few hours.

Near the best of the parks, on Beach Street, a few turn-of-the-nineteenth-century dwellings have been tidied up and turned into office space. At no. 252 S is the **Halifax Historical Museum** (Tues–Sat 10am–4pm; $3, free on Sat), which captures, with an absorbing stock of objects, models and photos, the frenzied growth of Daytona Beach and Halifax County. Amid the fine stash of prehistoric archeological artifacts and historic memorabilia, don't ignore the immense wall paintings of long-gone local landscapes.

One former Daytona Beach resident mentioned in the museum is better remembered by the **Mary McLeod Bethune Foundation**, a couple of miles north at 640 McLeod Bethune Blvd. Born in 1875 to freed slave parents, Mary McLeod Bethune was a lifelong campaigner for racial and sexual equality, founding the National Council of Negro Women and serving as a presidential advisor to Calvin Coolidge and Franklin Roosevelt on racial issues, especially the education of African-American women. In 1904, against the odds, she founded the state's first black girls' school here – with savings of $1.50 and five pupils. The white-framed **house** (Mon–Fri 9am–4pm; free), where Bethune lived from 1914 until her death in 1955, contains scores of awards and citations alongside furnishings and personal effects, and sits within the campus of Bethune-Cookman College, which has grown up around the original school.

If you're keen on paleontology and prehistory, stop off at the **Museum of the Arts & Sciences and Center for Florida History**, 1040 Museum Blvd (Tues–Fri 9am–4pm, Sat & Sun noon–5pm; $5), a mile south of International Speedway Boulevard (buses #6 and #7 pass close by), to scrutinize bones and fossils dug up from the numerous archeological sites in the area. These include the ferocious-looking reassembled remains of a million-year-old giant ground sloth (thirteen feet long). There is also a **Planetarium** ($3, children $2) that is only worth it if you desire a long nap under a virtual star-scape. The other sections of the constantly expanding museum are intriguingly diverse: a stash of American paintings, furnishings and decorative arts from the seventeenth century onwards illuminates early Anglo-American tastes. A major African collection displays domestic and ceremonial objects from thirty of the continent's cultures, including pieces donated – strangely enough – by some bygone television stars like Dirk Benedict (*A-Team*) and Linda Evans (*Dynasty*). Finally,

Cuban paintings spanning two centuries (donated by Cuba's former dictator, Batista, who spent many years of exile in a comfortable Daytona Beach house) provide a glimpse of the island nation's important artistic movements.

Daytona International Speedway

About three miles west along International Speedway Boulevard, at no. 1801 W (℡386/254-2700), accessible by bus #9A and #9B, stands an ungainly configuration of concrete and steel that has done much to promote Daytona Beach's name around the world: the **Daytona International Speedway**, home of the Daytona 500 stock-car meeting and a few other less famous races. When high speeds made racing on Daytona's sands unsafe, the solution was this 150,000-capacity temple to high-performance thrills and spills, which opened in 1959.

If you can't catch a race, **Daytona USA** (daily 9am–7pm; $12 to enter, $6 for speedway tours, $16 for a combo ticket; ℡386/947-6800; ⓦwww.daytonausa .com), located next to the speedway, is the next best thing. Though it doesn't quite capture the excitement of a race, the guided **trolley tour** (daily 9.30am–5pm, except on race days; every 30min) gives visitors a chance to see the sheer size of the place and the remarkable gradient of the curves, which help make this the fastest racetrack in the world – 200mph is not uncommon.

Inside, the interactive exhibits put you in the driver's seat: show the spectators how fast you can jack a race car off the ground during a sixteen-second pit stop; feel the engines revving in your chest as you watch the "thunder-round sound" Daytona 500 wide-screen movie; or call a race as it happens at the interactive commentator booth. Other exhibits showcase the history of NASCAR★ (National Association of Stock Car Auto Racing) and the evolution of the race car.

Klassix Auto Museum

A mile west of the Speedway, the **Klassix Auto Museum**, at 2909 W International Speedway Blvd (daily 9am–6pm; $8.50; ℡386/252-3800, ⓦwww.klassixauto.com), displays pristine examples of every Corvette design from 1953 to the present, in historically accurate settings. The museum also houses various other collector and "muscle" cars, as well as vintage motorcycles, all engagingly offset by a 1938 Woody Wagon that boasts a top speed of 50mph.

North to Tomoka State Park and the Bulow Ruins

At the meeting point of the Halifax and Tomoka rivers, just off Hwy-1 six miles north of International Speedway Boulevard (bus #1B, then a mile's walk), the attractive **Tomoka State Park** (daily 8am–sunset; cars $4.25, cyclists and pedestrians $1; ℡386/676-4050) comprises several hundred acres of marshes and tidal creeks, bordered by magnolias and moss-draped oaks. It's ripe for exploration by canoe ($3 per hour or $15 per day) or on foot along its many paths.

A 1972 addition to the park, the tiny **Fred Dana Marsh Museum** (9.30am–4.30pm; admission included in park entrance fee) details the life and work of the man who, in the 1910s, was the first American artist to create large-scale murals depicting "the drama and significance of men at work." In the 1920s, Marsh also designed a then (and in some ways still) futuristic home for himself and his wife in Ormond Beach. The house is located just north of Granada Boulevard on Hwy-A1A, though admission is not allowed. Within the park itself, don't miss Marsh's immense sculpture, *The Legend of Tomokie*.

★For the ultimate NASCAR racing experience, see p.284 for information on the **Richard Petty Driving Experience**, where you can do it yourself – for a price.

Daytona speed weeks and more

The Daytona Speedway hosts several major race meetings each year, starting in early February with the **Rolex 24**: a 24-hour race for GT prototype sports cars. A week or so later begin the qualifying races leading up to the biggest event of the year, the **Daytona 500** stock-car race in mid-February. Tickets (see below) for this are as common as Florida snow, but many of the same drivers compete in the **Pepsi 400**, for which tickets are much easier to get, held on the first Saturday in July. The track is also used for motorcycle races: **Bike Week**, in early March, sees a variety of high-powered clashes, highlighted by **American Motorcycle Association** championship racing, and **Biketoberfest**, held the third week in October, features the **Championship Cup Series races**.

Tickets (the cheapest are $45–50 for car-racing, $20–25 for bikes) for the bigger events sell out well in advance, and it's advisable to book accommodation at least six months ahead. For **information** and ticket details: ☎386/253-RACE or ⊛www.daytonainternationalspeedway.com.

Take full advantage of the park by camping overnight (see "Accommodation," p.221), which leaves time to visit the **Bulow Plantation Ruins** (daily 9am–5pm; $2; ☎386/517-2084) – scant and heavily vegetated remains of an eighteenth-century plantation destroyed by Seminole Indians (five miles north of the park off Route 201). Picnicking is encouraged and canoe rentals are available.

Eating

A visit to the principal pier is a must, and the *Mainstreet Pier Restaurant* (☎386/253-1212) is actually quite good, and good value, too. It's bustling, even chaotic, with ocean views and outdoor seating available. Try the great home-made clam chowder, and don't leave without sampling Florida's most extravagant Key Lime pie. Plus they have a Happy Hour daily from 3pm–7pm. Near the Sunglow Pier, at 3701 S Atlantic Ave, *Crabby Joe's* (☎386/788-3364) offers succulent all-you-can-eat seafood buffets for dinner at only $7.95.

Major appetites can be satisfied for a modest outlay at several other buffet **restaurants**, such as *Checkers*, 219 S Atlantic Ave (☎386/239-0010), which has buffet breakfasts and an all-you-can-eat dinner session. Seafood is the major lure in these parts, and two inexpensive restaurants that won't disappoint are the *Clocktower Restaurant*, inside the *Adams Mark Daytona Beach Resort* at 100 N Atlantic Ave (☎386/254-8200), and *Shells*, 200 S Atlantic Ave (☎386/258-0007). Other culinary favorites include the *St Regis Restaurant and Patio Bar*, 509 Seabreeze Blvd (☎386/252-8743); the strong Mexican flavors of the *Rio Bravo Cantina*, 1735 International Speedway Blvd (☎386/255-6500); and great burgers at *McK's Tavern*, 218 S Beach St (☎386/238-3321). Slightly pricier but with greater choices for lunch or dinner is *Julian's*, 88 N Atlantic Ave (☎386/677-6767), a dimly lit mock-Tahitian lounge with a good menu. Also definitely worth trying is the quirky and festive *Lighthouse Landing*, beside the Ponce Inlet Lighthouse (☎386/761-9271), offering the freshest seafood. Or try the more elegant *Inlet Harbor*, 133 Inlet Harbor Rd, Ponce Inlet (☎386/767-5590), where you can dine right on the marina while local bands play their hearts out. *Aunt Catfish's*, 4009 Halifax Drive, a few miles south of Daytona Beach in Port Orange (☎386/767-4768), has mighty portions of ribs and seafood prepared to traditional Southern recipes. If you have a sudden desire for Japanese food, head for *Sapporo*, 3340 S Atlantic Ave (☎386/756-0480).

Nightlife

Even without the Spring Break invasion of party-crazed students, it seems likely that Daytona Beach will retain its reputation as one of the best spots on Florida's east coast for merrymaking when the sun goes down. The nucleus of the beachside **nightlife** is *600 North*, at 600 N Atlantic Ave (☎386/255-4471; $3–10), with bars, discos, live rock, rave alternative and ceaseless wet T-shirt competitions. There's more rabble-rousing, accompanied by dazzling light shows, at *Razzles*, 611 Seabreeze Blvd (☎386/257-6236). *Ocean Deck*, 127 S Ocean Ave (☎386/253-5224), boasts live music; and *Kokomos on the Beach* and *Waves*, both at 100 N Atlantic Ave inside the *Adams Mark Daytona Beach Resort* (☎386/254-8200), have been known to offer a good time. A danceable **nightclub** with a less collegiate crowd is the *Checkers Café*, (see opposite), featuring occasional karaoke.

For a **drink**, the *Boot Hill Saloon*, across from the cemetery at 310 Main St (☎386/258-9506), can be enjoyable, but if you find its biker clientele threatening, an alternative is *The Oyster Pub*, 555 Seabreeze Blvd (☎386/255-6348), a sports bar where the beer is helped down by dirt-cheap oysters and a loud jukebox. For **live music**, look to the jazz of *Café Bravo Coffee Bar*, corner of Beach and Bay streets (☎386/252-7747); *Rockin' Ranch* in the Ellinor Village shopping center, 801 S Nova Rd (☎386/673-0904); the swaggering two-step line dancing of *Billy Bob's Race Country USA*, 2801 S Ridgewood Ave (☎386/756-0448); or the *Clocktower Lounge* in the *Adams Mark Daytona Beach Resort* (see opposite), an elegant piano bar with an ocean view.

North of Daytona Beach

Assuming you don't want to cut twenty miles inland along I-4 or Hwy-92 to DeLand and the Orlando area (see "Central Florida," p.268), keep on Hwy-A1A **northwards** along the coast towards St Augustine.

The first community you'll encounter is **Flagler Beach**, fourteen miles from Daytona Beach, comprising a few houses and shops, a pier and a very tempting beach. Nearby, at the **Flagler Beach State Recreation Area** (daily 8am–sunset; cars $4.25, cyclists and pedestrians $1), a good cross-section of coastal birdlife can be spotted, particularly at low tide when freshly exposed sands provide a feast for swift beaks. If the relative peace and solitude of Flagler Beach tempts you to stay, try the elegant, well-appointed *Topaz Motel/Hotel*, 1224 S Ocean Shore Blvd (☎1-800/555-4735; ❷). For delicious shrimp Wellington and other unusual recipes in a funky tropical island setting, go for *Caribbean Sin*, at no. 600 (☎386/439-0740), or nearby, at no. 500, the less eccentric *Fisherman's Net*, featuring stupendous combo seafood platters for as little at $12.95.

Further north, soon after passing the blazing blooms of **Washington Oaks State Gardens** (daily 8am–sunset; cars $4.25, pedestrians and cyclists $1), you can't miss the streamlined, yet crumbling, architecture of **Marineland** (daily 9.30am–4.30pm; $12; ☎386/460-1275), Florida's original sea-creature theme park. The state's biggest tourist draw when it opened in 1938, its status has been severely undermined by subsequent imitations, such as the far superior SeaWorld (see "Central Florida," p.289). Add to that the extensive damage done by a hurricane in 1999, and what you now see is a mere shadow of its former glory. Established as marine studios for underwater research and photography, the park's highlights are very limited now, but include sharks in a large viewing tank, performing porpoises and a 3-D film depicting sea creatures in their natural underwater habitats.

Hwy-A1A crosses a narrow inlet three miles beyond Marineland onto **Anastasia Island**, close to the Spanish-built seventeenth-century **Fort Matanzas** on Rattlesnake Island. Never conquered, partly due to the sixteen-foot-thick walls and the surrounding moat, the fort is accessible only by **ferry** (daily except Tues, 9am–4.30pm; every 15min; free), but it's of minor appeal in comparison to history-packed St Augustine.

A better stop might be the **St Augustine Alligator Farm** (daily 9am–6pm; $14.25), a few miles further north along Hwy-A1A. Visitors are greeted by shrieks from a vividly colored toucan and can take a walk through a wildlife-infested swamp. Time your visit to coincide with the alligator show (three shows daily; call ⓣ904/824-3337 for exact times), when a keeper drags an alligator around by its tail to demonstrate how the creature expresses anger: it bellows loudly, arches its back and displays a gaping jaw. It's heart-stopping stuff – not least when the handler, sitting on the creature's back, puts his fingers between the gator's teeth.

Once past the Alligator Farm, you're well within reach of St Augustine, whose old center is just across Matanzas Bay, three miles ahead.

St Augustine

With the size and even some of the looks of a small Mediterranean town, there are few places in Florida as immediately engaging as **ST AUGUSTINE**, the oldest permanent settlement in the US and one with much from its early days still intact. St Augustine's eminently strollable narrow streets are lined by carefully renovated buildings whose architecture carries evidence of Florida's broad European heritage and the power struggles that led up to its statehood. There's plenty here to fill a day or two, and for variation you can visit two alluring lengths of beach located just across the small bay on which the town stands.

Ponce de León, the Spaniard who gave Florida its name, touched ground here on *Pascua Florida* (Easter Sunday) in 1513, but it wasn't until Pedro Menéndez de Aviles put ashore on St Augustine's Day in 1565 that settlement began with the intention of subduing the Huguenots based to the north at Fort Caroline (see "The Jacksonville beaches," p.237). Repeated battles with the British began when Sir Francis Drake's ships razed St Augustine in 1586, but Spanish control was only relinquished when Florida was ceded to Britain in 1763, by which time the town was established as an important social and administrative center – soon to become the capital of East Florida. Spain regained possession twenty years later, and kept it until 1821, when Florida joined the US. Subsequently, Tallahassee became the capital of unified Florida, and St Augustine's fortunes waned. A railway and a posh hotel stimulated a turn-of-the-century tourist boom, but otherwise expansion bypassed St Augustine – which inadvertently made possible the restoration program that started in the Thirties. The current residential community is unsurprisingly proud of having flourished under five flags in its long history.

Arrival and information

From Anastasia Island, **Hwy-A1A** crosses over Mantanzas Bay into the heart of St Augustine; **Hwy-1** passes a mile west along Ponce de León Boulevard.

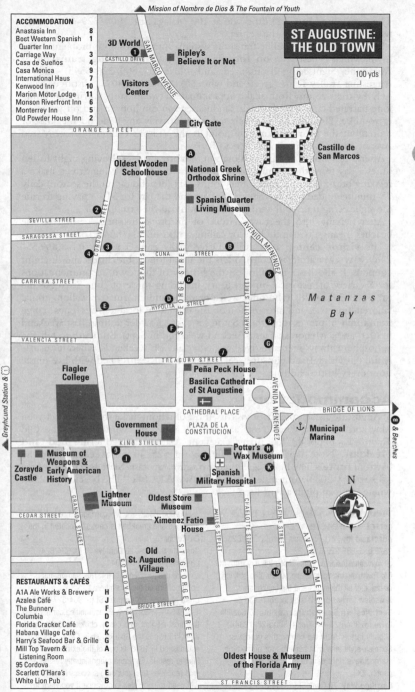

Mission of Nombre de Dios & The Fountain of Youth

ST AUGUSTINE: THE OLD TOWN

0   100 yds

ACCOMMODATION

Anastasia Inn	8
Best Western Spanish Quarter Inn	1
Carriage Way	3
Casa de Sueños	4
Casa Monica	9
International Haus	7
Kenwood Inn	10
Marion Motor Lodge	11
Monson Riverfront Inn	6
Monterrey Inn	5
Old Powder House Inn	2

RESTAURANTS & CAFÉS

A1A Ale Works & Brewery	H
Azalea Café	J
The Bunnery	F
Columbia	D
Florida Cracker Café	C
Habana Village Café	K
Harry's Seafood Bar & Grille	G
Mill Top Tavern & Listening Room	A
95 Cordova	I
Scarlett O'Hara's	E
White Lion Pub	B

3D World
Ripley's Believe It or Not
Visitors Center
City Gate
Castillo de San Marcos
Oldest Wooden Schoolhouse
National Greek Orthodox Shrine
Spanish Quarter Living Museum
Matanzas Bay
Flagler College
Peña Peck House
Basilica Cathedral of St Augustine
Government House
Plaza de la Constitucion
Bridge of Lions
Municipal Marina
Museum of Weapons & Early American History
Zorayda Castle
Potter's Wax Museum
Spanish Military Hospital
Lightner Museum
Oldest Store Museum
Ximenez Fatio House
Old St. Augustine Village
Oldest House & Museum of the Florida Army

Greyhound Station & (1)

8 & Beaches

N

4

THE NORTHEAST COAST | St Augustine

229

The Greyhound **bus** will drop you at 100 Malaga St (☎ 904/829-6401), a fifteen-minute walk from the center.

St Augustine has no public transport system, but this poses no problem in the town, which is best seen **on foot**. There are two **sightseeing trains**, the St Augustine Sightseeing Train (red and blue; ☎ 1-800/226-6545) and St Augustine Trolley Tours (green and white; ☎ 1-800/397-4071), distinguishable only by their colors. Both make approximately twenty stops during an hour-long narrated circuit of the main landmarks; you can hop on and off whenever you like. **Tickets** can be purchased from virtually any bed-and-breakfast or motel, but the primary purchase point is the Visitor's Center on San Marco Avenue (daily 8.30am–5pm; both $12).

After a few hours of hard exploration, **harbor cruises**, leaving eight to ten times a day from the Municipal Marina near the foot of King Street, make a relaxing break; Scenic Cruise offers four to six (depending on the season) daily 75-minute guided paddlewheeler trips around the bay for $10 – paying to ride the sightseeing train will earn you a discount on the cruise.

After delving into the town's trove of historical treasures, getting to the beaches means a two-mile hike or calling a **taxi** (☎ 904/824-8161).

The **visitor center**, 10 Castillo Drive (daily 8am–5.30pm; ☎ 1-800/653-2489, ⓦ www.visitoldcity.com), offers the usual tourist brochures and discount coupons. It also has a free film on the history of the town, recommendations for a variety of historical guided tours, including those of Tour St Augustine (☎ 1-800/797-3778), who offer well-organized and informative walking tours, tailored itineraries and information on the numerous local festivals. These range from torch-lit processions (third Sat in June) to chowder tastings (last weekend in Oct) and a Menorcan Fiesta (second weekend in Sept). But truth to tell, the atmosphere always seems festive here, especially on weekends, when it's usually full up with relaxed pleasure-seekers, and the air seems filled with live music from every bistro and café.

Accommodation

St Augustine attracts plenty of visitors, most of whom make short stays between May and October, when costs are $15–25 above the winter rates. The Old Town (see opposite) has many excellent restored inns offering **bed and breakfast**. Note that prices usually go up $25–40 on weekends for the bayfront **motels**. The best place to **camp** is the Anastasia State Recreation Area (☎ 904/461-2033), four miles south, off Hwy-A1A (see "The beaches," p.236), where you can pitch a tent for $17.

Hotels, motels and bed and breakfasts

Anastasia Inn, 218 Anastasia Blvd (☎ 904/825-2879 or 1-888/226-6181, ⓦ www.anastasiainn.com). Across the bay from the Old Town, on Anastasia Island, well within striking distance of all the sights and the beach, the *Anastasia Inn* has a waterside location. ❸

Best Western Spanish Quarter Inn, 6 Castillo Drive (☎ 904/824-4457 or 1-800/528-1234). Slightly farther from the center, this gracious Spanish-style villa with hot-tubs for night-time stargazing is right next to the main visitor center. ❹

Carriage Way, 70 Cuna St (☎ 904/829-2467 or 1-800/908-9832, ⓦ www.carriageway.com). This cozy bed and breakfast is centrally located in the Old Town. ❹

Casa de Suenos, 20 Cordova St (☎ 904/824-0887 or 1-800/824-0804, ⓦ www.casadesuenos.com). This sumptuous option offers all the amenities. ❺

Casa Monica, 95 Cordova St (☎ 904/827-1888 or 1-800/648-1888, ⓦ www.casamonica.com). By far the most elegant, and costly, choice in the heart of the Old Town is the Spanish-style *Casa Monica*, established in 1888 as one of the extravagant Flagler resorts. Fully and magnificently restored, it was reopened to resounding success in 1999. You will need to book well in advance if you want to

stay on a weekend. ⑥
International Haus, 32 Treasury St (check-in
times 8–10am and 5–10pm; $14; ☎904/808-
1999 or 1-877/463-8646, ⑩www.international-
haus.com). To cut costs considerably, this newly
renovated pirate-themed hotel has a giant kitchen
and common room stuffed with local guidebooks.
All rooms are air-conditioned and they offer an all-
you-can-eat pancake breakfast. ❶
Kenwood Inn, 38 Marine St (☎904/824-2116 or
1-800/824-8151, ⑩www.oldcity.com/kenwood).
This charming, immaculate, and inviting inn features its own pool. ❹
The Marion Motor Lodge, 120 Avenida
Menéndez (☎904/829-2261 or 1-800/258-2261,
⑩www.themarionmotorlodge.com). This bayfront
motel is one of the better-value options and features its own pool. ❸

Monson Riverfront Inn, 32 Avenida Menéndez
(☎904/829-2277). Bordering the Old Town on the
bayfront, this inn has its own pool. ❸
The Monterey Inn, 16 Avenida Menéndez
(☎904/824-4482, ⑩www.themontereyinn.com).
This is the least expensive of the motels that border the Old Town on the bayfront. ❷
Old Powder House Inn, 38 Cordova St
(☎904/824-4149 or 1-800/447-4149,
⑩www.oldpowderhouse.com). This historic and
colorful inn is centrally located in the Old Town. ❺
Seaway, 481 Hwy-A1A (☎904/471-3466). This
small motel is the most reliable of the family-ori-
entated establishments on busy St Augustine
Beach. ❸
Vilano Beach Motel, 50 Vilano Beach Rd
(☎904/829-2651). This laid-back motel is a great
base for enjoying the North Beach. ❷

The Old Town

St Augustine's historic area – or **Old Town** – along St George Street and
south of the central plaza, contains well-tended evidence of the town's various periods. Worth a look, too, are the lavish "Spanish Renaissance" structures
along King Street, just west of the plaza, remaining from the turn-of-the-
nineteenth-century resort era. Although St Augustine is small, there's a lot to
see: an early start, around 9am, will give you a lead on the crowds, and you
should ideally allow three days to explore the town fully.

The castle

Given the fine state of the **Castillo de San Marcos** (daily 8.45am–4.45pm;
$4), on the northern edge of the Old Town beside the bay, it's difficult to
believe that the fortress was started in the late 1600s. Its longevity is due to
the design: a diamond-shaped rampart at each corner maximized firepower,
and fourteen-foot-thick coquina (a type of soft limestone found on
Anastasia Island) walls reduced vulnerability to attack – as British troops
found when they waged a fruitless fifty-day siege in 1702. Time schedules
for the free twenty-minute **talks** on the fort and local history are indicated
in the courtyard.

Inside, there's not a lot to admire beyond a small museum and echoing rooms
– some of them with military and social exhibits – but venturing along the 35-
foot-high ramparts gives an unobstructed view over the low-lying city, which
the castle protected so successfully, and its waterborne approaches. Look for the
eerie graffiti on the walls, scrawled by prisoners in the 1600s.

Along St George Street

Leaving the castle, the little eighteenth-century **City Gate** marks the entrance
to **St George Street**, once the main thoroughfare and now a tourist-trampled
pedestrianized strip – but home to plenty of genuine history. At no. 14, the
Oldest Wooden Schoolhouse (daily 9am–5pm in winter, 9am–8pm in summer; $2.75; ☎1-888/653-7245, ⑩www.oldestschoolhouse.com) still has its
original eighteenth-century red-cedar and cypress walls and tabby floor (a mix
of crushed oyster shells and lime, common at the time). These architectural
points are the main interest: the building was put into use as a school some

years later, thereby inadvertently becoming, as the staff is quick to point out, the oldest wooden schoolhouse in the US. Pupils and teacher are now unconvincingly portrayed by speaking wax models.

Further along, at no. 41, an unassuming doorway leads into the petite **National Greek Orthodox Shrine** (daily 9am–5pm; free), where tapes of Byzantine choirs echo through the halls, and icons and candles stand alongside hard-hitting accounts of the experiences of Greek immigrants to the US – some of whom settled in St Augustine from New Smyrna Beach (see p.219) in 1777.

More directly relevant to the town, and taking up a fair-sized plot at the corner of St George and Cuna streets, the **Spanish Quarter Living Museum** (Sun–Thurs 9am–6pm, Fri & Sat until 7pm; $6.50; ☎ 904/825-5033) includes nine reconstructed homes and workshops. Volunteers disguised as Spanish settlers go about their daily tasks at spinning wheels, anvils and foot-driven wood lathes. The museum should be visited either early in the day or during an off-peak period; lines of camera-wielding tourists and rowdy school groups substantially lessen the effect. The main entrance is through the Triay House, on North St George Street.

For a more intimate look at local life during a slightly later period, head for the **Peña Peck House**, at no. 143 (Mon–Sat 10am–4.30pm, Sun 12.30–4.30pm; $4.50 suggested donation; ☎ 904/829-5064). Thought to have originally been the Spanish treasury, by the time the British took over in 1763 this was the home of a physician and his gregarious spouse, who turned the place into a high society rendezvous. The Pecks' furnishings and paintings, plus the enthusiastic spiel of the guide, make for an enjoyable tour.

Old St Augustine Village, 250 St George St (entrance on Bridge Street; daily 9am–5pm; $7; ☎ 904/823-9722), presents a group of ten period buildings that have been beautifully restored. They're from every period and cultural stripe, not just Spanish, and the detailed tours offered by the guides will easily hold your attention. Particularly fascinating is the **Prince Murat House**, 1790, briefly home to one of Napoleon's associates. Ravishing French Empire furniture graces its main room, and a glass case displays a letter penned by the emperor himself, along with one by the Revolutionary figure Lafayette, and one by Murat.

The Plaza

In the sixteenth century, the Spanish king decreed that all colonial towns had to be built around a central plaza, and St Augustine was no exception: St George Street runs into **Plaza de la Constitucion**, a marketplace dating from 1598 that nowadays attracts shade seekers and the occasional wino. On the north side of the plaza, the **Basilica Cathedral of St Augustine** (daily 7am–5pm; donation requested) adds a touch of grandeur, though it's largely a Sixties remodeling of the late eighteenth-century original, with murals by Hugo Ohlms depicting life in St Augustine. Periodic **guided tours** (times are sometimes pinned to the door) revel in the painstaking details of the rebuilding and the undistinguished stained-glass windows. Slightly more worthwhile, the ground floor of **Government House** (daily 9am–5pm; $2.50; ☎ 904/825-5033), on the west side of the plaza, contains small displays of objects from the city's various renovation projects and archeological digs. In contrast, on the south side of the square, seeking shelter from a thunderstorm might be the sole justification for entering **Potter's Wax Museum** (daily: summer 9am–9pm; winter 9am–5pm; $6.95; ☎ 904/829-9056 or 1-800/584-4781), populated by effigies of people you may have heard of but probably won't recognize.

South of the Plaza

Tourist numbers lessen as you cross south of the plaza into a web of quiet, narrow streets with as much antiquity as St George Street. At 4 Artillery Lane, the **Oldest Store Museum** (Mon–Sat 9am–5pm, Sun noon–5pm; $5; ☎ 904/829-9729) does an excellent job of recreating an 1880s general store, filled to the rafters with the produce of the time: curious foods and drinks, fiery medicinal potions and oversized consumer essentials such as apple peelers, cigar molders and wooden washing machines.

Close by, at 20 Aviles St, the **Ximenez Fatio House** (Mon–Thurs 11am–4pm, Sun 1–4pm; free; ☎ 904/829-3575) was built in 1797 for a Spanish merchant and proved popular with the travelers who predated the town's first tourist boom, drawn by the airy balconies added to the original structure. Although the upper floor is a bit rickety, a walk around is safe and quick in the company of a guide who points out illuminating details. At 3 Aviles St you can spend an interesting fifteen minutes in the small **Spanish Military Hospital** (Sun–Thurs 9am–7pm, Fri & Sat 9am–9pm; $3), built in 1791 and recreating the spartan care wounded soldiers could expect.

More substantial history is unfurled a ten-minute walk away at the **Oldest House**, 14 St Francis St (daily 9am–5pm; last admission 4.30pm; $5; ☎ 904/824-2872), occupied from the early 1700s (and, indeed, the oldest house in the town) by the family of an artillery hand at the castle. The second floor was grafted on during the British period, a fact evinced by the bone china crockery belonging to a former occupant, one Mary Peavitt, whose disastrous marriage to a hopeless gambler provided the basis for a popular historical novel, *Maria*, by Eugenia Price (the gift shop has copies). A smaller room shows the pine-stripped "sidecar" style made popular by the arrival of Flagler's railway: it copies the decor of a train carriage.

Entered through the back garden of the house, the less-than-riveting **Museum of the Florida Army** (entry included with admission to the Oldest House; same hours) gives an inkling, with its display of old uniforms, of the numerous conflicts that have divided Florida over the years. Anybody you might see striding by in modern military garb probably belongs to the Florida National Guard, whose headquarters are across the street.

West of the Plaza: along King Street

A walk west from the plaza along **King Street** bridges the gap between early St Augustine and its turn-of-the-nineteenth tourist boom. You'll soon notice, at the junction with Cordova Street, the flowing spires, arches and red-tiled roof of **Flagler College**. Now used by liberal arts students, a hundred years ago it was – as the *Ponce de León Hotel* – an exclusive winter retreat of the nation's rich and mighty. The hotel was an early attempt by entrepreneur Henry Flagler to exploit Florida's climate and coast, but as he developed properties further south and extended his railway, the *Ponce de León* fell from favor – not helped by a couple of freezing winters. There are free guided tours in the summer. You can **walk around** the campus and the first floor of the main building (daily 10am–3pm) to admire the Tiffany stained glass and the painstakingly restored painted ceiling in the dining room.

In competition with Flagler, the eccentric Bostonian architect Franklin W. Smith – seemingly obsessed with poured concrete and Moorish design (see the Zorayda Castle, overleaf) – built a rival hotel of matching extravagance directly opposite the *Ponce de León*. He eventually sold it to Flagler, who named it the *Alcazar*. Fronted by a courtyard of palm trees and fountains, the building now holds the **Lightner Museum** (daily 9am–5pm; last admission 4.30pm;

$6; ☎904/824-2874), where you can easily pass an hour poring over the Victorian cut glass, Tiffany lamps, antique music boxes and more. There's even a Russian malachite and ormolu urn from the Winter Palace in imperial St Petersburg. Much of the booty was acquired by publishing ace Otto C. Lightner from once-wealthy estates hard hit by the Depression.

A rather incongruous sight in St Augustine is Franklin W. Smith's recreation of the Alhambra. The architect was so impressed by the Moorish architecture he'd seen in Spain that he built a copy in the late nineteenth century of a wing of the thirteenth-century palace here, at a tenth of the original size. Called the **Zorayda Castle**, 83 King St, it is now a private residence and not visitable.

Just across the Zorayda's parking lot, a shack contains the **Museum of Weapons and Early American History** (daily 9.30am–5pm; $4). Reading the small collection of Civil War diaries gives an interesting personal view of the struggle, but this one-room cache will mainly appeal to survivalist types, with plenty of tools to shoot, stab and batter foes to death.

North of the Old Town: San Marco Avenue and around

Leading away from the tightly grouped streets of the Old Town, the traffic-bearing **San Marco Avenue**, beginning on the other side of the city gate from St George Street, passes the sites of the first Spanish landings and settlements as well as some remains of the Timucua Indians who greeted them. A couple of other potential stops are of much less relevance to the town but can be good for a laugh.

The **Ripley's Believe It or Not**, at 19 San Marco Ave (daily 9am–7pm; $9.95; ☎904/824-1606), isn't the best but contains a riveting collection of oddities gathered by Robert Ripley as he traveled around the world in the Twenties and Thirties. Among the oddities on display are a grandfather clock made from clothes pegs, the Lord's Prayer printed on the head of a pin and a toothpick model of the Eiffel Tower.

Directly across the street from Ripley's is **3–D World**, 28 San Marco Ave (Sun–Thurs 10am–6pm, Fri & Sat 10am–8pm, $10 for all three shows; ☎904/824-1220 or 1-800/998-4418), which shows three films ranging from the calming waters of "Blue Magic," where scores of colorful fish dart past your eyes, to action adventure films whose frenetic motion simulator pitches you headfirst into the "Castle of Doom" and then on to the "Curse of King Tut" – unadvisable for those susceptible to motion sickness.

Don't be discouraged, half a mile further along San Marco Avenue, by the dull, modern church that now stands in the grounds of **Mission of Nombre de Dios** (daily: summer 7am–8pm; rest of the year 8am–6pm; donation requested). This sixteenth-century mission was one of many established by Spanish settlers to convert Native Americans to Christianity, simultaneously exploiting their labor and seeking their support in possible confrontations with rival colonial powers.

A pathway leads to a 208-foot-tall stainless steel cross, glinting in the sun beside the river on the spot where Menéndez landed in 1565. Soon after, Father Francisco Lopez de Mendoza Grajales celebrated the first Mass in North America, recording that "a large number of Indians watched the proceedings and imitated all they saw," which was a bit unfortunate since the arrival of the Spanish signaled the beginning of the end for the Indians. A side-path takes a mildly interesting course around the rest of the squirrel-patrolled lawns, passing a few relics of the mission, on the way to a small, ivy-covered re-creation of the original chapel.

In addition to the prospect of finding gold and silver, it's said that Ponce de León was drawn to Florida by the belief that the fabled life-preserving "fountain of youth" was located here. Rather tenuously, this fact is celebrated at a mineral spring touted as **The Fountain of Youth**, 11 Magnolia Ave (daily 9am–5pm; $5.75; ℡1-800/356-8222) in a park at the end of Williams Street (off San Marco Avenue), very near the point where he landed in 1513, and about half a mile north of the old mission site; it's unlikely, however, you'll live forever after drinking the fresh water handed to you as you enter the springhouse. The expansive acres of the park have far more significance as an archeological site. Besides remains of the Spanish settlement, many Timucua Indian relics have been unearthed, and you'll also come across some of the wiry plants that were the base of the "Black Drink," a thick, highly potent concoction used by the Timucuans to help them achieve mystical states.

The beaches

If you've reached St Augustine with Hwy-A1A you'll need no introduction to the fine **beaches** that lie just a couple of miles from the Old Town. Few other people do either, especially on weekends when the bronzers, beachcombers and watersports fanatics descend in droves. A fine view of St Augustine and up and down the beaches is afforded by the **Lighthouse and Museum**, 81 Lighthouse Ave (daily 9am–5.30pm; $5; ℡904/829-0745; ⓦwww.lighthousestaug.com), which tells the story of the keepers and the lights they tended.

Across the bay on Anastasia Island, **St Augustine Beach** is family terrain, but here you'll also find the **Anastasia State Recreation Area** (daily 8am–sunset; cars $4.25, cyclists and pedestrians $1), offering a thousand protected acres of dunes, marshes, scrub and a wind-beaten group of live oaks, linked by nature walks – though most people come here to catch a fish dinner from the lagoon. In the other direction (take May Street, off San Marco Avenue), **Vilano Beach** pulls a younger crowd and marks the beginning of a dazzling strand continuing for twenty undeveloped miles all the way to Jacksonville Beach (see opposite).

Eating

The tourist throng on and around St George Street makes eating in the Old Town an often pricey affair, particularly for dinner. However, for coffee and economical **breakfasts,** follow your nose to *The Bunnery*, 121 St George St (℡904/829-6166), set up in an old Spanish bakery on a relaxing courtyard, where they serve very tempting homemade soups and sandwiches. Also good for **lunch**, and dinner as well, is the *Florida Cracker Cafe*, 81 St George St (℡904/829-0397), featuring eclectic combo salads, sandwiches, entrées and homemade desserts. Some of the local specialities featured here are hot artichoke and parmesan dip, blackened shrimp and spinach salad, and conch fritters. On the other side of the Plaza, at 4 Aviles St, there's the gourmet breakfast and lunch spot, the *Azalea Café* (9am–4pm, weekends 10am–4pm; ℡904/824-6465), offering traditional breakfasts and soups, sandwiches, pastas and salads.

For more upscale **dinner** choices, try two excellent local chains: *Harry's Seafood Bar & Grille*, 46 Avenida Menéndez (℡904/824-7765) with its lively New Orleans atmosphere and Cajun recipes, or the much more elegant *Columbia*, 98 St George St (℡904/824-3341), featuring a traditional Spanish/Cuban menu offered in a sumptuous setting, full of softly splashing fountains and candlelit arcades. The top choice for masterful nouvelle continental cuisine is the elegant and luxurious *95 Cordova* (℡904/810-6810), the restaurant at the *Casa Monica Hotel* (see p.230); reservations are a must.

Out at the beach, go for the excellent burgers at *The Oasis*, 4000 Ocean Trace Rd (also Hwy-A1A; ℡904/471-3424) – try the "Gonzo Burger," served with three kinds of cheese and piles of extras.

Nightlife

St Augustine's **nightlife** offers many establishments with live music, even in the afternoon and especially on weekends. In the Old Town, have a **drink** at the tavern-like *White Lion*, 20 Cuna St (℡904/829-2388); during the 5–7pm Happy Hours at *Scarlett O'Hara's*, 70 Hypolita St (℡904/824-6535), where you can also get full meals, specializing in barbecue, and hear a variety of live music; or by the millwheel of the *Milltop Tavern and Listening Room*, 19 1/2 St George St (℡904/829-2329), which has a terrific, funky atmosphere, live music in the afternoons and evenings and a great open-air view of the Castillo and the harbor. Near the Lion Bridge, where King Street meets the water, you'll find live Latin music to dance to, homemade sangria and yummy Cuban snacks to keep your evenings upbeat at *Habana Village Café*, 1 King St, #103 (music Thurs, Fri & Sat; ℡904/827-1700); It's open for lunch, too. In the same complex, right on the corner, the *A1A Ale Works & Brewery* (Happy Hour Mon–Fri, 4–7pm; ℡904/829-2977) is a fun place to while away some time raising brews, but its food is nothing special.

If drinking is not on your agenda, then consider indulging in "A Ghostly Experience," a more historical than scary guided **walking tour** that reveals local legends, tall tales, and haunted and spook-filled sites; tours start at 8pm in front of the Milltop Tavern (for tickets call ℡904/471-9010 or 1-888/461-1009; $6).

The Jacksonville beaches

However good the beaches around St Augustine may be, they're just the start of an unblemished coastal strip running northwards for twenty miles alongside Hwy-A1A, with nothing but the ocean on one side, and the swamps and marshes of the Talamato River (the local section of the Intracoastal Waterway) on the other. The scene begins to change when you near the sculptured golf courses and half-million-dollar homes of **Ponte Vedra Beach** – one of the most exclusive communities in northeast Florida. The crowd-free sands are prime beachcombing terrain – retreating tides often leave sharks' teeth among the more common ocean debris.

Four miles on, the much less snooty **Jacksonville Beach** (info at ℡904/249-3868, ⓦ www.jaxcvb.com) is an affable beachside community whose residents relax here and commute to work in the city of Jacksonville, twelve miles inland. Though much cleaner than Daytona, the place is inexplicably neglected by tourists outside of the summer months. The **pier** is the center of activity, and a fried-fish sandwich from its snack bar is the right accompaniment to observing novice surfers grappling with modest-sized breakers. If you start itching for some action of your own, you could do worse than visit **Adventure Landing**, 1944 Beach Blvd (Feb–May and Sept–Nov, Sun–Thurs 10am–midnight, Fri & Sat 10am–1am; ℡904/246-4386). Getting in is free, but you pay for the attractions that most strike your fancy: highlights include a water park ($18.99), a go-kart race track ($5.99), a game of laser-tag with pirates in the dark ($5.99), and baseball batting cages ($2). The "Nightflash" evening reduced-rate ticket will get you in for $13 between 4pm and 8pm Monday to Friday.

Once you cross Seagate Avenue, just under two miles north of the pier, Jacksonville Beach merges with the more commercialized **Neptune Beach**, which in turn blurs (at Atlantic Boulevard) with the identical-looking **Atlantic Beach**. These last two places are the best to visit for eating and socializing in this area. Just north of Atlantic Beach, downbeat **Mayport** is dominated by its naval station, berth to some of the biggest aircraft carriers in the US Navy. It's best seen through a car window on the way to the Mayport ferry, crossing the St Johns River, and the barrier islands beyond (see "Towards Amelia Island," p.243).

In contrast to the naval station is the **Kathryn Abbey Hanna Park**, 500 Wonderwood Drive ($1; ☎ 904/249-4700), just south of Mayport. Besides its mile and a half of unblemished beachfront, the park boasts 450 acres of woodland surrounding a large lake, around which wind ten miles of enjoyable biking and hiking trails. There's also a campground here (see "Sleeping, eating and nightlife," below).

Around the beaches

A few miles inland on Girvin Road (off Atlantic Boulevard), the **Fort Caroline National Memorial** (daily 9am–5pm; free; ☎ 904/641-7155, ⓦ www.nps.gov/foca) offers a historical interlude: a small museum here details the significance of the restored Huguenot fort here, which provoked the first Spanish settlement in Florida (see "St Augustine," p.228). Another reason to visit is the great view from the fort across the mile-wide St Johns River and its ocean-going freighters.

Sleeping, eating and nightlife

Along the coast there'll be plenty of bargains in winter, but during the summer be ready to spend $50–65 for a basic **motel** room, and book ahead. The

Sea Horse Oceanfront Inn, 120 Atlantic Blvd, Neptune Beach (☎904/246-2175 or 1-800/881-2330, ⓦwww.seahorseresort.com; ❸), is a two-story pink stucco hotel right on the beach without a pool, while the *Surfside*, 1236 N First St, Jacksonville Beach (☎904/246-1583; ❷), is right across from the beach and offers a pool and breakfast included. Of the more luxurious, and more expensive, options, the *Sea Turtle Inn*, 1 Ocean Blvd, Atlantic Beach (☎1-800/874-6000; ❻) and the *Best Western Oceanfront*, 305 N First St, Jacksonville Beach (☎1-800/897-8131; ⓔjaxbestwestern@hotmail.com; ❹), offer every amenity and comfort you might want. Your choice for homely hospitality is definitely the *Pelican Path B&B*, 11 N Nineteenth Ave, Jacksonville Beach (☎1-888/749-1177 or 904/249-1177, ⓦwww.pelicanpath.com; ❹), where hearty breakfasts are served in a beachside California-modern house – located in an optimal spot for shell-collecting. If you like roughing it and you have your own tent, you can **camp** at the Kathryn Abbey Hanna Park (see opposite) for $13.50.

For **eating**, Third Street at Jacksonville Beach offers the reliable local chain *Harry's Seafood Bar & Grille*, at no. 1018 N (☎904/247-8855), which features New Orleans-style fare. In the **Town Center** complex to the north, where Atlantic Boulevard meets the ocean, you'll find several sound choices, including the *Sun Dog Diner*, 207 S Atlantic Blvd, Neptune Beach (☎904/241-8221), with specials that might include pan-seared red snapper topped with avocado and mango salsa and blueberry cobbler à la mode for dessert; *Sliders Oyster Bar*, 218 First St, Neptune Beach (☎904/246-0881), where the fresh seafood is awesome; and the award-winning *Ragtime Tavern & Grill*, 207 Atlantic Blvd, Atlantic Beach (☎904/241-7877), which has a huge seafood menu and a tap room.

Nightlife on the beach is strong. Check out the live music every Thursday to Sunday from 9pm to 1.30am in the *Ragtime Tap Room* (see above). Down in the heart of Jacksonville Beach, slide into the *Firebird Café*, 200 N First St (☎904/246-2473), to take in the rough atmosphere and some solid Southern rock. For the hedonism of wet-T-shirt contests and the like, head for *Club H2O*, 2309 Beach Blvd (☎904/249-6992), inland from Jacksonville Beach on the Intracoastal Waterway. A slightly more sedate atmosphere can be found at *The Fly's Tie Irish Pub*, 177 E Sailfish Drive, Atlantic Beach (☎904/246-4293), where you can enjoy live Irish music on weekends.

Jacksonville

With long established lumber and coffee industries, and the deep St Johns River making it a major transit point for seaborne cargo, **JACKSONVILLE** has long been suspicious of anything liable to upset its hard-working traditions; pleasure-seeking visitors are expected to stick to the beaches, twelve miles east, and even the US film industry, when it came here seeking a base in the 1910s, was scared off by the religious zeal of the locals and settled instead in California. Lately, with a growing white-collar sector easing the visual blight of years of heavy industry, there have been efforts to enhance Jacksonville's appeal by creating parks and riverside boardwalks, but the sheer size of the city – at 841 square miles, the largest in the US – dilutes its character and makes it impossible to walk around and get a real feel for the city. For all that, Jacksonville, though not exactly geared up for tourism, is not an unwelcoming place, and will sufficiently consume a day – even if you spend most of it strolling the riverside downtown.

Information and transportation

In downtown Jacksonville, the **Convention and Visitors Bureau**, 201 E Adams St (Mon–Fri 8am–5pm; ℡904/798-9111 or 1-800/733-2668, Ⓦ www.jaxcvb.com), has plenty of tourist leaflets and discount vouchers (there are also affiliated information booths at the airport and in the Jacksonville Landing Mall), and is an easy walk from the Greyhound **bus** station at 10 N Pearl St (℡904/356-9976). The **train** station is an awkward six miles north-west of downtown at 3570 Clifford Lane (℡1-800/872-7245), from which a **taxi** (℡904/645-5466) downtown will cost around $8. The **local bus** service, JTA (℡904/630-3100, Ⓦ www.ridejta.net), no longer caters just to local commuters and is more user- and tourist-friendly.

Accommodation

The city's far-flung layout means that the best-value **accommodation** is represented by the motels around the perimeter. Of these, your best bets are the **chain hotels** near the airport, nine miles north of downtown Jacksonville.

Comfort Suites, 1180 Airport Rd (℡904/741-0505). This is one of the best options of the hotels situated right by the airport. ❸

Extended Stay America, 1413 Prudential Drive (℡904/396-1777). One of the cheapest of the downtown chains. ❸

The House on Cherry Street, 1844 Cherry St (℡904 384-1999). This cozy Colonial-style bed and breakfast overlooking the river about three miles south of downtown offers an expanded continental breakfast. ❹

Radisson Riverwalk Hotel, 1515 Prudential Drive (℡904/396-5100). Scenically situated on the south bank of the river, this high-rise hotel caters to businessmen but is suitable if you really want to experience downtown Jacksonville.

Red Roof Inn, 14701 Airport Entrance Rd (℡904/741-4488). Nine miles north of downtown Jacksonville, this chain is right by the airport. ❷

The Scottish Inn, 2300 Phillips Highway (℡1-800/251-1962). Near the junction of I-95 and Hwy-90, this bed and breakfast has its own spa and pool and is also a good option to consider if you're just passing through and have your own car. ❶

Downtown Jacksonville

Leaning on local businesses to divert some of their profits into area improvement schemes, an enlightened city administration has helped make **downtown Jacksonville** much less the forbidding forest of corporate high-rises and dreary slums that it initially resembles. For an overview of downtown Jacksonville, take the **Skyway monorail** (daily 6.30am–7.30pm; 35¢; ℡904/630-3100) from the Convention Center to Hemming Park, a ten-minute journey at eye-level with the high-rise offices. Another way to come to grips with this sprawling city is to gain a bird's-eye view of it by hitching a ride on a hot-air balloon, which reveals the broad, meandering St Johns River, the stadium, the city skyline and the islands to the north. Outdoor Adventures, 1625 Emerson St (℡904/393-9030; see p.242), can take you up for $225 round-trip. Otherwise, wander along the banks of St Johns River, which snakes through the city center, dividing downtown Jacksonville in two.

The north bank

Within four blocks of Bay Street on the **north bank** of the river, you'll find the few structures that survived a major fire in 1901 – which claimed much of early Jacksonville – as well as some of the more distinctive buildings from subsequent decades. These are best examined with the aid of the free *Downtown Walking* leaflet from the Convention and Visitors Bureau (see "Information and transportation" above). One noteworthy building is the **Florida Theater**, 128 E Forsyth St, which opened in 1927 and became a center of controversy thirty years later when Elvis Presley's pelvic thrusts shocked the city's burghers. Though rather nondescript from the outside, its interior has been restored with a dazzling gold proscenium arch, and the theater is now used for a variety of performances. The **Morocco Temple**, 219 N Newnan St, currently occupied by an insurance company, was built by Henry John Kluthco, a classically minded architect who arrived to rebuild Jacksonville after the 1901 fire but later converted to Frank Lloyd Wright–inspired Modernism and erected this sphinx-decorated curiosity in 1912.

The south bank

To cross to the **south bank** of the river, take the River Taxi ($2 one way, $3 round-trip) from the dock beside the gleaming **Jacksonville Landing** shopping mall, between Water Street and the river. You'll be dropped next to a mile-long pathway called the **Riverwalk**, a downtown boardwalk from where you can view the city's colorful bridges and its skyline. Three blocks on, you'll come to the oversized **Friendship Fountain**, best seen at night when colored lights illuminate its gushing jets. Finally, the **Museum of Science and History**, 1025 Museum Circle (Mon–Fri 10am–5pm, Sat 10am–6pm, Sun 1–6pm; $6; ☎904/396-7062) has educational hands-on exhibits primarily aimed at kids, plus a planetarium offering hi-tech trips around the cosmos.

In this city of commerce and industry, you might not expect much from the new **Jacksonville Museum of Modern Art** (Tues–Fri, 11am–2pm; $5; ☎904/366-6911), which you'll find at 333 N Laura St, in downtown Jacksonville. The museum's main purpose, however, is to provide support and studios for local artists and the workspaces are often open to the public; further details are available at the reception desk.

Beyond downtown

Scattered about Jacksonville's sprawl are a few diverting points of interest, including a couple of reasonable art collections; if you've got a car – and the time – aim to visit at least the Cummer Museum, the green fields of Metropolitan Park and the Jacksonville Zoological Gardens.

The Cummer Museum

Just south of the Fuller Warren river bridge (I-95) lies the **Cummer Museum of Art and Gardens**, 829 Riverside Drive (Tues & Thurs 10am–9pm, Wed, Fri&Sat 10am–5pm, Sun 2–5pm; $6, free Tues after 4pm; ☎904/356-6857), on the former estate of the wealthy Cummer family. The spacious rooms and sculpture-lined corridors contain works by prominent European masters from the thirteenth to nineteenth centuries, but American art is the strongest feature: Edmund Greacen's smoky cityscape *Brooklyn Bridge East River* and Martin Heade's *St Johns River* are particularly evocative. Afterwards, take a stroll through the flower-packed formal English and Italianate **gardens**, which roll down to the river's edge, providing an apt view of Jacksonville's steely industrial character.

The Jaguar Stadium and Metropolitan Park

In 1994 Jacksonville was awarded one of the new National Football League franchises, much to the delight of the town, and what was once college football's illustrious Gator Bowl is now the stamping ground of the Jaguars (www.jaguars.com). From all over Jacksonville you can see the floodlights of the 73,000-seat **Jacksonville Jaguar Stadium** (1 Altel Stadium Place), still the scene of the Florida-Georgia college football clash each November (an excuse for 48 hours of citywide drinking and partying; tickets for the actual match are notoriously hard to get) in addition to the equally exciting Jaguars' home games. Outside of match days, the main reason to visit is the neighboring **Metropolitan Park**, a plot of riverside greenery that provides a venue for enjoyable free events most weekends plus some big free rock concerts during spring and fall. In midweek it's often deserted and makes a fine spot for a quiet riverside picnic. The "Northside Connector" **bus** stops close by.

Jacksonville Zoological Gardens

Previously a depressing place with restrictive cages and poorly used space, **Jacksonville Zoological Gardens**, on Hecksher Drive, just off I-95 north of downtown Jacksonville (daily 9am–5pm; $8; T 904/757-4463), is hoping to develop into one of the better zoos around and affords its inmates plenty of space to prowl, pose and strut. A justifiable source of pride are the white rhinos, seldom bred in captivity, which live in the eleven-acre "African veldt." However, much of the zoo is under endless development, leaving serious gaps between animal displays and relegating the experience to a pricey nature hike. **Bus** #NS 10 stops outside – but only on weekends.

Anheuser-Busch Brewery

After trekking about the US's largest city, you'll inevitably have worked up a thirst, and the **Anheuser–Busch Brewery**, 111 Busch Drive (Mon–Sat 10am–4pm; free; T 904/751-8118), purveyor of Budweiser, would like to quench it for you. After taking the free tour, which follows the Germanic and Czech roots of America's most popular beer, including informative exhibits like a mural on the evolution of beer-can openers, visitors indulge in the main attraction: free beer.

Eating

At and near downtown's Jacksonville Landing Mall, you'll find the most tempting **breakfast** and **lunch** choices: *The Mill Bakery* is a health-conscious brew pub, with huge muffins, while *Biscotti's Espresso Café*, 3556 St Johns Ave (T 904/387-2060), serves up an eclectic blend any time of day. On the south bank, *The Loop*, 4000-21 St Johns Ave (T 904/384-7301), has good-priced general menus, specializing in Chicago- and California-style pizzas. For high-quality liquid refreshment, seafood and steaks, call at the *River City Brewing Co.*, 835 Museum Circle (T 904/398-2299), where you can sample home-brewed beer while listening to **live music**. The pick of the city's many stylish **dinner** restaurants is the *Wine Cellar*, 1314 Prudential Drive (T 904/398-8989), where a well-prepared fish or meat entrée costs upwards of $16.

Nightlife

Nightlife in Jacksonville is a pale shadow of the rave-ups at the beach (see "The Jacksonville beaches," p.237), but check out the *Milk Bar*, 128 W Adams St (℡904/356-MILK) – likely to have anything you could want, from house and reggae sounds to live punk bands and 25¢-beer nights; and *Havana-Jax*, 2578 Atlantic Blvd (℡904/399-0609), which has live rock groups and the occasional Latin band to spice up its Cuban-American cuisine.

Towards Amelia Island

Around thirty miles from Jacksonville lie the barrier islands, of which **Amelia Island** is particularly appealing, that mark Florida's northeast corner. To reach the islands, Hwy-105 will take you from Jacksonville along the north side of the St Johns River, but a much more enjoyable route is Hwy-A1A from the Jacksonville beaches, which crosses the river on the tiny **Mayport ferry** (6.20am–10pm; roughly every 30min; cars $2.75, cyclists and pedestrians $1). During this short voyage, pelicans can be seen swooping overhead to pluck morsels off the nearby shrimp boats.

The Kingsley Plantation

Near the ferry's landing point, Hwy-A1A combines with Hwy-105. Continuing north, you'll soon cross onto Fort George Island and, before long, encounter the entrance to the endless, tree-lined driveway of the **Kingsley Plantation** (daily 9am–5pm; free; ranger talks Mon–Fri 1pm, Sat & Sun 1pm & 3pm), the centerpiece of which is the elegant riverside house bought in 1817 by Scotsman Zephaniah Kingsley. The house and its 3000 acres were acquired with the proceeds from slavery, of which Kingsley was an advocate and dealer, amassing a fortune through the import and export of Africans. A pragmatic man, he wrote a treatise on the virtues of a patriarchal slave system more in keeping with the Spanish approach than the extremely brutal methods of the United States; he simply believed that well-fed, happier and freer (though not free) slaves made better workers. Nonetheless, the restored plantation reveals much about the plight of the forced arrivals and about Kingsley's remarkable wife, a Senegalese woman who ran the plantation and lived in extravagant style – perhaps compensating for her years as his servant. After returning to Hwy-A1A, keep an eye out for the **Huguenot Memorial Park** (daily 6am–sunset; 50¢ per person) on the east side of the road. Here there's a campground (℡904/251-3335), where you can pitch a tent for $5.63–7.88 per night, depending on whether you choose the interior or the riverfront sites.

The Talbot Islands

One mile further on from the park, Hwy-A1A runs through **Little Talbot Island State Park** (daily 8am–sunset; cars $4.25, cyclists and pedestrians $1), which consumes almost the whole of a thickly forested 3000-acre barrier island inhabited by 194 species of birdlife. The park has two tree-shaded, ocean-facing picnic areas and a superb four-mile **hiking trail**, which winds through a pristine landscape of oak and magnolia trees, wind-beaten sand dunes and a chunk of the park's five-mile-long beach. **Canoes** can be hired for $4 an hour ($15 a day) and **bikes** for $2 an hour ($10 a day). If you're smitten by the natural charms and want to save the bother of finding accommodation on Amelia Island (see below), use the **campground** (☎ 904/251-2321) on the western side of the park beside Myrtle Creek ($14).

Alternatively, carry on across the creek, onto tiny Long Island and over onto **Big Talbot Island**, which has three points of interest. First, **Bluffs Scenic Shoreline** (signposted off the road), where the bluffs have eroded, depositing entire trees on the beach, some of them still standing upright with all their roots intact. Second, the **Black Rock Trail**, a one-and-a-half-mile hike through woods onto the Atlantic coast, to rocks once made from peat. Finally, there's **BEAKS,** the Bird Emergency Aid and Kare Sanctuary, 12084 Houston Ave (Tues–Sun, noon–4pm; ☎ 904/251-2473, ⓦ www.beaks.org), which also provides emergency care for other wildlife, 365 days a year. Back on Hwy-A1A, the road continues for a few miles toward Amelia Island.

Amelia Island

Most first-time visitors to Florida would be hard-pressed to locate **AMELIA ISLAND**, at the state's northeastern extremity, which perhaps explains why this finger of land, thirteen miles long and never more than two across, is so peaceful and only modestly commercialized despite the unbroken silver swathe of Atlantic beach gracing its eastern edge. Matching the sands for appeal, **Fernandina Beach**, the island's sole town, was a haunt of pirates before transforming itself into an outpost of Victorian-era high society – a fact proven by its immaculately restored old center.

Some parts of the island are being swallowed by upmarket resorts (much of the southern half is taken up by the *Amelia Island Plantation*, a golf and tennis resort with private walking and biking trails, expensive restaurants and $200-a-night rooms), but it's still worth coming here. In Fernandina, at least, they still concern themselves more with the size of the shrimp catch than with pandering to tourists.

Fernandina Beach

Hwy-A1A runs more or less right into the effortlessly walkable town of **Fernandina Beach**, whose Victorian heyday is apparent in the restored painted wooden mansions with manicured lawns that line the short main drag, Centre Street. The English spelling reflects bygone political to-ing and fro-ing:

Amelia Island history: the eight flags

Amelia Island is the only place in the US to have been under the rule of **eight flags**. Following settlement by Huguenots in 1562, the Spanish arrived and founded a mission here. This was destroyed in 1702 by the British, who returned forty years later to govern the island (naming it in honor of King George II's daughter). The ensuing Spanish administration was interrupted by the US-backed "Patriots of Amelia Island," who ruled for a day during 1812; the Green Cross of the Florida Republic flew briefly in 1817; and, oddest of all, the Mexican rebel flag appeared over Amelia Island the same year. US rule has been disturbed only by Confederate occupancy during 1861.

These shifts reflect the ebb and flow of allegiances between the great sea-trading powers over many years, as well as the island's geographically desirable location: Amelia Island offered a harbor to ocean-going vessels outside US control but within spitting distance of the American border.

the Spanish named the town but the British named the streets. Beside the marina, at the western end of Centre Street and adjacent to a vintage train carriage, you'll spot the useful **visitor center** (Tues–Fri 9am–5pm, Sat 10am–2pm, Mon 10am–5pm; ⊕904/261-3248), where you can pick up a booklet produced by the Museum of History, highlighting driving and walking tours, as well as points of historical interest.

Remarkably, given the present calm, President James Monroe described Fernandina as a "festering fleshpot" after the 1807 US embargo on foreign shipping caused the Spanish-owned town to become a hotbed of smuggling and other illicit activities to circumvent the ban. The acquisition of Florida by the US in 1821 did not diminish Fernandina's importance – this time as a key rail terminal for freight moving between the Atlantic and the Gulf of Mexico. More recently, however, its charm has been impaired by the unfortunate proximity of two smelly paper mills across the Intracoastal Waterway – it can get bad when the winds are blowing the wrong way.

The Museum of History and walking around Centre Street

The obvious place to gain insights into the town is the **Museum of History**, 233 S Third St (Mon–Sat 11am–3pm; donation suggested; ⊕904/261-7378) – once the county jail – whose scattering of memorabilia is backed up by photographs and maps. The 45-minute **guided tours** (Mon–Sat at 11am & 2pm; recommended donation of $2.50) of the museum are excellent, informatively covering 4000 years of the island's varied history with humor. Also recommended are the longer **historical walks** (Thurs & Fri at 3pm from the visitor center; suspended June–Aug, except by appointment; $5), which feature many of the old buildings on and around Centre Street. Horse-drawn carriage tours are also on offer ($15, children $7.50; ⊕904/277-1555), covering downtown, Fort Clinch, and Old Town, the original, funky settlement just to the north.

Even if you miss the tours, **walking around** on your own is far from dull. Centre Street and the immediate area are alive with Victorian-era turrets, twirls and towers, plus many notable later buildings. Among them, **St Peter's Episcopal Church**, on the corner with Eighth Street, was completed in 1884 by New York architect Robert S. Schuyler, whose name is linked to many local structures and who never used the same style twice. The Gothic used for the church is a long way from the painted folly of the Italianate **Fairbanks House**, also by Schuyler, situated at the corner of Seventh and Cedar streets. This building, designed to look like a Florentine palace with a square tower rising above the center, was commissioned by a newspaper editor as a surprise for his wife, who hated it and refused to step over the threshold – at least according to local legend. Today it has been transformed into a sumptuous bed and breakfast (see overleaf).

The beach

Well suited to swimming and busy with beach sports, the most active of the island's **beaches** is at the eastern end of Fernandina's Atlantic Avenue, a mile from the town center. If you don't mind a long hike with sand between your toes, you can walk along the beach to Fort Clinch State Park, three miles north (see below). In the fall, you might be lucky enough to spot **whales** in the waters off Amelia Island. The right whale, an endangered species, moves into inland waterways to calve.

North to Fort Clinch State Park

After Florida came under US control in 1819, a fort was built on Amelia's northern tip, three miles from Fernandina, to protect seaborne access to

Georgia. The fort now forms part of **Fort Clinch State Park** (daily 8am–sunset; cars $4.25, pedestrians and cyclists $1), and provides a home for a gang of Civil War enthusiasts who pretend they're Union soldiers of 1864, the only time the fort saw action. Entrance to the fort itself costs $1, and the most atmospheric way to see it is with the soldier-guided **candle-lit tour** (most Fridays and Saturdays during summer; $2; reservations essential: ℡ 904/277-7274). With the pseudo–Civil War garrison moaning about their work and meager rations, the tour may sound like a ham job, but in fact it is a convincing, informative – and quite spooky – hour's affair.

The rest of the park can hardly be overlooked: by road, you have to go through three miles of it before reaching the fort, passing an animal reserve (from which overgrown alligators often emerge, so if you do fancy a spot of hiking, stick to the marked 30- and 45-minute **nature trails**) and a turn-off for the stunning 2.5-mile long **beach**, where legions of crab catchers cast their baskets off a long fishing jetty. From both jetty and fort there's an immaculate view of Cumberland Island (only accessible by ferry from St Mary's, on the Georgia mainland, or by canoe or kayak on organized trips run by Outdoor Adventures, ℡ 904/393-9030, see p.242), a Georgian nature reserve famed for its wild horses – if you're lucky, a few will be galloping over the island's sands. You might also catch a glimpse of a nuclear-powered submarine gliding towards Cumberland Sound and the massive Kings Bay naval base. **Camping** in the park is available for $17.

Accommodation

While the best way to savor Fernandina's unique historic atmosphere is by staying in one of the town's antique-filled **bed-and-breakfast inns**, more ordinary **accommodation** choices are the motels on the way to or on Fletcher Avenue (Hwy-A1A).

1735 House, 584 S Fletcher Ave (℡ 904/261-4148 or 1-800/872-8531, Ⓦ www.amelialodgings .com). To the east of the Old Town, right on Hwy-A1A and the sugary beach, lies this bed and breakfast, which offers a knotty-pine, nautical-theme ocean pad. ❺

Bailey House, 28 S Seventh St (℡ 904/261-5390 or 1-800/251-5390, Ⓦ www.bailey-house.com). One of the town's fabulous painted Victorian ladies with turrets and bay windows, this bed and breakfast has five large rooms. ❺

Fairbanks House ℡ 1-800/261-4838 or 904/277-0500, Ⓦ www.fairbankshouse.com). This is one of the most historic bed-and-breakfast inns (see above). Ask for the top-floor honeymoon suite, with private turret. ❺

Florida House Inn, 20 & 22 S Third St (℡ 904/261-3300 or 1-800/258-3301,

Ⓦ www.floridahouse.com). At the state's oldest hotel, you can sleep where Mary Pickford and Ulysses S. Grant stayed, and where children and pets are welcome. ❸

Hampton Inn & Suites, 19 S Second St (℡ 904/491-4911 or 1-800/426-7866, Ⓦ www.hamptoninn-suites.com). Fernandina's newest grand hotel, directly on the harbor, is harmoniously designed so as not to clash with the surrounding architecture. ❺

The Inn at Fernandina Beach, 2707 Sadler Rd (℡ 904/ 277-2300). This is one of the better budget inns, a little bit out from the center of town. ❹

The Lighthouse, 748 Fletcher Ave (℡ 904/261-5878). Book far in advance to secure a room in this small lighthouse with four rooms right on the sea. The top floor features a porch that wraps around the building. ❼

Eating and nightlife

For its size, the island has an exceptionally good number of places to **eat**, the bulk of them on and around Fernandina's Centre Street. *The Marina*, 101 Centre St (℡ 904/261-5310), is one of the island's oldest restaurants, with a seafood-based menu and a convivial atmosphere. It's renowned for "Fernandina Fantail Fried Shrimp" and as a **breakfast** hot spot, serving fried fish, eggs and cheese grits. But the not-to-be-missed choice for **Sunday brunch** ($10), or **lunch** and **dinner** Tuesday to Saturday is the *Florida House Inn* (see opposite), where the all-you-care-to-eat Southern cookin' served boarding-house-style is an unforgettable experience: homemade biscuits, cornbread, fried chicken, greens, gravy, the works, all washed down with iced tea – take it Southern-style, already sweetened, for the full experience.

In a more upmarket vein, *Brett's Waterway Café*, on the Fernandina Harbor Marina at the end of Centre Street (℡ 904/261-2660), has generous American meals, such as roast beef, and great views. For a slap-up gourmet **dinner** of the area's freshest seafood, try the classy *Beech Street Grill*, corner of Eighth and Beech streets (℡ 904/277-3662, ⓦ www.beechstreetgrill.com), or *Le Clos*, 20 S Second St (℡ 904/261-8100, ⓦ www.leclos.com), with its cordon bleu-level Provençale cuisine.

Simpler fare is available at *O'Kane's Irish Pub and Eatery*, 318 Centre St (℡ 904/261-1000), for lunch and dinner fish dishes and more, or at *27 North*, 27 N Third St (℡ 904/277-5269), an atmospheric coffee house that offers great breakfasts and creative sandwiches and wraps for lunch, as well as an excellent wine list. You'll also find a limited menu of plain and simple dishes at the *Palace Saloon*, 117 Centre St (℡ 904/261-6320), which claims to have the **oldest bar** in Florida, forty feet of hand-carved mahogany, built in 1878. You might prefer to save your visit for a night-time drink, not least because few other places warrant an after-dark investigation and the *Palace* has live music on weekends. This was the last tavern in the country to close after Prohibition began, taking two years to deplete its supply of spirits. If you're feeling brave, try the delicious "Pirate's Punch": lemon, lime, orange and pineapple with a gin-and-rum kick.

TRAVEL DETAILS

Trains (AMTRAK ℡ 1-800/872-7245)
Jacksonville to: Miami (3 daily; 10hr); Orlando (3 daily; 4hr); Pensacola (1 on Tues, Thurs, Sat; 9hr 30min); Tallahassee (same as Pensacola train; 4hr); Tampa (1 daily; 5hr).

Buses (GREYHOUND ℡ 1-800/231-2222)
Cocoa to: Daytona Beach (4 daily; 1hr 45min); Jacksonville (4 daily; 4hr); Melbourne (5 daily; 35min); New Smyrna Beach (4 daily;

1hr 15min); Titusville (4 daily; 30min).
Daytona Beach to: Jacksonville (10 daily; 1hr 40min–2hr); Orlando (7 daily; 1hr 5min–1hr 25min); St Augustine (7 daily; 1hr).
Jacksonville to: Miami (11 daily; 8–13hr); Orlando (11 daily; 3–5hr); St Petersburg (8 daily; 7hr–8hr 30min); Tallahassee (5 daily; 2hr 45min–3hr 45min); Tampa (11 daily; 5hr 30min–8hr).
St Augustine to: Jacksonville (5 daily; 55min)

Central Florida

CHAPTER 5

Highlights

* **Mount Dora** A Victoria-era town just north of Orlando, Mount Dora makes for a genteel break from the crowds. **P.267**

* **Blue Spring State Park** The St Johns River, which runs through the park, is a great place to watch manatees. **P.269**

* **Gatorland** Watch the alligators being fed – or wrestled – at this less-heralded theme park between Orlando and Kissimmee. **P.270**

* **Celebration USA** An easy day-trip from Orlando, this essay in urban planning, if not incredibly compelling in itself, has provoked a storm of controversy. **P.272**

* **Disney's Animal Kingdom** Climb into a jeep transport and be swept into a safari through African wildlands. **P.275**

* **Universal Studios** The rides don't get any better or more thrilling than here. **P.286**

* **Lake Okeechobee** The second largest freshwater lake within the United States offers plenty of outdoor activities, including cycling and fishing. **P.299**

Central Florida

Most of the broad and fertile expanse of **CENTRAL FLORIDA**, stretching between the state's east and west coasts, was self-sufficient farming country devoted to growing citrus and raising cattle when vacation-mania first gripped the beachside strips in the 1950s. Only the most adventurous of Florida's visitors then ferried by steamboat along the region's rivers and across its gushing springs. Over the last two decades, however, this picture of tranquillity has been largely shattered: no section of the state has been more dramatically affected by modern tourism.

The most visited part of Florida is also one of its ugliest: an ungodly clutter of freeway interchanges, motels, billboards and contrived tourist sights arching around the small and otherwise affable city of **Orlando**. The blame for the vulgarity lies with Orlando's near-neighbor, **Walt Disney World**, which, since the Seventies, has sucked millions of people into the biggest and cleverest theme park complex ever created – sparking off a tourist-dollar chase on its outskirts of Gold Rush proportions. The Disney parks are every bit as polished as their reputation, but their surrounds are no advertisement for Florida, and it's a tragedy that many visitors see no more of the state than this aggressive commercialism.

The rest of Central Florida is markedly less brash. The slow-paced towns of **South Central Florida** make excellent bases for cruising the Orlando circuit and offer plenty of relaxed diversions in their lake-filled vicinity. Much the same can be said of **North Central Florida**, where tiny villages, far more prevalent than towns, hold the century-old homes of Florida's pioneer settlers. **Gainesville**, an outpost of learning and liberalism containing one of the state's two major universities, is a surprising sight given its deeply rural setting.

Since Walt Disney World redefined the geography of the region, **getting around** Central Florida by **car** has become generally easy and quick – but take time to leave the charmless freeways and journey down some of the multitude of minor routes linking the lesser towns and villages. Non-drivers will find that

Accommodation price codes

All accommodation prices in this book have been coded using the symbols below. Note that prices are for the least expensive double rooms in each establishment. For a full explanation see p.29 in Basics.

❶ up to $40 ❸ $60–80 ❺ $100–130 ❼ $175–250
❷ $40–60 ❹ $80–100 ❻ $130–175 ❽ $250+

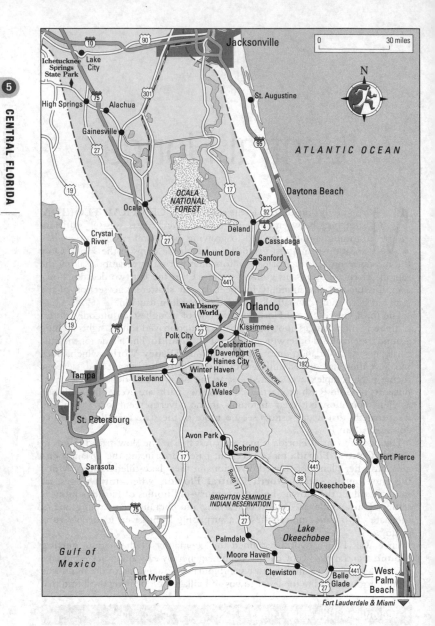

Fort Lauderdale & Miami ▼

Orlando's **bus system** extends quite a bit beyond downtown; many of the smaller centers have Greyhound **bus** connections, although they can take unbelievably long to get you from place to place; and twice-daily **trains** pass through some towns. Car-less visitors wanting to get to the Disney parks are dependent on the local **shuttle buses** (see "Getting Around," p.254).

Orlando and Disney World

It's highly ironic that **Orlando**, an insubstantial, quiet farming town in the heart of peninsular Florida just some thirty years ago, now has more people passing through its environs than any other place in the state. Reminders of the old Florida are still easy to find in and immediately north of Orlando, though most people get no closer to Orlando's heart than a string of cheap motels along Hwy-192, fifteen miles south of town. **International Drive** (five miles southwest of Orlando) – a long boulevard of posher motels, convention hotels, heavily themed shopping malls and schmaltzy restaurants – may be worth driving by just to see its buildings' extravagant yet utterly characterless exteriors.

The cause of the area's transformation is, of course, **Walt Disney World**, a group of state-of-the-art theme parks southwest of Orlando that lures 35 million people a year to a 43-square-mile plot of previously featureless scrubland. It's possible to pass through the Orlando area and not visit Walt Disney World, but there's no way to escape its impact – even the road system was reshaped to accommodate the place, and, whichever way you look, billboards tout more ways to spend your money there. Amid a plethora of fly-by-night, would-be tourist targets, only **Universal Studios** and **SeaWorld Orlando** (the second most expensive theme park in the world after Busch Gardens in Tampa; see p.329) offer serious competition to the most finely realized concept in escapist entertainment anywhere on earth.

Arrival and information

The region's primary **airport**, **Orlando International**, is nine miles south of downtown Orlando. Shuttle buses will carry you from the airport to any hotel or motel in the Orlando area for $10–15. If you're headed for downtown Orlando, use local bus #11 (a 45min journey), or #42 for International Drive (both buses depart from the airport's "A Side" concourse every 60 minutes between 6am and 9pm). A taxi to downtown Orlando, International Drive or the motels on Hwy-192 will cost a little more than $30.

A second airport, **Orlando Sanford International**, is a small but growing facility twenty miles north of downtown Orlando that receives a lot of charter flights from Great Britain. A taxi from Sanford to downtown Orlando costs about $55.

Arriving by **bus** or **train**, you'll wind up in downtown Orlando at the Greyhound terminal, 555 N John Young Parkway (T 407/292-3422), or the train station, 1400 Slight Blvd (T 407/843-7611). Other train stops in the area lie in Winter Park, 150 W Morse Blvd (T 407/645-5055), and Kissimmee, 111 E Dakin Ave (T 407/933-1170).

Free magazines, strewn virtually wherever you look, are packed with handy facts, but a better source of reliable **information** is the **Official Visitor Center**, 8723 International Drive, Suite 101 (daily 8am–7pm; T 1-800/643-

The area code for the Orlando area is T 407.

The major cross-Florida roads form a web-like mass of intersections in or around Orlando and Walt Disney World: I-4 passes southwest–northeast through Walt Disney World and continues in elevated form through downtown Orlando; Hwy-192 (the **Irlo Bronson Memorial Highway**) crosses I-4 in Walt Disney World and charts an east–west course fifteen miles south of Orlando; Hwy-528 (the **Beeline Expressway**) stems from International Drive and heads for the east coast; and **Florida's Turnpike** cuts northwest–southeast, avoiding Walt Disney World and downtown Orlando altogether.

9492, 407/363-5872 or 407/425-1234, ⓦwww.go2orlando.com), where you should pick up the free *Official Visitors Guide to Orlando*, plus hundreds of leaflets and discount coupons. If you're using the motels along Hwy-192, drop by the equally well-stocked **Kissimmee–St Cloud VC**, 1925 Billbeck Blvd in Kissimmee (daily 8am–5pm; ⓣ1-800/327-9159 or 407/847-5000, ⓦwww.floridakiss.com). The best entertainment guide to the area is the Friday "Calendar" section of the *Orlando Sentinel* newspaper.

Getting around

With most routes operating from 6.30am to 8pm on weekdays, 7.30am–6pm on Saturdays, and 8am–6pm on Sundays, **local bus lines** (ⓣ407/841-8240, ⓦwww.golynx.com) converge at the downtown Orlando terminal between Central and Pine streets. The system is known as the "Lynx," and bus-stop signs are cleverly marked with paw prints. You'll need **exact change** ($1 and 10¢ for a transfer from one route to another) if you pay on board; a weekly pass for $10 includes free transfers and is available from the terminal's information booth. The "Lynx" system makes about 4000 stops in three counties, and the **most-used bus routes** are #1 to Loch Haven and Winter Park; #11 to the airport; and #8 to International Drive, where you can catch a shuttle bus (see below) to Walt Disney World and the area's other major tourist parks, or link with #42 to **Orlando International Airport** (an hour-long journey). Along International Drive, between SeaWorld Orlando and Universal Studios, the **I-Ride** trolley service (ⓣ407/354-5656) operates every fifteen minutes daily from 7am to midnight, costing 75¢ one way (seniors 25¢); children 12 and under ride free.

Orlando **taxis** are expensive: rates begin at $3.25 for the first mile, plus $1.75 for each additional mile. For non-drivers, however, they're the only way to get around at night – try Town & Country (ⓣ407/827-6350) or Yellow Cab (ⓣ407/699-9999).

Cheaper than taxis, but more expensive and quicker than the I-Ride, are the **shuttle buses**, minivans or coaches run by private companies connecting the main accommodation areas, such as International Drive and Hwy-192 with Walt Disney World, SeaWorld Orlando, Universal Studios and the airports. You should phone at least a day ahead to be picked up, and confirm a time for your return. Mears Transportation Service (ⓣ407/423-5566) charges $10–12 for a round-trip ride from International Drive or Hwy-192 to all the major attractions, and $15 one way to Orlando International Airport.

All the main **car rental** firms have offices at or close to Orlando International Airport. Demand is strong despite the high rates,, so call in advance during busy seasons (the numbers are in "Getting around" in Basics).

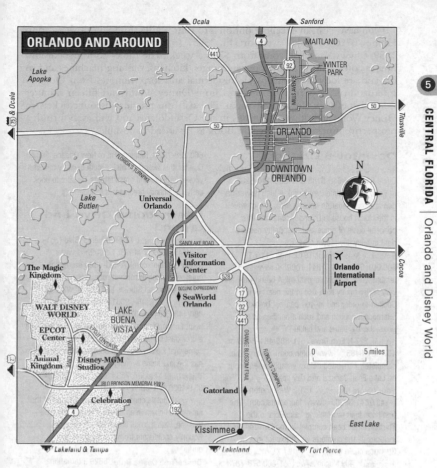

ORLANDO AND AROUND

Accommodation

Unless you're staying on Disney property and planning a Disney-only vacation, you'll need to be mobile wherever you stay in the far-flung Orlando area. Price, therefore, should be more of a concern than location when looking for **accommodation**. If you're dependent on public transport, however, downtown Orlando, where the old-fashioned B&Bs are practical options, is the best place to stay.

Genuinely budget-priced accommodation is offered only by the scores of cheap motels lined up **along Hwy-192** between Walt Disney World and Kissimmee; many offer special rates that are yours simply by picking up a discount coupon at one of the information offices mentioned above. **International Drive** is dominated by expensive chain hotels and is where you're likely to end up if you come on a package trip – but bargains can be found during the slower winter periods. The hotels in the Lake Buena Vista area just outside Disney World are pricey, but they also offer excellent accessibility to the theme parks. Accommodation, though expensive, is also available within Disney World itself (see p.274 for details). **Campgrounds** are plentiful on and around Hwy-192 close to Kissimmee.

If you have a car, an excellent option is to **rent a villa** from Sunsplash Vacation Homes, 3710 CR 54, Davenport, FL 33837 (☎863/424-6193 or 1-800/505-1359, ⓦwww.sunsplash.com; from $700 a week). The three- to four-bedroom houses come with their own pools, garages, kitchens, washing machines and so on, and are located in an upscale residential area forty minutes from Orlando International Airport, nine minutes from Disney World and fifteen minutes from Haines City, the nearest town. The staff can provide discount tickets to Disney World and other attractions in the Orlando area and will even furnish a prospective itinerary for your stay. Book as far ahead as possible.

Downtown Orlando

The Courtyard at Lake Lucerne, 211 N Lucerne Circle E (☎407/648-5188 or 1-800/444-5289, ⓦwww.orlandohistoricinn.com). A lush flower garden and four separate antique inns, one of which is the oldest house in Orlando, comprise this peaceful oasis of grace and hospitality nestled right in busy downtown area. ④

Embassy Suites Hotel, 191 E Pine St (☎1-800/601-6743 or 407/841-1000, ⓦwww.embassyorlandodowntown.com). A brand-new and very stylish luxury high-rise in the heart of it all. Cooked-to-order and all-you-can-eat breakfast, afternoon reception and such amenities as two pools, Jacuzzi baths and cable TV. ⑦

Eo Inn, 227 N Eola Drive (☎1-888/481-8488 or 407/481-8485, ⓦwww.eoinn.com). A very chic, completely converted deluxe establishment right on Lake Eola; Jacuzzi and day spa. ⑤

Four Points Sheraton, 151 E Washington St (☎407/841-3220, ⓦwww.fourpoints.com). The first hotel built overlooking Lake Eola in the Thirties, it has been completely modernized, and includes all the comforts you'd expect in a Sheraton chain entry. ④

Travelodge, 409 Magnolia Ave (☎1-800/578-7878 or 407/ 423-1671). Within walking distance of everything, with private pool, free HBO cable TV, newspaper and local calls, and non-smoking rooms. ②

The Veranda Bed & Breakfast Inn, 115 N Summerlin Ave (☎1-800/420-6822 or 407/849-0321, ⓦwww.theverandaBandB.com). Charming and friendly nine-room bed and breakfast located in four period buildings nestled around a courtyard garden, in Orlando's Thornton Park district, one block from Lake Eola. ⑤

Winter Park

The Fortnightly Inn, 377 E Fairbanks Ave (☎407/ 645-4440). A night or two at this personable five-room bed and breakfast makes for a relaxing break from the rampant commercialism of the Orlando area. Includes full breakfast and free use of bicycles. ④

Park Plaza, 307 Park Ave (☎407/ 647-1072 or 1-800/228-7220). Reminiscent of New Orleans' French Quarter, this Twenties hotel is stuffed with wonderful wicker furniture and brass fittings. Be sure to book early. Continental breakfast is included. ④

International Drive and around

Clarion Universal, 7299 Universal Blvd (☎1-800/445-7299 or 407/351-5009, ⓦwww.clarion-orlando.com). A mid-sized easygoing hotel with nicely furnished rooms. Handiest location for Universal Studios and Wet 'n' Wild. ③

Country Hearth Inn, 9861 International Drive (☎1-888/443-2784 or 407/352-0008, ⓦwww.country-hearth.com). Plain rooms at modest rates, a pool and a breakfast buffet are reasons for staying in this somewhat kitschy shrine to Southern Victoriana; also has live jazz some evenings. ④

Days Inn Lakeside, 7335 Sand Lake Rd (☎407/ 351-1900 or 1-800/777-3297, ⓦwww.thhotels.com). An enormous branch of the nationwide chain in an out-of-the-way lakeside location, with a small beach and three pools. Roughly equidistant from the big three theme parks. ③

DoubleTree Castle Hotel, 8629 International Drive (☎407/345-1511 or 1-800/952-2785, ⓦwww.doubletreecastle.com). This elaborate theme-hotel, complete with Renaissance music and medieval decor, such as armor, offers all the luxuries – plus complimentary chocolate chip cookies. ⑥

Howard Johnson, 7050 S Kirkman Rd (☎407/351-2000 or 1-800/327-3808, ⓦwww.allfloridaresorts.com). Good-sized rooms, three pools and free shuttle buses to the major theme parks make this a good base for non-drivers concentrating on the big attractions. ④

Peabody Orlando, 9801 International Drive (☎1-800/PEABODY or 407/352-4000, ⓦwww.peabodyorlando.com). Twenty-seven stories of opulent rooms primarily aimed at delegates using the massive Orange County Convention Center across the street. If money's no object and you like in-room luxuries, access to a fitness center and floodlit tennis courts, this one's for you. Ducks parade through the lobby twice a day. **❽**

Radisson Barcelo Hotel, 8444 International Drive (☎407/345-0505 or 1-800/333-3333, ⓦwww.radisson.com). While speed-swimming records have been set at the Olympic-sized pool here, those looking for relaxation will find the spacious rooms and the location, directly opposite the restaurants of the Mercado Mediterranean Shopping Village (see "Eating," p.264), a winning combination. **❹**

Red Roof Inn, 9922 Hawaiian Court (☎407/352-1507 or 1-800/THE-ROOF). Unelaborate but perfectly serviceable budget-range hotel with a pool and a coin-op laundromat. **❹**

Sandy Lake Towers, 6145 Carrier Drive (☎407/996-6000 or 1-877/996-6151, ⓦwww.sandylakesuites.com). Very close to Universal, this place is the apotheosis of Florida pink stucco. The eighteen-story twin tower stands out for miles around – good for getting your bearings. The hotel only offers suites, all two bedrooms and rather spartan, but it is a great choice for families and is proximate to everything. Pools, beach on the lake and steam room. **❺**

Lake Buena Vista

DoubleTree Club, 12490 Apopka Vineland Rd (☎1-800/222-TREE or 407/239-4646; ⓦwww.doubletreeclublbv.com). Newly renovated in very, very colorful yellow and red tones. Features thirteen Kids Club Suites – with two bunk beds and a king-size bed – and is located just outside the entrance to Downtown Disney. **❺**

Embassy Suites, 8100 Lake Ave (☎1-800/257-0483 or 407/239-1144, ⓦwww.embassysuites.com). Two-room suites including free cooked-to-order breakfast and in-room refrigerators and microwaves. Great pools and luxurious appointments. **❻**

Perri House Acres Estate B&B Inn, 10417 Vista Oaks Court (☎407/876-4830 or 1-800/780-4830). An eight-room bed and breakfast hidden on four wooded acres that is also a bird sanctuary, just outside Disney off State Road 535. The rooms are clean and bright and the atmosphere is friendly. Far from everything but Disney, but the perfect antidote to all the theme-park frenzy. Pool and hot-tub. **❺**

Westgate Lakes Family Resort, 10000 Turkey Lake Rd (☎407/345-0000 or 1-888/8087410, ⓦwww.westgateresorts.com). All rooms are suites that sleep at least eight, with full cooking facilities, and the resort is spread across a ninety-acre lakeside site. Paddleboats to Paradise Island and waterskiing available. **❽**

Along West Hwy-192 (Irlo Bronson Memorial Highway)

Best Western Eastgate, 5565 W Hwy-192 (☎1-800/223-5361 or 407/396-0707). Basic, comfortable and extremely convenient to Disney World, with its own pool and sheltered from the noise of the highway by a small lake. **❷**

Casa Rosa Inn, 4600 W Hwy-192 (☎407/396-2020, ⓦwww.hotel4you.com). A pleasant little Mediterranean-style place, with all the basics, plus free HBO cable TV and a large pool. **❸**

Comfort Inn Maingate West, 9330 W Hwy-192 (☎1-800/446-4473 or 407/424-8420). Brand-new and immaculate; includes continental breakfast and pool – microwave available; six minutes from Disney. **❶**

Comfort Suites Maingate Resort, 7888 W Hwy-192 (☎1-888/390-9888 or 407/390-9888). All suites here have every convenience, amid beautifully laid-out parklands with two pools. **❺**

DoubleTree Guest Suites, 4787 W Hwy-192, (☎1-800/222-TREE or 407/397-0555, ⓦwww.doubletree.com). Bi-level Mediterranean-style garden suites, within minutes of all the major attractions. **❺**

Econo Lodge Maingate East, 4311 W Hwy-192 (☎1-800/388-7698 or 407/396-7100, ⓦwww.econolodge.com). Spacious and clean, though basic, with two pools and free shuttles to Disney. **❷**

Grand Lake Resort, 7770 W Hwy-192 (☎1-800/527-9132 or 407/396-0564, ⓦwww.asitraveldirect.com). Book well in advance for a suite in this super-luxurious resort complex, located on Lake Wilson. Sports facilities available. **❺**

Holiday Inn Niki Bird Resort, 7300 W Hwy-192 (☎1-800/20-OASIS). This is the best hotel for children, with specially designed kid suites featuring bunks and playrooms. Just one mile from Disney. **❸**

Howard Johnson, 8660 W Hwy-192 (☎407/396-4500 or 1-800/638-7829, ⓦwww.orlandohojomaingate.com). Nice rooms with good amenities, including cable TV, a pool and a coin-op laundromat. **❷**

Larson Inn Family Suites, 6075 W Hwy-192 (☎1-800/327-9074 or 407/396-6100, ⓦwww.larsoninnfamilysuites.com). A good place for kids. The rates might be a touch higher than others in the vicinity, but under-18s stay for free in their parents' room and facilities include a game room, a small playground and a Jacuzzi. **❹**

Motel 6, 5731 W Hwy-192 (☎407/396-6333 or 1-800/4-MOTEL-6, ⓦwww.motel6.com). One of the nicer ones in the national chain, with two pools and a garden. **❷**

Just north of Universal Orlando, off Hiawassee Road and near Conroy-Windermere Road, lies **Turkey Lake Park** ($2, children $1), a quiet place to have lunch by a lake, take a short hike or let the kids run around a terrific playground. Five miles west of downtown Orlando off Hwy-50 is the **West Orange Trail**, 19 miles of scenic, paved walkways that run from historic Winter Garden to the hills of Lake County. West Orange Trail Bikes and Blades Co. (T 407/877-0600) provides bike ($5) and skate ($6) rentals.

Park Inn International Cedar Lakeside, 4960 W Hwy-192 (T 1-800/327-0072 or 407/396-1376). On Lake Cecile, four minutes from Disney. Pool, Jacuzzi, waterskiing, fishing, paddleboats, playground, laundry. ❶

Quality Suites, 4669 W Hwy-192 (T 1-800/848-4148 or 407/396-8040). Apartment-style accommodation is available in this hotel, which is constructed to look like a row of houses and shops, giving the impression of a small town. Several pools are nestled in its lush gardens, and free continental breakfast and shuttles are available. ❺

Sevilla Inn, 4640 W Hwy-192 (T 1-800/367-1363 or 407/396-4135, W www.sevillainn.com).

You can rely on this attractive Spanish-style place to be clean, tidy and well run; for down time from sightseeing, there's a pool in the spacious courtyard. ❷

Super 8 Motel, 1815 W Hwy-192 (T 1-800/325-4348 or 407/847-6121, W www.abcsuites.com). Comfort, a pool, and your choice of a designer room or mini-apartment suite, all in an attractive garden setting. Free continental breakfast. ❸

Wynfield Inn, 5335 W Hwy-192 (T 1-800/346-1551 or 407/396-2121, W www.orlando.com/wynfield). A tropically landscaped heated pool and large, homely rooms, plus free shuttle service to all the major attractions. ❷

Camping near Kissimmee

Numerous serviceable **campgrounds** stand beside Hwy-192, close to Kissimmee. The *KOA*, 4771 Hwy-192 (T 1-800/331-1453; $24.95 with water and electric, $21.95 without, $49.95 for cabins), is suited to tents. The site offers a large heated pool as well as a playground and game room for the kids. For a more peaceful setting, choose a site beside West Lake Tohopekaliga a few miles south of Kissimmee where the pace is leisurely and more fuss is made about fishing than visiting Mickey Mouse: pitch your tent at *Richardson's Fish Camp*, 1550 Scotty's Rd (T 407/846-6540; $19.59).

Orlando

Despite the enormous expansion of the Nineties, **ORLANDO** itself remains impressively free of the commercialism that surrounds it. Away from the small but growing crop of high-rise office buildings in downtown, the bulk of the city comprises smart residential areas adorned by parks and lakes. Visiting the historical leftovers and art collections spread throughout the city could fill a day – and, for those who thought that the state begins and ends with theme parks, Orlando offers a taste of Florida living without the mouse-ear hats.

Downtown Orlando

Except to sample the artificial charms of the Church Street Station entertainment center (see "Nightlife," p.266), few visitors make their way into **downtown Orlando**, which, despite the half-dozen corporate towers in its midst, is still redolent, in size and mood, of the tobacco-chewing cow-town that it used

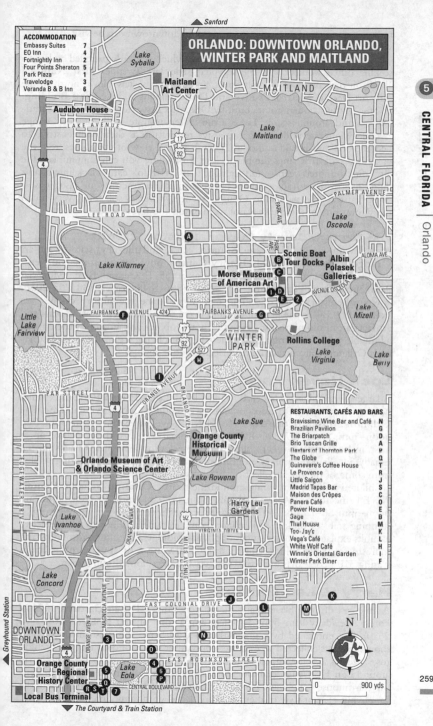

ACCOMMODATION
Embassy Suites 7
EO Inn 4
Fortnightly Inn 2
Four Points Sheraton 5
Park Plaza 1
Travelodge 3
Veranda B & B Inn 6

ORLANDO: DOWNTOWN ORLANDO, WINTER PARK AND MAITLAND

Sanford

Lake Sybalia

Maitland Art Center

MAITLAND

Audubon House

LAKE AVENUE

Lake Maitland

4

PALMER AVENUE

LEE ROAD

PARK AVE.

Lake Osceola

Lake Killarney

A

Scenic Boat Tour Docks

Albin Polasek Galleries

ALOMA AVE.

B

Morse Museum of American Art

C

AVENUE OSCEOLA

D

E

2

Lake Mizell

FAIRBANKS AVENUE (424)

F

FAIRBANKS AVENUE (426)

G

Little Lake Fairview

17

92

WINTER PARK

Rollins College

Lake Virginia

Lake Berry

527

H

PAR STREET

ORANGE AVENUE

ORLANDO AVENUE

I

4

Lake Sue

Orange County Historical Museum

RESTAURANTS, CAFÉS AND BARS
Bravissimo Wine Bar and Café N
Brazilian Pavilion G
The Briarpatch D
Brio Tuscan Grille A
Dexters of Thornton Park P
The Globe Q
Guinevere's Coffee House T
Le Provence R
Little Saigon J
Madrid Tapas Bar S
Maison des Crêpes C
Panera Café O
Power House E
Sage B
Thai House M
Too-Jay's K
Vega's Café L
White Wolf Café H
Winnie's Oriental Garden I
Winter Park Diner F

Orlando Museum of Art & Orlando Science Center

Lake Rowena

Harry Leu Gardens

EDGEWATER DRIVE

Lake Ivanhoe

ORANGE AVENUE

VIRGINIA DRIVE

MILLS AVENUE

Lake Concord

EAST COLONIAL DRIVE

J

L

M

K

N

DOWNTOWN ORLANDO

Orange County Regional History Center

MAGNOLIA AVENUE

ORANGE AVENUE

3

O

4

6

P

EAST ROBINSON STREET

N

Lake Eola

5

Q

R S T

7

CENTRAL BOULEVARD

Local Bus Terminal

Greyhound Station

The Courtyard & Train Station

0   900 yds

to be. Everything of consequence in the tiny downtown can be visited on foot within an hour.

Begin by dawdling along **Orange Avenue**, which is mostly patrolled by lunch-seeking office workers. Pass the Egyptian-style, late-Twenties **First National Bank** on the corner of Church Street, and continue a few blocks north to the early Art Deco of **McCrory's Five and Dime** building and the **Kress Building**.

Some of the wooden homes built by Orlando's first white settlers in the mid-1800s stand around scenic **Lake Eola**, a ten-minute walk east of Orange Avenue. Many are undergoing expensive restoration as their owners strive to become bed-and-breakfast moguls. There's a good view of the houses from the oak-filled park that rings the placid lake. From here you can contemplate the city's first hundred years – and the fact that Orlando's early black inhabitants didn't live in these leafy environs but in a much less picturesque district west of the railway line, parallel to Orange Avenue, which is still today very much the wrong side of the tracks – not to mention the freeway.

The Orange County Regional History Center

Also downtown, on **Heritage Square**, you'll find the new, state-of-the-art **Orange County Regional History Center**, now housed in the completely restored Orange County Courthouse at 65 E Central Blvd (Mon–Sat 9am–5pm, Sun 11am–5pm; $7; ☎ 407/836-8500 or 1-800/965-2030, Ⓦ www.thehistorycenter.org). The exhibitions trace the history of the area from 10,000 BC to the present day, and many of the most effective displays and artifacts, from old photos to recreated hotel lobbies and grocers' stores, do an admirable job of reviving a time when, far from being a global tourist destination, Orlando epitomized the American frontier town.

Loch Haven Park

A large lawn wedged between two small lakes, **Loch Haven Park**, three miles north of downtown Orlando, contains several buildings of varying interest. The **Orlando Museum of Art**, 2416 N Mills Ave (Tues–Sat 10am–5pm, Sun noon–5pm; $6; ☎ 407/896-4231, Ⓦ www.omart.org), is likely to take up at least an hour: a permanent collection of pre-Columbian pieces backs up the usually excellent temporary exhibitions of modern American paintings culled from some of the finest collections in the world.

Children will enjoy roaming around the nearby **Orlando Science Center**, 777 E Princeton St (Mon–Thurs 9am–5pm, Fri 9am–9pm, Sat noon–9pm, Sun noon–5pm; $6–12.50; ☎ 407/514-2000 or 1-888/672-4386, Ⓦ www.osc.org), a stunning state-of-the-art $44-million complex where hundreds of interactive exhibits explain the fundamentals of physics, biology, agriculture, astronomy and more to formative minds. The center's CineDome, a theater and planetarium seating 310 people, has the world's largest I-Works domed film screen.

Harry P. Leu Gardens

A mile east of Loch Haven Park, the 50-acre **Harry P. Leu Gardens**, 1920 N Forest Ave (daily 9am–5pm; $4, including a tour of Leu House; ☎ 407/246-2620), was purchased by a green-thumbed Orlando businessman in 1936 to show off plants collected around the world. After seeing and sniffing the orchids, roses, azaleas and the largest camellia collection in the eastern US, take a trip around **Leu House** (guided tours only; daily 10am–3.30pm), a nineteenth-century farmhouse bought and lived in by Leu and his wife, now maintained in the simple but elegant style of their time and laced with family mementos.

Winter Park

A couple of miles northeast of Loch Haven Park, **Winter Park** has been socially a cut above the rest of the city since it was launched in 1887 as "a beautiful winter retreat for well-to-do people." For all its obvious money – a mix of new yuppie dollars and old wealth – Winter Park is a very likeable place, with a pervasive sense of community and a scent of California-style, New Age affluence.

On Fairbanks Avenue, which brings traffic from Loch Haven into Winter Park, stand the 100-year-old Mediterranean Revival buildings of **Rollins College**, the oldest college in the state and a tiny but respected liberal arts college. Other than its neat landscaping, the campus has just one thing in its favor: the **Cornell Fine Arts Center** (Tues–Fri 10am–5pm, Sat & Sun 1–5pm; free; ☎ 407/646-2526, ⑩ www.rollins.edu/cfam), which offers a staid bundle of modest nineteenth-century European and American paintings, rather more interesting temporary shows and an eccentric collection of old watch keys.

You'll find a more personal art collection a mile east of the college on Osceola Avenue, at the **Albin Polasek Galleries**, no. 633 (Tues–Sat 10am–4pm, Sun 1–4pm; suggested donation $3; ☎ 407/647-6294, ⑩ www.polasek.org): the former home of Czech-born sculptor Albin Polasek, who arrived penniless in the US in 1901 and spent most of his time over the next fifty years winning big-money commissions. The profits were eventually channeled into the creation of this house and studio, which contain more than two hundred of his technically accomplished, realist works.

Park Avenue: the Morse Museum and boat tours

The showpiece of Winter Park's upmarket status is **Park Avenue**, a row of top-of-the-line outfitters, jewelers and spick-and-span restaurants, which meets Fairbanks Avenue close to Rollins. Worth a special stop are the Scott Laurent Galleries, 348 N Park Ave N (Mon–Sat 10am–6pm, Sun noon–5pm; ☎ 407/629-1488), a shop with an impressive collection of art, glass, ceramics and jewelry.

Should window-shopping not appeal, drop into the **Charles Hosmer Morse Museum of American Art**, 445 Park Ave N (Tues–Sat 9.30am–4pm, Fri to 8pm, Sun 1–4pm; $3; ☎ 407/645-5311), which houses the collections of its namesake, one of Winter Park's founding fathers. The major exhibits are drawn from the output of Louis Comfort Tiffany, a legend for his innovative Art Nouveau lamps and windows that furnished high-society homes around the turn of the last century. Great creativity and craftsmanship went into Tiffany's work. He molded glass while still soft, imbuing it with colored images of water lilies, leaves and even strutting peacocks. Tiffany's work is so stunning that the rest of the museum's possessions, including paintings by Norman Rockwell, pales in comparison.

To discover why those who can afford to live anywhere choose Winter Park, take the **scenic boat tour** from the dock at 312 E Morse Blvd (departures every hour daily 10am–4pm; $3.50; ☎ 407/644-4056). The forty-minute voyage provides a picture-postcard view, usually reserved exclusively for the owners of the big-buck waterside homes.

Eatonville

Just to the east of Winter Park is the small town of **Eatonville**, the first incorporated African-American municipality in the United States. The town was founded by three black men in 1875 so black Americans could "solve the great race problem by securing a home...in a Negro city governed by Negroes," according to an 1889 notice published in the local newspaper. Land was sold for $5–10 an acre, and renowned author Zora Neale Hurston, an Eatonville native, used the town as setting for novels such as *Their Eyes Were Watching God*. The town is worth a stop to see the **Zora Neale Hurston National Museum of Fine Arts**, 227 E Kennedy Blvd (Mon–Fri 9am–4pm; free; ☎ 407/647-3307), which rotates exhibits of artists of African descent, and also has documentary videos and a complete collection of her books.

Maitland

The luscious sunsets over Lake Sybelia in **Maitland**, directly north of Winter Park, inspired a young artist named André Smith to buy six acres on its banks during the Thirties. With the financial assistance of Mary Bok (wealthy widow of Edward Bok; see p.297), Smith established what is now the **Maitland Art Center**, 231 W Packwood Ave (Mon–Fri 9am–4.30pm, Sat & Sun noon–4.30pm; free; ☎ 407/539-2181), a collection of stuccoed studios, offices and apartments decorated with Aztec- and Mayan-style murals and grouped around garden courtyards. Smith invited other American artists to spend working winters here, but his abrasive personality scared many potential guests away. The colony continued in various forms until Smith's death in 1959, never becoming the aesthetes' commune he'd hoped for. There are temporary exhibitions and a permanent collection, but it's the unique design of the place that demands a visit. While here, spare a thought for Smith's ghost, which, according to a number of local painters and sculptors who claim to have felt its presence, dispenses artistic guidance.

A few steps from the Maitland Art Center are the **Maitland Historical Museum** and the **Telephone Museum**, 221 W Packwood Ave (Thurs–Sun noon–4pm; free; ☎ 407/644-2451). The front rooms of the combined museums house an ordinary collection of aging photos and household objects, but the back room is filled with wonderful vintage telephones, commemorating the day in 1910 when a Maitland grocer installed telephones in the homes of his customers, enabling them to place orders from their armchairs.

The only other thing to make you dally in Maitland is the **Florida Audubon Society's Center for Birds of Prey**, 1101 Audubon Way (Tues–Sun 10am–4pm; suggested donation $5, children $4; ☎ 407/644-0190), the headquarters of the Florida Audubon Society, the state's oldest and largest conservation organization. The house is primarily an educational center and gift shop, but the adjacent rehabilitation facility is the largest in the Southeast, treating injured and orphaned birds, such as ospreys, owls, hawks, eagles and falcons.

International Drive

Devoid of any of the traditional charm one might find in downtown Orlando and adjacent communities, **International Drive**, five miles southwest of Orlando and smack between Disney World, Universal Studios and SeaWorld Orlando, is still worth a short visit for those interested in gawking at big-budget tourism at its most obscenely creative. The strip boasts an **F.A.O. Schwartz** toy store, at no. 9101 (☎ 407/248-2838), whose location is marked by a 380-foot-high Raggedy Ann. Other wonders include a **Ripley's Believe It or Not Museum**, at no. 8201, housed in a dramatically lopsided building, and the **Skull Kingdom**, a haunted mansion built to look like a castle with a skeleton facade emerging from the front wall. A Belz outlet shopping complex (☎ 407/352-9611 or 352-9600)on International Drive's north end is good for heavily discounted Disney merchandise, Levi's and other name brands.

Eating: Orlando and around

Given the level of competition among restaurants hoping to attract hungry tourists, **eating** in Orlando is never difficult and – if you escape the clutches of the theme parks – need not be expensive. In **downtown Orlando**, choices are quite good, and the need to satisfy a regular clientele of lunch-breaking office workers keeps prices low. With a car, you might also investigate the local favorites scattered in the outlying areas away from downtown. Affluent **Winter Park** promises more variety, generally with higher standards and prices, though it does have a few serviceable low-cost diners.

Tourist-dominated **International Drive** offers a greater range, if less intimacy. The culinary hot spots are the gourmet ethnic restaurants, but strict-budget travelers will relish the opportunity to eat massive amounts at one of several buffet restaurants – all for less than they might spend on a tip elsewhere. Buffet eating reaches its ultimate expression along **Hwy-192**, where virtually every buffet restaurant chain has at least one outlet, leaving the discerning glutton spoilt for choice.

Discount coupons in tourist magazines bring sizeable reductions at many restaurants, including "Show Restaurants," where $40 per head not only buys a multi-course meal and (usually) limitless beer, wine and soft drinks but also entertainment ranging from cavorting ninja warriors to medieval knights jousting on horseback.

Orlando

Bravissimo Wine Bar & Cafe, 337 N Shine Ave (☎ 407/898-7333). Authentic yet rather expensive Italian cuisine, outdoor garden seating and aria-singing waiters in an out-of-the-way neighborhood about ten blocks from downtown.

Bubbalou's Bodacious Bar-B-Q, 5818 Conroy Rd (☎ 407/295-1212). One of a fun local chain, featuring smoked meat sandwiches and platters at down-home prices, just north of Universal Studios. Daily specials for under $5.

Dexters of Thornton Park, 808 E Washington St (☎ 407/648-2777). Priced-right, trendy foods and an extensive beer menu, which attracts a young, urban clientele.

The Globe, 25 Wall St Plaza (☎ 407/422-1669). Always packed with young artsy types, this is the perfect place for inexpensive Nouveau American snacks and light meals, such as pan-seared salmon salad and veggie burgers. Open 24 hours.

Guinevere's Coffee House, 37-39 S Magnolia Ave (☎ 407/992-1200). Light snacks near one of the city's newest, hippest art galleries.

India Palace, 8530 Palm Parkway, Vista Center (☎ 407/238-2322). Traditional Indian, offering tandoori and great seafood dishes for under $20, all in a quiet, appealing setting. Lunch buffet Tues–Sun, $6.95.

Le Coq au Vin, 4800 S Orange Ave (☎ 407/851-6980). French restaurant with surprisingly low prices for top-notch dishes, like bronzed grouper and oven-roasted salmon; closed Mon.

Le Provence, 50 E Pine St (☎ 407/843-1320). Well-presented, award-winning French cuisine, open for lunch and dinner. Fixed-price dinner menu for under $30; lunch averages under $20.

Little Saigon, 1106 E Colonial Drive (☎ 407/423-8539). Tempting Vietnamese treats – don't miss the summer rolls with peanut sauce.

Numero Uno, 2499 S Orange Ave (☎ 407/841-3840). A small, good-value Cuban restaurant, reputed to be the best Cuban food in town. Try the black beans and rice with grouper or the paella Valenciana for two at $39.95.

Panera Cafe, 227 N Eola Drive (☎ 407/481-1060). One of a great local chain, with a wonderful array of baked goods, plus soups, salads and sandwiches.

Thai House, 2117 E Colonial Drive (☎ 407/828-0820). Tasty Thai food priced under $10; wash the spicy dishes down with the Thai iced tea. Weekends, dinner only.

Too-Jay's, 2400 E Colonial Drive (☎ 407/894-1718). This casual Jewish-style deli is part of an attractive local chain with a big menu.

Vega's Café, 1835 E Colonial Drive (☎ 407/898-5196). Cuban diner with great-value lunches.

Winter Park

Brazilian Pavilion, 140 W Fairbanks Ave (☎ 407/740-7440). Sumptuous Brazilian creations; try the *peixe a Brasileira* (filet of snapper with tomatoes, scallions and coconut milk) or the *frango a Francesca* (chicken cutlet with fresh garlic and parsley). Closed Sun.

The Briarpatch, 252 Park Ave N (℡ 407/628-8651). Well-prepared eclectic lunches and dinners with salads that are especially huge. Try the waffles benedict for breakfast. Eat inside or on the terrace.

Brio Tuscan Grille, 480 N Orlando Ave (℡ 407/622-5611). A bright and bustling Italian restaurant that belies its location in a shopping mall. Wonderful *bruschetta* topped with shrimp and mozzarella.

Maison des Crêpes, Hidden Garden Shops, 348 Park Ave N (℡ 407/647-4469). Some people come here solely for the feather-light crêpes, but all the dishes are inventive and tasty, and under $20 except for the seafood. Closed Mon evening.

Power House, 109-111 E Lyman Ave (℡ 407/645-3616). Raise your energy levels with a vitamin-packed fruit juice, sample one of the tasty soups or try the Middle Eastern specialities.

Sage, 358 Park Ave N (℡ 407/647-4556). A rich, eclectic menu full of hidden treasures – try the wok-fried vegetables, the sesame-seared tuna salad, herb-marinated filet mignon – and the window seats are an excellent vantage point for people-watching.

White Wolf Café, 1829 N Orange Ave (℡ 407/895-5590). Down-to-earth café/antique store known for creative sandwiches and generous salads.

Winnie's Oriental Garden, 1346 Orange Ave (℡ 407/629-2111). Applauded by locals as the best Chinese restaurant in town with entrées ranging from $15 to $30. Its specialities include crispy sea bass and moo shoo vegetables.

Winter Park Diner, 1700 W Fairbanks Ave (℡ 407/644-2343). In business longer than most people can remember, and still serving generous portions of classic diner food at prices to please.

International Drive and around

Bahama Breeze, 8849 International Drive (℡ 407/248-2499). Decent Caribbean food in an upbeat atmosphere. Dinner only.

Bergamo's, Mercado Mediterranean Shopping Village, 8445 International Drive (℡ 407/352-3805). Good-quality and slightly expensive pasta and seafood dishes. Dinner only.

Boston Lobster Feast, 8731 International Drive (℡ 407/438-0607). Just what the name implies – all-you-can-eat lobster from $24.95 to $29.95.

Café Tu Tu Tango, 8625 International Drive (℡ 407/248-2222). Fill up on creative appetizers and pizza at this lively hot spot. The walls are decorated with artworks for sale, and some of the artists use the place as an atelier.

China Garden, Mercado Mediterranean Shopping Village, 8445 International Drive (℡ 407/226-9933). This spacious new venue offers an all-you-can-eat "super buffet" of authentic Chinese cuisine at great prices.

Christini's Ristorante Italiano, 7600 Dr Phillips Blvd (℡ 407/345-8770). One of the truly excellent tables in southwest Orlando. The menu, which includes linguini in white clam sauce and veal marsala, and service are so superb, it's worth the high prices, though it's a bit of a drive to get there.

The Crab House, 8291 International Drive (℡ 407/352-6140) & 8496 Palm Parkway, in the Vista Center (℡ 407/239-1888). Lively and packed seafood house specializing in many kinds of crab. Its all-you-can-eat seafood bar for $20 is very popular, so expect to wait for a table.

Cricketers Arms, Mercado Mediterranean Shopping Village, 8445 International Drive (℡ 407/354-0686). Fish and chips, pies and pasties complement a range of imported ales and lagers at this inexpensive nook. It has a cozy, authentic feel, the latest soccer scores – and sometimes the matches themselves on giant TV screens.

Damon's, Mercado Mediterranean Shopping Village, 8445 International Drive (℡ 407/363-9727). Try the St Louis-style barbecued ribs at this meat-lover's paradise.

Don Pablo, 8717 International Drive (℡ 407/354-1345). The decor will make you swear you're in a Tijuana cantina, and you'll find such Mexican favorites as enchiladas, fajitas and tostados, complemented by Mexican beer.

Hard Rock Cafe, at Universal CityWalk, 5800 S Kirkman Rd (℡ 407/351-7625). Orlando's outpost of the international chain known as much for its T-shirts and music memorabilia as its groovy hamburgers.

Italianni's, 8148 International Drive, Pointe Orlando (℡ 407/345-8884). Decent Italian food in a cavernous setting. The good make-your-own pizzas are a hit with kids.

Ming Court, 9188 International Drive (℡ 407/351-9988). Chinese cuisine of an exceptionally high standard makes this a good spot; less costly than you might expect when you see the fabulously flash decor.

Passage to India, 5532 International Drive (℡ 407/351-3456). Not-too-spicy Indian cuisine; the classic *thali* sampler is a house speciality, but the lunchtime buffet offers the best value.

Punjabi, 7451 International Drive (℡ 407/352-7887) & 3404 Hwy-192 (℡ 407/931-2449). Everything's spiced to your personal taste. There's a whole range of lunch specials at $5.95 each.

Race Rock Supercharged Restaurant, 8986 International Drive (☎407/248-9876). A race-car-themed restaurant with auto memorabilia on walls, serving such eclectic American choices as burgers, milkshakes and malts at super-reasonable prices.

Red Lobster, 5936 & 9892 International Drive (☎407/351-9313 or 345-0018) & at 1265 SR535, Lake Buena Vista (☎407/827-1095). This famous national chain will satisfy your lobster and seafood craving with the "Ultimate Feast," for under $20.

Timpano, 7488 W Sand Lake Rd (☎407/248-0429). A newish, clubby Italian bistro that offers roasted mussels, shrimp *fra diavolo* pasta with asparagus and veal osso bucco with balsamic sauce as well as a great wine list, all at good prices.

Lake Buena Vista

Bongo's Cuban Café, downtown Disney West Side, 1498 E Buena Vista Drive (☎407/828-0999). Gloria and Emilio Estefan's fair-but-fun Cuban cuisine. The decor is wildly fabulous and there are shows nightly.

The Brown Derby, Disney-MGM Studios (☎407/939-3463). A faithful re-creation of the mythic Hollywood landmark, with the famous original recipes to match. Try their famous Cobb Salad, invented by the Brown Derby's original chefs. One of Disney World's very best.

California Grill, inside Disney's *Contemporary Resort Hotel* (☎407/939-3463). Disney's culinary showpiece, with a menu from sushi to stews prepared in an open kitchen and served in a bustling dining room. One hundred wines available by the glass.

Chefs de France, the French Pavilion of Disney's EPCOT World Showcase (☎407/939-3463). Definitely the best, most authentic French cuisine around, served in perfect style. Fresh produce flown in daily from France. Wonderful wines, too.

Flying Fish Café, at Disney's Boardwalk Resort (☎407/939-3463). Excellent but pricey seafood in an energetic dining room. There's a notable sparkling wine menu. Considered Disney's best by many locals.

House of Blues, Downtown Disney West Side, 1490 E Buena Vista Drive (☎407/934-2583). Decent Creole- and Cajun-inspired food. Consider going during Sunday's popular Gospel brunch.

Pebbles, at Crossroads, 12551 SR535 (☎407/827-1111). Creative American cuisine with dishes priced within reach. Locals love it.

Planet Hollywood, Disney's Pleasure Island (☎407/827-7827). One of the world's top-grossing restaurants, serving burgers inside a giant globe.

Rainforest Café, two locations: Downtown Disney West Side and Disney's Animal Kingdom (☎407/827-8500 and 938-9100). Safari-themed restaurants with faux animals swinging through the trees and squealing. Walk through to see the creative decor then eat elsewhere.

Wolfgang Puck Café, Downtown Disney West Side, 1482 E Buena Vista Drive (☎407/938-9653). Moderately priced, truly creative meals in a multi-level setting. The food in the upstairs dining room is more refined but far more expensive.

Wolfgang Puck Express, two locations: Downtown Disney West Side and Disney's Marketplace (☎407/938-9653 and 828-0107). Fast-food restaurant serving up the famed *Spago* chef's gourmet pizzas, as well as rotisserie chicken, good sandwiches and other all-American fare at affordable prices.

Along Hwy-192

Buddy Freddy's Country Buffet, 4118 W Hwy-192 (also W Vine St; ☎407/343-0199). Down-home breakfasts, lunches and all-you-can-eat buffet dinners.

Cracker Barrel Old Country Store, 5400 W Hwy-192 (☎407/396-6521). Wholesome country cookin' in an Americana atmosphere, complete with country store.

Key W Kool's, 7225 W Hwy-192 (☎407/396-1166). For a break from buffets, sample the seafood and steaks served for lunch and dinner in this tropically themed restaurant.

Magic Mining Company, 7763 W Hwy-192 (☎407/396-1950). Colorful steak and seafood mountain-mining-themed joint.

Shoney's, 4150 W Hwy-192 (also W Vine St; ☎407/933-8818) & 7640 W Hwy-192; (☎407/397-2779). The dependable American chain serves up homestyle meals and features special buffets dinners on weekends.

Show restaurants

Aloha! Polynesian Luau, Bimini Bay Café, SeaWorld Orlando (☎407/327-2424 or 1-800/227-8048). So-so ethnic-style food, but a nonstop show that will captivate.

Arabian Nights, 6225 W Hwy-192 (☎407/239-9223 or 1-800/553-6116). Voted by Orlando locals as the best dinner theater. Fifty-plus live horses help tell a comic version of the classic story.

Capone's Dinner & Show, 4740 Hwy-192 (☎407/397-2378). Give the secret password and enter this Prohibition-era speakeasy for a Twenties-style song-and-dance revue and an Italian-food buffet – both of mediocre quality.

Hoop De Doo Musical Revue, Disney's Fort Wilderness Resort (T 407/939-3463). Hokey but tons of fun cowboy-themed dinner theater. Reserve early.

Medieval Times Dinner & Tournament, 4510 Hwy-192 (T 1-800/229-8300 or 407/239-0214). Knights joust on horseback as you feast inside this replica of an eleventh-century castle.

Pirate's Dinner Adventure, 6400 Carrier Drive (T 1-800/866-2469 or 407/248-0590). Shivering timbers, peg-leg buccaneers, scalawags, cannons, sword fights and a host of stunts will divert your attention from the ordinary food.

Polynesian Luau, Disney Polynesian Resort (T 407/939-3463). All the colorful and highly entertaining native dance performances you would expect and a fairly good outdoor barbecue.

Sleuth's Mystery Dinner Theater, 7508 Universal Blvd (T 407/363-1985 or 1-800/393-1985). If you know red herring isn't a seafood dish, you're well on the way to solving the murder mystery as you eat, played out in this Agatha-Christie-style set.

Nightlife

With such fun centers as the *Church Street Station* (see below), **nightlife** in downtown Orlando is pretty much stuck in permanent adolescence. Most of the after-dark action is focused along Orange Avenue, where the atmosphere still evokes the raunchy honky-tonk of a bygone era. Otherwise, area entertainment, like everything else, has been swallowed whole by **Downtown Disney** (see p.285) and **Universal CityWalk** (see p.289), and, as always with theme parks, the fun can seem somewhat artificial and predigested.

Downtown Orlando

Bonkers, 46 N Orange Ave (T 407/629-2665). A stand-up comedy showcase Fri & Sat.

Church Street Station, 129 W Church St (T 407/422-2434, W www.churchstreetstation.com). Don't let the crowds who flock here nightly fool you into thinking this complex of bars, restaurants and an 1890s-style music hall, *Rosie O'Grady's*, merits the $17.95 admission fee. You do get your choice of seeing live jazz, country or rock music, but the bands are mediocre and the drinks are consistently expensive.

Howl at the Moon Saloon, 55 W Church St (T 407/841-9118). It's hard to concentrate on your drink as dueling pianists whizz through a sing-along selection of rock and roll classics and show tunes.

Kit Kat Club, 25 Wall St Plaza (T 407/648-2777). "Billiards, cigars and live entertainment in red velvet swank," boasts the club, as well as being the alternative, psychedelic and indie rock hangout of the coolest youth in Orlando.

Sapphire Supper Club, 54 N Orange Ave (T 407/246-1599, W www.sapphiresupperclub.com). Southern, grunge and alternative rock, local bands, you name it. See the "Calendar" pullout from the *Orlando Sentinel* for the line-up.

Southern Nights, 375 S Bumby Ave (T 407/898-0424, W www.southern-nights.com). Orlando's main gay venue, Monday is Latin House Night and weekends feature lots of zany drag acts in the Spank Lounge.

Tabu, Sacred or Forbidden, 46 N Orange Ave (T 407/648-8363, W www.tabunightclub.com). Two venues in one, with a wide variety of music, from acid jazz to Latin American. Every Friday treat yourself to the Sushi Happy Hour, 5–8pm; Monday night is Gay Night.

North of Orlando

Back-to-back residential areas dissolve into fields of fruit and vegetables **north of Orlando**'s city limits. Around here, in slow-motion towns harking back to Florida's frontier days, farming still has the upper hand over tourism. Although it's easy to skim through on I-4, the older local roads connecting the major settlements have far more atmosphere.

Sanford and around

Its position on the south shore of Lake Monroe, fifteen miles north of Maitland on Hwy-92 (also known as Hwy-17 along this section), allows **Sanford** to take advantage of riverboat cruises for a fair share of its tourist dollars. Cruises (from $35; ⊤1-800/423-7401) embark from the marina on North Palmetto Avenue. For insight into the modestly sized town – and Shelton Sanford, the turn-of-the-nineteenth-century lawyer and diplomat who created it – dip inside the **Sanford Museum**, 520 E First St (Tues–Fri 11am–4pm; free;⊤407/302-1000). Once called "Celery City" on account of its major agricultural crop, Sanford hasn't had a lot going for it since the boom years of the early twentieth century, a period fondly chronicled in the museum. For more relics of the halcyon days, collect a self-guided tour map from the **Chamber of Commerce**, 400 E First St (Mon–Fri 9am–5pm; ⊤407/322-2212), and venture around 22 buildings of divergent classical architecture in the adjacent old downtown district, most of which are now doing business as drugstores and insurance offices. There's also a friendly, more tourist-orientated **Visitor Information Center** at 209B W First St (⊤407/322-5600, ⓦwww.sanfordmainstreet.com).

On the way back to Hwy-92 at Sanford's southwest corner, the **Seminole County Historical Museum**, 300 Bush Blvd (Tues–Fri 9am–noon & 1–4pm; free; ⊤407/321-2489), carries a multitude of objects from all over the county, including an intriguing selection of medicine bottles. You can also rummage around **Flea World** (Fri, Sat & Sun 8am–5pm; free), at the south end of town on Hwy-17-92 – a large-scale attempt to sell items that nobody in their right mind would ever buy.

If Sanford's historic buildings, antique shops and quiet charm appeal, consider **staying overnight** at *The Higgins House*, a Queen Anne Victorian B&B just a few blocks from downtown, at 420 S Oak Ave (⊤407/324-9238, ⓦwww.higginshouse.com; ❺); it features huge, healthy breakfasts – and homemade beer. A special place to **eat** lunch or dinner is *Morgan's Gourmet Café*, 112 E First St (⊤407/688-4745), with a fine middle-priced international menu.

Mount Dora

To see an authentic Victorian-era Florida village on a pristine lake, take Route 46 west of Sanford for seventeen miles and feast your eyes on the picket fences, wrought-iron balconies and fancy wood-trimmed buildings that make up **Mount Dora**. The **Chamber of Commerce**, 341 Alexander St (Mon–Fri 9am–5pm; ⊤352/383-2165, ⓦwww.mountdora.com), has a free guide to the old houses and the excellent antique shops that now occupy many of them. Of the stores that dot the hilly streets, visit The Jeweler's Studio, 432 N Donnelly St (⊤352/383-1883), and Double Creek Pottery, next door (⊤352/735-5579) for fine handmade creations. To get the most out of Lake Dora, you can rent a boat from Fun Boats (from $10/hr; bikes $8/hr; ⊤352/735-2669). One of the area's original railways is still operating here, too; take the 1920s-era *Dora Doodlebug* on a one-hour scenic spin (Mon–Fri; $10, children $6) or the *Mount Dora Cannonball*, dating from 1913, on a 75-minute run all round the lake (Sat & Sun; $20, children $10). The Mount Dora Trolley also offers narrated historic and scenic tours of the town's parks, monuments and significant buildings, lasting about an hour (daily, times vary; $7, children $5; ⊤352/357-9123, ⓦwww.mountdoratrolley.com).

A **stay** at Mount Dora's genteel *Lakeside Inn*, 100 N Alexander St (⊤1-800/ 556-5016 or 352/383-4101, ⓦwww.lakeside-inn.com; ❺) might just transport you back to Old Florida; the long front porch is excellent for sunset-watching. For casual **dining**, check out *Eduardo's Station*, 100 E Fourth Ave (℡ 352/735-1711), with a menu that veers towards Tex-Mex cuisine; the *Parrot Club* upstairs has music and dancing on weekends till 2am. In a more elegant vein, the *Palm Tree Grille*, 351 N Donnelly St (℡ 352/735-1936), offers fish and pasta specials.

Cassadaga

A village in the deep forest populated by spiritualists may conjure up images of beaded curtains and thumping tabletops in forbidding houses, but the few hundred residents of **Cassadaga**, just east of I-4, ten miles north of Sanford, are disarmingly conventional citizens in normal homes, offering to reach out and touch the spirit world for a very down-to-earth fee ($100 for a hour session). A group of northern spirit mediums bought this 35-acre site in 1875 and quickly caught the imagination of Florida's early settlers – for whom contacting the Other Side was a lot easier than communicating with the rest of the US.

Throughout the year, seminars and lectures cover topics ranging from UFO cover-ups to out-of-body traveling. For more details, visit the official **Cassadaga Camp Bookstore** in the Andrew Jackson Davis Building, on the corner of Route 4139 (Cassadaga Road) and Stevens Street (Mon–Fri 9.30am–5.30pm, Sat 9.30am–6pm, Sun noon–6pm; ℡ 904/228-2880), which doubles as an information center and psychic bookshop. Rival enclaves include The Universal Centre of Cassadaga, across the street at 460 Cassadaga Rd ($30 for 15 min, $100 for an hour; ℡ 904/228-3190, ⓦ www.universalcentre.net), which claims to be home to the finest psychics anywhere; and *The Cassadaga Hotel*, across the street at 355 Cassadaga Rd ($30 for 15 min, $100 for an hour; ℡ 904/228-2323, ⓦ www.cassadagahotel.com; ❷), which offers its own stable of seers – some with names like Philomena and Birdie. Yet another possibility is the Purple Rose, 1079 Stevens St ($30 for 15 min, $100 for an hour; ℡ 904/228-3315, ⓦ www.cassadaga-purplerose.com).

Just outside Cassadaga, on the way to nearby Lake Helen, *Clauser's Bed and Breakfast*, 201 E Kicklighter Rd (℡ 1-800/220-0310 or 904/228-0310, ⓦ www.clauserinn.com; ❺) makes a wonderful, woodsy getaway. The atmosphere is very friendly, and you'll find every comfort has been seen to in advance.

DeLand and around

Intended as the "Athens of Florida" when founded in 1876, **DeLand**, four miles north of Cassadaga, west off I-4, is really just an old-fashioned Central Florida town featuring a domed courthouse, an old theater and a welcoming atmosphere. It boasts the state's oldest private educational center, **Stetson University**, on Woodland Boulevard (℡ 904/822-8920, ⓦ www.stetson.edu), whose redbrick facades have stood since the 1880s. The school is partly funded by the profits of the cowboy hat of the university's name. Pick up a free tour map from the easily found DeLand Hall for a walk around the vintage buildings. Also on the campus, on the corner of Michigan and Amelia avenues, the **Gillespie Museum of Minerals** (Mon–Fri: June–Sept 10am–3pm; Oct–May 9am–4pm; suggested donation $2, students $1; ℡ 904/822-7330) displays Florida quartz, calcite and limestone, plus gemstones gathered from all over the world.

Around the corner from the town's Chamber of Commerce (see opposite) is the **Henry A. DeLand House Museum**, 137 W Michigan Ave (Tues–Sat noon–4pm; free), built in 1886 and refurbished in period style. Of particular note are a wood carving of The Lord's Prayer, antique kitchen appliances and an exhibit devoted to "Citrus Wizard" Lue Gim Gong, a Chinese botanist who lived in DeLand from 1888 until 1925.

DeLand activities and practicalities

If you're not rushing towards Daytona Beach twenty miles east on Hwy-92 or I-4 (see "The Northeast Coast," p.220) or hastening toward the Ocala National Forest, about 35 miles to the northwest (see "North Central Florida," p.302), **boating** on the St Johns River is reason enough to hang around the DeLand area. Safari River Tours, 1905 Hontoon Rd (T1-877/740-0333 or 904/740-0333, W www.safaririvertours.com; $14, children 6–10 $8), offers two nature-itinerary options that leave twice each day for one-and-a-half and two-hour trips. For general information, visit DeLand's super friendly **Chamber of Commerce**, 336 N Woodland Blvd (Mon–Fri 8.30am–5pm; T 1-800/749-4350 or 904/734-4331, W www.delandchamber .org), which provides detailed pamphlets of walking and driving tours in the area. Anyone spending the night in DeLand should stay at the pleasurable *DeLand Artisan Inn*, 215 S Woodland Blvd (T 904/736-3484; ❹), where each room has a different theme, such as Literary, Mediterranean or Tropical. You can also grab an ostrich burger for $7.95 at the hotel's lively restaurant. For dining in a lush garden setting, *The Original Holiday House*, 704 N Hwy-17/92, right across from Stetson University (T 904/734-6319), has great buffet deals.

DeLeon Springs, Lake Woodruff National Wildlife Refuge and Barberville

DeLeon Springs State Recreation Area (daily 8am–sunset; cars $4.25, pedestrians and cyclists $1; T 904/985-4212), ten miles north of DeLand on Hwy-17, is one of the better-known sites where thousands of gallons of pure water bubble continuously up from artesian springs. Fascination with the labyrinths of underground water that permeate North Central Florida is not limited only to tourists, however, for **DeLeon Springs** is a very popular place for locals, too. There's swimming, canoeing and picnicking in and beside the spring, and, when hungry, you can make your own pancakes in the *Old Spanish Sugar Mill & Griddle House* (weekdays 9am–4pm, weekends 8am–4pm; T 904/985-5644), which is set in a historic grist mill on the park grounds.

Following Hwy-17 a few miles west to Grand Avenue, you will find the stunning **Lake Woodruff National Wildlife Refuge** (open sunrise to sunset; free), a 22,000-acre section of untouched wetlands that is home to 200 species of birds, including the endangered Southern bald eagle, 68 species of fish and more. A good bet for dinner in DeLeon Springs is *Karling's Inn*, 4640 N Hwy-17 (Tues–Sat 5–9pm; T 904/985-5535), a continental restaurant featuring such entrées as crisp-roasted duck Montmorency and rainbow trout in lemon sauce from $11.95 to $21.95.

Seven miles further north on Hwy-17, the tiny crossroads community of **Barberville** celebrates rural Florida with its **Pioneer Settlement for the Creative Arts** (Mon–Fri 9am–3pm, Sat 9am–1pm; $2.50; T 904/749-2959), a small collection of turn-of-the-nineteenth-century buildings, including a train station, a log cabin, a turpentine still, a bridgehouse, and a general store. Here, an assembly of pottery wheels, looms, milling equipment and other tools are put to use during the informative 45-minute guided tour.

Blue Spring and Hontoon Island

The year-round 72°F waters at **Blue Spring State Park** (daily 8am–sunset; cars $4.25, pedestrians and cyclists $1), seven miles south of DeLand (off Hwy-17-92, on West French Avenue) in Orange City, attract **manatees** (the aquatic creatures affectionately known as "sea cows") between mid-November and mid-March. These best-loved of Florida's endangered animals swim here from the cooler waters of the St Johns River, and the colder it is there the more manatees you'll see here. Aside from staking out the manatees from several observation platforms (and watching a twenty-minute slide show describing their habits), there's also the chance to see **Thursby House**, a large frame dwelling built by pioneer settlers in 1872. **Accommodation** in the park includes a $16.65-a-night campground and $55.50-a-night cabins that sleep up to four people (℡904/775-3663).

Not far from Blue Spring is **Hontoon Island State Park**, a striking dollop of wooded land set within very flat and swampy terrain. Without a private boat, Hontoon Island is reachable only by the free **ferry**, which runs daily from 8am to sunset from a landing stage off Route 44 (the continuation of DeLand's New York Avenue). Unbelievably, the island once held a boatyard and cattle ranch, but today it's inhabited only by the hardy souls who decide to stay over in one of its six rustic **cabins** (reservations ℡904/736-5309; ❷), or at one of its very basic **campgrounds**.

South of Orlando

Not much fills the rough acres directly **south of Orlando**, though Gatorland, one of the area's oldest and, in its way, most amusing destinations, sits on what's called the **Orange Blossom Trail** (known variously as Hwy-92, Hwy-17 and Hwy-441), which runs the sixteen miles between Orlando and Kissimmee.

Gatorland

An oversized alligator mouth serves as the entrance for **Gatorland**, 14501 S Orange Blossom Trail (daily 9am–sunset; $16.93, children 3–12 $7.48; ℡1-800/393-JAWS or 407/855-5496, ⓦ www.gatorland.com), which has been giving visitors an up-close look at the state's most feared and least understood animals since the 1950s. Surprisingly lazy beasts, the residents of the park (actually a working farm, licensed to breed alligators for their hides and meat) only show signs of life at the organized feeding – the Gator Jumparoo show – when hunks of chicken are suspended from a wire and the largest alligators, using their powerful tail muscles, propel themselves out of the water to grab their dinner: a bizarre spectacle of heaving animals and ferociously snapping jaws. When you arrive, pick up a schedule for the three main shows: Gator Jumparoo, Gator Wrestling and Snakes of Florida. This last performance features some of Florida's most deadly reptiles – coral snakes, pygmy rattlesnakes, cottonmouth moccasins and diamond-back rattlesnakes – none of which you'd enjoy meeting in the wild, but the show serves as a handy recognition exercise just in case you ever do.

Kissimmee

A country-bumpkin counterpoint to the modern vacation developments that ring it, **Kissimmee**, at the end of Orange Blossom Trail, has most of its fun during the Wednesday lunchtime cattle auctions at the **Livestock Market**, 805 E Donegan Ave. The **motels** close to the town on Hwy-192 (see "Accommodation," p.255) make Kissimmee a cheap place to stay, and even without a car getting to the theme parks and elsewhere in the region is relatively simple: **trains** stop at 111 E Dakin Ave, Greyhound **buses** at 3501 W Vine St (℡407/847-3911), and there are frequent **shuttle bus** links to the

major Orlando area attractions (see "Getting around," p.254). For visitor information, call ☎ 1-800/327-9159 or 407/847-5000.

In shabby downtown Kissimmee, take a walk around the fifty-foot obelisk called **Kissimmee Monument of States**, on Monument Avenue. Comprising garishly painted concrete blocks adorned with pieces of stone and fossil from various American states and 21 foreign countries, this funky monument was erected in 1943 to honor the former president of the local All-States Tourist Club.

A peaceful, rural back street is the setting for **Green Meadows Petting Farm**, 1368 S Poinciana Blvd (daily 9.30am–5.30pm; $15; ☎ 407/846-0770, ⓦ www.greenmeadowsfarm.com). Take a leisurely (sometimes painfully slow) two-hour tour of this old-fashioned petting zoo, where kids can milk a cow and ride a pony. The farm is a refreshing change of pace from the major parks. The **JungleLand Zoo**, 4580 Hwy-192 (daily 9am–6pm; $11.95, children 3-11 $6.95; ☎ 407/396-1012), is fairly depressing, however – spend the extra money and go to Disney's Animal Kingdom. JungleLand's inhabitants have little more than a rubber ball for entertainment; and when the animals get riled up, they rattle their cages, creating a tense, get-me-out-of-here atmosphere.

Finding anything decent to **eat** in the town center can be a bit of a challenge at dinnertime, but for good home cooking at breakfast or lunch, there's *Mrs. Mack's Restaurant*, 215 Broadway (☎ 407/847-5771; closed Sat lunch and all day Sun).

Celebration

If you just can't get enough of the squeaky-clean Disney concept, you might consider buying a home in **Celebration** (☎ 407/566-2200, ⓦ www .celebrationfl.com), a 4900-acre town nestled between Kissimmee and Disney's theme parks (off Hwy-192) that was created by Disney and officially opened in 1996. The Disney people did massive sociological research before settling on the design they believed would capture the American ideal of community: old-fashioned exteriors, homes close to the road so neighbors are more likely to interact and a congenial old-fashioned downtown area. World-famous architects were brought in to design major buildings: Phillip Johnson, Ritchie & Fiore designed the Town Hall; Michael Graves the post office; Cesar Pelli the movie house; and Robert A.M. Stern the health center. The first 350 home sites sold out before a single model was even complete. Enthusiasts applaud Celebration's friendly small-town feeling, where new neighbors are greeted with home-baked brownies, each home is fully hooked up to all the others by an elaborate intercom system, town events are well attended, and children can walk care-free to school, all without being a gated community, as spokespersons are quick to point out. Detractors use words like "contrived" and "sterile," and point to stringent rules, such as the insistence that all window treatments facing the outside must be white. The town, though, is growing rapidly and is worth a short visit – and not only for the architecture and some of the best restaurants in the region. Stop by to determine for yourself whether this homogeneous blandness is an evolutionary stage of the American Dream, a touch of elitist Big Brother or some sort of smug cult.

Practicalities

The luxurious, neo-old-fashioned *Celebration Hotel*, 700 Bloom St (☎ 407/566-6000, ⓦ www.celebrationhotel.com; ❼), makes a pleasant base for exploring the area; and each of Celebration's restaurants, facing the town's small lake, can be recommended for its own reasons. The *Market Street Café*, 701 Front St (℡407/566-1144), is a classic inexpensive diner, featuring homemade potato chips and fried-chicken salad; *Café d'Antonio*, 691 Front St (℡407/566-2233), offers fine, fairly pricey Italian wood-fired specialities, such as bruschetta, *arugula* salad and mushroom ravioli; and the *Columbia Restaurant*, 649 Front St (℡407/566-1505), looks like an Iberian villa and serves moderately priced superb Spanish cuisine, featuring red snapper Alicante and paella Valenciana.

Walt Disney World

As significant as air-conditioning in making the state what it is today, **WALT DISNEY WORLD** turned a wedge of Florida grazing land into one of the world's most lucrative vacation venues within a decade of its opening in 1971. Bringing growth and money to central Florida for the first time since the citrus boom a century earlier, the immense and astutely planned empire (and Walt Disney World really *is* an empire) also pushed the state's profile through the roof: from being a down-at-heel and slightly seedy mixture of cheap motels, retirement homes and clapped-out alligator zoos, Florida suddenly became a showcase of modern international tourism and in doing so, some would claim, sold its soul for a fast buck.

Whatever your attitude toward theme parks, there's no denying that Disney World is the pacesetter: it goes way beyond Walt Disney's original "theme park" – Disneyland, which opened in Los Angeles in 1955 – delivering escapism at its most technologically advanced and psychologically brilliant in a multitude of ingenious guises across an area twice the size of Manhattan. In a crime-free environment where wholesome all-American values hold sway, and the concept of good clean fun finds its ultimate expression, Disney World often makes the real world – and all its problems – seem like a distant memory.

Here, litter is picked up within seconds of being dropped (by any of the "cast members," as all employees are called, who happen to spy it), subtle mind-games soften the pain of standing in line, the special effects are the best money can buy, and Disney minions grin merrily as snotty-nosed kids puke down their legs. It's not cheap, forward planning is essential, and there are times when you'll feel like a cog in a vast machine – but Walt Disney World unfailingly, and with ruthless efficiency, delivers what it promises.

Costs may come as a shock, especially to families (children under 3 are admitted free of charge, though note that little is designed specifically for their entertainment), but the basic admission fee allows unlimited access to all the shows and rides in a particular park – and you'll need *at least* a day per park to go on everything in each of the **four main parks**. Remember that Disney World comprises over 46 square miles in all and is not easy to take in, even if spread over a week. Restaurants and snack bars – each as clinically themed as the parks – are plentiful but pricey. No alcohol is served in the Magic Kingdom.

Disney Information: ℡407/824-4321

A brief history of Disney

When brilliant illustrator and animator Walt Disney devised the world's first theme park, California's **Disneyland** – which brought to life his cartoon characters, Mickey Mouse, Donald Duck, Goofy and the rest – he had no control over the hotels and restaurants that quickly engulfed it, preventing growth and raking in profits that Disney felt were rightfully his. Determined that this wouldn't happen again, the Disney Corporation secretly began to buy up 27,500 acres of Central Florida farmland, and by the late Sixties had acquired – for a comparatively paltry $6 million – a site a hundred times bigger than Disneyland. With the promise of a jobs bonanza for Florida, the state legislature gave the corporation – thinly disguised as the Reedy Creek Improvement District – the rights of any major municipality: empowering it to lay roads, enact building codes and enforce the law with its own security force.

Walt Disney World's first park, the **Magic Kingdom** (see p.278), opened in 1971; based, predictably, on Disneyland, it was an equally predictable success. The far more ambitious **EPCOT Center** (see p.279), unveiled in 1982, represented the first major break from cartoon-based escapism. Millions visited, but the rose-tinted look at the future received a mixed response. Partly because of this reaction, and some cockeyed management decisions, the Disney empire (Disney himself died in 1966) faced bankruptcy by the mid-Eighties.

Since then, clever marketing has brought the corporation back from the abyss, and it now steers a tight and competitive business ship, always looking to increase Walt Disney World's daily attendance figures of 100,000 visitors and stay ahead of its rivals. **Disney-MGM Studios**, for example, puts a sizeable dent in Universal Studios' trade (see p.286), while **Downtown Disney** is always finding new ways to wow you in order to keep ahead of the new Universal CityWalk (see p.289). It may trade in fantasy, but where money matters, the Disney Corporation's nose is firmly in the real world.

Accommodation

If you want to escape the all-pervasive influence and high prices of Walt Disney World for the night, refer to the accommodation listings under "Downtown Orlando" (p.256). If not, you'll be relieved to find a growing number of **hotels** on Disney property, most of which are, in fact, fully equipped resorts. Predictably, each follows a particular theme to the nth degree, and prices are much higher – sometimes more than $300 per night – than you'll pay elsewhere. *All-Star Resorts*, however, is specifically intended for the less affluent visitor, costing $79 to $109 a night, and staying on the property is, after all, the most convenient way of doing Disney World – if that is your primary goal in coming to the Orlando area.

Each resort occupies its own landscaped plot, usually encompassing several swimming pools and a beach beside an artificial lake, and has several restaurants and bars. The Disney resorts are located in several areas, and transport, be it by boat, bus or monorail, between them and the main theme parks is free. Disney guests can also use resort **parking** lots for free. Theme park admission tickets are also available at each resort, saving you valuable time otherwise spent lining up at park ticket booths. The standard of service should be excellent; if it isn't, make a stiff complaint and you'll probably be treated like royalty throughout the remainder of your stay.

At quiet times, rooms may be available at short notice, but with Disney resorts pitching themselves to convention-goers as much as vacationers, you may turn up to find that there is no space at all, even in 1000-room properties, such as the *Contemporary Resort*. To be assured of a room, book as far ahead as possible – nine months is not unreasonable. **Reservations** can be made by phone or on the net (℡ 1-800/828-0228 or 407/934-7639 from overseas, ⓦ www.disneyworld.com).

Disney's Animal Kingdom Resort Area

All-Star Resorts. The most affordable and garish of Disney's resorts, divided into the *All-Star Music Resort,* which is decorated with giant-sized, brightly colored cowboy boots, guitar-shaped swimming pools and the like; the *All-Star Sports Resort*, complete with huge Coca-Cola cups, American football helmets and so on; and the *All-Star Movies Resort*, featuring humongous reminders of Disney movies looming over you. Each complex has its own pools and over 1500 rooms. The much larger *All-Star Pop Century Resort* will be

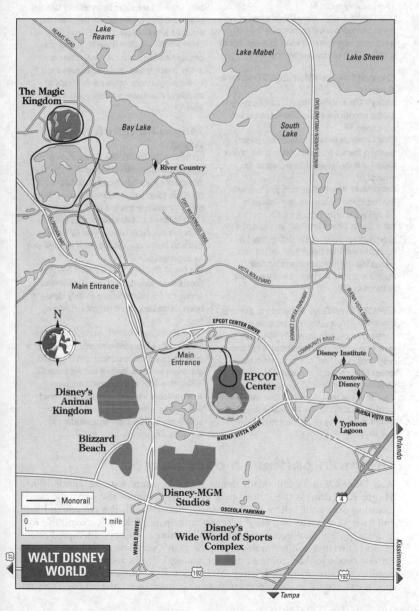

unveiled at the end of 2001, devoted to mammoth pop icons from each decade of the twentieth century. ⑤

Coronado Springs Resort. Disney's largest property to date and one of its more affordable, this hotel has 2000 Southwestern-style rooms built around a faux-Mayan pyramid. The food court is good for family meals. ⑥

Safari Lodge Resort. Disney World's newest luxury accommodation and its most over-the-top spectacular, where you can wake up to see African wildlife grazing outside your window. ⑧

Downtown Disney Resort Area

Disney's Old Key West Resort. Caribbean-style painted wooden homes available for rent when unoccupied. ⑧

Dixie Landings Resort. A moderately priced, Southern-themed hotel, with rooms in the "manor house" or in the "bayou cottages" set on the grounds. ⑥

Port Orleans Resort. Gaze from your wrought-iron balcony across the mini New Orleans re-created in this resort's courtyard. ⑥

The Villas at Disney Institute. An assortment of getaway options in a rustic setting, near the education-orientated Disney Institute. The town houses look like rustic treehouses but have modern amenities. The Institute also has its own luxurious spa. ⑦

EPCOT-MGM Resort Area

BoardWalk Inn. A complex on the scale of the *Contemporary* and the *Grand Floridian Beach* resorts (see "Magic Kingdom Resort Area," below), with rooms in the "inn" or – better value for groups of four or five – in studios. ⑦

Caribbean Beach Resort. Disney's first attempt at a budget-priced hotel still works rather well. Typical motel rooms at this plushly landscaped property are located in one of five lodges, each with its own pool. ⑥

The Dolphin. Topped by the giant sculpture of a dolphin and decorated in dizzying pastel shades and reproduction artwork from the likes of Matisse and Warhol. Although this property and its partner, *The Swan*, are on Disney property, they are the only hotels not owned by Disney. ⑦

The Swan. Intended as a partner to *The Dolphin*, from which it's separated by an artificial lake and beach, and likewise whimsically decorated and equipped with every conceivable luxury. ⑦

Yacht and Beach Club Resorts. Turn-of-the-century New England is the cue for these twin hotels, complete with clapboard facades and a miniature lighthouse. Amusements include all manner of waterborne activities and a croquet lawn. ⑧

Magic Kingdom Resort Area

Contemporary Resort. The Disney monorail runs right through the center of this hotel, which takes its exterior design from the futuristic fantasies of the Magic Kingdom's Tomorrowland but is disappointingly characterless inside. ⑦

Fort Wilderness Campground. Here you can pitch your tent ($47), hook up your RV ($65) or rent a six-berth cabin (around $279) – a good deal for larger groups.

The Grand Floridian Beach Resort & Spa. Gabled roofs, verandas and crystal chandeliers are among the frivolous variations on early Florida resort architecture at this elegant and relaxing base. ⑧

Polynesian Village Resort. An effective, if tacky, imitation of a Polynesian beach hotel; the concept is most effective if you spend your time on the lakeside beach under the shade of coconut palms. ⑧

Wilderness Lodge. This magnificent, over-sized replica of a frontier log cabin is furnished with massive totem poles, a wood-burning fire in the lobby, and Southern-style wooden rocking chairs. ⑧

The main parks: an overview

Walt Disney World's four main theme parks are quite separate entities. The **Magic Kingdom** is the Disney park everyone imagines, the signature castle towering over it all, where Mickey Mouse mingles with the crowds and the emphasis is on fantasy and fun – very much the park for kids. Recognizable for its giant, golfball-like geosphere, **EPCOT Center** is Disney's attempted celebration of science and technology, coupled with a very Disneyfied trip around various countries and cultures: dull for young kids, it's a sprawling area that involves a lot of walking. **Disney–MGM Studios** suits almost everyone; its special effects are enjoyable even if you've never seen the movies they're derived from, and the Backstage Tour, despite moments of tedium, at least visits *real* studios – reality being a rare commodity in Walt Disney World. Disney's newest theme park, the more relaxed **Disney's Animal Kingdom**, is part new-age zoo, part theme park, bringing remarkable African and Asian flavors to the swamplands of southwest Orlando.

Doing any kind of justice to all four parks will take at least five days – one should be set aside for rest – and you shouldn't tackle more than one on any single day. If you only have a day to spare, pick the park that appeals most and stick to it: day tickets are only valid for one location anyway. But if you insist on packing it all in in record time without spending so much on so many separate tickets, there is a more economical solution: the **Park-Hopper** ticket. With it, you can visit as many theme parks as many times as you like, in any order, over a four, five-, six- or seven-day period. **Park-Hopper Plus** is for those who want to include the water parks, Pleasure Island and the Wide World of Sports complex.

When to visit

While EPCOT Center in particular absorbs crowds easily, it's best to avoid the **busiest periods**: during summertime, and over Thanksgiving, Christmas and Easter. The busiest days vary from park to park (though, on average, Sunday is the least-crowded day), so plan your itinerary once you've arrived or contact Disney Information for help.

Provided you **arrive early** at the park (just before opening time is best), you'll easily get through the most popular rides before the mid-afternoon crush, when lines can become monstrously long. If you're staying at a Disney World resort, you may be offered early entrance to the parks (before opening time) to help beat the crowds. If you can't arrive early, don't show up until 5pm or 6pm, which in some seasons still leaves time to do plenty before the place shuts. Each park has regularly updated noticeboards showing the latest **waiting times** for each show and ride – at peak times often about an hour and a half for the most popular rides and up to forty minutes for others. However, there's a free **FastPass**, recently introduced, that minimizes waiting times. Once you have your ticket, you can actually reserve VIP treatment by simply inserting your ticket in a special turnstile. The system then prints out a special FastPass for you, indicating the time you should return. In effect, you get a reservation time to come back and enter the VIP line, which bypasses the regular line and gets you into the attraction in only a few minutes. If you're savvy enough, you can save lots of time booking ahead all day long, but only for the seventeen or so most popular attractions.

Opening times and tickets

The parks are open daily from 9am to midnight during holidays and summer, and from 9am to 6pm or later the rest of the year, with extended hours on holidays. Animal Kingdom opens at 8am, so you can catch the animals at their liveliest. During peak seasons the *Orlando Sentinel* lists each park's hours on the front page. A one-day, one-park ticket costs $48.76 (children 3–9 $39.22; under-3s get in free), is available from any park entrance, and allows entry to one park only.

For seeing multiple parks, spread your visits over four or five days using a **Park-Hopper** pass that permits entry to all four major parks and free use of the shuttle buses around the complex. A four-day pass costs $186.56 (children 3–9 $150.52), five-day $218.36 (children 3–9 $177.02). A few versions of the Park-Hopper, called Park-Hopper Plus passes, add on other Disney area attractions to the four major theme parks: a five-day pass costs $250.16 (children 3-9 $203.52); six-day $281.96 (children aged 3–9 $230.02); and seven-day $313.76 (children 3-9 $266.52). There's also a $350 year-long pass ($275 for children), strictly for fanatics. If you're staying at a Disney World resort, you are eligible for reductions on all these prices.

As obvious as it may sound, if you arrive by car be sure to follow the signs to the park you want to visit and use its **parking lot** ($6 a day, which covers you for all the Disney World parking lots free if you're staying at a Disney resort). These are enormous, so be sure to make a note of exactly where you're parked. Parking lots and hotels are linked to the main attractions by a comprehensive **transport system** of buses and a monorail (free to guests of the Disney World resorts).

The Magic Kingdom

Anyone who's been to Disneyland in LA will recognize much of the **MAGIC KINGDOM**. Like the original Disney theme park, it's divided into several themed sections, each with its own personality. Building facades, rides, gift shops, even the particular characters giving hugs contribute to the unique feel of each section. The areas are called **Adventureland**, **Tomorrowland**, **Fantasyland**, **Frontierland**, **Liberty Square** and **Mickey's Toontown Fair**. Some of the rides are identical to their Californian forebears, some are greatly expanded and improved – and a few are much worse. Like its older sibling, the place is best when it is reacted to enthusiastically: jump in with both feet and go on every ride you can.

A warning: don't promise the kids (or yourself) too much beforehand. Unless you cleverly use your FastPass option (see p.277), lines are sometimes so long that it may be better to pass up some attractions. Although waiting times are usually posted, lines can be deceiving: Disney masterfully disguises their true length and keeps you cool with shade, fans and air-conditioning wherever possible.

The park

From the main gates, you'll step into Main Street USA, a bustling assortment of souvenir shops selling the ubiquitous mouse-ear hats and other Disney paraphernalia in old-fashioned, town-square stores. Don't spend too much time here, as you can buy most of the same items throughout the park and in Disney hotels.

At the end of Main Street you'll see **Cinderella's Castle**, a stunning pseudo-Rhineland palace that looks like it should be the most elaborate ride in the park. In fact, it's merely a shell that conceals all the electronics and machinery that drive the whole extravaganza. You simply walk through a tunnel in its center, and use it as a reference point if you lose your bearings.

If you arrive early, beat the lines by heading immediately for the popular thrills-and-spills rides, which tend to draw the biggest crowds. The most nerve-jangling of these is **Space Mountain**, in essence an ordinary roller coaster, yet one whose total darkness makes every jump and jolt unexpected. The ride may last less than three minutes, but many breathe a sigh of relief once it's over. **Splash Mountain** employs water to great effect, culminating in a stunning 52-foot death-drop down a waterfall. Like most rides, you must be of adequate height to board Splash Mountain, so if you have a tot who's too tiny, there's a playground placed discreetly to the right of the ride. **Big Thunder Mountain Railroad** puts you on board a runaway train, which hurtles through Gold Rush California in about three minutes. There's also the kid-orientated **Barnstormer**, a milder attraction perfect for thrillseekers-in-training.

You don't have to be a roller-coaster junkie to enjoy the Magic Kingdom. Many of the best rides in the park rely on "AudioAnimatronic" characters – impressive vocal robots of Disney invention – for their appeal. The most up-to-date are seen in **ExtraTERRORestrial Alien Encounter**, which will especially appeal to those who are fans of the *Alien* films, though the sensation of being brushed by unseen things in the dark may be too close an encounter for others. A wonderful visual treat is **Timekeeper**, where you're taken on a trip through time by a zany robot (whose voice is provided by Robin Williams). A whole slew of realistic robots inhabit **Pirates of the Caribbean**, the classic boat ride through a pirate-infested Caribbean island complete with drunken debauchery and general mayhem.

Elsewhere, the **Haunted Mansion** is worth the wait, as much for the duration of the ride – one of the longest in the park – as for the clever special effects that include holograms: there's a sliding ceiling in the entrance room and macabre goings-on as your "doom buggy" passes through a spook-filled cemetery. The leisurely **Jungle Cruise** is narrated by a pun-loving guide, who takes you through waterfalls and cannibal camps in Africa's most "dangerous" territory. **Buzz Lightyear's Space Ranger Spin** is much like being inside a video game, as you try to help Buzz zap the enemy that threatens from every side.

Fantasyland is the one place where The Magic Kingdom shows its age (the park opened in 1971), but it also caters to the imaginations of its youngest visitors, making it one of the most-visited corners of the park. **It's a Small World** is a slow, pleasant boat ride past multi-ethnic childlike robots who sing the theme song over and over and over again. **Peter Pan's Flight** and **Snow White's Adventures** are creaky, low-tech amusements, still very popular with young kids, but which wouldn't be out of place in a fairground. **The Many Adventures of Winnie the Pooh** ride has replaced **Mr Toad's Wild Ride**, to the chagrin of many nostalgic Disney buffs, but it is suitable for small children. **The Enchanted Tiki Room (Under New Management)** has dozens of AudioAnimatronic tropical birds and Tiki-god statues that sing and whistle their way through a program of updated Broadway-show-style numbers – unfortunately, the infectious original melody that once sent visitors away humming is no more.

While in Fantasyland, head to the **Fantasyland Character Festival** area, set up between the **Mad Tea Party** and **Dumbo the Flying Elephant**, and where you can meet and greet Disney's myriad characters. Otherwise, visit **Mickey's Toontown Fair**, where you're guaranteed to see several, or stay for the character-saturated **parade**. Check for the parade times, as they change depending on the day and season. The best vantage point is from a bench in Frontierland. Hint: stake one out around an hour before the event.

EPCOT Center

Even before the new Magic Kingdom opened, Walt Disney was developing plans for the **EPCOT** (Experimental Prototype Community of Tomorrow) **CENTER**. It was conceived in 1966 as a real community that would experiment and work with the new ideas and materials of a technologically advancing US. The idea failed to take shape as Disney had envisaged: EPCOT didn't open its gates until 1982, when global recession and ecological concerns had put a damper on the belief in the infallibility of science. One drawback of this park is simply its immense size: twice as big as the Magic Kingdom and, ironically, given its futuristic themes, very sapping on mankind's oldest mode of transport – the feet.

The park

EPCOT's 180-foot-high **geosphere** (unlike a semi-circular geodesic *dome*, the geo*sphere* is completely round) provides information desks and souvenir shops and sits at the heart of the **Future World** section of the park, which keeps close to EPCOT's original concept of exploring the history and researching the future of agriculture, transport, energy and communication. Inside the geosphere is the **Spaceship Earth Ride**, a fifteen-minute look at communication, beginning with a pre-Cro-Magnon time tunnel and ending with a blast into the future to explore cutting-edge technologies.

Future World is divided into eight pavilions, each corporate-sponsored, and having its own rides, films, interactive computer exhibits and games. **Innoventions** highlights the newest trends in technological gadgetry, such as virtual-reality viewing helmets and computerized dwellings, with Innoventions **East** appealing mostly to adults, and Innoventions **West** to the kids. The **Wonders of Life** pavilion has the best of the rides, including **Body Wars**, an exciting, if rather wrenching, flight-simulator trip through a human body. While here, be sure to catch the entertaining **Cranium Command**, in which an AudioAnimatronic character is detailed to control the brain of a 12-year-old all-American boy, and **The Making of Me**, certainly one of the most sensitive and affecting treatments for younger visitors of conception and childbirth ever put together, including actual footage of a developing fetus.

Concentrate on beating the lines that often stretch outside the **Universe of Energy**, a celebration of the harnessing of the earth's energy. Its centerpiece is **Ellen's Energy Adventure**, starring actress Ellen DeGeneres, the highlight of which is a ride through the primeval forests where dinosaurs roamed and today's fossil fuels originated.

In the **Imagination!** pavilion, a 3-D cinematic thrill called **Honey I Shrunk the Audience** keeps you on the edge of your seat with the excellent "feelies," which add sensations of touch and smell to the state-of-the-art 3-D visuals and surround-sound effects (as imagined in Aldous Huxley's *Brave New World*). **The Living Seas**, the world's largest artificial saltwater environment, occupied by a multitude of dolphins, sharks and sea lions, also has a great deal to offer – not least of which is the chance to climb inside a diving suit. Kids love the **Seacabs** ride that takes them to **Sea Base Alpha**, which is a very popular, fully interactive learning center.

One of EPCOT's most successful new attractions is the **Test Track**, where you can experience firsthand what it might be like to be a test driver for a high-performance car. Reaching sixty miles per hour and lasting eight minutes, it's both the fastest and longest ride Disney World has to offer. **The Land** offers the very rich and informative **Living with the Land**, an experience of the world's various biomes and alternative means of food production, as well as **The Circle of Life**, with its powerful message about keeping the earth a viable habitat for all of its creatures, not just mankind. The newest pavilion, **Space**, opening in late 2001, will be a homage to the universe, space travel and astronauts.

Arranged around a forty-acre lagoon, the **World Showcase** section of EPCOT attempts to mirror the history, architecture and culture of the eleven nations that responded to Disney's worldwide appeal when the original idea of creating a futuristic ideal community using the latest technology was being developed in the 70s. Each section features an instantly recognizable landmark – Mexico has a Mayan Pyramid, France an Eiffel Tower – or a stereotypical scene, such as a British pub or a Moroccan bazaar. The elaborate reconstructions show careful attention to detail; highlights include the Viking longboat ride through Norway, Japan's gardens and cultural museum, and the *Wonders of China* film. Each country also offers its own cuisine in often excellent restaurants, and the staff are almost all natives. The most crowded place is usually **The American Adventure** inside a replica of Philadelphia's Liberty Hall, where AudioAnimatronic versions of Mark Twain and Benjamin Franklin give a somewhat sanitized account of two centuries of US history in under half an hour. It's worth staying on till late evening to see performances by many of the countries whose natives do a variety of singing and dancing acts for passing crowds. At night, the lagoon also transforms into the spectacular sound-and-light show, **IllumiNations**, which starts half an hour before closing.

Disney-MGM Studios

When the Disney Corporation began making films and TV shows for adults – most notably *Who Framed Roger Rabbit?* – it also began plotting the creation of a theme park geared as much towards adults as kids. Buying the rights to the gem-filled Metro-Goldwyn-Mayer (MGM) collection of films and TV shows, Disney acquired a vast array of instantly familiar images to mold into shows and rides. Opening in 1990, **DISNEY-MGM STUDIOS** overshadowed the opening of Florida's Universal Studios (see p.286) and at the same time found an extra use for the real film studios based here – the people you'll see laboring over storyboards on the Backlot Tour aren't there for show: they are genuinely making films.

The park

The first of several highly bowdlerized imitations of Hollywood's famous streets and buildings – which cause much amusement to anyone familiar with the seedy state of the originals – **Hollywood Boulevard** leads into the park, its length brightened with re-enactments of famous movie scenes, strolling film-star lookalikes and the odd Muppet.

Avoid a long wait in the sun by arriving early and going straight to the half-hour **Studios Backlot Tour**. A narrated tram-ride tour takes you behind the scenes, whisking you past the windows of animation studios and production offices (where you might see costumes and props being created) to the climax: the exploding **Catastrophe Canyon**, an ingenious set that demonstrates special effects at disturbingly close range. The tour's interest level rises and falls, depending on the movies in production at the time, but you won't feel as though you've had your money's worth if you miss it. The same applies to two other attractions that were previously part of the Studios Backlot Tour: **The Magic of Disney Animation**, a thirty-minute self-guided tour with a hilarious ten-minute instructional film, again featuring Robin Williams, and **Disney-MGM Studios PASS**, an entertaining special effects and production tour, which reveals the secrets behind the making of such movies as *101 Dalmatians* and *102 Dalmatians*. See how they created those realistic robotic puppies. Along the same lines and not to be missed, **The Indiana Jones Epic Stunt Spectacular** re-creates and explains many of the action-packed set pieces from the Steven Spielberg films.

Sharp turns and collisions with asteroids make **Star Tours**, a flight-simulator trip to the Moon of Endor piloted by *Star Wars* characters R2D2 and C-3PO, one of the most physical rides in the park – passengers' seatbelts are carefully checked before lift-off. But **Rock 'n' Roller Coaster** takes the prize for extreme edginess: a heavy-metal soundtrack, a breakneck-speed launch and any number of full inversion loop-the-loops – all in the pitch dark – make it a pure claustrophobic panic-attack at its finest. Another really scary ride is **The Twilight Zone Tower of Terror**, a thirteen-story drop that's enough to put you off elevators for life. For laughs, go to **Doug Live!**, which plucks volunteers from the crowd to serve as extras in a pleasurable mix of theatrics and animation. Also good fun is **Jim Henson's MuppetVision 4D**, a three-dimensional film whose special effects put you right inside the *Muppet Show*, with more of the "feelies" technology.

Adding a welcome dimension to the park are two theater productions: **Beauty and the Beast** and **The Hunchback of Notre Dame – A Musical**

5

Adventure. Both are live performances of shortened versions of the Disney movies. The costumes, sets and talents make them worth a visit.

Inside a replica of Mann's Chinese Theater in Hollywood is **The Great Movie Ride**, which repays the (usually) long line with a ride that allows visitors to enter scenes from classic movies, like *The Wizard of Oz* and *Casablanca*. This enjoyable, 22-minute voyage employs more than sixty AudioAnimatronic figures, which are surprisingly lifelike. Afterwards, consider refreshments at either the *Prime Time Café*, decorated with Fifties formica kitchen tables and other period pieces, or the *Sci-Fi Dine-In Theater*, where patrons are served in Fifties-style cars while watching science-fiction trailers and cartoons in a drive-in theater.

Disney's Animal Kingdom

DISNEY'S ANIMAL KINGDOM was opened in April 1998 as an animal-conservation park with Disney's patented over-the-top twist. The result is a 500-acre theme park, Disney World's largest by far, divided into six major "lands": **Africa**, **Camp Minnie-Mickey**, **DinoLand USA**, **Safari Village**, **Rafiki's Planet Watch** and **Asia**. The Animal Kingdom is a true tribute not only to wildlife but also to the versatility of concrete, which is colored, imprinted upon and formed into an endless variety of shapes to help create mock-authentic ambiences for each land. Note also that this park opens earlier than the others, at 8am.

The park

Upon entering, visitors find **The Oasis**, where they are greeted by flamingos and other exotic birds, reptiles and mammals. Just beyond is **Safari Village**, the center of which is **The Tree of Life**, a 145-foot-high concrete imitation tree. Depictions of animals are cleverly and intriguingly woven into the trunk and branches, and there's an amusing 3-D "feelie" **It's Tough to be a Bug!** shown inside.

The park's main thrill ride is in **DinoLand USA**, in which a roller-coaster-style vehicle makes small drops and short stops in the dark as dinosaurs pop out of nowhere and roar.

Disney's Animal Kingdom has four live shows, three for all ages and one particularly for younger visitors. Head to DinoLand USA for *Tarzan Rocks!*, in which amazing gymnast-actors swing to the high-energy rock music. Across the park at **Camp Minnie-Mickey** is the *Festival of the Lion King*, a participatory production of upbeat music with some nifty acrobatics, loosely based on its namesake film. Also in Camp Minnie-Mickey, for the kiddies, there's *Pocahontas and Her Forest Friends*, featuring the legendary Native American maid and a host of live animals. The *Flights of Wonder* bird show, on Asia's **Caravan Stage**, showcases falcons, vultures, owls and other wonderful birds that interact with the audience.

In **Africa**, you'll find one of the most involving and best-realized attractions: the **Kilimanjaro Safaris**. Climb into a good facsimile of a jeep transport and be swept into what feels very much like a real safari through African wildlands (local oak trees have been trimmed to look like African acacias). You not only view the many animals - giraffes, zebras, elephants, lions, gazelles and rhinos - but also take part in anti-poacher maneuvers. **Asia** offers the **Kali River Rapids Run** for thrills and wet chills, which compare favorably to those offered by Splash Mountain.

The remainder of the park requires no more than casual strolling, but all of its corners warrant exploration. **Rafiki's Planet Watch** features the **Conservation Station**, where you can observe as veterinarians treat animals, and where you'll find small booths in which sounds of the jungle come alive. Rafiki's is also the site of the **Affection Section**, a particularly well-run petting zoo. In Africa, don't miss the **Pangani Forest Exploration Trail**, home to a troop of lowland gorillas, hippos and innumerable exotic creatures; and Asia's **Maharajah Jungle Trek** gives you an astoundingly up-close look at Bengal tigers frolicking amidst ancient ruins, as well as a whole range of other creatures from that continent. Wander the **Safari Village Trails** to catch sight of lemurs, kangaroos and other exotica; and on the **Character Greeting Trails** in Camp Minnie-Mickey, you can track down classic Disney characters and get them to sign their autographs.

The rest of Walt Disney World

Several other **Disney-devised amusements** exist to keep people on Disney property as long as possible and to offer therapeutic recreation and relaxation to those suffering theme-park burn-out.

Blizzard Beach

Near Disney-MGM Studios and *All-Star Resorts* (see "Walt Disney World Accommodation," p.275). At peak times daily 9am–8pm, at other times hours vary; ☎ 407/560-3400; $28.57, children 3–9 $22.79.

An inviting and immensely popular water park, **Blizzard Beach** is a combination of sand and fake snow surrounding Melt Away Bay, which lies at the foot of a snow-covered "mountain," complete with a ski lift and water slides. The quickest way down is via **Summit Plummet**, designed to look like a ski jump, but in fact a steep water slide 120 feet high. If you don't want to get involved, you can lounge around and soak up some rays, then cool off in one of the pools rippled by wave machines. Arrive early in summer to beat the inevitable crowds.

River Country

At the Fort Wilderness Campground (see "Walt Disney World Accommodation," p.276). Daily 10am–5pm in low season, 10am–7pm in high season; ☎ 407/560-9283; $16.91, children 3–9 $13.25.

River Country, built around the **Ol' Swimming Hole**, is a rustic version of Typhoon Lagoon (see below), offering fewer and less exciting slides – and no wave machines. Yet it scores well with the high-speed, corkscrewing descents from **Whoop-'N-Holler Hollow**, and the enjoyable cruise on inner tubes down the **White Water Rapids**. With a small beach and a nature trail leading to a shady cypress hammock, River Country is more relaxing than Typhoon Lagoon and is a good place to unwind between touring the main parks.

Typhoon Lagoon

Just south of Pleasure Island (see "Nightlife: Downtown Disney," p.285). Daily 10am–5pm in low season, 9am–6pm or later in high season; ☎ 407/560-4141; $28.57, children 3–9 $22.79.

Typhoon Lagoon, busiest in the summer and on weekends (often reaching full capacity), consists of an imaginatively constructed "tropical island" around a two-and-a-half-acre lagoon, rippled every ninety seconds by artificial waves. Bodysurf the breakers, skim over them with a raft, or plunge into them from **Humunga Kowabunga**, a pair of speed-slides fifty feet up the "mountain" beside the lagoon. There are several smaller slides, too, and a saltwater **Shark Reef** where snorkelers fearful of the open seas can explore a "coral reef" and be sniffed by real (but not dangerous) nurse and bonnethead sharks. When you're exhausted, take an inner tube (provided at the start point) and float

Disney cruise line

Disney is also solidly in the cruise ship business. On the new *Disney Wonder* and the *Disney Magic*, you can book three- and four-day voyages along with land-based vacations. The elegant ships – the luxurious decor includes inlaid Italian woodwork – depart from Port Canaveral, an hour from the theme park (for Shuttle Info call ☏407/566-7000), and sail to Nassau and then Disney's own Bahamian island, Castaway Cay. Live shows are different every night, and separate entertainment areas are provided for children, adults, and families. Cabins in high season average about $1225 per person for seven nights, including three nights at a Disney resort and four nights on board. In general, rates run from $829 to $4799 per person, depending on accommodation choices and season. For a little more, not including airfare, you could also choose a seven-night cruise to various destinations in the Eastern Caribbean (☏1-800/939-2784).

around **Castaway Creek**, a half-hour meander through grottoes and caves, only interrupted by a sudden drenching from a tropical storm.

Unlike the major parks, you can bring **food** to Typhoon Lagoon, but no alcohol or glass containers.

The Richard Petty Driving Experience

Walt Disney World Speedway (at the south end of the Magic Kingdom Parking Lot) ☏1-800/237-3889). Feb–Sept daily 9am–5pm, limited times in Oct, Nov and Dec.

The **Richard Petty Driving Experience** offers race-car fanatics and wannabes two ways to fulfill their fantasies: they can take a three-lap stock-car ride around a one-mile tri-oval track driven by an expert for $105.99; or, for $423.99, an intensive three-hour "Rookie Experience" course, at the end of which participants drive eight laps themselves.

Every January, the speedway hosts the **Indy 200**, a 200-lap, 200-mile run that is one of a series of races leading up to the Indianapolis 500. For tickets call ☏1-800/822-INDY.

Disney's Wide World of Sports

Two miles east of Disney's Animal Kingdom on Osceola Parkway. Hours depend on daily events; $8, children $6.75; ☏407/363-6600.

Professional and amateur sporting events are frequently held at the Mediterranean-style **Disney's Wide World of Sports** complex, a collection of stadiums. Among them are the 7500-seat baseball field in which the Atlanta Braves hold their spring training; and the 30,000-square-foot, 5000-seat Fieldhouse, used for everything from basketball to badminton. Other features include a series of interactive football-related games called the NFL Experience, where amateurs can test passing, punting and kicking skills, using professional equipment; and a themed *All-Star Café* restaurant. Stop at the retail shop for stuffed Disney characters in athletic uniforms.

Disney Institute

Buena Vista Drive, north of Downtown Disney. ☏1-800/496-6337, ⓦwww.disney institute.com.

The **Disney Institute**, modeled on a university campus done in Florida-style architecture, is a combination resort, spa and educational facility, where guests (who don't have to stay there) can take short classes on subjects such as rock climbing, animation, photography, cooking, gardening and "Disney Behind the Scenes."

Nightlife: Downtown Disney

Around a half-hour before closing, most of the Walt Disney World parks hold some kind of bash, usually involving fireworks and fountains. For more solid night-time entertainment for adults, the corporation devised the six-acre **Pleasure Island**, exit 26B off I-4, and part of **Downtown Disney**, which also includes the **West Side** and **Marketplace**. On this remake of an abandoned island, pseudo-warehouses are the setting for a mixture of theme shops, bars and nightclubs. Admission to the island is free from 10am to 7pm; after 7pm a charge of $20.09, unless you have Park-Hopper Plus, is levied, which allows you limitless entry into the bars and clubs. Anyone under 18 must be accompanied by a parent, and alcohol will only be served to those who are 21 or over. Take your ID and be prepared to pay high prices for food and drink.

Five shows a night keep things lively at the *Comedy Warehouse*, where a handful of comedians do an improvisational act five times a week and are not afraid to send up Mickey Mouse. The *House of Blues Concert Hall*, built by the Blues Brothers themselves, now headlines top artists from the world of soul, blues and rock and roll. The *Pleasure Island Jazz Company* offers live combos and groups, with taped music between shows, plus a limited menu and a wine list. For dancing, *Mannequins Dance Palace* is a swish, and rather risqué by Disney standards, disco that doesn't get cracking until midnight; the less ostentatious *8 Trax* spins exclusively Seventies pop hits; and the *Rock N Roll Beach Club* jams to the all-time greatest hits, with both DJs and live bands.

The most original – and most enjoyable – place on Pleasure Island is the **Adventurers Club**, loosely based on a 1930s gentlemen's club and furnished with a motley collection of face masks (some of which unexpectedly start speaking), deer heads and assorted flea-market furniture. Between scheduled shows, actors and actresses move surreptitiously (despite their period attire) among the throng and strike up loud and eccentric conversations with unsuspecting audience members. New additions to Pleasure Island include the *Wildhorse Saloon*, a barbecue joint with live country music and line dancing, where you can get in for a $5 cover without paying the full Pleasure Island toll, and the *BET SoundStage Club*, owned by Black Entertainment Television and catering to the throngs that love rhythm and blues, soul and hip-hop music.

Orlando flexticket

In the hopes of prying tourists from Disney's clutches, competitors have teamed up to offer special multi-park passes. The **ORLANDO FLEXTICKET** offers unlimited admission for seven days to Universal Studios, SeaWorld Orlando and Wet'n'Wild (a water park) for $169.55 (adults), $135.63 (children 3–9). For $209.95 (adults) or $167.65 (children), you can throw Busch Gardens Tampa Bay (two hours away) into the deal, and the pass is good for ten days. Universal has also recently devised a system similar to Disney's FastPass to help get wily visitors around long waits in line. It's called **FastTrack**, it's free and it involves going to a ride entrance any time after 11am and picking up a card with a time on it. They also have a new program available, called **Express**, which allows multi-day ticket holders special access to most attractions 9–11am, with practically no waiting in line at all (℡ 407/363-8000).

Back on the mainland, next to Pleasure Island and glowing with neon lights, sits *Planet Hollywood*. Housed in a sphere, it seats 400 people and is the biggest branch in the restaurant chain to date. **Downtown Disney West Side** offers some interesting dining alternatives (see "Eating: Orlando and around," p.263). DisneyQuest ($27, children $21), a five-story, hi-tech arcade, is a bastion of virtual-reality games, including a canoe course where you paddle through a digital river – getting splashed with very real water. The Cirque du Soleil (T407/939-7600, Wwww.cirquedusoleil.com) has made Downtown Disney its permanent home, and they perform ten times a week in a 1600-seat theater – the shows are fascinating, but tickets are exorbitantly priced: $67 for adults, $46.85 for children. On the other side of Pleasure Island is **Marketplace**, a shopping emporium crammed with the world's largest Disney store, a Christmas shop and a Lego store, where kids can ogle massive Lego creations of, among others, a dragon and a spaceship, and also play with every type of Lego known.

Universal Orlando

For some years, it seemed that US TV and film production would be shifting away from expensive, demanding California to Florida, which, with its lower taxes and cheaper labor, was more amenable, and the opening of Universal Studios in June 1990 appeared to confirm that trend. So far, for various reasons, Florida has not proved to be a fully realistic alternative, but that hasn't stopped the Universal enclave here, now known as **Universal Orlando** (T1-888/331-9108, 1-800/837-2273 or 407/363-8000, Wwww.uescape.com), from expanding enormously and becoming even more successful.

The sequel to the long-established and immensely popular Universal Studios tour in Los Angeles, Florida's original Universal, like its rival Disney-MGM, is a working studio, filling over 400 acres with the latest in TV- and film-production technology. However, as the result of a multi-billion-dollar cash infusion, it is now much more than a glorified backlot and is competing with Disney World on more than one front. **Universal Studios** has added **Islands of Adventure**, which definitely has far zingier roller-coaster rides and zowier hi-tech special effects than Disney, and **CityWalk** (T407/224-2600), an earthier, more realistic lure for nightlife dollars that would otherwise go to Downtown Disney. In addition, Universal is also aspiring to full-fledged resort status with the recently opened *Portofino Bay Hotel*, with other on-property accommodations soon to follow.

Universal has proved to be extremely popular, becoming the fifth most visited theme park in the US. Overall, the mood is more hip and the rides are more spectacular than at Disney, but service can be snippy and the parks can feel less welcoming – as though almost everything is primarily aimed at hyper-energetic adolescent boys who want things louder, faster and with more attitude. For the overwhelming majority of visitors, two days will be sufficient.

Universal Studios

The first thing you'll encounter upon entering are street sets replicating New York, Los Angeles, San Francisco and Amity – the New England town where *Jaws* took place where the detail goes right down to the chewing gum painted onto the pavements. The park itself, arranged around a large lagoon, is nominally divided into several areas: the Front Lot, World Expo, Woody Woodpecker's KidZone, the cities named above and Production Central. But they are by no means that distinct, so there's no real need to follow a particular order in your explorations.

Universal Orlando practicalities

Half a mile north of exits 29B or 30A off I-4. Daily from 9am, with closing times varying by season. One-day studio pass $48.76 for adults, $39.22 for children 3–9; two-day **Escape Pass** $84.75 for adults, $68.85 for children; three-day, $121.85 for adults, $100.65 for children; five-day, $124.95 for adults, $99.95 for children.

⑤

For sheer excitement, nothing in the park compares to **Back to the Future**, a bone-shaking flight-simulator time-trip ranging from 2015 to the Ice Age. Next best is **Twister…Ride It Out**, a suffocating but gripping experience in which you stand beside an imitation tornado, complete with simulated lightning, flying objects and lots of rain (cover all camera equipment). **Jaws** owes its success to anticipation of horror and classy special effects, but the ride is over all too quickly. **Earthquake–The Big One** gives you an intensely claustrophobic two minutes of terror as you experience what it's like to be caught on a subway train when an 8.3 Richter-scale quake hits. **Terminator 2 3-D** offers second-to-none special effects – like the "plasma blasts" that reflect the heat and shock of its explosions – and is definitely worth the wait. The **Men in Black: Alien Attack** ride puts you smack inside a video game, where you rack up points zapping aliens – or being zapped – and return a hero, or a loser.

Moving on, the six-ton version of King Kong in **Kongfrontation**, which attacks your cable car amid cracks of thunder and lightning high above New York's East River, is neither particularly memorable nor worth the lengthy wait. Similarly, **ET's Adventure** is a rather dull ride on pretend bicycles to ET's home planet, although ET speaking your name (recorded earlier by a computer) as you leave is a pleasing touch. This and another tame ride, **Woody Woodpecker's Nuthouse Coaster**, are ideal for younger kids – and for adults who aren't into all the hyperactive jerks, spins and zooms. Nearby, **Curious George Goes to Town** provides an interactive aqua-playground, with special emphasis on splashing, squirting and getting drenched. Another playground option for tots or tots-at-heart is **Fievel's Playland**, where every piece of equipment is oversized and fun to climb on.

Obviously less fun for kids but often more enjoyable than the rides are the attempts to demystify TV- and film-production techniques. **Alfred Hitchcock's 3-D Theatre** explores some of the outrageous camera angles and visual tricks employed by the filmmaker to send shivers down the spines of millions. Apart from some rather tame efforts to frighten, the tour includes intriguing glimpses of some of his better films, a few startling scenes from the 3-D version of *Dial M for Murder*, and a group of actors playing out crucial scenes – including the shower scene from *Psycho* – using an unfortunate audience member.

At **The Funtastic World of Hanna-Barbera**, there's an excellent simulated cartoon chase from the creators of *The Flintstones* and *Yogi Bear*, which will have you shaking in your seat. Afterwards, using the interactive computers, you can create your own cartoon audio effects – bangs, whoops and crashes – to your heart's content. The kiddies might also go for **Nickelodeon Studios**, a peek behind the scenes at where most of the cable network programming is put together. You might want to spin by **Lucy: A Tribute** – snippets, clips, props, costumes, bits and bobs in memory of the zany, irrepressible redhead.

You'll also find a number of live stage shows on offer: *Beetlejuice's Graveyard Revue*, which is just plain wacky; the *Wild, Wild, Wild West Stunt Show*, a non-stop display of ribaldry and stunt-person prowess; the *Gory, Gruesome & Grotesque Horror Make-Up Show*, where movie makeup secrets are revealed amidst comic repartee; and *A Day in the Park with Barney*, a must if you've got preschoolers who adore the purple dinosaur.

Islands of Adventure

Billed as one of two Universal parks, **ISLANDS OF ADVENTURE** is really five superb miniparks, each with its own unique spin: **Seuss Landing**, fun for the little ones and those who grew up with the good Dr S's whimsical creations; **Lost Continent**, where ancient myth meets edgy technology; **Jurassic Park**, in which thunder lizards once again rule the earth; **Toon Lagoon**, whose classic cartoons come to giddy life; and **Marvel Super Hero Island**, which takes you into the supercharged comic-book world of your youth. The park has a truly remarkable number of amazing thrill rides and it must be said that it outshines anything Disney World has to offer in that department – even though no one has yet equaled Disney for the sheer seamless perfection of its imagined environments made real. There is also a live show, a field in which Disney still holds the edge, and a number of great hands-on play areas spread throughout.

The very best of the rides is also one of the newest: **The Amazing Adventures of Spider-Man**, which uses every trick imaginable – 3-D, sensory stimuli, motion simulation and more – to spirit you into another dimension that's not to be missed. **Dueling Dragons** may be the next most exciting ride – twin roller coasters engineered to provide harrowing near-misses that will literally have your hair standing on end at several points. A close second, too, is the **Incredible Hulk Coaster**, with its catapult start, seven full inversions, and two precipitous plunges. However, nothing, anywhere, gets more precipitous than the 85-foot drop you'll scream all the way through on the **Jurassic Park River Adventure**. Last, but not least, of the heavyweights is **Poseidon's Fury: Escape from the Lost City**, an unparalleled cataclysm of water and fire. The twin towers of **Doctor Doom's Fearfall** look frightening enough, but the ride, a controlled drop during which you experience a few seconds of weightlessness, doesn't really deliver that much to shout about; and **Storm Force Accelatron**, the newest ride for all ages, places visitors in tublike cars that spin and whirl in a domed space enveloped by a noisy light show.

In somewhat less adrenaline-pumping mode, you could go for **Dudley Do-Right's Ripsaw Falls**, a flume ride with its share of drops and lots of surprises; **Popeye & Bluto's Bilge-Rat Barges**, a river ride that's all about getting soaked; and the **Flying Unicorn**, a fanciful flight through an enchanted forest. **Caro-Seus-el**, the world's only animatronic merry-go-round, the adorable **Cat in the Hat**, and the interactive ride **One Fish, Two Fish, Red Fish, Blue Fish** are all tamer offerings for kiddies, and all located in Seuss Landing. Unless you have tons of time to kill, most of it waiting in line, give the **Pteranodon Flyers** gondola ride a miss.

Hands-on playgrounds and other attractions include **If I Ran the Zoo**, a Seussian maze full of buttons and splashes; **Triceratops Encounter** and the **Jurassic Park Discovery Center**, the former a petting zoo with a docile ten-foot-tall, 24-foot-long interactive robot, the latter a learning center where the focus is on, of course, more dinosaurs; **Me Ship, the *Olive***, in which kids of all ages can climb, crawl and scramble around to their heart's content; and the best, **Camp Jurassic**, an extensive, elaborate play area full of hidden treasures like bones and fossils. There's one live performance offered throughout the day: the *Eighth Voyage of Sinbad* stunt show, a nonstop extravaganza of swashbuckling adventure and pyrotechnics.

Universal Studios CityWalk

CITYWALK (☎407/224-2600) has actually surpassed both Downtown Disney and Church Street Station as a nightlife venue. Since it doesn't have the hyper-wholesome Disney image to live down, it's a much hipper place than Disney World could ever manage; and the downtown Orlando after-dark area simply doesn't seem to have the imagination, or the budget, to match it. Add to that the fact that one very reasonable price includes everything: the $7.95 all-club **Party Pass** (add $4 if you want to take in a movie). Free parking after 6pm makes the other two nightlife centers seem like the most abject tourist gougers.

CityWalk features a friendly mix of restaurants, live music, dance clubs, theaters, bars, eateries and shops. If you want to dance, try the drop-dead-hip **The Groove**, a huge, intense, multifaceted space filled with deafening decibels and pulsing photons, or the **Latin Quarter**, for devotees of every type of Latin beat. Live music abounds: **Bob Marley – A Tribute to Freedom** celebrates the "King of Reggae"; **CityJazz** offers a cooler, more sophisticated ambience and showcases all types of jazz; **Hard Rock Live**, a concert hall in-the-round, has live performers, occasionally famous ones, almost every evening; the **Nascar Café** features hard rock nightly; and **Jimmy Buffett's Margaritaville** has live island-style music that captures the famous laid-back Florida mood perfectly. A couple of other restaurant/bars complement the festive, musical atmosphere. at **Motown Café** the clientele creates its own music, singing and bopping along to the endless stream of great hits, and **Pat O'Brien's** perfectly re-creates the feel of Old New Orleans, with its dueling pianos and wrought-iron balconies. Check out the daily **Happy Hours**, which vary from bar to bar.

SeaWorld Orlando

Sea Harbor Drive, at the intersection of I-4 and the Central Florida Expressway, or I-4 and the Bee Line Expressway; exit 27A if you're coming from the west on I-4, exit 28 if you're coming from the east on I-4. Daily 9am–7pm in low season, longer hours in peak season; $50.83, children 3–9 $41.29.

It may have as many souvenir shops as fish, but **SEAWORLD ORLANDO** (☎1-800/327-2424 or 407/351-3600, ⊛www.seaworld.com) is the cream of Florida's sizeable crop of marine parks and as such shouldn't be missed. It's also now the second most expensive theme park in the world, after Busch Gardens, and both of them are now owned by Anheuser-Busch (which explains the incongruous homage to the brewery's Clydesdale horses, the company symbol, at SeaWorld's **Clydesdale Hamlet**). To see it all and get the best value for your money, you'll need to allocate a whole day and be certain to pick up the free map and show schedule at the entrance.

The big event is the *Shamu Stadium Show* – thirty minutes of tricks performed by a playful killer whale; the night show, *Shamu Rocks America,* is also terrific. Nearby **Shamu's Happy Harbor** is a paradise for children, offering inner tubes, slides, remote-control boats and even an area where they can catapult water balloons at each other. **Shamu Close-Up** is just what it sounds like, an unforgettable view of the private life of whales and their babies. The **Wild Arctic** complex (complete with artificial snow and ice) brings you close to beluga whales, walruses and polar bears, while a simulated ride takes you on a stomach-churning helicopter flight through an arctic blizzard. Be sure to check out the launch-pad viewing area (on your right as you exit through the gift shop) for insight into the mechanics of simulated rides.

The charming and funky **Key West** area invites visitors to pet slimy stingrays at **Stingray Lagoon**, or feed them smelt at $3 a tray; and the **Key West Dolphin Stadium** wows 'em with leaping dolphin and whale-riding shows. SeaWorld's first thrill ride, **Journey to Atlantis**, is part water slide, part roller coaster, and has a sixty-foot drop. You will get drenched – by the ride and by other tourists who pay for the privilege of spraying you. Inside the adjacent gift shop are two aquariums: a 25,000-gallon, underfoot aquarium filled with stingrays, and another one overhead (6000 gallons) with hammerhead sharks; odd-looking illuminated jellyfish are in tanks built into a nearby wall. **Kraken** is Orlando's latest contender in the roller-coaster sweepstakes, and it's a very strong entry; you'll be flung around, free-flying and looping-the-loop, at up to 65mph.

With substantially less razzmatazz, plenty of smaller tanks and displays around the park offer a wealth of information about the undersea world. Among the highlights, the **Penguin Encounter** attempts to re-create Antarctica with scores of the waddling birds scampering over a make-believe iceberg; the young occupants of the **Dolphin Nursery** assert their advanced intellect by flapping their fins and drenching passersby; and **Terrors of the Deep** includes a walk through a glass-sided tunnel, offering the closest eye-contact you're ever likely to have with sharks and other scary predators. As you might expect, in a park devoted to ocean life, there is a water adventure show called *Intensity Games–Water Ski Challenge*, at **Atlantis Bayside Stadium**, which involves daredevil waterskiing and diving. It is, however, genuinely spectacular and well worth waiting to see one of the three daily shows. The **Nautilus Theater** offers a different sort of live entertainment, which changes every year or so; be delighted and amazed at the current *Cirque de la Mer*, a fantastic blend of dance, gymnastics, mime, music and special effects. At **SeaWorld Theater** you'll be charmed by *Pets on Stage*, in which animals rescued by the local humane society do their best to win you over. Perhaps the best show takes place at the **Sea Lion & Otter Stadium**, where the stalwart mammals put on a grand entertainment entitled *Clyde and Seamore Take Pirate Island*. Just behind the stadium, at **Pacific Point Preserve**, check out more barking sea lions in a stunning replica of their natural Pacific Coast habitat.

If you've never been lucky enough to see a manatee in the wild, don't leave SeaWorld Orlando without taking in **Manatees: The Last Generation?**, a huge tank in which you can see a few of the endangered creatures and learn about the threat faced by their species. For wildlife buffs, the **Turtle Point** exhibit offers a behind-the-scenes look at how SeaWorld Orlando rescues and rehabilitates manatees, sea turtles and other marine life. One of the most successfully realized exhibits is **Tropical Reef**, a series of large aquariums offering dazzling, multihued re-creations of undersea worlds that are filled with marvelous and exotic sea creatures.

Discovery Cove

True adventure seekers now have SeaWorld's latest unique attraction to look forward to: **DISCOVERY COVE**, a multi-environment tropical paradise where the star turn is swimming with actual dolphins in the **Dolphin Lagoon**. After a training session, you enter the water and play with your new-found friends for thirty minutes. Other jungle treats are an **Aviary** that you have to swim under a waterfall to get to; a **Coral Reef** to snorkel through; the **Ray Lagoon**, where you can wade with hundreds of the fascinating creatures (all with their stingers safely removed); and a **Tropical River** and island-style **Beaches** to explore however you like. Access to Discovery Cove is limited to about 800 visitors a day, so you need to reserve at least a month in advance. Cost is $199 per person, which includes use of equipment, training and a meal (though not drinks), and also gives full seven-day access to SeaWorld. All the equipment you need is provided on the spot; and upon registering, you will be given an appointment to swim with the dolphins. Plan on spending a full day.

Other attractions around Orlando

The Orlando area's small-time entrepreneurs are nothing if not inventive. No end of tacky, short-lived, would-be attractions spring up each year and a large number of them swiftly sink without trace. The list below represents the best – or just the longest-surviving – of the thousand-and-one little places to visit **around Orlando**. Several other highly worthwhile attractions in the Orlando area, including Gatorland, Cypress Gardens and Bok Tower Gardens, are detailed on pp.270 and 296.

Airboat Rentals
Guide Marker 15, Hwy-192, Kissimmee. Daily 9am–5pm; 2-person canoes $5/hr; 6-person electric boats $22/hr; 4-5-person airboats $27/hr. ☎407/847-3672, ⊛www.airboatrentals.com.
Here's a chance to explore a pristine Florida cypress swamp on your own terms. All the boats are silent so as not to disturb any of the local fauna; you'll see alligators, otters, turtles, blue herons and countless other birds as you meander through their natural habitat.

Body Flight SkyVenture
On Visitors Circle, off International Drive, across from Wet 'n' Wild. Mon–Fri 4pm–midnight, Sat & Sun 1pm–midnight; $35, children 12 and under $25. ☎407/903-1150, ⊛www.skyventure.com.
Fly on a column of air without a parachute in this virtual reality freefall skydiving simulator. For $16 more you can have them video you in flight.

Flying Tigers Warbird Air Museum
231 N Hoagland Blvd, next to Kissimmee airport. Mon–Sat 9am–6pm, Sun 9am–5pm; $8, children 6–12 $6. ☎407/933-1942, ⊛www.warbirdmuseum.com.
The main hangar contains battle-weary Tiger Moths, Mustangs and assorted bombers and biplanes in various states of repair – all being commercially restored.

Guinness World Records Experience
8437 International Drive, in the Mercado. Sun–Thurs 10am–10pm, Fri & Sat 10am–11pm; $12.95, children under 12 $7.95. ☎407/248-8891.
Explore the wacky world of records and the obsessed humans who try to break them – try to set one yourself in this interactive, sense-surround,

multifaceted environment. This is well done, if you are into pointless trivia.

Helicopter Tours

8990 International Drive. Daily 9.30am, last flight varies with the season; $20–395/person, depending on the flight plan.☏407/354-1400.

Take in the area from your own private piloted helicopter. Nine different flight plans whisk you over the major attractions, even all the way out to the east coast of Florida, if you like.

Old Town

5770 W Hwy 192, Kissimmee. Daily 10am–11pm; free, rides $2 to $5. ☏1-800/843-4202 or 407/396–4888.

Old-fashioned amusement rides and 75 interesting, if slightly tacky, shops. The go-kart track and Ferris wheel are a hoot, as are the bumper cars and laser-tag game.

Pirate's Cove Adventure Golf

Two locations: in the Mercado, 8501 International Drive (☏407/352-7378) and Exit 27 off I-4 at Crosswoods, Lake Buena Vista (☏407/827-1242, ⓦwww.piratescove.net). Daily 9am–11.30pm; $7.42–12.19, children $6.89–11.66, depending on which course you choose; $15.90 for all day.

This is miniature golf at its inventive best: several challenging, fanciful courses to choose from.

Reptile World Serpentarium

5705 Hwy-192, just east of St Cloud. Tues–Sun 9am–5.30pm; $5.50, children 6–17 $4.50, children 3–5 $3.50. ☏407/892-6905.

A research center for the production of snake venoms, which are sold for research to produce anti-venoms. Visitors are introduced to a caged collection of poisonous and non-poisonous snakes from around the world, and are shown demonstrations of venom extraction at noon and 3pm.

Ripley's Believe It or Not!

8201 International Drive. Daily 9am–midnight; $12.95, children 4–12 $8.95. ☏1-800/998-4418 or 407/363-4418, ⓦwww.ripleysorlando.com.

A model of the world's tallest man, a chunk of the Berlin Wall and a Rolls-Royce built from a million matchsticks are among the innumerable oddities packed into these non-interactive displays in a building that is built to appear as if it is half-sunk into the earth.

Skull Kingdom

5933 American Way at International Drive, across from Wet 'n' Wild. Mon–Fri 6–11pm, Sat & Sun noon–11pm; $11.79. ☏407/354-1564, ⓦwww.skullkingdom.com.

A standard haunted house packaged in a nifty skull-faced castle. The scariest and most annoying part is having costumed pimple-faced teenagers yell in your face, "Do you have cooties?" Realistic-looking animatronic characters being tortured add a nice touch. Too scary for ages 7 and under.

Skycoaster

2850 Florida Plaza, on Hwy 192, next to Old Town. Daily noon–midnight; $27–37, depending on the number flying together (☏407/397-2509, ⓦwww.skyfun.com).

Bungee-jumping for one to three persons at a time, soaring between two joined poles; rather like skydiving and hang-gliding at once.

Splendid China

3000 Splendid China Blvd, two miles west of Disney World, off Hwy-192. Daily from 9.30am, with closing times varying by season; $26.99, children 5–12 $16.99. ☎1-800/244-6226 or 407/396-7111, ⓦ www.floridasplendidchina.com.

The best of the attractions, this park features over sixty authentic replicas celebrating 5000 years of Chinese architecture and history. Painstakingly reconstructed miniatures (including the Great Wall, the Forbidden City, the Leshan Buddha, and the Terracotta Warriors), plus museum exhibits, a variety of shows and fascinating displays, make this an intriguing place to spend the day. The best time to visit is towards evening when the park is beautifully illuminated. A food-and-gift area called Chinatown requires no admission and is a nice stop for dinner.

Titanic: Ship of Dreams

The Mercado, 8445 International Drive. Daily 10am–10pm; $16.95, children 6–12 $11.95. ☎ 407/248-1166 ⓦ www.titanicshipofdreams.com.

Full-scale replicas of the famous ship's Grand Staircase, authentic artifacts from the wreckage, and the stories of many of the ship's passengers and crew all await you at this new and well-researched attraction.

Wet'n'Wild

6200 International Drive. Daily 10am–5pm, longer hours in summer; $29.95, children 3–9 $23.95. After 2pm, you get $10 off regular prices. ☎ 1-800/992-9453 or 407/351-1800, ⓦ www.wetnwild.com.

A total of fifteen water slides, chutes, rapids, wave machines, bungee cords, and more – the perfect thing for a day when the thermometer soars. Since the water's well heated in winter, it's open all year round.

WonderWorks

9067 International Drive at Pointe Orlando. Daily 10 am–10pm; $14.95, children 3–12 $11.95. ☎ 407/351-8800, ⓦ www.wonderworksonline.com.

A collection of 85 hi-tech interactive gizmos housed cleverly inside an upside-down creaking house. Check out "Old Sparky," Florida's electric chair, which smokes just as the original did when it accidentally set a victim on fire. Also of interest: contraptions in which you experience earthquakes and hurricanes. Perfect for 13 year old boys.

A World of Orchids

2501 N Old Lake Wilson Rd, 1 mile S of Hwy-192, Kissimmee. Tues–Sun 9.30am–4.30pm. $4.50. ☎ 407/396-1881, ⓦ www.a-world-of-orchids.com.

An enthralling air-conditioned tropical raintorest garden that showcases thousands of rare, exotic and beautiful flowering orchids from around the world. Blooms all year round.

South Central Florida

Trapped between the vacation haunts of Orlando and the beaches of the Tampa Bay area, the main towns of **SOUTH CENTRAL FLORIDA** haven't been done any favors by decades of phosphate mining, which have left their surrounds pockmarked with craters. However, matters are gradually being improved. Many of the unsightly holes have been turned into man-made lakes (joining a large number of natural ones), and the prospect of boating, waterskiing and fishing on them is attracting visitors from the grip of Orlando. More interestingly, several of the region's small towns were formerly big towns around the turn of the nineteenth century, and are keen to flaunt their pasts – and near them can be found several refreshingly under-hyped attractions, which were bringing tourists into the state when Walt Disney was still in short trousers.

Lakeland and around

A logical place to begin touring the region, **LAKELAND**, fifty miles southwest of Orlando along I-4, plays the suburban big brother to its more rural neighbors and provides sleeping quarters for Orlando and Tampa commuters, who emerge on weekends to stroll the edges of the town's numerous lakes.

Aided by its busy railway terminal, Lakeland's fortunes rose in the Twenties, and a number of its more important buildings have been maintained as the **Munn Park Historic District** on and close to Main Street. Pay attention to the 1927 **Polk Theater**, 124 S Florida Ave, and the restored balustrades, lampposts and gazebo-style bandstand on the promenade around Lake Mirror, at the east end of Main Street. A few minutes' walk from the town center, the generous size of the **Polk County Museum of Art**, 800 E Palmetto St (Mon & Sat 10am–5pm, Tues–Fri 9am–5pm, Sun 1–5pm; free; ☎863/688-7743), suggests Lakeland is striving to raise its cultural profile: the spacious temporary galleries air the latest innovative pieces by up-and-coming Florida-based artists.

A stronger draw, and something of a surprise in such a tucked-away community, is the largest single grouping of buildings by **Frank Lloyd Wright**, who redefined American architecture in the Twenties and Thirties. Maybe it was the rare chance to design an entire communal area that appealed to Wright – the fee he got for converting an eighty-acre orange grove into **Florida Southern College** (ⓦ www.flsouthern.edu), a mile southwest of Lakeland's center, certainly didn't; the financially strapped college paid on credit and got its students to provide the labor.

Much of the integrity of Wright's initial concept has been lost: buildings have been crudely adapted and used for purposes other than those for which they were intended, and newer structures have distorted the college's overall harmony. Even so, the campus is an inventive statement and easily negotiated using the free **maps** provided in boxes along its covered walkways. Interestingly, Wright's contempt for air-conditioning caused him to erect thick masonry structures to shield the students from the Florida sun, and his desire to merge his work with the natural environment allowed the creeping vegetation of the orange grove (which has now given way to lawns) to wrap around the buildings and provide further insulation. For guided **tours** of the Wright buildings, call ☎863/680-4110.

Practicalities

Get a descriptive **walking tour map** of the Munn Park Historic District from the **Chamber of Commerce**, 35 Lake Morton Drive (Mon–Fri 8.30am–5pm; ☎863/688-8551). For **eating**, the *Reececliff*, 940 S Florida Ave (☎863/686-6661), a spartan diner in business since 1934, has ridiculously cheap breakfasts and lunches; *Harry's Seafood Bar & Grille*, 101 N Kentucky Ave

(ⓣ 863/686-2228), provides a large menu of Cajun and Creole-inspired food in a fern bar atmosphere; and the *Silver Ring Café*, 106 Tennessee Ave (ⓣ 863/687-3283), features sizeable Cuban sandwiches. But if you're in the mood for a posh meal, *The Terrace Grill*, in the newly restored, vintage 1924 *Terrace Hotel*, 329 E Main St (ⓣ 1-888/644-8400 or 863/688-0800, ⓦ www.terracehotel.com; ❻), offers superb dishes, such as the salmon with fresh *mozzarella di buffala* salad, in a chic Mediterranean Revival setting.

For further **accommodation** options, the atmospheric *Lake Morton Bed & Breakfast*, 817 S Blvd (ⓣ 863/688-6788; ❸), is an oak-decorated period boarding house near the campus and the main lake. There are inexpensive motels, such as the *Lake Mirror Inn*, 740 E Main St (ⓣ 863/688-5506; ❷), a walk around the lake from the historic center, or the *Scottish Inn*, 244 N Florida Ave (ⓣ 863/687-2530; ❷), a more basic choice, but near enough to everything of interest. Lakeland nightlife centers around *Lillian's Music Store*, 215 E Main St (ⓣ 863/616-9966), featuring live music on weekends.

Polk City: Fantasy of Flight

Ten miles northeast of Lakeland, near Polk City, **Fantasy of Flight**, 1400 Broadway Blvd SE (daily 9am–5pm; ⓣ 863/984-3500, ⓦ www.fantasyofflight

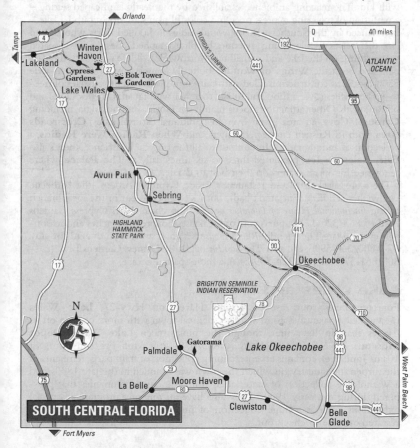

.com; $24.95, children $13.95), is trying to draw tourists and aviation enthusiasts. Part themed attraction and part private aircraft collection, Fantasy of Flight allows visitors to climb aboard a World War II B-17 Flying Fortress and pretend to drop bombs amid the sounds of anti-aircraft fire. You can be closed into "flight simulators" to get a somewhat realistic flavor of mid-air combat, or you can fly 500 feet into the air in an "Ultralight" airplane. Perhaps most interesting is the owner's collection of thirty-plus vintage planes, including the Lockheed Vega, which was the first plane ever flown around the globe.

Winter Haven and Cypress Gardens

Winter Haven, a few miles south of I-4, just off Hwy-27, struggles to hold onto passing traffic; the motels (see below) lining Cypress Gardens Boulevard exist for visitors to the long-popular **Cypress Gardens**, at the southeast corner of the town; daily, summer 9.30am–5.30pm, winter 9.30am–5pm; $34.93, one child free with each paying adult, otherwise $17.97 per child (℡1-800/282-2123 or 863/324-2111, ⓦwww.cypressgardens.com). Gouged from a sixteen-acre swamp by dollar-a-day laborers during the Depression, Cypress Gardens (now owned by the same people who run Busch Gardens, p.329, and SeaWorld, p.289) makes a good place to unwind after the tumult of the theme parks, especially with kids. The relaxing ambience established by the neatly landscaped setting – a profusion of towering cypress trees and colorful plants arching around a lake – is enhanced by the Southern Belles: young ladies in hooped skirts who sit and fan themselves while being relentlessly photographed. Besides syncopated **waterskiing** on the lake and a small but worthwhile wildlife sanctuary, the gardens also boast the **Wings of Wonder** butterfly conservatory, a Victorian-style 5500-foot glass construction filled with rainforest plants and fifty species of free-flying butterflies (over a thousand in all), together with iguanas, turtles, doves and button quails. Other attractions focus mainly on Florida and nostalgia, including **Carousel Cove**, an area given over to traditional carnival rides; **Crossroads Area**, with its Russian circus performers; and **When Radios Were Radios**, a collection of antique radios. In contrast to all the tropical luxuriance, there's also **Fairy Tales on Ice**, presented three to six times daily at **The Palace**, where renowned European skaters do their best to dazzle.

There are snack bars and restaurants inside Cypress Gardens (the barbecue sandwiches at *Village Fare* aren't bad), but it's cheaper to **eat** in the local branch of the *International House of Pancakes* coffee shop chain, 1915 Cypress Gardens Blvd (℡863/326-1772), purveyors of breakfasts, bounteous lunches and reasonable evening fare. The friendly *Ranch House* is a good spot for an **overnight stay** (℡1-800/366-5996; ❸), as is *The Scottish Inn*, 1901 Cypress Gardens Blvd (℡1-800/861-3777 or 863/324-5998; ❷), a more spartan choice.

Lake Wales and around

Fourteen miles southeast of Winter Haven on Hwy-27, **Lake Wales** (ⓦwww.cityoflakewales.com) is a lackadaisical town with more of note on its fringes than in its center, though the pink stucco **Lake Wales Depot Museum**, 325 S Scenic Highway (℡863/678-4209; Mon–Fri 9am–5pm, Sat 10am–4pm; free), contains an entertaining collection of train parts, remnants of the turpentine industry on which the town was founded in the late 1800s, and a Warhol-like collection of crate labels from the citrus companies that prospered during the early 1900s. They also have an ongoing program of special exhibitions, such as a huge collection of fine vintage quilts, and a recently restored caboose to check out.

At the museum, confirm directions to **Spook Hill**, an optical illusion that's been turned into a transparently bogus "legend" (which you can read about on a plaque), worth seeing as a unique example of local Florida kitsch (conveniently, it's on the way to Bok Tower Gardens, see below). By car, cross Central Avenue from the museum and turn right onto North Avenue, and then take a left at the T-intersection, following the one-way system. Just before meeting Hwy-17A, a sign indicates the spot to brake and put your vehicle into neutral. As you do so, the car appears to slide uphill. Looking back reveals the difference in road gradients that creates the effect.

Bok Tower Gardens

"A more striking example of the power of beauty could hardly be found, better proof that beauty exists could not be asked for," rejoiced landscape gardener William Lyman Phillips in 1956 upon visiting **Bok Tower Gardens**, two miles north of Lake Wales on Hwy-17A (daily 8am–6pm; last admission 5pm; $6, children 5–12 $2; ℡863/676-1408). As sentimental as it may sound, Phillips' comment was, and is, accurate. Whether it's the effusive entanglements of ferns, oaks and palms, the bright patches of magnolias, azaleas and gardenias, or just the sheer novelty of a hill (this being the highest point in peninsular Florida), Bok Tower Gardens is one of the state's most lush and lovely places.

Not content with winning the Pulitzer Prize for his autobiography in 1920, Dutch-born office-boy turned author and publisher **Edward Bok** resolved to transform the pine-covered Iron Mountain (as this red-soiled hump is named) into a "sanctuary for humans and birds," in gratitude to his adopted country for making his glittering career possible. President Coolidge, one of Bok's many famous friends, showed up to declare it open in 1929.

Marvelous though they are, these 128 acres would be just a glorified botanical garden were it not for the **Singing Tower** and the **mansion**. The tower, two hundred feet of marble and coquina, rises sheerly above the foliage, poetically mirrored in a swan- and duck-filled lily pond. Originally intended to conceal the garden's water tanks, the tower features finely sculpted impressions of Florida wildlife on its exterior and fills its interior with a 53-bell carillon: richly timbred chimes resound through the garden every half-hour. Only the 3pm recital is "live" (all the others are recordings), but you can discover more about its workings in the **visitor center**, which provides every detail imaginable about the garden and tower. Near the garden's entrance is an old "cracker" cottage. ("Cracker" was the nickname given to the state's early cattle farmers, perhaps because of the sound of the whips they handled with such precision.) The twenty-room Mediterranean-style mansion was renovated and opened in December 1995, its rooms decorated with 1920s furnishings. Guided tours last for one hour and cost $5.

A portion of the grounds has been left in its raw state, allowing wildlife to roam and be surreptitiously viewed through the glass front of a wooden hut. Hardier visitors can hack their way for twenty minutes along the **Pine Ridge Trail**, through the pine trees, saw-edged grasses and wild flowers that once covered the entire hill.

Chalet Suzanne

In 1931, gourmet cook and world traveler Bertha Hinshaw, recently widowed and made penniless by the Depression, moved to an isolated site two miles north of Lake Wales, beside Hwy-17, to open a restaurant called **Chalet Suzanne.** Armed with her own recipes and tremendous powers of culinary invention – adding chicken livers to grilled grapefruit, for instance – Bertha created what's now among the most highly rated meal stops in the country, and one that's still run by her family.

Aside from the food (a multi-course lunch costs upwards of $50, dinner costs upwards of $80; call for reservations ℡ 863/676-6011), the quirky architecture grabs the eye: part Arabic, part Renaissance, whimsical, Hobbit-like buildings painted in confectionery pinks, greens and yellows, topped by twisting towers and exotic turrets. Even if you're not dining or staying in one of the boudoir-like guest rooms (ⓦ www.chaletsuzanne.com; ❻), you're free to wander through the public rooms – whose furnishings are as loopy as the architecture, with decorative pieces picked up from Bertha's seven around-the-world trips.

The one conventional structure is the soup cannery, where "Romaine" soup – another of Bertha's creations – begins its journey to the nation's gourmet food stores. While here, don't be frightened by low-flying aircraft: a small run-way beside the cannery is where corporate execs and freeloading food critics breeze in by private plane for a slap-up meal.

Lake Kissimmee State Park

Nineteenth-century Floridian farming techniques may not seem the most inspiring subject in the world, but the 1876 Cow Camp section of **Lake Kissimmee State Park** (daily 7am–sunset; cars $3.25, pedestrians and cyclists $1; ℡ 863/696-1112), nine miles east of Lake Wales off Route 60, is an enjoyable and instructive re-creation of a pioneer-era cattle farm, complete with park rangers tending genuine cows and horses.

In the park picnic area, an observation platform above Lake Kissimmee can be utilized for bird- and alligator-spotting.

South of Lake Wales: along Hwy-27

The section of Hwy-27 that runs **south from Lake Wales** is among Florida's least eventful roads: a four-lane snake through a landscape of gentle hills, lakes, citrus groves and sleepy communities dominated by retirees. Busy with farm trucks, the highway itself is far from peaceful, but provides an interesting course off the beaten track if you're making for either coast: smaller roads branch off towards Fort Myers, on the west coast, and, after Hwy-27 twists around the massive Lake Okeechobee, to the big centers of the southeast coast.

Avon Park, Sebring and around

Twenty-two miles south of Lake Wales lies **Avon Park** (℡ 863/453-3350, ⓦ www.apfla.com), which acquired its name from an early English settler born in Stratford-upon-Avon. Information on her and the community's general history is available at the **Avon Park Museum**, 3 N Museum Ave (Tues–Fri; 10am–2pm, free; ℡ 863/453-3525), housed in yet another restored pink stucco train depot. Once **Downtown**, several miles away, spin by the quaint row of flea markets and antique shops on East Main Street, and have breakfast or lunch at the typical small-town eatery, the *Sandwich Depot*, 21 W Main St (℡ 863/453-5600). If you feel inclined to stay the night, the newly restored *Hotel Jacaranda*, 19 E Main St (℡ 863/453-2211; ❷), evokes the town in its glory days, and its *Palm Room* and *Citrus Room* (closed Sat) are elegantly appointed for dining, with Southern cooking buffets a specialty.

Leave Avon Park on Route 17 and trace a ten-mile path around a series of lakes to **Sebring**, where the unusual semicircular street plan was devised by its founder, George Sebring. He planted an oak tree here in 1912 to symbolize the sun, and declared that all the town's streets would radiate out from it. There's been no sign of the oak tree for decades, but Route 17 passes the small circular park, now sporting a commemorative plaque, just before reconnecting with Hwy-27.

As quiet as can be for eleven months of the year, Sebring's tranquillity is shattered each March and September when tens of thousands of motor-racing fans pack its motels and restaurants, arriving for a twelve-hour endurance contest, the **12 Hours of Sebring**, held at a race track about ten miles east – if you're passing through around this time, plan accordingly. Otherwise, if you decide to **stay**, for the area's lakes, unspoilt landscape or the race track, the historic *Kenilworth Lodge*, 836 SE Lakeview Drive (℡ 1-800/423-5939 or 863/385-0111, ⓦ www.kenlodge.com; ❸), is a mammoth Spanish-style hotel, newly restored to some of its former grandeur. For authentic American and local specialities, such as homemade burgers and lemon pepper grouper, the *Sebring Diner*, 4040 US 27 S (℡ 863/385-3434), comes through, in a snazzy replica of an old-fashioned Art Deco structure, all chrome and glass.

Well away from the sound of revving engines, the orange grove and cypress swamp trails inside **Highlands Hammock State Park**, six miles west of Sebring on Route 634 (daily 8am–sunset; cars $4.25, pedestrians and cyclists $1), add up to a well-spent afternoon. Keep an eye out for the white-tailed deer, and time your visit to coincide with the informative ranger-guided **tram tour** (for times, call ℡ 863/386-6094).

Gatorama and beyond

Just beyond Palmdale, forty miles south of Sebring, on Hwy-27, keep an eye out for **Gatorama** (Mon–Sat 8am–6pm, Sun 10am–6pm; $7.95, children under 56 inches $3.50), a working alligator farm, licensed to keep thousands of the toothy creatures for public viewing and for turning into handbags, boots and food; unlike Orlando's Gatorland (see "South of Orlando," p.270), this place has only one show – feeding time – otherwise, it's simply a self-guided tour around the raised wooden walkways.

Moving on from here, Route 29, off Hwy-27 at Palmdale, runs west to La Belle, from which Hwy-80 continues thirty miles to Fort Myers (see "The West Coast," p.371); Hwy-27 ploughs on around the southern edge of Lake Okeechobee.

Lake Okeechobee and around

For many years, one of the best-kept secrets in Florida was the outstanding natural beauty of **Lake Okeechobee**, the second largest freshwater lake entirely in the US. The former preserve of sugarcane, beef and dairy farmers, as well as fishermen in search of catfish or large-mouthed bass, the lake (whose name is the Seminole Indian for "Big Water") has started to draw tourists. This is the result of both a statewide push and the area's abundance of plants and **wildlife**. Birds feature strongly: over 120 varieties have been spotted, and this is one of the few places in the world where you can still sight a snail kite. Other inhabitants include bobcats, alligators, turtles, otters, snakes and, occasionally, manatees.

Home exclusively to Native Americans for centuries, the area's first farm settlers began arriving in 1910, encouraged by the work carried out by wealthy Philadelphian Hamilton Disston, who, in the nineteenth century, started dredging canals and draining the land for agriculture. Next came the railroads, extending around three-quarters of the lake by the late 1920s and providing easy access to the rest of the state. Today the area is also served by three major **highways**, which join to encircle the lake and allow access to the towns dotted around its shores (see below). Staying a few days in one of these will allow you to explore Lake Okeechobee and its environs at your leisure.

Lake Okeechobee

Covering 730 square miles and averaging fourteen feet in depth, **LAKE OKEECHOBEE** is fed by several rivers, creeks and canals, and has always played an important role not only in the lives of communities close to its shores but also in the life-cycle of the Everglades. Since the completion of the dike, it has served as both a flood-control safety valve during the hurricane season and as a freshwater storage reservoir. Traditionally, the lake's waters have drained slowly south to nourish the Everglades after the summer rains, but the disruption caused by extensive "reclaiming" of land for farming is one of the hottest environmental issues in Florida.

Visiting the lake

The lake itself is best enjoyed **by boat** or by **walking/cycling trails** (there is a 110-mile trail that runs along the top of the Hoover Dike, which surrounds the lake). For more information on the trails, call the Florida Trail Association (☎1-800/343-1882; ⓦ www.florida-trail.org), and to hire a bike, try Euler's Cycling Center, 50 Hwy-441 SE (☎863/357-0458). An exciting plan, now nearing realization, is to connect the Okeechobee Scenic Trail with the Appalachian National Scenic Trail, creating the longest trail in the US and joining Maine with Miami.

A sensitive and instructional way to learn about this habitat and its wildlife is a boat ride with **Swampland Tours**, based near the town of Okeechobee (see below) at the Kissimmee Bridge, 10375 Hwy-78 ($19 for two hours; daily 10am and 1pm, weather permitting; check times and book ahead on ☎863/467-4411 or 1-800/333-4264 ext 549). The 22-mile tours into the 28,000-acre wildlife sanctuary are run by Barry "Chop" Légé in association with the Florida Audubon Society, which owns the park. Barry's enthusiasm is infectious, and he will astonish you with his ability to spot all manner of creatures that you might otherwise miss; in any one trip, you're also likely to see at least 35 species of birds.

Okeechobee town

The largest lakeside community, **OKEECHOBEE** offers a base from which to explore and provides the most alternatives for accommodation, food and entertainment. The town was designed by the ubiquitous Henry M. Flagler (see "Palm Beach", p.191), whose grandiose plan demanded wide streets and wooden-framed buildings, some of which remain.

The town has a few places worthy of a visit for an hour or two, should the weather prevent you from more active pursuits: the **Historical Museum** (in the Historical Park; Thurs only 9am–1pm; free) and the 1926 **County Court House**, a pretty example of Mediterranean Revival architecture, a style much favored by Flagler. Details on these and other places of interest, as well as local events, can be found at the **Chamber of Commerce** at 55 S Parrott Ave (Mon–Fri 9am–4pm; ☎863/763-6464 or 1-800/871-4403).

If you're interested in **fishing**, still a primary activity in the area, go to Garrard Tackle Shop, 4259 Hwy-441 S (☎863/763-3416). They will supply all the gear and a guide to help ensure you catch something.

Practicalities

Although the town is easy to get to – Greyhound, 106 SW Third St (℡ 863/763-5328) and Amtrak, 801 N Parrot Ave (℡ 1-800/872-7245), both have depots – there is no local public transport system, and taxis stop running at 9pm. This means that if you don't have a car you'll be pretty much tied to the town in the evenings and may therefore want to limit your time to one or two nights. Of the places to **stay**, the quiet and unassuming *Wanta Linga Motel*, 3225 SE Hwy-441 (℡ 863/763-1020 or 1-800/754-0428; ❷), offers reasonably priced rooms and 45-foot boat-parking spaces. The *Motel Pier II*, 2200 SE Hwy-441 (℡ 1-800/874-3744 or 863/763-8003; ❸), offers standard, clean and comfortable accommodation, plus a pool, a five-story viewing tower and access to a fishing pier with a lounge. For **camping**, you'll find the largest *KOA* campground in **North America** just outside the town as you're heading towards the lake on Hwy-441 S (℡ 1-800/845-6846). A tent site costs $35, an RV site $45 and a one-room cabin (sleeping up to four) is $65. A nine-hole golf course is on the premises.

For **eating**, *Lightsey's Fish Co.*, 10435 Okee-Tantie Hwy-78 W (℡ 863/763-4276), serves a selection of fresh fish and homemade American fare at reasonable prices. Keep an eye out for their weekly specials. *Old Habits*, 4865 SE Hwy-441 (℡ 863/763-9924), offers Southern-style food and hospitality. Alternatively, gorge yourself on the all-you-can-eat breakfast, lunch or dinner at *Pogey's*, 1759 SE Hwy-441 (℡ 863/763-7222), or on the steak and seafood at *Michael's Restaurant*, 1001 S Parrott Ave (℡ 863/763-2069). The *Angus Restaurant*, 2054 Hwy-70 W at junction 98 (℡ 863/763-2040; closed Sun), specializes in steak and prime rib, for which the area is famous, plus a wide selection of seafood. They also run the *Club Angus* with live music or a DJ every night.

The west side of the lake

Leaving Hwy-27 just west of Moore Haven, Route 78 charts a 34-mile course along the **west side of the lake**, passing through Fisheating Creek and continuing into the treeless expanse of Indian Prairie, part of the 35,000-acre **Brighton Seminole Indian Reservation**.

The Seminole Indians migrated here in the eighteenth century from Georgia and Alabama, replacing the already decimated original Native American population. After they, too, became the target of aggression, a small number managed to establish themselves here on the western side of the lake, where about 450 remain, as successful cattle farmers. Although they live in houses rather than traditional Seminole *chickees*, or thatched huts, the current residents have remained faithful to long-held beliefs – handicrafts may be offered from the roadside, but you won't find any of the tacky souvenir shops common to reservations in more populous areas.

On this side of the lake, **accommodation** is limited to several well-equipped **campgrounds**, the best of which is *Twin Palms Resort* (℡ 863/946-0977), located thirteen miles from Moore Haven and twenty miles from the town of Okeechobee. This RV park offers self-contained cottages for $50 and tent sites for $16.50 per night.

Clewiston, Belle Glade and around

From Moore Haven, Hwy-27 is walled by many miles of sugar cane – half of all the sugar grown in the US, in fact – harvested between March and November by Jamaican laborers who are flown in, housed in hostels and notoriously underpaid for their physically demanding and even dangerous work.

Many in Florida, particularly the 43,000 locally employed in the sugar industry, seem content to turn a blind eye to the scandalous treatment of the migrants. Their plight is not a subject wisely brought up in **Clewiston**, fourteen miles from Moore Haven, which is dominated by the US Sugar Corporation and, through the company's multimillion-dollar profits, is enjoying the highest per capita income in the country. **Belle Glade**, a small town twenty miles east, has the biggest sugar mill in the country and numerous trailer parks aimed largely at attracting fishermen. In its otherwise quiet history, one event stands out: the loss of 2000 lives when the lake was whipped up by a hurricane in 1928. The Belle Glade **Chamber of Commerce** is at 540 S Main St (Mon–Fri 9am–5pm; ℡561/996-2745).

Acommodation is relatively plentiful, though squarely aimed at fishing folk – if that's not your scene you may as well stay away. On Torrey Island, two miles west of Belle Glade on Route 717, *The City of Belle Glade's Marina Campground* (℡561/996-6322) has lots of campervan space and a tent area ($16 a night), plus a miniature golf course.

Moving on from here, Hwy-27 swings south from just outside Belle Glade towards Miami, eighty miles distant, while Hwy-441 cuts east forty miles to West Palm Beach.

North Central Florida

Millions of people each year hammer through **NORTH CENTRAL FLORIDA** towards Orlando, almost all of them oblivious to the fact that a few miles east of the unrelentingly ordinary I-75 are the villages and small towns that typified Florida before the arrival of interstate highways and made-to-measure vacations. The region has just two appreciably sized towns, one of which, Gainesville, holds a major university, and a terrain that varies from rough scrub to resplendent grassy acres lubricated by dozens of natural springs. Giving this region a few days won't waste your time or break your budget: costs here are extremely low.

Ocala and around

Known throughout the US for the champion runners bred and trained at the thoroughbred horse farms occupying its green and softly undulating surrounds, **OCALA** itself is a town without much to shout about – though it makes an agreeable base for seeing more of the immediate area, which is noted for its pristine natural springs and for being Florida's premier horse country. The **Chamber of Commerce**, 110 E Silver Springs Blvd (Mon–Fri 8.30am–5pm; ℡352/629-8051), can supply local facts, issue walking maps of the town's mildly interesting historic districts and tell you which of the **horse farms** are open for free self-guided tours.

The area code for this part of North Central Florida is ℡352.

The Don Garlits and Appleton museums

Ten miles south of Ocala, exit 67 off I-75, the **Don Garlits Museum of Drag Racing** (daily 9am–5pm; $8 for the drag racing exhibit, $12 for that plus the antique car exhibit; ℡ 352/245-8661, Ⓦ www.1garlits.com) parades dozens of low-slung drag-racing vehicles, including the "Swamp Rat" machines that propelled local legend Don Garlits to 270mph over the drag tracks during the mid-Fifties. Yellowing press cuttings and grainy films chart the rise of the sport, and a subsidiary display of Chevys, Buicks and Fords – and the classic hits pumped out by a Wurlitzer jukebox – evoke an *American Graffiti* atmosphere.

An outstanding assembly of art and artifacts is found east of Ocala, inside the **Appleton Museum of Art**, 4333 NE Silver Springs Blvd (daily 10am–6pm; $6, under-18s free; ℡ 352/236-7100). Spanning the globe and five thousand years, the exhibits, collected by a wealthy Chicago industrialist, go together with remarkable cohesion, and there's barely a dull moment over two well-filled floors. Early Rembrandt etchings, a Rodin *Thinker* cast from the original mold and paintings by Jules Breton amid an exquisite stock of nineteenth-century French canvases are admirable enough, but the handicrafts are really special: look for the Turkish prayer rugs, the brightly colored Naxco ceramics, the wooden Tibetan saddle and the massed ranks of "Toggles" – Japanese *netsuke* figures carved from ivory.

Silver Springs

Approximately one mile east of Ocala at 5656 SR-40/Silver Springs Blvd, **Silver Springs** (Thurs–Sun 10am–5pm, daily in summer; $30.95, children $21.95; ℡ 1-800/234-7458 or 352/236-2121, Ⓦ www.silversprings.com) has been winning admirers since the late 1800s when Florida's first tourists came by steamboat to stare into the spring's deep, clear waters. Current visitors will find it less impressive than similar offerings in Orlando, yet cheaper and less crowded.

During the 1930s and 1940s, six of the original *Tarzan* films, starring Johnnie Weissmuller, were shot here. Today, the park operates as a highly commercial enterprise: a menagerie of imported animals, such as monkeys, giraffes and llamas, plus the inevitable petting zoo mar an otherwise attractive spot where you can happily while away the day. The admission fee, however, is high, especially considering the proliferation of springs all across Central and Northern Florida, some of them just a few miles east in the Ocala National Forest (see p.305) or north of Gainesville (see p.312). From a conservationist point of view, Wakulla Springs (near Tallahassee, see p.412) is a far better bet. However, if you do decide to visit Silver Springs, you'll get the most from the **Glass-Bottomed Boat Tour** (the best of several boat rides available), the **Jungle Cruise** and the **Jeep Safari**, all of which run regularly through the day. The **Big Gator Lagoon** attraction is fun during feeding time, when you get to throw hot dogs (three for $1) at the alligators and watch them jump for the food. **World of Bears** offers a glimpse of the creatures as well as an educational program about their lives at Silver Springs. The newest attractions are the **Panther Prowl**, an up-close look at the lives of these endangered felines, and the **Lost River Voyage**, which takes you around the Silver River and back into primeval Florida. Silver Springs also now offers a full schedule of popular music concerts, including big names from country to rock and roll. If you feel like cooling off, or have kids in tow, buy a combo ticket, allowing entry to the adjacent **Wild Waters** (March–Sept, daily 10am–5pm), a typical water park with slides, wave pools, amusement arcades and so on.

If you decide you want to spend a couple of days getting into Silver Springs and Wild Waters, the best choice for **lodging** is the *Holiday Inn*, right across from the entrance at no. 5751 (☏352/236-2575; ❸), an attractive establishment with two pools and an attached *Denny's* 24-hour restaurant.

Rainbow Springs State Park

A more natural setting for a walk and a swim is **Rainbow Springs State Park**, located about twenty miles west of Ocala and three miles north of Dunnellon, off Hwy-41 (daily 8am–sunset; walk-in only, $1 per person; ☏352/489-8503, camping ☏352/489-5201; $13 per night). From 1890 until the 1960s, this park rivaled Silver Springs as a commercial venture, but has thankfully been allowed to return to its natural state. A popular haunt for locals, it's busy on weekends, with families picnicking on the grass and splashing around in the springs. At other times you can enjoy exploring woodland **trails** in peace and quiet, keeping an eye out for bobcats, raccoons, wild pigs, otters and a great variety of birdlife, then have a swim in the cool, crystal-clear waters. Phone ahead to take advantage of the **ranger-led walks** and **snorkeling**. **Scuba diving** is also possible, but only for those camping. For daytrippers to the park, canoe and kayak rentals are $5 per hour. If you're camping, inner-tube rentals are also available for a leisurely drift down the Blue Run River.

Accommodation: Ocala and around

Motels line Silver Springs Boulevard between Ocala and Silver Springs: *Southland Motel*, no. 1260 E (☏352/351-0113; ❶); *Silver Springs Budget Motel*, no. 4121 E (☏352/236-4243; ❷); and the *Days Inn–Ocala East*, no. 5001 E (☏352/236-2891; ❸), are all worth trying. *The Ritz Historic Inn*, 1205 E Silver Springs Blvd (☏1-800/382-9390 or 352/671-9300,

---

Horseback riding

A visit to this area isn't really complete without seeing one of its numerous horse ranches, but you'll need a car to reach them. If you want to go horseback riding rather than just looking around, try Young's Paso Fino Ranch, four miles along SR-326, off I-75, at no. 8075 NW (☏352/867-5305; book ahead). One of the country's top ranches for breeding and training Paso Fino horses (the name means "fine gait" in Spanish), they offer instruction before taking you out on a trail ($26.50 for 1hr 30min, including instruction). The horses' easy disposition and exceptionally smooth gait make them an ideal choice for beginners as well as more advanced riders. If you're lucky, you'll meet Barbara Young, the owner, whose charm and enthusiasm know no bounds.

An ideal place to rest your saddle-sore butt after a hard day's horseback riding is the Heritage Country Inn, set in ranch country at 14343 W Hwy-40, off I-75 (☏352/489-0023). The $79 bed-and-breakfast is money well spent for the loving care and attention you'll receive. There are six unique bedrooms, ranging from the *Plantation Room* to the *English Thoroughbred Room*. A favorite among guests is the homebaked cinnamon bread.

West of Ocala, handy to Silver Springs, is another great option that combines horseback riding with a commodious B&B: Rosslor Manor, on Baseline Road/#35, just north of Wild Waters (☏1-800/404-2362 or 352/236-4219, ⊛www.rosslor.com; ❼). The friendly, urbane owners offer an extended continental breakfast, acres of trails, instruction for all levels, and pure luxury. You can bring your own horses or rent one from the Rosslor stables.

(℡352/236-1723; ❶), have considerably more charm and even historic appeal. For real luxury, try the *Seven Sisters Inn B&B* or its newly restored and more exotic theme-roomed neighbor, 820 SE Fort King St (℡1-800/250-3496 or 352/867-1170, Ⓦwww.7sistersinn.com; ❹). These B&Bs are unsurpassed for comfort, hospitality and old-fashioned charm – as well as for the owners' uniquely original touches. As a plus, the *Seven Sisters* is reputedly haunted – by a friendly ghost, of course. The only local **campground** (aside from camping in the Ocala National Forest) to allow tents is the *KOA* (℡352/237-2138), five miles southwest of Ocala on Route 200. You can pitch a tent for $19.95 or rent a cabin for $34.95.

Eating and drinking: Ocala and around

You'll seldom need to spend more than $5 for a filling **meal** in town, with a wide selection of eateries along East Silver Springs Boulevard. For lunch or dinner, *Piccadilly Cafeteria*, no. 1602 (℡352/622-7447), has homestyle foods served cafeteria-style, starting as low as $2.99 for a complete meal. *Sonny's*, no. 4102 (℡352/236-1012), specializes in barbecue, with $5.49-7.99 all-you-can-eat specials nightly. *Richard's Place*, no. 316, right in town (℡352/351-2233), is the place locals go for a full, American-style breakfast, while *Harry's*, 24 SE First Ave (℡352/840-0900), with outdoor seating directly on the central square, specializes in New Orleans cooking and has great seafood – and a fun-loving atmosphere, too. *Carmichael's*, 3105 E Silver Springs Blvd (℡352/622-3636), is one of the area's most elegant choices and features a large, eclectic menu for breakfast, lunch and dinner. Ocala **nightlife**, such as it is, is limited to the few nondescript bars and bistros grouped around the town square.

Ocala National Forest

Translucent lakes, bubbling springs and a splendid 65-mile hiking trail bring weekend adventurers to the 400,000-acre **OCALA NATIONAL FOREST** (free), five miles east of Silver Springs on Route 40. Steer clear of the busy bits, and you'll find plenty to savor in seclusion. Alternatively, if you only have time for a quick look, take a spin along Route 19 (meeting Route 40, 22 miles into the forest), running north–south in the shade of overhanging hardwoods near the forest's eastern edge.

Juniper, Alexander and Salt springs

For swimming, canoeing (rent on the spot, for $20-25 per one-way outing), gentle hiking and lots of other people, especially on weekends and holidays, the forest has three warm-water springs that fit the bill; and each of them has a campground. The easiest to reach from Silver Springs is **Juniper Springs** (℡352/625-2520; $3 per person; $13 per campsite), twenty miles ahead on Route 40, particularly suited to hassle-free canoeing with a seven-mile marked course. **Alexander Springs** (℡352/669-7495; $3 per person; $15 per campsite), on Route 445 off SR-19 about ten miles southeast of Juniper Springs, has good canoeing, too, and its see-through waters are perfect for snorkeling and scuba diving.

To the north of the forest, reachable with Route 314 or Route 19, the most developed site – it even has a gas station and laundromat – is **Salt Springs** (℡352/685-2048 or 685-3070; $3 per person; $13 per campsite). Despite the

Ocala National Forest information

The Ocala **Chamber of Commerce**, 110 E Silver Springs Blvd (daily 9am–5pm; ☎ 352/629-8051), has maps and general information, and visitor centers are located at three park entrances (daily 9am–5pm), offering details on every campground. The latest camping updates are available by phoning the camping areas at Juniper, Alexander and Salt springs (see p.305). For specialist hiking tips, call one of the district ranger offices – the northern and southern halves of the forest are administered respectively by the Lake George Ranger District, 17147 E Hwy-405, Silver Springs (☎ 352/625-2520), and the Seminole Ranger District, 40929 Route 19, Umatilla (☎ 352/669-3153).

name, the springs here flow with 52 million gallons of fresh water a day, and the steady 72°F temperature stimulates a semi-tropical landscape of vividly colored plants and palm trees. Swimming and canoeing are as good here as at the other two springs, but people come mainly for the **fishing**, casting off in anticipation of catfish, large-mouthed bass and speckled perch.

The Ocala Hiking Trail

The 67-mile **Ocala Hiking Trail** runs right through the forest, traversing many remote, swampy areas, and passing the three springs mentioned above. Very **basic campgrounds** appear at regular intervals (be warned that these are closed during the mid-November to early January hunting season). At the district rangers' offices (see the box above), pick up the excellent leaflet describing the trail, which is part of the Florida State Scenic Trail.

However keen you might be, you're unlikely to have the time or stamina to tackle the entire trail, though one exceptional area that merits the slog required

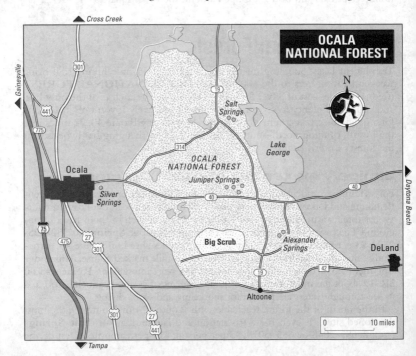

to get to it is **Big Scrub**, an imposingly severe landscape with sand dunes –
and sometimes wild deer – moving across its semi-arid acres. The biggest problem at Big Scrub is lack of shade from the scorching sun, and the fact that the
nearest facilities of any kind are miles away – don't come unprepared. Big
Scrub is in the southern part of the forest, seven miles along Forest Road 573,
off Route 19, twelve miles north of Altoona.

North of Ocala

From the monotonous I-75, you'd never guess that the thirty or so miles of
hilly, lakeside terrain just to the east contain some of the most distinctive and
insular villages in the state. Beyond the bounds of public transport, they can be
reached only by driving; head **north from Ocala** on Hwy-301.

Cross Creek and the Marjorie Kinnan Rawlings Home

Native Floridians often wax lyrical about Marjorie Kinnan Rawlings, author
of the international classic *The Yearling*, the Pulitzer Prize–winning tale of the
coming of age of a Florida farmer's son, and *Cross Creek*, which describes the
daily activities of country folk in **Cross Creek**, about twenty miles from Ocala
on Route 325 (off Hwy-301). Leaving her husband in New York, Rawlings
spent her most productive years writing and tending a citrus grove here during the 1930s – her experience being faithfully re-created in Martin Ritt's
1983 film, *Cross Creek*.

The restored **Marjorie Kinnan Rawlings Home** (Thurs–Sun 10–11am &
1–4pm; guided tours of up to ten people on the hour, with afternoon tours
often fully booked; $3, children $2; the grounds are open daily, free of charge,
9am–5pm; ☎352/466-3672) gives an eye-opening insight into the toughness
of the "cracker" lifestyle.

Micanopy, McIntosh and Paynes Prairie

Four miles north of Cross Creek, Route 346 branches off to meet Hwy-441
just outside **Micanopy**. A voguish vacation destination during the late 1800s,
Micanopy, named after a Seminole chief, has made an effort to win back
visitors by restoring many of its century-old brick buildings, and turning some
into antique and craft shops. The atmosphere is most evocative of the slowed-
down pace of the Old South, with its enormous live-oak trees and the Spanish
moss trailing down to the ground, and you may even be drawn to **stay**. Top
choice would certainly be the glorious Greek-revival *Herlong Mansion Bed &
Breakfast Inn*, 402 NE Cholokka Blvd (☎1-800/437-5664 or 352/466-3322,
ⓦwww.herlong.com; ❸), whose facade of Corinthian columns will make you
feel you've just come home to Tara. For great home cookin', try **lunch** on the
veranda of the *Old Florida Café*, right downtown (☎352/466-3663).

If you have time, you might want to travel a few miles south along Hwy-441 to
another village, **McIntosh**, whose 400-strong population dresses up every
October in Victorian costumes for the **1890 festival** to escort visitors around the
restored homes. There you'll find several antique stores and on the way, just four
miles south of Micanopy and two miles north of McIntosh, you can stop to check
out the Historic Harvest Village shops and its *Sisters 3 Café* (☎352/591-1191),
with its full range of international choices and great array of homemade desserts.

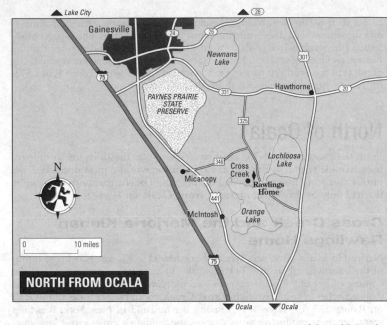

Lake City

Gainesville

Newnans
Lake

Hawthorne

PAYNES PRAIRIE
STATE
PRESERVE

Lochloosa
Lake

Cross
Creek
Micanopy

Rawlings
Home

McIntosh

Orange
Lake

N

0   10 miles

NORTH FROM OCALA

Ocala   Ocala

In contrast to the conviviality found in these quaint towns of the Old South, the marshy landscapes of the **Paynes Prairie State Preserve** (daily 8am–sunset; cars $3.25, cyclists and pedestrians $1), filling a broad sweep of land (18,000 acres) between Micanopy and Gainesville, can't help but strike a note of foreboding. It's an eerie place in many ways, though one well stocked with wildlife: cranes, hawks, waterfowl, otters, turtles and various wading birds all make homes here, as do many alligators. During weekends from October to March, **ranger-led hikes** (reservations ☎ 352/466-4100; free) uncover the fascinating natural history of the area – and some of the social history: habitations have been traced back to 10,000 BC. Without a guide, you can bone up on the background at the **visitor center** (daily 9am–5pm), four miles from Micanopy off Hwy-441, and peer into the moody wilderness from the nearby **observation tower**.

Gainesville and around

Without the University of Florida, **GAINESVILLE**, 35 miles north of Ocala, would be just another slow-paced rural community nodding off in the Florida heartland. As it is, the daintily sized place, once called Hogtown, is given a boost by its 40,000 students, who bring a lively, liberal spirit and account for the only decent **nightlife** in Central Florida outside Orlando. This, combined with a few low-key targets in and around the town, and reasonable accommodation, make Gainesville a deserving base for a day or two.

Accommodation

Although Gainesville has rows of low-cost **motels**, inconveniently located a couple of miles out of the center along Southwest Thirteenth Street, be warned that these fill quickly when the University of Florida Gators are playing at home. Gainesville also has two of the most pleasant **B&Bs** in the state. The closest tent-friendly **campground** is ten miles south at the Paynes Prairie State Preserve (see opposite; ℡352/466-3397).

Bambi, 2119 SW Thirteenth St (℡1-800/342-2624 or 352/376-2622). Slightly nearer to downtown than most of the inexpensive motels, this is an extremely rudimentary establishment. ❶
Comfort Inn, 2435 SW Thirteenth St (℡1-800/228-5150 or 352/373-6500). One of the better budget options, this inn has been recently refurbished. ❸
Econo Lodge, 2649 SW Thirteenth St (℡1-800/446-6900 or 352/373-7816). Reliable, though basic, chain motel. ❷
Gainesville Lodge, 413 W University Ave (℡1-800/637-1224 or 352/376-1224). Near downtown and the campus, so the most convenient location

of all the motels, but extremely spartan and uninviting. ❶
Magnolia Plantation B&B, 625 E University Ave (℡1-800/201-2379 or 352/375-6653, Ⓦwww.magnoliabnb.com). A romantic and dreamy historic mansion, with elegant yet cozy rooms decorated in a plush Victorian style, surrounded by lush gardens and waterfalls. ❹
Sweetwater Branch Inn B&B, 2649 SW Thirteenth St (℡1-800/595-7760 or 352/373-6760, Ⓦwww.sweetwaterinn.com). Spacious, beautifully laid out and convenient to everything the town has to offer, housed in two gracefully restored period homes. ❸

The town and university

Impressive sights are few in Gainesville's quiet center, where most of the people you'll see are office workers going to or from work or nipping out to lunch. At the junction of University Avenue and Northeast First Street you'll spot the **Clock Tower**, an undramatic relic culled from Gainesville's nineteenth-century courthouse. Inside are the clock workings and some photos from the old days. If these whet your historical appetite, explore northwards along Third Street, which reveals many of the showcase homes of turn-of-the-nineteenth-century Gainesville – Queen Anne, Colonial and various Revival styles dominate – and the palm-fronted **Thomas Center**, 306 NE Sixth Ave (Mon–Fri 9am–5pm, Sat & Sun 1–4pm; free), once a plush hotel and restaurant, which now hosts small-scale art and historical exhibitions.

The old buildings are easily tracked down with the *Historic Gainesville* brochure issued by the **Visitors and Convention Bureau**, at 30 E University Ave (Mon–Fri 8.30am–5pm; ℡352/374-5231, Ⓦwww.visitgainesville.net). From the town center, it's an easy fifteen-minute walk along University Avenue to the university; though if you're feeling very lazy, take a **bus** (any number from #1 to #10) from beside the Clock Tower. The Greyhound station is centrally placed, at 516 SW Fourth Ave (℡352/376-5252).

The University of Florida

Most of Gainesville's through traffic passes half a mile west of the town center along Thirteenth Street (part of Hwy-441), from which the **University of Florida (UF)** campus stretches three miles west from its main entrance by the junction with University Avenue. Call at the **information booth**, facing Southwest Second Street, for a free map, without which it's easy to get lost in the extensive grounds.

After it opened in 1906, the university's early alumni gave Florida's economy a leg-up by pioneering the state's fantastically successful citrus farms. These days, the curriculum is no longer devoted solely to agriculture and the university's modern buildings dominate the campus, though the first you'll see are the red-brick "Collegiate Gothic" structures favored by US turn-of-the-nineteenth-century academic institutions. In the center of the campus, the 1953 **Century Tower** serves as a navigational aid and a time-keeping device – its electric bells issue a nerve-shattering carillon every hour.

University sports venues

Beyond the tower, the 83,000-seat **Florida Field/Ben Hill Griffin Stadium**, nicknamed "The Swamp" – home of the Gators football team and a monument to the popularity of college sports in Florida – can hardly be missed, and neither can the adjacent **O'Connel Center** (☎352/392-5500), an indoor sports venue, entering which is akin to walking into a giant balloon. Aside from staging evening volleyball and basketball games, and entertaining design buffs, the building offers only a cool, refreshing breather.

University museums, gardens and cultural venues

For a quick respite from the sun, the temporary shows in the **University Gallery** (Mon–Sat 9am–5pm, Sun 1–5pm; free), inside the Fine Arts Building, capture the best student art. Head back outdoors and walk about a mile west along Museum Road to the tidy **University Garden**, where a concealed footpath leads to **Lake Alice**, overlooked by a wooden observation platform gradually losing its battle against the surrounding vegetation. You could come here for a picnic, but the roar of insects, the constant scampering of lizards and the knowledge that alligators are plentiful, means keeping your guard up as you gaze over the sizeable lake.

At the corner of Southwest 34th Street and Hull Road is the **University of Florida Cultural Complex**, where the **Florida Museum of Natural History** (Mon–Sat 10am–5pm, Sun 1–5pm; free; ☎352/846-2967, ⓦwww.flmnh.ufl.edu) focuses on Florida's prehistory and wildlife. The **Harn Museum of Art** (Tues–Fri 11am–5pm, Sat 10am–5pm, Sun 1–5pm; free) has an intriguing permanent collection with an emphasis on ethnic works and hosts about twelve temporary exhibitions per year. The nearby **Center for the Performing Arts**, 315 Hull Rd (☎1-800/905-2787 or 352/392-2787 for ticket information, ⓦwww.cpa.ufl.edu), brings in traveling Broadway plays, symphonies, popular music, family entertainment and educational programs.

Eating

Gainesville is not a difficult place in which to find a good **meal**, with plenty of restaurants around the town center and the university.

Cameo Tea Room, 230 NW Second Ave (☎352/379-5889, ⓦwww.cameotearoom.com). Experience the gentility and good eatin' of the Old South in these appealingly decorated rooms, where the artichoke and feta quiche or the chilled salmon with cucumber dill dressing will run about $10 for lunch.

Harry's Seafood Bar and Grill, 110 SE First St (☎352/372-1555). A sidewalk café serving New Orleans-style seafood, pasta, chicken, burgers and salads.

Leonardo's 706, 706 W University Ave (☎352/378-2001). California pizzas and lots of seafood offerings, and don't miss the made-to-order mid-priced Sunday brunch whose unusual items include French toast made from homemade

challah bread, filet mignon with eggs and hollandaise sauce.

Porter's, 1 W University Ave (☎352/372-0101). Classic steakhouse, ribs and seafood kind of establishment, which also features a champagne mimosa Sunday brunch.

The Top, 30 N Main St (☎352/337-1188). Young, arty and hip – a good choice if all you want is a pleasant spot to refuel on salads or sandwiches for about $5.

The Wine and Cheese Gallery, 113 N Main St (☎352/372-8446). An amazing selection of international wines and cheeses and all the fresh breads, hors d'oeuvres, crudités and pastries to go with them, in a warm, inviting setting. Prices range from $5 to $15.

Drinking and nightlife

The town's students keep a bright **nightlife** in motion, live rock music being especially easy to find. Check the "Scene" section of Friday's *Gainesville Sun*, or the free *Moon* magazine, found in most bars and restaurants, for details. You also may find some of the restaurants listed above suitable for a drink or two.

Lillian's Music Store, 112 SE First St (☏ 352/372-1010). A Gainesville institution, featuring live bands that play grunge, indie, Southern and acoustic rock, and a 2–8pm Happy Hour.

Lush, 6 E University Ave (☏ 352/381-9044). The hippest of Gainesville's clubs. Comics and acoustic acts early in the week, and house, acid, techno and classic disco grooves Thursday–

Sunday. Friday night is gay night.

Market Street Pub, 120 SW First St (☏ 352/377-2927). Brews its own beer and provides jazz, blues and rock to help it down.

The University Club, 18 E University Ave (☏ 352/378-6814, ⓦ www.ucclub.com). Downtown's no. 1 gay venue, three levels – a bar, club and disco – always crowded and lively, with a deck out back.

Kanapaha Botanical Gardens

Flower fanciers shouldn't miss the 62-acre **Kanapaha Botanical Gardens** (Mon, Tues & Fri 9am–5pm, Wed, Sat & Sun 9am–sunset; $3, children 6-13 $2, ☏ 352/372-4981), five miles southwest of central Gainesville on Route 24, reachable on bus #1. More than most, the summer months are a riot of color and fragrances, although the design of the gardens means there's always something in bloom. Besides vines and bamboos, and special sections planted to attract butterflies and hummingbirds, the highlight is the herb garden, whose aromatic bed is raised to nose-level to encourage sniffing.

The Fred Bear Museum

Across the road from the gardens, a signpost points to the **Fred Bear Museum** (daily 10am–6pm; $5, children 6–12 $3; ☏ 352/376-2411), a mass of mounted, skinned and stuffed animals, and some (such as the elephant's-ear table with hippo legs) turned into furniture. Many of the unfortunate creatures were caught and killed by Fred Bear himself, who runs the adjoining archery factory. Note: not a place for animal lovers.

The Devil's Millhopper

Of thousands of sinkholes in Florida, few are bigger or more spectacular than the **Devil's Millhopper**, set in a state geological site (daily 9am–5pm; cars $2, pedestrians and cyclists $1; free guided tour Sat 10am; ☏ 352/955-2008), seven miles northwest of Gainesville, at 4732 NW 53rd Ave. Formed by the gradual erosion of limestone deposits and the collapse of the resultant cavern's ceiling, the lower reaches of this 120-foot-deep bowl-shaped dent have a temperature significantly cooler than the surface, allowing species of alpine plant and animal life to thrive. A winding boardwalk delivers you into the thickly vegetated depths, where dozens of tiny waterfalls trickle all around you.

North of Gainesville

Traveling **north of Gainesville** puts you in easy striking distance of the Panhandle to the west, and Jacksonville, the major city of the Northeast Coast, but it's best not to be in a hurry. Choose to stop a night or two here and you'll

The area code for this part of North Central Florida is ☏ 904.

find yourself smack in the heart of some of the most pristine natural springs in the state – as well as some of the most charming, out-of-the-way towns of the Florida of yesteryear.

Alachua, High Springs and the Parks

Continuing about twelve miles north of Gainesville on Hwy-441, the town of **Alachua** is worth a stop for **lunch** and a bit of window-shopping. The restored old part of downtown has a broad selection of browsable shops, and *Govinda's*, 14603 Main St (℡904/462-4500) is a superb restaurant in a finely restored, enormous old home, run by the local Hare Krishna group, who do amazing things with vegetables.

Sticking to Hwy-441 for another six miles puts you in **High Springs** (Chamber of Commerce ℡904/454-3120), voted by the readers of *Florida Living* magazine Florida's friendliest small town and the state's best for antiquing. If you decide to experience it for yourself, top choice for a few nights' **stay** is the *Grady House*, 420 NW First Ave (℡904/454-2206, ⓦwww.gradyhouse.com; ❸), where the guys who own it have poured their hearts into creating one of the most attractive gazebo gardens of any B&B anywhere. Stroll around downtown, only a block away, and enjoy great **food** at the *Great Outdoors Trading Company & Café*, 65 N Main St (℡904/454-2900); the hot artichoke dip with raw veggies and chips is sensational. For less expensive accommodation, there's *The High Springs Country Inn*, along Hwy-441, 520 NW Santa Fe Blvd (℡904/454-1565; ❷), where the themed rooms all have kitchenettes. Enjoy diner food at the nearby *Alice's Parkside Restaurant*, 215 NW Santa Fe Blvd (℡904/454-1166), knockout 'rise 'n' shine' breakfasts a speciality.

The High Springs area is replete with crystal-clear sources: **Poe Springs** (9am–sunset; $4, children 6–13, $3; ℡904/454-1992), **Blue Springs** (9am–7pm; $6, children 5-14, $2; camping $10, children 5-14, $4; ℡904/454-1369) and **Ginnie Springs** ($8, children 7–14, $3; camping $14, children 7–14, $6; cottage $125 per night for two adults ℡1-800/874-8571 or 904/454-2202, ⓦwww.ginniesprings.com) just to the west along County Road 340. **O'Leno State Park** (8am–sunset; cars $4, pedestrians and cyclists $1; ℡904/454-1853) and **Ichetucknee Springs State Park** (daily 8am–sunset; cars $4.25, pedestrians and cyclists $1, ℡904/497-2511) to the north and northwest, off Hwy 441. All of these parks, both state and private, are endowed with springs, streams and rivers, waters that lend themselves to leisurely kayaking, canoeing or inner-tube rafting. **Canoes** can be rented in most of the parks for $15-25 a day. Weekdays, when beavers, otters and turtles sometimes share the river, are the best time to come to the area; weekend crowds scare much of the wildlife away. Ginnie and Ichetucknee springs both also offer the possibility of cave diving, using scuba equipment to explore the mysterious, labyrinthine domain of the underground rivers; at Ginnie Springs the cost is $25 a day for non-certified divers, plus the cost of renting whatever equipment you may need.-

There's no point in stopping in the unremarkable **Lake City**, thirteen miles north of the springs, nor in the **Osceola National Forest**, to the east of Lake City. This smallest of the state's three federally protected forests is mostly visited by hardened fishermen bound for its Ocean Pond, and you should aim instead for a couple of more fulfilling attractions in the near vicinity.

The Stephen Foster State Culture Center

Twelve miles north of Lake City, off Hwy-41, the **Stephen Foster State Culture Center** (daily 8am–sunset; cars $4, pedestrians and cyclists $1; ℡904/397-2733, ⓦwww.stepehnfostercenter.com) offers a tribute to the man who composed Florida's state song, *The Old Folks At Home*, immortalizing the waterway ("Way down upon the S'wanee river. . .") that flows by here on its 250-mile meander from Georgia's Okefenokee Swamp to the Gulf of Mexico. As it happens, Foster never actually saw the river but simply used "S'wanee" as a convenient Deep South–sounding allusion. Besides exploring Florida's musical roots, the center has a sentimental display about Foster, who penned a hatful of classic American songs including *Camptown Races, My Old Kentucky Home,* and *Oh! Susanna* – instantly familiar melodies, which ring out through the oak-filled park from a bell tower. Foster died in New York in 1863, at the age of 37.

The Olustee Battlefield Site

The **Olustee Battlefield Site**, thirteen miles west of Lake City beside Hwy-90 (daily 8am–sunset; free; ☎904/752-3866), is a sure sign you're approaching the Panhandle, a Confederate power base during the Civil War. The only major battle of the conflict in Florida took place here in February 1864, when 5000 Union troops pressing west from Jacksonville squared up to a similar-sized Confederate force. The five-hour battle, which left three hundred dead, nearly two thousand wounded and both sides claiming victory, is marked by a monument and a small interpretive center at the entrance (Thurs–Mon 9am–5pm), and by a trail around the respective troop positions. It's hard to imagine the carnage that took place in what is now – as it was then – a peaceful pine forest.

TRAVEL DETAILS

Trains (AMTRAK ☎1-800/872-7245)
Orlando to: DeLand (2 daily; 58min); Jacksonville (2 daily; 3hr 15min); Kissimmee (2 daily; 25min); Sanford (2 daily; 45min); Tampa (3–4 daily; 2hr 30min); Winter Park (2 daily; 18min).
Winter Haven to: Fort Lauderdale (3 daily; 3hr 30min); Miami (3 daily; 4hr 30min); Sebring (3 daily; 40min); West Palm Beach (3 daily; 2hr 30min).

Buses (GREYHOUND ☎1-800/231-2222)
Clewiston to: Belle Glade (1 daily; 25min); West Palm Beach (1 daily; 1hr 30min).
Lakeland to: Avon Park (1 daily; 2hr 30min);

Cypress Gardens (1 daily; 55min); Lake Wales (1 daily; 1hr 15min); Sebring (1 daily; 2hr 45min); West Palm Beach (6 daily; 5hr); Winter Haven (4 daily; 30min).
Orlando to: Daytona Beach (6 daily; 1–2 hrs); DeLand (4 daily; 1hr); Fort Lauderdale (9 daily; 5–7 hrs); Fort Pierce (7 daily; 2–6 hrs); Gainesville (8 daily; 2–6 hrs); Jacksonville (8 daily; 2–3 hrs); Lakeland (6 daily; 1–2 hrs); Kissimmee (6 daily; 40min); Miami (8 daily; 5–7 hrs); Ocala (7 daily; 1–2 hrs); Sanford (3 daily; 30min); Tallahassee (9 daily; 5–8 hrs); Tampa (6 daily; 2–3 hrs); West Palm Beach (8 daily; 4hr); Winter Haven (6 daily; 1hr 30min).

The West Coast

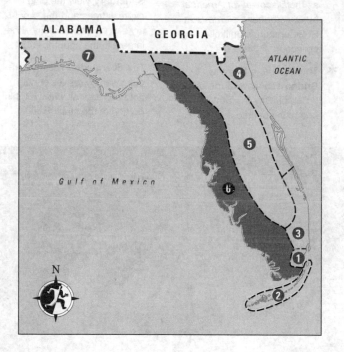

CHAPTER 6

Highlights

* **Ybor City** This neighborhood is ground zero for Tampa Bay's most exciting nightlife and dining; sample the Cuban music and flamenco dancing at *The Columbia*. **P.326**

* **The Salvador Dalí Museum** View Dalí masterpieces such as the *Discovery of America by Christopher Columbus* at St Petersburg's unlikeliest art collection. **P.338**

* **The Sunshine Skyway Bridge** The view of the ships in Tampa Bay from this bridge is spectacular. **P.357**

* **Cà d'Zan** Tour the Venetian-style mansion at the Ringling Museum Complex outside Sarasota. **P.364**

* **Sanibel Island** The shelling on this island is among the best in Florida. **P.376**

* **Corkscrew Swamp Sanctuary** View the bald cypress trees and the sanctuary's wood stork colony – the largest in the country. **P.380**

* **The Everglades** The mysterious swampy groves should hold allure for all who visit this portion of the state. **P.383**

6

The West Coast

S tretching three hundred miles from the state's southern tip to the border of the Panhandle, Florida's **WEST COAST** embraces a wide range of attractions, with buzzing, youthful towns abutting placid fishing hamlets, and mobbed holiday strips lying just minutes from desolate swamplands. Surprises are plentiful. Search for a snack bar and you'll stumble across a world-class art collection; doze off on an empty beach and you'll wake to find it packed with shell collectors. The West Coast's only constants are the Gulf of Mexico and sunset views rivaled only by those of the Florida Keys.

Served by an international airport and situated at the end of Interstate 4 from Central Florida, the diversely populated Tampa Bay area, midway along the coast, is the natural first stop. The West Coast's largest city, Tampa itself probably won't detain you long, though it has more to offer than its power-dressers and corporate towers suggest. Ybor City, for example, is Tampa's − and the entire coast's − hippest and most culturally eclectic quarter.

Directly across the bay, **St Petersburg** once took pride in being the archetypal Florida retirement community. In the past ten years, it has been recast in a younger mold and is riding high on its acquisition of a major collection of works by the surrealist Salvador Dalí. For most visitors, though, the Tampa Bay area begins and ends with the **St Petersburg beaches**, miles of sea, sun and sand fringed by uninspired vacation developments. The beaches are undiluted vacation territory, but are also a good base for exploring the Greek-dominated community of **Tarpon Springs**, just to the north.

The coast **north of Tampa** (known as the **Big Bend** for the way it curves toward the Panhandle) is consumed by flat, beachless marshes, large chunks of which are wildlife refuges with little public access. No settlement here boasts a population of more than a few thousand, and the area receives little attention from visitors bolting through on their way to the beach territories further south. It is, however, one of Florida's hidden treasures. Scattered throughout is

Accommodation price codes

All accommodation prices in this book have been coded using the symbols below. Note that prices are for the least expensive double rooms in each establishment. For a full explanation see p.29 in Basics.

❶ up to $40	❸ $60–80	❺ $100–130	❼ $175–250
❷ $40–60	❹ $80–100	❻ $130–175	❽ $250+

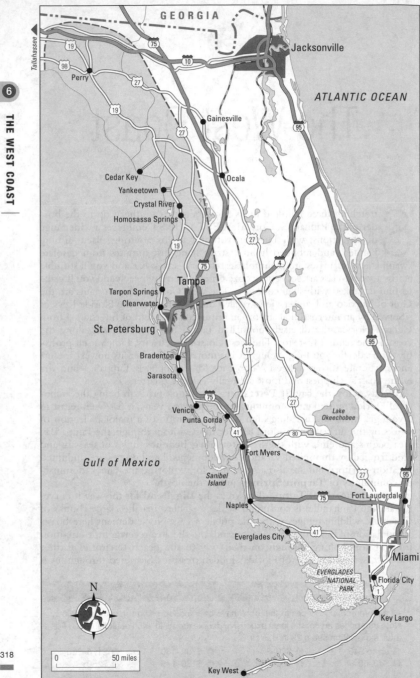

GEORGIA

Tallahassee

19

98

Perry

19

Jacksonville

ATLANTIC OCEAN

75

10

27

Gainesville

95

Cedar Key

Yankeetown

Crystal River

Homosassa Springs

19

Ocala

27

75

4

Tarpon Springs

Tampa

Clearwater

St. Petersburg

95

Bradenton

17

Sarasota

75

Venice

Punta Gorda

41

Lake
Okeechobee

27

Gulf of Mexico

80

Fort Myers

Sanibel
Island

27

95

Fort Lauderdale

Naples

75

Everglades City

41

Miami

EVERGLADES
NATIONAL
PARK

Florida City

1

Key Largo

N

0   50 miles

Key West

evidence of much busier and prosperous times, like the prehistoric sun-worshipping site at **Crystal River. Cedar Key**, which was a thriving port over a century ago, is now the perfect retreat. Locals here have preserved a laid-back way of life and the community is a time-warped enclave of excellent eating and rewarding sights. The wildlife park at **Homossasa Springs**, fifteen miles south of Crystal River, offers the chance to view some of Florida's beautiful, yet endangered animals.

A string of barrier-island beaches runs the length of the gulf **south of Tampa**. And while it may be the beaches that draw the crowds, the mainland towns that provide access to them have a lot in their favor as well. The first of any consequential size is **Sarasota**, the custodian of an arts legacy passed down at the turn of the nineteenth century by John Ringling, the circus entrepreneur. Further south, Thomas Edison was one of a number of scientific pioneers who took a fancy to palm-studded **Fort Myers**, which neighbors two atmospheric islands – **Sanibel** and **Captiva**. As you reach the end of the southwest coast and pass over the tropic of Cancer, take the opportunity to strike inland and explore the national parks that form the **Everglades**, the largest subtropical wilderness in America. Here you will discover vast expanses of swamps, prairies, mangrove islands and sawgrass marshes, all brimming with wildlife. Most can be explored by walking trails or canoe. If you feel adventurous, try spending a night at one of the backcountry campgrounds with only alligators for company.

The West Coast is easy to **get around**. The region's **major roads** and **I-4** from Central Florida all converge close to Tampa. From Tampa through the Big Bend, **Hwy-19** is the only route, served by two Greyhound **buses** daily in each direction. **Hwy-41** connects the main southwest coastal settlements and is often known as the **Tamiami Trail**, a nickname incorporating Tampa and Miami, from its time as the only road link crossing the Everglades between the two cities. These days, the bland **I-75** is a faster alternative to the trail. Greyhound services number five daily each way through the southwest coast and a few towns are also connected by Amtrak buses from Tampa. The bigger centers have adequate **public transport**, though the barrier islands and Big Bend towns do not. Visitors arriving from Key West can arrive at Marco Island and Naples by ferry (see p.382).

The Tampa Bay area

The geographic and economic nerve center of the region, with a population greater than Miami's, the **Tampa Bay area**, consisting of Tampa and St Petersburg, is easily the busiest and most congested part of the West Coast. But people do live here for reasons other than work. The wide waters of the bay provide a scenic backdrop for Tampa itself, which is a stimulating city. And the barrier-island beaches along the coast let the locals swap metropolitan bustle for luscious sunsets and miles of glistening sands. With sun, sand and sea, however, comes the inevitable span of chain restaurants and accommodations for the touring masses.

The area code for the Tampa Bay and Ybor City areas is ☎813; St Petersburg, Clearwater, Gulfport and Tarpon Springs have a ☎727 area code.

Tampa

TAMPA is a small city with an infectious, upbeat mood. You'll only need a day or two to explore it thoroughly, but you'll depart with a lasting impression of a city on the rise. The West Coast's undisputed business hub, it has been one of the major beneficiaries of the flood of people and money into Florida. Yet despite cultural and artistic offerings envied by many larger communities and an international airport in its back yard, Tampa rarely gets more than a passing glance. Tourists speed through to Busch Gardens, a theme park on the city's outskirts, and the Gulf Coast beaches half an hour's drive west – missing out totally on one of Florida's most youthful and energetic urban communities.

Tampa began as a small settlement beside Fort Brooke (a US Army base built to keep an eye on local Seminole Indians during the 1820s), and remained tiny, isolated and insignificant until the 1880s, when the railway arrived and the Hillsborough River – on which the city stands – was dredged to allow sea-going vessels to dock. It became a booming port and simultaneously acquired a major tobacco industry as thousands of Cubans moved north in 1886 from Key West to the new cigar factories of neighboring Ybor City. Although the Depression stalled the economic surge, the port remained one of the busiest in

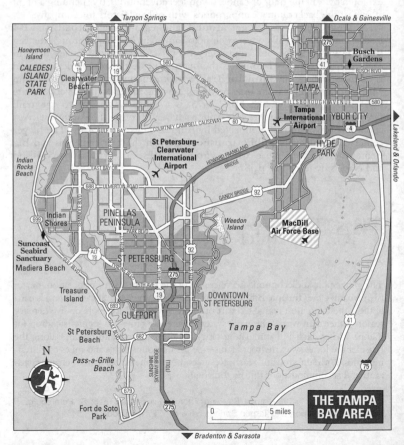

▲ Tarpon Springs   ▲ Ocala & Gainesville

THE TAMPA BAY AREA

0   5 miles

▼ Bradenton & Sarasota

the country. And while the social problems that blight any decent-sized US city are evident, Tampa continues to emerge as a forward-thinking, financially secure community.

Regardless of the deals being struck in its towering office blocks, which are surprisingly thoughtfully designed, **downtown Tampa** is quiet and compact. An art museum, a sensational Spanish Revival film house and the *Tampa Bay Hotel* – one of the few reminders of earlier times – form the basis for a half-day ramble. What downtown may lack in atmosphere and history is made up for three miles northeast in the **Ybor City** quarter, whose Latin American character derives from migrant cigar workers. Ybor now boasts a plethora of historical markers to the heady days of the struggle for Cuban independence.

Venture a mile south of downtown into **Hyde Park**, and you will find the homes of Tampa's wealthiest early settlers. **Busch Gardens** and the **Museum of Science and Industry** are also worth a stop, or you could just amble into the wilds of the open country that appears remarkably quickly just north of the busy city.

Arrival, information and getting around

The city's international **airport** (☏813/870-8700, ⓦwww.TampaAirport .com) is five miles northwest of downtown Tampa. Local bus #30 is the least costly connection ($1.15) to downtown Tampa, or use the around-the-clock Limo Inc vans (☏813/572-1111 or 1-800/282-6817, ⓦwww.supershuttle .com), whose representatives have desks outside, at either end of the baggage claim area. They also cover St Petersburg, Clearwater and the beaches. The flat fare is $15 per person, or $28 for a round-trip ticket.

If you arrive **by car** from St Petersburg, the main route into Tampa is I-275, which crosses Old Tampa Bay and ends up in the west of downtown. From east or central Florida, you'll come in on the I-4, which intersects with I-75. Be advised that from I-75, it's essential to exit at Hwy-60 (signposted Kennedy Boulevard) for downtown Tampa. There are seven less convenient exits and if you miss this one and end up in north Tampa, the city's fiendish one-way system will keep you in your car for hours.

Taxis – the main firms are United (☏813/253-2424) and Yellow (☏813/253-0121) and they are abundant but expensive. The fare to downtown Tampa or a Busch Boulevard motel is $13–24; to St Petersburg or the St Petersburg beaches, $30–45. All the major **car rental** companies have desks at the airport.

Long-distance public transport terminates in downtown Tampa: Greyhound **buses** at 610 Polk St (☏813/229-2174 or 1-800/231-????) and **trains** at 601 N Nebraska Ave (☏813/221-7600 or 1-800/872-7245).

Information

In downtown Tampa, collect vouchers, leaflets and general information at the **Visitors Information Center**, 400 N Tampa St, Suite 1010 (Mon–Sat 9am–5pm; ☏1-800/44-TAMPA or 813/223-2752, Ⓕ229-6616, ⓦwww .tampa.com). In Ybor City, visit the **Ybor City Chamber of Commerce**, 1800 E Ninth Ave (Mon–Fri 9am–5pm; ☏813/248-3712, ⓦwww.ybor.org). Opposite Busch Gardens, the **Tampa Bay Visitor Information Center**, 3601 E Busch Blvd (daily 10am–6pm; ☏813/985-3601), has local and state-wide information. For **nightlife** listings, try the Friday edition of the *Tampa Tribune*, the free *Weekly Planet*, or call the free Nightlife phone service at ☏813/854-8000.

Getting around

Although downtown Tampa and Ybor City are easily covered on foot, to travel between them – or to reach Busch Gardens or the Museum of Science and Industry – without a car, you'll need to use **local buses** (HARTline ☎813/254-4278, 🌐www.Hartline.org), whose routes fan out from Marion Street in downtown Tampa. **Useful bus numbers** are the #8 to Ybor City; #5, #18 or #39 to Busch Gardens; #6 to the Museum of Science and Industry; and #30 to the airport. Starting in 2002, a free **Uptown–Downtown Connector** trolley service is scheduled to run Monday to Friday 6am–6pm; check at the Visitor Information Center (see above) for more details. Rush-hour commuter (express) buses run **between Tampa and the coast**: #100X to St Petersburg (for schedule information for this bus only, call ☎813/530-9911) and #200X to Clearwater. Alternatives are the numerous daily Greyhound buses or the twice-daily Amtrak bus. Another way to travel between downtown Tampa and Ybor City is on the **Tampa-Ybor Trolley** (☎813/254-4278), which runs daily 7.30am–5.30pm, several times an hour. The route takes you via Harbor Island and the Florida Aquarium (see p.324), and costs 50¢ one way.

Accommodation

Except for the area around Busch Gardens, Tampa is not generously supplied with low-cost **accommodation**. Within Tampa, the cheaper **motels** are all on East Busch Boulevard close to Busch Gardens. Other than the site at the Hillsborough River State Park (see "Around Tampa," p.330), the only local **campground** where tents are welcome is the *Camp Nebraska RV Park*, 10314 N Nebraska Ave/Hwy-41 (☎ 813/971-3460 or 1-800/998-6025), which lies a mile and a half north of Busch Gardens.

Hotels, motels and inns

Best Western Resort, 820 E Busch Boulevard (☎ 813/933-4011). This chain serves as a reasonable base for seeing the city by car. It's so close to Busch Gardens that the parrots escape into their trees. Features a Happy Hour every afternoon and free breakfast each morning. ❹ –❺

Days Inn, 2522 N Dale Mabry Hwy (☎ 1-800/448-4373). This chain is ten minutes' walk from downtown and provides a shuttle bus to the airport. Features two pools, one with a waterfall, and a tropical fish garden. ❸ –❺

Days Inn Busch Gardens, 2901 E Busch Blvd (☎ 813/933-6471). The closest hotel to Busch Gardens, it has a 24-hour restaurant and is within walking distance of plenty of others. ❸ –❹

Don Vincente de Ybor Historic Inn, 1915 Avenida Republica de Cuba (☎ 813/241-4545, 🌐 www

.donvincente.com). The most luxurious B&B option in Ybor City, it features sixteen one-bedroom suites, a fine restaurant and a cigar and martini bar that features live entertainment most nights. ❻

Gram's Place, 3109 North Ola Ave (☎ 813/221-0596, 🌐 www.grams-inn-tampa.com). Named after music legend Gram Parsons, this inn has a relaxed, laid-back atmosphere and both private rooms, themed in different musical styles (complete with music to match the room), and youth-hostel-style accommodation in a simulated train carriage. With a recording studio in the basement and the strains of jazz, blues, folk, country and rock and roll everywhere, it's a music lovers' paradise. ❶ –❹

Riverside, 200 N Ashley Drive (☎ 813/223-2222). If you're dependent on public transport, this downtown business-traveler-oriented hotel is highly convenient. ❹ –❻

Downtown Tampa

Downtown Tampa's prosperity is demonstrated by its office towers, especially at **Lykes Gaslight Square**, where massive, mirrored structures jut into the sky. But, aside from the riverside warehouses in various states of dilapidation around the northern end of pedestrian-friendly **Franklin Street** (once a pulsating main drag and still the best place to get your bearings), any hint of the city's past is left largely to text-bearing plaques that detail everything from the passage of sixteenth-century explorer Hernando De Soto to the site of Florida's first radio station. The single substantial relic of the past is the **Tampa Theatre**, 711 Franklin St (Mon–Sat 10.30am–5.30pm; ☎813/274–9981, ⓦwww.tampatheatre.org), one of the few surviving "atmospheric theaters" erected by designer John Eberson during the Twenties. When silent movies enthralled the masses, Eberson's movie houses heightened the escapist mood: ceilings became star-filled skies, balconies were chiseled to resemble Moorish arches, gargoyles leered from stuccoed walls, and replica Greek and Roman statuary filled every nook and cranny. Having fallen on hard times with the arrival of TV, the Tampa Theatre is now enjoying a new lease on life as the home of the Tampa Theatre Film Society and boasts a full program of movies. Paying $6.25 for a ticket (see "Nightlife," p.332) is one way to gain access to the splendidly restored interior. Another is the "Balcony to Backstage" guided tours ($5), which are highly entertaining but are held only twice a month (call theater for dates and times). In addition to the theater's magnificent lighting system that cultivates the feel of an open auditorium at night, a Wurlitzer organ rises from the orchestra pit fifteen minutes before each screening to serenade the crowd.

Tampa Museum of Art

None of the contemporary buildings in downtown Tampa better reflects the city's striving for cultural recognition than the **Tampa Museum of Art**, on the

▲ Busch Gardens and Museum of Science & Industry

RESTAURANTS, CAFÉS & BARS

Baker's Billiards	G
Bernini	E
Café Cohiba	C
Café Firenze	J
Castillo's Café	H
Cephas	I
Columbia Restaurant	F
Don Vicente de Ybor Historic Inn	A
Gladstone's Grilled Chicken	L
Jazz Cellar	B
Joffrey's Coffee Company	D
Manhattan Bagel Bar	K

DOWNTOWN TAMPA & YBOR CITY

▼ Harbor Island

banks of the Hillsborough River at 600 N Ashley Drive (Tues, Wed, Fri & Sat 10am–5pm, Thurs 10am–8pm, Sun 1–5pm; guided tours Wed & Sat 1pm, Sun 2pm; ☎ 813/274-8130, www.ci.tampa.fl.us/dept_Museum). The highly regarded museum specializes in an incongruous mix of classical antiquities and twentieth-century American art. Selections from the permanent modern stock are cleverly blended with loaned pieces from the cream of contemporary US painting, photography and sculpture. A third gallery is devoted to major traveling exhibitions. The sculpture gallery, which houses a collection of not-so-thrilling contemporary pieces, affords lovely views of the *Tampa Bay Hotel* across the river. On the second Saturday of each month, the museum also runs **guided walking tours** of downtown Tampa departing from the entrance of the museum at 10am. For more information call ☎ 813/274-8130.

Harbor Island and the Aquarium

Continuing south, you'll feel like an insignificant speck at the feet of the city's tallest structures. For a better view of them – and their surroundings – take the short monorail ride (from the terminal on top of the Fort Brooke Parking Garage on Whiting Street; 50¢ each way) to **Harbor Island**, a large shopping mall on a small island dredged from the Hillsborough Bay. If strapped for time, walk through the concrete walkway of the Nations Bank Plaza and take the elevator to the 31st floor – the view is an exquisite vista of the whole city.

The **Florida Aquarium**, 701 Channelside Drive (daily 9.30am–5pm; $13.75; audio wands an extra $2; parking $4; ☎ 813/273-4000 or 1-800/353-4741, ⓦ www.flaquarium.com) houses lavish displays of Florida's fresh- and salt-water habitats, ranging from springs and swamps to beaches and coral reefs. The permanent residents include an impressive variety of exotic fish and native creatures like otters, turtles, baby alligators and countless species of bird.

Northeast from downtown Tampa

Far from the glamorous skyscrapers, the northeast section of the city has an unsafe reputation. If you're heading to Ybor City (see p.326) on foot, this rather desolate area is on the route, and though there isn't much reason to linger in this part of town, it's worth a detour to **Oaklawn Cemetery**, on the junction of Morgan and Harrison streets, just north of downtown, which was set aside to bury the town's dead ("whites and slaves alike") in 1850. Along with the bones of one Florida governor and two Supreme Court judges, the picturesque graveyard guards the remains of soldiers from the Second Seminole War, the Mexican War, the Billy Bowlegs Indian War, the Civil War, the Spanish American War and both World Wars. Hidden away at the far end of the cemetery, in the shadow of the faceless Morgan Street Penitentiary, is the tomb of the **Ybor family** – whose name lives on in Tampa's most exotic quarter, Ybor City.

The only other attractions back in downtown that might warrant a look are two churches. Built in 1898, **Sacred Heart Catholic Church**, at 509 Florida Ave (☎ 813/229-1595), has a gleaming facade of mottled marble and a rich interior illuminated by stained glass. **St Paul African Methodist Church**, at 1100 Marion St, just a few minutes' walk north, cannot match Sacred Heart's grandeur, but its Victorian-style red-brick and vivid stained glass are worth a visit.

Across the river: the Tampa Bay Hotel

From Harbor Island you can't miss the silver minarets, cupolas and domes of the main building of the University of Tampa – formerly the **Tampa Bay Hotel**. A fusion of Moorish, Turkish and Spanish building styles and financed

6

to the tune of $2 million by steamship and railway magnate **Henry B. Plant**, the structure is as bizarre a sight today as it was on its opening in 1891, when its 500 rooms looked out on a community of just 700 people. For a good look, walk across the river on Kennedy Boulevard and climb down the steps leading into Plant Park.

Plant had been buying up bankrupt railways since the Civil War and steadily inching his way into Florida to meet his steamships unloading at Tampa Harbor. Like Henry Flagler, whose tracks were forging a trail along Florida's east coast and whose upscale resorts in St Augustine (see "The Northeast Coast") were the talk of US socialites, Plant was wealthy enough to realize his fantasy of creating the world's most luxurious hotel. While the hotel boosted the prestige of the town, Plant's intention of "turning this sandheap into the Champs Elysées, the Hillsborough into the Seine" was never accomplished, and the hotel stayed open for less than ten years. Neglect (the hotel was only used during the winter months and left to fester during the scorching summer), and Plant's death in 1899, hastened its transformation from the last word in comfort to a pile of musty, crumbling plaster. The city authorities bought the place in 1905 and halted the rot, before leasing the building to the fledgling University of Tampa 23 years later.

In a wing of the main building, the **Henry B. Plant Museum**, 401 W Kennedy Blvd (Tues–Sat 10am–4pm, Sun noon–4pm; $5; ☏813/254-1891, Ⓦwww.plantmuseum.com), has several rooms, including an original suite containing what's left of the hotel's furnishings. This is a gorgeous clutter of Venetian mirrors, elaborate candelabras, ankle-deep rugs, Wedgwood crockery and intricate teak cabinets – all the fruits of a half-million-dollar shopping expedition undertaken by Plant and his wife across Europe and Asia. Incredibly, when the hotel was closed up for five years, it was left unlocked and many of the antiques disappeared.

The hotel was Florida's first electric building, and low-wattage Edison carbon filters are used today to ensure the original, authentic gloom, which is perfect for taking in the richness of the Cuban mahogany doors. You can almost imagine guests calling room service for a grand piano (there were twelve). Note the reassembled *Rathskellar*, a gentleman's social room previously in the hotel basement (now a student snack bar), complete with a German wine cooler and billiard tables. The final room reveals Mrs Plant's affection for oversized ornamental swans.

A few strides from the museum, the former lobby is a popular rendezvous point for the university's three thousand students, who display their tans from the hotel's overstuffed leather chairs surrounded by antique French statuary. You can roam around much of the building at will and a self guided tour brochure is available to help the details of the building and its history fall into place. Make sure you see the evocative photographs of society life from the hotel's heyday in the long corridors. As for the furniture, though, there's precious little left – what human looters left behind, the termites finished off.

Hyde Park

If they don't ensconce themselves in bay-view condos, Tampa's yuppies snap up the old wooden homes of **Hyde Park**, a mile southwest of downtown Tampa just off Bayshore Boulevard. Attracted by the glamour of the *Tampa Bay Hotel*, well-heeled arrivals in the 1890s duplicated the architectural mold that defined the wealthier sections of the turn-of-the-century's American towns: a mishmash of Mediterranean, Gothic, Tudor and Colonial revival jobs, interspersed with Queen Anne cottages and prairie-style bungalows – rocking-chair-equipped porches being the sole unifying feature. Such complete "blasts from the past" are rare in Tampa and, provided you're driving (they don't justify a slog around on foot), the old homes are easy to appreciate on a twenty-minute drive on and around Swann and Magnolia avenues and Hyde Park and South boulevards. Even Tampans who prefer modern living quarters descend on Hyde Park to lay waste to their wages in the fashionable stores of **Olde Hyde Park Village**, beside Snow Avenue, where several classy restaurants offer affordable refreshment (see "Eating," p.330). "Tow Away Zone" signs pepper Hyde Park, so if you want to browse or lunch here, go to the free parking garage right in the village at the corner of Bristol Avenue and South Rome Avenue.

Continuing south from Hyde Park, incidentally, brings you to the gates of **Mac Dill Air Force Base**. The nerve center of US operations during the 1991 Gulf War; this was where the Queen of England knighted General "Stormin' Norman" Schwarzkopf later the same year.

Ybor City

In 1886, as soon as Henry Plant's ships (see p.325) ensured a regular supply of Havana tobacco into Tampa, cigar magnate Don Vincente Martínez Ybor cleared a patch of scrubland three miles northeast of present-day downtown Tampa and laid the foundations of **Ybor City**. Around 20,000 immigrants – mostly Cubans drawn from the strife-ridden Key West cigar industry, joined by a smattering of Spaniards and Italians – settled here, creating an enclave of Latin American life and producing the top-class hand-rolled cigars that made Tampa the "Cigar Capital of the World" for forty years. Mass-production, the popularity of cigarettes and the Depression proved a fatal combination for skilled cigar makers. Ybor City lost its *joie de vivre* and, while the rest of Tampa expanded, its twenty tight-knit blocks of cobbled streets and red-brick buildings were engulfed by drab and dangerous low-rent neighborhoods.

Today, Ybor City is in the midst of a revival; it buzzes with tourists and at night the atmosphere reaches carnival proportions, especially on weekends. It is trendy, culturally diverse and a terrific place to wander at will. Yet commercialism is taking hold fast. Shops still sell hand-rolled cigars, but, owing to rising rents, the little hole-in-the-wall cafés that once doled out freshly baked Cuban bread and fresh-brewed coffee have all but disappeared, replaced by a new breed of stylish but essentially generic café-bars and restaurants. There are still some sensational, authentic places to savor Cuban cooking, but they are being forced further and further off the main drag.

Ybor City State Museum

Ybor City's Cuban roots are immediately apparent and explanatory background texts adorn many buildings. Soak up the atmosphere during the day, but don't expect the place to really get going until the evening. The **Ybor City State Museum**, 1818 Ninth Ave (Tues–Sat 9am–5pm; $2; ☎813/247-6323, Ⓦwww.ybormuseum.org), offers just enough to help you grasp the main points of Ybor City's creation and its multi-ethnic make-up. Enormous wall photographs show cigar rollers at work: thousands sat in long rows at bench-tables making 25¢ per cigar and cheering or heckling the *lector* (or reader), who recited the news from Spanish-language newspapers. On the grounds lies a cigar worker's cottage, which you can enter to get a taste of the simple domestic arrangements – more interesting than riveting. The museum also offers cigar-rolling demonstrations on Fridays and Saturdays 10am–1pm, historic walking tours (Fri 11am) and walking ghost tours of Ybor City (Sat 10.30am; $4).

Ybor Square and the local brewery

The old Stemmenzy-Zago building, where cigar rolling actually took place, at 1901 Thirteenth St on the corner of Eighth Avenue (Mon–Sat 10am–6pm, Sun noon–5.30pm), is now called **Ybor Square**. This cavernous structure – three stories supported by sturdy oak pillars – has been converted into a collection of tourist-aimed shops and restaurants, a depressingly commercialized market of fairy lights draped over T-shirt shops, and cafés without a local in sight. Standing on the factory's iron steps in 1893, the famed Cuban poet and independence fighter José Martí spoke to thousands of Ybor City's Cubans, calling for pledges of money, machetes and manpower for the country's anti-Spanish, pro-independence struggles.★ It's estimated that expatriate Cuban cigar workers contributed ten percent of their earnings, most of which was spent on the illicit purchase and shipment of arms to rebels in Cuba. A stone marker at the foot of the steps records the event and, across the street, the **José Martí Park** remembers Martí with a statue.

Ybor City even has its own brewery whose beers – the most famous of which is Ybor Gold – can be found all over Florida. The **Ybor City Brewing Company**, 2205 N Twentieth St, (☎813/242-9222, ⊚www.ycbc.com), housed in what used to be a storage warehouse for the Hava–Tampa Cigar Company, runs daily guided tours (11am–1pm; $2), where you can learn how the beer is brewed and give it an all-important taste test.

Ybor's social clubs

From the earliest days, each of Ybor City's ethnic communities ran its own **social clubs**, published newspapers, and even organized a medical insurance scheme which led to the building of two hospitals. The hospitals still function today, as do several of the social centers. Stepping inside one of the centers (opening hours vary wildly) reveals patriotic paraphernalia and sometimes, in the basement, men-only dens of dominoes and drinking. If you can, visit *Centro Español*, at 1526 E Seventh Ave, *The Cuban Club*, 2010 Avenida Republica de Cuba N, or *Centro Asturiano*, 1913 N Nebraska Ave, for a look at Ybor City life that most visitors miss. One Ybor City institution out-of-towners invariably do find is the *Columbia* restaurant, 2117 E Seventh Ave (see "Eating," p.331). Now filling a whole block, the *Columbia* opened in 1905 as a humble coffee stop for tobacco workers; inside, newspaper cuttings plaster the walls and recount the restaurant's lustrous past.

Around Tampa

The collar of suburbia around downtown Tampa offers few reasons to stop, though the city's least expensive motels cluster around the **Busch Gardens** theme park, which ranks among the state's top tourist attractions. While as enjoyable as any of its ilk, you might be inclined to skip the park and divide your attentions between the **Lowry Park Zoo**, the **Museum of Science and Industry,** and (provided you're driving, for it's unreachable by public transport) the 3000 pristine acres of the **Hillsborough River State Park**. On the way, don't be tempted by the Seminole Indian Village (5221 N Orient Rd), part of a Seminole reservation where a token collection of Native American arts and crafts is on sale to tourists, and high-stakes bingo is played.

★ A few years after Martí's speech, Tampa became the embarkation point for the US's Cuban Expeditionary Forces. Thousands of US soldiers were housed in tents here waiting to join the Spanish-American War. On January 1, 1899, the Spanish pulled out of Cuba, and the island acquired its independence.

Busch Gardens

Incredible as it may seem, most people are drawn to Tampa by a theme-park re-creation of colonial Africa in the grounds of a brewery, at 3000 E Busch Blvd (two miles east of I-275 or two miles west of I-75, exit 54, signposted Fowler Avenue). In glossing over a period of imperial exploitation in the name of entertainment – compounding this insensitivity with the garden's subtitle, "The Dark Continent," which caused outrage within the local black community – **Busch Gardens** (daily 9.30am–6pm; longer hours in high season; $48.76, children $39.22; ℡813/987-5082, ⓦwww.buschgardens.com), which opened in 1959 as a brewery and was devloped into a theme park six years later, brazenly reshapes world history just as much as its archrival, Walt Disney World. It costs a packet and is as tacky as hell, but if you do come you'll need to stick around all day to get your money's worth. Go on everything in the park (all the rides are included in the admission fee), and try to love the kitsch without dwelling on its implications.

Traversable on foot or by pseudo-steam train, the 300-acre park divides into several areas. You'll first enter **Morocco**, where Moroccan crafts are sold at un-Moroccan prices, snake-charmers and belly dancers weave through the crowds, and the Mystick Sheiks Marching Band blast their trumpets into the ears of passers-by. Then comes the **Myombe Reserve**, where a collection of chimps and gorillas are kept in a tropical environment complete with waterfall. Follow the signs to **Nairobi** and you'll find small gatherings of elephants, giant tortoises, alligators, crocodiles and monkeys in varying states of liveliness, and the Animal Nursery and children's zoo inhabited by cute, cuddly creatures that are happy to be stroked by kids. Directly ahead in **Timbuktu**, animals are less in evidence than amusement rides: a small roller coaster and a children's fairground ride called "Sandstorm," neither of which can match "Kumba" (see below). If the Ubanga-Banga bumper cars in the **Congo** don't hold lasting appeal, gird your loins for the swirling raft trip around the Congo River Rapids – which may induce you to cross Stanleyville Falls on a roller coaster, the best feature of neighboring **Stanleyville**. Whatever you do, don't miss the Congo's devastating "Kumba," the largest and fastest roller coaster in the southeastern US. The biggest single section of the gardens, the eighty-acre **Serengeti Plain**, roamed by giraffes, buffaloes, zebras, antelopes, black rhino and elephants, is the closest the place gets to showing anything genuinely African; see the beasts from the all-too-brief monorail ride. After all this, retire to the Hospitality House of the Anheuser-Busch Brewery, purveyors of Budweiser and owners of the park, where the beer is free but limited to two drinks (in a paper cup) per person.

The Lowry Park Zoo

Two miles southwest of Busch Gardens and just west of I-275, the **Lowry Park Zoo**, 1101 Sligh Ave (daily 9.30am–5pm; $9.50; ℡813/935-8552), established in the 1930s, was Tampa's first zoo. Today it is home to about 1500 animals, kept on 41 acres of natural habitats; many of them are rare and endangered. There are five major exhibits: the Florida Manatee and Aquatic Center, Native Florida Wildlife Center, Asian Domain, Primate World and the Free-Flight Aviary, as well as a hands-on Discovery Center and a small insect zoo, all of which are supported by regular educational events held in an outdoor amphitheater. This is a good place to learn about Florida's wildlife, especially if most of your trip centers around the beaches and theme parks.

The Museum of Science and Industry

Two miles northeast of Busch Gardens, at 4801 E Fowler Ave, the **Museum of Science and Industry** (daily 9am, closing times seasonal; $13; ℡813/987-

6100, ⓦ www.mosi.org) will entertain adults as much as it does kids. Intended to reveal the mysteries of the scientific world, the hands-on displays and machines will easily fill half a day. To get the most from your visit, study the program schedule carefully upon arrival: the main – and most interesting – features run at fixed times throughout the day. Plan your time around the Challenger Learning Center, an engrossing simulated spacecraft and mission control. The Gulf Coast Hurricane is a convincing demonstration that allows begoggled participants to feel the force of the strongest winds known. Energy Pinball, a massive walk-through pinball machine, lets you follow a ball along 700 feet of track. Finally, the Saunders Planetarium houses the unmissable MOSIMAX, Florida's first IMAX (or "maximum image") film theater in a dome, which shows films of outstanding visual and audio quality. The entrance fee includes admission to a single IMAX screening.

Hillsborough River State Park

Twelve miles north of Tampa on Hwy-301, shaded by live oaks, magnolias and sable palms, the **Hillsborough River State Park** (daily 8am–sunset; cars $3.25, pedestrians and cyclists $1; ⓣ 813/987-6771) holds one of the state's rare instances of rapids – outside of a theme park. The Hillsborough River tumbles over limestone outcrops before pursuing a more typical meandering course. Rambling the sizeable park's walking trails and canoeing the gentler sections of the river could fill a day nicely (and the park makes an enjoyable place for **camping**; $8–19 to pitch a tent; ⓣ 813/986-1020), but on weekends you should devote part of the afternoon to the **Fort Foster Historic Site**, a reconstructed 1836 Seminole War fort that can only be seen with one of the **guided tours** which depart at regular intervals. Stemming from the US attempts to drive Florida's Seminole Indians out to reservations in the Midwest and make the state fit for the white man, the Seminole Wars raged throughout the nineteenth century and didn't officially end until 1937 (see "History" in Contexts). Period-attired enthusiasts occupy the fort and recount historical details, not least the fact that more soldiers died from tropical diseases than in battle. Not surprisingly, the Seminoles tell a somewhat different account of the conflict, and both sides make for interesting listening. For an extra $1 you can also swim in the new pool (summer Fri–Sun 10am–5pm, winter daily 10am–5pm).

Eating

Eating in Tampa means good quality and lots of choice – except in **downtown**, where street stands dispensing snacks to lunching office workers are the culinary norm. Some of the best and most interesting meals are served in Ybor City, whose Latin heritage and hip reputation have made it a restaurant haven.

Canoeing on the Hillsborough River

To spend two hours or a whole day gliding past the alligators, turtles, wading birds and other creatures which call the Hillsborough River home, contact Canoe Escape, 9335 E Fowler Ave (ⓣ 813/986-2067, ⓦ www.canoeescape.com), who have devised a series of novice-friendly routes along the tea-colored river. Prices range between $8 and $32 depending on length of trip, and you should make a reservation at least 72 hours in advance.

Downtown

Bern's Steak House, 1208 S Howard Ave (☎813/251-2421). Starting from $20, these are the most unforgettable charcoal-broiled steaks you'll ever have.

Café Firenze, 719 N Franklin St (☎813/228-9200). Lovely little moderately priced Italian restaurant near the Tampa Theatre, it features authentic homemade pastas and unbelievable desserts, such as *zuccotto fiorentino*, a chocolate-covered amaretto mousse.

Café Pepé, 2006 W Kennedy Blvd (☎813/253-6501). This moderately priced restaurant has been a Tampa landmark for years. Enjoy favorites like *filete salteado* and paella.

Gladstone's Grilled Chicken, 502 Tampa St (☎813/221-2988). You'll definitely be glad you tried the poultry here.

Manhattan Bagel Bar, 602 Franklin St (☎813/307-0555). Basic but a good choice for a quick bite before heading to the Tampa Theatre (see p.332).

Ole Style Deli, 110 E Madison St (☎813/223-4282). A worthy address where businessmen devour $4 sandwiches. Service can be very slow, but breakfasts and salads are good.

Hyde Park

Blackhawk Coffee Café, 1628 W Snow Circle (☎813/258-1600). Favorite haunt of locals, this café offers great coffee and is open late every night except Sundays.

Cactus Club, 1601 W Snow Ave (☎813/251-4089). Good selection of Mexican and American favorites – famous for its unbeatable margaritas. Evening highlights include Happy Hours (see nightlife below).

Café DeSoto, 504 E Kennedy Blvd (☎813/229-2566). The Cuban lunch specials, like roast chicken, black beans, rice and Cuban bread – all for $3.95 – are a steal.

Ybor City

Bernini, 1702 Seventh Ave (☎813/248-0099). An Italian joint serving up wood-fired pizza and pasta in the lovely old Bank of Ybor City (note the giant-insect door handles).

Café Cohiba, 1430 E Seventh Ave (☎813/248-0357). Named for a renowned Cuban cigar, this is a chic place with prices to match. Original fare, like baked Brie with guava glaze, is served to patrons willing to spend upwards of $35.

Café Creole, 1330 E Ninth Ave (☎813/247-6283). Good Creole food at reasonable prices – the Creole Sampler Platters will give you a taste of everything for $12.25.

Castillo's, 1823 Seventh Ave (☎813/248-1306). One of the few places left to sample real Cuban sandwiches and invigorating Cuban coffee on Seventh Avenue.

Cephas, 1701 E Fourth Ave (☎813/247-9022). A funky Jamaican restaurant run from the political-poster decorated front room of Cephas Gilbert, who arrived in Ybor via Birmingham, England. He serves jerk chicken, curry goat chicken and fish while regaling guests with his vivid life story.

The Columbia, 2117 E Seventh Ave (☎813/248-4961, ⊛www.columbiarestaurant.com). Serving refined yet moderately priced Spanish and Cuban food, this Tampa institution – the city's oldest restaurant – has become a fixture on the tourist circuit. Its eleven rooms hold nearly 2000 people, who are entertained six nights a week by flamenco dancers. Reservations recommended.

Joffrey's Coffee House, 1616 Seventh Ave (☎813/248-5282). The delectable aromas of fruit, coffee and chocolate are always thick in the air at this reasonably priced coffee house.

La Teresita Cafeteria, 3246 W Columbus Drive (☎813/879-4909). Cuban sandwiches go for $2, and dishes like *patas de cerdo* (pigs' feet) and *rabo encendido* (oxtail) are served with superb Cuban coffee. Locals chat and often break into fits of singing and guitar playing at the bar.

St Frances Cafe, 1811 N Sixteenth St (☎813/247-6993). The owner, a secular Franciscan woman whose aim is to feed the hungry, serves gorgeous falafel, humus, homemade cheesecake and chocolate-butter-pecan shortbread – and you pay only what you feel you can afford.

Nightlife

Tampa **at night** may have the reputation of being strong on drinking and live rock music, but there are more cultural alternatives for those who are looking for more from a night out. For details on upcoming arts and cultural events, phone the Artsline at ☎813/229-ARTS; general nightlife listings are available for free on the Nightlife line ☎813/854-8000. For tickets to any major event, call Ticketmaster at ☎813/287-8844. For a list of all things nightlife-related, pick up a copy of the free *Weekly Planet* (every Thursday), or try their Web site ⓦwww.weeklyplanet.com, or the Friday edition of the *Tampa Tribune*.

Performing arts and film

Tampa's cultural profile is improved by regular high-quality shows at the **Tampa Bay Performing Arts Center** (box office open Mon–Fri 10am–6pm, Sat & Sun noon–6pm and ninety minutes prior to performances; ⓣ813/222-1054, ⓦwww.tbpac.org), a state-of-the-art performance venue that features top US and international names. The **Gorilla Theatre**, 4419 N Hubert Ave (tickets $14–20; ⓣ813/879-2914, ⓦwww.gorilla-theatre.com) is a more intimate, but just as professional, theater with a program including contemporary comedies and dramas, as well as the classics. For a full list of **films** playing around the city, read the Friday edition of the *Tampa Tribune*. Foreign-language, classic or cult films crop up only at the **Tampa Theatre**, 711 Franklin St (see "Downtown Tampa," p.323); pick up a schedule from the building itself or phone the 24-hour information line ⓣ813/223-8981; tickets are $6.25.

Drinking

Many live music venues and nightclubs have tempting **drink** reductions, though the most cost-effective way to booze, as ever, is at the **Happy Hours** taking place all over the city – just watch for the signs. For later drinking, head to Ybor City's *Irish Pub*, 1721 E Seventh Ave (ⓣ813/248-2099), or the Gothic-inspired *Castle*, 2004 Sixteenth St at Ninth Ave (ⓣ813/247-7547). In addition to daily Happy Hours – and there are twenty draft beers to choose from – the *Cactus Club* in Hyde Park (see "Eating," p.331) has screen viewing of many sporting events. For **sports bars,** try *Grand Slam* at the *Sheraton Grand Hotel* (ⓣ813/286-4400), or *Baker's Billiards*, 1811 N Tampa St (ⓣ813/226-6541), which has fourteen full-sized pool tables.

Live music and nightclubs

Ybor City is brimming with clubs and music bars and many of the area's restaurants also offer entertainment, such as the famous *Columbia* (see "Eating" p.331), which has live music every night in its *Cigar Bar*, plus live Spanish flamenco dance performances in the main restaurant. Outside of Ybor, Tampa's most dependable **live music** club is the blues- and reggae-dominated *Skipper's Smokehouse*, 910 Skipper Rd (ⓣ813/971-0666). Jazz lovers should head for the *Jazz Cellar,* 1916 Fourteenth St, which has good live music most nights. Another live music favorite, ranging from retro to techno, is the *Amphitheater*, 1609 E Seventh Ave (ⓣ813/248-2331, ⓦwww.amphitheaterybor.com). For big-name bands and big crowds keep an eye on Tampa's **major venues**: the USF Sun Dome, 4202 S Fowler Ave (ⓣ813/974-3002), and Tampa Stadium, 4201 Dale Mabry Hwy (ⓣ813/872-7977). Among Tampa's **nightclubs**, the *Green Iguana*, 1708 E Seventh Ave (ⓣ813/248-9555), and the *Rain Lounge,* 302 S Nebraska Ave (ⓣ813/229-7246), are the best bets. Cover varies from nothing to $10.

Comedy clubs

Tampa has two notable **comedy clubs**. *Side Splitters*, 12938 N Dale Mabry Hwy (ⓣ813/960-1197), is one of the best in the area and has a line up featuring national and regional comedians. The other is the *Improv Comedy Theater*, 1600 E Eighth Ave (ⓣ813/864-4000). Cover charges vary between $8 and $14 at both venues.

Gay and lesbian Tampa

With the constant addition of more bars, clubs and resource centers, **gay and lesbian** life in Tampa is improving all the time, and it's a very gay-friendly city. Get general information by calling The Line (T813/586-4297), which features the very informative What's Gay in Tampa Bay, or contact the Gay and Lesbian Community Center at 3708 W Swann Ave (T813/875-8116, Wwww .tampacenter.org). The Florida-wide *Encounter* magazine, 1222 S Dale Mabry Hwy, is another good source of information on Tampa's gay life. A good bookstore to try is Tomes & Treasures, 408 S Howard Ave (T813/251-9368). Every October, Tampa hosts the Gay and Lesbian Film Festival; check Wwww .pridefilmfest.com for up-to-date information.

Gay and lesbian bars and clubs

The Pleasure Dome, 1430 E Seventh Ave in Ybor City (T813/247-2711), is one of the most popular **nightspots**. A gay and straight crowd drinks and dances on and about the two dance-floors and three bars. Drag shows and high energy music abound, so don't be put off by the crumbling exterior. Other pulsating gay clubs include *Tampa Eagle*, 302 S Nebraska Ave (T813/223-2780), a very leather club; *Mecca*, on the corner of Ninth Avenue and Sixteenth Street in Ybor City, which features a huge dance-floor and drink specials and welcomes men and women; *Rascals*, 105 W Martin Luther King Blvd (T813/237-8883), a dance club particularly packed on Thursdays; *Angel's*, 4502 S Dale Mabry Hwy (T813/831-9980), is friendly and unpretentious – and has nightly strippers. Close by is *Baxters*, 4010 S Dale Mabry Hwy (T813/258-8830), which has live jazz. *The Cherokee Club*, 1320 E Ninth Ave (T813/247-9966), is primarily geared towards lesbians.

Listings

Airport Five miles northwest of downtown Tampa (T 813/870-8700); reach it with local bus #30, see "Arrival, information and getting around"). St Petersburg-Clearwater International Airport is the only other airport close by (T 813/535-7600).
Buses Greyhound bus lines T 813/229-2174 or 1-800/231-2222. **Local bus information** T 813/254-4278.
Car rental Avis, at Tampa Airport T 813/396-3500; Budget T 1-800/527-0700; Dollar T 1-800/882-1181.
Dentists For referral: T 813/886-9040.
Directory enquiries (local only) T 411.
Doctor For referral: T 813/870-4444.
Hospital Tampa General on Davis Island T 813 /251 7000. Emergency room T 813/251-7100.
Left luggage At the Greyhound station, 610 Polk St; the train station, 601 Nebraska Ave. There is no left luggage at the airport.
Pharmacy Eckerd Drugs, 11613 N Nebraska Ave (T 813/978-0775), is open 24hr.
Police Emergencies T 911. To report something lost or stolen: T 813/223-1515. General police information: T 813/276-3200.
Post Office 5201 W Spruce St or 925 N Florida Ave. In Ybor City, 1900 E Twelfth Ave.

Sports The city's professional football team, the Tampa Bay Buccaneers (W www.buccaneers.com), plays at Raymond James Stadium, 4201 N Dale Mabry Hwy (box office and information T 813/870-2700); cheapest tickets are $15–35. The local baseball team, the Tampa Bay Devil Rays (W www.devilrays.com), actually play in St Petersburg; see p.336. Tampa's hockey team, the Tampa Bay Lightning (T 813/229-8800, W www.tampabaylightning.com), play at the Ice Palace; cheapest tickets cost $16. Tampa's soccer team, the Rowdies (T 813/877-7800), play outdoor matches at Tampa Stadium and indoors at the Bayfront Center in St Petersburg, 400 First St; tickets are $8–50.
Taxis Yellow Cab T 813/253-0121; Tampa Bay Cab T 813/251-5555 or United Cab Co T 813/253-2424.
Thomas Cook Nearest branch is in St Petersburg: Paragon Crossing, 11300 Fourth St N (T 813/577-6556).
Ticketmaster Branches around the city: T 813/287-8844.
Trains Amtrak T 813/221-7601 or 1-800/872-7245.
Travelers Aid T 813/273-5936.
Weather information T 813/645-2323.

St Petersburg

Situated on the eastern edge of the Pinellas Peninsula, **ST PETERSBURG** (named by a homesick Russian) may be physically close to Tampa, but location is about the only thing the cities share. St Petersburg holds the world record for the number of consecutive days of sunshine – 768 in total, set in 1967–69 – and enjoys on average 361 days of sunshine a year. It should come as no surprise that this city wasted no time in attracting the recuperating and the retired to its climate. At one point, the city put five thousand green benches on its streets to take the weight off elderly backsides, and by the early 1980s, few people under 50 lived in the town. Although it remains a mecca for the retired, St Petersburg has worked hard to attract young blood. In addition to the rejuvenated pier, which now offers something for every age, its diverse selection of museums and plethora of art galleries has contributed to its emergence as one of Florida's richest cultural cities. The mixture of old and new architecture and the landscaped parks around the seafront make this city a good option if you are looking for a break from the beaches nine miles west on the Gulf Coast (see "The St Petersburg beaches," p.341).

Arrival, information and getting around

St Petersburg-Clearwater International Airport (☎727/535-7600) is served by several major carriers as well as charters. The main route **by car** into St Petersburg is I-275 and don't get off before the "Downtown St Petersburg" exit or you'll face a barrage of traffic lights. The Greyhound **bus** station is centrally located at 180 Ninth St N (☎1-800/231-2222). A daytrip to Tampa is difficult without a car; there are no trains between Tampa and St Petersburg, just a twice-daily Amtrak bus link (☎727/221-7600 or 1-800/872-7245), which drops you at the Pinellas Square Mall at 7200 Hwy-19 N. The only **bus** service to Tampa is the 100X commuter service which runs between the out-of-town Gateway Mall, on Ninth Street and 77th Avenue, and downtown Tampa and is both inconvenient to reach and infrequent during the day. Most bus services arrive at and depart from the Williams Park terminal, at the junction of First Avenue North and Third Street North, where an information booth (open Mon–Sat 7am–5.45pm, Sun 8–11.30am & 12.30–4pm) gives route details. Most bus journeys cost $1 (except the 100X which is $1.50). The best option if you're planning to take several buses in one day is to purchase a Go Card pass, which allows unlimited travel for a day. It costs $2.50 and can be purchased on board. You can reach the St Petersburg beaches on PSTA local buses (☎727/530-9911, ⬤www.psta.net), though these are not always direct (see the "Buses between St Petersburg and the beaches" box on p.342). There is also a **Trolley** to the beaches which is probably your best option. The **Looper** is a pink trolley bus which runs every 30 minutes, daily 11am–5pm, connecting all the museums and attractions. It cost 50¢ a ride and there are pink Looper stops all around the downtown area.

Gather the usual tourist **information** and discount coupons from the **Chamber of Commerce**, 100 Second Ave N (Mon–Fri 8am–5pm; ☎727/821-4715, ⬤895-6326, ⬤www.stpete.com), and look out for the "Weekend" section of the *St Petersburg Times* for entertainment and nightlife listings, also available on their website (⬤www.stptimes.com), which contains a great deal of information on walking tours and exhibits. The first floor of the pier (see p.337) also has a well-stocked tourist counter.

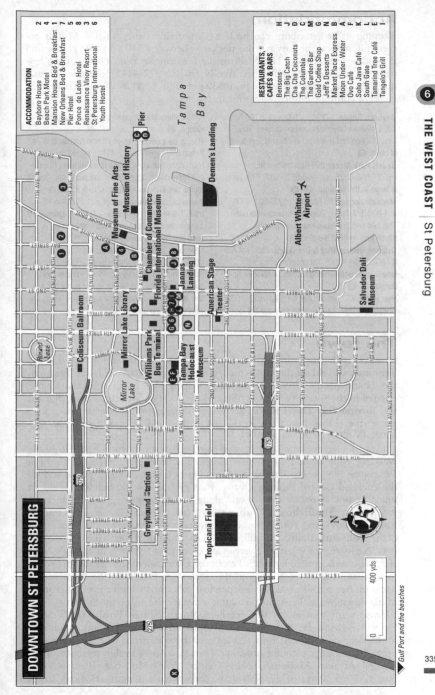

DOWNTOWN ST PETERSBURG

ACCOMMODATION

Bayboro House	2
Beach Park Motel	4
Mansion House Bed & Breakfast	1
New Orleans Bed & Breakfast	7
Pier Hotel	5
Ponce de León Hotel	8
Renaissance Vinoy Resort	3
St Petersburg International Youth Hostel	6

RESTAURANTS, CAFÉS & BARS

Bensons	H
The Big Catch	J
Cha Cha Coconuts	D
The Columbia	C
The Garden Bar	M
Gold Coffee Shop	G
Jeff's Desserts	N
Market Place Express	B
Moon Under Water	A
Ovo Café	F
Soho Java Café	K
South Gate	L
Tamarind Tree Café	E
Tangelo's Grill	I

Coliseum Ballroom

Mirror Lake Library

Williams Park

Tampa Bay Bus Terminal

Tampa Bay Holocaust Museum

Museum of Fine Arts

Museum of History

Pier

Chamber of Commerce

Florida International Museum

Jannus Landing

American Stage Theater

Demen's Landing

Albert Whitted Airport

Salvador Dalí Museum

Tropicana Field

Greyhound Station

Round Lake

Mirror Lake

Tampa Bay

Gulf Port and the beaches

0   400 yds

Accommodation

Sleeping in St Petersburg can be less costly than at the beaches. **Motels** are plentiful and can be easy on the pocket – between $40 and $80 year-round depending on location. The *St Petersburg International Youth Hostel*, in the historic *Bay Park Arms*, at 326 First Ave N (℡727/822-4141), charges $15, and double rooms are also available from $39 per night or $125 a week. There's free coffee, a communal microwave and Internet access.

Bayboro House, 1719 Beach Drive (℡727/823-4955, ⊛www.bayborohousebandb.com). This beautiful bed and breakfast is situated just south of town. ❺

Beach Park Motel, 300 Beach Drive NE (℡727/898-6325 or 1-800/657-7687). This motel is close to the seafront. ❸–❹

Mansion House, 105 Fifth Ave (℡727/821-9391 or 1-800/274-7520, ⊛www.mansionbandb.com) This bed and breakfast lies in a charming house just north of the pier. ❹

Orleans Bishop Bed & Breakfast, 256 First Ave N (℡727/894-4312). This cosy building with ornate, cast-iron verandas offers a choice of fine breakfasts. ❹

Pier Hotel, 253 Second Ave N (℡727/822-7500, ⊛www.pierhotel.net). This luxury, centrally located option offers guests evening cocktails in the piano lounge. ❺

Ponce de León Hotel, at Central Avenue and Beach Drive (℡727/822-4139). In addition to a room once occupied by the late President Nixon, this hotel offers a restaurant and piano bar. Double rooms are $65 per night or $215 a week. ❸

Renaissance Vinoy Resort, 501 Fifth Ave NE (℡727/894-1000 or 1-800/468-3571, ⊛www.renaissancehotels.com). If you want to stay in style you have to experience this pink hotel opened in 1925 as a haven for the rich and famous. Now beautifully restored, it offers guests two swimming pools, twelve tennis courts, golf course, bike hire and health spa to name but a few. It also offers special package rates which are worth checking out. ❼–❽.

The town

However you reach downtown St Petersburg, the first thing you'll see is **Tropicana Field** on the western edge of town at 1 Stadium Drive. Formerly the Thunderdome, this huge building, shaped like a half-collapsed soufflé, opened in the spring of 1998 as home to the local major league baseball team, the **Tampa Bay Devil Rays** (⊛www.devilrays.com). To reserve tickets for a game (the season lasts from April to October) call the visitor line at ℡1-800/345-6710 or 727/825-3250.

If your preferences run more toward culture than sports, consider a self-guided **walking tour** around the town's historic buildings; pick up the *St Petersburg Preservation Program* brochure at the Chamber of Commerce (see p.334) and use the enclosed Central Business District map. Not all the old buildings listed are much to look at, but be sure to walk along **Fourth Avenue**, passing the grandstands of the **Shuffleboard Club**, no. 536 N, the original home of this popular game. Directly across Fourth Avenue North, is the Mediterranean Revival facade of the **Coliseum Ballroom**, built in 1924 and still throbbing to big-band sounds (see "Nightlife," p.339). If art galleries are more your style try *Take a Walk on the Art Side*, a walk created by the St Petersburg Downtown Arts Association, which incorporates the 27 art galleries in the downtown area, from the Salvador Dalí Museum (see p.338) to smaller independent galleries. Pick up a free leaflet at any of the downtown galleries and set a side a day for the entire tour.

If you want a swim, try the excellent **North Shore Pool**, 901 N Shore Drive NE (Mon–Fri 9am–4pm, Sat 10am–4pm and Sun 1–4pm); in addition to the large pool, there is a sun terrace near the waterfront where you can soak up St Petersburg's plentiful sunshine. Though a considerable trek west along Central Avenue, **Haslam's**, 2025 Central Ave (Mon–Sat 10am–6.30pm, Sun 12.30–5.30pm; ℡727/822-8616, ⊛www.haslams.com), Florida's largest bookstore, will keep browsers occupied for hours. Opened in the Depression to provide avid readers with used magazines and books at bargain prices, the store stocks over 300,000 new and used books on all topics. If it's virtual information you need, your best option for Internet access is the **Mirror Lake Library**, 280 Fifth St N (Mon–Fri 9am–6pm, Sat 9am–5pm; ☎727/893-7268, ⓦwww.stpetersburg.org), which offers free use of online computers.

The pier and around

The focus point of downtown St Petersburg is its quarter-mile-long **pier** (open Mon–Thurs 10am–9pm, Fri & Sat 10am–10pm and Sun 11am–7pm, ⓦwww.stpete-pier.com), which juts from the end of Second Avenue North. Pier parking is $2 and there is a shuttle tram that runs between the parking lots and the front of the pier. Arts and crafts exhibitions often line the pier and you'll find stacks of tourist information at the **Chamber of Commerce** desk (Mon–Sat 10am–8pm, Sun noon–6pm; ☎727/821-6164), which is near the entrance. The five-story, inverted-pyramid-like building is packed with restaurants, shops, fast-food counters and an aquarium. Outside at the bait house, you can buy fish to feed the many pelicans or hire bikes from Bayside Rentals (☎727/363-0000), for $5 an hour, $10 half a day and $15 full day. The pier is also home to **Great Explorations** (Mon–Sat 10am–8pm, Sun 11am–6pm; $4; ☎727/821-8992, ⓦwww.greatexplorations.org), a hands-on science museum, which, like Tampa's much larger Museum of Science and Industry (see p.329), strives to make the rudiments of science accessible with inventive games. Although aimed more at children than adults, this attraction can be both fun and educational for all ages and new exhibits are regularly added.

Opposite the entrance to the pier is the **Museum of History**, 335 Second Ave NE (Mon–Sat 10am–5pm, Sun 1–5pm; $5; ☎727/894-1052, ⓦwww.museumofhistoryonline.org). Modest displays recount St Petersburg's early twentieth-century heyday as a winter resort (which lasted until the wider and sandier Gulf Coast beaches became accessible), and the inaugural flight of the world's first commercial airline, which took off from St Petersburg in 1914. There's documentation, too, on **Weedon Island**, five miles north of the town and once the base of a small film industry. Significant pottery finds were unearthed from Native American burial mounds here, but they were ransacked by looters in the 1960s. Now a state-protected wildlife refuge, the island is mostly used for fishing.

One block west of the pier, a group of Mediterranean Revival buildings houses the **Museum of Fine Arts**, at 255 Beach Drive NE (Tues–Sat 10am–5pm, Sun 1–5pm; $6, $10 or more for special exhibitions, free Sun; regular free guided tours; ☎727/896-2667, ⓦwww.fine-arts.org). This elegant Mediterranean-villa-style building, set in a landscaped park with sculptures and banyan trees, is a work of art in itself. Opened in 1965, its twenty galleries hold more than four hundred objects from antiquity to the present day. Inside, the works of seventeenth-century art are competent but not imposing; more inspiring is the section on modern European art, featuring drawings by Kandinsky, Monet's *Houses of Parliament* and Daumier's amusing *Connoisseur of Prints*. Also on display are pre-Columbian pieces, plus ceramics, glasswork and antiquities from Europe and Asia. The American contemporary room displays include Georgia O'Keeffe's vibrant *Poppy* and George Luks' *The Musician*.

A short walk south of the Museum of Fine Arts is the massive **Florida International Museum**, 100 Second St N (during exhibition periods only, Mon–Sat 9am–6pm, Sun noon–6pm; $13.95, students $7; ☎1-800/777-9882, ⓦwww.floridamuseum.org), which encompasses an entire block. The museum opened in 1995 with the first of its exhibitions, "Treasures of the Czars," which contained works from the Moscow Kremlin museums. Grand in scale, with subject matter ranging from Ancient Egypt to John F. Kennedy, the exhibitions each last for about a year and are some of the best in the country.

The Salvador Dalí Museum

Few places make a less likely depository for the biggest collection of works by maverick artist Salvador Dalí than St Petersburg. However, the **Salvador Dalí Museum**, 1000 S Third St (Mon–Sat 9.30am–5.30pm, Sun noon–5.30pm; $8; ☎ 727/822-6270, Ⓦ www.salvadordalimuseum.org), a mile and a half south of the pier, stores more than a thousand Dalí works from the collection of a Cleveland industrialist who struck up a friendship with the artist in the Forties, bought stacks of his works and ran out of space to show them – until this specially built gallery opened in 1982.

Hook up with the **free tours** that run continuously throughout the day. They trace a fact-filled path around the chronologically arranged paintings (some shown on rotation), from early experiments with Impressionism and Cubism to the ectoplasmic watches of the seminal surrealist canvas *Persistence of Memory*, and on to works from Dalí's "Classic" period in the Forties, which play upon the fundamentals of religion, science and history. Some canvases – such as the overwhelming *Discovery of America by Christopher Columbus*, and the *Hallucinogenic Toreador*, with its multiple double-images – are so big they have been hung in a specially deepened section of the gallery.

Tampa Bay Holocaust Museum

Dedicated to providing public awareness, education and understanding of the Holocaust, the emotionally wrenching **Tampa Bay Holocaust Museum**, at 55 Fifth St (Mon–Fri 10am–5pm, Sat & Sun noon–5pm, $6; ☎ 727/820-0100, Ⓦ www.flholocaustmuseum.org), chronicles the genocide of Europe's Jewish population with sensitive and intelligent clarity, and puts the history of anti-Semitism, from the first anti-Jewish legislation in Europe in 1215 AD, into context. The museum has both permanent and temporary exhibits, including an expansive second-floor gallery focusing on Holocaust art, and eleven eternal flames – symbolizing the eleven million victims of the Nazis – form part of the building's facade.

The brainchild of local businessman and World War II veteran Walter Loebenberg, who escaped Germany in 1939, the center achieves its objective of understanding for future generations. Most dramatic is a massive, original boxcar – #1130695-5 – that carried thousands of starving victims to their deaths and is the only one of its kind in the US. Upstairs, the work of artists Judy Chicago and Donald Woodman explore how with horrifying ease Holocaust imagery can be superimposed on America in the 1990s. There are also some stunning sculptures on Jewish and secular themes, though for the best of these, head for the superb annual show at Temple Beth El, 400 Pasadena Ave S (☎ 727/347-6136, www.templebeth-el.com), which takes place during the last week of January.

The Sunken Gardens

If you've had your fill of museums, head for the **Sunken Gardens**, 1825 Fourth St N (Wed–Sun 10am–4pm; $5, daily tours 10.30am & 1.30pm; ☎ 727/551-3100), a mile north of the pier. In 1935, a water-filled sinkhole was drained and planted with thousands of tropical plants and trees; this now forms four acres of shady and sweet-scented gardens. Fifteen feet below street level, lush tropical gardens are combined with flowing ponds and waterfalls. For a crash-course in exotic botany, scrutinize the texts along the pathway that descends gently through bougainvillaea, hibiscus and staghead ferns. Only the parrot shows, alligator show and the depressingly small cages housing some of the resident animals dim an hour's unhurried pleasure.

Eating

As the atmosphere in St Petersburg grows increasingly hipper, so does the choice of places to **eat**. Creative cuisines spiced with Cuban and Spanish accents are especially prevalent near the pier and good food can be found anywhere in town at a reasonable price.

Bensons, 244 First Ave N (℡727/823-6065). It may be pricey, but *Bensons* has superb sandwiches, good salads and great coffee.

Cha Cha Coconuts, 800 Second St, 5th Floor (℡727/822-6655). Inexpensive Caribbean dishes, such as blue mountain voodoo ribs, tropical tuna salad and Caribbean steak, accompanied by tall, frosty island drinks and live entertainment.

The Chattaway, 358 22nd Ave (℡727/823-1594). A one-time grocery store, gas station and trolley stop, *The Chattaway* is now a great and inexpensive American diner, famous for its Chattaburger, with all the trimmings.

Columbia, 800 Second St, Third Floor (℡727/822-8000). High-quality Cuban and Spanish food for $10–15.

Gold Coffee Shop, 336 First Ave N (℡727/822-4922). Inexpensive and simple, this is a good bet for an all-American breakfast.

Jeff's Desserts, 300 Central Ave (℡727/896-9866). Inexpensive spinach-and-feta pie, sandwiches and salads are just warm-ups before the relaxed, young crowd tackles the serious chocolates, pastries and cream creations for dessert.

Market Place Express, 284 Beach Drive (℡727/894-3330). Open at 7am weekdays, this delightful deli with outside terrace is a great place for breakfast. It also sells good-quality deli-style food and wine.

Moon Under Water, 332 Beach Drive NE (℡727/896-6160). Overlooking the waterfront, this inexpensive British Colonial tavern is well known for its cocktails, curries and baked salmon. Try the killer Key Lime pie for dessert.

Ovo Cafe, 515 Central Ave (℡727/895-5515). A blast of pure chic, but if you keep to salads and drinks, you can enjoy the minimalist, classic decor without smashing your budget.

SoHo Java Café, 2105 Central Ave (℡727/502-9445). Situated next door to Haslam's bookstore (see p.336), this art gallery and café offers a tranquil retreat for lunch and speedy Internet access.

South Gate Restaurant, 29 Third St N (℡727/823-7071). Family-style fare at reasonable prices. Try the blueberry waffles for breakfast or the lamb and beef gyros at dinner time.

Tamarind Tree, 537 Central Ave (℡727/898-2115). Vegetarian cuisine, such as tabouli salad, lasagna and avocado and salsa sandwiches – and plenty of it – for under $5.

Tangelo's Grill, 226 First Ave N (℡727/894-1695). Excellent Cuban café offering hearty economical food, such as fantastic black beans and rice, sweet potato fries and Cuban sandwiches, and great music.

Ted Peters' Famous Smoked Fish, 1350 Pasadena Ave (℡727/381-7931). Indulge in hot smoked-fish dinners with all the trimmings. Expensive but worth it.

Nightlife

It's been said that if you fire a cannon down Central Avenue after 9pm on any night, you won't hit a soul. This may have been true in the past, but enough bars and cafés have opened to make it a bit more of a risk. For information on events at St Petersburg's major entertainment venues call the 24-hour hotline ℡727/893-9500 ext 106. If you're at the pier, go up to roof level to hear the free band playing at *Cha Cha Coconut's* (℡727/822-6655) – the cool ocean breeze and St Petersburg skyline make the lightweight rock sounds palatable. Another restaurant, offering live **jazz** and a Martini Lounge at the weekends, is *The Garden*, 217 Central Ave (℡727/896-3800), a Mediterranean bistro open every night until 2am. **Country music** enthusiasts should head for *The Bull Pen Lounge*, 3510 34th St N (℡727/526-3366). Elsewhere, a steady procession of **rock** bands appear at *Jannus Landing*, 19 Second St N (℡727/896-1244), and *The Big Catch*, 9 NE First St (℡727/821-6444). Turn up with your own booze (there's no bar) at the *Coliseum Ballroom*, 535 Fourth Ave (℡727/892-5202, ⓦwww.stpete.org/coliseum), a **big band** venue for decades that boasts one of the biggest dance-floors in the US; weekend cover is $15, less during the week, and $5 for the Wednesday tea dances (1–3.30pm). The **American Stage,** 211 Third St (℡727/823-7529, ⓦwww.americanstage.org is the oldest **theater** in the Tampa Bay area. A nonprofit organization with a mission to "entertain, educate and enlighten," it presents American classics and Broadway shows. Each spring it stages a Shakespeare in the Park Festival at **Demen's Landing**, a waterfront park facing the pier. Ticket prices range from $7 to $28.

Gay and lesbian bars and clubs

There are a couple of friendly, dependable **gay bars** in town. *Golden Arrow*, 10604 Gandy Blvd (℡727/577-7774), is at exit 15 off I-275. It's a dark neighborhood place that rarely sees a tourist. To the south of St Petersburg is the livelier *Sharp A's Lounge*, 4918 Gulfport Blvd S (℡727/327-4897), just north of the Skyway Bridge. For more information on events pick up a copy of *Encounter* or *Womyn's Word* at Affinity Books, 2435 Ninth St N (℡727/823-3662), a gay and lesbian bookstore.

Gulfport

Absent from most tourist brochures and unseen by the thousands of visitors who hustle between downtown and the St Petersburg beaches, **Gulfport** (ⓦwww.ci.gulfport.fl.us) is a charming enclave of peaceful eateries, interesting art galleries and unusual shops. There's little glamour to this former fishing community, but without a high-rise hotel in sight, it's one the best places to stay (see below) in the area if you want to get off the tourist trail.

From downtown St Petersburg, travel a few miles south on I-275 to exit 6, then turn right at the bottom of the exit onto Gulfport Boulevard (22nd Avenue South), which, after about two miles, serves as the central axis for the town. If you are traveling by bus, catch either the #15 or #23 from the Williams Park terminal to Shore Boulevard. Much of Gulfport is an unpretentious and rather bland mix of weather-beaten houses, coin laundries and little grocery stores. Turn off Gulfport Boulevard onto Beach Boulevard, however, and you'll discover a stretch of antique shops and restaurants shaded by oak trees dripping with Spanish moss. At the end of the road is the **Gulfport Casino**, 5500 Shore Blvd (℡727/893-1070), where **ballroom dancing** to a live orchestra has the locals strutting their stuff on Sundays, Mondays, Tuesdays and Thursdays (country dancers have it their way on Wednesdays).

Practicalities

The *Sea Breeze Manor*, 5701 Shore Blvd (℡727/343-4445 ⓕ343-4447; ❺–❽), is a gloriously restored, seaside house with sumptuous beds, antique furnishings and homebaked breakfasts which makes a great alternative to staying in St Petersburg proper. There are many **eating** options as well. Renowned as one of the best Cuban restaurants in the Tampa Bay area, *Habana Café*, at 5402 Gulfport Blvd (℡727/321-8855), serves shrimp of all sorts (Guantanamo Bay, Creole butterfly, *ajillo*), all for around $5. Try *H.T. Kanes* (℡727/347-6299), which faces the casino at the end of Beach Boulevard, for inexpensive grouper, clam, ribs and catfish; or *La Côte Basque*, at 3104 Beach Blvd (℡727/595-995), which specializes in moderately priced flounder and roast lamb. For **nightlife** *O'Maddy's*, 5405 Shore Blvd (℡727/323-8643), has a cool view of the sea and a Happy Hour between 3pm and 8pm.

The Pinellas Trail

If you're looking for an intriguing alternative to the usual beach-hopping paths of tourists up or down the coast, take the **Pinellas Trail,** a 34-mile hiking/cycling track that runs between St Petersburg and Tarpon Springs. You can pick up a free, informative and highly portable guide to the trail at any of the Chambers of Commerce or visitor centers between these two destinations. The guide describes the route and picks out points of interest, providing easy-to-manage maps. Numerous exit and entry points encourage a leisurely approach, so allow yourself time to meander off the well-marked confines of the trail and, if you don't feel inclined to tackle its entirety, you can take a bus or drive to various pre-selected areas for day excursions. Despite some uglier sections through urban centers (tricky on a bike), the trail offers enjoyable scenery along its rural portions and a chance for contemplation away from tanning and watersports. (See "The pier and around" on p.337 for details of bike rental.) Florida law says that everyone under 16 has to wear a helmet when they ride a bike – no matter where they ride.

The St Petersburg beaches

Framing the gulf side of the Pinellas Peninsula – a bulky thumb of land poking out between Tampa Bay and the Gulf of Mexico – is 35 miles of barrier islands that form the **St Petersburg beaches**, a convenient name for one of Florida's busiest coastal strips. Although each beach area has a name of its own, they are often collectively referred to as "the Holiday Isles," or the "Pinellas County Suncoast," and in reality merge together in one long, built-up strip of tourism at its tackiest. When the famed resorts of Miami Beach lost their allure during the Seventies, the St Petersburg beaches grew in popularity with Americans and have since evolved into an established destination for package-holidaying Europeans. There's no denying that the beaches themselves are beautiful, the sea is warm and the sunsets are fabulous, yet in no way is this Florida at its best. That said, staying here can be very cost-effective (especially during the summer) and if you're prepared to travel beyond the major built-up areas, you will find that some of the islands deserve exploration. It's quite feasible to combine lazing on the beach with daytrips to the more interesting inland areas. A word of warning – alcohol is prohibited on all municipal beaches in Florida, and glass containers are also illegal. Police in this area are particularly vigilant in chucking the drunk and disorderly in jail.

Information

Several beach areas have **Chambers of Commerce** readily dispensing handy information: St Petersburg Beach, 6990 Gulf Blvd (Mon–Fri 9am–5pm; ☎727/360-6957, ℱ360-2233, ⓦwww.gulfbeaches-tampa.com); Treasure Island, 152 108th Ave (Mon–Fri 9am–5pm; ☎727/367-4529, ℱ360-1853); Madeira Beach, 501 150th Ave (Mon–Fri 9am–5pm; ☎727/391-7373, ℱ391-4259). In Clearwater Beach, visit the booth at Pier 60, 1 Causeway Blvd (Mon–Fri 9am–5pm; ☎727/477-7600), or the Clearwater Welcome Center, 3350 Gulf-to-Bay Blvd (daily 9am–5pm; ☎727/726-1547). At any of the above and in shops, restaurants and motels, look for **free magazines** such as the *St Petersburg Official Visitors Guide* and *See St Pete and Beaches*. If you want the latest nightlife listings, check the Friday edition of the *St Petersburg Times*.

Buses between St Petersburg and the beaches

The best way to access the beaches by bus is the **Suncoast Trolley** service. A beach trolley (PSTA service #3) operates daily from the Williams Park terminal in St Petersburg to **Treasure Island Beach** (Mon–Sat hourly 5.50am–7.50pm, Sun hourly 6.50am–6.50pm). Change here for the Suncoast Trolley which travels along Gulf Boulevard and connects all the beaches from **Sand Key** to **Pass-a-Grille** (daily every half-hour 5.05am–10.10pm). Alternatively, there's a direct connection from Williams Park to **Indian Rocks Beach** with #59, **St Pete Beach** with #35, and to **Clearwater** with #18 and #52, where #80 continues **to Clearwater Beach**. PSTA bus fares are $1 one way. If you are making a number of journeys in one day, a daily Go Card can be purchased on board for $2.50 and provides unlimited trips on any PSTA vehicle for one day, while $12 buys a Seven-Day Unlimited pass – a real bargain if you're planning to explore the beaches over a number of days. Bicycles can be taken on buses. For further transport details, see "Buses around Clearwater Beach," p.345.

Accommodation

With the exception of camping, your choices are limited when seeking somewhere to sleep around the beaches. **Hotels** are plentiful, but tend to be filled with package tourists and are pricier than motels. Two unusual options are the luxurious *Don Cesar*, 3400 Gulf Blvd (☏727/360-1881, ⓦwww.doncesar.com; ❼–❽), described opposite, and the restored *Clearwater Beach Hotel*, 500 Mandalay Ave (☏727/441-2425 or 1-800/292-2295, ⓔcbhotel@msn.com, ⓦwww .clearwaterbeachhotel.com; ❹–❻).

Better value can be had at the **motels** that line mile after mile of Gulf Boulevard and the neighboring streets – typically $50–75 in winter, $15–20 less during the summer, though if you're staying long enough, many offer discounted weekly rates. Some also offer **self-catering** accommodation (basic amenities like a fridge and stove) for $5–10 above the basic room rate. Remember that a room on the beach side of Gulf Boulevard costs $5–10 more than an identical room across the street.

Lack of competition causes prices in **Pass-a-Grille** to be around $10 higher than you might pay a few miles north, but the district is much less built up than other areas and makes an excellent base. Try the *Pass-a-Grille Beach Motel*, 709 Gulf Way (☏727/367-4726; ❹), or, for a lengthy stay, opt for the cottages at *Island's End Resort*, 1 Pass-a-Grille (☏727/360-5023, ⓦwww.islandsend.com; ❺–❻). For the best deals in **St Petersburg Beach**, check out the *Florida Dolphin*, 6801 Sunset Way (☏727/360-7233; ❹), a secluded old hotel that features shuffleboard, a pool and a kitchen in each room or the *Ritz*, 4237 Gulf Blvd (☏727/360-7642, ⓦwww.rask.com/ritz; ❹), where guests can enjoy a marina, a waterfront picnic area and a pool. Further north on **Treasure Island**, try the *Beach House*, 12100 Gulf Blvd (☏727/360-1153; ❹); *Green Gables*, 11160 Gulf Blvd (☏727/360-0206; ❸); *Jolly Roger*, 11525 Gulf Blvd (☏727/360-5571; ❹); or *Sunrise*, 9360 Gulf Blvd (☏727/360-9210; ❹). In **Madeira Beach**, try the *Skyline*, 13999 Gulf Blvd (☏727/391-5817, ⓦwww.skylinemotel.com; ❹), across the street from the beach, which features a pool, a boat deck and cable TV.

In **Clearwater Beach**, you'll find the West Coast's only IYHA youth hostel at 606 Bay Esplanada (☏727/443-1211; ⓔmagillr1@juno.com), which has a pool, volleyball and tennis and offers free use of canoes and bike rental. Dorm beds cost $13 and private rooms are available from $75 a week. Reservations are advisable in December–April and August–September. Low-cost accommodation is also available at the adjacent *Sands Motel and Apts* (☏727/433-1211; ❷). Otherwise, the lowest rates are at *Bay Lawn*, 406 Hamden Drive (☏727/443-4529; ❹); *Cyprus Motel Apts*, 609 Cyprus Ave (☏727/442-3304; ❹); *Gulf Beach*, 419 Coronado Drive (☏727/447-3236; ❹), and *Olympia Motel*, 423 E Shore Drive (☏727/446-3384; ❹).

Camping

There are no **campgrounds** along the main beach strip, though the nearest and nicest spot, at Fort de Soto Park (see overleaf; ☏727/582-2267; ❶), is adjacent to sand and sea; no reservations can be made at this site. An inland alternative is *St Petersburg KOA*, 5400 95th St W (☏1-800/562-7714). Situated five miles east of Madeira Beach and tucked away on a mangrove bayou, this campground rents "kamping kabins" from $55 a night or tent sites for $38. Canoe and bike rentals are also available. *Clearwater/Tarpon Springs KOA*, 37061 Hwy-19 N (☏727/937-8412), six miles north of Clearwater, is handier for Clearwater Beach and charges $24 to pitch a tent.

The southern beaches

In twenty or so miles of heavily touristed coast, just one section has the feel of a genuine community with a history attached to it. The slender finger of **Pass-a-Grille**, at the very southern tip of the barrier island chain, was discovered in the early 1500s by Spanish explorers and became one of the first beach communities on the West Coast. Settled by fishermen in 1911, it is now recognized in the National Historic Registry. Named by French fishermen – "la passe aux grilleurs" because they grilled their catch at this pass – modern Pass-a-Grille comprises two miles of tidy houses, well-kept lawns, small shops and a cluster of bars and restaurants. On weekends, informed locals come to Pass-a-Grille's beach to enjoy one of the area's liveliest stretches of sand and the unobstructed views of the tiny islands that dot the entrance to Tampa Bay. **The Gulf Beaches Historical Museum**, 115 Tenth Ave (Thurs & Sat 10am–4pm, Sun 1–4pm; free; ☏727/360-2491), is situated here in what was the first church built on the barrier islands. The museum traces the history of the islands, from the 1500s to the present day, through photographs, news clippings and artifacts. For food in this area all the locals eat at *The Wharf*, 2001 Passe-a-Grille Way (☏727/367-9469), which forms part of the marina – an enormous bowl of fantastic clam chowder costs $3. Another popular option is *Sea Critter's Café*, 2007 Pass-a-Grille Way (☏727/360-3706), where patrons can feed the catfish from the docks. **The Suncoast Beach Trolley** serves Pass-a-Grille (see Buses between St Petersburg and the beaches, opposite).

The Don Cesar Hotel and around

A mile and a half north of Pass-a-Grille, at St Petersburg Beach, you won't need a signpost to locate the **Don Cesar Hotel**, 3400 Gulf Blvd (free guided tours Fri 11.30am; ☏727/360-1881). Contrasting sharply with the turquoise sea, this grandiose pink castle with white-trimmed arched windows and vaguely Moorish turrets rising above Gulf Boulevard and filling seven beachside acres was conceived by a Twenties property speculator, Thomas J. Rowe. The *Don Cesar* opened in 1928, but its glamour was shortlived. The Depression forced Rowe to use part of the hotel as a warehouse and later drove him to allow the New York Yankees baseball team to make it their spring training base. After decades as a military hospital and then as federal offices, the building received a $1-million facelift during the Seventies and regained its hotel function (see p.342 for details) – a vacation base for anyone with upwards of $200 a night to spare. The present interior bears little resemblance to its original appearance, but you should stride past the marble columns and crystal chandeliers of the lobby into the lounge, where you can soak up the understated elegance from the depths of a sofa or, just outside, from the poolside. The hotel offers live music every night, both inside and outside, and of course great sunsets.

Just beyond the *Don Cesar*, Pinellas County Bayway cuts inland and makes a good route to take to Fort de Soto Park (see below). Keeping to Gulf Boulevard brings you into the main section of **St Petersburg Beach**, a series of uninspiring rows of hotels, motels and eating places grouped along Gulf Boulevard and continuing for several miles. A very short break in the monotony is provided by a batch of pseudo-English shops around Corey Avenue. Further north, **Treasure Island** is even less varied, but does offer watersports galore for those bored with lying in the sun. An arching drawbridge crosses over to **Madeira Beach** and the wood-walled, tin-roofed shops, restaurants and bars of **John's Pass Village**, 12901 Gulf Blvd. Linked by a creaking boardwalk, the shops and the local fishing and pleasure-cruising fleet moored close by are mildly entertaining if you're at a (very) loose end. Madeira Beach itself is another sleepy place and if you can't make it to Pass-a-Grille, the local beach justifies a weekend fling. **Hubbard's Marina** (℡727/393-1947 or 1-800/755-0677, ⓦwww.hubbardsmarina.com, offers deep-sea fishing and the adjacent *Friendly Fisherman Seafood Restaurant* (daily 7am–11pm; ℡727/391-6025;) will cook the fish caught from their boats for you.

Suncoast Seabird Sanctuary
Four miles north of Madeira Beach, at **Indian Shores**, the **Suncoast Seabird Sanctuary**, 18328 Gulf Blvd (daily 9am–sunset; donations suggested; free guided tours Wed & Sun 2pm; ℡727/391-6211), offers a break from bronzing. The sanctuary is the largest wild-bird hospital in North America, treating between 400 and 600 convalescing birds, including pelicans, herons and turkey vultures at any one time. These birds, commonly injured by fishing lines or environmental pollution, are released back into their natural habitat once well.

Fort de Soto Park
If you have a car, you can soak up some of the history surrounding the St Petersburg beaches by heading across the Pinellas County Bayway, immediately north of the *Don Cesar*, then turning south along Route 679 to spend a day on the five islands comprising **Fort de Soto Park** (sunrise–sunset; free; ℡727/866-2484, ⓦwww.fortdesoto.com). The Spaniard credited with discovering Florida, Juan Ponce de León, is thought to have anchored here in 1513 and again in 1521 when the islands' indigenous inhabitants inflicted on him what proved to be a fatal wound. Centuries later, the islands became a strategically important Union base during the Civil War, and in 1898 a fort was constructed to forestall attacks on Tampa during the Spanish-American War. The remains of the fort – which was never completed – can be explored on one of several **walking trails**, which wind through an impressively untamed, thickly vegetated landscape featuring Australian pines and oaks, with plenty of palm-shaded picnic tables along the way. Pick up a leaflet for the self-guided walking tour of the fort, or join in a guided walking tour offered on Saturdays at 10am. Free nature tours through the park are also available at 10am at various locations.

Buses around Clearwater Beach

Clearwater Beach is good news for travelers without cars. **Around the beach strip,** the Jolly Trolley (☎727/445-1200) runs daily (Sun–Thurs 10am–10pm, Fri & Sat 10am–midnight) between Sand Key (from the *Sheraton Sand Key Resort*) and Clearwater Beach (along Gulfview Boulevard, Mandalay Avenue and Acacia Street); fares are 50¢. **To the mainland,** another JollyTrolley runs between the beach and downtown Clearwater for 50¢. Alternatively, catch bus #80, which operates between Clearwater Beach and Clearwater's Park Street terminal (info: ☎727/530-9911). **Useful routes** from the terminal are: #80 to Honeymoon Island Sand Quay; #18 and #52 to St Petersburg; #66 to Tarpon Springs; and #200X (weekdays and rush hours only) to Tampa. A much less frequent mainland link is provided by two daily Amtrak buses, running from Tampa in lieu of trains; they stop in Clearwater at 657 Court St, and at Clearwater Beach's Civic Center. The Greyhound station in Clearwater is at 2811 Gulf-to-Bay Blvd (☎727/796-7315).

Three miles of swimmer-friendly **beaches** line the park, which possess an intoxicating air of isolation during the week – a far cry from the busy beach strips. The best way to savor the area is by **camping**, see "Accommodation," p.343.

The northern beaches

Much of the **northern section** of **Sand Key**, the longest barrier island in the St Petersburg chain, is lined by stylish condos and time-share apartments – this is one of the wealthier bits of the coast. It ends with the pretty **Sand Key Park**, where tall palm trees frame a scintillating strip of sand. The classic beach vista is a good spot to watch dolphins, though the view is marred by the nearby high-rises.

The 65 acres of Sand Key Park occupy one bank of Clearwater Pass, across which a belt of sparkling white sands characterize **Clearwater Beach**, another community devoted to the holiday industry. Motels fill its side streets, while more expensive accommodation overlooks the Gulf. The endearing small-town ambience makes this a pleasant place to spend a couple of days, certainly preferable to Clearwater's dull downtown. For information about accommodation, try the **Chamber of Commerce**, 100 Coronado Drive (Mon–Fri 9am–5pm; ☎727/447-7600, ⓕ 443-7812, ⓦwww.beachchamber.com). A crucial plus for non-drivers is the regular bus links between Clearwater Beach and the mainland town of **Clearwater** – reached by a two-mile causeway where you'll find connections to St Petersburg and Tarpon Springs, and a Greyhound station (see box above). Clearwater has its own **information point** separate from that of Clearwater Beach at 1130 Cleveland St (Mon–Fri 8.30am–5pm; ☎727/461-0011, ⓕ449-2889).

The Clearwater Marine Aquarium, 249 Windward Passage (Mon–Fri 9am–5pm, Sat 9am–4pm, Sun 11am–4pm; $7.75; ☎727/441-1790, ⓦwww.CMAquarium.org), is well worth a break from the beach. At this non-profit working aquarium, injured marine mammals, sea turtles and river otters are rescued and rehabilitated. Visitors can learn ways to help protect these animals and visit exhibits on Florida's coastal ecology and tanks of stingrays and sharks. Beyond its sands and two long piers, there's not much else to do in Clearwater Beach: if the brine beckons, board a mock pirate vessel for a two-hour *Captain Memo* "pirate cruise" (daily 10am & 2pm, $28; evening Champagne Cruises at varying times through the year, $30; ☎727/446-2587,

more adventurously, make a daytrip to the Caladesi or Honeymoon islands, a
few miles north.

Listed on the National Register of Historic Places and a short trip inland
from the intracoastal waterway, the **Belleview Biltmore Resort Hotel**, 25
Belleview Blvd, Clearwater (℡ 727/442-6171, ⓦ www.belleviewbiltmore.com;
❸–❻), is a beautiful wooden construction dating from 1897. It sits high on a
bluff and consists of 145 rooms. Originally owned by the railroad magnate
Henry B. Plant, who entertained important shippers and celebrities here, the
Belleview has been immaculately preserved and is well worth a look inside and
out. You can explore the hotel by joining one of the **historic tours** (daily
11am; $5, or $15 including lunch).

Honeymoon and Caladesi islands

These islands were created in 1921 when a hurricane tore the aptly named
Hurricane Pass out of what was a single, five-mile island. These islands are
now protected state parks (each $4 per car; $1 pedestrians and cyclists) that
offer a chance to see the jungle-like terrain that covered the whole coast
before the bulldozers arrived. Of the two, only **Honeymoon Island** can be
reached by road; take Route 586 off Hwy-19 just north of Dunedin (or bus
#80 from Clearwater). The island earned its name when Paramount newsreels
and *Life* magazine gave away all-expenses-paid honeymoons on the island as
a grand prize in a 1940s contest. Today the condos that sprout from
Honeymoon Island dent its natural impact, but a wild pocket at the end of the
road is well worth exploring on the walking trail that runs around the edge
of the entire island.

For a glimpse of what these islands must have looked like before the onset of
mass tourism, make for **Caladesi Island**, just to the south. From a signposted
landing stage beside Route 586 on Honeymoon Island, the **Caledesi
Connections** ferry ($6 round-trip) crosses between the islands daily on the
hour every hour on weekdays and every half-hour at weekends, between 10am
and 4.30pm (hours may vary, ℡ 727/734-5263). A ferry service also runs from
the Clearwater marina. Once ashore at Caladesi's mangrove-fringed marina,
boardwalks lead to a beach of unsurpassed tranquillity: perfect for swimming,
sunbathing and shell collecting. While here, though, summon up the strength
to tackle the three-mile **nature trail**, which cuts inland through saw palmetto and slash pines to an observation tower. Be certain to bring food and drink
to the island, as the poorly stocked snack bar at the marina is the sole source
of sustenance.

Eating

It's easy to find a decent place to **eat** around the beaches. At 807 Gulf Way, the
Hurricane Restaurant (℡ 727/360-9558; you can also pitch a tent here for
$16.50) sports a well-priced menu of the freshest seafood. It also features some
of the area's top **jazz** musicians; further north, the *Sea Horse*, 800 Pass-a-Grille
(closed Tues; ℡ 727/360-1734), is strong on sandwiches; *Pep's Sea Grille*, 5895
Gulf Blvd (℡ 727/367-3550), creates inspired combinations of moderately
priced pasta and seafood; *Debby's*, 7370 Gulf Blvd (℡ 727/367-8700), serves
substantial breakfasts and lunches at insubstantial prices; *46th South Beach*, 46
46th Ave, St Pete's Beach (℡ 727/360-9414), offers nightly specials, such as the
"one-pound you-peel-em shrimp dinner," and Bloody Marys for just $1; and
O'Malley's Bar, 7745 Blind Pass Way (℡ 727/360-2050), grills the thickest,

juiciest burgers around at reasonable prices. If you're feeling wealthy, and inordinately hungry, on a Sunday, show up in smart attire for the lunch **buffet** at the *Don Cesar*, 3400 Gulf Blvd (☏727/360-1881), which starts at 10.30am and costs $28.95 per person.

In Clearwater Beach, *Alex*, 305 Coronado Drive (☏727/447-4560), and *Coca Cabana Motel*, 669 Mandalay Ave (☏727/446-7775), are good for cheap breakfasts, as is the always-packed *IHOP (International House of Pancakes)* attached to the *Quality Inn* at 655 South Gulfview Blvd. The moderately priced *Frenchy's Shrimp and Oyster Café*, 41 Baymont St (☏727/446-3607), cooks up grouper burgers and shrimp sandwiches; *Seafood & Sunsets*, 351 S Gulfview Blvd (☏727/441-2548), provides inexpensive seafood, ideally consumed while watching the sun sink. Larger appetites should be sated by the **dinner buffets** for $11.95 spread out at the *Holiday Inn Sunspree,* 715 S Gulfview Blvd (☏727/447-9566).

Nightlife

As you'd expect, most **nightlife** is aimed at tourists, though there are exceptions. Many hotel and restaurant bars have lengthy **Happy Hours** and lounges designed for watching the sunset while sipping a cocktail – look for the signs and ads in the free tourist magazines. For more cut-rate boozing, investigate *Jammins*, 470 Mandalay Ave (☏727/441-2005), or the *Beach Bar*, 454 Mandalay Ave (☏727/446-8866). *Pier 60* on Clearwater Beach (☏727/449 1036) hosts a free daily street festival in celebration of the sunset (weather permitting), featuring live music and entertainment.

Bland pop bands are two-a-penny in the hotels. For better **live music**, aim for one of the following: the *Harp and Thistle*, 650 Corey Ave (☏727/360-4104), hosting Irish folksters most nights; *Shephards,* 601 S Gulfview Blvd (☏727/441-6875), for the **reggae** bands on the weekend. In Clearwater Beach, there's reggae of fluctuating standards at *Cha Cha Coconuts*, 1241 Gulf Blvd (☏727/569-6040). **Country** music can be heard every night at *Joyland*, 11225 Hwy-19 S (☏727/573-1919).

In downtown Clearwater, the Royalty Theatre, 405 Cleveland St (☏727/441-8868, ⓦwww.royaltytheatre.org), offers country music and jazz, and all proceeds from ticket sales are used to further renovate this beautiful historic building. Those wanting to club the night away should head for the *Liquid Blue* nightclub, 22 N Fort Harrison.

Tarpon Springs

Greek sponge-divers driven out of Key West by xenophobic locals during the early 1900s resettled in **TARPON SPRINGS**, ten miles north of Clearwater off Hwy-19 (use Alt 19 – called Pinellas Avenue here – to arrive in the center and have a map on hand). These early migrants began what has become a sizeable Greek community in a town previously the preserve of wealthy wintering northerners. Demand for sponges was unprecedented during World War II (among other attributes, sponges are excellent for mopping up blood), but the industry was later devastated by a marine blight and the development of synthetic sponges. The Greek presence in Tarpon Springs remains strong, however, and is most evident each January 6 when around 30,000 participate in the country's largest Greek Orthodox Epiphany celebration. Each year, an even greater number of visitors traipse around the souvenir shops lining the old

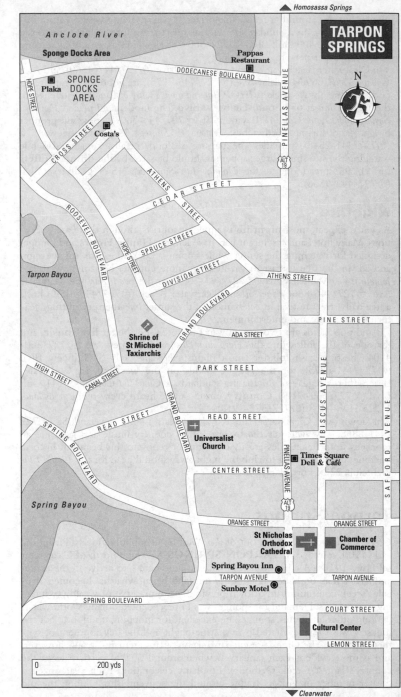

Homosassa Springs

TARPON SPRINGS

N

Anclote River

Sponge Docks Area

Pappas Restaurant

DODECANESE BOULEVARD

PINELLAS AVENUE

ALT 19

Plaka

SPONGE DOCKS AREA

Costa's

CROSS STREET

ATHENS STREET

CEDAR STREET

ROOSEVELT BOULEVARD

HOPE STREET

SPRUCE STREET

Tarpon Bayou

DIVISION STREET

GRAND BOULEVARD

ATHENS STREET

PINE STREET

Shrine of St Michael Taxiarchis

ADA STREET

PARK STREET

HIBISCUS AVENUE

SAFFORD AVENUE

HIGH STREET

CANAL STREET

READ STREET

READ STREET

SPRING BOULEVARD

Universalist Church

Times Square Deli & Café

CENTER STREET

PINELLAS AVENUE

ALT 19

Spring Bayou

ORANGE STREET

ORANGE STREET

St Nicholas Orthodox Cathedral

Chamber of Commerce

Spring Bayou Inn

Sunbay Motel

TARPON AVENUE

TARPON AVENUE

SPRING BOULEVARD

COURT STREET

Cultural Center

LEMON STREET

0   200 yds

Clearwater

sponge docks, largely neglecting the rest of the small town which – from restored buildings to weeping icons – has much more to offer.

The town

Greek names appear on virtually every shop front throughout Tarpon Springs, and although most of the shops lining the busy Pinellas Avenue bill themselves as antique dealers, their displays gleam with newness. Don't stop here, but follow the "docks" signs. On the right you'll see the strongest symbol in this Greek community: the resplendent Byzantine-Revival **St Nicholas Orthodox Cathedral**, on the corner of Pinellas Avenue and Orange Street (daily 10am–4pm; free; ☎727/937-3540), partly funded by a half-percent levy on local sponge sales and finished in 1943. The full significance of the cathedral's ornate interior is inevitably lost on those not of the faith, though the icons and slow-burning incense create an intensely spiritual atmosphere.

After leaving the cathedral, drop into the nearby **Tarpon Springs Cultural Center**, 101 S Pinellas Ave (Mon–Fri 8am–5pm, Sat 10am–5pm; free except for special events; ☎727/942-5605), a facility which identifies, preserves and promotes the city's heritage and cultural and natural resources. It regularly stages imaginative exhibitions about Tarpon Springs' past and present, as well as art exhibitions. For $2, you can also pick up a forty-page pamphlet detailing a self-guided walking tour of historic Tarpon Springs, which has to be one of the best ways to absorb the history and architecture of this area. This Neoclassical building has served as the city hall since 1915, when Tarpon Avenue, a street away, was a bustling commercial strip. This is where butchers, bakers and grocers once plied their trades from stumpy masonry structures, many of which still stand. Several have now been converted into curio filled antique shops, which make for a good half-hour's walk.

The Universalist Church and George Innes Junior Collection

Walking west along Tarpon Avenue takes you downhill to **Spring Bayou**, a crescent-shaped lake ringed by the opulent homes of Tarpon Springs' pre-sponge-era residents, who were primarily a mix of tycoons and artists.

Universalist Church, 57 Read St (Oct–May Tues–Sun 2–5pm, donations suggested; ☎727/937-4682), is known for its collection of whimsical paintings by the early-twentieth century landscapist George Innes Junior. To mark what would have been the 100th birthday of his late father (George Innes Senior, also a renowned artist), Innes painted a delicate rendition of the Spring Bayou, now the centerpiece of the church's collection. Innes spent much of his career mired in depression and mediocrity, but this singular work seemed to ignite a creative spark and prompted the series of hauntingly beautiful paintings that dominate the church's walls today. The paintings once hung in the Louvre, but after George Junior's death, his widow paid for their safe return. Helpful locals guide you through the collection; of particular note are the murals Innes painted to stop up the church's windows, which were blown out by a hurricane in 1918.

Keeping to a religious theme and just a few minutes' walk from the Universalist Church, the simple wooden **Shrine of St Michael Taxiarchis**, at 113 Hope St (always open), was erected by a local woman in gratitude for the unexplained recovery of her "terminally ill" son in 1939. Numerous instances of the blind regaining their sight and the crippled throwing away their walking sticks after visiting the shrine have been reported, all detailed in a free pamphlet.

The sponge docks

Along Dodecanese Boulevard, on the banks of the Anclote River, the **sponge docks** are a disappointing conglomeration of one-time supply stores turned into restaurants and gift shops touting cassettes of Greek "belly-dancing music" and, of course, sponges ($4 for a small specimen). A boat departs regularly throughout the day on a half-hour **sponge-diving trip** from the St Nicholas Boat Line, 693 Dodecanese Blvd ($5; ℡727/942-6425). The trip includes a cruise through the sponge docks, a talk on the history of sponge-diving and a demonstration of harvesting performed in a traditional brass-helmeted diving suit; these days only a few sponge boats still operate commercially.

You'll pay less, and learn more about the local community and sponge-diving, in a group of shops at 510 Dodecanese Blvd, whose **Spongerama Exhibit Center** (Mon–Sat 10am–6pm, Sun noon–4pm; free; ℡727/942-3771) includes the Museum of Sponge Diving and a half-hour film detailing where sponges grow and how they are harvested. It also traces the history of Tarpon Springs' Greek settlers and shows the primitive techniques still used in the industry. Some of the museum exhibits are showing signs of aging, and sponging terminology sounds much more raunchy than it really is – "nude sponging" and "thrusting hookers" are two themes explored in the displays. A shop sells alligator heads with their mouths held open, but the only real reason to hang around is the free **sponge-diving shows**, which run roughly half-hourly from 10am to 4.30pm just outside Spongerama.

Once you've had your fill of sponges and tourist shops, the **Konger Tarpon Spring Aquarium**, 850 Dodecanese Blvd (Mon–Sat 10am–5pm, Sun noon–5pm; $4.75; ℡727/938-5378), is a small aquarium with a simulated coral reef, complete with native plants and tropical fish, while a tidal pool offers a closer look at such creatures as starfish and hermit crabs. For a really lazy and very pleasurable half-day, you can take a **boat tour** to nearby **Anclote Key** with Island Wind Tours from 600 Dodecanese Blvd (℡727/934-0606). One hour is $5, half a day is $20.

Practicalities

Collect general **information** and a map guide to historical sites and points of interest in downtown from the **Chamber of Commerce**, 11 E Orange St, opposite the cathedral (Mon–Fri 8.30am–5pm; ℡727/937-6109, ⓦwww.tarponsprings.com). On weekends, head for the **visitor center** at the City Marina (Tues–Sun 10.30am–4.30pm; ℡727/937-9165).

Tarpon Springs makes a sensible **overnight stop** if you're continuing north. A number of motels dot the junctions with Hwy-19, and the most central is the *Sunbay Motel*, 57 W Tarpon Ave (℡727/934-1001; ❷); or, for bed and breakfast, try the *Spring Bayou Inn*, 32 W Tarpon Ave (℡727/938-9333). The *Gulf Manor Motel*, 548 Whitcomb Blvd (℡727/937-4207; ❸), is in a beautiful setting overlooking Spring Bayou.

For **eating**, check out *Pappas Restaurant*, 10 W Dodecanese Blvd (℡727/937-5101), whose large parking garage is a blessing in itself (there aren't many places to leave your car in the center of town), and the large if rather pricey portions of seafood are very satisfying. For excellent syrupy pastries, or to stock up on homemade Greek breads, head to *Apollo Bakery* at the docks, and don't forget their chocolate baklava ($1.99). Cheap breakfasts can be found at *Bread and Butter Deli*, 1880 Pinellas Ave (℡727/934-9003). In the Arcade at 210 Pinellas Ave, the *Times Square Deli & Café* (℡727/934-4026) has sandwiches and snacks to eat in or take away. For a fuller sit-down meal, sample the inexpensive Greek dishes at *Costa's*, 510 Athens St (℡727/938-6890), or *Plaka*, 769 Dodecanese Blvd (℡727/934-4752), which specializes in seafood, salads and souvlaki.

The Big Bend

Popularly known as the **BIG BEND** for the way it curves towards the Panhandle, Florida's **northwest coast** is one of its best-kept secrets. Far from the tourist beaches and theme parks, this sparsely populated coastline offers thousands of mangrove islands and marshlands, wide spring-fed rivers and quiet roads leading to small communities. Here you will find some of the best wildlife Florida has to offer and – in one instance – an outstanding Native American ceremonial site. Sand-crazy visitors miss it all by barreling towards the Tampa Bay beaches on Hwy-19, the region's only major road, ignoring the Big Bend. For the more inquisitive visitor, this area will reward you with a taste of the real Florida.

Homosassa Springs and around

The main highway out of Tampa Bay, Hwy-19, is a roadside clutter of filling stations and used-car lots and something of a parking lot, until you reach New Port Richey – an uninteresting series of condos and time-share properties. A quicker route out of the area is to take I-275, which becomes I-75 after it leaves Tampa, then head west on Hwy-98 at junction 61. By the time you reach Hwy-19, after approximately twenty miles, it has become a more soothing, if often monotonous, landscape of hardwood and pine forests along with expanses of swamp. Those taking this route to the Big Bend who are planning a visit to **Weeki Wachee Springs Waterpark** should join Hwy-50 at Brooksville, while those on Hwy-19 will remain on it until the junction with Hwy-50, about thirty miles north of Clearwater. Weeki Wachee Springs (daily 9.30am–5.30pm in winter, longer hours in summer; $16.95, children 3–16 $12.95; ☎ 352/596-2062 or 1-800/678-9335, ⓦ www.weekiwachee .com) opened in 1947 and has attracted numerous celebrities – including Elvis – to its thoroughly kitsch underwater shows performed by "mermaids" in one of the Big Bend's many natural springs. The park also offers a Wilderness River Cruise, a petting zoo and bird shows and is now part of its own city. There are plenty of places to stay, although it can be visited as a daytrip from Clearwater. During the summer months it is possible to buy a combination ticket which allows access to the adjacent **Buccaneer Bay Water Park** (☎ 352/596-2062), where you can swim and play on the water slides to your heart's content.

The desire to see animals and (real) sea life is better satisfied twenty miles north at **HOMOSASSA SPRINGS**, the first community of any size on Hwy-19. The **Homosassa Springs State Wildlife Park** (daily 9am–5.30pm; $7.95; ☎ 352/628-2311, ⓦ www.homosassasprings.org), is a showcase of Florida's native wildlife, offering a chance to see animals, birds and plants in their natural setting. Squirrel-infested walking trails lead to a gushing spring and an underwater observatory where you can see numerous fish and manatees firsthand. Daily educational programs offer the opportunity of learning more about the wildlife on show. The park also serves as a rehabilitation center and refuge for endangered West Indian manatees that have been orphaned or injured in the wild. To get a feel for the town, go a couple of miles west along the oak-lined Route 490, passing the crumbling walls and rusting machinery of the **Yulee**

Sugar Mill, originally owned by David Yulee, Florida's first congressman and the financier of the 1860s Cedar Key to Fernandina Beach rail line (see "Cedar Key," p.354), which he extended to Homosassa Springs. With the railway long gone this tranquil town's old wooden houses are finding favor with young artists: drop into the Riverworks Gallery, 10844 W Yulee Drive (☎352/628-0822), to see some of the better works, or the Old Mill House Printing Museum, 10466 W Yulee Drive, (☎352/628-0822), which, in addition to an art gallery, has antique printing presses on display.

Practicalities

Homosassa Springs is a good option if you're seeking somewhere to **stay** off the beaten track. Avoid the usual chain motels on Hwy-19 and spend a night at *Homosassa Riverside Resort*, 5297 S Cherokee Way (☎352/628-2474 or 1-800/442-2040, ⓦwww.homosassariverside.com; ❷–❸). In addition to a pool and riverside **bar** and **restaurant**, this established resort on the banks of the Homosassa River, offers boat rentals and the chance to swim with the manatees. **Campers** should head for the centrally located *Nature Resort Campground and Marina*, 10359 W Halls River Rd (☎352/628-9544 or 1-800/301-7880), which charges $19.44 per night to pitch a tent.

Crystal River and around

Seven miles further north along Hwy-19, **CRYSTAL RIVER** is among the region's larger communities – its population is a whopping four thousand. Many residents are retirees, fearful of the crime in Florida's urban areas and unable to afford the more southerly sections of the coast. You'd never guess it from the drab Hwy-19, but quite a few arrivals are also drawn here by the sedate beauty of the clear river from which the town takes its name. **Manatees** take a shine to it as well: they can be seen all year round, but during the winter greater numbers are found at the **Chassahowitzka National Wildlife Refuge** (Mon–Fri 7.30am–4pm; ☎352/563-208), accessible by turning west

---

Manatees

Manatees are one of Florida's most beloved creatures, but sadly also one of their most endangered. More closely related to elephants and aardvarks than to other sea life, it's hard to believe that these large – they can grow up to thirteen feet and weigh up to 3500 pounds – docile animals are the source of the mermaid myth. Manatees are harmless and love to graze on seagrasses in shallow water, surfacing every three to four minutes to breathe. They have been on the endangered species list since 1973, and there are only an estimated 2000 left in Florida waters. With no natural predators, a third of manatee deaths have human-related causes, such as accidents with boats, pollution and flood control gates that automatically close. Although scientists believe that manatees can live to 60 or longer, their slow development to sexual maturity and low birth rate does little to compensate for their disproportionately high death rate. Manatees may be endangered, but Florida law prohibits breeding them; resources, they say, are better spent on the care and rehabilitation of wild manatees who have suffered the blows of ship's propellers or river poisoning. You should never approach, feed or touch manatees in the wild and if you see an injured or dead one, a calf with no adult around, or see anyone harassing one, call the Florida Marine Patrol on ☎1-800/342-5367.

on Hwy-19 at Paradise Point Road in Crystal River. Here you can also swim, snorkel and scuba dive and there are also plenty of boat trips in the area. The American Pro Diving Center, 821 SE Hwy-19 (☎352/563-0041 or 1-800 /291-3483, ⓦwww.americanprodiving.com), offers all kinds of guided dives starting at $30 and rents great waterfront villas from $70 a night, so you can step right out into a boat in the morning.

Crystal River's present dwellers are by no means the first to live by the waterway. It provided a source of food for Native Americans from at least 200 BC. To gain some insight on Indian culture, take State Park Road off Hwy-19 just north of the town to the **Crystal River State Archeological Site**, 3400 N Museum Point (daily 8am–sunset; cars $2, pedestrians and cyclists $1; ☎352/795-3817), where the temple, burial and shell midden mounds are still visible. Inside the **visitor center** (daily 9am–5pm), there is an enlightening assessment of finds from the 450 graves discovered here, indicating trade links with tribes far to the north. More fascinating, however, are the connections with the south. The site contains two *stele*, or ceremonial stones, much more commonly found in Mexico. The engravings – thought to be faces of sun deities – suggest that large-scale solar ceremonies were conducted here. The sense of the past and the serenity of the setting make the site a highly evocative educational experience. Don't pass it by.

Practicalities

Other than diving and visiting the archeological site, Crystal River doesn't have much to justify a long stop, though if you're traveling by Greyhound (the station is at 200 N Hwy-19; ☎352/795-4445), it's useful for an overnight rest. The cheapest **accommodation** is provided by *Days Inn*, just north of the town on Hwy-19 (☎352/795-2111; ❷); more expensive but more relaxing is the *Plantation Inn*, on Route 44 (☎1-800/632-6662 or 352/795-4211; ❺–❽). If you're planning some diving and an overnight stay, check out the dive-and-accommodation packages offered by the *Best Western*, 614 NW Hwy-19 (☎352/795-3171; ❸). The closest **campground** is *Rock Crusher Canyon*, 275 Rock Crusher Rd (☎352/795-3878, ⓦwww.rockcrushercanyon.com), where it costs $35 a night to pitch a tent. The site is also home to Florida's largest natural amphitheater, where a wide variety of live music is regularly performed. For **food**, try the basic but dependable *Crystal Paradise Restaurant*, 508 Citrus Ave (☎352/563-2620). The **Chamber of Commerce**, 28 NW Hwy-19 (Mon–Fri 9am–4pm; ☎352/795-3149), can supply general facts on Crystal River and around.

Yankeetown and around

Ten miles north of Crystal River, Hwy-19 spans the **Florida Barge Canal**. Conceived in the 1820s to provide a cargo link between the Gulf and Atlantic coasts, work on the canal only started in the 1930s and – thanks largely to the efforts of conservationists – was abandoned in the 1970s with just six miles completed. The bridge offers a view of the Crystal River nuclear power station, the area's major employer and the reason why local telephone books carry instructions on how to survive a nuclear catastrophe.

Further on, taking any left turn off Hwy-19 will invariably lead to some tiny, eerily quiet community, where fishing on the local river is the only sign of life. One such place is **YANKEETOWN**, five miles west of Inglis on Route 40, reputedly named for some Yankee soldiers who moved here following the Civil War. Yankeetown's claim to fame is that in 1961 Elvis filmed *Follow That Dream* in several locations around the area: the bridge over Bird Creek was the main set, and Route 40 is also known as Follow That Dream Parkway. Those who follow it to the very end will be rewarded with a large stretch of serene, isolated water, populated only by herons and the ubiquitous fishermen.

This area contains many parks and preserves, most with something to recommend them. Two of the largest are **Withlacoochee State Forest** (south of Route 44) and **Chassahowitzka National Wildlife Refuge** (west of Hwy-19, see p.352). Further north, the protected wildlife habitats of the **Wacassassa State Preserve** cover the salt marshes and tidal creeks on the coastal side of Hwy-19 as you travel on from Yankeetown. A breeding ground for deer and turkey, and sometimes visited by black bear and Florida panthers, these swampy lands are intended to allow the state's indigenous creatures to replenish their numbers. Humans are not allowed free rein, though there are periodic ranger-guided **canoe trips** through the area; call ☎ 352/543-5567 for details. More information can be found at the **Chamber of Commerce**, 167 Follow That Dream Parkway (Mon–Fri 10am–1pm; ☎ 352/447-3383). For motel **accommodation** try the Withlacoochee Motel, 66 Hwy-19 S (☎ 352/447-2211), or you can **camp** on the banks of the Withlacoochee River at *B's Marina*, 6621 Riverside Drive (☎ 352/447-5888, ✉ dbmarin@citrus.infi.net).

Cedar Key

Whatever you do on your way north, don't deny yourself a day or two at the splendidly isolated and charmingly scenic community of **CEDAR KEY**. To find it, turn west on Hwy-19 onto Route 24 at the hamlet of Otter Creek and drive for 24 miles until the road ends. In the 1860s, the railroad from Fernandina Beach (see "The Northeast Coast" p.244) ended its journey here, turning the community – which occupies one of several small islands – into a thriving port. When ships got bigger and moved on to deeper harbors, Cedar Key began cutting down its cypress, pine and cedar trees to fuel a pencil-producing industry. Inevitably, the trees were soon gone, and by 1900 Cedar Key was all but a ghost town. The few who stayed eked out a living from fishing and harvesting oysters, as many of the thousand-strong population still do. Cedar Key has, however, undergone a revival. Many decaying, timber-framed warehouses have been turned into restaurants and shops, and more holiday homes are appearing. Given the town's remoteness, however (there's no public transport from other communities in the area), it's unlikely that Cedar Key will ever be deluged with visitors – the only remotely busy periods are during the Seafood Festival sponsored by the Cedar Key Lions Club (☎ 352/543-5600) in October and the arts and crafts show during April – and the place remains a fascinating example of the Old South.

The island and around

With its rustic, ramshackle galleries, old wooden houses on Second Street, and the glittering reflections off the waters of Cedar Key's unspoilt bay, the island is perfect for exploring. The **Cedar Key State Museum,** 1710 Museum Drive (Thurs–Mon 9am–5pm; $1; ☏352/543-5350), exhibits household items from the past and boasts an enormous collection of exotic shells from around the region. The **Historical Society Museum,** on the corner of D and Second streets (Mon–Sat 11am–4pm, Sun 2–4pm; $1; ☏352/543-5549), reveals the fact that this, in fact, is not the original Cedar Key. The uninhabited island cloaked in foliage across the water bore the town's name until the end of the nineteenth century, when a hurricane tore every building to pieces. The devastated ruins of a bed-and-breakfast still sulk near the dock, and now serve as the adopted home of a troupe of pelicans. The birds' presence has helped make this Cedar Key's most popular postcard scene. The museum also supplies various leaflets, including a 50¢ map of Cedar Key, and a **historic walking tour** guide for $2.

If you're staying for several days, take a boat trip out to the twelve islands within a five-mile radius of Cedar Key – set aside in 1929 by President Hoover as the **Cedar Keys National Wildlife Refuge**. *Island Hopper,* at the City Marina on Dock Street (☏352/543-5904, ⓦwww.cedarkeyislandhopper.com), operates daily cruises to **Seahorse Key** for $12 and boat rentals. Seahorse Key boasts a pretty lighthouse built in 1851. At 52 feet, it is the highest point of land on the Gulf Coast. Landing is prohibited on the key between March and June when the island becomes a sanctuary for nesting birds; during this time the *Island Hopper* lands at another key in the area. For a more personalized tour of the area, consider the **kayak tours** run by Wild Florida Adventures (☏352/528-2741 or 1-888/247-5070, ⓦwww.wild-florida.com), which explore much of the Big Bend as well as the lower Suwannee River. Their half-day tours cover the **Lower Suwannee National Wildlife Refuge**, which fronts 26 miles of the Gulf of Mexico and is an ideal place to see the nesting grounds of a multitude of birds, including white ibis, egret, blue herons, ospreys and brown pelicans. They also offer a sunset/moonrise tour from which you can watch the moon rise over the water and maybe even spot a dolphin in the moonlight. Both tours cost $50.

Practicalities

The **Chamber of Commerce**, next door to the former city hall on Second Street (Mon, Wed & Fri 10am–1pm; ☏352/543-5600, ⓦwww.cedarkey.org), has a cozy visitor's center with all the usual neighborhood information. When this is closed, try the Cedar Key State Museum (see above) or Cedar Key Bookstore on Second Street for information. There's no shortage of **accommodation** on offer, and the visitor's center has a useful color-picture guide detailing what's available. The 140-year-old *Island Hotel,* at the corner of Second and B streets (☏352/543-5111 or 1-800/432-4640, ⓦwww.islandhotel -cedarkey.com; ❹–❺), has sloping wooden floors, overhanging verandas and sepia murals dating from 1915. For huge, comfortable suites on the waterfront, head to the luxurious *Island Place* by the dock (☏352/543-5307; ⓕ543-9141 or 1-800/780-6522, ⓦwww.islandplace-ck.com; ❺–❻). For a standard room or a cottage with a kitchen, try the *Faraway Inn,* on the corner of Third and G streets (☏352/543-5330; ❷–❸); or *Pirates' Cove,* half a mile from the center on Route 24 (☏352/543-5141, ⓦwww.crestcomm.com/pirates-cove; ❷–❸). **Tents** can be pitched at *Sunset Isle RV Park,* three miles away on Route 24 (☏352/543-5375; $12).

Eating freshly caught seafood is a great way to while away a few hours in Cedar Key: oysters, smoked mullet and fried trout are among the local, rather expensive specialities. Three likely spots to sample the goods are close to each other along Dock Street (and too conspicuous to have street numbers). *The Captain's Table* (☏352/543-5441) serves sandwiches of flounder, oyster or

> ### Bikes, cars and Cedar Key's slow pace
>
> The island is made for walking, but renting a **bike** from the dock on Third Street
> (☎ 352/543-9143) is also an enjoyable option. If you're driving, the one thing
> you're sure to notice is the absurdly slow speed limits – sometimes down to fifteen
> miles per hour despite the absence of traffic. Don't be lulled into thinking the traf-
> fic police don't bother. They do.

crabcake for around $5. Lunches of fried shrimp, scallops or mullet go for $8,
and dinner consists of bigger portions of the same for $14–20. The *Brown Pelican*
(☎ 352/543-5428) has devilled and soft claw crab, oysters, perch and flounder
for around $17. Next door, the *Sunset Room Restaurant* (☎ 352/543-5428) has a
big model manatee outside and boasts having the "highest view in Cedar Key"
– a dubious claim considering the island is pancake-flat. A cheap alternative,
away from the dock, is *Annie's Café*, on the corner of Hwy-24 and Sixth Street
(☎ 352/543-6141), serving good, homestyle breakfasts and lunches. For cheap,
wholesome eats, try the plain-looking *Cook's Café* (☎ 352/543-5548) on
Second Street; the fresh fish special of grouper, mullet and shrimp is a bargain.

North towards the Panhandle

Back on Hwy-19, there's a featureless ninety-mile slog to the next noticeable town,
Perry. The lumber industry for which the place is famous is celebrated in the
Forest Capitol State Museum, one mile south of the town, at 204 Forest Park
Drive (Thurs–Mon 9am–5pm; $1; ☎ 352/584-3227); exhibits include an 1860 fur-
nished "cracker" home of limited interest. The only reason to stay in Perry is if
you're too tired to travel any further, and there are a number of motels on Hwy-19
set up for just that, the best deal being the *Villager Lodge*, 2238 S Hwy-19
(☎ 352/584-4221; ❶). Otherwise, nothing breaks the journey **north towards the
Panhandle**, fifty miles distant. Gas stations are less frequent and more expensive on
this stretch of road, so if you're driving fill up in advance. To reach Tallahassee, stick
to Hwy-19 (from here also known as Hwy-27), or, for the Panhandle coast, branch
west with Hwy-98. The Panhandle is fully detailed in Chapter Seven.

The Southwest Coast

Flavoring the 150 miles of coast south of Tampa Bay are several unique towns
with origins dating back to the early days of Florida's incorporation into the
US. Residents here lead more tranquil lives away from the bustle of the big city,
and until the last few decades had an easy job preserving their seclusion.
Nowadays, newer communities in the vicinity are beginning to expand at a
colossal rate and large-scale tourism is prevalent. Accommodation prices double in high season – December to April – and can be hard to find on the weekends in more popular areas. However, for those prepared to venture off the
tourist trail, there is more to Florida's southwest coast than sun, sand and sea.
A mixture of history, culture and wildlife awaits discovery in this fine balance
of mainland sights and beaches begging for exploration, and the **Everglades
National Park** at the region's southernmost border is the grand finale.

South from Tampa Bay

Taking I-275 south from St Petersburg (a preferable route to the lackluster I-75 or Hwy-41 from Tampa), you'll soar over Tampa Bay on the **Sunshine Skyway Bridge**, high enough to allow ocean-going ships to pass beneath and for the outlines of land and sea to become blurred in the heat haze. The original Sunshine Skyway was rammed by a phosphate tanker during a storm in May 1980, causing the central span of the southbound section to collapse. With visibility reduced to a few feet, drivers on the bridge failed to spot the gap, and 35 people, including the occupants of a Greyhound bus, plunged 250 feet to their deaths; this tragedy was the worst of several fatal accidents on the Sunshine Skyway. The southern and northern sections of the remains have now been turned into the longest fishing piers in the world (access costs $3 per vehicle), while the central section, submerged in the waters at the mouth of Tampa Bay, creates an artificial reef. The Sunshine Skyway Bridge, which cost $215 million to build, is rife with tales of phantom hitchhikers who thumb rides across only to vanish into thin air before reaching the other side. For the dollar toll, it rivals anything at Walt Disney World.

Palmetto and the Gamble Plantation

Frequently dismissed in favor of Bradenton (see overleaf), the little town of **Palmetto**, five miles south of the Sunshine Skyway Bridge, makes for a pleasant foray and is untouched by the commercialism of the bigger towns and beaches beyond. Perched on the northern shore of the Manatee River, Palmetto's prettiest section is Riverside Drive, an avenue of grand old mansions. The 1889 **J.A. Lamb House** at no. 1100, a stunning villa carved from heart pine with fairytale-like features in its twenty rooms, is probably the most impressive – though it's a private residence and not open to the public.

Next door, *The Palmetto House*, at no. 1102 (℡941/723-1236 or 1-800/658-4167, ⒲www.thepalmettohouse.com), is a fine **place to stay** (rooms start at $100), and serves as a good base for visiting Bradenton and the beaches. Built in 1910, the house's interior has graceful arches, elegant silver and, if you stay, breakfast and cocktails served on a sweeping veranda.

If you have time to spare, veer east from Palmetto along Tenth Street (Hwy-301) to **Ellenton**, a riverside settlement where the 1840s **Gamble Plantation**, 3708 Patten Ave (℡941/723-4536), is one of the oldest homes on Florida's West Coast and the only slave-era plantation this far south. Composed of thick, tabby walls (a mixture of crushed shell and molasses) and girded on three sides by sturdy columns, the house belonged to a Confederate major, Robert Gamble, a failed Tallahassee cotton planter who ran a sugar plantation here before financial uncertainty caused by the impending Civil War forced him to leave. In 1925, the mansion was designated the **Judah Benjamin Confederate Memorial** in remembrance of Confederate Secretary Benjamin, who took refuge here in 1865 after the fall of the Confederacy. With Union troops in hot pursuit, he hid here until friends found him a boat in which he sailed from Sarasota Bay to England, where he joined the English Bar and practiced law. A showcase of wealthy (and white) Old South living, the house – stuffed to the rafters with period fittings – is open Thursday to Monday

---

The area code for the section of the Florida coast south of Tampa Bay to Naples is ℡941.

9am–5pm; however, admission is only by **guided tour** which costs $3 and runs approximately every hour through the day. Besides describing the building, its contents and owners, the tour offers a very Confederate view of the Civil War.

Bradenton and around

A major producer of tomato and orange juice, **BRADENTON**, across the broad Manatee River from Palmetto, is a hard-working town whose center comprises several unlovely miles of office buildings along the river's south bank. While mainland Bradenton is far from exciting, **Anna Maria Island** (the northernmost point of a chain of barrier islands running from here to Fort Myers) and the **Bradenton beaches** eight miles west of downtown make up for Bradenton proper's lack of charm. It's well worth traveling along Route 789, known along Lido Key as Gulf of Mexico Drive, for a more picturesque (if slightly longer) route to Sarasota than the inland options.

The town and around

In central Bradenton, the **South Florida History Museum, Bishop Planetarium and Parker Manatee Aquarium**, 201 Tenth St (Mon–Sat 10am–5pm, Sun noon–5pm; $7.50 – extra fees for astronomy presentations; ☎941/746-4131, ⓦ www.sfmbp.org), are well worth time away from the beaches. The museum takes a wide-ranging look at the region's past. If you're around in April, it sponsors a month-long **Florida Heritage Festival**, which culminates with a ceremonial crowning of a local as the new Hernando de Soto. The most popular attraction here is not, however, the museum artifacts, but the **aquarium**, home to manatees Snooty and Mo. Born in 1948, Snooty is the oldest manatee born in captivity, while the considerably younger Mo was rescued in 1994 from Crystal River after being orphaned. Ten minutes of watching them glide about is enough, but the aquarium is intelligently laid out to provide varying views of the creatures. Feeding times – 12.30pm, 2pm and 3.30pm – are more lively and included in the entry price. The **Bishop Planetarium** is open throughout the day – weekday mornings, however, are reserved for school visits. Daily Starshows, which take you on an educational tour of the universe, are on offer at 1pm and 4pm, while at 2.30pm the laser light show is more spectacular than informative. On Fridays and Saturdays at 7pm live astronomy presentations are given, and at 9pm and 10.30pm, a remarkable rock and roll laser light show does dramatic things to the music of Pink Floyd, Jimi Hendrix, Pearl Jam and Led Zeppelin. In addition, weather permitting, on Saturday mornings between 11.30am and 1pm, you can view the sun through a large telescope from the rooftop observatory.

Further knowledge of turn-of-the-nineteenth-century's settlers can be acquired at the **Manatee Village Historical Park**, on the corner of Manatee Avenue East and Fifteenth Street East (Mon–Fri 9am–4.30pm; free; ☎941/749-7765), which has a courthouse, church, general store and "cracker" cottage dating from Florida's rough-and-ready frontier days.

Five miles west of central Bradenton, Manatee Avenue (the main route to the beaches) crosses 75th Street West, at the northern end of which is the **De Soto National Memorial** (daily 9am–5pm; free; ☎941/792-0458, ⓦ www.nps.gov /deso). This is believed to mark the spot where Spanish conquistador Hernando de Soto came ashore in 1539. The three-year de Soto expedition, hacking through Florida's dense subtropical terrain and wading through its swamps, led to the European discovery of the Mississippi River – and numerous pitched battles with Native Americans. The visitor center contains artifacts and exhibits explaining the expedition's effect on American Indians, and a film depicting the expedition is shown hourly. From December to April, park rangers dressed as sixteenth-century Spaniards add informative pointers to the lifestyles of Florida's first adventurers (hourly 10.30am–3.30pm); for more about the de Soto expedition, see "History" in Contexts.

Anna Maria Island and the Bradenton beaches

In contrast to central Bradenton's grayness, the ramshackle beach cottages, seaside snack stands and beachside bars on **Anna Maria Island** are bright and convivial. From the end of Manatee Avenue, turn left along Gulf Drive for **Coquina Beach**, where the swimming is excellent and the weekend social life

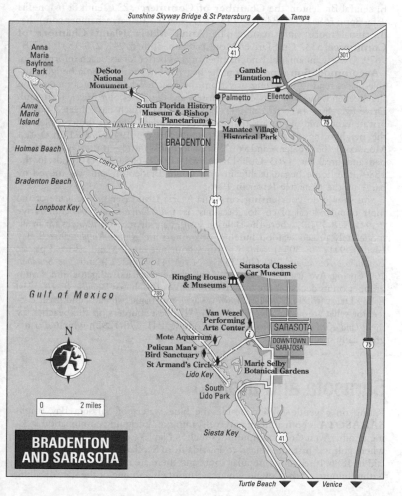

is youthful and merry; with a quieter time in mind, take a right turn along Marina Drive for the calm **Anna Maria Bayfront Park**. For a break from the beach, the **Anna Maria Island Historical Museum** 402 Pine Ave (May–Sept Tues–Thurs & Sat 10am–1pm; Oct–April daily; 10am–3pm; ☎941/778-1514), exhibits interesting old photos, islands artifacts and videos of interviews with early residents. Further down the road, bikes can be hired from Neumann's Island Beach Store, 427 Pine Ave (☎941/778-3316).

South of Anna Maria Island, **Longboat Key** is all about privacy: its pricey homes are shielded by rows of tall Australian pines and, while all the sands along this nineteen-mile-long island are public property, access points are few and far between, making the beach almost impossible to reach for non-residents. Not until you reach Lido Key, further south, are there more useable beaches (see "The Sarasota beaches," p.365).

Practicalities

In central Bradenton, the **Chamber of Commerce**, 222 Tenth St (Mon–Fri 9am–5pm; ☎941/748-3411 ⓕ745-1877, ⓦwww.manateechamber.com), has the usual tourist information. The **Anna Maria Island Chamber of Commerce**, 5337 Gulf Drive (Mon–Fri 9am–5pm; ☎941/778-1541; ⓕ778-9679, ⓦwww.annamariaislandchamber.org), is better for its beach information.

Accommodation is prolific on the beaches but for those on a budget suitable places tend to be a long way from the beach. While the rates increase on the weekend, the best bets of the motels are the *Silver Surf Motel*, 1301 Gulf Drive (☎1-800/441-7873 or 941/778-6626; ❺), which has a heated pool, a private beach and big rooms that can accommodate three or four people; and the neighboring *Queen's Gate*, 1101 Gulf Drive (☎941/778-7153; ❺–❻). More costly but cozier – and you'll need to book ahead – is the *Duncan House* bed and breakfast, 1703 Gulf Drive (☎941/778-6858; ❺–❻); built in the 1880s, the house began its life in downtown Bradenton and was moved by barge up the Manattee River in 1946.

You should do your **eating** on Anna Maria Island (see p.359). One of the most popular local places for breakfast is *Gulf Drive Café*, 900 Gulf Drive (☎941/778-1919), where the Belgian waffles are divine. Top choices for fresh, moderately priced seafood lunches or dinners are *Rotten Ralph's*, 902 S Bay Blvd (☎941/778-3953), which features gourmet omelets and assorted pastas; *Beachhouse Restaurant*, 200 Gulf Drive N (☎941/779-2222) and *The Sandbar*, 100 Spring Ave (☎941/778-0444), which serves fried alligator and Cajun grouper on its decks on the beach. On Holmes Beach, try *Paradise Bagels*, 3210 E Bay Drive (☎941/779-1212), for a variety of bagles, spreads, and great coffee; for what are justly advertised as the "baddest" burgers on the beaches try the *Island Kitchen & Market*, 414 Pine Ave (☎941/778-7295), which also has great daily specials.

Sarasota and around

Rising on a gentle hillside beside the blue waters of Sarasota Bay, bright **SARASOTA** is both affluent and welcoming, an intriguing combination lacking in other West Coast communities such as Naples (see p.381). This is the city where golf was first introduced to Florida from Scotland – the first course was laid in 1886. It remains a popular sport and there are more than thirty courses within minutes of the downtown area. Sarasota is also one of the state's leading cultural centers: home to numerous writers and artists, and the base of several respected performing arts companies. This is a place where opera and theater-goers in formal attire join hip students in coffee bars, and the tone of the town is intelligently upbeat. The community is far less stuffy than its wealth might suggest, and downtown Sarasota is fairly lively, with cafés, bars and eateries complementing the excellent grouping of bookstores for which the place is known. A few miles north up the Tamiami Trail (Hwy-41), the **Ringling Museum Complex** – home of the late art-loving circus magnate – is a fine diversion. And the barrier-island **beaches**, a couple of miles away across the bay, are the lounger's paradise.

Arrival, transport and information

Whether you're arriving from north or south, **Hwy-41** (always referred to here as the Tamiami Trail) zips through Sarasota, passing the main causeway to the islands just west of downtown and skirting the Ringling estate in the north. I-75 runs parallel to the Tamiami, and while it's not as enticing, it's a lot quicker. Downtown Sarasota is an easy grid of streets mostly named for fruits, though Main Street contains most of the eating and nightlife venues.

Local **bus** routes on the Sarasota County Area Transit (4.30am–8.30pm, except Sun; ☎941/316-1234) radiate out from the downtown Sarasota terminal on Lemon Avenue, between First and Second streets. **Useful routes** are #2 or #10 to the Ringling estate; #4 to Lido Key; #18 to Longboat Key; #11 to Siesta Key; and #13 to Venice Beach. Fares are 50¢ per journey; there are no transfers and no Sunday service. The Amtrak bus from Tampa also pulls into the Lemon Avenue station, but all passengers arriving on Greyhound buses are dropped at 575 N Washington Blvd (☎941/955-5735). The Sarasota Tampa Express provides a direct connection with Tampa airport and runs frequently throughout the day (☎941/727-1344 or 1-800/326-2800). If you're around for a week or more, a good way to explore the town and the islands is by **renting a bike** for around $25 per day from Sarasota Bicycle Center, 4048 Bee Ridge Rd (☎941/377-4505); or the Backyard Bike Shop, on Longboat Key at 5610 Gulf of Mexico Drive (☎941/383-5184). In addition to bikes, Siesta Sports Rental, 6551 Midnight Pass Rd, Siesta Key (☎941/346-1747; ⓦwww .siestasportsrentals.com), also rent out kayaks and beach equipment. For a **taxi**, try Diplomat Taxi (☎941/355-5155) or Yellow Cabs of Sarasota (☎941/955-3341). A good option for getting around the area is the Trolley service (☎941/316-1234; Mon–Sat 5am–8pm). One route runs to Lido Island and costs $2, the other is the free Main Street Trolley, which serves the downtown area.

To see all the islands cheaply and with the minimum of exertion, take the trolley ($2, you can hop on and off as many times as you like), which runs three times a day (9.30am, 12.30pm & 3.30pm), starting at the *Best Western Siesta Beach Resort* (schedule info ☎941/346-3115, ⓦwww.tsatrolley.com).

Information

For **information** in Sarasota, call at the **Visitors and Convention Bureau**, 655 N Tamiami Trail (Mon–Sat 9am–5pm, Sun 11am–3pm; ☎1-800/522-9799, ⓦwww.sarasotafl.org), or the **Chamber of Commerce**, 1819 Main St (Mon–Fri 9am–5pm; ☎941/955-8187). On **Siesta Key**, you'll find a Chamber of Commerce at 5100 Ocean Blvd (Mon–Fri 9am–5pm; ☎941/349-3800). Besides the customary discount coupons and leaflets, look for the free magazines, *Sarasota Visitors Guide* and *See*, and the Friday edition of the *Sarasota Herald Tribune*, whose pullout section, "Ticket," has entertainment listings.

Accommodation

On the **mainland**, motels run the length of Hwy-41 between the Ringling estate and downtown Sarasota, typically charging $40–60. Prices are higher at the **beaches**.

Hotels and motels

Best Western Golden Host Resort, Hwy-41 (☎1-800/722-4895 or 941/355-5141). This chain is a good bet for reasonable off-season rates. ❹–❺

Flamingo Colony Motel, 4703 Hwy-41 (☎ 941/355-5135). The Flamingo has a pool and guest laundry. ❸

Gulf Beach Travel Trailer Park, 8862 Midnight Pass Rd (☎941/349-3839). The only budget alternative on Gulf Beach, it consists almost exclusively of RV sites. Be prepared to pay upwards of $25 for a tent. ❶

Gulf Sun Apartments & Motel, 6722 Midnight Pass Rd (☎ 941/349-2442). Set in an acre of tropical gardens, it has a heated pool and private access to Crescent Beach. ❺

Lido Vacation Rentals, 528 S Polk Drive (☎ 941/388-1004 or 1-800/890-7991). The best rates on Lido Key are at *Lido Vacation Rentals*, which has friendly service, access to an Olympic-sized pool and a fine location. ❹

Sunset Terrace, 4644 Hwy-41 (☎ 941/355-8489). This is slightly more upscale and has a pool, family apartments, complimentary breakfast and shuttle service from Tampa airport. ❸

Downtown Sarasota

Visitors who ogle the Ringling estate and nearby beaches without making a foray into **downtown Sarasota**, will miss one of the most enticing towns on the coast. Restored architectural oddities, excellent theater and some of the best art galleries in Florida give the city a very upbeat aura. Anyone bemoaning the lack of decent **bookstores** in Florida should take heart: here you'll find the biggest and most varied selection in the state. The best-filled shelves are at the Main Bookshop, 1962 Main St (Ⓦ www.mainbookshop.com), which has thousands of books on virtually every subject as well as comics, records and old easy chairs that foster a relaxed atmosphere. Other good bets are Book Bazaar, 1488 Main St (☎ 941/336-1373), and Parker's, at the same address (☎ 941/366-2898). Don't miss a visit to the amazing **Selby Public Library**, 1331 First St (Mon–Thurs 9am–9pm, Fri & Sat 9am–5pm, Sun 1–5pm; ☎ 941/316-1181, Ⓦ http://suncat.co.sarasota.fl.us/selby/selby.html, which from the outside looks like it belongs in a grandiose Hollywood epic, while inside it's a clean, functioning library, complete with a fishtank and loads of computers with free **Internet** access. Opposite the library on the corner of First Street and Pineapple Avenue is the **Sarasota Opera House**, (☎ 941/953-7030, Ⓦ www .sarasotaopera.org). Opened in 1926, this Mediterranean Revival building hosted the Ziegfeld Follies and a young Elvis Presley (see "Nightlife"). Opposite the Selby Public Library, it's hard to miss the enormous purple building of the brand-new **Van Wezel Performing Arts Hall**, 777 N Tamiami Trail (☎ 941/953-3368 or 1-800/826-9303, Ⓦ www.vanwezel.org). Named one of the five hundred most notable buildings in the United States, its program includes musicals, dance, comedy and plays (see "Nightlife," p.367). For those who wish to explore behind the scenes, backstage tours are on offer (call for times and cost).

South of Main Street a few blocks past the pretty Methodist Church is **Burns Court**, a hidden enclave of 1920s bungalows, each with Moorish details. Almost all the Spanish/Mediterranean buildings in town were built just before the Depression, when the style was most in vogue. At the end of this lane stands the startlingly pink **Burns Court Cinema**, a great alternative film house run by Sarasota Film Society. For tickets and schedule call the box office between noon and 5pm at ☎941/955-3456 or 955-9338.

Follow the curve of the bay for half a mile south to the **Marie Selby Botanical Gardens**, 811 S Palm Ave (daily 10am–5pm; $8; ☎ 941/336-5731,

@www.selby.org), whose walled perimeter hides a small but startling gathering of growths inside. Internationally recognized for its plant and rainforest educational displays, the garden can't fail to improve the mood of anyone who spends time meandering along the fragrant pathways.

The Ringling Museum Complex

Two miles north of downtown Sarasota lies the **Ringling Museum Complex**, containing the house and art collections of John Ringling, a multimillionaire who not only poured money into the fledgling community beginning in the 1910s, but also gave it a taste for fine arts that it's never lost. One of the owners of the fantastically successful Ringling Brothers Circus, which began touring the US during the 1890s, Ringling – an imposing figure over six feet tall and weighing nearly 280 pounds – ploughed the circus's profits into railways, oil and land. By the Twenties, he had acquired a fortune estimated at $200 million. Charmed by Sarasota and recognizing its investment potential, Ringling built the first causeway to the barrier islands and made the town his circus's winter base, saving a fortune in northern heating bills and generating tremendous publicity for the town in the process. His greatest gift to Sarasota, however, was a Venetian Gothic mansion – a combination of European elegance and American-millionaire extravagance – and an incredible collection of European Baroque paintings, displayed in a museum built for the purpose beside the house. Grief-stricken following the death of his wife in 1927 and losing much of his wealth through the Wall Street crash two years later, Ringling died in 1936, reportedly with just $300 to his name.

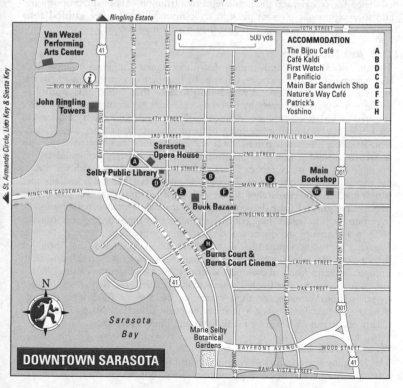

6

The Ringling House: Cà d'Zan

Begin your exploration of the Ringling estate by walking through the gardens to the former Ringling residence, **Cà d'Zan** ("House of John," in Venetian dialect). A lavish though not tasteless piece of work serenely situated beside the bay, it was the inappropriate setting for the 1998 film adaptation of *Great Expectations*. The multitude of attractive trees was a gift from Thomas Edison, who nurtured the young seeds at his Fort Myers Home. The most dramatic, a Chinese banyan, shades the circular *Banyan Café* (℡ 941/359-3183), where you can grab lunch for around $8. Completed in 1925, reputedly at a cost of $1.5 million, the house was planned around an airy, two-story living room marked on one side by a fireplace of carved Italian marble and on the other by a $50,000 organ belonging to Ringling's musically inclined wife. The other rooms are similarly filled with expensive items, but unlike their mansion-erecting contemporaries elsewhere in Florida, John and Mable Ringling knew the value of restraint. Their spending power never exceeded their sense of style, and the house remains a triumph of taste and proportion – and an exceptionally pleasant place to walk around. Take the free **guided tour** departing regularly from the entrance, then roam on your own.

The Art Museum

The mix of inspiration and caution that underpinned Ringling's business deals also influenced his art purchases. On trips to Europe to scout for new circus talent, Ringling became obsessed with **Baroque art** – then wildly unfashionable – and over five years, led largely by his own sensibilities, he acquired more than five hundred Old Masters, a collection now regarded as one of the finest of its kind in the US. To display the paintings, many of them as epic in size as they were in content, Ringling selected a patch of Cà d'Zan's grounds and erected a spacious **museum** around a mock fifteenth-century Italian palazzo, decorated by his stockpile of high-quality replica Greek and Roman statuary. As with Cà d'Zan, the very concept initially seems absurdly pretentious but, like the house, the idea works: the architecture matches the art with great aplomb. Here also, you should take the free **guided tour** departing regularly from the entrance, before wandering around at your leisure. Five enormous paintings by **Rubens**, commissioned in 1625 by a Hapsburg archduchess, and the painter's subsequent *Portrait of Archduke Ferdinand*, are the undisputed highlights of the collection, though they shouldn't detract from the excellent canvases in succeeding rooms: a wealth of talent from Europe's leading schools of the mid-sixteenth to mid-eighteenth centuries. Watch out, in particular, for the finely composed and detailed *The Rest on the Flight to Egypt*, by Paolo Veronese, and the entertaining *Building of a Palace* from Piero de Cosimo. Contemporary works include sculpture from Joel Shapiro and John Chamberlain, and paintings by Frank Stella and Philip Pearlstein.

The Circus Gallery

The Ringling fortune had its origins in the big top, and the **Circus Gallery** is worth a brief visit. The cuttings and memorabilia of famous dwarfs and freakshow performers are more intriguing than the standard-issue tiger cages and costumes. Among the most diverting tidbits is the account of Tom Thumb's wedding in New York, which actually took the Civil War off the front pages. Thumb (his real name was Charles Stratton) stopped growing at 35 inches. His wife, Lavinia, was three inches shorter. There's also a display on Chang and Eng, the mid-nineteenth century Siamese twins who came here from Siam in 1829 and during their 62 years joined at the ribs married sisters in 1843, had 22 children and died within three hours of each other in 1874.

The Asolo Theater and Asolo Center for the Performing Arts

Ringling transported an eighteenth-century, Italian-court playhouse from the castle of Asolo to the grounds of his estate. Its interior is fascinating, though it is only open for special events and conferences; inquire at the reception (☏941/355-7115) for a schedule. The **Asolo Center for the Performing Arts**, not to be confused with the Asolo Theater, is right next door and has a strong program of theatrical events throughout the year. The main stage was brought over from Dunfermline, Scotland, where it was built in 1903. While not as enticing as the off-limits Asolo Theater, the center has an elegant, gilded interior. Free backstage tours are available (see "Nightlife" for performance details).

Sarasota Classic Car Museum

Vintage car enthusiasts and devotees of old music boxes will love the **Sarasota Classic Car Museum**, across Hwy-41 from the entrance to the Ringling Museum Complex (daily 9am–6pm; $8.50; ☏941/355-6228, ⓦwww.sarasotacarmuseum.org). Nearly 200 aged vehicles – including John Lennon's Mercedes and Stephen King's "Christine" – are gathered together with hurdy-gurdies, cylinder discs, an enormous Belgian pipe organ and nickelodeons. There's also an antique game room filled with arcade games from the 1930s and 1940s. Real car buffs should take the detailed guided tours, which are a little detailed for those who just want to wander. Even if you don't pay to enter the museum, check out the gift shop for some unusual souvenirs and collectibles.

The Sarasota beaches

Increasingly the stomping ground of European package tourists spilling south from the St Petersburg beaches, the powdery white sands of the **Sarasota beaches** – fringing two barrier islands, which continue the chain beginning off Bradenton – haven't been spared the attentions of property developers either and have lost much of their scenic appeal to towering condos. For all that, the Sarasota beaches are worth a day of anybody's time – either to lie back and soak up the rays, or to seek out the few remaining isolated stretches. And the sunsets alone make them worth a visit. Both islands, **Lido Key** and **Siesta Key**, are accessible by car or bus from the mainland, though there's no link directly between them. If you are traveling by car, the beach roads are very busy in high season and the tailbacks to leave the beach towards the end of the day can ruin any relaxation you might have gained throughout the day.

Lido Key

Financed by and named for Sarasota's circus-owning sugar daddy, the Ringling Causeway – take buses #4 or #18 – crosses the yacht-filled Sarasota Bay from the foot of Main Street to **Lido Key** and flows into **St Armand's Circle**. This roundabout ringed by upmarket shops and restaurants is dotted with some of Ringling's replica classical statuary – musclebound torsos emerging surrealistically from behind palm fronds. The shops aren't cheap, but there is plenty of parking and it's worth having a stroll around, especially as this is a handy transfer point between the #4 bus to the beach and the #18 to the Mote Aquarium and Pelican Man's Bird Sanctuary (see below). After a look around – head to the north end of Lido Key beach, which is relatively condo-free, and then trek south along Benjamin Franklin Drive. This route passes more accessible beaches, fine in and of themselves though overrun by the holiday-making set. After two miles, you'll find the more attractive **South Lido Park** (daily 8am–sunset; free), a belt of dazzlingly bright sand beyond a large grassy park, with walking trails shaded by Australian pines. Busy with barbecues and tanned bodies on Saturday and Sunday, the park is a delightfully subdued spot for weekday rambles.

Away from the beaches the only place of consequence on Lido Key, the **Mote Marine Aquarium**, 1600 Ken Thompson Parkway (daily 10am–5pm; $8; ☎ 941/388-4441, ⓦ www.mote.org) on Lido Key, is a mile north of St Armand's Circle. The public off-shoot of a marine laboratory studying the ecological problems threatening Florida's sea life such as the ride tide—a mysterious algae that blooms every few years devastating sea life—the aquarium has an assortment of live creatures, from seahorses to loggerhead turtles. The centerpiece of the 22 aquariums is a massive outdoor shark tank, wherein you can view several species up close through underwater windows.

Adjacent to the Mote Aquarium, you'll find **Pelican Man's Bird Sanctuary**, 1708 Ken Thompson Parkway (daily 10am–5pm; $3; ☎ 941/388-4444, ⓦ www.pelicanman.org). Injured and sick migratory birds from all over the world, together with native Floridian species, are cared for here by over two hundred volunteers. You'll come away with facts about the various ways our feathered friends come to grief (usually at the hands of man) and how they are nursed back to health before being released into the wild.

Siesta Key

Far funkier and more laid-back than Lido or Longboat keys **Siesta Key** (arrive via Siesta Drive off Hwy-41 about five miles south of downtown Sarasota) attracts a younger crowd and has less-manicured surroundings than other spots on the coast. The affluent, however, have not ignored Siesta Key – this is, after all, where Paul Simon has a condo. Beach-lovers should hit **Siesta Key Beach**, beside Ocean Beach Boulevard, a wide white strand that can – and often does – accommodate thousands of partying sun-worshippers. To escape the crowds, continue south past Crescent Beach, which meets a second road (Stickney Point Road) from the mainland, and follow Midnight Pass Road for six miles to **Turtle Beach**, a small body of sand that has the islands' only campground; see p.362.

Eating

Owing to the increase in evening entertainment venues and the resurgence of a youthful downtown scene, Sarasota's **restaurant** and **café culture** has taken off. Exquisite restaurants with prices to match are popping up everywhere, but every taste and budget is still easily catered to. If you're staying on Hwy-41, especially in a motel closer to the airport than downtown, good places to eat can be hard to find and what is available is usually closed by 9pm. St Armand's Circle in Lido Key makes a viable option, a bit touristy but lively, with shops and a wide range of restaurants open late.

Downtown

The Bijou Cafe, 1287 First St (℡ 941/366-8111).
Expensive lunch and dinner menus of seafood,
fowl and meat served in surprisingly basic surroundings.

Café Kaldi, 1568 Main St (℡ 941/366-2326).
Terrific coffee house turned cyber café, where students sip an incredible range of coffees and wince
as would-be musicians practice their art.

First Watch, 1395 Main St (℡ 941/954-1395).
There isn't much character to the joint, but the
excellent American-style breakfast and inexpensive lunch offerings assure there's always a
line.

Il Panificio, 1703 Main St (℡ 941/366-5570).
Italian deli and coffee shop with superb (and huge)
homemade pizzas, sandwiches and strong espres-
sos.

Main Bar Sandwich Shop, 1944 Main St (no
phone). Great and reasonably priced sandwiches
have been served here since 1958.

Nature's Way Café, 1572 Main St
(℡ 941/954-3131). A good vegetarian option
known for its sandwiches, fresh-fruit salads
and frozen yogurt.

Patrick's, 1400 Main St (℡ 941/952-1170). A
sports bar/restaurant serving steaks and chops
($12–17) and burgers ($6).

Yoder's, 3434 Bahia Vista St (℡ 941/955-7771).
There are thriving Mennonite and Amish communities in the Sarasota area and this local favorite has
won awards for the homemade goodness of its
old-fashioned Amish cuisine.

Yoshino, 417 Burns Court (℡ 941/366-8544).
Good Japanese food served in what looks like a
private home at moderate prices.

St Armand's Circle

Cha Cha Coconuts, 717 St Armand's Circle
(℡ 941/388-3300). A young crowd spills out of the
very busy, very loud bar. The inexpensive menu
claims to feature "Caribbean cuisine," but it's really
just fish sandwiches and burgers and live music on
some nights.

Hemingway's, 325 Ringling Blvd (℡ 941/388-
3948). Seafood is a speciality and a cocktail Happy
Hour is held every night.

Hungary Fox Tree Top Bistro, 419 Ringling Blvd
(℡ 941/388-2222). A tropically decorated bistro
with a menu bursting with such American favorites
as hamburgers and stuffed sandwiches.

Watson's Pump, 328 Ringling Blvd (℡ 941/388-
0155). British-style pub, with a menu featuring fish
and chips and bangers and mash, plus the usual
American favorites – and plenty of draught ale to
wash it all down.

At the beaches

The Broken Egg, 210 Avenida Madera
(℡ 941/346-2750). A favorite with locals looking
for a filling, inexpensive all-American breakfast or
lunch. Try the broken egg breakfast for $5.29 or
the homemade soups for $2.99.

The Old Salty Dog, 5023 Ocean Blvd
(℡ 941/349-0158). Inexpensive English-style fish
and chips alongside regular seafood and hot dogs.
Famous for the Salty Dog Hot Dog.

Surfrider, 6400 Midnight Pass Rd (℡ 941/346-
1199). For a taste of Peru and a menu including
seafood, steaks, ribs pasta and decadent desserts,
this is an excellent option.

Turtles, 8875 Midnight Pass Rd (℡ 941/346-
2207). Outstanding seafood dinners for under $15.

Nightlife

There's no shortage of arts in Sarasota, and the Visitors and Convention Bureau
(see p.361) has full details of events on offer at any one time; also check out the
Sarasota County Arts Council Web site (ꞷ www.sarasota-arts.org). Some of the
state's top small theatrical groups are based in Sarasota. **Drama** devotees should
scan local newspapers for play listings or phone the theaters directly. For **opera**
buffs, the Sarasota Opera House has been staging grand performances since the
1920s, and, though not known for his arias, Elvis Presley also performed here
in his younger days. For information and tickets call ℡ 941/366-8450; the box
office is open daily, 10am–4pm. Check out *Elipse*, and the daily *Sarasota Herald
Tribune* for entertainment information.

Theaters and cinemas

Asolo Center for the Performing Arts, 5555 N
Tamiami Trail (℡ 941/351-8000 or 1-800/361-
3833, ꞷ www.asolo.org). The major repertory, the
Asolo Theater Company, has a strong program

throughout the year (tickets $30–$40, gallery
seats $13, students $6; $7 tickets are sometimes
available on the day).

The Burns Court Cinema, Burns Court
(℡ 941/364-8662). Cinema that hosts Sarasota's

film festival in November, showing over forty of the best international films of the year.

Florida Studio Theater, 1241 N Palm Ave (Mon 9am–6pm, Tues–Sat 9am–9pm, Sun 10am–9pm; tickets $16–30; ☏ 941/366-9000, ⊛ www.fst2000 .org. Sarasota's most contemporary theater.

Golden Apple Dinner Theater, 25 N Pineapple Ave (☏ 941/366-5454). For theater with cocktails and candlelit dining.

Hollywood 20, 1993 Main St (☏ 941/365-2000). All mainstream films are shown at this striking (and popular) pure Art Deco theater. Inside, a neon-lilac glow bathes the popcorn-devouring crowds.

The Van Wezel Performing Arts Hall, 777 N Tamiami Trail (Mon–Sat, 9am–4.30pm, 1pm–5pm Sun; ☏ 941/953-3368 or 1-800/826-9303, ⊛ www .vanwezel.org. Built in 1968, the hall has a varied program of musicals and dance.

Bars and nightclubs

On weekend evenings, Main Street attracts both students looking to chill and a more rough-and-ready, good-old-boys crowd.

Daiquiri Deck, 5350 Ocean Blvd (☏ 941/349-8697). This Siesta Key bar specializes in frozen daiquiris and is hugely popular as an after-beach venue.

The Gator Club, 1490 Main St. (☏ 941/366-5969). The *Gator* is trying to challenge the *Main Street Depot* for loudest-bar honors. Set in a big, flaking warehouse, it has rhythm and blues Mondays to Saturdays at 9.30pm and jazz on Sundays at 8pm.

Main Street Depot, at the corner of Main St and Lemon Ave. Local bands jam outside the *Depot* while an inebriated horde listens from plastic tables.

Old Salty Dog, 5023 Ocean Blvd (☏ 941/349-0158). This is one of the more popular bars on Siesta Key.

Ristorante Bellini Jazz Club, 1551 Main St (☏ 941/365-7380). For jazz on weekdays try this club – you don't have to eat at the restaurant to listen to the music.

Gay nightlife

The gay and lesbian information line (☏ 941/923-4636) provides details of **gay nightlife** in the area. Try the long-established *Rowdy's*, 1330 Dr Martin Luther King Way (☏ 941/953-5945), which has a chatty, mostly local crowd. Out of the downtown area 2941 N Tamiami Trail offers *Big Daddy* upstairs and *Twisted Sister* downstairs. **Films** of gay interest are most likely to appear at the Burns Court Cinema.

Inland from Sarasota: Myakka River State Park

Should your knowledge of Florida be limited to beaches and theme parks, broaden your horizons by traveling fourteen miles inland from Sarasota on Route 72. Here you'll find a great tract of rural Florida barely touched by humans, whose marshes, pinewoods and prairies form **Myakka River State Park**, 3715 Jaffa Drive (daily 8am–sunset; $2 for one person, $4 for two to eight people; ☏ 941/365-0100, ⊛ www.myakka.sarasota.fl.us). On arrival, drop into the **interpretive center** for an insight into this fragile (and threatened) ecosystem. Begin exploring it by walking along the numerous paths or canoeing on the calm expanse of the Upper Myakka Lake. Myakka Wildlife Tours (☏ 941/365-0100) offer narrated tram and air-boat tours through the wildlife habitats, which explain the ecology of the area and provide views of the animals; both tours cost $7 and run at regular intervals throughout the day. If you're equipped for **hiking**, following the forty miles of trails through the park's **wilderness preserve** is a better way to get close to the cotton-tailed rabbits, deer, turkey, bobcats and alligators which live in the park; before commencing, register at the entrance office and get maps and check weather conditions – be ready for wet conditions during the summer storms. Other than the five basic campgrounds on the hiking trails ($11–15), park **accommodation** (details and reservations: ☎941/361-6511) comprises two well-equipped **campgrounds** and a few four-berth **log cabins** ($55 a night); these are very popular so it's a good idea to book in advance.

South from Sarasota: Venice and around

In the Fifties, the Ringling Circus moved its winter base twenty miles south from Sarasota to **Venice**, a pleasant small town with Italianate architecture surrounded by water that was modeled on its European namesake. Parking at the beachfront is limited, but it's a lovely walk from downtown along a palm-lined avenue; the parking time is limited away from the beaches. The downtown area itself has a more relaxed, friendly feel than many other tourist destinations on this coastline, but most people come for the gorgeous **beaches**, which are used by a range of people, from watersports enthusiasts to pensioner sunbathers. Swimming is a pleasure in the ocean here, but beware of the jellyfish – if there's a blue flag flying on the beach it means that there are lots of them around. Even if this is the case and swimming is out of bounds, you can always entertain yourself by watching flocks of pelicans dive into the waves, or by searching for the sharks' teeth commonly washed ashore. To see a shark you have to get above water, either on a helicopter ride or by parasailing. Anyone with their own transport can also explore the underexploited coastline around **Englewood beaches**, south of Venice on Route 775, pockmarked by small islands and creeks.

Practicalities

If you're arriving in Venice by Greyhound bus, you'll be dropped at 225 S Tamiami Trail (☎941/485-1001), from which your first port of call might be the **Chamber of Commerce**, 257 N Tamiami Trail (Mon–Fri 8.30am–5pm; Nov–March also Sat 9am–noon; ☎941/488-2236, ⓦwww.venice.fla.com), for local information. **Local buses** (SCAT; ☎94/316-1234) #13 and #16 (25¢ fare) link Venice with the beaches and surrounding areas.

Spending a night in this quiet community might seem an attractive proposition, though prices can be steep: of the motels, try the *Kon-Tiki*, 1487 Tamiami Trail (☎941/485-9696; ❹), or the *Gulf Tide*, 708 Granada Ave (☎941/484-9709, ❺). More luxurious is the *Inn at the Beach Resort*, 101 The Esplanade (☎1-800/255-8471; ❺). The *Venice Campground* is at 4085 E Venice Ave ($24–30; ☎941/488-0850, ⓦwww.campvenice.com), in an oak hammock by the river.

For **eating**, don't miss the *Soda Fountain*, 349 W Venice Ave (☎941/412-9860), whose milkshakes are not to be missed; *The Frosted Mug*, 1856 S Tamiami Trail (☎941/497-1611), has been here since 1957 and serves the best root beer and burgers in the area; *TJ Carney's Pub and Grill*, 231 W Venice Ave (☎941/480-9244), has evening entertainment as well as inexpensive to moderately priced food throughout the day.

Continuing south: Punta Gorda

Punta Gorda, about thirty miles from Venice, is easily dismissed as one of the retirement communities that populate the West Coast and, although there is not much here to detain you for long, it does warrant exploring. Don't expect to find impressive beaches here, but you will find large, Southern-style houses facing the sea and an unhurried pace of life that directly contrasts with the frantic Hwy-41 which runs through it. One of the surprises of Punta Gorda is its excellent public art. Large murals adorn walls and a plethora of small statues appear at frequent intervals along its main street. Situated on the banks of the Peace River, the **Fishermen's Village**, a quaint collection of unusual shops and a working marina housed in the old city docks, was established by Cuban fishermen. A collection of boat-tour operators line the pier offering trips around the harbor and further afield to Cayo Costa Island and Cabbage Key (see p.379). **King Fisher Cruises** (℡ 941/639-0969, ⓦ www.kingfisherfleet .com) runs full- and half-day cruises and shorter sunset boat trips, starting at $6. **The Florida Adventure Museum**, 260 W Retta Esplanade (Mon–Fri 10am–5pm, Sat & Sun 10am–3pm; $2; ℡ 941/639-3777), features exhibits of state and local history, as well as Florida's natural history, but won't detain you for more than an hour.

Telegraph Cypress Swamp

For anyone interested in untamed Florida, but lacking the desire to traipse through the wild for days, **Babcock Wilderness Adventures**, 8000 State Rd 31 at Punta Gorda (℡ 1-800/500-5583, ⓦ www.babcockwilderness.com), is a must. Forty miles inland and northeast of Fort Myers (take exit 26 on I-75), the Babcock crew offer you a choice of either a ninety-minute swamp-buggy tour or a three-hour off-road bike tour through the Babcock Ranch and **Telegraph Cypress Swamp** (Nov–April 9am–3pm, May–Oct 9am–noon, reservations essential; swamp-buggy tours $17.95, children $9.95; bike tours $35, $30 children). Excellent guides lead the tours through this vast ranch (it's three times the size of Washington DC), which was bought in 1914 by Edward Babcock and adapted as a wildlife refuge by his son Fred. From open fields with wild pigs and bison to swamp areas where alligators carpet the pathway, the tours will take you through a wild, ever-changing terrain. Among the highlights – and there are plenty – is the **bald cypress swamp**, a primeval scene of stunning trees and blood-red bromeliads reflected in still, tea-colored water. Another highlight is the gold Florida panthers, although they're not pure-bred. Only around fifty true Florida panthers are left, and inbreeding has caused most of the young to be stillborn. You'll also be offered the opportunity to stroke the surprisingly dry, smooth belly of a baby alligator, and learn about how trade in the reptile's meat and skin is carried out – an unexpected aspect to this essentially very caring establishment. There's also a museum where visitors can learn more about the history of the ranch and take a break from the wilderness by viewing all the Florida memorabilia.

Practicalities

If you are charmed enough by Punta Gorda to want to stay the night, ignore the motels on Hwy-41 and try one of the waterfront **accommodation** options in the town itself. Villas are available for rent at the *Fishermen's Village* (℡ 1-800/639-0020, ⓦ www.fishville.com; ❹), whose amenities include a beach area, tennis courts, free use of bikes and heated pool; you'll get all the same amenities with a bit more glamour at the *Best Western Waterfront* (℡ 941/639-1165 or 1-800/525-1002, ⓦ www.bestwestern.com/waterfront; ❹-❺). The *Banana Bay Waterfront Motel*, 23285 Bayshore Rd (℡ 941/743-4411, ⓦ www.bananabaymotel.com), is a more private option, tucked away beside the Fisherman's Village.

Harpoon Harry's (℡ 941/637-1177) at the end of the pier, is a great restaurant and bar, renowned for its raw oysters, clams and its special firehouse chili. Another good **eating** option is *Salty's Harborside Restaurant*, 5000 Burnt Shore Rd (℡ 941/639-3650), where cocktails are served in cozy surroundings and Sunday brunch is a speciality. The terrace dining area offers a brilliant view of Charlotte Harbor, excellent food and entertainment on the weekend.

Fort Myers

Though lacking the sophistication of Sarasota (fifty miles north) and the exclusivity of Naples (twenty miles south), **FORT MYERS** is one of the up-and-coming communities of the southwest coast. The town took its name from Abraham Myers, who helped establish a fort here in 1860 after the Seminole War. During the war, the town was activated as a base where cattle were rounded up to supply beef to Federal gunboats patrolling the gulf off Sanibel Island (see p.375). Fortunately, most of the town's late-twentieth-century growth occurred on the north side of the wide Caloosahatchee River, leaving the traditional center relatively unspoiled. The workplace of inventor Thomas Edison, who lived in Fort Myers for many years, provides the strongest interest in a town that otherwise relies on its scenery. Its riverside setting and regimental lines of palm trees along the main thoroughfares are arresting enough to delay your progress towards the local beaches, fifteen miles south, or the islands of Sanibel and Captiva, a similar distance west.

Arrival and information

Fort Myers, like many south Florida towns, sprawls farther than you initially imagine. East of I-75, Southwest Florida International Airport lies on Daniels Parkway. Hwy-41 is known here as Cleveland Avenue. Hwy-80 runs through downtown Fort Myers and curves into McGregor Boulevard to the west, where you'll find the Edison home. Most tourist maps fail to refer to downtown and the wider city on the same map, and the fact that there's only a mile between Edison's house and downtown is not always clear. If you're arriving from Hwy-41, the exit for McGregor Boulevard is clearly marked and, for those on mass transit, it's covered by the #20 **local bus** (☎941/275-8726, ⒲www.lee-county.com/leetran) and a trolley service. To get from downtown Fort Myers to the beaches, take the #140 south to Bell Tower and then change to the #50 to Fort Myers beach. Fares are $1 and there's no local public transport on Sundays. The Greyhound station is at 2275 Cleveland Ave (☎941/334-1011), just south of downtown Fort Myers. Stacks of **information** await you at the **Visitor and Convention Bureau**, 2180 W First St (Mon–Fri 8am–5pm; ☎1-800/237-6444, ⒡334-1106), and the **Chamber of Commerce**, 2301 Edwards Drive (Mon–Fri 8am–5pm; ☎941/332-3624, ⒡332-7276, ⒲www.fortmyers.com).

Accommodation

Accommodation costs are low in and around Fort Myers between May and mid-December, when 40–50 percent is lopped off the standard rates. In high season, however, not only do prices skyrocket, but available spare rooms are few and far between. There's a good selection of chain motels on Hwy-41 north of downtown which are an economical option. **At the beaches**, seek a room along the motel-lined Estero Boulevard and be prepared to spend $120 in season ($70 otherwise). Of the **campgrounds**, only *Red Coconut*, 3001 Estero Blvd (☎941/463-7200), is right on the beach. Two others further inland are *Fort Myers Campground*, 16800 S Tamiami Trail (☎941/267-2141), and *San Carlos*, 18701 San Carlos Blvd (☎941/466-3133).

Hotels and motels

Beacon, 1240 Estero Blvd (☎941/463-5264). Midweek, you may find cheaper deals at this beachside motel. ❹

Homewood Suites Hotel, 5255 Big Pine Way (☎941/275-6601). For considerable luxury without pomp, and sharp reductions out of season, try the *Homewood Suites*, which features a whirlpool, exercise equipment and a babysitting service. **❼**

Island, 201 San Carlos Blvd (☎ 941/463-2381). This inexpensive option lies a few miles inland. **❸**

Sea Chest, 2571 First St (☎ 941/332-1545). This riverfront motel has a pier and heated pool. **❷**

Ta Ki-Ki, 2631 First St (☎ 941/334-2135). On the banks of the Caloosahatchee, this hotel is very friendly, with a family feel. Barbecue by the pool is available for guests. **❸**

Downtown Fort Myers

Crossing the Caloosahatchee River, Hwy-41 hits **downtown Fort Myers**, which is picturesquely nestled on the river's edge. Aside from a few restored homes and storefronts around Main Street and Broadway, modern office buildings predominate. However, time exploring downtown is well spent. The Patio de León is a quaint courtyard just off First Street – the central downtown street – and here you'll find unusual shops and good eating places (see "Practicalities," opposite). Pay a visit to *Flowers to Fifties*, 2229 Main St (Mon–Thurs 11am–5.30pm, Fri 11am–8pm, Sat 11am–5.30pm; ☎ 941/334-2443): from 50s clothing to 70s furniture, this rambling vintage department store is filled to the brim with American "antiques" and odd collectibles. For more serious shopping, *Shakespeare Beethoven* (☎ 941/332-8300) in the attractive Collier Arcade, on Broadway between Main and First streets, has a good selection of books and music and stocks European newspapers. For a thorough insight into the town's past, stop by the **Fort Myers Historical Museum**, 2300 Peck St (Tues–Sat 9am–4pm; $2.50; ☎ 941/332-6125), for exhibits including details on the exploits of Doctor Franklin Miles, the Fort Myers inhabitant who developed Alka Seltzer. The invention of the world's great hangover cure was overshadowed, however, by the deeds of Thomas Edison, comprehensively recalled a mile west of downtown Fort Myers on McGregor Boulevard – also the route to the Fort Myers beaches and the Sanibel Island causeway.

The Edison Winter Home

In 1885, six years after inventing the light bulb, workaholic **Thomas Edison** collapsed from exhaustion and was instructed by his doctor to find a warm working environment or face an early death. While on holiday in Florida, the 37-year-old Edison noted a patch of bamboo sprouting from the banks of the Caloosahatchee River and bought fourteen acres of it. Having cleared a section, he established what became the **Edison Winter Home**, 2350 McGregor Blvd (Mon–Sat 9am–5pm, Sun noon–5pm; guided tours every 30min; $12; an extra $2 allows entrance to the Ford Winter Home, see opposite; ☎ 941/334-3614, ⊛ www.edison-ford-estate .com), where he spent each winter until his death in 1931.

A liking for bamboo was no idle fancy: Edison was a keen horticulturist and often used the chemicals produced by plants and trees in his experiments. The **gardens** of the house, where the tour begins (get a ticket from the signposted office across McGregor Boulevard), are sensational and provided Edison with much raw material: a variety of tropical foliage, from the extraordinary African sausage tree to a profusion of wild orchids, intoxicatingly scented by frangipani, that the inventor nurtured. By contrast, Edison's **house** is an anticlimax: a palm-cloaked wooden structure with an ordinary collection of period furnishings glimpsed only through the windows. A reason for the plainness of the abode may be that Edison spent most of his waking hours inside the **laboratory**, attempting to turn the latex-rich sap of *solidago Edisoni* (a giant strain of goldenrod weed that he developed) into rubber. A mass of test tubes, files and tripods are scattered over the benches, unchanged since Edison's last experiment, performed just before his death.

Not until the tour reaches the **museum** does the full impact of Edison's achievements become apparent. A design for an improved ticker-tape machine provided him with the funds for the experiments that led to the creation of the phonograph in 1877 and financed research into passing electricity through a vacuum that resulted in the incandescent lightbulb two years later. Scores of cylinder and disc phonographs with gaily painted horn-speakers, bulky vintage lightbulbs, and innumerable spin-off gadgets, make up an engrossing collection. Here, too, you'll see some of the ungainly cinema projectors derived from Edison's Kinetoscope – bringing the inventor a million dollars a year in patent royalties from 1907.

The Ford Winter Home

Henry Ford, a close friend of Edison's since 1896, when the latter had been one of the few people to speak admiringly of his ambitious car ideas, bought the house next door to Edison's in 1915, by which time he was established as the country's top automobile manufacturer. Unlike the Edison home, you can go inside the **Ford Winter Home** (Mon–Sat 9am–5pm, Sun noon–5pm; guided tours every 30min; $12), though the interior, restored to the style of Ford's time but lacking the original fittings, hardly justifies the admission price: despite becoming the world's first billionaire, Ford lived with his wife in modest surroundings.

Before leaving the old homes, pause to admire the sprawling **banyan tree** outside the ticket office: grown from a seedling given to Edison by tire-king Harvey Firestone in 1925, it's now the largest tree in the state.

The Fort Myers beaches

Still being discovered by the holidaying multitudes, the **Fort Myers beaches**, fifteen miles south of downtown Fort Myers, are appreciably different in character from the West Coast's more commercialized beach strips, with a cheerful seaside mood that's worth getting acquainted with. Accommodation (see p.371) is plentiful on and around Estero Boulevard – reached by San Carlos Boulevard, off McGregor Boulevard – which runs the seven-mile length of **Estero Island**; the hubs of activity are the short fishing pier and the **Lynne Hall Memorial Park** at the island's northern end.

Estero Island becomes quieter and increasingly residential as you press south. Estero Boulevard eventually swings over a slender causeway onto the barely developed **San Carlos Island**. A few miles ahead, at **Lovers Key** (daily sunrise to sunset; cars $3.25, pedestrians and cyclists $1), a footpath picks a trail over a couple of mangrove-fringed islands and several mullet-filled creeks. Although this area has recently experienced some build-up, it remains one of the quietest and prettiest beaches in the region – the perfect base for stress-free beachcombing and sunbathing, although canoes and kayaks are available to rent for those who want to be a bit more active. If you don't fancy the half-mile walk, a free trolleybus will transport you between the park entrance and the beach.

Practicalities

Restaurants and cafés

Bara Bread, 1520 Broadway (℡941/334-8216). Try the fresh pastry at this inexpensive downtown bakery and bistro that has been in the Bara family for five generations.

Café du Monde, 1740 Estero Blvd (℡941/463-8088). This laid-back beachside café offers tempting homemade recipes.

The Casa De Guereto, 2225 First St (℡941/332-4674). Features favorites from old

Mexico from $9 and up.

Chocolate Schmooze, 1530 Jackson St (℡ 941/337-3400). For a sweet treat, try the wonderful *Chocolate Schmooze*.

D' Patio Café, in the patio de León (℡ 941/226-007). This café offers great Cuban food and stays open until 9pm most nights.

Farmers' Market Restaurant, 2736 Edison Ave (℡ 941/334-1687). Despite the grim appearance and 1950s signs, try the reasonably priced *Farmers'* for such good country cooking as smoked ham hocks and barbecued ribs.

The French Connection Café, 2288 First St (℡ 941/332-4443). This convivial place for an evening bite serves inexpensive French onion soup, crepes and excellent reuben sandwiches.

Graveyard Rock 'n' Comedy Grill, 1502 Hendry St (℡ 941/334-8833). Glamorous dining can be had at this funky grill (see below), where entrées are $13–19. It gets mobbed, so be sure to reserve.

Oasis Restaurant, 2222 McGregor Blvd (℡ 941/334-1566). For cheap breakfast, specials and large burger lunches, head for this super-friendly place, wedged into the Edison Ford Square Shopping Center.

The Reef, 2601 Estero Blvd (℡ 941/463-4181). If you have a massive appetite, go to this beachside restaurant for all-you-can-eat nightly specials, ranging from catfish to frogs' legs.

Top O' The Mast, 1028 Estero Blvd (℡ 941/463-9424). This restaurant by the beach is a solid bet for seafood.

Bars, clubs and theaters

The Arcade Theater, 2267 First St (℡ 941/332-4488; box office Mon–Sat 10am–5pm and 1 hour before performances; tickets start at $11). One of Fort Myers historic buildings, this is home to the Florida Repertory Theater.

The Cigar Bar, 1502 Hendry St (℡ 941/337-4662). This is the most laid-back yet stylish bar in town, filled with leather chesterfields, a black grand piano and the mounted heads of bison, oryx and bears with cigars protruding from their lips. Everyone indulges in the huge range of bourbons and single malts and, unsurprisingly, smokes. An attached speciality cigar shop stocks everything from $1 cigarillos to pre-embargo Cuban cigars that cost $35 each.

Graveyard Rock 'n' Comedy Grill, 1502 Hendry St (℡ 941/337-4662). One of the more unusual joints, the *Grill* is on the site of the old city mortuary. It has a huge bar shaped like a coffin and stand-up comedians doing their schtick while you dine (see above).

The Liquid Cafe, in the Patio de León (℡ 941/461-0444). For a relaxed drink and live guitar music on Saturday nights this is a cool place with blue light and steel columns. It also has a good casual food menu and is open until 2am every night except Sunday.

Peter's La Cuisine, 2224 Bay St (℡ 941/332-2228). Very costly for eating, *Peter's* has a separate floor that functions as an open-air nightclub. Below, a jazz bistro is cheaper and less formal than the first-floor restaurant.

Gay and lesbian bars and clubs

For **gay nightlife,** an unusual bar and club is *The Bottom Line*, 3090 Evans Ave (℡ 941/337-7292), a cavernous place isolated in a desolate stretch of downtown. For a drink in a friendly if gloomy, unlit pub, try *The Office*, at 3704 Grove St (℡ 941/936-3212), in the Pizza Hut Plaza opposite the Red Lobster sign. More gregarious and inviting is *Apex*, at 4226 Fowler St. Apart from table-top dancers and drag acts, this is a very friendly locals' bar. There's a different theme every night.

Inland from Fort Myers: the Calusa Nature Center

Just as the beaches are kept in good condition, so is much of the eastern perimeter of the town, which is protected by a series of parks that make scenic spots for picnicking, canoeing and walking. For a more informative look at the local landscape, spend a couple of hours at the **Calusa Nature Center and Planetarium**, 3450 Ortiz Ave, five miles west of I-75 from junction 22 (Mon–Sat 9am–5pm, Sun 11am–5pm; $4, planetarium shows $3; ℡ 941/275-3435, ℗ www.calusanature.com), and trek the boardwalk trails through cypress and pine woods. Cast an eye, too, around the aviary where injured birds regain their strength before returning to the wild, and the indoor **museum**. Here, alongside general geological and wildlife exhibits, you'll find a caged specimen of each of the state's four varieties of poisonous snakes; the facial expressions of the mice, fed to each snake once a day, are not a sight for the faint-hearted. The museum also features a recreation of a Seminole Indian village as well as exhibitions on the history of this area of Florida.

Lee County Manatee Park

One creature you won't find at Babcock's is a manatee. Fortunately, just one stop further north on I-75, they're the center of attention at the **Lee County Manatee Park** (winter 8am–5pm, summer 8am–8pm; free; ☏941/432-2004). Here, along the banks of the Orange River, large information boards explain how manatees are identified by their scar patterns, which are caused by collisions with boat propellers. Those most often sighted – and, therefore, the most scarred – are given names. Due to its proximity to the Interstate and the Fort Myers Power Company, the park isn't too aesthetically pleasing. Still, the manatees seem to like it and if you wander to the first inlet, where they congregate in the calm, shallow waters you are likely to see them. Although they are easiest to spot in the early morning, there's a good chance you'll see at least a couple at any time of day.

ECHO

For more eco-tourism pay a visit to **ECHO** (Educational Concerns for Hunger Organization), 17430 Durrance Rd, (Mon–Sat 9am–noon; donations suggested; ☏941/543-3246, ⓦwww.echonet.org), a twenty-one acre farm devoted to the development of Third World farming techniques. Greenhouses simulate different environments in which workers experiment with plants to find out which ones thrive in them, while gardens in such unlikely settings as old tires and rooftops prove that it is possible to create a garden anywhere. Free tours are available on Tuesdays, Fridays and Saturdays at 10am.

Sanibel and Captiva islands

Hailed as paradise by many package-tours operators, Sanibel and Captiva islands, 25 miles southwest of Fort Myers, have more of a sense of paradise lost than the perfect holiday destination. The lack of public transport both to and on the islands makes daytrips virtually impossible without a car. When the Lee County authorities (who are responsible for the whole Fort Myers area) decided to link **Sanibel Island**, the most southerly of an island grouping around the mouth of the Caloosahatchee River, by road to the mainland in 1963, Sanibel's thousand or so occupants fought tooth and nail against the scheme, but eventually lost. A decade later, they got their revenge by seceding from the county, becoming a self-governing "city" and passing strict land-use laws to prevent their island sinking beneath holiday homes and hotels. To its credit, there are no high resorts to mar the view; however, much of the island is dominated by motels and restaurants, and visitors always outnumber the not-always-welcoming residents. Sizeable areas are set aside as nature preserves, so that when these are combined with all the resort-dominated territory, day visit can leave you with the sense that you've seen little of the island. North of Sanibel, a road continues to **Captiva Island**. Even less populated, its only concession to modern economics is an upmarket holiday resort at its northern tip, from which you can take boat trips to some of the otherwise inaccessible neighboring islands.

Arrival and information

To reach Sanibel and Captiva from mainland Fort Myers, take College Parkway west off of Hwy-41, turning almost immediately onto Summerlin Road. Summerlin winds its way to Sanibel Causeway, which links to the island. There's a $3 vehicle **toll** to get onto Sanibel.

Your first stop on Sanibel should be the **Visitor Center**, 1159 Causeway Blvd (Mon–Sat 9am–7pm, Sun 10am–5pm; ℡941/472-1080, ℻472-1070, ⓦwww.sanibel-captiva.org), which is packed with essential **information** and numerous free publications. There is no public transport on the island so without a car, you'll have to rent a **bike**: Finnimore's Cycle Shop, 2353 Periwinkle Way (℡941/472-5577) and The Bike Rental Inc, 2330 Palm Ridge Rd (℡941/472-2241), offer a good selection; bike rental is around $5 an hour. Billy's Rentals, 1470 Periwinkle Way (℡941/472-5248), also provides a good cycle guide with rentals at the same prices, and it's worth bearing in mind that no bikes are allowed on the beaches. There are no organized tours on the island and a rather unsatisfactory alternative is buying a **self-guide tape** for $12.95 from the visitor center.

Accommodation

Accommodation on the islands is always more expensive than on the mainland, though rates are relatively lower between May and November. *Kona Kai*, 1539 Periwinkle Way, Sanibel (℡941/472-1001, ⓦwww.konakaimotel.com; ❺), is set in quiet gardens and has one of the largest pools on the island. If you'd rather be on the beach, try *West Wind Inn*, 3345 W Gulf Drive, Sanibel (℡941/472-1541, ⓦwww.westwindinn.com; ❼), which has complimentary tennis and a poolside bar overlooking the sea, or *Best Western*, 3287 W Gulf Drive, Sanibel (℡941/472-1700, ⓦwww.bwsanibel.com; ❽), which has shuffleboard, barbecue grills and a picnic area. A good alternative to standard rooms are the wooden cottages, sleeping two to four, at *Seahorse*, 1223 Buttonwood Lane, Sanibel (℡941/472-4262, ⓦwww.seahorsecottages.com; ❹). Sanibel also has a **campground**, *Periwinkle Trailer Park*, 1119 Periwinkle Way ($25 to pitch a tent; ℡941/472-1433; ℮dick1312@aol.com).

Sanibel Island

People visit **Sanibel Island** for its beaches and although there are a number of them, public access is limited and they are not always as spectacular as the glossy brochures would have you believe. Signs prohibit parking wherever you look and the parking lots at the main beaches are clogged with vacationers lining up for a precious, and sometimes expensive, space. The further west and north you travel the more likely you are to find space; however, by this time you can be fairly frazzled and wishing you'd opted for the free roadside beaches before the toll bridge, where the sea, sun and views are pretty much the same.

The first sight you'll come across on the island is the undramatic **Sanibel Lighthouse** (erected in 1884), a relic most arrivals feel obliged to inspect (from the outside only) before spending a few hours on the presentable beach at its foot. After the beach, trace your way along Periwinkle Way and turn right into Dunlop Street, acknowledging the island's tiny city hall on the way to the **Island Historical Museum** (mid-Oct to mid-Aug Wed–Sat 10am–4pm, Dec–March also Sun 1–4pm; donations suggested). The museum is a century-old, pioneer settler's home with furnishings and photos of early Sanibel arrivals – those who weren't seafarers tried agriculture until the soils were ruined by saltwater blown up by hurricanes – and displays on the Caloosa Indians,

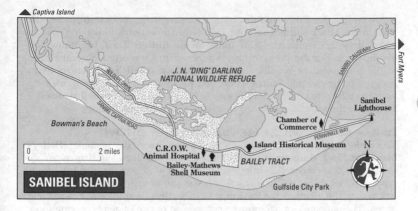

including a thousand-year-old skeleton. Continuing along Periwinkle Way, Tarpon Bay Road cuts west to the coast, passing the rampant vegetation of the **Bailey Tract**, a jungle-like rectangle of untamed land in the midst of a residential area; poorly marked trails – for the careful and courageous only – will take you deep among the alligators and the wildfowl. In either direction from the end of Tarpon Springs Road, resorts and tourists mark the beaches. Turning left along Casa Ybel Road and Algiers Lane leads to the more promising **Gulfside City Park**, a slender sandy strip shaded by Australian pines and bordered by a narrow canal, with a nicely secluded picnic area. Before you leave, follow the bike path off Algiers Road for a few yards to a tiny **cemetery**, where a few wooden markers remember those who perished in their attempts to forge an existence on the then inhospitable island some hundred years ago.

The J. N. "Ding" Darling National Wildlife Refuge
In contrast to the smooth beaches along the Gulf side of Sanibel island, the opposite edge comprises shallow bays and creeks, and a vibrant wildlife habitat under the protection of the **J. N. "Ding" Darling National Wildlife Refuge** (daily except Fri sunrise–sunset; cars $5, cyclists and pedestrians $1; ℡941/472-1100); the main entrance and **information center** are just off Sanibel-Captiva Road. Alligators, brown pelicans and ospreys are usually easy to spy, but much of what you'll see at the refuge is determined by when you come: during the fall, migrating songbirds are plentiful, thousands of wintering ducks show up in subsequent months, and in spring, graceful roseate spoonbills sweep by just before sunset. The five-mile **Wildlife Drive** requires slow speeds and plenty of stops if you're to see the well-camouflaged residents by car. If

Shelling on Sanibel and Captiva islands

Something Sanibel and Captiva share are **shells**. Literally tons of them are washed ashore with each tide, and the popularity of shell collecting has led to the bent-over condition known as "Sanibel Stoop." The potential ecological upset of too many shells being taken away has led to laws forbidding the removal of any live shells (ones with a creature living inside), on pain of a $500 fine or a prison sentence. Novices and seasoned conchologists alike will find plenty to occupy them on the beaches; to identify your find, use one of the shell charts drawn in most of the giveaway tourist magazines – or watch the experts at work during the **Sanibel Shell Festival** in early March.

you're cycling, heed the wind direction before entering; you'll usually keep the wind at your back and not in your face by pedaling north to south. You'd do better, though, to plod the four miles of the **Indigo Trail**, beginning just beyond the information center. There's a second, much shorter, foot route close to the north end of Wildlife Drive; the **Indian Shell Trail**, which twists between mangrove and buttonwood, and passes a few lime trees (remaining from the efforts to cultivate the island) to a Native American **shell mound** – a hump in the ground, much less spectacular than you might hope.

Bailey-Matthews Shell Museum and CROW

Taking the local love of shells to its logical conclusion, the nonprofit **Bailey-Matthews Shell Museum**, at 3075 Sanibel-Captiva Rd (Tues–Sun 10am–4pm; $5; ℡ 941/395-2233), is devoted entirely to molluscs from all over the world. A cornucopia of colors, shapes and sizes is spread before you in such a way as to inform as well as entertain, revealing the formation of shells, their diversity and uses, past and present. The museum's several rooms merit an hour or two of quiet contemplation.

Still on Sanibel-Captiva Road, near the entrance to the J. N. "Ding" Darling Wildlife Refuge (see p.377), you'll find a "hospital" for injured, orphaned and sick native wildlife from all over southwest Florida. Since most of the several thousand patients treated here each year are there due to interaction with humans, **CROW** (Care and Rehabilitation of Wildlife Inc) puts some of its energy into educating the public about the threats we often unwittingly pose. This ten-acre sanctuary, established thirty years ago and largely staffed by volunteers, offers **guided tours** for small groups (Mon–Fri at 11am, Sun at 1pm; $3; book ahead on ℡ 941/472-3644). A short but enlightening talk on the dangers posed by carelessly discarded fishing lines and other detritus, is followed by a walk around the sanctuary's outdoor enclosures, which house a multitude of mammals, birds, amphibians and reptiles until they are (hopefully) ready for release back into the wild. It all serves as a poignant reminder of man's impact on the environment, as well as the healing powers of nature.

Bowman's Beach

Sanibel's loveliest, but most popular swathe of sand is **Bowman's Beach,** which lies to the north of the island; to reach it, watch for Bowman's Beach Road off Sanibel-Captiva Road just prior to Blind Pass. Attracting shell-hunters and suntan-seekers it offers showers and a shady picnic spot and spectacular sunsets. **Naturists** seeking to perfect their all-over tans should beware: as the visitor center will remind you, nude sunbathing is forbidden by Florida state law.

Captiva Island

Immediately north of Bowman's Beach, Sanibel-Captiva Road crosses Blind Pass by bridge and reaches **Captiva Island**, markedly less developed than Sanibel and inhabited by only a few hundred people. If you're not going to call on one of them, the sole site of note is the tiny **Chapel-by-the-Sea**, at 11580 Chapin (down Wiles Drive). Mostly used for weddings, the chapel is unlikely to be open and you should walk instead around the unusual **cemetery**, just opposite, where many of the island's original settlers are buried. With crashing waves a shell's throw away and the graves protected from the sun by a roof of seagrape, it's a fitting final resting place for an islander. A few miles further, Captiva's northern tip is covered by the tennis courts, golf courses and Polynesian-style villas of the ultra-posh *South Sea Plantation*, where the cheapest beds are $150 a night in season. There's no point in hanging around here, except for the **boat trips** to the neighboring islands.

Boat trips from Captiva Island

Several organized **boat trips** begin from the docks at the *South Sea Plantation*. The trips on offer include dolphin-spotting cruises and shelling trips, but the best of them is the lunch cruise, departing at 10.30am and returning at 3.30pm, allowing two hours ashore at either Cabbage Key (see below) or at a gourmet restaurant on Useppa Island; cost is $27.50. The price does not include food while ashore – there's no obligation to eat once you land, but taking your own food on the boat isn't allowed. Another option is the six-hour cruise to Boca Grande or Cayo Costa; prices range from $17.50 to $35. Whenever you sail, you're likely to see **dolphins**: many of them live in the warm waters around the islands, sometimes leaping above the water to turn somersaults for your benefit. For further **details** and to make **reservations** for all sailings, contact Captiva Cruises (℡941/472 5300, Ⓦ www.captivacruises.com).

Eating and drinking

For **eating**, the best coffee house is *The Bean Café*, at 2240 Periwinkle Way in Sanibel Square (℡941/395-1919), serving a huge range of goodies, including incredible cappuccino cheesecake. The *Lighthouse Café*, 362 Periwinkle Way, Sanibel (℡941/472-0303), serves good-value meals throughout the day, and *Cheeburger Cheeburger*, 2413 Periwinkle Way, Sanibel (℡941/472-6111), has a variety of burgers. For a more substantial lunch or dinner, you'll find a wide selection of seafood at *The Mucky Duck*, Andy Rosee Lane (closed Sun; ℡941/472-3434), and at *Pippins Bar & Grill*, 1975 Periwinkle Way, Sanibel (℡941/395-2616). Alternatively, mouthwatering pasta and Cajun dishes are a speciality at the slightly more expensive *Jacaranda*, 1223 Periwinkle Way, Sanibel (℡941/472-1771).

Beyond Captiva Island: Cabbage Key

Of a number of small islands just north of Captiva, **Cabbage Key** is the one to visit. Even if you arrive on the lunch cruise from Captiva (see the box above), skip the unexciting food in favor of prowling the footpaths and the small marina: there's a special beauty to the isolated setting and the views across Pine Island Sound. Take a peep into the **restaurant**, though, to see the most expensive wallpaper in Florida: an estimated $25,000 worth of dollar bills, each one signed by the person who left it pinned up in observance of a Cabbage Key tradition. The lunchtime menu is reasonable, but if you're planning to stay for dinner expect to pay about $100 for the works. If you get the urge **to stay** longer, the inn has six simple rooms on offer at $65 a night and a few two-bedroomed rustic cottages in the grounds at $145; reserve at least a month in advance (℡941/283-2278).

South of Fort Myers

While Sanibel and Captiva islands warrant a few days of exploration, there's less to keep you occupied on the mainland on the seventy-mile journey **south of Fort Myers** towards the Everglades National Park. The towns you'll pass will hold less appeal than the nearby beaches, or the vistas of Florida's interior lying at the end of inland detours. Set aside a few hours, however, to examine one of the stranger footnotes to Florida's history: the oddball religious community of the Koreshans.

The Koreshan State Historic Site

Around the turn of the nineteenth century, some of the nation's radicals and idealists began viewing Florida as the last earthly wilderness – a subtropical Garden of Eden where the wrongs of modern society could be righted. Much to the amusement of hard-living Florida farmers, some of the idealists came south to experiment with utopian ways, though few braved the humidity and mosquitoes for long. One of the more significant arrivals was also the most bizarre: the **Koreshan Unity** community, which came from Chicago in 1894 to build the "New Jerusalem" on a site now preserved as the **Koreshan State Historic Site**, 22 miles from Fort Myers, just south of Estero beside Hwy-41 (daily 8am–sunset; cars $3.25, pedestrians and cyclists $1; ☎941/992-0311).

The flamboyant leader of the Koreshans, **Cyrus Teed**, was an army surgeon when he witnessed the "great illumination": an angel appearing and informing him that the Earth was concave, lining the inner edge of a hollow sphere, at the center of which was the rest of the universe. Subsequently, Teed changed his name to "Koresh," which is Hebrew for Cyrus, meaning "the anointed of God," and gained a following among Chicago intellectuals who, like him, were disillusioned with established religions and sought a communal, anti-materialistic way of life. Among the tenets of the Koreshan creed were celibacy outside marriage, shared ownership of goods, and gender equality. The aesthetes who came to this desolate outpost, accessible only by boat along the alligator-infested Estero River, quickly learned new skills in farming and house building and marked out thirty-foot-wide boulevards, which they believed would one day be the arteries of a city inhabited by ten million enlightened souls. In fact, at its peak in the three years after 1904, the community numbered just two hundred. After Teed's death in 1908, the Koreshans fizzled out, the last member – who arrived in 1940, fleeing Nazi Germany – dying in 1982. Ranger-led tours are available and there are over forty **campgrounds** available in the pine lands along the river at $21 a night.

The Koreshan library and museum

The Koreshan site will be a disappointment unless you first call at the **Koreshan library and museum**, 8661 Corkscrew Rd (tours Mon–Fri at 1pm, 2pm, 3pm & 4pm; $1; four-person minimum; ☎941/992-0311), for some background on the Koreshans' beliefs, plus the chance to see numerous photos and portraits of Teed, some of his esoteric books and copies of the Koreshan newspaper, *The American Eagle*. Along the broad thoroughfares at the neighboring **site**, several of the Koreshan buildings have been restored. Among them are Teed's home; the Planetary Court, meeting place of the seven women – each named for one of the seven known planets – who governed the community; and the Art Hall, where the community's cultural evenings were staged, where Koreshan celebrations (such as the solar festival in October and the lunar festival in April) still occur and where the rectilinator, a device which "proved" the Koreshan theory of the concave Earth, can be seen.

Bonita Springs and the Corkscrew Swamp Sanctuary

A fast-growing residential community, **Bonita Springs**, seven miles south of the Koreshan site, has negligible appeal aside from providing access to **Bonita Beach**, along Bonita Beach Road, and the less impressive **Everglades Wonder Gardens**, on the corner of Terry Street and Hwy-41 (daily

9am–5pm; $9), keeping a multitude of the state's indigenous creatures in cramped confinement.

Make more of an effort and you'll get a better impression of natural Florida twenty miles **inland** on Route 846 (branching from Hwy-41 a few miles south of Bonita Springs) at the National Audubon Society's **Corkscrew Swamp Sanctuary,** 375 Sanctuary Rd, Naples (May–Nov daily 8am–5.30pm; Dec–April 7am–5.30pm; $8; ☎941/348-9151), an enormous gathering of Spanish-moss-draped cypress trees rising through a dark and moody swamp landscape. Tempering the initial impression is the knowledge that all of the much larger area – presently safeguarded by the Big Cypress National Preserve (see "The Everglades," p.388) – used to look like this; uncontrolled logging felled the 500-year-old trees, partly for war efforts, and severely reduced Florida's population of wood stork, which nest a hundred feet up in the tree tops. The remaining wood stork colony is still the largest in the country, but is now faced with the threat of falling water levels. The two-and-a-quarter-mile **self-guided boardwalk tour** is excellent; leaflets are available from the visitor center. A unique facet of this park, though, is found at the outset, on the way to the rest rooms. Here an ingenious, though remarkably simple "living machine" aids water management in the park by recycling waste matter from the rest rooms through a purely natural environment to produce purified water. Within a visually pleasing plant-filled glasshouse construction, the cycle relies on sunlight, bacteria, algae and snails to break down the waste, a process that is later continued by vegetation, such as alligator flag, arrowhead, and small insects and animals. The result is purified water that fulfills the statutory hygiene standard. It's mildly amusing to think that if you avail yourself of the facilities in Corkscrew Swamp, a part of you will remain here for some time to come, helping to preserve it.

Naples

Twenty miles south of Corkscrew, **Naples** is cushioned in wealth. Hardly a soul walks and the most action in town is the sprinklers that spray the obsessively manicured lawns. You'll get the hang of the place on Fifth Avenue, where the boatyards have been turned into upscale clothes shops, art galleries and restaurants. The many miles of public **beaches**, however, are lovely and make the pervading social snobbishness more than bearable. **Lowdermilk Park,** about two miles north of the pier, is the most gregarious of the local sands, especially on weekends.

A good way to explore Naples and learn of its history is to take a **Naples Trolley Tour.** Running daily 8.30am–5.30pm (☎941/262-7300), these entertaining and educational tours last nearly two hours, departing from the Old Naples General Store and Trolley Depot downtown. The tour passes such sights as **Palm Cottage,** at 137 Twelfth Ave, one of the few houses left in Florida built of tabby mortar (made by burning seashells), and the building which now houses **Fantozzi's Café** (see overleaf), a 1922-built cube which has been everything to Naples – from its first town hall, to a courthouse, drugstore, movie theater, Presbyterian church, Catholic church, tap-dance shop and zoo. Fares are $15 for the trolley, including an all-day boarding pass.

To ogle the fruits of Naples' money, head north up Hwy-41 to the *Ritz Carlton Hotel* (☎941/598-3300, ⓦ www.ritzcarlton.com) at the end of Vanderbilt Beach Road. While you'd need $3500 for a night in the presidential suite, sweeping through the grand entrance for a coffee at the bar is an inexpensive way to appreciate the hotel's towering splendor. The building looks like a 1930s vision of classical decadence, but it actually appeared in the late 1980s.

Getting to the Everglades from Naples

There's no public transport to the Everglades, so if you don't have transport of your own a good option for visiting them is to take a daytrip from Naples or Marco Island (see opposite). **Everglades Excursions** (℡941/262-1914 or 1-800/592-0848, ⊛www.everglades-excursions.com), runs full- and half-day tours, and trips include safari guided transportation, a jungle cruise through the Everglades National Park, and a tour of Everglades city. Half-day tours cost $59, and full-day $79 – including lunch. It is possible to pick up discount coupons of up to $5 from the tourist booklets at the Chamber of Commerce (see below).

Information and accommodation

For **information**, try the **Chamber of Commerce**, 895 Fifth Ave S (daily 9am–5pm; ℡941/262-6141; ℻435-9910, ⊛www.naples.org) or the **Golden Gate Visitor Center** at 3847 Tollgate Blvd (daily 9am–5pm; ℡941/352-0508). They're not the most friendly of offices, but if you push hard enough, they'll supply you with local bus schedules. Greyhound **buses** stop in Naples at 2669 Davis Blvd S (℡941/774-5660 or 1-800/231-2222 for schedules).

Accommodation, not surprisingly, is more expensive the closer you get to the beach. Between December and April even expensive accommodation can be hard to find and it's worth making the Chamber of Commerce (see above), your first stop as they have a list of all available accommodation when it's in high demand. The nearest campground is the *KOA* site, 1700 Barefoot Williams Rd (℡941/774-5455 or 1-800/562-77340, ℮naples@koa.net), where you can pitch a tent for $31 a night, or rent a Kamping Kabin for $47.

The Cove Inn, 900 Broad Ave S (℡941/598-3300). This reasonably priced inn is convenient for walking everywhere in Old Naples. ❹

Flamingo Apartment Motel, 383 Sixth Ave S (℡941/261-7017, wwwwflamingonaplesfl.com). This old-style Fifties motel is set in a cozy tropical courtyard and features a pool, shuffleboard and picnic tables. ❷-❹

The Lemon Tree Inn, 250 Ninth St (℡941/262-1414, ⊛www.lemontreeinn.com). This friendly B&B offers free lemonade in the lobby and bike rental for guests. ❸-❼

Lighthouse Inn, 9140 Gulfshore Drive, (℡941/597-3345). This small and friendly inn has a riverside restaurant, boats and sun decks and a large pool. ❷-❹

The Olde Naples Inn, 801 Third St (℡941/262-5194). Though it isn't old at all, the rooms are large, there's a pool and breakfast is included. ❹-❺

Eating

Cafe Plantain, 947 Third Ave N. A trek from the beaches, this café serves good sandwiches, chorizopan, blackbean veggie burgers and plantains.

Cheeburger Cheeburger, 505 Fifth Ave (℡941/435-9796). For a real classic cheeseburger and other American favorites.

Fantozzi's Café, on the corner of Broad Ave and Third St South. Convenient for the old town and beach, this popular café serves frozen yogurts and gourmet sandwiches.

McCabe's Irish Pub and Grill, Almost opposite *Zoe's*, this bar and grill attracts a younger crowd.

Riverside Fish and Ale House, 1200 Fifth Ave S (℡941/263-2734). This great seafood restaurant by the water has a wide range of beers and exotic cocktails.

Spanky's Speakeasy, 1550 Airport Pulling Rd. It's worth seeking out for its unique atmosphere of old America, complete with 1924 model-T Truck and antiques in every nook and cranny. Try the fried catfish sandwich or the Louisiana barbecue shrimp.

Zoe's, 101 Fifth Ave. This eclectic menu features smoked Thai chicken, Gulf shrimp and lots of noodle dishes. You can order half-portions to cut costs; main courses run from $9 to $27. *Zoe's* is open until 10pm as a restaurant, but the bar and live music go on until late.

Marco Island

There's not all that much reason to visit **Marco Island** (directly south of Naples), where artificial bald eagle nests are among the techniques dreamed up by property developers to bring back the wildlife their high-rise condos have driven away. A good way to see the island is on a trolley tour, which runs daily 10am–5pm (℡ 941/394-1600); the complete narrated journey takes about ninety minutes, but you can hop on and off as many times as you like. At the northern end of the island, the old village of Marco has some charm, and **Tigertail Beach Park**, at the end of a boardwalk from Hernando Drive, is a fine place to relax – though neither really makes the journey (seven miles along Route 951 off Hwy-41) worthwhile. Also, a few fairly authentic **fish shacks** are located near the eastern edge of the island – worth a stop if you're hungry. Still, the Everglades, within easy striking distance, are a far superior target.

Seventeen miles south of Naples on Hwy-41, the landscape becomes an unbroken swathe of forest. **Collier-Seminole State Park**, at 20200 E Tamiami Trail (8am–sunset; cars $3.25, cyclists or pedestrians $1; ℡ 941/394-3397), is a tropical hammock filled with Florida royal palms and a six-and-a-half-mile walking trail; a hiking guide is available at the park's main office. Boat tours run throughout the day taking passengers along the Black Water River, which runs through the park; fares are $10. If you want to camp here (and it's not a bad base from which to explore the Everglades), there are two sites, one for tents where it costs $8-13 a night, the other for RVs (enquire at the office at the above number).

The Everglades

Nothing anywhere else is like them: their vast glittering openness, wider than the enormous visible round of the horizon, the racing free saltness and sweetness of their massive winds, under the dazzling blue heights of space. They are unique also in the simplicity, the diversity, the related harmony of the forms of life they enclose. The miracle of the light pours over the green and brown expanse of saw-grass and of water, shining and slow-moving below, the grass and water that is the meaning and the central fact of the Everglades of Florida. It is a river of grass.

Marjory Stoneman Douglas, *The Everglades: River of Grass*

Whatever scenic excitement you might anticipate from one of the country's more celebrated natural areas, no mountains, canyons or even signposts herald your arrival in the **Everglades**. From the straight and monotonous ninety-mile course of Hwy-41, the most dramatic sights are small pockets of trees poking above a completely flat sawgrass plain that stretches to the horizon. It looks dead and empty; you wonder what all the fuss is about. Yet these wide-open spaces resonate with life, forming part of an immensely subtle and ever-changing ecosystem that has evolved through a unique combination of climate, vegetation and wildlife.

Originally encompassing everything south of Lake Okeechobee, throughout the last century the Everglades' boundaries have steadily been pushed back by human demands for farmland, fresh water and urban development. Only a comparatively small section around Florida's southeastern corner is under the federal protection of the **Everglades National Park**. It's here, where public access is designed to inflict minimum damage, that the vital links holding the Everglades together become apparent: the all-important cycle of wet and dry seasons; the ability of alligators to discover water and dig for it with their tails; and the tree islands providing sanctuaries for animals during the flood period. None of this can be comprehended from a car window, or with a half-hour ride through the sawgrass on an airboat: noisy, destructive contraptions touted all along Hwy-41, but banned inside the park.

Don't expect to fathom it all: the Everglades is a constant source of surprise, even for the few hundred people who live in them. Use the visitor centers, read the free material, take the guided tours and, above all, explore slowly. It's then that the Everglades begin to reveal themselves and you'll realize you're in the middle of one of the natural world's most remarkable ecosystems.

Some geology and natural history

Appearing as flat as a tabletop, the oolitic limestone (once part of the seabed) on which the Everglades stands actually tilts very slightly – a few inches over seventy miles – towards the southwest. For thousands of years, water from summer storms and the overflow of Lake Okeechobee has moved slowly through the Everglades towards the coast. The water replenishes the sawgrass, which grows on a thin layer of soil – or "marl" – formed by decaying vegetation on the limestone base, and gives birth to the algae at the foot of a complex food chain that sustains much larger creatures, most importantly alligators.

Alligators earn their "keepers of the Everglades" nickname during the dry winter season. After the summer floodwaters have reached the sea, drained through the bedrock or simply evaporated, the Everglades is barren except for the water accumulated in ponds or "gator holes" – created when an alligator senses water and clears the soil covering it with its tail. Besides nourishing the alligator, the pond provides a home for other wildlife until the summer rains return.

Sawgrass covers much of the Everglades, but where natural indentations in the limestone fill with marl, tree islands – or "hammocks" – appear, just high enough to stand above the flood waters and fertile enough to support a variety of trees and plants. Close to hammocks, often surrounding gator holes, you'll find wispy green-leafed willows. Smaller patches of vegetation, like small green humps, are called "bayheads." Pinewoods grow in the few places where the elevation exceeds seven feet and, in the deep depressions that hold water the longest, dwarf cypress trees flourish, their treetops forming a distinctive "cypress dome" when large numbers cover an extensive area.

Human habitation and exploitation

Before dying out through contact with Europeans, several Native American tribes lived hunter-gatherer existences in the Everglades. The shell mounds they built can still be seen in sections of the park. In the nineteenth century, Seminole Indians, who'd fled white settlers in the north, also lived peaceably in the area (for more on them, see "Miccosukee Indian Village," p.390). By the late 1800s, a few white settlements – such as those at Everglades City and Flamingo – had sprung up, peopled by fugitives, outcasts and loners who, unlike the Indians, looked to exploit the land rather than live in harmony with it.

As Florida's population grew, the damage caused by uncontrolled hunting, road building and draining the Everglades for farmland gave rise to a significant conservation lobby. In 1947, a section of the Everglades was declared a national park, but unrestrained commercial use of nearby areas continued to upset the Everglades' natural cycle. The problem was acknowledged – if hardly alleviated – by the preservation in the Seventies of the Big Cypress Swamp, just north of the park.

As human understanding increases, so the severity of the problems faced by the Everglades becomes ever more apparent. The 1500 miles of canals built to divert the flow of water away from the Everglades towards the state's expanding cities, the poisoning caused by agricultural chemicals from the farmlands around Lake Okeechobee, and the broader changes wrought by global warming, could yet turn Florida's greatest natural asset into a wasteland – with wider ecological implications that can only be guessed at.

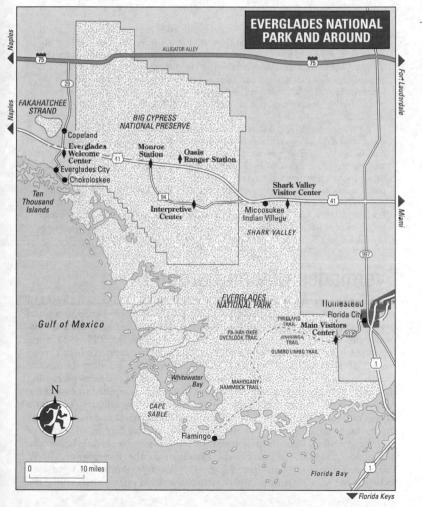

EVERGLADES NATIONAL PARK AND AROUND

Naples

75 ALLIGATOR ALLEY 75

Fort Lauderdale

29

FAKAHATCHEE STRAND

Naples

BIG CYPRESS NATIONAL PRESERVE

Copeland

Everglades Welcome Center

Monroe Station

Oasis Ranger Station

41

Everglades City

Chokoloskee

94

Interpretive Center

Shark Valley Visitor Center

41

Miami

Miccosukee Indian Village

Ten Thousand Islands

SHARK VALLEY

997

EVERGLADES NATIONAL PARK

Homestead

Florida City

Gulf of Mexico

PINELAND TRAIL

Main Visitors Center

PA-HAY-OKEE OVERLOOK TRAIL

ANHINGA TRAIL

9336

GUMBO LIMBO TRAIL

1

N

Whitewater Bay

MAHOGANY HAMMOCK TRAIL

CAPE SABLE

Flamingo

0   10 miles

Florida Bay

1

Florida Keys

Orientation

A busy two-lane road, not the scenic drive you might expect, **Hwy-41** (the **Tamiami Trail**) runs east from Naples around the northern edge of the park, providing the only land access to the Everglades City, Shark Valley and Chekika (at the end of Richmond Drive, nine miles south of Hwy-41, on Route 997) park entrances, and to Fakahatchee Strand, the Big Cypress National Preserve and the Miccosukee Indian Village. To reach the Flamingo entrance, touch the edge of Miami and head south via Florida City. **No public transport** of any kind runs along Hwy-41 or to any of the park entrances, though daytrips are available from Miami (see p.128) and Naples (see p.382). Between Naples and Fort Lauderdale, Greyhound buses use "Alligator Alley," the popular title for Route 84, twenty miles north of Hwy-41, recently converted into a section of I-75.

When to visit

Though open all year, the park changes completely between its **wet** (summer) and **dry** (winter) seasons. The best time to visit is **winter** (Nov to April), when receding floodwaters cause wildlife, including migratory birds, to congregate around gator holes and sloughs (freshwater channels); ranger-led activities – such as guided walks, canoe trips and talks – are frequent and the mosquitoes are bearable. However, accommodation prices soar to practically double summer prices and at certain times it is advisable to book ahead, especially on the weekends.

The picture is entirely different in **summer** (May to Oct), when afternoon storms flood the sawgrass prairies and pour through the sloughs, leaving only the hammocks visible above water. Around this time, mosquitoes become a severe annoyance, rendering the backcountry campgrounds almost uninhabitable, organized activities are substantially reduced, migratory birds have gone and the park's wildlife spreads throughout the park due to a plentiful supply of food.

A clever compromise is a visit **between the seasons** (late April to early May or late Oct to early Nov), which avoids the worst of the mosquitoes and the winter tourist crowds, but at the same time reveals plenty of wildlife and the park's changing landscapes.

Everglades City and around

Purchased and named in the Twenties by an advertising executive dreaming of a subtropical metropolis, **EVERGLADES CITY** not only serves as a good base from which to explore the Everglades, it also warrants investigating in its own right. Thirty miles from Naples and three miles south off Hwy-41 along Route 29, it has a population of under five hundred in summer, which rises to around 1500 in winter. Everglades City took a direct hit from Hurricane Donna in the Sixties. As a result, many of its buildings were destroyed, causing the town's whole infrastructure to collapse. As the city is reputed to have some of best fishing in the country, New York businessmen regularly fly down for a day on the water. Everglades City has lost none of its charm and sense of identity in its re-creation. Some of the properties left standing in the wake of Hurricane Donna have been restored, offering a glimpse of life before the destruction. One such building is the **Museum of the Everglades**, 105 W Broadway (Tues– Sat 11am–4pm; $2; ☎ 941/695-0008), housed in what used to be the old laundry. It now displays artifacts and old photographs telling the

Entering the park and accommodation

Entering the park is free at Everglades City (though you can only see it by boat or canoe). At Shark Valley, Flamingo and Chekika it's $10 per car, $5 pedestrians and cyclists; tickets are valid for seven days and can be used at all sites. Only Shark Valley closes for the night. With the exception of the wilderness waterway canoe trail between Everglades City and Flamingo, you can't travel from one section of the park into another.

Apart from the two organized campgrounds and a hotel at Flamingo, park **accommodation** is limited to backcountry campgrounds. In most cases these are raised wooden platforms with a roof and chemical toilet accessible by boat or canoe. To stay, you need a permit, issued free from the relevant visitor center. One backcountry site at Flamingo, Pearl Bay, is accessible to **disabled visitors**.

Ten miles outside the park in Florida City, the *Everglades International Hostel*, 20 SW Second Ave (☎941/248-1122 or 1-800/372-3874; ✉gladeshostel@hotmail.com), may be the best option for budget-minded travelers who want to maximize their time in the Everglades. Beds go for $13 a night (private rooms are available) and the hostel is perfectly situated for continuing on to the Florida Keys or to Miami International Airport. The hostel provides bike and kayak rental and the very friendly staff will lend you racks to transport equipment on your car, or give you a lift to the park entrance. *Rosita's*, 199 W Palm Drive, is a great Mexican restaurant opposite the hostel. The food is excellent and reasonably priced and they are even open for breakfast.

Practical tips

In the park, wear a hat, sunglasses and loose-fitting clothes with long sleeves and long trousers, and carry plenty of **insect repellent**. Aside from anticipating the hazards of sunburn (there's very little shade) and mosquitoes, you need take no special measures for the walking trails, most of which are short trots along raised boardwalks.

Traveling and camping in the **backcountry** requires more caution. Most exploration is done by boat or canoe along marked trails, with basic campgrounds situated on the longer routes. Take a **compass**, **maps** (available from visitor centers) and ample provisions, including at least a **gallon of water** per person per day. Supplies should be carried in **hard containers**, as raccoons can chew through soft ones. Be sure to leave a **detailed plan** of your journey and its expected duration with a park ranger. Finally, pay heed to the latest **weather forecast** and note the tidal patterns if you're canoeing in a coastal area.

story of two thousand years of human habitation in the southwest Everglades. It's hard to miss the large, wooden triangular building that houses the Everglades **Chamber of Commerce Welcome Center** (daily 8.30am–5pm; ☎941/695-3941, ⓦwww.florida-everglades.com) at the junction of Route 29 (signposted Everglades City) and Hwy-41. Many of the visitors are here for the fishing, especially around the numerous mangrove islands arranged like jigsaw-puzzle pieces along the coastline – aptly titled **Ten Thousand Islands**. For a closer look at the mangroves that safeguard the Everglades from surge tides, ignore the ecologically dubious tours advertised along the roadside and take one of the park-sanctioned **boat trips**. Try either Everglades National Park Boat Tours (☎941/695-2591 or 1-800/445-7724) or Everglades Rentals and Eco Adventures (☎941/695-4666, ⓦwww.evergladesadventures.com), located at the *Ivey House* B&B (see "Accommodation" overleaf). The full- and half-day trips depart from the dock on Chokoloskee, a blob of land – actually an Indian shell mound – marking the end of Route 29. Two to six guided adventures are also available, departing daily at intervals between 8.30am and 5pm, with fares starting at $16. Canoes and kayaks can also be rented for those who want to explore on their own. The dockside **visitor center** (daily 8.30am–5pm; ☎941/695-3311) provides information on the cruises and the excellent ranger-led **canoe trips.** Anybody adequately skilled with the paddle, equipped with rough camping gear and with a week to spare, should have a crack at the hundred-mile **wilderness waterway**, a marked trail through Whitewater Bay to Flamingo (see p.392), with numerous backcountry campgrounds en route. A way to sit back and see the Everglades is to take an **Everglades City Trolley Tour** (☎941/695-1557 or 1-888/667-3600). Picking up outside the *Captain's Table* (see below), these narrated tours last an hour and run daily at 11am, 1.30pm and 3.30pm. In addition to taking you around the city they also venture into the surrounding area, offering panoramic views and a chance to see wildlife in its natural habitat.

Accommodation

Other than boat-accessed camping, there's no **accommodation** inside this section of the park. In Chokoloskee you can rent an RV by the night for $50–70 at *Outdoor Resorts* (☎941/695-2881), or, back in Everglades City, there's a range of good accommodation to choose from. For the budget-minded traveler, the *Ivey House*, 107 Camellia St (☎941/695-3299, ⓦwww.iveyhouse.com; open Nov–April – booking advisable; ❷), is charming and clean, breakfast is included with the room rate and evening meals are also served daily at 6pm for an extra $10-15. *The Captain's Table,* 102 E Broadway (☎941/695-4211 or 1-800/741-6430; ❷-❹), has a great heated pool overlooking a lake and guests get a good discount at the *Everglades Seafood Depot* restaurant (see below). *The Banks of the Everglades*, a listed building located at 201 W Broadway (☎941/695-3151 or 1-888/431-1977, ❷-❺); is an eccentric B&B housed in what used to be the first bank in Collier County. Breakfast is served in the old walk-in vault and the whole place is crammed full of artifacts from the building's previous life. The *Rod & Gun Lodge*, 200 Riverside Drive (☎941/695-4211; ❹-❻), used to be an exclusive club whose members included presidents, but now anyone can stay here; for an extra $10–20 you can eat at their restaurant. There are also basic motel rooms (and RV space) in the cheap, but shabby *Barron River Resort* on Route 29 (☎941/695-3331 or 1-800/535-4961; ❷-❹). Camping is available at the **Big Cypress Trail Lakes Campground**, Ochoppe, Hwy-41 (☎941/695-2275), where it costs $12 a night to pitch a tent.

Eating and drinking

It's no surprise that there's plenty of **seafood** to be eaten in the area. Situated in the old train depot, *The Everglades Seafood Depot*, 102 Collier Ave, offers a good selection of Mexican and Caribbean dishes as well as seafood, and will cook any fish that you have caught from one of their trips. At the *Oyster House*, Chokoloskee Causeway, you can watch the sunset over the ten thousand islands while you eat, and enjoy a full cocktail lounge – "Glades Margarita" a speciality – and entertainment on the weekends. If pizza is more your style, try *Guido's Pizzeria* in the middle of Everglades City, open noon–8pm.

Big Cypress National Preserve

The completion of Hwy-41 in 1928 led to the destruction of thousands of towering bald cypress trees – whose durable wood is highly marketable – that lined the roadside sloughs. By the Seventies, attempts to drain these acres and turn them into saleable residential plots had caused enough damage to the national park for the government to create the **Big Cypress National Preserve** – a massive chunk of protected land mostly on the northern side of Hwy-41. Sadly, neither the bald cypress trees nor the wood storks that once flourished here are present in anything like their previous numbers (a better place to observe both is the Corkscrew Swamp Sanctuary, see p.381). Although this stretch of the highway has frequent warning signs reminding drivers to be careful of panthers on the road, you're as likely to see one as you are to win the Florida lottery. When Miami started to grow in the late 1800s these timid cats were seen as a threat and now, due to over-hunting, it is estimated that there are only between thirty and fifty of this official state mammal of Florida left alive.

Seeing the preserve

The only way to traverse the Big Cypress Swamp is on a very rugged 29-mile hiking trail, beginning twenty miles east on Hwy-41 at the **Oasis Visitor Center** (daily 8.30am–4pm; ☏ 941/695-4111). Near the Visitor Center is the **Big Cypress Gallery**, 52388 Tamiami Trail (Mon–Sat 10am–5pm; ☏ 941/695-2428, ⓦ www.clydebutcher.com), which exhibits the work of Everglades photographer Clyde Butcher. His pictures are amazing and capture all the beauty and magic of the area. Framed pictures are on the expensive side, but they also come as smaller cards which make perfect souvenirs. There's also a convenient gator hole beside the gallery where you can take your own close-up photos of alligators. While it's not actually part of the national preserve, be sure to visit the nearby **Fakahatchee Strand**, directly north of Everglades City on Route 29. This water-holding slough sustains dwarf cypress trees (much smaller than the bald cypress; gray and spindly during the winter, draped with green needles in summer), a stately batch of royal palms, and masses of orchids and spiky-leafed air plants. If possible, see it on a **ranger-guided walk** (details on ☏ 941/695-4593).

Dragonfly Expeditions (☏ 941/774-9010 or 1-888/9-WANDER, ⓦ www.dragonflyexpeditions.com/daygladesgallery_body.htm) offer brilliant backwater day treks in which small groups are led off the beaten track – which in summer means wading waist-deep in water – right into the heart of the Everglades. More of an adventure than a hike these treks are led by highly informed field guides who offer loads of information on the environment and wildlife in it. A gourmet lunch under a canopy of Spanish moss is also included in the price – as are the use of water shoes and walking sticks (which you may need to pull yourself out of the mud!). Tours start at $75 per person and tour guides will either meet you at the Big Cypress Gallery (see above), or provide transport to the start of the walk. They also offer Miccosukee Indian Heritage Tours where a Native American guide leads groups to the Miccosukee/Seminole island camp, offering the chance to learn about both the wildlife and the history and culture of the Miccosukee; tours start at $45 per person.

If your car's suspension is dependable, turn right at Monroe Station, travel four miles west of the Oasis Ranger Station onto Loop Road, a gravel road that's potholed in parts and prone to sudden flooding. This winds its way through cypress and pinewoods to Pinecrest where an **interpretive center** makes sense of the varied terrains all around. The road rejoins Hwy-41 at Forty Mile Bend, just west of the Miccosukee Indian Village.

The Miccosukee Indian Village

Driven out of central Florida by white settlers, several hundred Seminole Indians retreated to the Everglades during the nineteenth century to avoid forced resettlement in the Midwest. They lived on hammocks in open-sided *chickee* huts built from cypress and cabbage palm, and traded, hunted and fished across the wetlands by canoe. Descendants of the Seminoles and a related tribe, the **Miccosukee** still live in the Everglades, though the coming of Hwy-41 – making the land accessible to the white man – brought another fundamental change in their lifestyle as they set about grabbing their share of the tourist dollars.

Four miles east of Forty Mile Bend, the **Miccosukee Indian Village** (daily 9am–5pm; $5; ☎941/223-8380) symbolizes the tribe's uneasy compromise. In the souvenir shop good-quality traditional crafts and clothes stand side by side with blatant tat, and in the "village" men turn logs into canoes and women cook over open fires. Despite the authentic roots, it's such a contrived affair that anyone with an ounce of sensitivity can't help but feel uneasy – the arrow-shooting gallery and the awful alligator-wrestling don't help. Since it's the only chance you're likely to get to discover anything of Native American life in the Everglades, it's hard to resist taking a look, though a plateful of traditional pumpkin bread from the *Miccosukee Restaurant* (☎305/223-8388) across the road and a look at the *Seminole Tribune* newspaper, describing modern concerns, might serve you better.

Shark Valley

In no other section of the park does the Everglades' "River of Grass" tag seem as appropriate as it does at **Shark Valley** (daily 8.30am–6pm; cars $8, pedestrians and cyclists $4), a mile east of the Miccosukee Indian Village. From here the sawgrass plain stretches as far as the eye can see, dotted by hardwood hammocks and the smaller bayheads. It's here, too, that the damage wrought by humans on the natural cycle can sometimes be disturbingly clear. The thirst of Miami coupled with a period of drought can make Shark Valley resemble a stricken desert.

Seeing Shark Valley

Aside from a few simple walking trails close to the **visitor center** (winter daily 8.30am–5.15pm; reduced hours during the summer; ☎305/221-8455), you can see Shark Valley only from a fourteen-mile loop road. Too lengthy and lacking in shade to be covered comfortably on foot, and off limits to cars, the

Airboat tours

Airboat tours are synonymous with the Everglades and all along Hwy-41 operators will try and tempt you onto one of their trips. In the hands of a responsible operator they are not a problem; however, not all operators are so inclined and these tours have a damaging impact on the environment. Oil and gas from the boats pollute the rivers and constant use of the same routes leaves scars in the environment. Many will give passengers marshmallows to feed the alligators, thus ensuring you get to see one. Feeding wild animals is not the best of ideas and is discouraged by the authorities as it makes animals lose their natural fear of humans and become aggressive and dangerous. If you do want to take an airboat tour, be careful which operator you choose.

loop is ideally covered by **bike** (rental costs $3.25 an hour; return by 4pm). Alternatively, a highly informative two-hour **tram tour** (daily in summer; $9.50; reservations necessary March–July; ☎ 305/221-8455) will get you around and stop frequently to view wildlife, but won't allow you to linger in any particular place.

Set out as early as possible (the wildlife is most active in the cool of the morning), ride slowly and stay alert: otters, turtles and snakes are plentiful but not always easy to spot, and the abundant alligators often keep uncannily still. During September and October you'll come across female alligators tending their young; the brightly striped babies often sun themselves on the backs of their extremely protective mothers; watch them from a safe distance. More of the same creatures – and a good selection of birdlife – can be seen from the **observation tower** overlooking a deep canal and marking the far point of the loop.

It may seem hard to believe, but Shark Valley is only seventeen miles from the western fringes of Miami. To **see more of the park**, continue east on Hwy-41, turn south along Route 997, and head west for eleven miles along Route 9336 from Florida City to the park's main entrance.

Pine Island

Everglades City has the islands and Shark Valley has the sawgrass, but the **Pine Island** section of the park – the entire southerly portion, containing Cape Sable and Flamingo (see overleaf) – holds virtually everything that makes the Everglades tick: spend a well-planned day or two here and you'll quickly grasp the fundamentals of its complex ecology. From the **park entrance** (always open; cars $8, pedestrians and cyclists $4), the road passes the **main visitor center** (daily 8am–5pm; ☎ 305/242-7700) and continues for 38 miles to the tiny coastal settlement of Flamingo, a one-time pioneer fishing colony now comprising a marina, hotel and campground. There's no compulsion to drive the whole way, and the short walking trails (none more than half a mile) along the route will keep you engaged for hours; sensibly, though, you should devote one day to walking and another to the canoe trails close to Flamingo.

Accommodation

There are well-equipped **campgrounds** at Long Pine Key, near the main visitor center, and Flamingo, as well as many backcountry sites (free) on the longer walking and canoe trails. Reservations are not accepted for any of the campgrounds: spare space at Flamingo (which invariably fills first) or Long Pine Key can be checked on the board just inside the park entrance. If there is space and the visitor center is closed, you can use the site, but should pay at the visitor center before 10am the following day. For the backcountry sites, you will, of course, need a permit. These are issued free at the visitor centers. The only **rooms** within the park are at *Flamingo Lodge* (☎ 941/695-3101 or 1-800/600-38131, ⊛ www.flamingolodge.com; ❸-❹), which offers a large continental breakfast. You'll need to make a reservation months in advance if arriving between November and April.

Towards Flamingo: walking trails

A good place to gather information on the Everglades' various habitats is the Royal Palm **visitor center** (daily 8am–5pm) down the Royal Palm turn-off, a mile from the main park entrance. Apparently unimpressed by the multitudinous forms of nature and animal life throughout the Everglades, large numbers of park visitors simply want to see an alligator, and most are satisfied by walking the **Anhinga Trail**, a mile from the main visitor center. Turtles, marsh rabbits and the odd raccoon are also likely to turn up on the route, but you should watch for the bizarre anhinga, a black-bodied bird resembling an elongated cormorant, which, after diving for fish, spends ages drying itself on rocks and tree branches with its white-tipped wings fully spread. Beat the crowds to the Anhinga Trail and then peruse the adjacent, but very different **Gumbo Limbo Trail** (much of the vegetation along the trail was destroyed by Hurricane Andrew in 1992 and is now beginning to grow back), a hardwood hammock packed with exotic sub-tropical growths: strangler figs, gumbo limbos, royal palms, wild coffee and resurrection ferns. The latter appear dead during the dry season, but "resurrect" themselves in the summer rains to form a lush collar of green.

By comparison, the **Pinelands Trail**, a few miles further, by the Long Pine Key campground (T305/242-7700), offers an undramatic ramble through a forest of slash pine, though the solitude comes as a welcome relief after the busier trails. The hammering of woodpeckers is often the loudest sound you'll hear. More birdlife – including egrets, red-shouldered hawks and circling vultures – is viewable six miles ahead from the **Pa-hay-okee Overlook Trail**, which emerges from a stretch of dwarf cypress to face a great tract of sawgrass – a familiar sight if you've arrived from Shark Valley.

Although related to California's giant redwoods, the mahogany trees of the **Mahogany Hammock Trail**, eight miles from the Overlook, are disappointingly small despite being the largest of the type in the country. A greater draw is the colorful snails and golden orb spiders lurking amongst their branches. The sight of the red mangrove trees – recognizable by their above-ground roots – rising from the sawgrass is a sure indication that you're approaching the coast.

Flamingo and around

A century ago, the only way to reach **Flamingo** was by boat, a fact that failed to deter a small bunch of settlers who came here to fish, hunt, smuggle and get paralytic on moonshine whisky. It didn't even have a name until the opening of a post office made one necessary: "The End of the World" was favored by those who knew the place, but "Flamingo" was eventually chosen due to an abundance of roseate spoonbills – pink-plumed birds, killed for their feathers – wrongly identified by locals. The completion of the road to Homestead in 1922 was expected to bring boom times to Flamingo, but as it turned out, most people seized on this as a chance to leave. None of the old buildings remains, and present-day Flamingo does a brisk trade servicing the needs of sportsfishing fanatics. On land, the **visitor center** (8am–5pm; T941/695-2945) and the marina of the *Flamingo Lodge* (see p.391) are the activity bases.

There are several walking trails within reach of Flamingo, but more promising are the numerous **canoe trails**. Rent a canoe ($22 half a day, $32 a full day) from the marina, and get maps and advice from the visitor center. Obviously, you should pick a canoe trail that suits your level of expertise. A likely one for novices (though not alone if you've no experience whatsoever) is the three-mile **Noble Hammock Trail**, passing through sawgrass and around mangroves, using a course pioneered by makers of bootleg booze. For polished paddlers, the hundred-mile **wilderness waterway** to Everglades City (see p.386), lined by plentiful backcountry campgrounds, is the trip you've been waiting for.

If you lack faith in your own abilities, take one of the **guided boat trips** from the marina. The most informative, the **Pelican Backcountry Cruise** (daily; $16; reservations on ☎305/253-2241), makes a two-hour foray around the mangrove-enshrouded Whitewater Bay, offering good views of **Cape Sable**, a strip of deserted beach and rough prairie hovering uncertainly between land and sea.

TRAVEL DETAILS

Trains

Tampa to: Bradenton (2 daily; 1hr 10min); DeLand (2 daily; 3hr 14min); Jacksonville (3 daily; 5hr 28min); Lakeland (1 daily; 32min); Orlando (2 daily; 2hr 20min); Palatka (2 daily; 5hr 34min); Sanford (2 daily; 3hr); Sarasota (1 daily; 1hr 50min); St Petersburg (1 daily; 30min); Winter Park (2 daily; 3hr 25min).

St Petersburg to: Tampa (2 daily; 35min).

Buses

Tampa to: Avon Park (1 daily; 3hr 35min); Bradenton (5 daily; 1hr 20 min); Clearwater (7 daily; 30min); Crystal River (2 daily; 3hr 13min); Fort Lauderdale (8 daily; 7hr 45min); Fort Myers (6 daily; 2hr 50min); Lake Wales (1 daily; 2hr 25min); Lakeland (4 daily; 1hr); Miami (6 daily; 8hr 55min); Naples (3 daily; 5hr 35min); Orlando (7 daily; 2hr); Sarasota (5 daily; 1hr 50min); Sebring (1 daily; 3hr 55min); St Petersburg (7 daily; 35min); Tallahassee (4 daily; 6hr 35min); Venice (5 daily; 2hr 30min); West Palm Beach (1 daily; 6hr 50min); Winter Haven (3 daily; 1hr 30min).

St Petersburg to: Clearwater (6 daily; 30min–1hr 50min); Tampa (7 daily; 35min–1hr).

7

The Panhandle

CHAPTER 7

Highlights

* **The Old City Cemetery**
Perhaps the starting point
for learning about African-
American history in
Tallahassee. **P.405**

* **Havana** It may not be the one
in Cuba, but this former
tobacco plantation town has
its own charms, like numerous
worthy antique shops. **P.409**

* **Apalachicola National
Forest** The great outdoors
reasserts itself in these woods
- rent a canoe or hike some
trails to explore. **P.412**

* **Wakulla Springs** The best
way to take the waters here
is on a glass-bottomed boat
tour. **P.412**

* **Florida Caverns State Park**
The deep caverns here, used
by Seminole Indians to hide
from Andrew Jackson's
army, hold magnificent
calcite formations. **P.416**

* **Seaside** The dollhouse
architecture and incredibly
manicured streets and
lawns of this resort should
be seen to be believed.
P.427

* **National Heritage
Coastline** The stretch of
highway between Pensacola
and Navarre beaches holds
scenic reef dunes and other
visual delights. **P.439**

7

The Panhandle

Butting up against the southernmost borders of both Alabama and Georgia, the long, narrow **Panhandle** has much more in common with the Deep South than it does with the rest of the state. Cosmopolitan sophisticates in Miami and Tampa tell countless jokes lampooning the folksy lifestyles of the people here – undeniably more rural and down-to-earth than their counterparts around the rest of the state – but the Panhandle has more to offer than many give it credit for. You certainly won't get a true picture of Florida without seeing at least some of it.

A century ago, the Panhandle actually *was* Florida. When Miami was still a swamp, **Pensacola**, at the Panhandle's western edge, was a busy port. Fertile soils lured wealthy plantation owners south and helped establish **Tallahassee** as a high-society gathering place and administrative center – a role that, as the state capital, it retains. The great Panhandle forests fueled a timber boom that brought new towns and an unrivaled prosperity, but the decline of cotton, the felling of too many trees and the building of the East Coast Railroad eventually left the Panhandle high and dry.

Today, the region divides neatly in two. Much of the **inland Panhandle** consists of small farming towns that see few visitors, despite their friendly rhythm, fine examples of Old South architecture and proximity to springs, sinkholes and the **Apalachicola National Forest** – perhaps the best place in Florida to disappear into the wilderness. The **coastal Panhandle**, on the other hand, is inundated with tourists who flock in from the southern states and wreak havoc during the riotous student Spring Breaks. Much of the coastline is marked by rows of hotels and condos, but there are also protected areas that are home to some of the finest stretches of unspoilt sand anywhere in the state. The blinding white sands are almost pure quartz, washed down over millions of years from the Appalachian mountains, and they squeak when you walk on them. Not to be outshone, the Gulf of Mexico's waters here are two-tone: emerald green close to the shore and deep blue further out.

Accommodation price codes

All accommodation prices in this book have been coded using the symbols below. Note that prices are for the least expensive double rooms in each establishment. For a full explanation see p.29 in Basics.

❶ up to $40	❸ $60–80	❺ $100–130	❼ $175–250
❷ $40–60	❹ $80–100	❻ $130–175	❽ $250+

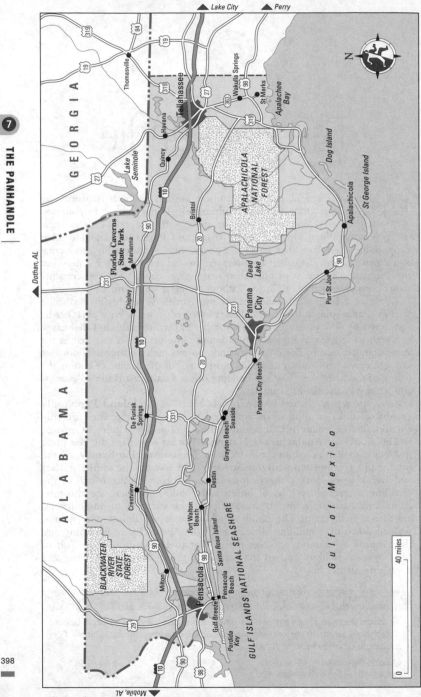

Provided you're driving, **getting around** presents few problems. Across the inland Panhandle, **I-10** carries the through traffic, and **Hwy-90** links the little places and many of the natural sights between Tallahassee and Pensacola. It's easy, too, to turn south off I-10 or Hwy-90 and get to the coast in under an hour. The main route along the coast is **Hwy-98**, with a number of smaller, scenic roads leading off it. Several daily Greyhound buses connect the bigger centers, but rural and coastal services are fewer, and some parts see no bus services at all. The Los Angeles–Jacksonville Amtrak train service crosses the Panhandle, stopping at Tallahassee and Pensacola three times a week going eastward and four times going westward.

The Inland Panhandle

Vast tracts of oak and pine trees, dozens of winding rivers and a handful of moderately sized agricultural bases make much of the **inland Panhandle** powerfully evocative of Florida in the days before mass tourism took hold. Despite the presence of the sociable state capital, **Tallahassee**, it's the insular rural communities strung along Hwy-90 – between Tallahassee and the busy coastal city of **Pensacola** – that set the tone of the region. These small towns, including **Marianna**, **Chipley** and **De Funiak Springs**, all grew rich from the turn-of-the-century timber industry and now pull their earnings by working some of the richest soil in Florida. Thanks to some architectural gems, they warrant a look as you pass through to the area's compelling natural features, which include the state's only explorable caverns and two massive forests.

Tallahassee and around

State capital it may be, but **TALLAHASSEE** is a provincial city of oak trees and soft hills that won't take more than two days to explore in full. Around its small grid of central streets – where you'll find plenty of reminders of Florida's formative years – briefcase-clutching bureaucrats mingle with some of Florida State University's 25,000 students, who brighten the mood considerably and keep the city awake late into the night.

Though built on the site of an important prehistoric meeting place and taking its name from Apalachee Indian (*talwa* meaning "town", and *ahassee* meaning "old"), Tallahassee's **history** really begins with Florida's incorporation into the US and the search for an administrative base between the former regional capitals, Pensacola and St Augustine. Once this site was chosen, the local Native Americans – the Tamali tribe – were unceremoniously dispatched to make room for a trio of log cabins in which the first Florida government sat in 1823.

The area code throughout the Panhandle is ☎ 850.

The scene of every major wrangle in Florida politics – including the controversial "dimpled ballot" recount of the 2000 presidential election – and the home of an ever-expanding white-collar workforce handling the paperwork of the country's fourth fastest-growing state, Tallahassee's own fortunes have been hindered by the lightning-paced development of south Florida. Oddly distanced from most of the people it governs, the city has a slow tempo and a strong sense of the past.

Arrival, getting around and information

I-10 cuts across Tallahassee's northern perimeter; turning off along Monroe Street takes you into downtown Tallahassee. **Hwy-90** (known as Tennessee Street) and **Hwy-27** (Apalachee Parkway) are more central – arriving in or close to downtown. Coming by **bus** presents few problems. The Greyhound terminal is at 112 W Tennessee St (℡850/222-4249 locally or 1-800/231-2222 for reservations), within walking distance of downtown and opposite the local bus station. The **train** station is housed in an 1855 building at the intersection of Gaines Street and Railroad Avenue (℡850/224-2779 or 1-800/872-7245), one block from Railroad Square in downtown Tallahassee. Tallahassee's **airport** is twelve miles southwest of the city (℡850/891-7800); frustratingly, no public transport services link it to the town. Annett Bus Lines provides an airport shuttle service (℡850/877-2163 or 1-800/328-6033), while a **taxi** to the center will cost around $15 (try City Taxi ℡850/562-4222, or Yellow Cab ℡850/580-8080); some motels offer a free pick-up service.

Getting around

Downtown Tallahassee can easily be seen **on foot. Local buses** (TalTran ℡850/891-5200 or 1-800/955-8771; $1 per journey) need only be used to reach outlying destinations. Collect a route map and timetable from the bus station (officially known as Transfer Plaza) at the corner of Tennessee and Duval streets. You can get a **free ride** into downtown Tallahassee from the bus station with the **Old Town Trolley**, which runs to the Civic Center (near the New Capitol Building) and back at ten-minute intervals on weekdays between 7am and 6pm; hop on at any of the "Trolley Stop" signs. The *Old Town Trolley Tour Guide* leaflet also gives a brief history of each of the eighteen stops and their surrounds. Despite the area's hills, there is plenty of good **cycling** terrain. Rent a bike from Tec's Pro Shop, 672 Gaines St (℡850/681-6979; $20 per day), or St Mark's Trail Bikes and Blades, 4780 Woodville Hwy (℡850/656-0001; $4.50 per hour).

Information

The **Chamber of Commerce**, 100 N Duval St (Mon–Fri 8.30am–5pm; ℡850/224-8116), has a limited amount of leaflets relating to the city and the surrounding area. A better option is the **Visitor Information Center**, 106 E Jefferson St (Mon–Fri 8am–5pm, Sat 9am–1pm; ℡850/413-9200 or 1-800/628-2866, ⓦwww.seetallahassee.com) which stocks large amounts of leaflets and guides for the city. For material covering the rest of the Panhandle, and much of the rest of the state, use the **Tallahassee Area Visitor Information Center** (Mon–Fri 8am–5pm, Sat & Sun 8.30am–4.30pm; ℡1-800/628-2866 or 850/413-9200) on the first floor of the New Capitol Building – see "Downtown Tallahassee," p.402. While there, be sure to pick up the engaging *Walking Guide to Historic Downtown Tallahassee* booklet (free), a comprehensive guide to the buildings and history of the area. Tallahassee's main

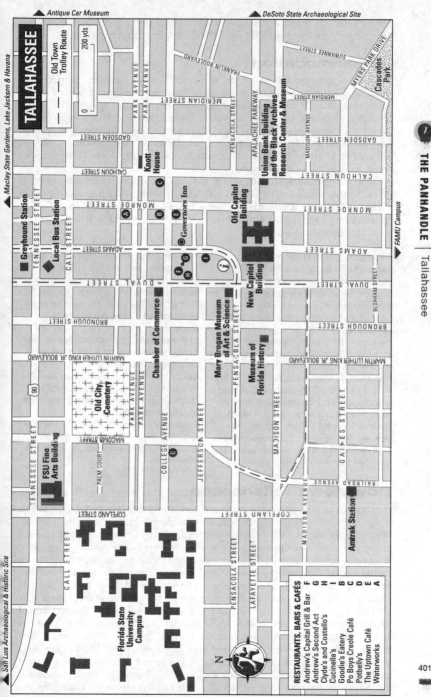

TALLAHASSEE

Old Town
Trolley Route

200 yds

0

▲ Antique Car Museum

▲ DeSoto State Archaeological Site

◀ Maclay State Gardens, Lake Jackson & Havana

Greyhound Station

Local Bus Station

Tennessee Street

Knott
House

Union Bank Building
and the Black Archives
Research Center & Museum

PARK AVENUE

PARK AVENUE

FRANKLIN BOULEVARD

MERIDIAN STREET

PENSACOLA STREET

GADSDEN STREET

CALHOUN STREET

MONROE STREET

ADAMS STREET

CALL STREET

DUVAL STREET

BRONOUGH STREET

MARTIN LUTHER KING JR. BOULEVARD

SUWANNEE STREET

MYERS PARK DRIVE

Cascades
Park

MERIDIAN STREET

MADISON AVENUE

GADSDEN STREET

CALHOUN STREET

MONROE STREET

ADAMS STREET

DUVAL STREET

BLOXHAM STREET

BRONOUGH STREET

MARTIN LUTHER KING JR. BOULEVARD

APALACHEE PARKWAY

Governors Inn

Old Capitol
Building

New Capitol
Building

Chamber of Commerce

Mary Brogan Museum
of Art & Science

Museum
of Florida History

▲ FAMU Campus

A
B
C
E
F G
H
I
i

Old City
Cemetery

FSU Fine
Arts Building

Florida State
University Campus

◀ San Luis Archaeological & Historic Site

Tennessee Street

Call Street

Copeland Street

Copeland Street

Palm Court

Macomb Street

Park Avenue

Park Avenue

College Avenue

Jefferson Street

Pensacola Street

Madison Street

Gaines Street

Railroad Avenue

Pensacola Street

Lafayette Street

Madison Street

D

Amtrak Station

N

RESTAURANTS, BARS & CAFÉS
Andrew's Capital Grill & Bar   F
Andrew's Second Act   G
Clyde's and Costello's   H
Cucinella's   I
Goodie's Eatery   B
Po Boys Creole Café   C
Potbelly's   D
The Uptown Café   E
Waterworks   A

401

library, 200 W Park Ave (Mon–Thurs 10am–9pm, Fri 10am–6pm, Sat 10am–5pm, Sun 1–6pm; ℡850/487-2665), has free **Internet access**.

Accommodation

Finding **accommodation** in Tallahassee is only a problem during two periods: the sixty-day sitting of the state legislature beginning with the first Tuesday in March – if you're arriving then, try to turn up on a Friday or Saturday when the power-brokers have gone home—and on fall weekends when the Seminoles (Florida State University's immensely well-supported football team) are playing at home. If you can't avoid these periods, book well ahead. The cheapest **hotels** and **motels** are on North Monroe Street about three miles north of downtown.

There are no **campgrounds** within the city. The nearest place you can pitch a tent is the *Tallahassee RV Park*, 6504 Mahan Drive, which is also Hwy-90 (℡850/878-7641; $20). Alternatively, try the *Tallahassee East KOA* in Monticello (℡850/997-3890), where you can either pitch a tent for $15 or rent a Kamping Kabin for $28.

Hotels and motels

Calhoun Street Inn, 525 N Calhoun St (850/425-5095). Set in a Colonial Revival-style house on a tree-lined, historic street, this bed and breakfast is only a short walk from downtown. Each room features antique furniture, pine floors and original fireplaces. ❸–❹

Days Inn, 3100 Apalachee Parkway (Hwy-27) (℡1-800/877-6121). This chain has decent rooms and a large pool. ❶

Econo Lodge, 2681 N Monroe Street (℡850/385-6155 or 1-800/424-4777). This basic chain motel offers complimentary continental breakfasts. All rooms have a microwave and a refrigerator. ❸

Governors Inn, 209 S Adams St (℡850/681-6855 or 1-800/342-7717). This luxurious downtown inn, offering free cocktails and newspapers, is well worth splurging for. The rooms are decorated with antique furniture, reflecting the period of the governor each is named for. Book in advance. ❼

La Quinta North, 2905 N Monroe St (℡850/385-7172 or 1-800/687-6667). This motel has much bigger and better rooms than the exterior suggests. ❹

La Quinta South, 2850 Apalachee Parkway (Hwy-27) (℡850/878-5099). The hotel includes continental breakfast. ❶–❷

Quality Inn, 2020 Apalachee Parkway (Hwy-27) (℡850/877-4437). This recently renovated inn features bright and modern rooms and offers free evening cocktails. ❷

Super 8, 2702 N Monroe St (℡850/386-8818, or 1-800/800-8000). A good option for the budget traveler, this motel offers simple rooms with basic amenities. ❸

Downtown Tallahassee

The soul of Tallahassee is the mile-square downtown area, where the main targets – the two Capitol Buildings, the Museum of Florida History and the two universities – are within walking distance of Adams Street. The street is a peaceful and partly pedestrianized main drag whose restored Twenties storefronts more often than not conceal attorneys' offices. A unique and charming feature of downtown Tallahassee is the **canopy roads**, thoroughfares lined with oak trees, whose branches, heavy with Spanish moss, arch across the road. Next to the allure of these splendid tree corridors – the best examples being Miccosukee, Centerville, Old St Augustine, Meridian and Old Bainbridge roads – the **New Capitol Building**, at the junction of Apalachee Parkway and Monroe Street (Mon–Fri 8.30am–5pm; free; Visitor Information Center open in lobby Sat & Sun 8.30am–4.30pm), is an eyesore. Vertical vents make the seat of Florida's legal system resemble a gigantic air-conditioning unit. The only way to escape the sight of the structure, unveiled to much outrage in 1977, is to go inside, where the 22nd-floor observation level provides an unobstructed view over Tallahassee and its environs. If you're visiting from mid–February to April, stop off at the fifth floor for a glance at the state house of representatives or the senate in action. Should you feel the need to learn more about the building, there is a self-guided tour as well as a free 45-minute **guided tour** (ask Visitor Information for more details), not particularly exciting but full of information.

Florida's growing army of bureaucrats made the New Capitol Building necessary. Previously, they'd been crammed into the 90-year-old **Old Capitol Building** (Mon–Fri 9am–4.30pm, Sat 10am–4.30pm, Sun noon–4.30pm; free; main entrance facing Apalachee Parkway), which stands in the shadow of its replacement. Designed on a more human scale than its modern counterpart, with playful red and white awnings over its windows, it's hard to imagine that the Old Capitol's walls once echoed with the decisions that shaped modern Florida. Proof is provided, however, by the political history displays in the side rooms: absorbing exhibits lifting the lid on the state's juiciest scandals and controversies. There's also a small art gallery to provide a bit of creative relief from all the politics.

One of the best ways to discover downtown is on a walking tour. If the free self-guided tour leaflets available from the Visitor Information Center (see opposite) don't interest you, there are a number of companies that organize guided tours. Both **Historic Tallahassee Tours**, 729 E Tennessee St (℡850/222-4143), and **Tours of Tallahassee**, 209 E Brevard St (℡850/513-1000), run a selection of walking and van tours lasting from two hours to a whole day, which cover different aspects of the city's history.

Along Apalachee Parkway from the Old Capitol's entrance is the nineteenth-century **Union Bank Building**. The bank's past has been unsteady: going bust in the 1850s after giving farmers too much credit, reopening to administer the financial needs of emancipated slaves after the Civil War, and later serving variously as a shoe factory, a bakery and a cosmetics shop.

Black Archives Research Center and Museum at the Union Bank

Today, the Union Bank Building serves as an extension to the Florida Agricultural and Mechanical University's **Black Archives Research Center and Museum** (Mon–Fri 9am–4pm; free; ℡850/561-2603), and chronicles the history and persecution of Florida's black community. The first black Floridians arrived with Spanish explorers in the sixteenth century, and many more came as runaways in the early nineteenth century, taking refuge among the Creek and Seminole Indians. The museum explores these stories and the many facets of black culture through documents and displays. Among the most intriguing are a collection of black piggy banks depicting derogatory images of African Americans, which were popular in some white households until the 1960s. Another exhibit charts the rise of Madame C.J. Walker, the first black female millionaire, whose line of beauty products, among other things, helped African-American women straighten their hair. In addition to tributes to such black American entertainers as Josephine Baker, the museum has some chilling Ku Klux Klan memorabilia, including an original Klan sword and a fairly recent application for membership, which proves the Klan is far from being ancient history; in 1997, the Klan won permission to march through town, but was turned back by protesting students on Monroe Street.

The Mary Brogan Museum of Art and Science

Situated one block behind the Capitol buildings is the **Mary Brogan Museum of Art and Science**, 350 Duval St (Mon–Sat 10am–5pm, Sun 1–5pm; $6; ℡850/513-0700, ⓦwww.thebrogan.org), a unique museum offering a hands-on science center combined with rotating exhibitions of national art. There aren't many places where you can explore freshwater and marine fish in an Eco Lab one minute and view an exhibition of Impressionist art the next. In addition, the museum receives touring science exhibitions and has a very active educational program providing lots of opportunities to learn more about the displays. There's also a brilliant gift shop where you can buy everything from a crystal radio set to paint brushes.

The Museum of Florida History

For a well-rounded history – easily the fullest account of Florida's past anywhere in the state – visit the **Museum of Florida History**, 500 S Bronough St (Mon–Fri 9am–4.30pm, Sat 10am–4.30pm, Sun noon–4.30pm; free; ☎850/488-1484, Ⓦ www.flheritage.com). Detailed accounts of Paleo-Indian settlements and the significance of their burial and temple mounds – some of which have been found on the edge of Tallahassee (see "Around Tallahassee," p.408) – are valuable tools in comprehending Florida's prehistory. The colonialist crusades of the Spanish, both in Florida and across South and Central America, are also outlined by means of copious finds. However, other than portraits of hard-faced Seminole chiefs, whose Native American tribes were driven south into Florida backcountry, there's disappointingly little on the nineteenth-century Seminole Wars – one of the sadder and bloodier skeletons in Florida's closet. There's plenty, though, on the railroads that made Florida a winter resort for wealthy northerners around the turn of the century, and on the subsequent arrival of the "tin can tourists," whose nickname refers to the rickety Ford camper vans (forerunners of the modern Recreational Vehicles) they drove to what had by then been named "the Sunshine State."

Florida State University

West from Adams Street, graffiti-coated fraternity and sorority houses along College Avenue line the approach to **Florida State University (FSU)**. This has long enjoyed a strong reputation for its humanities courses, taught from the late 1800s in the Collegiate Gothic classrooms you'll see as you enter the wrought-iron gates, but has recently switched emphasis to science and business, and the newer buildings on the far side of the campus have far less character. Shady oaks and palm trees make the grounds a pleasant place for a stroll, but there's little cause to linger. The student art of the **University Gallery and Museum** (Mon–Fri 9am–4pm; free; ☎850/644-6836), in the Fine Arts Building, might consume a few minutes, but you'd be better occupied rummaging around inside Bill's Bookstore, just across Call Street at 107 S Copeland St (☎850/224-3178), where the large stock includes many student cast-offs at reduced prices.

Despite being poorer, the more interesting of Tallahassee's universities is the Florida Agricultural and Mechanical University (Ⓦ www.famu.edu), about a mile south of the Capitol Buildings on Wahnish Avenue and Gamble Street. Founded in 1887 as the State Normal College for Colored Students, the university remains a major black educational center. Housed in the historic Carnegie Library on campus is the **Black Archives Research Center and Museum** (see p.403).

The Knott House

Another important landmark in Florida's black history, and one of the city's best-restored Victorian homes, is the **Knott House Museum**, 301 E Park Ave (Wed–Fri 1–3pm, Sat 10am–3pm; free; ☎850/922-2459). It was built by a free black in 1843 and later became home to Florida's first black physician. Florida's slaves were officially emancipated in May 1865 by a proclamation read from the steps of this very house. The house takes its name, however, from the Knotts, a white couple who bought it in 1928. State treasurer during a period of economic calamity (Florida had been devastated by two hurricanes just as the country entered the Depression), William Knott became one of Florida's most respected and influential politicians until his retirement in 1941. His wife, Luella, meanwhile, devoted her energies to the temperance movement (partly through her efforts, alcohol was banned in Tallahassee for a fifty-year period) and to writing moralistic poems, many of which you'll see attached to the antiques and furnishings that fill this intriguing relic and which give it the nick-name of "the house that rhymes." The absence of intrusive ropes cordoning off the exhibits allows for an unusually intimate visit of the house and its history. Guided tours are available on the hour.

Old City Cemetery

A somewhat different perspective on Tallahassee's past is provided by a walking tour around the **Old City Cemetery**, between Macomb Street and Martin Luther King Jr Boulevard (daily sunrise–sunset; free), which was established outside the city's original boundaries in 1829 and restored in 1991. Its layout, consisting of four quadrants, is a striking testament to segregation, even in death. Graves of Union soldiers lie in the southwest quarter, while those of Confederates are kept at a distance in the southeast portion; slaves and free blacks were consigned to the western half of the ground, while whites occupied the eastern part. Among the names marked on gravestones, you'll find many of Tallahassee's former leading figures: their stories are told in an informative leaflet, *A Walking Tour of Old City Cemetery*, available at Tallahassee's Visitor Information Center (see p.400).

Restaurants and Cafés

Andrew's Capital Grill & Bar, 228 S Adams St (℡850/222-3444). This is a great lunch option, serving a variety of burgers, chicken and pasta as well as a weekday lunch buffet.
Andrew's Second Act, at the same address as *Andrew's Capital Grill & Bar*, is an elegant restaurant that also offers more expensive dinners.
Barnacle Bill's, 1830 N Monroe St (℡850/385-8734). Offers low-cost seafood – with a riotous atmosphere and live Fifties music.
Café Cabernet, 1019 N Monroe St (℡850/224-1175). For light, inexpensive California-style eating, this café has the biggest wine selection in town. Live jazz can be heard here in the evening.
Cucinella's, 124 W Jefferson St (℡850/222-1522). Munch on gourmet sandwiches and sip coffee at this laid-back bakery and café that has a good range of different breads and classic Italian light meals.
Goodies, 116 E College Ave (℡850/681-3888). One of the few places to get breakfast in downtown, *Goodies* also serves sandwich specials and big salads for lunch.
Kool Beanz Café, 921 Thomasville Rd (℡850/224-2466). *Kool Beanz* offers original and pricey starters like smoked rabbit and andouille gumbo and follows with entrées like spice-rum

seared mahi with pineapple-black bean salsa and plantain fries. Service is variable and be warned – the spice levels are set on hot.
La Fiesta, 911 Apalachee Parkway (℡850/656-3392). Try this eatery for the for very best Mexican food in the city. The number of cars outside at lunchtime gives away how good the food is.
Mom and Dad's, 4175 Apalachee Parkway (℡850/877-4518). Delicious and affordable homemade Italian food is available at this restaurant just outside downtown. Closed Mon.
Paradise Grill, 1406 N Meridian Rd (℡850/224-2742). This cheap to moderately priced eatery is a fun place to go for seafood, gumbo and British beer.
Po' Boys Creole Café, 224 E College Ave (℡850/224-5400, ⓦwwwpoboys.com). A range of Creole delights, such as jammin' jambalaya and Carmen's red beans and rice, as well as a good selection of seafood is available here, generally for under $10. This restaurant is also one of Tallahassee's most popular live music venues (see overleaf).
The Uptown Café, 111 E College Ave (℡850/222-3253). Reasonably priced sandwiches and salads at lunchtime and bagels for breakfast are available here.

Nightlife

Bolstered by its students, Tallahassee has a strong **nightlife**, with a leaning to social drinking and live rock music (see below). There's also **comedy** at the *Comedy Zone*, Ramada Inn North, 2900 N Monroe St (☎850/386-1027, or call ☎850/386-5653 for a full program), and a fair amount of **drama**, headed by the student productions at the University Theater on the FSU campus (☎850/644-6500), and the Tallahassee Little Theater, 1861 Thomasville Rd (☎850/224-8474). The Warehouse, 706 W Gaines St (☎850/222-6188), is famous for its poetry readings on Tuesdays and open-mic nights on Thursdays. Literary events are regularly held at Borders Bookshop, 1302 Apalachee Parkway, which is also a great place to shop for books and music until 11pm. Find out **what's on** from the "Limelights" section of the Friday *Tallahassee Democrat* newspaper; the *Florida Flambeau*, the FSU student paper, contains listings and recommendations; *Break* is another free local paper with nightlife listings and articles; or, for live music details, listen to radio station WFSU at 89.7 FM.

Bars

B. Merrell's, 1433 E Lafayette St (☎850/660-1995). Try taking the "World Beer Tour" here or enjoy the daily Happy Hour.

Calico Jack's, 2745 Capitol Circle NE (☎850/385-6653). Beer, oysters and stomping southern rock and roll records are featured here.

Clyde's & Costello's, 210 S Adams St (☎850/224-2173). Pulls a smart and very cliquey crowd, which grows a bit rowdy during Thursday's four-for-one drink offer.

Halligan's, 1700 Halstead Blvd in Oak Lake Village (☎850/668-7665). This joint is popular for its pool tables and chilled mugs of beer.

Late Night Library, 809 Gay St (☎850/224-2429). The jazz on Friday nights here creates a groovy mood as students mingle in a sultry setting.

Po' Boys Creole Café, 224 E College Ave (☎850/224-5400). Creole and acoustic music sets nicely complement the drink specials in this collegiate bar.

SoMo International Café, 104 1/2 S Munroe St (☎850/599-9293). This popular wine bar offers a large selection of wines and international beers. With a hanging rope chair in one corner and an upright piano in another, partying and fun are in no short supply.

Live music and clubs

American Legion Hall, 229 Lake Ella Drive (☎850/222-3382). For a taste of the past, try this venue, which hosts a big-band dance night every Tuesday and old-fashioned country the rest of the week.

Bullwinkle's, 620 W Tennessee St (☎850/224-0651). Rock and blues dominate in this log-cabin-like setting.

Cow Haus, 469 St Francis St (☎850/425-2697),. Showcases known and unknown indie rock acts.

Late Night Library, 809 Gay St (☎850/224-2429). At the apex of the nightclub scene, this cool dance-music club caters to a college crowd.

Leon County Civic Center, at the corner of Pensacola Street and Martin Luther King Jr Boulevard (☎850/222-0400, ⊛wwwtlcc.org). Major touring acts play here – as does the Arena Football League every weekend during the summer.

The Moon, 1020 E Lafayette St (☎850/222-6666 for recorded info). Big-name live bands appear here.

Paradise Grill, 1406 Meridian Rd (☎850/224-2742). Popular with the 25-plus age group and offers live bands Thurs–Sat.

Top Flite Club, 623 Osceola St (☎850/425-2697). Offers live jazz and blues and is always good for a drink, dance or laugh.

Gay clubs and bars

Brothers, 926 W Tharpe St (☎850/386-2399). The most popular of Tallahassee's several bar/clubs, this is a design-conscious venue with a friendly crowd that's almost exclusively gay on Sundays, Thursdays and Fridays. The rest of the week pulls in a mixed clientele.

Club Park Ave, 115 Park Ave (☎850/681-6880). A bit more slick than *Brothers*, *Club Park Ave* is gay-only on Saturday nights.

Listings

Art galleries Tallahassee has a credible arts scene centered around Railroad Square, close to the junction of Springhill Road and Gaines Street near the FSU campus, where there are some innovative galleries, and several local artists have open studios. Other contemporary art showcases are: Nomads, 508 W Gaines St; The 621 Gallery, 567 Industrial Drive, and Signature Gallery, 2779 NE Capital Circle.

Car rental Most companies have branches at the airport (see p.400), and at the following locations: Avis, 3300 Capitol Circle (☎ 850/331-1212); Budget, 628 Monroe St (☎ 850/915-0600); Lucky's, 2539 W Tennessee St (☎ 850/575-0632); Thrifty Car Rental, 1385 Blountstown Hwy (☎ 850/576-RENT).

Dentist Dental Information Service: ☎ 1-800/282-9117.

Hospital Non-emergencies: Tallahassee Regional Medical Center, 1300 Miccosukee Rd (☎ 850/681-1155).

Pharmacy Walgreens, in the Tallahassee Mall, 2415 N Monroe St (☎ 850/385-7145), open Mon–Sat 10am–9pm, Sun 12.30–5.30pm.

Sports Tickets for FSU baseball (March–May) and football (Sept–Nov) matches are on sale at the stadiums two hours before the games begin: ☎ 850/644-1073 and ☎ 850/644-1830 respectively. For info on FAMU sports teams, all known as the Rattlers, call ☎ 850/599-3200. There's a full fixture list in the local telephone book.

Western Union The most convenient locations are Easy Mail West, Inc at 1717 Apalachee Parkway and 3491 Thomasville Rd; Mail Boxes Etc,1350 E Tennessee St; and Winn Dixie, 813 N Monroe St. Call ☎ 1-800/325-6000 for other locations.

Around Tallahassee

Scattered around the fringes of Tallahassee, half a dozen diverse spots deserve brief visits: a remarkable antique car museum, prehistoric mounds, archeological sites and lakeside gardens. All are easily accessible by car, though most are much harder to reach by bus.

The Tallahassee Antique Car Museum

The **Tallahassee Antique Car Museum**, 3550 Mahan Drive (Mon–Sat 10am–5pm, Sun noon–5pm; $7.50, children $4; ☎ 850/942-0137, ⓦ www.tacm .com), is well worth the three-mile drive east along Tennessee Street, which changes to Mahan Drive. The museum's owner, DeVeo Moore, began his career modestly by shoeing horses. But through quiet determination, which inspires admiration or distaste depending on who you ask in Tallahassee, he is now one of the region's richest men: selling just one of his businesses in early 1998 netted $37.5 million. The biggest crowd-puller in the collection is the gleaming 21-foot-long Batmobile from the Tim Burton *Batman* movie, bought for $500,000 and complete with Batman's suits and gloves and a flame-thrower attachment. While the most valuable car in the collection is a $1.2 million 1931 Duesenberg Model J, the most intriguing specimen is an 1860-built horse-drawn hearse believed to have carried Abraham Lincoln to his final resting place. The consummate collector, Moore didn't limit his collecting to automobiles. Among the eclectic exhibits are "anti-colic" baby bottles and whole rooms of scooters and cash registers.

The San Luis and de Soto archaeological sites

Slowly being unearthed at the **San Luis Archaeological and Historic Site**, 2020 W Mission Rd, about three miles west of downtown Tallahassee (bus #21), the village of San Luis de Talimali was a hub of the seventeenth-century Spanish mission system, second only to St Augustine. At its zenith in 1675, its population numbered 1400. Stop by the **Visitor Center** (Mon–Fri 9am–4.30pm, Sat 10am–4.30pm, Sun noon–4.30pm; free; ☎ 850/487-3655) for a general explanation and to see some of the finds – or join the hour-long **guided tour** (Mon–Fri at noon, Sat at 11am & 3pm, Sun at 2pm; free) to appreciate the importance of the place. On some weekends, period-attired individuals re-enact village life – it sounds tacky but can be fun.

The **de Soto State Archaeological Site**, two miles east of downtown Tallahassee at the corner of Goodbody Lane and Lafayette Street, is where Spanish explorer Hernando de Soto is thought to have set up camp in 1539 and held the first Christmas celebration in North American history. The historical associations are more dramatic here than at the San Luis site, but there's much less tangible evidence of the past and the site is in fact closed to the public except for special events. All there is to see is a few holes in the ground and it's not at all an essential stop even when it's open. For more information on the de Soto expedition, which was the first European team to cross the Mississippi River, see "History" in Contexts.

Tallahassee Museum of History and Natural Science

Three miles southwest of the city, the **Tallahassee Museum of History and Natural Science** (Mon–Sat 9am–5pm, Sun 12.30–5pm; $6; ⊤850/576-1636, ⓦwww.tallahasseemuseum.org), off Lake Bradford Road (bus #15) at 3945 Museum Drive, is aimed primarily at kids, though it could fill an hour even if you don't have young minds to stimulate. The centerpiece is a working nineteenth-century-style farm, complete with cows and wandering roosters. Elsewhere, there's a short nature walk, a few cases of snakes and a couple of old buildings of moderate note: a 1937 Baptist Church and a vintage schoolhouse.

Maclay State Gardens

For a lazy half-day, journey four miles northeast of downtown Tallahassee to **Maclay State Gardens**, set in a lakeside park at 3540 Thomasville Rd, north of I-10, exit 30 (park: daily 8am–sunset, cars $3.25, pedestrians and cyclists $1; garden: daily 9am–5pm, Jan–April $3, rest of year free; ⊤850/487-9910). New York financier and amateur gardener Alfred B. Maclay bought this large piece of land in the Twenties and planted flowers and shrubs in order to create a blooming season from January to April. It worked: for four months each year the gardens are alive with the fragrances and fantastic colors of azaleas, camellias, pansies and other flowers, framed by dogwood and redbud trees and towered over by huge oaks and pines. Guided tours of the gardens are conducted on weekends around mid-March (call ⊤850/487-4556 for details and times), but they're worth visiting at any time, if only to retire to the lakeside pavilion for a snooze as lizards and squirrels scurry around your feet. The admission fee to the gardens also gets you into the **Maclay House** (open Jan–April only), which is filled with the Maclays' furniture and countless books on horticulture. While you're here, take your time to explore the rest of the park and Lake Hall. A picnic area gives great views of the lake, as does the short **Lake Overstreet Trail**, which meanders through the wooded hillside overlooking it. There is also a swimming area close to the parking area nearest the park's entrance.

Lake Jackson and the Indian Mounds

Most boat-owning locals moor their vessels beside the sizeable **Lake Jackson**, five miles north of downtown Tallahassee. On an inlet known as Meginnis Arm is the **Lake Jackson Mounds State Archaeological Site**, off Hwy-27 at Crowder Road (daily 8am–sunset; free), where rich finds, such as copper breastplates and ritual figures, suggest that this eighty-acre site was once an important Native American ceremonial center. Other than large humps of soil and a sense of history, all that's here now are a few picnic tables and an undemanding nature trail over a small ravine. By car, follow the signs off Monroe Street; on foot, the site's a three-mile trek from the #1 bus stop.

North of Tallahassee

There's a wide range of roads that snake **north from Tallahassee** and a surprising number of them offer low-key but enjoyable forays. The Georgia border is only twenty miles away, and the most direct route is the Thomasville Road (Route 319) to, unsurprisingly, **Thomasville** (ⓦwww.thomasvillega .com) a sleepy little town just across the Georgia border that was a winter haven for wealthy northerners who built magnificent plantations on the Florida side of the border. Five miles south of Thomasville (and still in Georgia), the **Pebble Hill Plantation** (Tues–Sat 10am–5pm, Sun 1–5pm, closed Sept; hour-long guided tour of house, with the last tour leaving at 4pm; $7, grounds only $3; ☎229/226-2344, ⓦwww.pebblehill.com) remains from the time of cotton picking and slavery and shows how comfortable things were for the wealthy whites who ran the show. Much of the original Pebble Hill burnt down in the Thirties and what you see now is a fairly faithful rebuilding of the sumptuous main house, complete with the extensive fine art, antique, crystal and porcelain collections that belonged to the house's final owner, Elisabeth Ireland Poe, and was rescued from the fire. Note that babies and children aged 6 or under are not allowed in the house. Each April, the house comes back to life as people throng to a spring plantation ball.

If you're feeling carnivorous, take Centerville Road north from Tallahassee (Route 151), which, after twelve miles, leads to **Bradley's Country Store** (Mon–Fri 9am–6pm, Sat 9am–5pm). For seventy years, Bradley's has been peddling Southern-style food, specializing in smoked sausages and unusual delicacies like country-milled grits, hogshead cheese and liver pudding.

Havana

Twelve miles northwest of Tallahassee along Monroe Street (Route 27), tiny **Havana** (pronounced "Hey-vannah"), is defiantly worth time off the beaten track to explore. Providing an authentic taste of Americana, this historic little town takes a pride in its history and, although it has a number of shops catering for the tourist trade, tourism has done nothing to damage this community's sense of identity. The town even has a railroad running through it, and when a train passes, blowing its horn, for a moment those pioneering days of the past seem closer than the history books would have us believe. The town's name came from its tobacco plantations that once supplied cigar-making factories in Cuba. Following the embargo against Cuba in 1958, the town could no longer sell tobacco leaves to Havana and went into decline, only to be rejuvenated again in 1984 when the first antique center opened and the community discovered that history can mean business.

The main body of shops and cafés huddle around Second Street; however, don't miss a detour to the **Havana Cannery** on East Eighth Avenue (Wed, Thurs & Sun 10am 6pm, Fri & Sat 10am 10pm; ☎850/539 3800). Once a burgeoning fruit-canning business, packing seven million pounds of fruit during World War II, the company lost out to larger rivals and shifted to honey-packing until shutting down in 1994. Like the rest of the town, the cannery has been given a new lease of life and is now a maze of antique and curio stores where you can buy everything from fried green tomato mix to antique furniture. Nestled between the antique shops, you'll find a couple of small art galleries, an Amish furniture store and the wonderful Historical Bookshop, 101 W Seventh Ave (☎850/539-5040). This shop used to be the old town bank and when the new owner dug into the floor to install an access ramp, the old brick road from Havana to Bainbridge, Georgia, was unearthed.

The **McLauchlin House**, at the corner of Seventh Avenue and Second Street (Wed–Sat 10am–5.30pm, Sun noon–5pm; ☎850/539-0901) is the home of six more antique shops. This 150-year-old farmhouse is a gem with its wrap-round porch, sloping floors and uneven doors. There's not much else

to see in Havana, but if you hit town in April, look for the **MusicFest**, a three-day jazz and blues event (call ☏850/353-3309 for information).

Eating in Havana is never a problem. You're sure to come across *Bella's*, 211 NW First St, situated amongst a plethora of antique shops; this fine Italian restaurant has a beautiful outdoor courtyard for eating al fresco when the weather allows. For a better deal and more fun, try *Dolly's Expresso*, 206 NW First St (☏850/539-6716). The owners are from Key West, and serve Cuban sandwiches, luscious desserts (try a wicked chocolate-cheese cannoli) and great coffee. At *Confetti's Ice Cream Shoppe*, 102 E Seventh Ave (☏850/539-3355), you can eat ice cream in big, wide booth seats straight from the 50s.

Unfortunately, there is no accommodation in Havana. The nearest places to stay are the motels along North Monroe Street in Tallahassee (see p.402), or one of the bed and breakfasts in Quincy 12 miles west (see p.415).

South of Tallahassee

On weekends, many Tallahassee residents head south to the Panhandle's beaches (see "The Coastal Panhandle," p.419). If you're not eager to join them, make a slower trek **south** along Routes 363 or 61, tracking down a few isolated pockets of historical or geological significance; or take Hwy-319 and lose yourself in the biggest and best of Florida's forests.

One of the most enjoyable ways to explore is by **cycling or rollerblading** the sixteen-mile Tallahassee–St Marks Historic Railroad Trail, a flat and straight course through placid woodlands following the route of a long-abandoned railroad. Bikes and blades can be rented from one hour to a full day from Tec's Pro Bike Shop, 4780 Woodville Hwy (from $4.50 an hour; ☏850/656-0001).

Leon Sinks Geological Area

Seven miles south of Tallahassee on Route 319 is the **Leon Sinks Geological Area** (8am–8pm; free), a fascinating karst (terrain that has been altered by rain and ground water dissolving underlying limestone bedrock). The area contains several prominent sinkholes, numerous depressions, a natural bridge and a disappearing stream, all of which give a unique glimpse of the area before man's interference. There are three manageable trails of between half a mile and three miles, described in a guide available from the ranger station at the entrance.

The Natural Bridge Battlefield Site and St Marks

Ten miles southeast of Tallahassee, a turn off Route 363 at Woodville leads after six miles to the **Natural Bridge Battlefield Site** (daily 8am–sunset; free; ☏850/922-6007), where, on March 4, 1865, a motley band of Confederate soldiers saw off a much larger group of Union troops, preventing Tallahassee from falling into Yankee hands. Not that it made much difference – the war ended a couple of months later – but the victory is celebrated by a monument and an annual re-enactment on or close to the anniversary: several hours of shouting, loud bangs and smoke.

Twelve miles south of Woodville, Route 363 expires at the hamlet of **St Marks**, where the **San Marcos de Apalache Historic Site** (Thurs–Mon 9am–5pm; free, museum $1; ☏850/925-6216) offers decent pickings for students of Florida history – this sixteenth-century Spanish-built fort was visited by early explorers such as Pánfilo de Narváez and Hernando de Soto, and two hundred years later became Andrew Jackson's headquarters when he waged war on the Seminole Indians. Round off a visit at one of the nearby fishcamp eating places, such as *Posey's* (no phone), on Old Fort Drive.

If you prefer wildlife to history, backtrack slightly along Route 363 and turn east along Hwy-98. Three miles on you'll find the main entrance to **St Marks National Wildlife Refuge** (daily sunrise–sunset; cars $3, pedestrians and cyclists $1), which spreads out over the boggy outflow of the St Marks River. Bald eagles and a few black bears reside in the refuge, though from the various roadside lookout points and observation towers you're more likely to spot otters, white-tailed deer, raccoons and a wealth of birdlife. A drive to the end of the road leads to the picturesque St Marks Lighthouse. Just inside the entrance, a **visitor center** doles out useful information (Mon–Fri 8.15am–4.15pm, Sat & Sun 10am–5pm).

Wakulla Springs

Fifteen miles south of Tallahassee, off Route 61 on Route 267, **Wakulla Springs State Park** (daily 8am–sunset; cars $3.25, pedestrians and cyclists $1; ☎ 850/224-5950, Ⓦ www.wakullacounty.org) contains what is believed to be one of the biggest and deepest natural springs in the world, pumping up half a million gallons of crystal-clear pure water from the bowels of the earth every day – difficult to guess from the calm surface. The principal reason for visiting Wakulla Springs is to enjoy the barely touched scenery and to appreciate a part of Florida that is still intact after hundreds of years.

It's refreshing to **swim** in the cool waters, though it's somewhat disconcerting that the marked areas are just inches from those where swimming is prohibited due to alligators. To learn more about the spring, you should take the fifteen-minute narrated **glass-bottomed boat tour** ($4.50) and peer down to the swarms of fish hovering around the 180-foot-deep cavern through which the water comes. Join the forty-minute **river cruise** ($4.50) for glimpses of some of the park's other inhabitants: deer, turkeys, turtles, herons and egrets – and the inevitable alligators. If *déjà vu* strikes, it may be because a number of films have been shot here, including several of the early *Tarzan* movies and parts of *The Creature from the Black Lagoon*. To see the alligators and snakes at their most active, take the **moonlight cruise** at twilight ($4.50).

You shouldn't leave without strolling through the **Wakulla Lodge**, 550 Wakulla Park Drive (☎ 850/224-5950; ❸–❹), a hotel built beside the spring in 1937, which retains many of its original features: Moorish archways, stone fireplaces and fabulous hand-painted Toltec and Aztec designs on the lobby's wooden ceiling. Take the opportunity, also, to pay your respects to the stuffed carcass of "Old Joe," one of the oldest and largest alligators ever known, who died in the Fifties, measuring eleven feet long and supposedly aged 200; he's in a glass case by the reception desk. The lodge and its surrounds have a relaxing ambience that can prove quite addictive. An added bonus is that once the daytrippers have departed, you'll have the springs and wildlife all to yourself.

Further south: the Apalachicola National Forest

With swamps, savannahs and springs dotted liberally about its half-million acres, the **Apalachicola National Forest** is the inland Panhandle at its natural best. Several roads enable you to drive through a good-sized chunk and

Apalachicola National Forest information

Always equip yourself with maps, a weather forecast and advice from a ranger's office before setting off on a hike or canoe trip through the forest (for more on how to travel in the backcountry safely, see Basics). The Ochlockonee River divides the forest into two administrative districts and the following offices are responsible for the west and east sides of the forest respectively:

Apalachicola Ranger District, Hwy-20, near Bristol; ☏850/643-2282
Wakulla Ranger District, Route 6, near Crawfordville; ☏850/926-3561

many undemanding spots offer a rest and a snack, but to see more of the forest than its picnic tables and litter bins you'll have to make an effort. Leave the periphery and delve into the pristine interior and explore at a leisurely pace, following hiking trails, taking a canoe on one of the rivers, or simply spending a night under the stars at one of the basic campgrounds.

Practicalities

The northeast corner of the forest almost touches Tallahassee's airport, fanning out from there to the edge of the Apalachicola River, about 35 miles west. Most of the northern edge is bordered by Hwy-20, the eastern side by Hwy-319 and Hwy-98, and to the south lies the gruesome no-man's-land of Tate's Hell Swamp (see overleaf).

The main **entrances** are off Hwy-20 and Hwy-319, and three minor roads, Routes 267, 375 and 65, form cross-forest links between the two highways. **Accommodation** is limited to camping. With the exception of Silver Lake

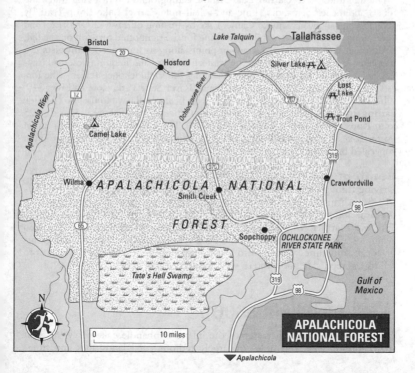

▼ *Apalachicola*

and Lost Lake (see below), all the sites are free and have basic facilities – usually just toilets and drinking water. For more information, call ☎850/643-2282. The only place to **rent a canoe** near the forest is TNT Hideaway (☎850/925-6412), on Route 2 near Crawfordville, on Hwy-319.

One section of the forest, Trout Pond (April–Oct only; cars $2), on Route 373, near Tallahassee airport, is intended for **disabled visitors** and their guests, with a wheelchair-accessible lakeside nature trail and picnic area.

The edge of the forest: Lost Lake and Silver Lake

For a brief taste of what the forest can offer, make for **Lost Lake**, seven miles from Tallahassee along Route 373, where there's little except a few picnic tables beside a small lake. The area's well suited to a nibble and a waterside laze, and is less busy than the campervan-infested **Silver Lake**, nine miles east of the city, off Hwy-20. Swimming or camping at Silver Lake will cost you $2 and $5 respectively; anticipate the company of too many other people.

Deeper into the forest: hiking and canoeing

Several short, clearly marked **nature walks** lie within the forest, but the major **hiking trail**, strictly for ardent and well-equipped backpackers, is the thirty-mile **Apalachicola Trail**, which begins close to Crawfordville, on Hwy-319. This passes through the heart of the forest and includes a memorable (and sometimes difficult, depending on the weather conditions and water level) leg across an isolated swamp, the Bradwell Bay Wilderness. After this, the campground at Porter Lake, just to the west of the wilderness area, with its toilets and drinking water, seems the epitome of civilization.

The trail leads on to **Camel Lake**, whose campground has drinking water and toilets, and the less demanding nine-and-a-half-mile **Camel Lake Loop Trail**. By vehicle, you can get directly to Camel Lake by turning off Hwy-20 at Bristol and continuing south for twelve miles, watching for the signposted turn-off on the left.

Although there are numerous put-in points along its four rivers, **canoeists** can paddle right into the forest from the western end of Lake Talquin (close to Hwy-20), and continue for a sixty-mile glide along the Ochlockonee River – the forest's major waterway – to the Ochlockonee River State Park, close to Hwy-319. Obviously, the length of trip means that to do it all you'll have to use the riverside **campgrounds** (info from the Supervisor's Office, National Forests Florida, 325 John Knox Rd, Tallahassee; ☎904/942-9300). Those with drinking water are at Porter Lake, Whitehead Lake and Mack Landing; be warned that these are often concealed by dense foliage, so study your map carefully.

South of the forest: Tate's Hell Swamp

Driving through the forest on Route 65 or Route 67, or around it on Hwy-319 (which merges with Hwy-98 as it nears the coast), you'll eventually pass the large and forbidding area called **Tate's Hell Swamp**. According to legend, Tate was a farmer who pursued a panther into the swamp and was never seen again. It's a breeding ground for the deadly water moccasin snake, and gung-ho locals sometimes venture into the swamp hoping to catch a few snakes to sell to less reputable zoos; you're well advised to stay clear.

West of Tallahassee

To discover the social character of the inland Panhandle, take Hwy-90 **west from Tallahassee**: 180 miles of largely tedious rural landscapes and time-locked farming towns that have been down on their luck since the demise of the timber industry fifty years ago. When it gets too much to bear, you can easily switch to the speedier I-10, or cut south to the coast. But the compensations are the endless supply of rustic eating places, low-cost accommodation, several appealing natural areas – and a chance to see a part of Florida that the travel brochures rarely reveal.

Quincy

Twenty miles west of Tallahassee on Hwy-90 is a sign that says "Welcome to Quincy City." With a fleeting glance at the surroundings – thick forest and not a building in sight – most tourists barrel on by without a second thought. The capital of Gadsden County, **Quincy** was one of the first towns to strike it rich because of Coca-Cola. The Atlanta-based pharmacist who patented the fizzy drink sold company stock to friends in Quincy, who made a mint and built grandiose villas throughout the town at the beginning of the twentieth century. From the square on **Madison Street**, observe the immaculate **Court House**, surrounded by topiary, and a grand marble memorial to slain Confederate soldiers, erected by the "Ladies of Gadsden" in 1884. Just opposite, on East Jefferson Street, the wall of Padgett's jewelry store is covered with the original Coke ad. Painted here in 1905, it espouses coke as "delicious and refreshing, five cents at fountains and bottles." Quincy is served by three Greyhound **buses** a day from Tallahassee that arrive opposite the **Chamber of Commerce**, 203 E Jefferson St (☏850/627-9231). It's hard to believe that this building is the Chamber of Commerce as there's no sign outside and this big old Southern-style house looks nothing more than a private residence. Inside, however, there is lots of **information** about the town, including an excellent leaflet detailing a walking tour of the town's historic district.

Most of the central square is unremarkable, looking like a dowdy film set from a B-grade cowboy movie. Take time to explore the **Gadsden Arts Center**, 13 N Madison St (Tues–Sat 10am–5pm; ☏850/875-4866, ⓦwww.gadsdenarts.com). One of the finest art galleries in the area, it hosts major traveling exhibitions as well as the work of local and regional artists. If you walk to its north side, you'll see what Quincy was once all about – tobacco, the substance that made Quincy prosperous before the arrival of Coca-Cola. The **Leaf Theater**, 118 E Washington St (Mon–Fri 9.30am–1pm; ☏850/875-9444), is a 1930s tribute to the tobacco leaf with tiles and motifs riddled with shade-leaf tobacco emblems. Near the theater is one of the best places to **eat**, the *Gadsden Carriage House Restaurant*, 104 E Washington St (☏850/875-4660), fabulous for its local fare and Celtic music nights. For a café-style meal try the *Gucchidadi Deli & Bakery*, 7 N Madison St (☏850/627-6660); it has a great home-town, old-fashioned feel and a good selection of sandwiches, salads and cakes.

Wealthy Quincy, with its bungalow homes of delicate trellises and sweeping verandas, begins on East Washington Street. The most exquisite mansions, though, are between Love and King streets. The finest of all also happens to be the **bed and breakfast** *McFarlin House*, 305 E King St (☏850/875-2526, ⓔmcfarlin@www.tallahassee.net; ❹–❺), an exquisite, turreted mansion whose sumptuous interior and 42-pillar porch were created for John McFarlin, Quincy's richest tobacco planter, in 1895. If this is out of your price range try the *Allison House Inn*, 215 N Madison St (☏850/875-2511, ⓔinnkeepeer@tds.net; ❸–❹), an English-style bed and breakfast in another of the oldest houses in town.

Lake Seminole and the Three Rivers State Recreational Area

Fifty miles west of Tallahassee, close to the Georgia border, Hwy-90 reaches Sneads, a small town dominated by the large **Lake Seminole**, created by a Fifties hydroelectric project. On the lake's Florida side (other banks are in Georgia and Alabama), spend an enjoyable few hours in the **Three Rivers State Recreational Area** (daily 8am–sunset; cars $3.25, pedestrians and cyclists $1), two miles from Sneads on Route 271. A mile-long **nature walk** from the park's **camping area** (℡850/482-9006) leads to a wooded, hilly section where squirrels and alligators are two-a-penny, and white-tailed deer and gray foxes lurk in the shrubbery. The lake is popular for its massive and abundant catfish, bream and bass. To spend a night by the lake without camping, use the ten-room *Seminole Lodge* (℡850/593-6886; ❶), just outside Sneads at the end of Legion Road.

Marianna and the Florida Caverns State Park

Twenty-five miles west along Hwy-90, **Marianna** is one of the larger inland Panhandle settlements, despite only having a four-figure population for whom the twice-monthly horse sale is the only source of excitement. There isn't much to recommend the place, except that it tries to sell itself (rather unsuccessfully) as "The Belle of the Panhandle" and that it has been the seat of Jackson County since 1829. The **Chamber of Commerce**, 2928 Jefferson St (Mon–Fri 8am–5pm; ℡850/482-8061), will give you a walking-tour map of the town's elegant Old South homes (the Chamber of Commerce itself sits inside one).

There's a collection of motels on Hwy-90 after exit 21 off the I-10, however, if you want to **stay** in town. The delightful, if strange, *Hinson House* bed-and-breakfast, 4338 Lafayette St (℡850/526-1500, ℮ hinson@phonl.com; ❸–❹), is a beautifully restored villa with authentic furnishings, and breakfasts served in a formal dining room. The owner has created a permanent sense of Christmas, with not only a year-round lit-up tree in the hallway, but twinkling lights on the stairs, windows patterned with fake frost and golden reindeer all over the fireplace.

For **eating**, your best bet is the *Red Canyon Grill*, 3297 Caverns Rd (℡850/482-4256), which features such dishes as fajitas, mesquite-grilled shrimp and a hearty corn soup at moderate prices. *Jim's Buffet & Grill*, 4473 Lafayette St (℡850/526-3300), offers a lunch buffet for $5.95 and a steak and catfish buffet on weekends for $8.99, while *Captain D's Seafood Restaurant*, 4253 Lafayette St (℡850/482-6230), serves inexpensive chicken and seafood dishes. A popular eatery is the traditional and moderately priced *Old Mexican Restaurant*, 4434 Lafayette St (℡850/482-5552).

Crossing the time zone

Crossing the Apalachicola River, which flows north–south across the inland Panhandle, roughly 45 miles west of Tallahassee, takes you into the **Central Time Zone**, an hour behind Eastern Time and the rest of Florida. In the coastal Panhandle, the time shift occurs about ten miles west of Port St Joe, on the boundary between Gulf and Bay counties.

Florida Caverns State Park

The best thing about Marianna is its proximity to **Florida Caverns State Park** (daily 8am–sunset; cars $3.25, pedestrians and cyclists $1), three miles north on Route 167, where hourly **guided tours** (9am–5pm; $4) venture through 65-foot-deep caverns filled with strangely shaped calcite formations. Far from being new discoveries, the caves were mentioned in colonial Spanish accounts of the area and used by Seminole Indians to hide from Andrew Jackson's army in the early 1800s. Back in the sun, the park has a few other features to fill a day comfortably. From the **Visitor Center** (℗850/482-1228) by the caverns' entrance, a **nature trail** leads around the flood plain of the Chipola River. The river curiously dips underground for several hundred feet as it flows through the park. At the **Blue Hole Spring**, at the end of the park road, you can canoe (rental is $10 for half a day), swim, snorkel or scuba-dive – and sleep at its **campground** ($14).

Chipley and Falling Waters State Recreation Area

Continuing west, the next community of any size is **Chipley**, 26 miles from Marianna. The town takes its name from William D. Chipley, who put a railroad across the Panhandle in the mid-1800s to improve the timber trade, which in turn gave rise to little sawmill towns such as Chipley. The railroad is still here (restricted locally to freight), but the boom times are long gone. The town itself is, for the most part, unexciting and the Neoclassical bulk of the **Washington County Court House** on Hwy-90 (also called Jackson Avenue) seems very out of place. The only other building of interest is the large and elegant **First United Methodist Church**, built in 1910 and set on hand-hewn log foundations. If you can find someone to let you in, the interior is most unexpected. Towering over the vast, curved golden-oak pews are a huge pipe organ and semi-opaque stained glass that is especially radiant on a sunny day.

Chipley's historic district is on South Third Street, down the western side of the Court House. The houses here date from 1900 to 1920 and are not worth more than a cursory glance. More interesting, if only as a well-preserved example of the inland Panhandle's ubiquitous Main Streets, is the area just north of Hwy-90, a charming row of old brick-faced shops along the railroad tracks. **Antique shops** abound here, and Chipley's best are at the Historic Chipley Antique Mall, 1368 Railroad Ave N (℗850/638-2535).

The Falling Waters State Recreation Area

Leave town along Route 77 and head for **Falling Waters State Recreation Area** (daily 8am–sunset; cars $3.25, pedestrians and cyclists $1), three miles south and the home of Florida's only **waterfall**. The fall is in fact a 100-foot drop into a tube like sinkhole topped by a viewing platform. A trail passes several other sinks (without waterfalls), and another leads to a decaying oil well – remaining from an unsuccessful attempt to strike black gold in 1919. The park has a **campground** (℗850/638-6130; $10), but for **accommodation** under a roof, head back to Chipley where there are a number of chain motels on Hwy-90, including the dull but cheap *Budget Hotel*, 700 Hwy-90 (℗850/638-1850; **❶–❷**), or *Chipley Motel*, 404 Hwy-90 (℗850/638-1322; **❶–❷**). For **food**, try the *Chinese Garden Restaurant*, next to the *Chipley Motel* at 1320 Hwy-90 (℗850/638-3080). Local farmers pack into *Granny's Country Kitchen*, 1284 W Jackson Ave, open daily until 2pm, for hearty breakfasts and lunch buffets.

De Funiak Springs

A real jewel of the inland Panhandle, **De Funiak Springs**, forty miles west of Chipley on Hwy-90, was founded as a fashionable stop on the newly completed Louisville–Nashville railroad in 1882. Drawn to the large, naturally circular lake, nineteenth-century socialites built fairy-tale villas to fringe the waters here, and three years later the Florida Chautauqua Alliance – a benevolent religious society espousing free culture and education for all – made the town its southern base. The alliance was headquartered at the grandiose Hall of Brotherhood, which still stands on Circle Drive – an ideal cruising lane to view the splendid villas, painted in gingerbread-house style with white or wedding-cake blue trim. With the death of its founders and the coming of the Depression, the alliance faded away, and in 1975 their 4000-seat auditorium was demolished by Hurricane Eloise. There has been renewed interest in the Chautauqua ethos, however, and a **Chautauqua Assembly Revival** is now held here around the first week of March (call ☎ 850/892-4300 for details). In addition to putting on workshops and craft activities, the town also opens up its historic houses so you can view the interiors. If you miss that, the only building open to the public is the smallest, the **Walton–De Funiak Library**, 3 Circle Drive (Mon 9am–7pm, Tues & Fri 9am–6pm, Sat 9am–3pm; free), which has been lending books since 1886 and recently acquired a small stash of medieval European weaponry, donated by a local collector.

Another unlikely find is the **Chautauqua Vineyards** (☎ 850/892-5887), on Hwy-331 just north of the junction with I-10, whose diverse wines may not be the world's finest, but have picked up a few awards in their ten years of existence (free tours and tastings, Mon–Sat 9am–5pm, Sun noon–5pm).

Stopping over in De Funiak Springs is a sound move if you're aiming for the more expensive coastal strip 25 miles south along Hwy-331. The *Days Inn*, 1325 S Freeport Rd (☎850/892-6115; ❷–❸), has good rates but is closer to I-10 than the town. To stay in step with the town's historical mood, opt instead for *Hotel de Funiak*, 400 E Nelson Ave (☎850/892-4383, ⓦwww.hoteldefuniak.com; ❸–❹), a charmingly restored hotel in the old business district that is still close to the lake. Alternatively, you can rent a log cabin at *Sunset King Lake Resort*, 366 Paradise Island Drive (☎850/892-7229 or 1-800/774-5454, ⓦwww.sunsetking .com; ❸), where there's also an outdoor pool and boat rentals. While in town, make sure to **eat lunch** amid the antiques at the delightful *Busy Bee Café*, 35 Seventh St (☎850/892-6700). For **dinner**, the restaurant at *Hotel de Funiak* (above) serves regional and ethnic food in the cozy atmosphere of its Chautauqua dining room. For cheaper eats try the *McLains Family Steakhouse*, on Hwy-331 (☎850/892-2402), for a good selection of steaks, seafood and salads, or head back to I-10 for the usual array of quick-stop restaurants.

The Blackwater River State Forest

Between the sluggish towns of Crestview and Milton, thirty miles west of De Funiak Springs, the creeks and slow-flowing rivers of **Blackwater River State Forest** are jammed each weekend with waterborne families enjoying what's officially dubbed "the canoe capital of Florida." In spite of the crowds, the forest is by no means over-commercialized, being big enough to absorb the influx and still offer peace, isolation and unruffled nature to anyone intrepid enough to hike through it. Alternatively, if you're not game for canoeing or hiking, but just want a few hours' break, the **Blackwater River State Park** (daily 8am–sunset; cars $3, pedestrians and cyclists $1), within the forest four miles north of Harold off Hwy-90, has some easy walking trails.

From Milton, Hwy-90 and I-10 both offer a mildly scenic fifteen-mile drive over Escambia Bay to the hotels and freeways on the northern fringes of Pensacola, the city marking Florida's western extremity (see p.431).

Accommodation in the forest

With the exception of the restored 1800s "cracker" **cabins** and an *Old School House Inn* rented through **Adventures Unlimited** at Tomahawk Landing (see below; **❶**–**❺**, depending on the comfort level), forest accommodation is limited to **camping** ($10–12). There are fully equipped sites at the Krul Recreation Area (℡850/957-4201), near the junction of Forest Road 4 and Route 19, and at the Blackwater River State Park (see opposite; ℡850/623-2363). Free basic sites intended for hikers are dotted along the main trails.

Hiking and canoeing

Hardened **hikers** carrying overnight gear can tackle the 21-mile **Jackson Trail**, named after Andrew Jackson who led his invading army this way in 1818, seeking to wrest Florida from Spanish control. On the way, two very basic shelters have handpumps for water. The trail runs between Karick Lake, off Hwy-189, fourteen miles north of Hwy-90, and the Krul Recreation Area. The shorter **Sweetwater Trail** is a good substitute if your feet aren't up to the longer hike. An enjoyable four-and-a-half-mile walk, it leaves the Krul Recreation Area and crosses a swingbridge and the Bear Lake Dam before joining the Jackson Trail.

Canoeing in the forest is offered by Adventures Unlimited, at **Tomahawk Landing** on Coldwater Creek (℡850/623-6197 or 1-800/239-6864, Ⓦwww.adventuresunlimited.com), twelve miles north of Milton on Hwy-87. Here you can rent tubes, canoes and kayaks for around $8, $13 and $20 respectively per day. Two- and three-day trips, with overnight gear and food provided, can also be arranged from $16 to $62 per person.

The Coastal Panhandle

Lacking the glamour and international renown of Florida's other beach strips, the **coastal Panhandle** is nonetheless no secret to residents of the Southern states who descend upon the region by the thousands during the summer. Consequently, a few sections of the region's 180-mile-long coastline are nightmarishly overdeveloped: **Panama City Beach** revels in its "redneck Riviera" nickname, and smaller **Destin** and **Fort Walton Beach** are only marginally more refined. By contrast, little **Apalachicola**, and the **South Walton beaches**, both easily reached by car (they're inaccessible by bus) but out of the main tourist corridor, have much to recommend them as they have beautiful unspoilt sands and off-shore islands where people are a rarer sight than wildlife.

Apalachicola and around

A few miles south of the Apalachicola National Forest (p.412), and the first substantial part of the coast you'll hit on Hwy-98 from central Florida, the **Apalachicola area** contains much of value. Mainland beaches may be few, but sand-seekers are compensated by the brilliant strands of three barrier islands, and the small fishing communities you'll pass through are untainted by the aggressive tourism that scars the coast fifty miles west in Panama City Beach.

Apalachicola

Now a tiny port with an income largely derived from harvesting oysters (nine out of every ten eaten in Florida are farmed here), **Apalachicola** once rode high on the cotton industry, which kept its dock busy and its populace affluent during the early 1800s. A number of stately columned buildings attest to former wealth; one, at 99 Market St, is occupied by the **Chamber of Commerce** (Mon–Fri 9.30am–4pm, Sat 10am–3pm; ☎850/653-9419, ⓦ www.apalachicola.com), where you can pick up a map to find the attractions along an enjoyable half-hour's stroll.

To reach Apalachicola take Hwy-98 which crosses the four-mile Gorrie Memorial Bridge, named for a physician held in high regard by Floridians. Arriving in the town in 1833, John Gorrie was seeking a way to keep malaria patients cool when he devised a machine to make ice (previously transported in large blocks from the north). Gorrie died before the idea took off and became the basis of modern refrigerators and air-conditioners. The **John Gorrie State Museum**, on the corner of Sixth Street and Avenue D (Thurs–Mon 9am–5pm; $1; ☎850/653-9347), remembers the man and his work, as well as the general history of Apalachicola. The museum contains a replica of the cumbersome ice-making device – the original is in the Smithsonian Institute in Washington DC.

Accommodation and eating

There isn't a lot to Apalachicola, but the town makes a good base for visiting the barrier islands (see opposite) and there's plenty of good **accommodation**

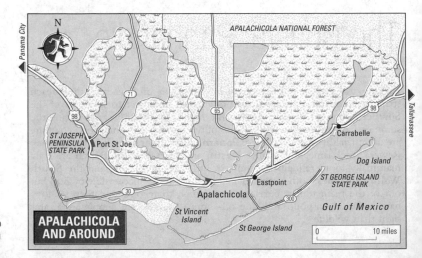

to chose from. Good bed and breakfast is available at the *Apalachicola River Inn*, 123 Water St (℡ 850/653-8139, Ⓦwww.apalachicolariverinn.com; ❸-❻), all of whose rooms have river views; the lovely *Coombes House Inn*, 80 Sixth St (℡850/653-9199, Ⓦwww.coombeshouseinn.com; ❹-❻), which is in a Victorian-style mansion filled with antiques and oriental carpets; and the *Gibson Inn*, 57 Market St (℡850/653-2191, Ⓦwww.gibsoninn.com; ❸-❺), which offers murder-mystery weekends and a full lunch and dinner menu in their own somewhat pricey restaurant. You'll find lower prices just outside town (one and a half miles west) at the *Rancho Inn*, 240 Hwy-98 (℡850/653-9435; Ⓦwww.ranchoinn.com; ❷).

Good places to **eat** in town include the inexpensive *Apalachicola Seafood Grill and Steakhouse*, 100 Market St (℡850/653-9510), for a wide range of lunch and dinner specials; and the *Boss Oyster Bar*, 123 Water St (℡850/653-9364), where you can tuck into fresh Apalachicola oysters. The motto of this place is "shut up and shuck," and it prepares its oysters in thirty different ways. Try the boss oyster combo for $12.25. Adjacent to the *Rancho Inn* (see above) you'll find the *Red Top Café* (℡850/653-8612), which serves inexpensive, Southern cooking for lunch and dinner; while also on Hwy-98, *That Place on 98* at no. 500 (℡850/670-9898) serves fresh seafood, pasta and homemade desserts on a dining deck overlooking the Apalachicola Bay.

The barrier islands: St George, Dog and St Vincent

A few miles off the coast, framing the Apalachicola Bay and the broad, marshy outflow of the Apalachicola River, the three Apalachicola **barrier islands** are well endowed with beaches and creatures – including thousands of birds which use them as resting stops during migration – and two of them hold what must qualify as the most isolated communities in Florida. It's worth seeing one of the islands if you have the chance, but only the largest island, St George, is accessible by road – Route 1A, which leaves Hwy-98 at Eastpoint. Once here you can visit the rest with Journeys of St George's Island, 240 E Third St (℡850/927-3259, Ⓦwww.sgislandjourneys.com), which provides a variety of instructional guided canoe trips and hikes.

Twenty-seven miles of powdery white sands and Gulf vistas are not the only reason to come to **St George Island**, where shady live-oak hammocks and an abundance of osprey-inhabited pine trees add color to a day's lazy sunning. A few restaurants, beach shops, the eight-room *St George Inn*, 135 Franklin Blvd (℡850/927-2903, Ⓦwww.stgeorgeinn.com; ❸-❻), a beautiful wooden beachfront motel with its own heated pool, and the *Buccaneer Inn* (℡850/927-2585, Ⓔcastaway@gtcom.net; ❹), with basic rooms and proximity to the island's restaurants and shops, occupy the island's central section. The eastern sector is dominated by the raccoon-infested **St George Island State Park** (daily 8am–sunset; cars $3.25, pedestrians and cyclists $1), where a three-mile **hiking trail** leads to a very basic **campground**, ($4; there's a better-equipped site at the start of the hike, $10; ℡850/927-2111).

A couple of miles east of St George, **Dog Island**, accessible only by boat (signs advertising crossings are all over the marina in Carrabelle, on Hwy-98), has a small permanent population living in little cottages nestled among Florida's tallest sand dunes. Several footpaths lead around the windswept isle, which won't take more than a few hours to cover. The only **accommodation** is the pricey bed and breakfast at the *Pelican Inn* (℡1-800/451-5294; Ⓦwww.pelicaninn.com; ❻); reservations are essential.

The freshwater lakes and saltwater swamps of **St Vincent Island** (Ⓦwww .stvincentisland.com), almost within a shell's throw of St George's western end, form a protected refuge for loggerhead turtles, wild turkeys and bald eagles, among many other creatures. Trips to the island are available year-round with St Vincent Island Shuttle Services (Ⓣ 850/229-1065) from $10; they also organize bike rental for those who want to cycle their way around the twelve-acre island.

St Joseph Peninsula State Park and Port St Joe

For a final taste of virgin Florida coast before hitting heavily commercial Panama City Beach, take Route 30 – eighteen miles from Apalachicola, off Hwy-98 – to the **St Joseph Peninsula State Park** (daily 8am–sunset; cars $3.25, pedestrians and cyclists $1). A long finger of sand with a short **nature trail** at one end and a spectacular nine-mile **hiking route** at the other, the park has rough **camping** ($8) at its northern tip and better-equipped sites ($19) and **cabins** ($55–$70; Ⓣ 850/227-1327) about halfway along near Eagle Harbor.

The peninsula wraps a protective arm around **Port St Joe** on the mainland, another dot-on-the-map fishing port that has seen better days. One such day came in 1838 when a constitution calling for statehood (which Florida didn't acquire until seven years later) and liberal reforms was drawn up here★ – only to be deemed too radical by the legislators of the time. At the **Constitution Convention State Museum** (Thurs–Mon 9am–noon & 1–5pm; $1; Ⓣ 850/229-8029), signposted from Hwy-98 as you enter the town, you'll find battery-powered waxworks that re-enact the deed. There are also more credible mementos of the town's colorful past, including an explanation of how the town's reputation for pirate pursuits earned it the title "Wickedest City in the Southeast" during its early years.

Panama City Beach

An orgy of motels, go-kart tracks, mini-golf courses and amusement parks, **PANAMA CITY BEACH** is entirely without pretensions, capitalizing as blatantly as possible on the appeal of its 27-mile-long beach. The place is entirely commercial, but with the shops, bars and restaurants all trying to undercut one another, there are some great bargains to be found – from airbrushed T-shirts and cut-price sunglasses to cheap buffet food. With everybody out to have a good time, there's some fine cruising to be done, too; not least during the Spring Break months of March and April when thousands of students – predominately from the Deep South – descend upon Panama City Beach to drink and dance themselves into oblivion. Party town it may be, but Panama City Beach has zero drug tolerance and there are big signs along the beach to constantly remind you of this fact. As vulgar and crass as it often is, Panama City Beach cries out to be seen. Come here once, if only as a voyeuristic day trip – you may well be tempted enough by its tacky charm to stay longer.

Seasons greatly affect the mood. Throughout the lively **summer** (the so-called "100 Magic Days"), accommodation costs are high and advance bookings essential. In **winter**, prices drop and visitors are fewer; most are Canadians and – increasingly – northern Europeans, who have no problems sunbathing and swimming in the relatively cool (typically around 65°F) temperatures.

★ Strictly speaking, the constitution was drawn up in the town of St Joseph (later devastated by yellow fever, two hurricanes and a fire), whose site Port St Joe now occupies.

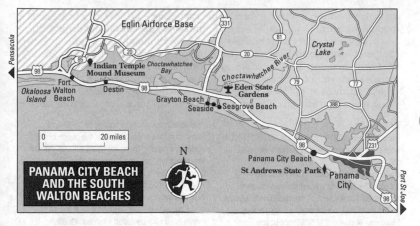

What Panama City Beach doesn't have is any **history** worth mentioning. It began as an off-shoot of **Panama City**, a dull place of docks and paper mills eight miles away over the Hathaway Bridge (which Hwy-98 crosses). Today there's little love lost between the two communities; they have nothing in common besides a name.

Arrival, getting around and information

Since Panama City Beach is essentially a very long beach, **getting your bearings** could hardly be simpler, even if there are only two real, if rather similar landmarks (City Pier to the west, County Pier to the east). Much of the two piers was destroyed during Hurricane Opal in 1996, but restoration plans were quickly enforced and they're pretty much back to normal now. **Front Beach Road** (part of Hwy-98A, which starts at the foot of the Hathaway Bridge) is the main track, a two-lane highway, often called "the Strip," that's very much the place to cruise on weekends. The speedier, four-lane **Middle Beach Road** loops off Front Beach Road for a few blocks around County Pier from the junction with **Thomas Drive** (which links the eastern extremity of the beach). If you don't want to see gaudy Panama City Beach at all, **Back Beach Road** (Hwy-98) will take you straight through its anonymous residential quarter.

Greyhound **buses** pick up and drop off at the Shell station, 17325 W Hwy-98, leaving a fifteen-minute walk to the nearest motels. Traveling by other bus lines, however, you may well end up in Panama City (917 Harrison Ave; ⊕850/785-7861), rather than Panama City Beach, and you'll need to use one of the four daily Greyhound services linking them.

Panama City Beach is incredibly bad for **walking**; **public transport** is non-existent and **taxis** are prohibitively expensive, even for a short journey. Without a car, rent a **bicycle** (around $15 per day) or a **scooter** (around $30 per day; driver's license necessary) from any of the myriad beach shops. For free news-sheets, magazines and discount coupons, drop into the **Visitors Information Center**, 12015 Front Beach Rd (Mon–Sun 8am–5pm; ⊕1-800/722-3224, Ⓦwww.panamacitybeachfl.com).

Accommodation

Visitors to Panama City Beach outnumber residents, and though there are plenty of **places to stay**, these fill with amazing speed, especially on weekends. **Prices** are higher than you'll pay elsewhere in the Panhandle – $70–90 for a basic motel room in summer – so if you're counting the bucks, stay inland and drive to the beach. In winter prices drop by 30–40 percent, with monthly rentals being even cheaper. **Campgrounds** sites are rarely more expensive than their equivalents elsewhere, though only a couple are good for tents. As a very general rule, **motels** at the eastern end of the beach are smarter and slightly pricier than those in the center, and those at the western end are quiet and family-orientated. That said, you're unlikely to find much to complain about at any place that takes your fancy.

Motels

Blue Dolphin, 19919 Front Beach Rd (☎ 850/234-5895). A simple motel with a beachfront location. ❹

Driftwood Lodge, 15811 Front Beach Rd (☎ 850/234-6601, ⓦ www.driftwoodpcb.com). Shuffleboard and volleyball are available to guests at this motel, centered around a courtyard. ❸

Flamingo Motel, no. 15525 Front Beach Rd (☎ 850/234-2232, ⓦ www.flamingomotel.com). This large motel is situated in the center of the beach half a mile east of the pier. It features a tropical garden on the beach. ❷–❹

Impala, 17751 Front Beach Rd (☎ 850/234-6462). This cozy, basic beachfront motel offers inexpensive rooms, a sundeck with beach chairs and barbecue pit. ❸

Marriott's Bay Point Resort Village, 4200 Marriott Drive (☎ 850/236-6000, ⓦ www.marriottbaypoint.com). Located on 1100 acres. Every room has a view of either the beach or the wildlife sanctuary. There are four pools, whirlpools, exercise room, golf and tennis on offer. ❻

Osprey Motel, 15801 Front Beach Rd (☎ 850/234-0303, ⓦ www.theaospreymotel.com). This relatively inexpensive, large beachfront motel offers heated pool, hot-tub and beach bar. All rooms have fully equipped kitchens. ❷–❹

Sea Witch, 21905 Front Beach Rd (☎ 850/234-5722, ⓦ www.seawitchmotel.com). Situated in a secluded part of the beach known as Sunnyside, this motel has a large gulfside pool, jet-ski hire, gift shop and a game room. ❸

Sugar Sands Motel, 20723 Front Beach Rd (☎ 1-800/367-9221, ⓦ www.sugarsands.com). The facilities offered by this motel include shuffleboard, a heated pool and a hot-tub. Beach activities, such as volleyball and jet skiing, are also available. ❸

Campgrounds

Several large and busy **campgrounds** cater mainly to RVs. The most central are *Miracle Strip RV Resort*, 10510 Front Beach Rd ($25; ☎ 850/234-3833), and *Raccoon River*, 12405 Middle Beach Rd ($20; ☎ 850/234-0181). For quieter confines that are better for **tents**, try *Magnolia Beach*, 7800 Magnolia Beach Rd ($18; ☎ 850/235-1581), and the waterfront *St Andrews State Recreation Area*, 4415 Thomas Drive ($9–20 with electricity; ☎ 850/233-5140). Also on Thomas Drive is *KOA* at no. 8800 ($15–25; ☎ 850/234-5731).

Around the beach

Getting a tan, running yourself ragged at beach sports and going wild at night are the main concerns in Panama City Beach – you'll get very strange looks indeed if you go around demanding history, art and culture.

If you remain dissatisfied, try go-karting (around $10 for ten minutes), visiting one of the amusement parks (usually $18 for an all-inclusive day ticket), going on a fishing trip (take your pick of the party boats on the Thomas Drive Marina, from around $30 a day), scuba diving (several explorable shipwrecks litter the area; details from any of the numerous dive shops), a waverunner trip to Shell Island (see opposite; $79), parasailing ($35 for a ten-minute ride), bungee jumping ($18) or a four-mile helicopter ride (starting at $30 for two people). Otherwise, the following provide the only variation.

Gulf World Marine Park

15412 Front Beach Rd. Open daily 9am, closing times vary throughout the year; $17.56; ☎ 850/234-5271, ⓦ www.gulfworldmarinepark.com.

Allow about three hours to wander around the 20,000 square feet of this indoor tropical garden, where you can see a dolphin, sea lion and tropical bird shows as well as view otters, alligators and penguins, among others. Further attractions include the nightly "Splash Magic" laser show and the chance to become a dolphin trainer for the day.

Museum of Man in the Sea
17314 W Hwy-98. Daily 9am–5pm; $5; ☎ 850/235-4101.

All you ever needed to know about diving is contained in this large collection that includes enormous eighteenth-century underwater helmets, bulky air pumps, bodysuits, deep-sea cutting devices, and torpedo-like propulsion vehicles. A separate display documents *Sealab*, the US Navy's underwater research vessels, the first of which was fitted out in Panama City and now stands outside the museum. This entertaining stop makes an ideal prelude to a day's snorkeling.

St Andrews State Recreation Area
4415 Thomas Drive. Daily 8am–sunset; cars $3.25, pedestrians and cyclists $1; ☎ 850/233-5140.

Get here early and you'll spot a variety of hopping, crawling and slithering wildlife by following one of the nature trails around the pine forest and salt marshes within the park. By noon the hordes have arrived to swim, fish and prepare picnics. If you're with kids, they'll enjoy splashing in the shallow lagoon sheltered by an artificial reef known as The Jetties. Clean enough that locals catch their dinner here, these crystal waters are ideal for swimming, snorkeling, diving, canoeing and kayaking. Take advantage of the campground to enjoy the quietest times in this spot.

Shell Island
Half an hour by ferry from the Captain Anderson Marina, at the foot of Thomas Drive. Boat departures every 30min from 10am–3pm; return ticket $12. Alternatively, five minutes from St Andrews State Recreation Area, departing every 30min 9am–5pm in summer, and 10am–3pm in winter.

This seven-mile strip of sand is a haven for shell collectors and sun worshippers alike. With little shade on the undeveloped island, sunglasses are essential; the glare off the sands can be blinding. There are numerous boat trips from Captain Anderson Marina, most of which include a brief stop at Shell Island. Prices vary wildly among tour operators, so shop around.

Zoo World
9008 Front Beach Rd. Daily 9am–dusk; $8.95; ☎ 850/230-1243.

If you're not opposed to animals being incarcerated, you'll enjoy this small collection of lions, tigers, orang-utans and other creatures. Many of the inmates prefer to sleep through the midday heat, so try to time your visit for early morning or late afternoon.

Restaurants and Cafés

Bishop's Family Buffet, 12628 Front Beach Rd (☎ 850/234-6457). Features substantial buffet meals three times daily for $5–10.

Cajun Inn, at the Edgewater Beach Resort Shopping Center (☎ 850/235-9987). Mouthwatering and inexpensive selection of Cajun and Creole American cuisine, such as crawfish *étouffée*, are available here.

Golden Anchor, 11800 Front Beach Rd (☎ 850/234-1481). Buffet meals for $5–10 are available here, as well as sizeable seafood lunches and dinners.

Hamilton's, 5711 N Lagoon Drive (☎ 850/234-1255). Blackened alligator nuggets stand out among the more regular dishes. Dinner only.

Katman'du, at the intersection of Hwy-79 and Front Beach Road (℡ 850/235-9866). Offers cheap and tasty breakfasts and catfish to die for.

Mikato, 7724 Front Beach Rd (℡ 850/234-1388). Watching the knife-throwing chefs is part of the show at this moderately priced sushi bar.

Mike's Diner, 17554 Front Beach Rd (℡ 850/234-1942). This coffee shop opens early, closes late and is great value throughout the day.

Ruthie T's, two blocks east of Joan Avenue on Thomas Drive (℡ 850/234-2111). Moderately priced soul food with heart and a house special of blackened prime rib with attitude. The wine list is first rate.

Shuckum's Oyster Pub & Seafood Grill, 15618 W Hwy-98 (℡ 850/235-3214). Cheap oysters in many styles are available here, including fried in a sandwich.

Sweet Basil's, 11208 Front Beach Rd (℡ 850/234-2855). Classy Italian food and the freshest seafood are offered at this moderately priced eatery.

The Treasure Ship, 3605 Thomas Drive (℡ 850/234-8881). A seafood restaurant built to resemble a wooden sailing ship, with pirates hopping around the tables.

Nightlife

Even if you only stay a few minutes, you should visit one of the two beachside **nightlife** fleshpots: *Club La Vela*, 8813 Thomas Drive (℡ 850/234-3866), or *Spinnaker*, 8795 Thomas Drive (℡ 850/234-7822) – both open 10am to 4am, with free entry. Each has dozens of bars, several discos, live bands and a predominantly under-25 clientele eagerly awaiting the weekend bikini and wet T-shirt contests, and thrice-weekly "hunk shows." Because competition between the two clubs is so intense, there'll often be free beer in the early evening. During the day, the action is by the clubs' open-air pools, where you're overdressed if covering anything more than your genitalia.

Everywhere else is tranquil by comparison. Although they may also have live music, a number of **bars** are worth a call simply for a drink. Check out: *Pineapple Willy's Jazz Club* , 9875 S Thomas Drive (℡ 850/235-0928), famous for their jazz; or *Y Bar*, 17190 Front Beach Rd (℡ 850/234-6770), for live music and Happy Hours.

West of Panama City Beach: the South Walton beaches

West of Panama City Beach, the motels eventually give way to the more rugged and less developed **beaches of South Walton County**: fifty miles of some of Florida's best-kept coastline. With a few exceptions, accommodation here is in resort complexes with sky-high rates, but it's a great area to spend a day. **Route 30A** (far superior to Hwy-98, which takes an inland route) is an eighteen-mile scenic road linking the region's small beach communities. For **general information** on the South Walton beaches and surrounding area, phone the South Walton Tourist Development Council (℡ 1-800/822-6877), or visit their offices at the junction of Route 331 and Hwy-98, twenty miles west of Panama City Beach and ten miles east of San Destin.

Deer Lake Park and Seagrove Beach

Deer Lake Park, ten miles west of Panama City Beach on Route 30A, is a dramatic stretch of creamy-white sand dunes on a coastline studded with smooth driftwood. The best beach of the South Walton bunch, it somehow goes almost without mention in the area's tourist brochures. The road signposted "Deer Lake Park" ends at a parking lot, and a five-minute walk through scrubland leads to the beach, a favorite hideout for nude sunbathing – officially, it's forbidden, but the rules are enforced infrequently.

A few miles west, **Seagrove Beach** shares the same attractive shoreline as Deer Lake Park, and is also home to the *Granola Girls Gourmet Bakery*, 4935 E Hwy-30 (℡850/231-2023; closed Mon), perfect for fresh muffins, bagels, filled croissants and granola. For more upmarket dining, try the stylish *Café Thirty A*, Hwy-30A (℡850/231-2166), a rotisserie and bar serving mainly fish and meat dishes. *Cocoons*, Hwy-30A (℡850/231-4544), is a great deli that offers take out sandwiches for the beach.

If you wish to **stay**, the *Sugar Beach Inn Bed and Breakfast*, 3501 E Scenic 30A, at Seagrove Beach (℡850/231-1577, www.sugarbeachinn.com; ❺–❼), is a luxurious Victorian-inspired inn with Gulf views within walking distance of the sea. There's limited tent **camping** at Seagrove Beach's *RV Resort* ($15; ℡850/231-2826). Whether you camp or not, the *RV Resort* is a good place to rent a **bike** ($13 a day, with big reductions for weekly rentals) and they provide a useful free pick-up and delivery service. Seagrove Cycles, 4042 Hwy-30 A (℡850/231-4000), also rents out cycles and scooters, while Butterfly Beach Rentals, 3657 Hwy 30 A (℡850/231-2826), rents canoes and kayaks as well as bikes.

Seaside and Grayton Beach

An exception to the casual, unplanned appearance of most South Walton beach towns, **Seaside** (Ⓦwww.seasidefl.com) just west of Seagrove Beach, is an experiment in urban architecture begun in 1981 by a rich, idealistic developer called Robert Davies. The theory was that Seaside's pseudo-Victorian cottages, all gleaming white and incredibly well kept, foster village-like neighborliness and instill a sense of community. In reality, they do nothing of the sort, and it's basically a wealthy and sterile resort these days. Still, as elitist and economically discriminating as this place is, there's no escaping the unique appeal of the streets; you won't see houses like this anywhere else, and though you'll never feel like you belong, it's well worth stopping to explore. The shops are interesting and unusual, offering high-quality arts and crafts, gourmet food and expensive clothing, and the beach is fantastic. Everything is expensive, though (the fine for dropping litter is $500), and there's no shortage of pricey places to eat or stay. *Bud and Alley's*, Route 30A (℡850/231-5900), is widely renowned for its carpetbagger steak, a filet mignon stuffed with pan-fried oysters. *Blue Luna Café*, 52 Upper Town, Grayton Circle (℡850/231-0530), has a good dinner menu that won't break the bank; while at lunchtime try *Spiazzia*, 183 Central Square (℡850/231-1950), whose dishes use fresh ingredients, and the coffee is great. For luscious cakes and an earful of Seaside's local gossip, head for *Modica Market*, 53 Central Square (℡850/231-1214), a fabulous gourmet grocery store. If you decide to splash out and stay in Seaside, *Josephine's*, 38 Seaside Ave (℡850/231-1940 or 1-800/848-1840, Ⓦwww.josephinesfl.com; ❼), is the most elegant bed and breakfast on the Gulf Coast. The owners even offer a massage followed by a glass on the veranda and more than likely a beautiful sunset for the final touch of perfection.

Fortunately, the antidote to Seaside's sterility is just a few miles further along Route 30A at **Grayton**, whose secluded position (it's hemmed in by protected land) and ramshackle wooden dwellings have taken the fancy of a number of artists who now reside here. Some of their work is regularly on show at the beachside Gallery at Grayton (Tues–Sat 9.30am–5pm). For more information on the area visit the **Chamber of Commerce** at the junction of Hwy-331 and Hwy-98 (daily 8.30am–4.30pm; ℡850/267-3511). Accommodation is much cheaper here than at Seaside. One unusual option is *Hibiscus Coffee and Guesthouse*, 85 De Funiak St (℡850/231-2733; Ⓦwww.hibiscusflorida.com; ❸–❺), which is a coffee house that also serves basic snack food during the day.

For more formal dining *Criolla's*, Hwy-30A (☎850/267-1267), has excellent seafood served in Creole style.

Many who come to Grayton skip straight through to the **Grayton Beach State Recreation Area** (daily 8am–sunset; cars $3.25, pedestrians and cyclists $1), just east of the village. The recreation area is walled by sand dunes and touches the banks of a large brackish lake. A night at the park's **campground** ($14) leaves plenty of time for a slow exploration of the village and its natural surrounds. Route 30A rejoins Hwy-98 seven miles west of Grayton.

Blue Mountain Beach and Santa Rosa Beach

Just west of Grayton the relatively undiscovered **Blue Mountain Beach** is a welcome escape from the Spring Break crowds that zip past without a second glance. Don't make the same mistake; the quiet beach is an expanse of creamy white sand bordered by unpretentious vacation homes. There's a gourmet grocery store at *Blue Mountain Plaza*, though for delicious, health-conscious lunches, wander across the street to *For the Health of It*, no. 2217 on Scenic Route 30A, where lime-bean chowder and sesame pastas are served amid a huge selection of organic everything.

A mile further west is **Santa Rosa Beach**. Slightly more developed than Blue Mountain, Santa Rosa has one of the better places to **stay** in the region: *A Highlands House Bed & Breakfast*, 4193 W Scenic 30A (☎850/267-0110, ⓦwww.ahighlandshousebbinn.com; ❹), an excellent, well-furnished lodging with panoramic views and a perfect beachside setting, all for considerably less than the selection of characterless new hotels that dot the area. A couple of good – though not cheap – places to **eat** here are *Goatfeathers Seafood Market & Restaurant,* 3865 W County Hwy-30 (☎850/267-3342; closed Wed), which has excellent seafood, and *Café Tango* (☎850/267-0054; closed Sun–Tues), down a tiny track called Vicki Street and serving Cajun and Deep South dishes in a pretty red and green cottage.

Hidden up Satinwood Road, just opposite *Goatfeathers*, is *The S. House* (Tues–Sat 10am–4pm; ☎850/267-2194 or 267-2551), an **antique** shop dealing in a cache of vintage clothes, furniture and collectable oddities from the region. If you ask, the friendly owner will show you his orchid house, which is dripping with color just outside.

Inland: Eden State Gardens

Away from the coast road, only **Eden State Gardens** (Thurs–Mon 8am–sunset; free), reached by Route 395 from Seagrove Beach a mile east of Seaside, are worth a visit. The gardens, now disturbed only by the buzz of dragonflies, were once the base of the Wesley Lumber Company, which helped decimate Florida's forests during the 1890s timber boom. Impressed with the setting, the company's boss pinched some of the wood to build himself a grandiose two-story plantation-style home, the **Wesley House** (guided tours on the hour Thurs–Mon 9am–4pm; $1.50; ☎850/231-4214). After the death of the last Wesley, the house stood empty for ten years until Lois Maxon, a journalist with an interest in antiques, bought it in 1963 as a showcase for her collections, which include a Chippendale cabinet and a Louis XVI mirror.

Destin and around

Heading west from Panama City, six miles before you encounter **DESTIN**, you will pass through San Destin, its newer, more resort-like cousin. San

Destin is an exclusive and somewhat soulless collection of high resorts and is best given a wide berth. The real Destin, once a small fishing village and a cult name among anglers for the fat marlin and tuna lurking in an undersea canyon a few miles offshore, is a less pristine version of San Destin. Towering condos emerge through the heat haze as you approach on Hwy-98 and bear witness to more than two decades of unrestrained exploitation that have stripped away much of the town's character. Pick up tourist information at the **Visitors Center**, 1021 Hwy-98 (Mon–Fri 9am–5pm; ℡ 850/837-6241, ⓦ www.destin .com), signposted to your right as you arrive on Hwy-98.

Accommodation

Most of the **accommodation** consists of rather monolithic hotels in central Destin, so head four miles east to the **motels** along Route 2378, also known as Old Hwy-98 or Beach Road. *Surf High*, no. 3000 (℡ 850/837-2366; ❼, though more reasonable prices are available in low season), is situated on the Gulf front and offers good accommodation and a heated pool. For groups planning a **long stay**, *Surfside*, no. 4701 (℡ 850/837-4700; ❻) is a good option. A more expensive alternative is the *Henderson Park Inn*, 2700 Hwy-98 E (℡ 850/654-0400 or 1-800/336-4853, ⓦ www.hendersonparkinn.com; ❺), an elegant beachside hotel that provides bed and breakfast in style and, for added romance, the restaurant offers candlelit dining. Another more reasonably priced option, the *Silver Beach Motel & Cottages*, eight miles east of Fort Walton Beach (see overleaf), 1050 Hwy-98 (℡ 850/837-6125; ❸ for motel rooms).

Of the **campgrounds**, only two accept tents: *Destin RV Resort*, 150 Regions Way (℡ 850/837-6215, ⓦ www.destinrvresort.com) and, in central Destin, *Destin Campground*, 209 Beach Drive ($26; no reservations; ℡ 850/837-6511).

The town and beach

Evidence of Destin's sudden expansion can be found amid the fading photos of bygone days in the **Old Destin Post Office Museum** (Mon & Wed 1.30–4.30pm; free, ℡ 850/837 8572), opposite the library on Stahlman Avenue. The **Fishing Museum**, at 20009 Emerald Coast Parkway (Mon–Sat 11am–4pm; $2), with its mounted record-breaking catches, and thousands of pictures of landed fish with their grinning captors, is proof of Destin's high esteem among hook-and-line enthusiasts.

An escape from the condo overkill is provided by enticing white sands situated just east of Destin. The **beach** here is family territory, but it offers relaxation, excellent sea swimming and classic Gulf coast sunsets. To reach it, take **Route 2378**, lined by unobtrusive motels and beach shops, which makes a coast-hugging loop off Hwy-98, starting about four miles from Destin.

Eating and nightlife

On Hwy-98, *The Back Porch,* at no. 1740 (℡ 850/837-2022), is Destin's oldest seafood and oyster house and one of the few places open late (until midnight). Otherwise, the 24-hour *Destin Diner*, 1083 Hwy-98 (℡ 850/654-5843), dishes up hearty and economical breakfasts, burgers and frothy milkshakes in surroundings of neon and chrome. Later in the day, there's a buffet at the *Flamingo Café*, 414 Hwy-98 (℡ 850/837-0961), which is famous for its sea view and "Mango Coladas"; *Nigel Manley's World Grill & Microbrewery*, 14051 Emerald Coast Parkway (℡ 850/650-7854), has reasonable prices and unique microbrews. Along Route 2378, you can munch a fish sandwich or shrimp salad at *Captain Dave's*, no. 3796 (℡ 850/837-2627), while gazing over the ocean.

Destin's **nightlife** has little vigor: a few of the beachside bars and restaurants offer nightly drinks specials – look for the signs – or you can drink to the accompaniment of undistinguished rock bands at the *Hog's Breath Saloon*, 1239 Siebert St (☎850/244-2199). Dance the night away at *Nightown*, 140 Palmetto Ave (☎850/837-6448), two blocks east of the Destin Bridge (see below), or enjoy the floor shows accompanied by Fifties and Sixties music at *Yesterday's*, 1079 E Hwy-98 (☎850/837-1954), easy to spot with its classic Chevy and Thunderbird out front.

Okaloosa Island and Fort Walton Beach

Hwy-98 leaves Destin by rising over the **Destin Bridge**, giving towering views of the two-tone ocean and intensely white sands, before hitting the crazy-golf courses and amusement parks of **OKALOOSA ISLAND**. The island's **beaches**, immediately west, are a better sight, kept in their unspoiled state by their owner – the US Air Force – and making a lively weekend playground for local youths and high-spirited beach bums.

A mile west, the neon motel signs that greet arrivals to **FORT WALTON BEACH** offer no indication that this was the site of a major religious and social center during the Paleo-Indian period – so important were the finds made here that the place gave its name to the "Fort Walton Culture" (see "History" in Contexts for more). These days it's military culture that dominates, as the town is home to Eglin, the country's biggest Air Force base. Aside from a few crewcuts and topless bars, however, you'll see little evidence of the base close to Hwy-98 and much of Fort Walton Beach has a more downbeat and homely feel – and slightly lower prices – than Destin. The local **Visitors Center**, 1540 Hwy-98 E (Mon 9am–5pm, Tues–Fri 8am–5pm; ☎1-800/322-3319, Ⓦwww.fwb.org), has abundant information on eating and accommodation.

Fort Walton Beach is home to the world's oldest marine show aquarium. The **Gulfarium,** 1010 Miracle Strip Parkway (daily: June–Aug 9am–8pm; Sept–May 9am–6pm; last admission two hours before closing time; $16; ☎850/244-5169, Ⓦwww.gulfarium.com, opened in 1958 and today is one of the best aquariums in the area, with all kinds of sea life on show. Sharks, moray eels and sea turtles are displayed in their natural habitat and other exhibits include penguins and alligators. A program of dolphin and sea lion shows, each lasting about twenty minutes, is scheduled throughout the day and for an extra fee you can even get into the pool with the dolphins.

Accommodation

Cayo Grande Suites Hotel, 214 Racetrack Rd (☎850/862-7440 or 1-800/827-9908, Ⓦwww.cayogrande.com; ❺-❼), is a luxury hotel with three pools, two saunas, tennis, a fitness center and a putting green. Prices include breakfast and there is a good café on site. Most of the **motels** are along Miracle Strip Parkway (the local section of Hwy-98). *Super 8,* no. 333 SW (☎850/244-4999; ❸), is a very basic two-story motel with a small pool. Some rooms have fridges and mircowaves. *Travel Lodge*, no. 209 (☎850/244-5137; ❹), does not have a pool, but features a restaurant. *Greenwood*, 1340 Hwy-98 (☎850/244-1141; ❸), is good economical accommodation with a heated pool.

The nearest **campground** is the RV-only *Playground RV Park*, four miles north on Hwy-189 (☎850/862-3513); campers with **tents** should make for *Gulf Winds Park*, ten miles west on Hwy-98 (☎850/939-3593), which charges

$12 per night, or, slightly further on, *Navarre Beach Family Campground* (℡ 850 /939-2188, Ⓦ www.gocampingamerica.com/navarrebeach), just outside Navarre, which also rents cabins from $65.

The Indian Temple Mound and Air Force Armament museums

If you were inspired by the sizeable temple mound standing incongruously beside the busy highway into Fort Walton Beach, then you might wish to inspect the small **Indian Temple Mound Museum** (Mon–Fri 11am–4pm, Sat 9am–4pm; $2; ℡ 850/833-9595), at the junction of Hwy-98 and Route 85, which is crammed with over four thousand elucidating relics.

For an insight into more contemporary culture, the **Air Force Armament Museum**, 100 Museum Drive, Eglin (daily 9.30am–4.30pm; free; ℡ 850/882-4062), six miles north of Fort Walton Beach on Route 85, has a large stock of what the local Air Force base is famous for – guns, missiles and bombs, and the planes that carry them. The first guided missiles were put together here in the Forties, and work on developing and testing (non-nuclear) airborne weaponry has continued unabated ever since.

Eating and nightlife

Old Bay Steamer, 1310 Hwy-98 (℡ 850/664-2795), serves good, fresh seafood and pasta dishes, while *Thai Saree*, 163 Eglin Parkway (℡ 850/244-4600), serves excellent Thai food for lunch and dinner at reasonable prices. The pricier *Royal Orchid*, 238 N Eglin Parkway (℡ 850/864-3344), dishes up great Indian dinners. Latin American cuisine is served at *Tapas Etc*, 99 Eglin Parkway (℡ 850/243-1044), but best of all are the high-quality steak and seafood dinners at the *Coach-N-Four*, 1313 Lewis Turner Blvd (℡ 850/863-3443).

Fort Walton Beach **nightlife** amounts to little more than the usual **beachfront bars**, mostly on Okaloosa Island, with some good Happy Hours. The best are *Pandora's*, 1120 Santa Rosa Blvd (℡ 850/244-8669), which draws tourists and locals to its nightly specials; and *Fudpucker's On the Island*, 108 Santa Rosa Blvd (℡ 850/243-3833), with live entertainment on "The Deck." A good **gay bar/club** (actually the only gay club between Panama City and Pensacola) is *Frankly Scarlet's*, 223 Hwy-98 (℡ 850/664-2966), a friendly, lively place equally as welcoming to lesbians as to gay men.

West from Fort Walton

If you're driving, travel **west from Fort Walton** along Hwy-98 and branch off on Route 399 for sixty scenic miles along **Santa Rosa Island** to the Gulf Islands National Seashore, near Pensacola Beach (see "Pensacola and around", below). The parallel route, the continuation of Hwy-98, is much duller, but is the one the daily Greyhound **bus** takes from the station at 101 SE Perry Ave (℡ 850/243-1940). A worthy stop for tasty food at rock-bottom prices is the friendly, yet idiosyncratic *Hazel's Country Kitchen*, 223 Hwy-98 (℡ 850/664-2966).

Pensacola and around

Tucked away at the western end of the Panhandle, **PENSACOLA** is built on the northern bank of the broad Pensacola Bay, five miles inland from the nearest

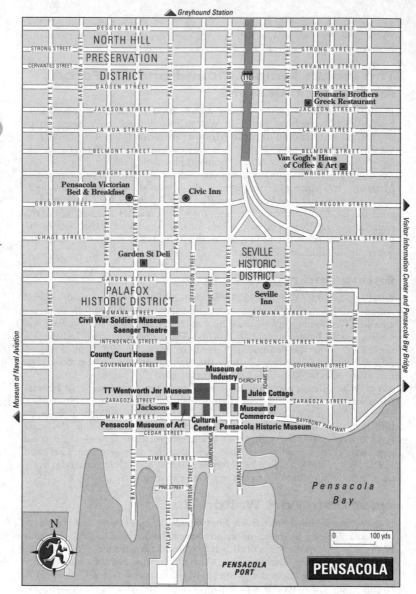

Greyhound Station

DESOTO STREET

NORTH HILL
PRESERVATION
DISTRICT

STRONG STREET

CERVANTES STREET

GADSEN STREET

Founaris Brothers
Greek Restaurant

JACKSON STREET

LA RUA STREET

BELMONT STREET

Van Gogh's Haus
of Coffee & Art

WRIGHT STREET

Pensacola Victorian
Bed & Breakfast

Civic Inn

GREGORY STREET

CHASE STREET

Garden St Deli

SEVILLE
HISTORIC
DISTRICT

GARDEN STREET

PALAFOX
HISTORIC DISTRICT

Seville
Inn

ROMANA STREET

Civil War Soldiers Museum
Saenger Theatre

INTENDENCIA STREET

County Court House

GOVERNMENT STREET

Museum of
Industry

CHURCH ST.

TT Wentworth Jnr Museum

Julee Cottage

ZARAGOZA STREET

Jacksons

Museum of
Commerce

Pensacola Museum of Art

Cultural
Center

Pensacola Historic Museum

CEDAR STREET

GIMBLE STREET

PINE STREET

Pensacola
Bay

N

0   100 yds

PENSACOLA
PORT

PENSACOLA

Museum of Naval Aviation

Visitor Information Center and Pensacola Bay Bridge

beaches. Although its primary features are a naval aviation school and some busy dockyards, Pensacola is also a historic center.   In 1559, Spanish soldiers and colonists established a settlement at Pensacola that lasted two years before being destroyed by a hurricane. A permanent settlement was not established here until 1698, when Fort San Carlos was built. The fort repeatedly changed hands between the Spanish, French and British before becoming the venue where Florida was officially ceded by Spain to the US in 1821. The city has retained enough evidence of its mercurial history to warrant a short visit, but it also makes a good base for exploring one of the prettiest and least-spoilt parts of the coastal Panhandle. Just cross the Bay Bridge to the coast, you'll find Pensacola Beach neighboring the wild, protected beaches of the Gulf Islands National Seashore.

Arrival, information and getting around

Pensacola Regional Airport, 2430 Airport Blvd (ⓦ www.flypensacola.com), is a fifteen-minute drive from downtown. Unless you're arriving from the inland Panhandle on I-10 or Hwy-90, aim to take the scenic route to Pensacola, along Santa Rosa Island on **Route 399** (also known here as Via De Luna Drive). Doing this, you'll first strike Pensacola Beach, from which Pensacola Beach Road swings north, crossing the Santa Rosa peninsula and joining **Hwy-98** before crossing the three-mile-long Pensacola Bay Bridge into the city. At the foot of the bridge, on the city side, is the **Visitor Information Center** (daily 8am–5pm; ⓣ 1-800/874-1234, ⓕ 434-7626, ⓦ www.visitpensacola.com), packed with the usual worthwhile handouts.

Unfortunately, the Greyhound **bus** station is far from central, being seven miles north of the city center at 505 W Burgess Rd (ⓣ 850/476-4800); bus #10A links it to Pensacola proper. **Local buses** (for information call ⓣ 850/595-3228, ext 611, ⓦ www.ecat.pensacola.com) serve the city, but not the beach; the main terminal is at the junction of Gregory and Palafox streets. The downtown area is easy to get around on foot, otherwise the best way of seeing everything is on a trolleybus. The red Palafox line is the downtown service and a 45-minute round-trip only costs 25¢. There is also a beach trolley which only operates Friday to Sunday between May and September, which will take you up and down the beaches, but does not connect to downtown. To get from the city to the beach without your own transport, take a **taxi** (Cross Town Taxi ⓣ 850/456-8294, or Yellow ⓣ 850/433-3333); the fare will be roughly $12–14. For **bike** hire on the beach try Dinah's Shore Shop, 715A Pensacola Beach Blvd (ⓣ 850/934-0014), which also rents rollerblades.

Accommodation

The main approach roads from I-10, North Davis Boulevard and Pensacola Boulevard are both lined with unmissable billboards advertising **budget chain hotels** for $35–55 a night.

The closest **campground** is the *Fort Pickens Campground* (ⓣ 1-800/365-2267), on the Gulf Islands National Seashore, a few miles west of Pensacola Beach (see p.438). Further out, options are *Big Lagoon*, ten miles southwest on Route 292A on Perdido Key ($15; ⓣ 850/492-1595) and *Navarre Beach Campground*, 9201 Navarre Parkway Hwy-98 (ⓣ 850/939-2188 or 1-888/639-2188, ⓔ campnbc@aol.com), who also rent kamping kabins from $65 a night.

On **Perdido Key**, accommodation is pricey unless you choose to camp. The best hotel option is the *Best Western*, 13585 Perdido Key Drive (ⓣ 850/492-2755; ⓹).

Pensacola

Days Inn, 710 N Palafox St (ⓣ 850/438-4922). This chain offers a large pool, bar, full complimentary breakfast and rooms have coffee makers, fridges and microwaves. ⓷

Howard Johnson, 6911 Pensacola Blvd (ⓣ 850/479-3800 or 1-800/446-4656). This chain is one of the cheaper motel options. ⓵

Noble Manor, 110 W Strong St (ⓣ 850/434-9544, ⓦ www.noblemanor.com. This bed and breakfast does special packages and has a great location in the North Hill District. There is a pool and two hottubs and breakfast is served in either the formal dining room or front porch. ⓷–⓸

Pensacola Grand Hotel, 200 E Gregory St (ⓣ 850 /433-3336, ⓦ www.pensacolagrandhotel.com).

This modern high-rise hotel offers modern luxury in a downtown setting. It features a luxurious pool, gym, library, restaurant and cocktail lounge. ❺–❽

Pensacola Victorian, 203 W Gregory St (☎ 850/434-2818 or 1-800/370-8354, ⓦ www .pensacolavictorian.com). Charming and comfortable, this bed and breakfast is in a Queen Anne-style home that was originally built for a captain who also founded the Pensacola Symphony Orchestra. ❸–❹

Seville Inn, 223 E Garden St (☎ 1-800/277-7275). This inn offers very good low-priced accommodation in a central location. ❷

Pensacola Beach

Gulf Aire, 21 Via De Luna Drive (☎ 850/932-2319, ⓦ wwwparadisebeachhomes.com). The *Gulf Aire* features a private beach, picnic area, BBQ and a pool. ❸

The Hampton Inn, 2 Via De Luna Drive (☎850/932-6800, ⓦwww.hamptonbeachresort .com). This extremely comfortable inn includes continental breakfast in the cost. ❺

Sandpiper Inn, 23 Via De Luna Drive (☎ 850/932-2516). A basic motel offering guests use of its pool. ❸

The city

While not as lively as it once was, Pensacola still warrants exploration due to a number of buildings of architectural merit and a relaxing atmosphere. The city is grouped in three distinct, adjoining **districts**: the south-central Palafox District, North Hill in the northern section of the city, and the Seville District in Pensacola's southeast quarter. The Palafox and Seville districts are the most interesting historically. The streets of Seville are flanked by house after house of interest. The only other attraction that might delay serious sunbathing at Pensacola Beach is a naval aviation museum.

The Palafox District

Pensacola was already a booming port at the turn of the nineteenth century, and the opening of the Panama Canal was expected to further boost the city's fortunes. Sadly, the surge in wealth never came, but the optimism of the era is apparent in the delicate ornamentation and detail in the buildings around the **Palafox District**.

Take a look first at the **County Court House**, at the junction of Palafox and Government streets, which, besides its legal function, has also seen service as a customs house, a post office and tax offices. Opposite, the slender form and vertically aligned windows of the **Seville Tower** exaggerate the height of what, in 1909, was the tallest building in Florida. A block further north, at 118 S Palafox Place, the Spanish Baroque **Saenger Theater** (see "Nightlife", p.437), is now the base of the Pensacola Symphony Orchestra. If the door is open, take the opportunity to have a peek at the interior – twice as opulent as the outside.

Also meriting a look is the **Civil War Soldiers Museum**, 108 S Palafox Place (Tues–Sat 10am–4.30pm; $5; ☎ 850/469-1900, ⓦ www.cwmuseum.org), which houses a collection of uniforms, weaponry and many unsettling medical tools – all of which saw action in the Civil War – a graphic illustration of the conditions endured by soldiers during the conflict between the states. Ask at the entrance, which doubles as a well-stocked bookstore specializing in the Civil War, about the thirty-minute video that puts the exhibits into context.

North Hill

Between 1870 and 1930, Pensacola's professional classes took a shine to the **North Hill** area, just across Wright Street from the Palafox District, and commissioned elaborate homes in a plethora of fancy styles. Strewn across the tree-studded fifty-block area are pompous Neoclassical porches, cutesy Tudor Revival cottages, low-slung California-style bungalows, and rounded towers belonging to fine Queen Anne homes. These are private residences not open to the public and the best way to see them is by driving around Palafox, Spring, Strong and Brainerd streets.

The clamor to build houses in this fashionable neighborhood led to the dismantling of **Fort George**, which had once barracked two thousand British troops before falling to the Spanish at the Battle of Pensacola in 1781. Only an imitation cannon and a plaque at the corner of Palafox and LaRua streets commemorates the original location of the fort.

The Seville District: Historic Pensacola Village

As a commercial center, Pensacola kicked into gear in the late 1700s with a cosmopolitan mix of Native Americans, early settlers and seafaring traders gathering here to swap, sell and barter on the waterfront of the **Seville District**, about half a mile east of Palafox Street. Those who did well took up permanent residence and many of their homes remain in fine states of repair, forming – together with several museums – the **Historic Pensacola Village** (Tues–Sat 10am–4pm; $6; ℡850/595-5985, ⓦwww.historicpensacola.org). Each ticket is valid for two days and allows access to all of the museums and former homes (and you should see them *all*, the effect of the whole is far greater than any of its parts) in an easily navigated four-block area. Start at the **Museum of Commerce**, next door to the visitor center on the corner of Zaragoza and Tarragona streets, an entertaining indoor recreation of Palafox Street in its turn-of-the-century heyday, displaying many of the original storefronts and shop fittings. Much of the prosperity of Pensacola was based on the timber industry, a point celebrated by a noisy, working sawmill in the **Museum of Industry**, just across Zaragoza Street.

To catch up on earlier local history, cross Church Street to the sedate **Colonial Archaeology Trail**, where bits of pottery and weapons suggest the lifestyles of the city's first Spanish inhabitants and a marked path leads around the site of the Government House, an outpost of the British Empire which collapsed in the 1820s. Virtually next door, the 1809 **Julee Cottage** belonged to Julee Panton, a "freewoman of color," who had her own land, business and even her own slave. The building's exhibits record her life and deeds as well as the achievements of later black people with Pensacola associations.

Other **restored homes** in the vicinity signify the mishmash of architectural styles, from Creole to Greek Revival, favored by wealthier Pensacolians in the late 1800s. Filled with period furnishings, they make for an enjoyable browse – despite the somewhat twee attendants who sit in them, dressed in period costume during the summer season.

If you have neither the energy nor the inclination to visit all the museums and old homes of the Historic Village, head instead to the **Pensacola Historic Museum**, 115 Zaragoza St (Mon–Sat 9am–4.30; $1; ℡850/433-1559), which will return, once restoration is completed, to its usual home: the Old Christ Church at 405 S Adams St, easily spotted by its sturdy masonry tower. Built in 1832, the church now keeps an imposing clutter, from fossils and Native American pottery to cut-glass ornaments owned by the well-to-do settlers of the early 1900s.

The **T. T. Wentworth Jr Museum**, on Plaza Ferdinand (Mon–Sat 10am–4pm; $6, free admission with Historic Pensacola Village ticket; ⓦwww.dos.state.fl.us/dhr/pensacola), contains the random, garage-sale-like collections that once belonged to Mr Wentworth, who intended to create a museum of oddities. Thankfully, his ambitions were thwarted. The existing ephemera are briefly diverting, though it's the yellow-brick Renaissance building (constructed as the city hall in 1907) itself that is the real attraction. The upstairs has been converted to a museum of the local history, which is comprehensive, but not over-exciting. In the Plaza Ferdinand stands a statue to Andrew Jackson, the state's first governor, commemorating the fact that this is the spot where

Florida was accepted into the US and, for the first time, an American flag was planted on US soil. If you want to learn more about the exhibits join one of the tours which run regularly throughout the day.

Museum of Art

Cleverly incorporated into the old jailhouse, Pensacola's **Museum of Art**, opposite the Cultural Center at 407 S Jefferson St (Tues–Fri 10am–5pm, Sat 10am–4pm; $2, free Tues; ☎ 850/432-6247, ⓦwww.artsnwfl.org /pma), was built in 1906 on what was once the shoreline of Pensacola Bay (after ships started dumping their ballast stones, the shoreline was pushed out by half a mile). The art isn't of any particular distinction, but the building itself is worth exploring: old prison cells have been preserved as exhibition space, classrooms for children now occupy the former women's incarceration area and temporary exhibits fill the upstairs all-male cell block.

The Museum of Naval Aviation and Fort Barrancas

You don't have to be a military fanatic to enjoy the **Museum of Naval Aviation** (daily 9am–5pm; free; ☎1-800/247-6289, ⓦwww.naval-air.org), inside the US naval base on Navy Boulevard, about eight miles southwest of downtown Pensacola and accessible by bus #14, though having a good imagination will help. Visitors can climb into many of the full-sized training cockpits and play with the controls. The main purpose of the museum, however, is to collect and display US naval aircraft, from the first flimsy seaplane acquired in 1911 to the Phantoms and Hornets of more recent times. Among them are a couple of oddities: a small Vietnamese plane, which carried a Vietnamese family onto a US carrier during the fall of Saigon, and the Command Module from the first Skylab mission in 1973, whose crew were naval pilots. It's all rather impressive and serves to underline Pensacola's role as the home base of US naval aviation. The base trains thousands of new pilots each year. Don't miss the seven-story-tall IMAX movie screen, on which a pilot's-eye view of flight makes for quite a visual sensation (tickets $5.50).

On the other side of the road lies the visitor center for **Fort Barrancas** (daily 9.30am–5pm; guided tours Sat & Sun 2pm; free), part of the National Seashore area (see p.438). It's worth spending an hour or so at this well-preserved 1698 Spanish fort, whose design includes a fascinating system of connecting interior vaults.

Eating

Pensacola boasts a large number of restaurants and cafés largely concentrated on Main Street.

Pensacola

Founaris Brothers Greek Restaurant, 1015 N Ninth Ave (☎850/432-0629). Dishes up cheap and cheerful Greek entrées.

Garden St Deli, 236 W Garden St (☎850/470-0305). For cheap speciality sandwiches, try this deli which serves excellent inexpensive meals at checkered-table-clothed tables. You'd never know it without asking, but as a young man, the owner began the city's biggest annual party (see "Memorial Day," p.438).

Hall's Catfish & Seafood, 920 E Gregory St (☎850/438-9019). This eatery has has fish-laden

dinner buffets at reasonable prices .

Jacksons, 400 S Palafox St (☎850/469-9898). Open for dinner only, this elegant restaurant, which offers such delicacies as wood-fired salmon or pan-seared beef tenderloin with crab, is housed is a restored 1860 building overlooking the Plaza Ferdinand.

McGuire's Irish Pub, 600 E Gregory St (☎850 /433-6789). Serves immense portions and draft porter in a lively atmosphere.

Van Gogh's Haus of Coffee & Art, 610 E Wright St (☎850/429-0336). Enjoy light snacks and sandwiches in this Seventies-inspired interior that is the frequent setting for poetry readings.

Pensacola Beach

Chan's Market Café & Bakery, 16 Via de Luna Drive (℡ 850/932-8454). Despite its basic diner decor, *Chan's* serves exceptionally good seafood sandwiches and homebaked side orders of okra, corn fritters and great pancakes and cookies. Look to the end of the room for a remarkable 1880 photo of the Indian chief Geronimo.

Flounder's Chowder & Ale House, 800 Quietwater Beach Rd (℡ 850/932-2003). This pricey alehouse offers hearty seafood dinners.

The Great Brit Inn, 49 Via De Luna Drive (℡ 850/916-1288). Enjoy the standard pub fare while you gaze at the front ends of a Triumph TR6, a white MG and an old Jag that jut from the walls.

Olliejava, next door to the *Hampton Inn* on Via De Luna Drive, serves great breakfasts and dinner in a laid-back environment. Evening specialities include sautéed shrimp, burritos, fries and salsa and great crawfish soup.

Sundae's, 37 Via De Luna Drive. A cheerful place serving good gourmet coffees and rich ice creams.

Nightlife

Pick up a copy of *The Real Paper*, Pensacola's free weekly news and entertainment paper for more nightlife information.

Theater

Little Theatre, 400 S Jefferson St (box office Tues–Sat 10am–3pm and one hour before curtain; tickets $14; ℡ 850/432-2042, ⊛ www.pensacolalittletheatre.com). Housed in the Pensacola Cultural Center, the *Little* shows a program of musicals and plays. Even if you don't see a production here it's worth going inside just to look around.

Saenger Theater, 118 S Palafox Place (box office Mon–Fri 10am–4pm and two hours before curtain; ℡ 850/444-7686, ⊛ www.pensacolasaenger.com). More architecturally impressive than the *Little*, the *Saenger* offers cheap daytime shows, often classic plays for $5–6, and more expensive evening productions for $25–46.

Bars and nightclubs

Pensacola

McGuire's Irish Pub, 600 E Gregory St (℡ 850/433-6789; see "Eating," opposite). This pub serves home-brewed ale.

Seville Quarter, 130 E Government St (℡ 850/434-6201). This tourist-orientated bar and disco decked out to reflect Pensacola's history is a bit more expensive than you might pay elsewhere, but it has atmosphere and can be fun.

Pensacola Beach

The Dock (℡ 850/934-3314). Beside the pier, this hangout is packed every Friday and Saturday night.

Flounder's Chowder & Ale House, 800 Quietwater Beach Rd (℡ 850/932-2003; see "Eating," above). Possibly the most hyped place to drink, this bar draws as many drinkers as diners and has live music about once a week.

Olliejava (see "Eating," above). At the funkiest place to sip beer, long-haired locals strum guitars and tell tales late into the night.

Paddy O'Leary's Irish Pub, 49 Via De Luna Drive (℡ 850/916-9808). This is the place for a spot of traditional Irish music on the beach.

Sandshaker Lounge, 731 Pensacola Beach Blvd (℡ 850/932-2211). This lounge is ideal for rum cocktails.

Gay nightlife

For a city with a conservative reputation, Pensacola has a lively **gay scene** and a wild gay Mardi Gras celebration that annually envelopes the city (see overleaf). The best gay **coffee house** is *Cup N Saucer*, 7 E Gregory St (℡ 850/435-9228), which serves the gooiest cheesecake and cinnamon rolls to a mixed clientele. It's also the only after-hours coffee house in town. Next door is *Pride,* a store selling all the usual gay-orientated merchandise For a friendly local pub, head to *The Round Up*, 706 E Gregory St (℡ 850/433-8482), which has a pleasant covered veranda, but a strict ID policy – take official ID (like a passport) if you could be taken for under 30. The biggest club is *Riviera*, on Main Street, behind the Pensacola Cultural Center.

The Memorial Day party

Every year between the Friday and Monday of the last week of May, Pensacola is consumed by a gay and lesbian party, which began when a 20-year-old local, Dickie Carr, threw a party at the *San Carlos Hotel* (recently demolished to build the courts of law). Dickie's father, who managed the hotel in the Seventies, said he would foot the bill for any of the five hundred rooms which weren't taken. They all were. The party took place on Memorial Day, and has become an annual event involving most of the town and drawing large numbers of outsiders. Despite a brief and quickly squashed homophobic reaction from local businesses in 1985, the party gets bigger every year, pulling Americans from every state. If you're about, the party begins at Navarre Beach on Friday morning and heads back into town at around 4pm, and repeats over the next two days.

Around Pensacola

On the other side of the bay from the city, the glistening quartz beaches of two **barrier islands** are ideal for sunbathing. Santa Rosa Island runs fifty miles from Fort Walton and contains Pensacola Beach while Perdido Key sits to the west of Santa Rosa. The **Gulf Islands National Seashore**, a generic name for several parks, each with a specific point of interest (natural or historical), stretches 150 miles along the coast from here to Mississippi and includes the Naval Live Oaks Reservation, the western section of Santa Rosa Island, Fort Barrancas, and the eastern section of Perdido Key.

Gulf Breeze and the Naval Live Oaks Reservation

En route to Santa Rosa Island, via the three-mile-long Pensacola Bridge, you'll pass through **Gulf Breeze**, a well-scrubbed, well-off community that's going all-out to attract homebuyers. Besides a few supermarkets, the only reason to give it more than a passing thought is the **Naval Live Oaks Reservation** (daily 8am–sunset; free), about two miles east along Hwy-98. In the 1820s, part of this live-oak forest was turned into a tree farm, intended to ensure a supply of shipbuilding material for years to come. Precise calculations were made as to how many trees would be needed for a particular ship, and the requisite number of acorns then planted – followed by a fifty-year wait. Problems were plentiful: the oak was too heavy for road transportation, wood rustlers cut down trees and sold them to foreign navies, and the final blow for the farm was the advent of iron-built ships.

The **visitor center** (daily 8.30am–4.30pm), near the entrance, has exhibits and explanatory texts on the intriguing forest, where fragments from Native American settlements from as far back as 1000 BC have been found. To escape the glare of the sun for an hour or so, take one of the short but shady **forest trails**, which include a two-mile section of what was, in the early 1800s, Florida's major roadway, linking Pensacola and St Augustine.

Pensacola Beach

From Gulf Breeze, another (shorter) bridge ($1 toll) leads across a narrow waterway to Santa Rosa Island and the epitome of a Gulf Coast strand, **Pensacola Beach** (Ⓦwww.visitpensacolabeach.com). Featuring mile after mile of fine white sands, rental outlets for beach and watersports equipment, a pier lined with fishermen, beachside bars and snack stands, it's hard to beat for uncomplicated oceanside recreation. With its sprinkling of motels and hotels (see p.434), Pensacola Beach also makes an alternative – if pricier – base to mainland Pensacola.

Fort Pickens and Navarre Beach

From Pensacola Beach, it's just two and a half miles along the Fort Pickens Toll Road (9am–sunset; cars $6, pedestrians and cyclists $3) to the western end of Santa Rosa Island and the entrance to a part of the Gulf Islands National Seashore. Here, vibrant white sands are walled by a nine-mile stretch of high, rugged dunes, and the only reminder of civilization – other than the road – is a foliage-encircled campground. Hoofing over the dunes is strictly forbidden (as are bottles on the beach), but several tracks lead from the road to the beach. Once on the beach, you'll find plenty of space and seclusion – and sometimes even dolphins. To learn more about the dunes and the curious ecology of the island, join one of the frequent **ranger-led walks**; for details call ☎ 850/934-2622, or read the bulletin boards situated around the park.

At the western tip of the island are the substantial remains of **Fort Pickens** (daily 9.30am–4pm; free), which was built by slaves in the early 1800s to protect Pensacola from seaborne attack. There's plenty to be gleaned by walking around the fort's creepy passageways and rooms on your own: pick up the free tour leaflet at the visitor center. A small **museum** explains the origins of the structure, details the flora and fauna of the national seashore area and records the travails of the seventeen Apache Indians who were imprisoned here in 1886. Among their number was a chief, Goyahkla, better known as **Geronimo**, who served his sentence roaming the sands. The Apaches, whose tribal lands covered much of the southwestern US, were one of the last Native American tribes to surrender to the advancing white settlers, signing a peace treaty with the sympathetic General Crook in 1886. Soon after, the higher-ranking General Sheridan reneged on the terms of the surrender and incarcerated Geronimo and his fellows, leading Crook to resign from the army in protest.

Beside the fort, some crumbling concrete walls remain from seacoast batteries erected in the Forties, which, together with the pillboxes and observation posts that litter the area, are a reminder that the fort's defensive function lasted until the end of World War II and only became obsolete with the advent of guided missiles.

If you head back east along Route 399, the stretch of sand between Pensacola Beach and Navarre Beach is clean and pristine. There are no developments (the area is part of the National Heritage Coastline) and inspirational vistas are plentiful. **Navarre Beach** itself (Ⓦ www.navarrefl.com), unfortunately, is an explosion of unpleasant development, neither as pretty as Seaside nor as impersonally glamorous as San Destin. Yet just beyond where Route 399 curves north to cross the Pensacola Sound is one of the loveliest stretches of reef dunes and sand on the coast. In some places along this stretch there are no lifeguards, so swim in the sea at your own risk. Hurricane Opal did its best to raze the dunes to nothing in 1996, but impressive conservation work has restored much of the coast. Use the parking lot near the *Juana's Pagodas* tiki hut, a popular grill and bar. However, for the best and most popular food on the beach you have to pay a visit to the *Sailor's Grill,* 1451 Navarre Beach Causeway (☎ 850/929-1092), where the breakfasts are amazing and the Key Lime Pie is legendary.

Perdido Key

Another barrier island, to the west of Santa Rosa, **Perdido Key** offers more pristine beaches. Its eastern section, protected as part of the Gulf Islands National Seashore, provides five miles of island untouched by roads. A one-and-a-quarter-mile nature trail allows you to explore the area and if you're smitten with the seclusion, stick around to swim or pitch your tent at one of the primitive campgrounds. Note that you need a permit to use the island's parking lot and camp ($4 for up to seven days; arrange for one by calling ☎850/492-1595. The remainder of Perdido Key is much like Santa Rosa Island, a hotbed of sport, drinking and suntanning rituals.

TRAVEL DETAILS

Trains

Pensacola to: Jacksonville (Mon, Wed, Fri; 10hr 15min); Tallahassee (Mon, Wed, Fri; 6hr).
Tallahassee to: Jacksonville (Mon, Wed, Fri; 4hr 20min); Pensacola (Tues, Thurs, Fri, Sun; 4hr 20min).

Buses

Panama City Beach to: Destin (2 daily; 50min); Fort Walton Beach (2 daily; 1hr 10min); Panama City (2 daily; 30min); Pensacola (2 daily; 2hr 15min).

Pensacola to: Destin (2 daily; 1hr 45min); Fort Walton Beach (4 daily; 1hr 5min); Mobile (7 daily; 1hr 5min); New Orleans (6 daily; 5hr); Panama City Beach (2 daily; 2hr 15min); Tallahassee (10 daily; 4hr 50min).

Tallahassee to: Chipley (2 daily; 2hr 15 min); De Funiak Springs (2 daily; 3hr); Gainesville (6 daily; 2hr 30min); Jacksonville (7 daily; 3hr 45min); Marianna (6 daily; 1hr 15min); Miami (5 daily; 12 hr); New Orleans (7 daily; 9hr); Orlando (11 daily; 6hr 30min); Panama City Beach (2 daily; 2hr 20min); Pensacola (7 daily; 5hr); Tampa (7 daily; 6hr); Thomasville (3 daily; 1hr).

contexts

contexts

The Historical Framework

Contrary to popular belief, Florida's history goes back far beyond Walt Disney World and motel-lined beaches. For thousands of years, its aboriginal inhabitants lived in organized social groupings with contacts across a large section of the Americas. During the height of European colonization, it became a Spanish possession and, for a time, was under British control. Only in the nineteenth century did Florida become part of the US: the beginning of a period of unrestrained exploitation and expansion and the start of many of the problems with which the state continues to grapple today.

Origins of the land

Over billions of years, rivers flowing through what's now **northern Florida** carried debris from the Appalachian mountains to the coast, and their deposits of fine-powdered rock formed the beaches and barrier islands of the Panhandle. Further south, the highest section of a seabed plateau – the **Florida peninsula** – altered in shape according to the world's ice covering. The exposed land sometimes measured twice its present size; during other periods, the coastline was far inland of its current position, with wave action carving out still-visible bluffs in the oolitic limestone base. In the **present era**, beginning about 75 million years ago, rotting vegetation mixed with rainfall to form acid that burned holes in the limestone, and natural freshwater springs emerged; the underground water accumulated from heavy rains which preceded each Ice Age. Inland forests of live oak and pine became inhabited 20,000 years ago by mastodons, mammoths and saber-toothed tigers, thought to have traveled – over many generations – across the ice-covered Bering Strait from Siberia.

First human habitation

Two theories exist regarding the origins of Florida's **first human inhabitants**. It's commonly believed that the earliest arrivals followed the same route as the animals from Siberia, crossing North America and arriving in northern Florida around 10,000 years ago. A minority of anthropologists takes the alternative view that the first Floridians were the result of migration by aboriginal peoples in South and Central America. Either way, the **Paleo** (or "Early") **Indians** in Florida lived hunter-gatherer existences – the spear tips they used are widely found across the central and northern parts of the state.

Around 5000 BC, social patterns changed: settlements became semi-permanent and diet switched from meat to shellfish, snails and mollusks, which were abundant along the rivers. Traveling was done by dugout canoe and, periodically, a community would move to a new site, probably to allow food supplies to replenish themselves. Discarded shells and other rubbish were piled onto the **midden mounds** still commonly seen in the state.

Though pottery began to appear around 2000 BC, not until 1000 BC was there a big change in lifestyle, as indicated by the discovery of **irrigation canals**, patches of land cleared for **cultivation**, and cooking utensils used to prepare grown food. From the time of the Christian era, the erection of **burial mounds** – elaborate tombs of prominent tribes people, often with sacrificed kin and valuable objects also placed inside – became common. These suggest strong religious and trading links across an area stretching from Central America to the North American interior.

Spreading east from the Georgian coastal plain, the **Fort Walton Culture** became prevalent from around 200 AD. This divided society into a rigid caste system and people lived in villages planned around a central plaza. Throughout Florida at this time, approximately 100,000 inhabitants formed several distinct tribal groupings: most notably the **Timucua** across northern Florida, the **Caloosa** around the southwest and Lake Okeechobee, the **Apalachee** in the Panhandle and the **Tequesta** along the southeast coast.

European settlement

After Christopher Columbus located the "New World" in 1492, Europe's great sea powers were increasingly active around the Caribbean. One of them, Spain, had discovered and plundered the treasures of ancient civilizations in Central America, and all were eager to locate other riches across these and neighboring lands. The **first European sighting** of Florida is believed to have been made by John and Sebastian **Cabot** in 1498, when they set eyes on what is now called Cape Florida, on Key Biscayne in Miami.

In 1513, the **first European landing** was made by **Juan Ponce de León**, a Spaniard previously employed as governor of Puerto Rico (a Spanish possession) and who was eager to carve out a niche for himself in the expanding empire. While searching for Bimini, Ponce de León sighted land during *Pascua Florida*, the Spanish Easter "Festival of the Flowers," and named what he saw **La Florida** – or "Land of Flowers." After landing somewhere between the mouth of the St Johns River and present-day St Augustine, Ponce de León sailed on around the Florida Keys, naming them *Los Martires*, for their supposed resemblance to the bones of martyred men, and *Las Tortugas* (now the Dry Tortugas), named for the turtles he saw around them.

Sent to deal with troublesome natives in the Lower Antilles, it was eight years before Ponce de León returned to Florida, this time with a mandate from the Spanish king to **conquer and colonize** the territory. Landing on the southwest coast, probably somewhere between Tampa Bay and Fort Myers, Ponce de León met a hostile reception from the Caloosa Indians and was forced to withdraw, eventually dying from an arrow wound received in the battle.

Rumors of gold hidden in Apalachee, in the north of the region, stimulated several Spanish incursions into Florida, all of which were driven back by the aggression of the indigenes and the ferocity of the terrain and climate. The most successful undertaking – even though it ended in death for its leader – was the **Hernando de Soto expedition**, a thousand-strong band of war-hardened knights and treasure seekers, which landed at Tampa Bay in May 1539. Recent excavations in Tallahassee have located the site of one of de

Soto's camps, where the first Christmas celebration in North America is thought to have taken place before the expedition continued north, later making the first European crossing of the Mississippi River – for a long time marking Florida's western boundary.

Written accounts of the expeditions are a major source of information about the aboriginal life of that period, though anthropology was not a major concern of the Spanish, and the news that Florida did not harbor stunning riches caused interest to wane. Treasure-laden Spanish ships sailing off the Florida coast between the Americas and Europe proved attractive to pirate ships, however, many of them British and French vessels hoisting the Jolly Roger. The Spanish failure to colonize Florida made it a prime base for attacks on their vessels, and a small group of **French Huguenots** landed in 1562, building Fort Caroline on the St Johns River.

The French presence forced the Spanish into a more determined effort at settlement. Already commissioned to explore the Atlantic coast of North America, **Pedro Menéndez de Aviles** was promised the lion's share of whatever profits could be made from Florida. Landing south of the French fort on August 28, 1562, the day of the Spanish Festival of San Augustín, Menéndez named the site **St Augustine** – founding what was to become the longest continuous site of European habitation on the continent. The French were quickly defeated, their leader **Jean Ribault** and his crew massacred after being driven ashore by a hurricane; the site of the killing is still known as *Matanzas*, or "Place of Slaughter."

The first Spanish period (1585–1763)

Only the enthusiasm of Menéndez held Florida together during the early decades of Spanish rule. A few small and insecure settlements were established, usually around **missions** founded by Jesuits or Franciscans bent on Christianizing the Indians. It was a far from harmonious setup: homesick Spanish soldiers frequently mutinied and fought with the Indians, who responded by burning St Augustine to the ground. Menéndez replaced St Augustine's wooden buildings with "tabby" (a cement-like mixture of seashells and limestone) structures with palm-thatched roofs, a style typical of early European Florida. While easily the largest settlement, even St Augustine was a lifeless outpost unless a ship happened to be in port. Despite sinking all his personal finances into the colony, Menéndez never lived to see Florida thrive, and he left in 1571, ordered by the king to help plan the Spanish Armada's attack on Britain.

Fifteen years later, as war raged between the European powers, St Augustine was razed by a naval bombardment led by **Francis Drake**, a sign that the **British** were beginning to establish their colonies along the Atlantic coast north of Florida. Aware that the Indians would hold the balance of power in future colonial power struggles, a string of Spanish missions were built along the Panhandle from 1606; besides seeking to earn the loyalty of the natives, these were intended to provide a defensive shield against attacks from the north. By the 1700s the British were making forays into Florida, ostensibly to capture Indians to sell as slaves. One by one, the missions were destroyed, and only the timely arrival of Spanish reinforcements prevented the fall of St Augustine to the British in 1740.

With the French in Louisiana, the British in Georgia and the Spanish clinging to Florida, the scene was set for a bloody confrontation for control of North America. Eventually, the **1763 Treaty of Paris**, concluding the Seven Years' War in Europe, settled the issue: the British had captured the crucial Spanish possession of Havana, and Spain willingly parted with Florida to get it back.

The British period (1763–83)

Despite their two centuries of occupation, the Spanish failed to make much impression on Florida. It was the British, already developing the colonies further north, who grafted a social infrastructure onto the region. They also divided Florida (then with only the northern section inhabited by whites) into separate colonies: **East Florida** governed from St Augustine, and **West Florida** governed from the growing Panhandle port of **Pensacola**.

By this time, aboriginal Floridians had largely died out through contact with European diseases, to which they had no immunity, and Florida's Indian population was becoming composed of disparate tribes arriving from the west, collectively known as the **Seminoles**. Like the Spanish, the British acknowledged the numerical importance of the Indians and sought good relations with them. In return for goods, the British took Indian land around ports and supply routes, but generally left the Seminoles undisturbed in the inland areas.

Despite attractive grants, few settlers arrived from Britain. Those with money to spare bought Florida land as an investment, never intending to develop or settle on it, and only large holdings – **plantations** growing corn, sugar, rice and other crops – were profitable. Charleston, to the north, dominated sea trade in the area, though St Augustine was still a modestly important settlement and the gathering place of passing British aristocrats and intellectuals. West Florida, on the other hand, was driven by political factionalism and was also often the scene of skirmishes with the Seminoles, who received worse treatment than their counterparts in the east.

Being a new and sparsely populated region, the discontent that fueled the **American War of Independence** in the 1770s barely affected Florida, except for St Augustine, which served as a haven for British Royalists fleeing the war, many of whom moved on to the Bahamas or Jamaica. Pensacola, though, was attacked and briefly occupied in 1781 by the Spanish, who had been promised Florida in return for helping the American rebels defeat the British. As it turned out, diplomacy rather than gunfire signaled the end of British rule in Florida.

The second Spanish period (1783–1821)

The **1783 Treaty of Paris**, with which Britain recognized American independence, not only returned Florida to Spain, but also gave it Louisiana and the prized port of New Orleans. Spanish holdings in North America were now larger than ever, but with Europe in turmoil and the Spanish colonies in Central America agitating for their own independence, the country was ill-equipped to capitalize on them. Moreover, the complexity of Florida's melting pot, comprising the British, smaller numbers of ethnically diverse European settlers, and the increasingly assertive Seminoles (now well established in fertile central Florida, and often joined by Africans escaping slavery further north), made it impossible for a declining colonial power to govern.

As fresh European migration slowed, Spain was forced to **sell land to US citizens**, who bought large tracts, confident that Florida would soon be under Washington's control. Indeed, in gaining Louisiana from France in 1800 (to whom it had been ceded by Spain), and moving the Georgia border south, it was clear the US had Florida in its sights. Fearful of losing the commercial toehold it still retained in Florida, and aligned with Spain through the Napoleonic wars, Britain landed troops at Pensacola in 1814. In response, a US general, **Andrew Jackson**, used the excuse of an Indian uprising in Alabama to march south, killing hundreds of Indians and pursuing them – unlawfully and without official sanction from Washington – into Pensacola, declaring no quarrel with the Spanish but insisting that the British depart. The British duly left, and Jackson and his men withdrew to Mobile (a Floridian town that became part of Alabama as the Americans inched the border eastwards), soon to participate in the Battle of New Orleans, which further strengthened the US position on the Florida border.

The First Seminole War

Jackson's actions in 1814 had triggered the **First Seminole War**. As international tension heightened, Seminole raids (often as a result of baiting on the US side) were commonly used as excuses for US incursions into Florida. In 1818, Jackson finally received what he took to be presidential approval (the "Rhea Letter," thought to have been authorized by President Monroe) to march again into Florida on the pretext of subduing the Seminoles but with the actual intention of taking outright control.

While US public officials were uneasy with the dubious legality of these events, the American public was firmly on Jackson's side. The US government issued an ultimatum to Spain, demanding that either it police Florida effectively or relinquish its ownership. With little alternative, Spain formally **ceded Florida to the US** in 1819, in return for the US assuming the $5 million owed by the Spanish government to American settlers in land grants (a sum which was never repaid). Nonetheless, it took the threat of an invasion of Cuba for the Spanish king to ratify the treaty in 1821; at the same time Andrew Jackson was sworn in as Florida's first American governor.

Territorial Florida

In territorial Florida it was soon evident that the East and West divisions were unworkable, and a site midway between St Augustine and Pensacola was selected as the new administrative center: **Tallahassee**. The Indians living on the fertile soils of the area were rudely dispatched towards the coast – an act of callousness that was to typify relations between the new settlers and the incumbent Native Americans for decades to come.

Under Spanish and British rule, the Seminoles, notwithstanding some feuding between themselves, lived peaceably on the productive lands of northern central Florida. These, however, were precisely the agriculturally rich areas that US settlers coveted. Under the **Treaty of Moultrie Creek** in 1823, most of the Seminole tribes signed a document agreeing to sell their present land and resettle in southwest Florida. Neither side was to honor this agreement: no time limit was imposed on the Seminole exodus, and those who did go found the new land to be unsuitable for farming. The US side, meanwhile, failed to provide promised resettlement funds.

Andrew Jackson spent only three months as territorial governor, though his influence on Florida continued from the White House when he became US president in 1829. In 1830 he approved the **Act of Indian Removal**, decreeing that all Native Americans in the eastern US should be transferred to reservations in the open areas of the Midwest. Two years later, James Gadsden, the newly appointed Indian commissioner, called a meeting of the Seminole tribes at Payne's Landing on the Oklawaha River, near Silver Springs, urging them to cede their land to the US and move west. Amid much acrimony, a few did sign the **Treaty of Payne's Landing**, which provided for their complete removal within three years.

The Second Seminole War (1821–42)

A small number took what monies were offered and resettled in the west, but most Seminoles were determined to stay, and the **Second Seminole War** ensued, with the Indians repeatedly ambushing the US militiamen who had arrived to enforce the law. The natives also ransacked the plantations of white settlers, many of whom fled and never returned. Trained for set-piece battles, the US troops were rarely able to deal effectively with the guerrilla tactics of the Seminoles. It was apparent that the Seminoles were unlikely to be defeated by conventional means and in October 1837 their leader, **Osceola**, was lured to St Augustine with the promise of a truce – only to be arrested and imprisoned, eventually to die in jail. This treachery failed to break the spirit of the Seminoles, though a few continued to give themselves up and leave for the west, while others were captured and sold into slavery.

It became the policy of the US to drive the Seminoles steadily south, away from the fertile lands of central Florida and **into the Everglades**. In the Everglades, the Seminoles linked up with the long-established "Spanish Indians" to raid the Cape Florida lighthouse and destroy the white colony on Indian Key in the Florida Keys. Even after bloodhounds were – controversially – used to track the Indians, it was clear that total US victory would never be achieved. With the Seminoles confined to the Everglades, the US formally **ended the conflict** in 1842, when the Seminoles agreed to stay where they were – an area earlier described by an army surveyor as "fit only for Indian habitation."

The war crippled the Florida economy but stimulated the growth of a number of **new towns** around the army forts. Several of these, such as Fort Brooke (Tampa), Fort Lauderdale, Fort Myers and Fort Pierce, have survived into modern times.

Statehood and secession (1842–61)

The Second Seminole War forestalled the possibility of Florida **attaining statehood** – which would have entitled it to full representation in Washington and to appoint its own administrators. Influence in Florida at this time was split between two camps. On one side were the wealthy slave-owning plantation farmers, concentrated in the "cotton counties" of the central section of the Panhandle, who enjoyed all the traditions of the upper rung of Deep South society. They were eager to make sure that the balance of power in Washington did not shift towards the non-slave-owning "free" states, which would inevitably bring a call for the abolition of slavery. Opposing statehood were the smallholders scattered about the rest of the territory – many of whom were Northerners, already ideologically against slavery and fearing the imposition of federal taxes.

One compromise mooted was a return to a divided Florida, with the West becoming a state while the East remained a territory. Eventually, based on a narrowly agreed **constitution** drawn up in Port St Joseph on the Panhandle coast (on the site of present-day Port St Joe), Florida **became a state** on March 3, 1845. The arrival of statehood coincided with a period of material prosperity: the first railroads began spidering across the Panhandle and central Florida; an organized school system became established; and Florida's 60,000 population was doubled within twenty years.

Nationally, things were less bright. The issue of slavery was to be the catalyst that led the US into civil war, though it was only a part of a great cultural divide between the rural Southern states – to which Florida was linked more through geography than history – and the modern industrial states of the North. As federal pressure intensified for the abolition of slavery, Florida formally **seceded from the Union** on January 10, 1861, aligning itself with the breakaway Confederate States in the run up to the Civil War.

The Civil War (1861–65)

Inevitably, the **Civil War** had a great effect on Florida, although most Floridians conscripted into the Confederate army fought far away from home, and rarely were there more than minor confrontations within the state. The relatively small number of Union sympathizers generally kept a low profile, concentrating on protecting their families. At the start of the war, most of Florida's **coastal forts** were occupied by Union troops as part of the blockade on Confederate shipping. Lacking the strength to mount effective attacks on the forts, those Confederate soldiers who remained in Florida based themselves in the interior and watched for Union troop movements, swiftly destroying whatever bridge, road or railroad lay in the invaders' path – in effect creating a stalemate, which endured throughout the conflict.

Away from the coast, Florida's primary contribution to the war effort was the **provision of food** – chiefly beef and pork reared on the central Florida farms – and the transportation of it across the Panhandle towards Confederate strongholds further west. Union attempts to cut the supply route gave rise to the only major battle fought in the state, the **Battle of Olustee**, just outside Live Oak, in February 1864: 10,000 participated in an engagement that left nearly 3000 dead or injured and both sides claiming victory.

The most celebrated battle from a Floridian viewpoint, however, happened in March 1865 at **Natural Bridge**, when a youthful group of Confederates defeated the technically superior Union troops, preventing the fall of Tallahassee. As events transpired, it was a hollow victory: following the Confederate surrender, the war ended a few months later.

Reconstruction

Following the cessation of hostilities, Florida was caught in an uneasy hiatus. In the years after the war, the defeated states were subject to **Reconstruction**, a rearrangement of their internal affairs determined by, at first, the president, and later by a much harder-line Congress intent on ensuring the Southern states would never return to their old ways.

The Northern ideal of free-labor capitalism was an alien concept in the South, and there were enormous problems. Of paramount concern was the future of the **freed slaves**. With restrictions on their movements lifted, many emancipated slaves wandered the countryside, often unwittingly putting fear into all-white communities that had never before had a black face in their midst. Rubbing salt into the wounds, as far as the Southern whites were concerned, was the occupation of many towns by black Union troops. As a backlash, the white-supremacist **Ku Klux Klan** became active in Tennessee during 1866, and its race-hate, segregationist doctrine soon spread into Florida.

Against this background of uncertainty, Florida's **domestic politics** entered a period of unparalleled chicanery. Suddenly, not only were black men allowed to vote, but there were more black voters than white. The gullibility of the uneducated blacks and the power of their votes proved an irresistible combination to the unscrupulous and power-hungry. Double-dealing and vote-rigging were practiced by diverse factions united only in their desire to restore Florida's statehood and acquire even more power. Following a constitution written and approved in controversial circumstances, Florida was **readmitted to the Union** on July 21, 1868.

Eventually, in Florida as in the other Southern states, an all-white, **conservative Democrat government** emerged. Despite emancipation and the hopes for integration outlined by the Civil Rights Act passed by Congress in 1875, blacks in Florida were still denied many of the rights reasonably regarded as basic. In fact, all that distanced the new administration from the one that led Florida into secession was awareness of the power of the federal government and the need to at least appear to take outside views into account. It was also true that many of the former slave-owners were now the employers of freed blacks, who remained very much under their white masters' control.

A new Florida (1876–1914)

Florida's bonds with its neighboring states became increasingly tenuous in the years following Reconstruction. A fast-growing population began spreading south – part of a gradual diminishing of the importance of the Panhandle, where ties to the Deep South were strongest. Florida's identity was forged by a new **frontier spirit**. Besides smallholding farmers, loggers came to work the abundant forests, and a new breed of wealthy settler started putting down roots, among them Henry DeLand and Henry S. Sanford, who each bought large chunks of central Florida and founded the towns that still bear their names.

As northern speculators invested in Florida, they sought to publicize the region, and a host of articles extolling the virtues of the state's climate as a cure for all ills began to appear in the country's newspapers. These early efforts to promote **Florida as a tourist destination** brought the wintering rich along the new railroads to enjoy the sparkling rivers and springs, and naturalists arrived to explore the unique flora and fauna.

With a fortune made through his partnership in Standard Oil, **Henry Flagler** opened luxury resorts on Florida's northeast coast for his socialite friends, and gradually extended his Florida East Coast Railroad south, giving birth to communities such as **Palm Beach** and making the remote trading post of **Miami** an accessible, expanding town. Flagler's friendly rival, **Henry Plant**, connected *his* railroad to **Tampa**, turning a desolate hamlet into a thriving port city and a major base of cigar manufacturing. The **citrus industry** also revved into top gear: Florida's climate enabled oranges, grapefruits, lemons, and other citrus fruits to be grown during the winter and sold to an eager market in the cooler north. The **cattle farms** went from small to strong, Florida becoming a major supplier of beef to the rest of the US: cows were rounded up with a special wooden whip which made a gunshot-like sound when used – hence the nickname "**cracker**," which was applied to rural settlers.

One group that didn't benefit from the boom years was the blacks. Many were imprisoned for no reason, and found themselves on chain gangs building the new roads and railroads; punishments for refusing to work included severe floggings and hanging by the thumbs. Few whites paid any attention, and those who were in a position to stop the abuses were usually too busy getting rich. There was, however, the founding of **Eatonville**, just north of Orlando, which was the first town in Florida – and possibly the US – to be founded, governed and lived in by black people.

The Spanish-American War

By the 1890s, the US was a large and unified nation itching for a bigger role in the world. As the drive in **Cuba** for independence from Spain gathered momentum, an opportunity to participate in international affairs presented itself. Florida already had long links with Cuba – the capital, Havana, was just ninety miles from Key West, and several thousand Cuban migrants were employed in the Tampa cigar factories. During 1898, tens of thousands of US troops – the Cuban Expeditionary Force – arrived in the state, and the **Spanish-American War** was declared on April 25. As it turned out, the fighting was comparatively minor. Spain withdrew, and on January 1, 1899, Cuba attained independence (and the US a big say in its future). But the war was also the first of several major conflicts that were to prove beneficial to Florida. Many of the soldiers would return as settlers or tourists, and improved railroads and strengthened harbors at the commercially significant ports of Key West, Tampa and Pensacola did much to boost the economy.

The Broward era

The early years of the 1900s were dominated by the progressive policies of **Napoleon Bonaparte Broward**, who was elected state governor in 1905. In a nutshell, Broward championed the small man against corporate interests, particularly the giant land-owning railroad companies. Among Broward's aims were an improved education system, a state-run commission to oversee new railroad construction, a tax on cars to finance road building, better salaries for teachers and the judiciary, a state-run life insurance scheme, and a ban on newspapers – few of which were well disposed towards Broward – knowingly publishing untruths. Broward also enacted the first **conservation laws**, protecting fish, oysters, game and forests; but at the same time, in an attempt to create new land to rival the holdings of the rail barons, he conceived the drainage program that would cause untold damage to the Everglades.

By no means did all of Broward's policies become law, and he departed Tallahassee for a US Senate seat in 1910. Nonetheless, the forward-thinking plans of what became known as the **Broward era** were continued through subsequent administrations – a process that went some way toward bringing a rough-and-ready frontier land into the twentieth century.

World War I and after

World War I continued the tradition of the Spanish-American War by giving Florida an economic shot in the arm, as the military arrived to police the coastline and develop sea-warfare projects. Despite the influx of money and the reforms of the Broward years, there was little happening to improve the lot of Florida's blacks. The Ku Klux Klan was revived in Tallahassee in 1915, and the public outcry that followed the beating to death of a young black on a chain gang was answered only by the introduction of the sweatbox as punishment for prisoners considered unruly.

Typically, most visitors to Florida at this time were more concerned with getting drunk than social justice. The coast so vigilantly protected from advancing Germans during the war was left wide open when **Prohibition** was introduced in 1919; the many secluded inlets became secure landing sites for spirits from the Caribbean. The illicit booze improved the atmosphere in the new resorts of **Miami Beach**, a picture-postcard piece of beach landscaping replacing what had been a barely habitable mangrove island just a few years before. Drink was not the only illegal pleasure pursued in the nightclubs: gambling and prostitution were also rife, and were soon to attract the attention of big-time **gangsters** such as Al Capone, initiating a climate of corruption that was to scar Florida politics for years.

The lightning-paced creation of Miami Beach was no isolated incident. Throughout Florida, and especially in the southeast, new communities appeared almost overnight. Self-proclaimed architectural genius **Addison Mizner** erected the "million dollar cottages" of Palm Beach and began fashioning **Boca Raton** with the same mock-Mediterranean excesses, on the premise: "get the big snob and the little snob will follow;" visionary **George Merrick** plotted the superlative **Coral Gables** – now absorbed by Miami – which became the nation's first pre-planned city and one of the few schemes of the time to age with dignity.

In the rush of prosperity that followed the war, it seemed everyone in America wanted a piece of Florida, and chartered trains brought in thousands of eager buyers. The spending frenzy soon meant that for every genuine offer there were a hundred bogus ones: many people unknowingly bought acres of empty swampland. The period was satirized by the Marx Brothers in their first film, *The Cocoanuts*.

Although millions of dollars technically changed hands each week during the peak year of 1925, little hard cash actually moved. Most deals were paper transactions with buyers paying a small deposit into a bank. The inflation inherent in the system finally went out of control in 1926. With buyers failing to keep up payments, banks went **bust** and were quickly followed by everyone else. A **hurricane** devastated Miami the same year – the city's house-builders never thought to protect the structures against tropical storms – and an even worse hurricane in 1928 caused Lake Okeechobee to burst its banks and flood surrounding communities.

With the Florida land boom well and truly over, the **Wall Street Crash** in 1929 proceeded to make paupers of the millionaires, such as Henry Flagler and Sarasota's **John Ringling**, whose considerable investments had helped to shape the state, and who would later found the **Ringling Brothers Barnum and Bailey Circus**.

The Depression and World War II

At the start of the Thirties, even the major railroads that had stimulated Florida's expansion were in receivership, and the state government only avoided bankruptcy with a constitutional escape clause. Due to the property crash, Florida had had a few extra years to adjust to grinding poverty before the whole country experienced the Depression, and a number of recovery measures – making the state more active in citizens' welfare – pre-empted the national New Deal legislation of President Roosevelt.

No single place was harder hit than **Key West**, which was not only suffering the Depression but hadn't been favored by the property boom either. With a population of 12,000, Key West was an incredible $5 million in debt, and had even lost its link to the mainland when the Overseas Railroad – running across the Florida Keys between Key West and Miami – was destroyed by the 1935 Labor Day hurricane.

What saved Key West, and indeed brought financial stability to all of Florida, was **World War II**. Once again, thousands of troops arrived to guard the coastline – off which there was an immense amount of German U-boat activity – while the flat inland areas made a perfect training venue for pilots. Empty tourist hotels provided ready-made barracks, and the soldiers – and their visiting families – got a taste of Florida that would bring many of them back.

In the immediate **postwar period**, the inability of the state to plan and provide for increased growth was resoundingly apparent, with public services – particularly in the field of education – woefully inadequate. Because of the massive profits being made through illegal gambling, corruption became endemic in public life. State governor **Fuller Warren**, implicated with the Al Capone crime syndicate in 1950, was by no means the only state official suspected of being in cahoots with criminals. A wave of attacks against blacks and Jews in 1951 caused Warren to speak out against the Ku Klux Klan, but the discovery that he himself had once been a Klan member only confirmed the poison flowing through the heart of Florida's political system.

A rare upbeat development was a continued commitment to the conservation measures introduced in the Broward era, with $2 million allocated to buying the land that, in 1947, became the **Everglades National Park**.

The 1950s and 1960s

Cattle, citrus and tourism continued to be the major components of Florida's economy as, in the ten years from 1950, the state soared from being the twentieth to the tenth most populous in the country, home to five million people. While its increased size raised Florida's profile in federal government, the demographic changes within the state – most dramatically the shift from rural life in the north to urban living in the south – went unacknowledged, and **reapportionment** of representation in state government became a critical issue. It was only resolved by the **1968 constitution**, which provided for automatic reapportionment in line with population changes.

The fervent desire for growth and the need to present a wholesome public image prevented the state's conservative-dominated assembly from fighting as hard as their counterparts in the other Southern states against **de-segregation**, following a ruling by the federal Supreme Court on the issue in 1956. Nonetheless, blacks continued to be banned from Miami Beach after dark and from swimming off the Palm Beach coast. In addition, they were subject to segregation in restaurants, buses, hotels, and schools – and barely represented at all in public office. As the **Civil Rights** movement gained strength during the early Sixties, bus boycotts and demonstrations took place in Tallahassee and Daytona Beach, and a march in St Augustine in 1964 resulted in the arrest of the movement's leader, Dr Martin Luther King Jr. The success of the Civil Rights movement in ending legalized discrimination did little to affect the deeply entrenched racist attitudes among much of Florida's longer-established population. Most of the state's blacks still lived and worked in conditions that would have been intolerable to whites: a fact that, in part, accounted for the **Liberty City riot** in August 1968, which was the first of several violent uprisings in Miami's depressed areas.

The ideological shift in Florida's near-neighbor, **Cuba** – declared a socialist state by its leader Fidel Castro in 1961 – came sharply into focus with the 1962 **missile crisis**, which triggered a tense game of cat and mouse between the US and the USSR over Soviet missile bases on the island. After world war was averted, Florida became the base of the US government's covert anti-Castro operations. Many engaged in these activities were among the 300,000 **Cuban immigrants** who had arrived following the Castro-led revolution. The Bay of Pigs fiasco in 1961 proved that there was to be no quick return to the homeland, and while not all of the new arrivals stayed in Florida, many went no further than Miami, where they were to totally change the social character – and eventually the power balance – of the city.

Another factor in Florida's expansion was the basing of the new civilian space administration, **NASA**, at the military long-range missile testing site at Cape Canaveral. The all-out drive to land a man on the moon brought an enormous influx of space industry personnel in the early Sixties – quadrupling the population of the region soon to become known as the **Space Coast**.

The 1970s and 1980s

Florida's tourist boom truly began with the opening of **Walt Disney World** in 1971, which had actually been in development since the mid-1960s. The state government bent over backwards to help the Disney Corporation turn a sizeable slice of central Florida into the biggest theme park complex ever known, even though throughout its construction debate raged over the commercial and ecological effects of such a major undertaking on the rest of the region. Undeterred, smaller businesses rushed to the area, eager to capitalize on the anticipated tourist influx, and the sleepy cow-town of **Orlando** suddenly found itself the hub of one of the state's fastest-growing population centers – soon to become one of the world's best-known holiday destinations.

Around the same time, Florida's other multi-billion dollar business – the **drug trade** – also began taking off. Indeed, Florida's proximity to various Latin and South American countries with large drug production operations perfectly positioned the state as a gateway for drug smuggling and money-laundering; estimates suggest that at least a quarter of the cocaine entering the US still arrives through the state. The inherent violence of the drug trade, along with lax Florida gun laws, helped Miami earn the unflattering designation "murder capital of the US" in the late 1980s, a label it has largely shaken off, though some incidents of **violence against tourists** in the early 1990s resullied its reputation.

Despite the social problems engendered, much money was being made by the US–Latin American trade, both legal and contraband, and poured into the coffers of a burgeoning **banking** industry, which set up shop in gleaming high towers just south of downtown Miami.

Contemporary Florida

Time, plus Disney's success and Miami's rise to prominence, has only helped solidify Florida's place in the **international tourist market**. Directly or indirectly, one in five of the state's twelve million inhabitants now makes a living from tourism. Simultaneously, the general swing from heavy to **hi-tech industries** has resulted in many American corporations forsaking their traditional northern bases in favor of Florida, bringing their white-collar workforces with them.

Increased protection of the state's **natural resources** has been another positive feature of the last decade, especially since a huge Everglades Restoration bill passed Congress in 2000. Impressive amounts of land are under state control and, overall, wildlife is less threatened now than at any time since white settlers first arrived. Most spectacular of all has been the revival of the state's alligator population.

Behind the optimistic facade, however, lie many problems. For starters, much of southern Florida's resurgent landscape – and its dependent animals – could still be destroyed by south Florida's ever-increasing need for land and drinking water. And, **nature** itself often poses a serious threat. In August 1992, **Hurricane Andrew** brought winds of 168mph tearing through the southern regions of Miami, blowing down the radar of the National Hurricane Center in the process and leaving an estimated $30 billion worth of damage in its wake. In the summer of 1999, another storm, **Hurricane Floyd**, came blowing through, leading to the evacuation of millions of residents all along the southeast US coast and causing considerable damage, though fortunately less than feared.

The lack of state spending, due in part to low **taxes** kept that way to stimulate growth, has reduced funding for public services, leaving the apparently booming state with appalling levels of adult illiteracy, infant mortality and crime. Ironically, the switch in Florida's "war of drugs" from capturing dealers to clamping down on **money-laundering** has begun to threaten many of its financial institutions, built on – and it's an open secret – the drug trade. And, a further cause for concern is the broadening **gap** between the relative liberalism of the big cities and the arch-conservatism of the Bible Belt rural areas. While Miami is busy promoting its modernity and multicultural make-up, the

Ku Klux Klan holds picnics in the Panhandle, a children's storybook is removed from a north Florida school's reading list for containing the words "damn" and "bitch," and in Pensacola a doctor is shot dead by anti-abortion activists.

Elián, the election and beyond

As the worn-out millennium wound down, two major news stories whipped through Florida with Hurricane Andrew-like force. The first was the heart-rending story of **Elián González**, the six-year-old Cuban boy whose mother perished at sea in her attempt to bring her son to the US (González was rescued and brought to shore by an American fisherman). Elián's father demanded his son's return to Cuba, and was at odds with the boy's Miami-based, Cuban-American relatives, who felt he should stay. The debate raged for weeks, eventually escalating to a clash between governments. The impasse was finally resolved only when US Attorney General Janet Reno, a Floridian, ordered a SWAT-team-like raid by the Justice Department on the relatives' Little Havana home, in which Elián was spirited away from them at gunpoint and returned to his father.

Just as things appeared to be cooling down in the last weeks of 2000, Florida made international news for another all-too-familiar kind of public mess – **election irregularities**. The political maneuvering whereby **George W. Bush** became the 43rd President of the US cast a shadow over the Sunshine State, which it – as well as the entire country – will doubtless take a long time to live down.

The election itself was a virtual dead heat. **Al Gore**, the Democratic Party's nominee, won the country's **popular vote** by around half a million, but Bush led in the **electoral college** tally – with Florida too close to call. Bush's margin was so narrow – he led by less than 1000 votes out of a total of nearly six million cast – that a recount was called for. And although Bush's **brother**, **Governor Jeb Bush**, officially recused himself during the controversy, his Secretary of State – and Bush's campaign chairman for the state of Florida – **Katherine Harris** didn't. Instead, Ms Harris, in what many feel was a blatant display of partisanship, disallowed a full count, shutting down normal **recount** operations while her man was leading by only a few hundred votes and calling him the winner. Thousands of Florida voters felt disenfranchised, since, in effect, their votes were never counted. Add to that the accusations of illegal police roadblocks keeping **African-American**s – who overwhelmingly supported Al Gore – from even getting to the polls, and it's not hard to fathom the protests and demonstrations that took place throughout the state, especially in Miami and Palm Beach.

Attempts by the **Florida Supreme Court** to overturn the Harris decision were summarily quashed by the right-leaning **US Supreme Court**, who shot the Florida Court down and simply allowed the peremptory decision to stand. As a result of all the irregularities, Florida and many other states have promised to modernize and streamline their voting procedures. But it remains to be seen if the rips and tears in the state's and the nation's political fabric will be stitched up any time soon.

Natural Florida

The biggest surprise for most people in Florida is the abundance of undeveloped, natural areas throughout the state and the extraordinary variety of wildlife and vegetation within them. From a rare hawk that eats only snails to a vine-like fig that strangles other trees, natural Florida possesses plenty that you've probably never seen before, and which – due to drainage, pressures from the agricultural lobby, and the constant need for new housing – may not be on view for very much longer.

Background

Many factors contribute to the unusual diversity of **ecosystems** found in Florida, the most obvious being **latitude**: the north of the state has vegetation common to temperate regions, which is quite distinct from the subtropical flora of the south. Another crucial element is **elevation**: while much of Florida is flat and low-lying, a change of a few inches in elevation drastically affects what grows, due in part to the enormous variety of soils.

The role of fire

Florida has more thunderstorms than any other part of the US, and the resulting lightning frequently ignites **fires**. Many Florida plants have adapted to fire by developing thick bark or the ability to regenerate from stumps. Others, such as cabbage palmetto and sawgrass, protect their growth bud with a sheath of green leaves. Fire is necessary to keep a natural balance of plant species – human attempts to control naturally ignited fires have contributed to the changing composition of Florida's remaining wild lands.

Human intervention was desperately needed in July 1998, when Florida suffered one of its most severe summer droughts. In an instant, devastating wildfires roared out of control in Volusia County, and raged on a head-on course for downtown Daytona and the beaches. Over 140,000 acres of forested lands were destroyed – approximately ten percent of the land in Volusia County. The total loss attributed to the fires was estimated at $379 million. Weary firefighters from across the country came to fight the fires, and due to billowing smoke, a long stretch of I-95 was shut down. For the first time in history, the Daytona International Speedway canceled a major race because of the close proximity of the fires, and turned its massive steel structure into a temporary shelter for displaced residents. The good thing is that there were very few casualties; what's more, the destruction of the underbrush will in fact promote a healthy rejuvenation of the forest floor.

Forests and woodlands

Forests and woodlands aren't the first thing people associate with Florida, but the state has an impressive assortment, ranging from the great tracts of upland pine common in the north to the mixed bag of tropical foliage found in the southern hammocks.

Pine flatwoods

Covering roughly half of Florida, **pine flatwoods** are most widespread on the southeastern coastal plain. These pine species – longleaf, slash and pond – rise tall and straight like telegraph poles. The Spanish once harvested products such as turpentine and rosin from Florida's flatwood pines, a practice that continued during US settlement, and some trees still bear the scars on their trunks. Pine flatwoods are airy and open, with abundant light filtering through the upper canopy of leaves, allowing thickets of shrubs such as saw palmetto, evergreen oaks, gallberry and fetterbrush to grow. **Inhabitants** of the pine flatwoods include white-tailed deer, cotton rats, brown-headed nuthatches, pine warblers, eastern diamondback rattlesnakes and oak toads. Many of these creatures also inhabit other Florida ecosystems, but the **fox squirrel** – a large and noisy character with a rusty tinge to its undercoat – is one of the few mammalian denizens more or less restricted to the pine flatwoods.

Upland pine forests

As the name suggests, **upland pine forests** – or high pinelands – are found on the rolling sand ridges and sandhills of northeastern Florida and the Panhandle, conditions that tend to keep upland pine forests dryer and therefore even more open than the flatwoods. Upland pine forests have a groundcover of wiregrass and an overstory of (mostly) longleaf pine trees, which creates a park-like appearance. Redheaded woodpeckers, eastern bluebirds, Florida mice, pocket gophers (locally called "salamanders," a distortion of "sand mounder") and gopher tortoises (amiable creatures often sharing their burrows with gopher frogs) all make the high pine country their home. The latter two, together with scarab beetles, keep the forest healthy by mixing and aerating the soil. The now-endangered red-cockaded woodpecker is symbolic of old-growth upland pine forest; logging and repression of the natural fire process have contributed to its decline.

Hammocks

Wildlife tends to be more abundant in hardwood **hammocks** than in the associated pine forests and prairies (see below). Hammocks consist of narrow bands of (non-pine) hardwoods growing transitionally between pinelands and lower, wetter vegetation. The make-up of hammocks varies across the state: in the south, they chiefly comprise tropical hardwoods (see "The south Florida rocklands," opposite); in the north, they contain an overstory of oaks, magnolia and beech, with a few smaller plants – red-bellied woodpeckers, red-tailed and red-shouldered hawks and barred owls nest in them, and you can also find eastern wood rats, striped skunks and white-tailed deer.

Scrubs and prairies

Scrub ecosystems once spread to the southern Rocky Mountains and northern Mexico, but climatic changes reduced their distribution and remnant stands are now found only in northern and central Florida. Like the high pines, scrub occurs in dry, hilly areas. The vegetation, which forms an impenetrable mass, consists of varied combinations of drought-adapted evergreen oaks, saw palmetto, Florida rosemary and/or sand pine. The **Florida bonamia**, a morning glory with pale blue funnel-shaped blossoms, is one of the most attractive plants of the scrub, which has more than a dozen plant species officially listed as endangered. Scrub also harbors some unique animals, including the Florida mouse, the Florida scrub lizard, the sand skink and the Florida scrub jay. The **scrub jay** has an unusual social system: pairs nest in co-operation with offspring of previous seasons, who help carry food to their younger siblings. Although not unique to scrub habitat, other inhabitants include black bear, white-tailed deer, bobcats and gopher tortoises.

Some of Florida's inland areas are covered by **prairie**, characterized by love grass, broomsedge and wiregrass – the best examples surround Lake Okeechobee. Settlers destroyed the bison that roamed here some two hundred years ago, but herds are now being reintroduced to some state parks. A more diminutive prairie denizen is the **burrowing owl**: most owls are active at night, but burrowing owls feed during the day and, equally unusually, live in underground dens and bow nervously when approached – earning them the nickname the "howdy owl." Eastern spotted skunks, cotton rats, black vultures, eastern meadowlarks and box turtles are a few other prairie denizens. Nine-banded **armadillos** are also found in prairie habitats and in any non-swampy terrain. Recent invaders from Texas, the armadillos usually forage at night, feeding on insects. Due to poor eyesight, they often fail to notice a human's approach until the last minute, when they will leap up and bound away noisily.

The south Florida rocklands

Elevated areas around the state's southern tip – in the Everglades and along the Florida Keys – support either pines or tropical hardwood hammocks on limestone outcrops collectively known as the **south Florida rocklands**. More jungle-like than the temperate hardwood forests found in northern Florida, the **tropical hardwood hammocks** of the south tend to occur as "tree islands" surrounded by sparser vegetation. Royal palm, pigeon plum, gumbo-limbo (one of the most beautiful of the tropical hammock trees, with a distinctive smooth red bark) and ferns form dense thickets within the hammocks. The **pine forests** of the south Florida rocklands largely consist of scraggly-looking slash pine. Wet prairies or mangroves surround the hammocks and pine forests.

Epiphytic plants

Tropical hammocks contain various forms of **epiphytic plants** – which use other plants for physical support but don't depend on them for nutrients. In southern Florida, epiphytes include orchids, ferns, bromeliads (**Spanish moss** is one of the most widespread bromeliads, hanging from tree branches throughout the state and forming the "canopy roads" in Tallahassee, see "The Panhandle," p.399). Seemingly the most aggressive of epiphytes, **strangler figs**, after germinating in the canopy of trees such as palms, suffocate their host tree. They then send out aerial roots that eventually reach the soil and then tightly enlace the host, preventing growth of the trunk. Finally, the fig produces so many leaves that it chokes out the host's greenery and the host dies leaving only the fig.

Other plants and vertebrates

The south Florida rocklands support over forty plants and a dozen vertebrates found nowhere else in the state. These include the crenulate lead plant, the Key tree cactus, the Florida mastiff bat, the Key deer and the Miami black-headed snake. More common residents include **butterflies and spiders** – the black and yellow yeliconia butterflies, with their long paddle-shaped wings and a distinctive gliding flight pattern, are particularly elegant. Butterflies need to practice careful navigation as hammocks are laced with the foot-long webs of the banana spider. Other wildlife species include sixty types of land snail, green tree frogs, green anoles, cardinals, opossums, raccoons and white-tailed deer. Most of these are native to the southeastern US, but a few West Indian bird species, such as the mangrove cuckoo, gray kingbird and white-crowned pigeon, have colonized the south Florida rocklands.

Swamps and marshes

Although about half have been destroyed due to logging, peat removal, draining, or sewage outflow, swamps are still found all over Florida. Trees growing around swamps include pines, palms, cedars, oaks, black gum, willows and bald cypress. Particularly adapted to aquatic conditions, the bald cypress is ringed by knobby "knees," or modified roots, providing oxygen to the tree, which would otherwise suffocate in the wet soil. Epiphytic orchids and bromeliads are common on cypresses, especially in the southern part of the state. Florida's official state tree, the sabal palm, is another swamp/hammock plant: "heart of palm" is the gourmet's name for the vegetable cut from its insides and used in salads.

Florida swamps also have many species of **insectivorous plants**; sticky pads or liquid-filled funnels trap small insects, which are then digested by the nitrogen-hungry plant. Around the Apalachicola National Forest is the highest diversity of carnivorous plants in the world, among them pitcher plants, bladderworts and sundews. Other swamp-dwellers include dragonflies, snails, clams, fish, bird-voiced tree frogs, limpkins, ibis, wood ducks, beavers, raccoons and Florida panthers.

Wetlands with relatively few trees, **freshwater marshes** range from shallow wet prairies to deep-water cattail marshes. **The Everglades** form Florida's largest marsh, most of which is sawgrass. On higher ground with good soils, sawgrass (actually a sedge) grows densely; at lower elevations it's sparser, and often an algae mat covers the soil between its plants. Water beetles, tiny crustaceans such as amphipods, mosquitoes, crayfish, killifish, sunfish, gar, catfish, bullfrogs, herons, egrets, ibis, water rats, white-tailed deer and Florida panthers can all be found. With luck, you might see a **snail kite**: a brown or black mottled hawk with a very specialized diet, entirely dependent on large apple snails. Snail and snail kite numbers have drastically fallen following the draining of marshes for agriculture and flood control. So far, over sixty percent of the Everglades has been irreversibly drained.

Wetland denizens: alligators and wading birds

Alligators are one of the most widely known inhabitants of Florida's wetlands, lakes and rivers. Look for them on sunny mornings when they bask on logs or banks. If you hear thunder rumbling on a clear day, it may in fact be the bellow of territorial males. Alligators can reach ten feet in length and primarily prey on fish, turtles, birds, crayfish and crabs. Once overhunted for their hides and meat, alligators have made a strong comeback since protection was initiated in 1973; by 1987, Florida had up to half a million of them. They are not usually dangerous – only a handful of fatal attacks have been registered since 1973. Most at risk are people who swim at dusk and small children playing unattended near water. To many creatures, alligators are a life-saver: during the summer, when the marshes dry up, they use their snouts, legs and tails to enlarge existing pools, creating a refuge for themselves and for other aquatic species. In these "gator holes," garfish stack up like cordwood, snakes search for frogs, and otters and anhingas forage for fish.

Wading birds are conspicuous in the wetlands. Egrets, herons and ibis, usually clad in white or grey feathers, stalk frogs, mice and small fish. Turn-of-the-nineteenth-century plume-hunters decimated these birds to make fanciful hats, and during the last few decades habitat destruction has caused a ninety-percent reduction in their numbers. Nonetheless, many are still visible in swamps, marshes and mangroves. Cattle egrets, invaders from South America, are a common sight on pastures, where they forage on insects disturbed by grazing livestock. Pink waders – roseate spoonbills and, to a much lesser extent, flamingoes – can also be found in southern Florida's wetlands.

Lakes, springs and rivers

Florida has almost 8000 freshwater **lakes**. Game fish such as bass and bluegill are common, but the waters are too warm to support trout. Some native fish species are threatened by the introduction of the **walking catfish**, which has a specially adapted gill system enabling it to leave the water and take the fish equivalent of cross-country hikes. A native of India and Burma, the walking catfish was released into southern Florida canals in the early Sixties and within twenty years had "walked" across twenty counties, disturbing the indigenous food chain. A freeze eliminated a number of these exotic fish, though enough remain to cause concern.

Most Florida **springs** release cold fresh water, but some springs are warm and others emit sulfur, chloride or salt-laden waters. Homosassa Springs (see "The West Coast," p.351), for example, have a high chloride content, making them attractive to both freshwater and marine species of fish.

Besides fish, Florida's extensive **river** system supports snails, freshwater mussels and crayfish. Southern river-dwellers also include the lovable **manatee**, or sea cow, which inhabits bays and shallow coastal waters. The only totally aquatic herbivorous mammal, manatees sometimes weigh almost a ton but only eat aquatic plants. Unable to tolerate cold conditions, manatees are partial to the warm water discharged by power plants, taking some of them as far north as North Carolina. In Florida during the winter, the large springs at Crystal River (see "The West Coast," p.352) attract manatees, some of which have become tame enough to allow divers to scratch their bellies. Although they have few natural enemies, manatees are on the decline, often due to powerboat propellers injuring their backs or heads when they feed at the surface.

The coast

There's a lot more than sunbathing taking place around Florida's **coast**. The sandy beaches provide a habitat for many species, not least sea turtles. Where there isn't sand, you'll find the fascinating mangrove forests, or wildlife-filled salt marshes and estuaries. Off-shore, coral reefs provide yet another exotic ecosystem, and one of the more pleasurable to explore by snorkeling or diving.

Sandy beaches

Waves bring many interesting creatures onto Florida's **sandy beaches**, such as sponges, horseshoe crabs and the occasional sea horse. Florida's **shells** are justly famous – fig shells, moon snails, conches, whelks, olive shells, red and orange scallops, murex, cockles, pen and turban shells are a few of the many varieties. As you beachcomb, beware of stepping barefoot on purplish fragments of **man-of-war** tentacles: these jellyfish have no means of locomotion, and their floating, sail-like bodies often cause them to be washed ashore – their tentacles, which sometimes reach to sixty feet in length, can deliver a painful sting. More innocuous beach inhabitants include wintering birds such as black-bellied plovers and sanderlings, and nesting black skimmers.

Of the seven species of **sea turtle**, five nest on Florida's sandy beaches: green, loggerhead, leatherback, hawksbill and olive ridley. From February to August, the female turtles haul out at night, excavate a beachside hole and deposit a hundred-plus eggs. Not many of these will survive to adulthood: raccoons eat a lot of the eggs, and hatchlings are liable to be crushed by vehicles on the coastal highways when they become disorientated by their lights. Programs to hatch the eggs artificially have helped offset some of the losses. The best time to view sea turtles is during June – peak nesting time – with one of the park-ranger-led walks offered along the southern portion of the northeast coast (see Chapter Four, "The Northeast Coast," p.216).

Mangroves

Found in brackish waters around the Florida Keys and the southwest coast, Florida has three species of **mangrove**. Unlike most plants, mangroves bear live young: the "seeds," or propagules, germinate while still on the tree; after dropping from the parent, the young propagule floats for weeks or months until it washes up on a suitable site, where its sprouted condition allows it to put out roots rapidly. Like bald cypress, mangroves have difficulty extracting oxygen from their muddy environs and solve this problem with extensive aerial roots, which either dangle finger-like from branches or twist outwards from the lower trunk. Various fish species, such as the mangrove snapper, depend on mangroves as a nursery; other **mangrove inhabitants** include frogs, crocodiles, brown pelicans, wood storks, roseate spoonbills, river otters, mink and raccoons.

Salt marshes and estuaries

Like the mangrove ecosystem, the **salt marsh and estuary** habitat provides a nursery for many fish species, which in turn fodder larger fish, herons, egrets and the occasional dolphin. **Crocodiles**, with narrower and more pointed snouts than alligators, are seldom sighted, and confined to salt water at the state's southernmost tip. In a few southern Florida salt marshes, you might find a **great white heron**, a rare and handsome form of the more common great blue heron. Around Florida Bay, great white herons have learned to beg for fish from local residents, each of these massive birds "working" a particular neighborhood – striding from household to household demanding fish by rattling window blinds with their bills or issuing guttural croaks. A less appealing salt marsh denizen is the **mosquito**: unfortunately, the more damaging methods of mosquito control, such as impounding salt water or spraying DDT, have inflicted extensive harm on the fragile salt marshes and estuaries.

The coral reef

A long band of living **coral reef** frames Florida's southeastern corner. Living coral comes in many colors: star coral is green, elkhorn coral orange, and brain coral red. Each piece of coral is actually a colony of hundreds or thousands of small, soft animals called **polyps**, related to sea anemones and jellyfish. The polyps secrete limestone to form their hard outer skeletons, and at night extend their feathery tentacles to filter seawater for microscopic food. The filtering process, however, provides only a fraction of the coral's nutrition – most is produced via the photosynthesis of algae that live within the polyps' cells. In recent years, influxes of warmer water, possibly associated with global warming, have killed off large numbers of the algae cells. The half-starved polyp then often succumbs to disease, a phenomenon known as "bleaching." Although this has been observed throughout the Pacific, the damage in Florida has so far been moderate; the impact of the tourist industry on the reef has been more pronounced, though reef destruction for souvenirs is now banned.

Coral reefs are home to a kaleidoscopic variety of brightly colored fish – beau gregories, porkfish, parrot fish, blennies, grunts and wrasses – which swirl in dazzling schools or lurk between coral crevices. The **damselfish** is the farmer of the reef: after destroying a polyp patch, it feeds on the resultant algae growth, fiercely defending it from other fish. Sponges, feather-duster worms, sea fans, crabs, spiny lobsters, sea urchins and conches are among the thousands of other creatures resident in the coral reef.

Florida on film

The Silver Screen and the Sunshine State have one vital thing in common: escapism. Both on film and off, Florida has always represented the ultimate getaway. For nineteenth-century homesteaders, Cuban refugees, New York retirees, libido-laden college kids, or criminals on the lam, the state has always beckoned as some kind of paradise. Hollywood has also used Florida as an exotic backdrop for everything from light-hearted vacation flicks to black-hearted crime yarns, and the state has made the most of its movie-tinted charms. Henry Levin's phenomenally successful teen flick *Where the Boys Are* (1960), for instance, not only spawned a cinematic sub-genre, but also made Fort Lauderdale the country's top Spring Break resort. And Miami's rejuvenation in the Eighties can be attributed at least in part to the glamour imparted by filmmaker Michael Mann's TV series, *Miami Vice*.

To immerse yourself in Florida's cinematic history, where images of palm trees, beaches and luxury hotels predominate, is to take a virtual vacation. And though there are plenty of mediocre Florida flicks (most of them sun-addled Spring Break romps or Elvis Presley showcases), there are many that convey the unique and varied qualities of the state. Here are some of the best.

Drama and history

Any Given Sunday (Oliver Stone, 1999). Overblown football saga where aging old-school coach Al Pacino wrestles with cut-throat corporate owner Cameron Diaz for control of the fictional Miami Sharks, all while trying win the big game with a cocky rookie quarterback – ably played by Jamie Foxx.

Beneath the 12 Mile Reef (Robert Webb, 1953). In this beautiful travelogue, Greek sponge fishermen from Tarpon Springs venture south to fish the "Glades" and tangle with the Anglo "Conchs" of Key West. Robert Wagner plays a young Greek Romeo named Adonis, who dares to dive the "12 mile reef" for his sponge-worthy Juliet.

Distant Drums (Raoul Walsh, 1951). One of many movies that have focused on Florida's Seminole Indians (the first was made by Vitagraph in 1906), *Distant Drums*, set in the midst of the Seminole Wars in 1840, stars Gary Cooper as a legendary Indian fighter

who finds himself and his men trapped in the Everglades. Cooper and his band encounter snakes, alligators, and hordes of Seminole braves as they attempt to reach dry land.

Reap the Wild Wind (Cecil B. De Mille, 1942). A stirring account of skullduggery in the Florida Keys of the 1840s. Spunky Paulette Goddard vacillates between sea salt John Wayne and landlubber Ray Milland while trying to outwit pirates, gangs and a giant squid off the deadly coral reefs.

Ruby in Paradise (Victor Nunez, 1993). Ashley Judd plays Ruby, who leaves her home in the Tennessee mountains and hitches a ride south to taste life in the Florida Panhandle. Settling in Panama City, Ruby finds work in a tourist shop selling tacky souvenirs. She fends off the boss's son and finds herself along the way. The film was sensitively directed by Florida's own Victor Nunez, a true regional independent who has been making movies in northern Florida since 1970.

Salesman (The Maysles Brothers, 1968). The second half of this brilliant and moving documentary follows four Bible Salesmen to Opa-Locka on the outskirts of Miami. It's not a tale of beaches and luxury hotels, but rather low-rent apartments, cheap motels and the quiet desperation of four men trying to sell overpriced illustrated Bibles door to door.

Seminole (Budd Boetticher, 1953). Set five years before *Distant Drums* (see opposite) and far more sympathetic to the Seminoles' plight, Boetticher's Western stars Rock Hudson as a US dragoon and Anthony Quinn as his half-breed childhood friend who has become the Seminole chief Osceola. Attempting to claim even the swamps of Florida for white settlers, a power-hungry general sends a platoon into the Everglades to flush out the Seminole and drive them out west.

★ **Stranger than Paradise** (Jim Jarmusch, 1984). Jarmusch's austere indie masterpiece about two laconic hipsters and their Hungarian cousin. The trio travels from snow-bound Ohio to a lifeless, out-of-season Florida. The movie's Florida

scenes consist of a cheap motel room and a deserted stretch of beach, proving the main characters' theory that everywhere starts to look the same after a while.

★ **Ulee's Gold** (Victor Nunez, 1997). Twenty-two years after *92 in the Shade*, Peter Fonda gave the best performance of his career as Florida beekeeper Ulee, a stoical Vietnam vet raising his granddaughters while his son is in jail. Florida auteur Nunez (*Ruby in Paradise*) knows and captures northern Florida better than any filmmaker, and despite a strained plot about a couple of ne'er-do-wells and a stash of money, this meditative, measured movie is a triumph.

★ **The Yearling** (Clarence Brown, 1946). A Technicolor classic about a family struggling to eke out a living in the scrub country of northern Florida (in the vicinity of Lake George and Volusia) in 1878. Oscar-winner Claude Jarman Jr plays the son of Gregory Peck and Jane Wyman who adopts a mighty troublesome fawn. The movie was shot on location and based on Florida scribe Marjorie Kinnan Rawlings' Pulitzer Prize-winning novel of the same name.

Crime stories

★ **Aileen Wuornos: The Selling of a Serial Killer** (Nick Broomfield, 1993). British documentarian Broomfield, in his inimitably fearless, in-your-face style, stumbles into a swamp of avarice and exploitation in his search for the true story of Aileen Wuornos, a woman convicted of murdering seven men on a Florida Interstate. That America's first female serial killer comes across as more sympathetic than most of the people around her makes this portrait of backwoods Florida all the more chilling.

Black Sunday (John Frankenheimer, 1976). Palestinian terrorists, with the aid of disgruntled Vietnam vet Bruce

Dern, plan to wipe out 80,000 football fans, including President Jimmy Carter, in the Orange Bowl on Superbowl Sunday. Though the first half of the movie unfolds in Beirut and LA, the heart-stopping climax results in some fine aerial views of Miami.

Blood and Wine (Bob Rafelson, 1997). Jack Nicholson plays a dodgy Miami wine dealer with access to the cellars of southern Florida's rich and famous. He enlists a wheezy expat safe-breaker (Michael Caine), and a feisty Cuban nanny (Jennifer Lopez) in his scheme to snag a million-dollar necklace. When the jewels end up in the hands of his jilted wife (Judy

Davis) and perpetually pissed-off stepson (Stephen Dorff) the action heads south to the Florida Keys.

Body Heat (Lawrence Kasdan, 1981). Filmed just south of Palm Beach in the small coastal town of Lake Worth, Kasdan's directorial debut makes the most of the sweaty potential of a southern Florida heatwave. Shady lawyer William Hurt falls for the charms of wealthy Kathleen Turner and plans to bump off her husband for the inheritance.

Illtown (Nick Gomez, 1995). Depending on whom you ask, Nick Gomez's movie has been described as stylish, strange and ambitious or a pretentious mess. This mystical indie film features Tony Danza as a gay mob boss, and a gaggle of familiar indie stars (Michael Rapaport, Adam Trese, Lili Taylor and Kevin Corrigan) as an unlikely bunch of Miami drug dealers.

Key Largo (John Huston, 1948). Though shot entirely on Hollywood sets, Huston's tense crime melodrama about an army veteran (Humphrey Bogart) and a mob boss (Edward G. Robinson) barricaded in a Key Largo hotel during a major hurricane has the credible feel of a muggy summer in the Florida Keys.

Miami Blues (George Armitage, 1990). Adapted from Charles Willeford's fiction, this quirky crime story about a home-loving psychopath (Alec Baldwin), the naive hooker he shacks up with (Jennifer Jason Leigh), and the burnt-out homicide detective who's on their trail (Fred Ward), is set in a seedy back-street Miami that glitters with terrific characters, gritty performances, and delicious offbeat details.

Night Moves (Arthur Penn, 1975). In one of the great metaphysical thrillers of the post-Watergate Seventies, Gene Hackman plays a weary LA private eye with marital problems who is hired to track down a young and underdressed Melanie Griffith in the Florida Keys.

Out of Sight (Steven Soderbergh, 1998). Flip-flopping between past and present and between a jazzy, sun-drenched Florida and a snow-peppered Detroit, Soderbergh's movie is a hugely satisfying adaptation of Elmore Leonard's novel. The action is set in motion when George Clooney's urbane bank-robber tunnels out of a Pensacola penitentiary and into the life of Federal Marshal Jennifer Lopez.

Palmetto (Volker Schlondorff, 1998). Woody Harrelson returns from jail to the Sarasota beach town of Palmetto and becomes Florida's number one patsy when a bleach-blonde Elisabeth Shue walks into his life and proposes a little fake kidnapping. Perfectly exploiting Florida's sultry charms, *Palmetto* is a somewhat clichéd neo-noir, but has some satisfying twists and turns.

Scarface (Brian De Palma, 1983). Small-time Cuban thug Tony Montana arrives in Miami during the 1980 Mariel boatlift and murders, bullies and snorts his way to the top of his profession, becoming Miami's most powerful drug lord. One of the great Florida movies, De Palma's seductive and shocking paean to excess and the perversion of the American Dream stars Al Pacino in a legendary, go-for-broke performance.

Tony Rome (Gordon Douglas, 1967). Wise-cracking, hard-living private eye Frank Sinatra tangles with pushers, strippers, gold diggers and self-made millionaires on the wild side of Miami (the town his love interest Jill St John calls "Twenty miles of beach looking for a city"). The movie is a run-of-the-mill detective yarn, but Frank was entertaining enough to warrant a sequel: *Lady in Cement*.

Wild Things (John McNaughton, 1997). A cartoonish, noir fantasy about handsome high-school counselors, lubricious schoolgirls, and wealthy widows in a well-heeled community in the Everglades. Beautifully shot and played to the hilt by Matt Dillon, Kevin Bacon, Denise Richards and Neve Campbell, though it fails to live up to the promise of its campy setup.

Comic capers

92 in the Shade (Thomas McGuane, 1975). A nutty, laid-back comedy about rival fishing guides in Key West, starring a potpourri of Hollywood's greatest oddballs: Peter Fonda, Harry Dean Stanton, Warren Oates, Burgess Meredith and William Hickey. Ripe with local color but somewhat lacking in affect, the movie was based on Thomas McGuane's acclaimed novel of the same name.

Ace Ventura, Pet Detective (Tom Shadyac, 1994). The movie that launched Jim Carrey's thousand faces. Carrey stars as a bequiffed investigator on a quest to recover Snowflake, the Miami Dolphins' kidnapped mascot, on the eve of the Superbowl. The Miami Dolphins and their quarterback Dan Marino appear as themselves.

The Bellboy (Jerry Lewis, 1960). This movie was shot almost entirely within Miami Beach's ultra-kitsch pleasure palace *The Fontainebleau* (the same hotel where James Bond sunbathes at the beginning of 1964's *Goldfinger*). Jerry Lewis, in his debut as writer-director, plays Stanley, the bellhop from hell, and cameos as vacationing movie star "Jerry Lewis" in one of the most site-specific movies ever made.

The Birdcage (Mike Nichols, 1996). Nichols' Miami remake of *La Cage Aux Folles* makes playful use of South Beach's burgeoning gay scene, portraying the rejuvenated Art Deco playground as a bright paradise of pecs, thongs and drag queens. Impresario Armand (Robin Williams) and reigning Birdcage diva Albert (Nathan Lane) are happily cohabiting in kitsch heaven until the day Armand's son brings his ultra-conservative future in-laws to dinner.

The Cocoanuts (Joseph Santley & Robert Florey, 1929). Set during Florida's real-estate boom, the Marx Brothers' first film stars Groucho as an impecunious hotel proprietor attempting to keep his business afloat by auctioning off land (with the usual interference from Chico and Harpo) in Cocoanut Grove, "the Palm Beach of tomorrow." Groucho expounds on Florida's climate while standing in what is really a sand-filled studio lot.

The Heartbreak Kid (Elaine May, 1972). An underrated comic masterpiece written by Neil Simon, in which Charles Grodin marries a nice Jewish girl, and then, on the honeymoon drive down to Florida, starts to regret it. His doubts are compounded when goddess Cybill Shepherd starts flirting with him on the beach while his sunburnt bride lies in bed.

A Hole in the Head (Frank Capra, 1959). Frank Sinatra plays an irresponsible Miami Beach hotel owner who has dreams of striking it rich by turning South Beach into "Disneyland." The breezy opening titles in this musical comedy are pulled on airborne banners across the Miami Beach skyline.

Miami Rhapsody (David Frankel, 1995). Sarah Jessica Parker (kvetching like a female Woody Allen) weighs commitment against the marital dissatisfaction and compulsive infidelity of her extended family in an otherwise picture-perfect, upscale Miami: "I guess I look at marriage the same way I look at Miami: it's hot and it's stormy, and it's occasionally a little dangerous...but if it's really so awful why is there still so much traffic?"

Moon Over Miami (Walter Lang, 1941). Gold-digging, Texas-hamburger-stand waitress Betty Grable takes her sister and aunt to Miami, "where rich men are as plentiful as grapefruit, and millionaires hang from every palm tree." Grable has little trouble snagging herself a couple of ripe ones in this colorful, sappy musical comedy (the theme song "Oh Me, Oh Mi...ami!" sets the tone). On-location shooting took place in Winter Haven and Ocala, a few hundred miles north of Miami.

The Palm Beach Story (Preston Sturges, 1942). In this madcap masterpiece, Claudette Colbert takes a train from Penn Station to Palm Beach ("the best place to get a divorce," a cabbie tells her) to free herself from her penniless dreamer of a husband and find herself a good millionaire to marry.

Porky's (Bob Clark, 1981). The *Citizen Kane* of randy teen movies, the notorious (and Canadian) *Porky's* is set in fictional Angel Beach near Fort Lauderdale in the mid-Fifties. A group of high-school guys with only one thing on their minds venture into Florida's backcountry in the hopes of getting laid at "Porky's," a licentious redneck bar.

⭐ **Some Like it Hot** (Billy Wilder, 1959). Wilder's classic

farce starts in 1929 in Chicago. Jazz musicians Tony Curtis and Jack Lemmon escape retribution for witnessing the St Valentine's Day massacre by disguising themselves as women and joining an all-girl jazz band on a train to Miami. Though *Some Like it Hot* could be a candidate for the best movie ever set in Miami, it was actually shot at the *Hotel del Coronado* in San Diego.

⭐ **There's Something About Mary** (The Farrelly Brothers, 1998). Years after a heinous pre-prom disaster (involving an unruly zipper), Rhode Island geek Ben Stiller tracks down Mary, the eponymous object of his affection, to her new home in Miami. Once there he finds he's not the only one suffering from obsessive tendencies. The Farrelly boys have created a hysterical, gross-out masterpiece.

Fantasy lands

Cocoon (Ron Howard, 1985). Even extra-terrestrials vacation in Florida. This sentimental, Spielbergesque fantasy centers around residents of a Florida retirement community who discover a local swimming pool with alien powers of rejuvenation. Nearly half a century after he danced with Betty Grable in *Moon Over Miami*, Don Ameche won a Best Supporting Actor Oscar for this film.

Dumbo (Ben Sharpsteen, 1941). In the opening sequence of this Disney animated classic there is a wonderful stork's-eye view of the entire state of Florida, where the circus has hunkered down for the winter. Though the show eventually goes on the road, this eyeful of Florida seems prescient considering Disney's role in the state some quarter of a century later.

Revenge of the Creature (Jack Arnold, 1955). Transported comatose

from the Upper Amazon, the Creature from the Black Lagoon is brought to Marineland's oceanarium to create the "greatest scientific stir since the explosion of the Atomic Bomb." He creates an even bigger stir when he cuts loose and heads for the beach, crashing a swing party at a seafront oyster house.

The Truman Show (Peter Weir, 1998). The picture-perfect, picket-fence community of Seahaven that Jim Carrey's Truman Burbank calls home turns out to be nothing more than a giant television studio, where Truman is watched every minute of the day in the world's longest-running soap opera. The false paradise of Seahaven is actually the real, but equally artificial, Florida Gulf Coast town of Seaside, a planned vacation community (built in 1981) that looks like it's stuck in the Fifties.

Books

Florida's perennial state of social and political flux has always promised rich material for historians and journalists eager to pin the place down. Rarely have they managed this, though the picture of the region's unpredictable evolution that emerges can make for compulsive reading. Many established fiction writers spend their winters in Florida, but few have convincingly portrayed its characters, climate and scenery. Those who have succeeded, however, have produced some of the most remarkable and gripping literature to emerge from any part of the US.

History

Edward N. Akin, *Flagler: Rockefeller Partner & Florida Baron.* Solid biography of the man whose Standard Oil fortune helped build Florida's first hotels and railroads.

Charles R. Ewen and John H. Hann, *Hernando de Soto Among the Apalachee.* A history and description of the archeological site (located in downtown Tallahassee) believed to be a campsite used by Hernando de Soto in the sixteenth century.

John T. Foster and Sarah Whitmer Foster, *Beechers, Stowes and Yankee Strangers.* An entertaining and relatively brief account about a group of Yankee reformers who lived in Florida at the end of the Civil War – including Harriet Beecher Stowe, author of *Uncle Tom's Cabin* – and their designs on a postwar Florida.

John J. Guthrie Jr, Philip Charels Lucas and Gary Monroe, *Cassadaga: The South's Oldest Spiritual Community.* A "metaphysical mecca," this book examines the history, people and religious beliefs of Cassadaga, a small town between Orlando and Daytona Beach, established more than a hundred years ago on the principle of continuous life.

★ **Carl Hiaasen,** *Team Rodent.* A native of Florida, Hiaasen has been a firsthand witness to Disney's domination of Orlando, and this book is a scathing attack on the entertainment conglomerate, exposing Disney for what Hiaasen thinks it is: evil. As he says in this book, "Disney is so good at being good that it manifests an evil; so uniformly and courteous, so dependably clean and conscientious, so unfailingly entertaining that it's unreal, and therefore is an agent of pure wickedness." Like Hiaasen's fiction work (see p.473), the prose is a mix of sharp wit, informed research and a lot of humor.

Stetson Kennedy, *The Klan Unmasked.* A riveting history of the Klan's activity in the post-World War II era, including specific references to Florida.

Robert Kerstein, *Politics and Growth in Twentieth Century Tampa.* A history of the politics and growth in Tampa from the coming of the railroads and cigar industry to the mid-1990s.

Howard Kleinberg, *The Way We Were.* Oversized overview of Miami's history: colorful archival photos and text by a former editor-in-chief of the city's dominant newspaper, *The Miami News.*

Stuart B. McIver, *Dreamers, Schemers and Scalawags*. An intriguing mix of biography and storytelling that tells Florida's history through its mobsters and millionaires. This is the first volume in a continuing series.

Jerald T. Milanich, *Florida's Indians, from Ancient Times to the Present*. A comprehensive history spanning 12,000 years of Indian life in Florida.

Gary R. Mormino and George E. Pozzetta, *The Immigrant World of Ybor City*. Flavorful accounts of the Cuban, Italian and Spanish immigrants who built their lives around Ybor City's cigar industry at the turn of the nineteenth century.

Helen Muir, *Miami, USA*. An insider's account of how Miami's first developers gave the place shape during the land boom of the Twenties.

John Rothchild, *Up for Grabs: A Trip Through Time and Space in the Sunshine State*. An irreverent look at Florida's checkered career as a vacation spa, tourist trap and haven for scheming ne'er-do-wells.

Charlton W. Tebeau, *A History of Florida*. The definitive academic tome, but not for casual reading.

Victor Andres Triay, *Fleeing Castro*. An emotional account of the plight of Cuba's children during the missile crisis. With their parents unable to obtain visas, 14,048 children were smuggled from the island; many never saw their families again.

Garcilaso de la Vega, *The Florida of the Inca*. Comprehensive account of the sixteenth-century expedition led by Hernando de Soto through Florida's prairies, swamps and aboriginal settlements. Extremely turgid in parts, but overall an excellent insight into the period.

David C. Weeks, *Ringling*. An in-depth work chronicling the time spent in Florida by circus guru John Ringling.

Patsy West, *The Enduring Seminoles*. A history of Florida's Seminole Indians, who, by embracing tourism, found a means to keep their vibrant cultural identity alive.

Lawrence E. Will, *Swamp to Sugarbowl: Pioneer Days in Belle Glade*. A "cracker" account of early times in the state, written in first-person redneck vernacular. Variously oafish and offensive – but never dull.

Natural history

Mark Derr, *Some Kind of Paradise*. A cautionary history of Florida's penchant to mishandle its environmental assets, from spongers off the reefs to Miami's ruthless hotel contractors.

★ **Marjory Stoneman Douglas**, *The Everglades: River of Grass*. Concerned conservationist literature by one of the state's most respected historians, describing the nature and beauty of the Everglades from their beginnings. A superb work that contributed to the founding of the Everglades National Park. Douglas passed away in 1998 at the age of 108.

Jon L. Dunn and Eirik A.T. Blom, *Field Guide to the Birds of North America, (2nd ed)*. The best country-wide guide, with plenty on Florida, and excellent illustrations throughout.

Harold R. Holt, *Lane's "A Birder's Guide to Florida."* Detailed accounts of when and where to find Florida's birds, including maps and seasonal charts. Aimed at the expert but excellent value for the novice bird-watcher.

David McCally, *The Everglades: An Environmental History*. For both general readers and environmentalists, this book examines the formation, development and history of the Everglades – believed to be the most endangered ecosystem in North America.

Joe Schafer and George Tanner, *Landscaping for Florida's Wildlife*. Step-by-step advice on how to replicate a sliver of Florida's wildlife in your own garden.

Glen Simmons with Laura Ogden, *Gladesmen*. Entertaining accounts of the "swamp rats:" rugged men and women who made a living wrestling alligators and trekking the "Glades."

Travel impressions

★ **William Bartram**, *Travels*. The lively diary of an eighteenth-century naturalist rambling through the Deep South and on into Florida during the period of British rule. Outstanding accounts of the indigenous people and all kinds of wildlife.

Edna Buchanan, *The Corpse Had a Familiar Face*. Sometimes sharp, often sensationalist account of the author's years spent pounding the crime beat for the *Miami Herald* – five thousand corpses and gore galore. The subsequent *Vice* is more of the same.

Joan Didion, *Miami*. A riveting though ultimately unsatisfying voyage around the impenetrably complex and wildly passionate *el exilio* politics of Cuban Miami.

Lynn Geldof, *Cubans*. Passionate and rambling interviews with Cubans in Cuba and Miami, which confirm the tight bond between them.

Henry James, *The American Scene*. Interesting waffle from the celebrated novelist, including written portraits of St Augustine and Palm Beach as they thronged with wintering socialites at the turn of the nineteenth century.

Norman Mailer, *Miami and the Siege of Chicago*. A rabid study of the American political conventions of 1968, the first part frothing over the Republican Party's shenanigans at Miami Beach when Nixon beat Reagan for the presidential ticket.

Kevin McCarthy, *Alligator Tales*. This intriguing collection of both actual and slightly overblown encounters with alligators is illustrated with the photographs of John Moran.

Roxanne Pulitzer, *The Prize Pulitzer: The Scandal that Rocked Palm Beach*. A small-town girl who married into the jet-set lifestyle of Palm Beach describes the mud-slinging in Florida's most moneyed community when she seeks a divorce.

Alexander Stuart, *Life on Mars*. "Paradise with a lobotomy" is how a friend of the author described Florida. This is an often amusing series of snapshots of the empty lives led by both the beautiful people of South Beach and the redneck "white trash" of up-state.

John Williams, *Into the Badlands: A Journey through the American Dream*. The author's trek across the US to interview the country's best crime writers begins in Miami, "the city that coke built," its compelling strangeness all too briefly reveled in.

Architecture

Barbara Baer Capitman, *Deco Delights*. A tour of Miami Beach's Art Deco buildings by the woman who championed their preservation, with definitive photography.

Laura Cerwinske, *Miami: Hot & Cool*. Coffee-table tome with text on high-style south Florida living and glowing, colour pics of Miami's beautiful homes and gardens. By the same author, *Tropical Deco: The Architecture & Design of Old Miami Beach* delivers a wealth of architectural detail.

Donald W. Curl, *Mizner's Florida: American Resort Architecture*. An assessment of the life, career and designs of Addison Mizner, the self-taught architect responsible for the "Bastard Spanish Moorish Romanesque Renaissance Bull Market Damn the Expense Style" structures of Palm Beach and Boca Raton.

Hap Hatton, *Tropical Splendor: An Architectural History of Florida*. A readable, informative and effectively illustrated account of the wild, weird and wonderful buildings that have graced and disgraced the state over the years.

Nicholas N. Patricios, *Building Marvelous Miami*. The architectural development of Florida's favorite city documented by 250 photos.

Art and photography

Todd Bertolaet, *Crescent Rivers*. Ansel Adamsesque photos of the dark, blackwater rivers that wind through Florida's Big Bend.

Anne Jeffrey and Aletta Drever, *Art Lovers Guide to Florida*. A comprehensive guidebook featuring 86 of the most dynamic and exciting art groupings in Florida.

Gary Monroe, *Life in South Beach*. A slim volume of monochrome photos showing Miami Beach's South Beach before the restoration of the Art Deco district and the arrival of globetrotting trendies.

Tom Shroder and John Barry, *Seeing the Light – Wilderness and Salvation: A Photographer's Tale*. An attractive book describing the story of photographer Clyde Butcher's long connection with the Everglades and showcasing his wonderful pictures of the area.

Woody Walters, *Visions of Florida*. Black-and-white photos, but ones which still convey the richness and beauty of Florida's terrain, from misty mornings in Tallahassee to shocks of lightning over the Everglades.

William Weber, *Florida Nature Photography*. A glossy, pictorial look at Florida's many state parks, recreation areas and nature preserves.

Millard Wells, *Florida Key Impressions*. An illustrated journal describing a journey through the Florida Keys, highlighted by the author's original watercolor paintings.

Fiction

Pat Booth, *Miami*. Miami's South Beach is used as a backdrop to a pot-boiling tale of seduction and desire.

Liza Cody, *Backhand*. London's finest female private investigator, Anna Lee, follows the clues from Kensington to the West Coast of Florida – highly entertaining.

Harry Crews, *Florida Frenzy*. A collection of tales relating macho outdoor pursuits like 'gator poaching and cockfighting. "[It] will hit you right between the eyes," says the *Chicago Tribune*.

Kate Di Camillo, *Because of Winn-Dixie*. When a stray dog appears in the midst of the produce section of the Winn-Dixie grocery store, it leads 10-year-old India Opal Buloni from one new friend to the next in a small Florida town. The stories India gathers in this award-winning children's book help her to piece together a new definition of family.

Tim Dorsey, *Florida Roadkill*. This dark, and at times violent, first novel memorably – and often comically – recounts the lives of Florida's criminal lowlife.

Edward Falco, *Winter in Florida*. Flawed but compulsive story of a cosseted New York boy seeking thrills on a central Florida horse farm.

Connie May Fowler, *Before Women Had Wings*. Set in and around Tampa in the 1960s, this powerful novel tells the story of the youngest daughter of a family crippled by poverty and the effects of alcohol, violence and broken dreams.

James Hall, *Under Cover of Daylight; Squall Line; Hard Aground*. Taut thrillers with a cast of crazies that make the most of the edge-of-the-world landscapes of the Florida Keys.

Ernest Hemingway, *To Have and Have Not*. Hemingway lived and drank in Key West for years but set only this moderate tale in the town, describing the woes of fishermen brutalized by the Depression.

Carl Hiaasen, *Double Whammy*. Ferociously funny fishing thriller that brings together a classic collection of warped but believable Florida characters, among them a hermit-like ex-state governor, a cynical Cuban cop and a corrupt TV preacher. By the same author, *Skin Tight* explores the perils of unskilled plastic surgery in a Miami crawling with mutant hitmen, bought politicians and police on gangsters' payrolls, and *Native Tongue* delves into the murky goings-on behind the scenes at a Florida theme park.

★ **Zora Neale Hurston**, *Their Eyes Were Watching God*. Florida-born Hurston became one of the bright lights of the Harlem Renaissance in the Twenties. This novel describes the founding of Eatonville – her home town and the state's first all-black town – and the labourers' lot in Belle Glade at the time of the 1928 hurricane. Equally hard to put down are *Jonah's Gourd Vine* and the autobiography, *Dust Tracks on a Road*.

★ **Elmore Leonard**, *Stick; La Brava; Gold Coast*. The pick of this highly recommended author's Florida-set thrillers, respectively detailing the rise of an opportunist ex-con through the money, sex and drugs of Latino Miami; lowlife on the seedy South Beach before the preservation of the Art Deco district; and the tribulations of a wealthy gangster-widow alone in a Fort Lauderdale mansion.

★ **Peter Matthiessen**, *Killing Mister Watson*. The first in a thoroughly researched trilogy on the early days of white settlement in the Everglades. Slow-paced but a strong insight into the Florida frontier mentality.

Thomas McGuane, *Ninety-Two in the Shade*. A strange, hallucinatory search for identity by a young man of shifting mental states who aspires to become a Key West fishing guide – and whose family and friends are equally warped.

Theodore Pratt, *The Barefoot Mailman*. A Forties account of the long-distance postman who kept the far-flung settlements of pioneer-period Florida in mail by hiking the many miles of beach between them.

Marjorie Kinnan Rawlings, *Short Stories*. A collection of 23 of Rawlings' most acclaimed short pieces, which draw heavily on Florida's natural surroundings for inspiration.

John Sayles, *Los Gusanos*. Absorbing, if long-winded novel set around the lives of Cuban exiles in Miami – written by a cult movie director.

Edmund Skellings, *Collected Poems: 1958–1998*. A "best of" collection of work by Florida's poet laureate. Of Skellings' poems, Norman Mailer says, "At their best, they shine like silver in the sun."

Patrick D. Smith, *A Land Remembered*. This historical novel is an epic portrayal of the lives of an American pioneering family, set against the rich and rugged history of Florida.

Randy Wayne White, *Sanibel Flats*. First in a series of Doc Ford detective novels, this book tells the story of a murder committed on a deserted mangrove island on Florida's West Coast.

Charles Willeford, *Miami Blues*. Thanks to an uninspired movie, the best-known but not the best of a highly recommended crime fiction series starring Hoke Mosely, a cool and calculating, but very human, Miami cop. Superior titles in the series are *The Way We Die Now, Kiss Your Ass Goodbye* and *Sideswipe*.

Cookbooks

Linda Gassenheimer, *Keys Cuisine*. A collection of recipes which captures the flavor of the Florida Keys.

Sue Mullin, *Nuevo Cubano Cooking*. Easy-to-follow instructions and mouthwatering photographs of recipes fusing traditional Cuban cooking with *nouvelle cuisine*.

Dawn O'Brien and Becky Roper, *Florida's Historic Restaurants and Their Recipes*. Featuring a variety of cuisines, this book contains fifty recipes from Florida's best-known restaurants.

Ferdie Pacheco and Luisita Sevilla Pacheco, *The Christmas Eve Cookbook*. A collection of over 200 holiday recipes and stories that illustrates the melting pot of immigrants that settled in Ybor City.

Steven Raichleu, *Miami Spice*. Latin American and Caribbean cooking meets Florida and the "Deep South," resulting in some of the tastiest dishes in America. Clear recipes and interesting background information.

index

and small print

Index

Map entries are in color

INDEX

Ⓘ

Twenty Years of Rough Guides

In the summer of 1981, Mark Ellingham, Rough Guides' founder, knocked out the first guide on a typewriter, with a group of friends. Mark had been traveling in Greece after university, and couldn't find a guidebook that really answered his needs. There were heavyweight cultural guides on the one hand – good on museums and classical sites but not on beaches and tavernas – and on the other hand student manuals that were so caught up with how to save money that they lost sight of the country's significance beyond its role as a place for a cool vacation. None of the guides began to address Greece as a country, with its natural and human environment, its politics and its contemporary life.

Having no urgent reason to return home, Mark decided to write his own guide. It was a guide to Greece that tried to combine some erudition and insight with a thoroughly practical approach to travelers' needs. Scrupulously researched listings of places to stay, eat and drink were matched by careful attention to detail on everything from Homer to Greek music, from classical sites to national parks and from nude beaches to monasteries. Back in London, Mark and his friends got their Rough Guide accepted by a farsighted commissioning editor at the publisher Routledge and it came out in 1982.

The Rough Guide to Greece was a student scheme that became a publishing phenomenon. The immediate success of the book – shortlisted for the Thomas Cook award – spawned a series that rapidly covered dozens of countries. The Rough Guides found a ready market among backpackers and budget travellers, but soon acquired a much broader readership that included older and less impecunious visitors. Readers relished the guides' wit and inquisitiveness as much as the enthusiastic, critical approach that acknowledges everyone wants value for money – but not at any price.

Rough Guides soon began supplementing the "rougher" information – the hostel and low-budget listings – with the kind of detail that independent-minded travellers on any budget might expect. These days, the guides – distributed worldwide by the Penguin group – include recommendations spanning the range from shoestring to luxury, and cover more than 200 destinations around the globe. Our growing team of authors, many of whom come to Rough Guides initially as outstandingly good letter-writers telling us about their travels, are spread all over the world, particularly in Europe, the USA and Australia. As well as the travel guides, Rough Guides publishes a series of dictionary phrasebooks covering two dozen major languages, an acclaimed series of music guides running the gamut from Classical to World Music, a series of music CDs in association with World Music Network, and a range of reference books on topics as diverse as the internet, pregnancy and unexplained phenomena. Visit www.roughguides.com to see what's cooking.

Rough Guide Credits

Text editors: Richard Koss
Series editor: Mark Ellingham
Editorial: Martin Dunford, Jonathan Buckley, Jo Mead, Kate Berens, Ann-Marie Shaw, Helena Smith, Judith Bamber, Orla Duane, Olivia Eccleshall, Ruth Blackmore, Geoff Howard, Claire Saunders, Gavin Thomas, Alexander Mark Rogers, Polly Thomas, Joe Staines, Richard Lim, Duncan Clark, Peter Buckley, Lucy Ratcliffe, Clifton Wilkinson, Alison Murchie, Matthew Teller (UK); Andrew Rosenberg, Stephen Timblin, Yuki Takagaki, (US)
Production: Susanne Hillen, Andy Hilliard, Link Hall, Helen Prior, Julia Bovis, Michelle Draycott, Katie Pringle, Mike Hancock, Zoë Nobes, Rachel Holmes, Andy Turner

Cartography: Melissa Baker, Maxine Repath, Ed Wright, Katie Lloyd-Jones
Picture research: Louise Boulton, Sharon Martins
Online: Kelly Cross, Anja Mutic-Blessing, Jennifer Gold, Audra Epstein, Suzanne Welles, Cree Lawson (US)
Finance: John Fisher, Gary Singh, Edward Downey, Mark Hall, Tim Bill
Marketing & Publicity: Richard Trillo, Niki Smith, David Wearn, Chloë Roberts, Birgit Hartmann, Claire Southern, Demelza Dallow (UK); Simon Carloss, David Wechsler, Kathleen Rushforth (US)
Administration: Tania Hummel, Julie Sanderson (UK); Hunter Slaton (US)

Publishing Information

This fifth edition published October 2001 by Rough Guides Ltd,
62–70 Shorts Gardens, London WC2H 9AH
4th Floor, 345 Hudson St, New York, NY 10014

Distributed by the Penguin Group
Penguin Books Ltd,
80 The Strand, London WC2R ORL
Penguin Putnam, Inc.
345 Hudson Street, NY 10014, USA
Penguin Books Australia Ltd,
487 Maroondah Highway, PO Box 257,
Ringwood, Victoria 3134, Australia
Penguin Books Canada Ltd,
10 Alcorn Avenue, Toronto, Ontario,
Canada M4V 1E4
Penguin Books (NZ) Ltd,
182–190 Wairau Road, Auckland 10,
New Zealand
Typeset in Bembo and Helvetica to an original design by Henry Iles.
Printed in Italy by LegoPrint S.p.A

520pp – Includes index
A catalogue record for this book is available from the British Library

ISBN 1-85828-724-3

The publishers and authors have done their best to ensure the accuracy and currency of all the information in The Rough Guide to Florida, however, they can accept no responsibility for any loss, injury, or inconvenience sustained by any traveler as a result of information or advice contained in the guide.

Help us update

We've gone to a lot of effort to ensure that the fifth edition of The Rough Guide to Florida is accurate and up to date. However, things change – places get "discovered", opening hours are notoriously fickle, restaurants and rooms increase prices or lower standards. If you feel we've got it wrong or left something out, we'd like to know, and if you can remember the address, the price, the time, the phone number, so much the better.

We'll credit all contributions, and send a copy of the next edition (or any other Rough Guide if you prefer) for the best letters. Everyone who writes to us and isn't already a subscriber will receive a copy of our full-color thrice-yearly newsletter. Please mark letters: "Rough Guide Florida Update" and send to: Rough Guides, 62–70 Shorts Gardens, London WC2H 9AH, or Rough Guides, 4th Floor, 345 Hudson St, New York, NY 10014. Or send an email to: mail@roughguides.co.uk or mail@roughguides.com

SMALL PRINT

Acknowledgments

Jeffrey Kennedy Thanks to Paul Auld, Marge and Tom Clauser, Stormy Coleman, Kerrianne and Mark Constant, Blake Gardner, Elizabeth Geoghegan, Rebekah Gimenez, Leigh Anne Hoberg, Joan and Tom Hubbard, Carolyn Johnston, Jean Kennedy, Jason L. Laseck, Clare Merlo, Martha and Chuck Nighswonger, Joan K. O'Steen, Angi and Nick Perri, Hector Palacios, Jim Stigall, Erin Sullivan, John Turk, Roseanne and Jim Ullman,
Lesley Rose I would like to thank my husband, Martin, for his steadfast support and research and editing assistance; Mark Holland for his hospitality; Michael Cushing for showing me the Everglades and Nikki Beare for sharing her knowledge of Florida's history.

Charles Young Thanks to Christian (D.A.M.E.), Saori, Beach-Boy, Pieter, all the shark-brothers (Messers Sweden, Morocco, Canada, Germany and Argentina), the Argies, and all the people I met at the Bungalow, Mr Two Crows, Bob the night porter (you kept me sane), las muchachas de la Rumba and Tom.

Heartfelt thanks go to Melissa Baker for her mapmaking expertise, Arabella Bowen, for her masterful index, Derek Wilde for his diligent proofreading, Andrew Rosenberg for his astute guidance and Link Hall for his seamless production work.

Readers' letters

Tony Boothby and Kirk Eppenstein, Barbara Burton, Paul Clements and Jason Peck, Keith and Virginia Du Quette, Kimberly Feazell, Ann Feltham, Judy Griffiths, Karen Hughes, Jay Humphreys, Andrew Jones, Marianne Loggia, Tom McClelland, J.B. Medley, Gloria Muroff, Linda M. Parker, Dr and Mrs. D.J. Payne, Kathleen Stafford, Bill Taylor, Leslie Williams

SMALL PRINT

Photo credits

Cover Credits

front small top picture, Tampa © Robert
Harding Picture library

front small lower picture, South Beach, Miami
© Robert Harding Picture Library

back top picture, Art Deco, Miami © Neil
Setchfield

back lower picture, EPCOT geosphere, Walt
Disney World © Robert Harding Picture
Library

Colour Introduction

Beaches of South Walton © J. Greenberg
Ocean Drive © Robert Harding Picture Library
Biscayne bay Miami, Pelicans © T. Why/Trip
Tampon Springs, stall © Visit Florida
Disney World, EPCOT centre © J. Greenberg/Trip
Little Havana © Neil Setchfield
The Kumba – Busch Gardens, Tampa, Florida
© Chris Parker/Axiom Photographic Agency
Walt Disney resort © James Morgan/Axiom
Bougainvillea © Visit Florida
Scuba Keys © Visit Florida
Clearwater Beach © Visit Florida
Air plant, the Everglades © Picturesque/Trip
Beaches of South Walton © J. Greenberg
Mallory Dock at sunset © J. Greenberg/Trip
St Augustine, Lightner Museum © Viesti
Collection © Trip

Things not to miss

1. Ocean Drive © F. and M. Hall
2. Art Deco © Nigel Francis/Robert Harding
3. Lowe Art Museum © Courtesy of Brian A.
Dursum, Lowe Art Museum
4. The Causeway of Miami © J. Greenberg/
Robert Harding Picture Library
5. Conch fritters © Trevor Wood/Robert
Harding Picture Library
6. Captain Tony's Saloon © Fraser Hall/
Robert Harding Picture Library
7. Sea turtle viewing © Robert Harding
Picture Library

8. Key deer © J. Greenberg/Trip
9. Boca Raton Resort © J. Greenberg/Trip
10. Fantasy Fest © Fantasy Fest Media
11. Sunset at Sebastian Inlet © J. Greenberg/
Trip
12. Beachcombing © Fraser Hall
13. Space Shuttle launches, Cape Canaveral
© Visit Florida
14. Ponce Inlet Lighthouse © J. Greenberg/
Trip
15. Back to the Future, Universal Studios ©
Universal Studios
16. Disney's Animal Kingdom © James
Morgan/Axiom
17. St Augustine's Old Town © J. Greenberg/
Trip
18. Corkscrew Swamp Sanctuary © Fraser
Hall
19. Chalet Suzanne © Chalet Suzanne
20. Ca d'zan © Fraser Hall
21. Apalachicola National Forest © Visit
Florida
22. Seaside © Visit Florida
23. Fishing © Ann Curtis/Travel Ink
24. Canoeing in the Everglades © Richard
Crawford/Axiom
25. Alligator encounters © Amanda Hall

Black and White Photos

Sea World, Orlando, Florida © M. MacKenzie/
Trip

Boats by River © Visit Florida
Jacksonville Landing © Visit Florida
Jacksonville Fountain © Visit Florida
Fort Lauderdale © Visit Florida
Miami Beach © Visit Florida
Biscayne Bay © Visit Florida
Marathon Keys © Visit Florida
Scuba Keys © Visit Florida
West Coast © Visit Florida
Tampa Skyline Bridge © Visit Florida
The Panhandle © Visit Florida
The Panhandle © Visit Florida

SMALL PRINT

The ideas expressed in this code were developed by and for independent travellers.

Learn About The Country You're Visiting

Start enjoying your travels before you leave by tapping into as many sources of information as you can.

The Cost Of Your Holiday

Think about where your money goes - be fair and realistic about how cheaply you travel. Try and put money into local peoples' hands; drink local beer or fruit juice rather than imported brands and stay in locally owned accommodation. Haggle with humour and not aggressively. Pay what something is worth to you and remember how wealthy you are compared to local people.

Embrace The Local Culture

Open your mind to new cultures and traditions - it will transform you experience. Think carefully about what's appropriate in terms of your clothes and the way you behave. You'll earn respect and be more readily welcomed by local people. Respect local laws and attitudes towards drugs and alcohol that vary in different countries and communities. Think about the impact you could have on them.

Exploring The World – The Travellers' Code

Being sensitive to these ideas means getting more out of your travels - and giving more back to the people you meet and the places you visit.

Minimise Your Environmental Impact

Think about what happens to your rubbish - take biodegradable products and a water filter bottle. Be sensitive to limited resources like water, fuel and electricity. Help preserve local wildlife and habitats by respecting local rules and regulations, such as sticking to footpaths and not standing on coral.

Don't Rely On Guidebooks

Use your guidebook as a starting point, not the only source of information. Talk to local people, then discover your own adventure!

Be Discreet With Photography

Don't treat people as part of the landscape, they may not want their picture taken. Ask first and respect their wishes.

We work with people the world over to promote tourism that benefits their communities, but we can only carry on our work with the support of people like you. For membership details or to find out how to make your travels work for local people and the environment, visit our website.

www.tourismconcern.org.uk

TourismConcern
Campaigning for Ethical and Fairly Traded Tourism

WHY ROUGH IT

Confirmed online reservations with Hostelworld.com

Prebook your beds with hostelworld.com giving you much more time to **experience** your destination.

For real-time confirmed reservations at over 1000 hostels worldwide
visit **www.roughguides.com/hostelworld**

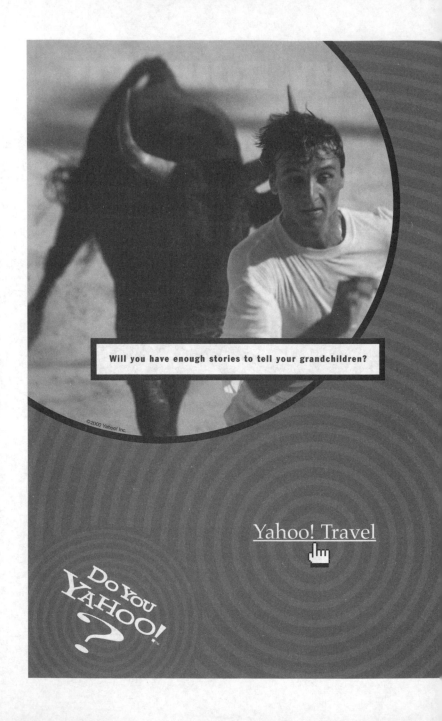

Will you have enough stories to tell your grandchildren?

©2000 Yahoo! Inc.

Yahoo! Travel